THE
COLONIAL CLERGY
AND THE
COLONIAL CHURCHES
OF
NEW ENGLAND

By
Frederick Lewis Weis

CLEARFIELD

Originally published
Lancaster, Massachusetts
1936

Copyright © 1936
Frederick L. Weis
All Rights Reserved

Reprinted with the permission of the
Society of the Descendants of the Colonial Clergy
and Mr. Robert P. Weis
Genealogical Publishing Co., Inc.
Baltimore, Maryland
1977

Library of Congress Catalogue Card Number 77-82296

Reprinted for Clearfield Company by
Genealogical Publishing Company
Baltimore, Maryland
1991, 1992, 1995, 1997, 2010

ISBN 978-0-8063-0779-4

Made in the United States of America

PREFACE

FOR the first time a complete list of New England colonial churches and clergymen of all denominations is herein presented. Obviously there must be mistakes and omissions because of the very nature and extent of the subject matter. Thus, in some instances, the births or deaths of individuals vary with the sources: church records give one date, gravestones another, town records another, while diaries, journals and family histories give still others. To quote all is impossible because of limited space. The compiler has often been forced to choose the most likely source as probably the correct one. Likewise there are notable discrepancies in dates of foundations of churches and of ordinations and dismissions. But even more provoking still is the absence of any records at all, due to neglect, carelessness, hard usage or fire. Finally the compiler himself, being human, is prone to err, and though many of the dates have been checked a dozen times from as many original or secondary sources, it is inevitable that others will prove to be wrong even though backed by the most competent authorities.

Any correction or any additional information will be gratefully received by the compiler and duly noted for a future edition.

Our sincere thanks are due to the American Antiquarian Society, the Connecticut Historical Society, the Worcester Art Museum, Miss Louisa Dresser, Miss Marie Johnson, Mr. Clarence S. Brigham, Mrs. Samuel E. Staines, and Mr. Fred G. May, Jr. for permission to use the illustrations which add so much to the attractiveness of this book.

WILLIAM DEXTER,
DUDLEY HUNTINGTON DORR
GEORGE CHEEVER GUILD,
EDWARD CRARY LORD,
THOMAS TEMPLE POND,
DUNCAN FORBES THAYER,
FREDERICK LEWIS WEIS,

Publication Committee.

The Fifth Meeting House of the First Church of Christ in Lancaster, founded 1653.

Designed by Charles Bulfinch and built in 1816.

(Drawn by Phila Linville Staines)

THE SOCIETY
OF THE DESCENDANTS OF THE COLONIAL CLERGY.

OFFICERS OF THE SOCIETY.

Governor
REVEREND HENRY WILDER FOOTE, D. D.

Deputy-Governors
COLONEL JOHN ELIOT THAYER*
WILLIAM CROWNINSHIELD ENDICOTT

Secretary
DUDLEY HUNTINGTON DORR

Historian
REVEREND FREDERICK LEWIS WEIS, Th.D.

Treasurer
WILLIAM DEXTER

Chaplain
REVEREND LOUIS CRAIG CORNISH, D. D.

Chancellor
HONORABLE HERBERT PARKER, LL.D.

Marshal
MAJOR GEORGE ALANSON PARKER

Surgeon
FRANKLIN GREENE BALCH, M. D.

Signet
REVEREND RICHARD ALLEN DAY

Members of the Council

1935-1938	HONORABLE CHARLES FRANCIS ADAMS, LL.D.
1936-1939	REVEREND ALFRED WILLIAMS ANTHONY, D.D., LL.D.
1936-1939	JOHN WASHBURN BARTOL, M.D.
1933-1935	HENRY FORBES BIGELOW
1934-1937	REVEREND CHRISTOPHER RHODES ELIOT, LL.D.
1933-1936	FRANCIS ABBOT GOODHUE
1933-1936	REVEREND CHARLES EDWARDS PARK, D.D.
1935-1938	REVEREND HOWARD CHANDLER ROBBINS, D.D.
1934-1937	MRS. BAYARD THAYER
1933-1934	DUNCAN FORBES THAYER
1934-1934	MRS. NATHANIEL THAYER*
1933-1934	GEORGE WILLIAM WHEELWRIGHT
1933-1935	REVEREND JOHN HENRY WILSON

*Deceased.

Honorary Member

ABBOTT LAWRENCE LOWELL, LL.D., Ph.D., Litt.D.

MEMBERS OF THE SOCIETY
OF THE DESCENDANTS OF THE COLONIAL CLERGY.

Hon. Charles Francis Adams, LL.D.
Mrs. William Porter Allen
Rev. Alfred Williams Anthony, D.D., LL.D.
Mrs. Edward Austin
Rev. Everett Moore Baker
Miss Lucy Myrtle Baker
Miss Mary Leona Baker
Franklin Greene Balch, M.D.
John Washburn Bartol, M.D.
Miss Ann Batchelder
Mrs. S. Westray Battle
Henry Forbes Bigelow
Francis Millet Booth
Mrs. William Harris Booth
Jeffrey Richardson Brackett, Ph.D.
Miss Marjorie Cross Bradford
Mrs. Benjamin Thomas Burley
Philip Raymond Calder
Christopher Millet Carey
Mrs. Arthur Graham Carey
Miss Hilda Carey
Miss Joan Graham Carey
Mrs. Clovis Leon Carpenter
Mrs. Miles Leach Carter
John Chandler
Mrs. Lewis Williamson Cherry
Richard Fletcher Clapp
Mrs. Russell Charles Collin
Miss H. Elizabeth Coolidge
Eugene Smith Cooper
Rev. Louis Craig Cornish, D.D.
Miss Frances Cordis Cruft
Mrs. Fred William Culver
Mrs. Alexander Griswold Cummins
Rev. Richard Allen Day
Mrs. Richard Allen Day

Edward Henry Dewson
Miss Mary Williams Dewson
Miss Constance Van Rensselaer Dexter
Miss Mary Ann Dexter
Nathaniel Thayer Dexter
Philip Dexter
William Dexter
Mrs. William Dexter
Prof. Robert Cloutman Dexter, Ph.D.
Mrs. Robert Cloutman Dexter, Ph.D.
Mrs. H. Louis Dorman
Dudley Huntington Dorr
Dudley Huntington Dorr, Jr.
Rev. Christopher Rhodes Eliot, LL.D.
Rev. Samuel Atkins Eliot, D.D., LL.D.
Miss Amy Ethel Emery
William Crowninshield Endicott
Edgar Conway Felton
Rev. Dan Huntington Fenn
Roland Willard Fletcher
Walter Weston Folger
Rev. Henry Wilder Foote, D.D.
Mrs. Glenville C. Frissell
Mrs. Claude Moore Fuess
Eben Howard Gay*
Mrs. George L. Gilmore
Francis Abbot Goodhue
Mrs. Francis Abbot Goodhue
Miss Marion Adelaide Green
Elbridge Gerry Greene
Mrs. Elbridge Gerry Greene
George Cheever Guild
Richard Walden Hale
Mrs. Frank E. Harter
Joseph Alfred Harwood
Miss Jessica Lauvenia Hawthorne
Mrs. John G. Henry
Mrs. Stephen J. Herben
Mrs. Willis Kennedy Hodgman, Jr.

Mrs. Warren H. Hollinshed
George Eli Howe
Mrs. George Eli Howe
Mrs. Robert James Johnston
Mrs. Edward Harte Jones
Eliot Norris Jones
Mrs. Hermann August Knorr
Major Paul Mayer La Bach
Mrs. William Grinnell Landon
Mrs. Edward Lawrence Lepper
Mrs. Richard James Leupold
Rev. Augustus Mendon Lord, D.D.
Edward Crary Lord
Miss Elizabeth Wellington Lord
Abbott Lawrence Lowell, LL.D., Ph.D., Litt.D.
Miss Lucy Buckminster Lowell
Mrs. Jerome Morley Lynch
Mrs. Gilbert A. Mackenzie
Miss Helen Cartwright McCleary
Rev. Edward Webster McGlenen, Jr.
Mrs. Edward Webster McGlenen
Mrs. William Wallace McPherson
Frederick Goddard May, Jr.
George Henry May
Mrs. George Henry May
Mrs. H. Frazer Meiklejohn
Mrs. Paul Adams Merriam
Mrs. Josiah Byram Millet
Mrs. George Parsons Milmine
Lester Dunbar Morris
Miss Esther Crafts Morse
Rev. Morgan Phelps Noyes
Rev. Charles Edwards Park, D.D.
Major George Alanson Parker
Mrs. George Alanson Parker
Miss Harriet Felton Parker
Haven Parker
Mrs. Haven Parker
Hon. Herbert Parker, LL.D.

Mrs. Herbert Parker
Miss Katherine Vose Parker
Mrs. Ismay Graham Pattinson
Rev. Endicott Peabody, D.D.
Franklin Haskins Perkins, M.D.
Mrs. Franklin Haskins Perkins
Rev. Howard Delvon Perkins
Mrs. George Frederick Pierce
Miss Cora Eliza Pierce
Thomas Temple Pond
Mrs. Murray Anthony Potter
Rev. Howard Chandler Robbins, D.D.
Harry Browning Russell*
Rev. Vincent Brown Silliman
Frederick Johnson Simmons
Donald Kennedy Snow
Rev. Sydney Bruce Snow, D.D.
Mrs. Edwin Erle Sparks
Samuel Edgar Staines
Roger Pomeroy Stone
Miss Virginia Stone
Mrs. Elbridge Fernald Stoneham
Mrs. Richard Cutts Storey, Jr.
Miss Catherine Coolidge Tatnall
Mrs. Bayard Thayer
Duncan Forbes Thayer
Mrs. Duncan Forbes Thayer
Col. John Eliot Thayer*
Mrs. John Eliot Thayer
Hon. John Eliot Thayer, Jr.
Mrs. Nathaniel Thayer*
Bennett Edwin Tousley
Mrs. George Fuller Tuttle
Rev. Frederick Lewis Weis, Th.D.
Mrs. Frederick Lewis Weis
Robert Pomeroy Weis
Miss Virginia Stone Weis
Mrs. Arthur Clement Wescott
George William Wheelwright

Mrs. George William Wheelwright
Lester James Williams, M.D.
Rev. John Henry Wilson
Mrs. Byron K. Worrall
Howard Harlan Paige Wright
Mrs. Howard Harlan Paige Wright
Mrs. Milburn Edgar Yeager

PARTIAL LIST OF AUTHORITIES:

Addison: Life and Times of Edward Bass
Allen: History of the Worcester Association
American Antiquarian Society, Proceedings
Amidown: Historical Collections
Backus: History of the Baptists
Barber: Historical Collections
Batchelder: History of the Eastern Diocese
Baxter: Trelawny Papers
Baylies: Churches of Taunton
Belknap: Historical Collections
Benedict: General History of the Baptist Denomination
Blake: History of the Mendon Association
Blake: Separates or Strict Congregationalists of New England
Burrage: History of the Baptists of Maine
Calamy: Account of Ejected Ministers
Callender: History of Rhode Island
Carter: Native Ministry of New Hampshire
Clark: History of the Congregational Churches of Maine
Clarke: Congregational Churches of Massachusetts
Colonial Society of Massachusetts, Proceedings
Congregational Quarterly
Congregational Churches of New Hampshire
Connecticut Historical Society, Proceedings
Contributions to the Ecclesiastical History of Connecticut
Dexter: Biographies and Annals of Yale College
Dexter: Congregationalism
Dictionary of American Biography
Ecclesiastical Records of the State of New York
Eliot: Biographical Dictionary
Eliot: Heralds of a Liberal Faith
Essex Institute, Proceedings
Evans: American Bibliography
Family Histories and Genealogies
Farmer: First Settlers of New England
Farmer: Historical Collections
Farmer: List of Graduates of New England Colleges
Felt: Ecclesiastical History of New England
Fiske: Beginnings of New England

Foote: Annals of King's Chapel
Foster: Alumni Oxoniensis
Fothergill: List of Emigrant Ministers to America
Genealogical Dictionary of Maine and New Hampshire
Gillett: History of the Presbyterian Church
Goodwin: Pilgrim Republic
Greenleaf: Ecclesiastical Sketches of Maine
Hayward: Gazeteer of Massachusetts
Hazen: Ministers and Churches of New Hampshire
Hazen: Pastors of New Hampshire
History of the American Episcopal Church
Histories of Churches, Towns, Counties and States of New England
Holland: History of Western Massachusetts
Johnson: Wonder Working Providence
Maine Historical Society, Proceedings
Mather: Magnalia Christi
Massachusetts Historical Society, Proceedings
Meade: Old Churches and Families of Virginia
Memorials of the Dead in Boston
Morton: New England Memorial
Nason: Gazeteer of Massachusetts
Neal: History of the Puritans
New England Historic Genealogical Register
New Hampshire Historical Society, Proceedings
Pope: Pioneers of Massachusetts
Prince: Chronology
Rhode Island Historical Society, Publications
Quinquennial Catalogue of Harvard University
Savage: Genealogical Dictionary of New England
Sewall: Diary
Sibley: Biographies of Harvard Graduates
Sketches of Some Historic Churches of Greater Boston
Smalley: Worcester Pulpit
Sprague: Annals of the American Pulpit
Winsor: Memorial History of Boston
Updike: Narragansett Church
Venn: Alumni Cantabrigiensis
Vital Records of New England Towns
Weis: Colonial Churches of Massachusetts

Winthrop: Journal
Worcester Magazine
Year Books, Congregational Christian Churches, Unitarian Congregational Churches and Universalist Churches.
Young: Chronicles of the Pilgrim Fathers
Young: Chronicles of Massachusetts
Historical Catalogues of Brown, Columbia, Dartmouth, Harvard, Princeton and Williams Colleges

THE COLONIAL CHURCHES OF NEW ENGLAND:

Denomination	Me.	N.H.	Vt.	Mass.	R.I.	Ct.	Total	Less*	Total	%
Congregational	48	101	12	344	15	200	720	—	720	72
Baptist	5	11	2	63	41	26	148	—	148	15
Episcopal	4	3	—	22	7	40	76	1	75	7.5
Separatist	—	1	—	18	—	26	45	3	42	4
Presbyterian	10	14	—	9	—	1	34	25	9	1
Huguenot	—	—	—	2	—	—	2	—	2	
Lutheran	1	—	—	—	—	—	1	—	1	
Moravian	—	—	—	—	1	—	1	—	1	
Sandemanian	—	1	—	1	—	2	4	—	4	
Total	68	131	14	459	64	295	1031	30	1001	
Less*	9	11	—	7	1	2	30			
Total	59	120	14	452	63	293	1001			
Percent	6	12	1	45	6	29				
*Counted Twice.										
Became Unitarian	6	9	—	125	1	1			142	14
Became Universalist	—	—	—	12	—	1			13	1

THE COLONIAL CLERGY OF NEW ENGLAND:

	Total	Per cent	Non-graduates	Per cent
Congregationalists	1586	77	79	05
Baptists	217	11.5	192	89
Episcopalians	127	6		
Separatists	64	3	52	81
Presbyterians	51	2.5		
Sandemanians	7			
Huguenots	6			
Moravians	4			
Lutherans	1			
Universalists	1			
Total	2064			

The college trained, degree holders or graduates among the Colonial Clergy of New England numbered   1676
    Percentage of the whole   85

Colonial Clergymen of New England received degrees, graduated from or attended the following Colleges and Universities:

	Number	Per cent
Harvard	946	57
Yale	436	26
Cambridge	96	6
Princeton	50	3
Oxford	43	2.5
Edinburgh	13	
Dartmouth	10	
Brown	9	
Glasgow	6	
Dublin	5	
Pennsylvania	3	
Aberdeen	2	
Columbia	1	
Geneva	1	
Unidentified	55	3
Total	1676	—

Colonial Clergymen of New England received honorary doctor's degrees from the following Colleges and Universities:

	Number	Per cent
Harvard	38	24
Yale	25	16
Princeton	22	14
Dartmouth	18	11
Edinburgh	14	9
Brown	11	7
Oxford	7	6
Aberdeen	6	3
Glasgow	3	2
Williams	3	2
Pennsylvania	3	2
Cambridge	3	2
Columbia	3	2
Padua	2	1
Dublin	1	
Union	1	
South Carolina	1	
Total	160	—

Clergymen receiving doctor's degrees	142*	
Congregational	118	83
Episcopal	17	12
Baptist	5	
Presbyterian	2	

*Some of these possessed more than one doctor's degree, — thus 142 recipients received 160 degrees, as noted above.

THE COLONIAL CLERGY OF NEW ENGLAND. 1620-1776.

HULL ABBOT, A.M., b. Boston, June 15, 1702, son of Moses and Rebecca (Knight) Abbot; H. C., 1720, A.B., A.M.; Ord. Charlestown, Feb. 5, 1724; sett. Charlestown, 1724-1774; Artillery Election Sermon, 1735; Convention Sermon, 1756; Dudleian Lecture, 1764; d. Charlestown, Apr. 19, 1774, a. 72.

THOMAS ABBOT, A.M., b. Charlestown, May 2, 1745, son of Rev. Hull and Mary (Bradstreet) Abbot; H. C., 1764, A.B., A.M.; Ord. West Roxbury, Sept. 29, 1773; sett. West Roxbury, 1773-1783; dism. Mar. 10, 1783; d. Nov. 1, 1789.

ROBERT ABERCROMBIE, A.B., b. Edinburgh, Scotland, 1712; educ. at Edinburgh; came to N. E., ca. 1740; Ord. Pelham, Aug. 30, 1744; sett. Pelham, 1744-1755; Presb.; d. Pelham, Mar. 7, 1780.

AMOS ADAMS, A.M., b. Medfield, Sept. 1, 1728, son of Henry and Jemimah (Morse) Adams; H. C., 1752, A.B., A.M.; Ord. Roxbury, Sept. 12, 1753; sett. Roxbury, 1753-1775; Chaplain, Col. David Brewer's Cont. Regt., 1775; Artillery Election Sermon, 1759; Dudleian Lecture, 1770; d. Dorchester, Oct. 5, 1775, a. 48.

BENJAMIN ADAMS, A.M., b. Newbury, May 8, 1719, son of Capt. Abraham and Anne (Longfellow) Adams; H. C., 1738, A.B., A.M.; Ord. Lynnfield, Nov. 5, 1755; sett. Lynnfield, 1755-1777; d. Lynnfield, May 4, 1777, a. 57.

ELIPHALET ADAMS, A.M., b. Dedham, Mar. 26, 1677, son of Rev. William and Mary (Manning) Adams; H. C., 1694, A.B., A.M.; preached at Little Compton, R. I., 1696-1698; Indian Missionary, 1698-1700; sett. Boston, (Brattle St. Chh., asst. min.), 1701-1704; Ord. New London, Ct., Feb. 9, 1708/9; sett. New London, Ct., 1708-1753; worked among the Indians, 1725-1746; Trustee, Y. C., 1720-1738; Ct. Election Sermons, 1710, 1734; d. New London, Ct., Oct. 4, 1753, a. 77.

HUGH ADAMS, A.M., b. Limerick, Ireland, May 7, 1676, son of John and Avis Adams; H. C., 1697, A.B., A.M.; preached in South Carolina, 1698-1705; Ord. Braintree, Sept. 10, 1707; sett. Braintree, (first min. of 2nd Chh.), 1707-1710; left. Aug. 22, 1710; sett. Chatham, 1711-1715; inst. Durham, N. H., Mar. 26, 1718; sett. Durham, N. H., 1717-1739; dism. Jan. 23, 1739; physician; d. Durham, N. H., Oct. 1748, a. 72.

JEDEDIAH ADAMS, A.M., b. Braintree, Jan. 21, 1710, son of Capt. Peter and Mary (Webb) Adams; H. C., 1733, A.B., A.M.; Ord. Stoughton, Feb. 19, 1746; sett. Stoughton, 1745-1795; liberal; d. Stoughton, Feb. 25, 1799, a. 89.

JOHN ADAMS, A.M., bapt. Boston, Mar. 26, 1704/5, son of Lt. Gov. John and Hannah (Checkley) Adams; H. C., 1721, A.B., A.M.; Ord. Newport, R. I., (2nd Cong. Chh.), Apr. 11, 1728, as the first minister; sett. Newport, R. I., 1728-1730; dism. Feb. 25, 1729/30; sett. Philadelphia, Pa.; d. Cambridge, Jan. 1740, a. 36.

JOHN ADAMS, A.B., b. Boston, June 19, 1725, son of Matthew and Katherine (Brigden) Adams; H. C., 1745, A.B.; Ord. Durham, N. H., Mar. 25, 1748/9; sett. Durham, N. H., 1748-1778; removed to Newfield, Me., where he practiced medicine at Newfield, Limington, Parsonsfield and Limerick; d. Newfield, Me., June 4, 1792, a. 67.

JOSEPH ADAMS, A.M., b. Braintree, Jan. 4, 1688/9, son of Joseph and Hannah (Bass) Adams; H. C., 1710, A.B., A.M.; Ord. Newington, N. H., Nov. 16, 1715; sett. Newington, N. H., 1710-1783; d. Newington, N. H., May 26, 1783, a. 95.

JOSEPH ADAMS, A.B., b. Boston, June 1, 1720, son of John and Mary (Boomer) Adams; H. C., 1742, A.B., A.M.; Ord. Stratham, N. H., Mar. 20, 1747; sett. Stratham, N. H., 1742-1783; dism. Oct. 26, 1783; New Light preacher; d. Stratham, N. H., Feb. 24, 1785, a. 66.

PHINEAS ADAMS, A.M., b. Georgetown, Mar. 3, 1742/3, son of Abraham and Mary (Coleman) Adams; H. C., 1762, A.B., A.M.; Ord. Haverhill, (3rd or West Chh.), Jan. 9, 1771; sett. Haverhill, 1771-1801; d. Haverhill, Nov. 15, 1801.

WILLIAM ADAMS, A.M., b. Ipswich, May 27, 1650, son of William and Elizabeth (Stacy) Adams; H. C., 1671, A.B., A.M.; Ord. Dedham, Dec. 3, 1673; sett. Dedham, 1672-1685; Artillery Election Sermon, 1680; Election Sermon, 1685; d. Dedham, Aug. 17, 1685, a. 35.

WILLIAM ADAMS, A.M., b. New London, Ct., Oct. 7, 1710, son of Rev. Eliphalet and Lydia (Pygan) Adams; Y. C., 1730, A.B., A.M.; Tutor, Y. C., 1732-1734; not ordained; preached for 60 yrs.; sett. New London, Ct., (North Parish); Ledyard, Ct.; Shelter Island, L. I.; New London, Ct., 1753-1756; d. New London, Ct., Nov. 28, 1798, a. 88, unm.

ZABDIEL ADAMS, A.M., b. Braintree, Nov. 5, 1739, son of Capt. Ebenezer and Anne (Boylston) Adams; H. C., 1759, A.B., A.M.; Ord. Lunenburg, Sept. 5, 1764; sett. Lunenburg, 1764-1801; double cousin to President John Adams; Election Sermon, 1782; Dudleian Lecture, 1794; d. Lunenburg, Mar. 1, 1801.

SAMUEL ALBRO (Aldborough or Alborough), sett. North Kingston, R. I., 1760; Bapt.

NOAH ALDEN, b. Middleborough, May 30, 1725, son of John and Hannah (White) Alden; Ord. Stafford, Ct., June 5, 1755; sett. Stafford, Ct., 1755-1765; inst. Bellingham, Nov. 12, 1766; sett. Bellingham, 1766-1797; delegate, Const. Convent. of Mass.; Bapt.; d. Bellingham, May 5, 1797, a. 72.

TIMOTHY ALDEN, A.M., b. Bridgewater, Nov. 24, 1736, son of Eleazer and Martha (Shaw) Alden; H. C., 1762, A.B., A.M.; Ord. Yarmouth, Dec. 13, 1769; sett. Yarmouth, 1769-1828; d. Yarmouth, Nov. 13, 1828, a. 92.

BENJAMIN ALLEN, A.M., b. Tisbury, 1680, son of James

and Elizabeth (Perkins) Allen; Y. C., 1708, A.B., A.M.; Ord. Bridgewater, July 9, 1718; sett. Bridgewater, 1717-1730; inst. South Portland, Me., (2nd Parish in Falmouth at Cape Elizabeth), Nov. 10, 1734; sett. South Portland, Me., 1730-1754; d. Cape Elizabeth, Me., May 6, 1754.

JAMES ALLEN, A.M., b. Hampshire, Eng., June 24, 1632, son of a Hampshire minister; matric. Magdalen Hall, Oxford, Mar. 16, 1649/50; Chaplain, New Coll., Oxford, 1649; New Coll., Oxford, 1652, A.B.; A.M., 1654; Fellow at New Coll., 1650; Fellow, H. C., 1700; ejected for non-conformity, 1662; came to N. E., June 10, 1662; inst. Boston, (1st Chh.), Dec. 9, 1668; sett. Boston, 1668-1710; Election Sermon, 1679; d. Boston, Sept. 22, 1710, a. 78.

JAMES ALLING, A.M., b. New Haven, Ct., June 24, 1657, son of Dea. Roger and Mary (Nash) Alling; H. C., 1679, A.B., A.M.; Ord. Salisbury, May 4, 1687; sett. Salisbury, 1682-1696; d. Salisbury, Mar. 3, 1695/6, a. 39.

JAMES ALLEN, A.M., b. Roxbury, June 5, 1692, son of Peter and Mary Allen; H. C., 1710, A.B., A.M.; Ord. Brookline, Nov. 5, 1718; sett. Brookline, 1718-1747; Artillery Election Sermon, 1731; Election Sermon, 1744; d. Brookline, Feb. 18, 1747.

JOHN ALLIN, A.M., bapt. Colby, Norf., Eng., May 22, 1597, son of Reginald Allin of Colby, Gent.; Gonville & Caius Coll., Camb., A.B., 1616, A.M., 1619; Ord. Sept. 20, 1619; Curate at Denton, Norfolk, and at Wrentham, Suffolk, Eng.; came to N. E., 1637; Ord. Dedham, Apr. 24, 1639, as the first minister; sett. Dedham, 1637-1671; Overseer, H. C., 1654; Artillery Election Sermon, 1664; d. Dedham, Aug. 26, 1671, a. 75.

PARK ALLYN, b. Ledyard, Ct., 1733; Ord. Ledyard, Ct., (North Groton Separatist Chh.), ca. 1755; deposed; d. Ledyard, Ct., Feb. 13, 1804.

PAUL ALLYN, Ord. North Groton, Ct., (Separatist Chh.), June 1, 1775.

PETER ALLYN, Ord. North Groton, Ct., (Separatist Chh.), Sept. 1, 1765.

THOMAS ALLEN, A.M., b. Norwich, Eng., 1608, son of John Allen; Gonville & Caius Coll., Camb., 1627/8, A.B., A.M.; Ord. by the Bishop of Norwich, Mar. 2, 1633/4; sett. St. Edmonds, Norwich, 1633-1638; silenced by Bishop Wren; came to N. E., 1638; Ord. Charlestown, Feb. 1639/40; sett. Charlestown, 1638-1651; returned to St. George's, Norwich, Eng., where he preached, 1651-1660; d. Norwich, Eng., Sept. 21, 1673, a. 65.

THOMAS ALLEN, A.M., b. Northampton, Jan. 17, 1743, son of Joseph and Elizabeth (Parsons) Allen; H. C., 1762, A.B., A.M.; Ord. Pittsfield, Apr. 18, 1764; sett. Pittsfield, 1763-1810; Chaplain at White Plains, 1776; Ticonderoga, 1777; fought at Bennington; father of Rev. William Allen, D.D., President of Bowdoin Coll.; Election Sermon, 1808; d. Pittsfield, Feb. 11, 1810, a. 67.

TIMOTHY ALLEN, A.M., b. Lisbon, Ct., Aug. 31, 1715, son of Timothy and Rachel (Bushnell) Allen; Y. C., 1736, A.B., A.M.; Ord. West Haven, Ct., Oct. 10, 1738; sett. West Haven, Ct., 1738-1742; dism. May 27, 1742; sett. Maidenhead and Hopewll, N. J., 1748-1752; inst. New Providence, N. J., Mar. 26, 1753; sett. New Providence, N. J., 1752-1756; inst. Ashford, Ct., Oct. 12, 1757; sett. Ashford, Ct., 1757-1764; dism. Jan. 13, 1764; sett. Granville, Mass., ca. 1782; inst. Chesterfield, June 15, 1785; sett. Chesterfield, 1785-1796; d. Chesterfield, Jan. 12, 1806, a. 90.

WILLIAM ALLEN, A.M., b. Boston, Mar. 1676, son of Bozoun Allen; H. C., 1703, A.B., A.M.; Ord. Greenland, N. H., July 15, 1707; sett. Greenland, 1707-1760; d. Greenland, N. H., Sept. 8, 1760, a. 84.

SAMUEL ALLIS, A.M., b. Hatfield, Dec. 12, 1705, son of Ichabod and Mary (Belden) Allis; H. C., 1724, A.B., A.M.; schoolmaster at Northampton, 1725; Ord. Somers, (East Enfield), Ct., Mar. 1727; sett. Somers, Ct., 1727-1747; d. Somers, Ct., Dec. 16, 1796, a. 91.

PRESIDENT SAMUEL ANDREW, A.M., b. Cambridge, Jan. 29, 1656, son of Samuel and Elizabeth (White) Andrew; H. C., 1675, A.B., A.M.; Fellow, H. C., 1679-1684; Founder and Trustee, Y. C., 1699-1738; Rector. (i. e. Pres.), pro. tem., 1707-1719; Ord. Milford, Ct., Nov. 18, 1685; sett. Milford, Ct., 1685-1738; d. Milford, Ct., Jan. 24, 1737/8, a. 82.

SAMUEL ANDREWS, A.M., b. Meriden, Ct., Apr. 27, 1737, son of Samuel and Abigail (Tyler) Andrews; Y. C., 1759, A.B.; A.M., Columbia; Ord. Eng., Aug. 24, 1761; sett. Wallingford, Ct. and New Haven, Ct., (Epis. Chh.), 1762-1786; sett. St. Andrews, New Brunswick, May 1786, as the first minister; Epis.; d. St. Andrews, N. B., Sept. 26, 1818, a. 82.

EZEKIEL ANGELL, b. North Providence, R. I., 1722, son of Daniel and Hannah (Winsor) Angell; Ord. North Providence, R. I., June 23, 1765; sett. North Providence, R. I., 1765-1782; Bapt.; d. North Providence, R. I., Sept. 27, 1782.

JOHN ANGIER, A.M., b. Waltham, July 1, 1701, son of Rev. Samuel and Hannah (Oakes) Angier; H. C., 1720, A.B., A.M.; Ord. East Bridgewater, Oct. 28, 1724; sett. East Bridgewater, 1724-1787; d. East Bridgewater, Apr. 14, 1787, a. 86.

SAMUEL ANGIER, A.M., b. Cambridge, Mar. 17, 1654/5, son of Edmund and Ruth (Ames) Angier; H. C., 1673, A.B., A.M.; Tutor; Fellow; Ord. Rehoboth (Seekonk), Oct. 15, 1679; sett. Rehoboth (Seekonk), 1679-1693; inst. Waltham, May 25, 1697, as first minister; sett. Waltham, 1697-1719; d. Waltham, Jan. 21, 1718/19, a. 65.

SAMUEL ANGIER, A.M., b. East Bridgewater, Mar. 20, 1743, son of Rev. John and Mary (Bourne) Angier; H. C., 1763, A.B.,

A.M.; Ord. East Bridgewater, Dec. 23, 1767; sett. East Bridgewater, 1763-1805; d. East Bridgewater, Jan. 18, 1805.

NATHANIEL APPLETON, D.D., b. Ipswich, Dec. 9, 1693, son of Judge John and Elizabeth (Rogers) Appleton; H. C., 1712, A.B., A.M.; S.T.D., 1771, (second D.D. conferred at H. C.); Fellow, 1717-1779; Ord. Cambridge, Oct. 9, 1717; sett. Cambridge, 1717-1784; Artillery Election Sermon, 1733; Election Sermon, 1742; Convention Sermon, 1743; Dudleian Lecture, 1758; d. Cambridge, Feb. 9, 1784, a. 91.

EAST APTHORP, D.D., b. Boston, 1733, son of Charles and Grizel (Eastwick) Apthorp; Jesus Coll., Camb., 1755, A.B., A.M.; D.D., 1780; sett. Cambridge, Mass., (Christ Chh.), Mar. 1759-1765; ret. to Eng.; sett. as Vicar of Croydon, St. Mary le Bow, London, Eng., 1780-1793; Prebend, St. Paul's London, 1790; Fellow of Jesus Coll.; Epis.; d. Cambridge, Eng., Apr. 16, 1816, a. 83.

JONATHAN ARNOLD, A.M., b. Haddam, Ct., Jan. 11, 1700/1, son of Jonathan and Elizabeth Arnold; Y. C., 1723, A.B., A.M.; A.M., Oxford, 1736; Ord. West Haven, Ct., (Cong. Chh.), 1725; sett West Haven, Ct., (Cong. Chh.), 1725-1734; dism. 1734; became an Epis.; Ord. Eng., 1735; sett. West Haven, Ct. and Derby, Ct., (Epis. Chhs.), 1736-1740; sett. Staten Island, N. Y., (St. Andrew's Chh.), 1740-1745; Epis.; d. 1752.

SAMUEL ARNOLD, b. England, 1622; was at Sandwich, 1643; later lived at Yarmouth where he was Rep. Gen. Ct., 1654-1656; original proprietor at Marshfield; Ord. Marshfield, 1658; sett. Marshfield, 1657-1693; d. Marshfield, Sept. 3, 1693, a. 71.

SAMUEL ARNOLD, JR., b. Yarmouth, May 9, 1649, son of Rev. Samuel and Elizabeth Arnold; Ord. Marion (1st Chh., Rochester), Oct. 13, 1703; sett. Marion, (1st Chh., Rochtster), 1684-1707; d. Rochester, Feb. 11, 1708/9.

JONATHAN ASHLEY, JR., A.M., b. Westfield, Nov. 11, 1712, son of Lieut. Jonathan and Abigail (Stebbins) Ashley; Y. C., 1730, A.B., A.M.; Ord. Deerfield, Nov. 8, 1732; sett. Deerfield, 1729-1780; published many sermons; own cousin to Rev. Jonathan Edwards; brilliant and liberal preacher; d. Deerfield, Aug. 28, 1780, a. 67.

JOSEPH ASHLEY, A.M., b. Westfield, Oct. 11, 1709, son of Samuel and Sarah (Kellogg) Ashley; Y. C., 1730, A.B., A.M.; Ord. Winchester, N. H., Nov. 12, 1736, as first minister there; sett. Winchester, N. H., 1736-1747, until the town was broken up by the Indian menace; inst. Sunderland, Nov. 1, 1747; sett. Sunderland, 1747-1784; emeritus, 1784-1797; Tory; d. Sunderland, Feb. 8, 1797, a. 87.

HOPE ATHERTON, A.M., bapt. Dorchester, Aug. 30, 1646, son of Major-General Humphrey and Mary (Wales) Atherton; H. C., 1665, A.B.; Ord. Hatfield, Mar. 1671, as the first minister; sett. Hatfield, 1669-1677; wounded as Chaplain under the command of Capt.

William Turner, of Boston, at the Turner's Falls Fight with the Indians, May 18, 1676; d. Hatfield, June 8, 1677, a. 30.

MR. AVERY, Ord. Montville, Ct., (Chesterfield Cong. Chh.), Mar. 22, 1775; sett. Montville, Ct., 1775-1776; dism. June 25, 1776.

DAVID AVERY, A.M., b. Norwich, Ct., Apr. 5, 1746, son of John and Lydia (Smith) Avery; Y. C., 1769, A.B., A.M.; A.M. (Hon.), Dart. Coll., 1773; Ord. as missionary to the Oneida Indians, Aug. 29, 1771; inst. Windsor, Mar. 25, 1773; sett. Windsor, 1773-1777; dism. Apr. 14, 1777; Chaplain, Cont. Army, 1777, and during war; inst. Bennington, Vt., May 3, 1780; sett. Bennington, Vt., 1779-1783; dism. June 17, 1783; inst. Wrentham, Mass., May 25, 1786; sett. Wrentham, 1786-1794; dism. Apr. 21, 1794; d. Middleton, Va., Feb. 16, 1818, a. 72.

EPHRAIM AVERY, A.M., b. Truro, 1712 (bapt. Apr. 26, 1713), son of Rev. John and Ruth (Little) Avery; H. C., 1731, A.B., A.M.; Ord. Brooklyn, Ct., (2nd Chh., Pomfret), Sept. 24, 1735; sett. Brooklyn, Ct., 1735-1754; d. Brooklyn, Ct., Oct. 20, 1754, a. 42.

JOHN AVERY, A.M., b. Dedham, Feb. 4, 1685/6, son of Robert and Elizabeth (Lane) Avery; H. C., 1706, A.B., A.M.; Ord. Truro, Nov. 1, 1711; sett. Truro, 1711-1754; physician; d. Truro, Apr. 23, 1754, a. 69.

JOSEPH AVERY, A.M., b. Berks., Eng., ca. 1600; matric., Queen's Coll., Oxford, 1615, a. 15; St. Edmund Hall, Oxford, A.B., 1618; A.M., 1621; Vicar of Romsey, Hants., 1626; came to N. E., 1634; sett. Newbury, 1634-1635; had been called to Marblehead and was drowned in a storm with his wife and eight children en route from Newbury to that place; d. off Thatcher's Woe, Aug. 16, 1635.

JOSEPH AVERY, A.M., b. Dedham, Apr. 9, 1687, son of Lieut. William and Elizabeth (White) Avery; H. C., 1706, A.B., A.M.; min. at Freetown, ca. 1710; Ord. Norton, Oct. 28, 1714; sett. Norton, 1710-1749; dism. Jan. 30, 1748/9; d. Norton, Apr. 23, 1770, a. 83.

JOSEPH AVERY, A.M., b. South Parish, Dedham, Oct. 14, 1751, son of Dea. William and Bethia (Metcalf) Avery; H. C., 1771, A.B., A.M.; Ord. Holden, Dec. 21, 1774; sett. Holden, 1774-1824; liberal; d. Holden, Mar. 5, 1824, a. 74.

NATHAN AVERY, b. Groton, Ct., Mar. 10, 1712, son of Christopher and Abigail (Parke) Avery; Ord. North Stonington, Ct., (Separatist Chh.), Apr. 25, 1759; sett. North Stonington, Ct., 1759-1780; d. North Stonington, Ct., Sept. 7, 1780.

PARKE AVERY, b. Groton, Ct., Dec. 9, 1710, son of Col. Ebenezer and Dorothy (Parke) Avery; sett. Groton, Ct. (Separatist Chh.), ca. 1750-1797; deputy, 1776; moderator, town meeting, 1780, 1781; constable and surveyor, 1748; d. Groton, Ct., May 4, 1797, a. 87.

OLIVER BABCOCK, b. Westerly, R. I., July 27, 1738, son of Rev. Stephen and Anna (Thompson) Babcock; Ord. Westerly, R. I.,

Sept. 18, 1776; sett. Westerly, R. I., 1775-1784; Capt., Westerly militia, 1768-1769; Rep., 1770; J. P., 1776; Bapt.; d. Westerly, R. I., Feb. 13, 1784.

STEPHEN BABCOCK, b. Westerly, R. I., May 2, 1706, son of Capt. John and Mary (Champlin) Babcock; Ord. Westerly, R. I., (Bapt. Chh., first min.), Apr. 5, 1750; sett. Westerly, R. I., 1750-1764; sett. Westerly, R. I., (Chh. of Christ in Stonington (Ct.) and Westerly (R. I.) in Union (Bapt.)), J. P., 1735-1738; Deacon, 1742; Bapt.; d. Westerly, R. I., Dec. 22, 1775.

SAMUEL BACHELLOR, A.M., b. Reading, May 11, 1707, son of John and Sarah (Poore) Bachellor; H. C., 1731, A.B., A.M.; Ord. Haverhill, (West Parish), Nov. 3, 1735; sett. Haverhill, 1735-1761; dism. Oct. 9, 1761; Rep. Gen. Ct. from Haverhill, 1769, 1770; d. Royalston, Mar. 19, 1796, a. 90.

STEPHEN BACHILLER, A.B., b. Eng., 1561; St. John's Coll., Oxford, 1585/6, A.B.; sett. as Vicar, Chh. of the Holy Cross and St. Peter, Wherwell, Hampshire, Eng., 1587/8-1605; deprived, 1605, for Calvanistic opinions; perhaps in Holland, 1607-1620; Newton Stacey, 1622-1631; came to N. E., 1632; sett. Lynn, Aug. 1632-1636, as first minister; sett. Yarmouth, 1637; sett. Newbury, 1638; sett. Hampton, N. H., 1638-1641, as first minister; returned to Eng., ca. 1650; d. Hackney, London, Eng., ca. 1660, a. 101 yrs.

CHARLES BACKUS, D.D., b. Norwich, Ct., Oct. 25, 1749, son of Jabez and Eunice (Kingsbury) Backus; Y. C., 1769, A.B., A.M.; S.T.D., Williams, 1801; Ord. Somers, Ct., Aug. 10, 1774; sett. Somers, Ct., 1773-1801; dism. Aug. 1801; Ct. Election Sermon, 1793; d. Somers, Ct., Dec. 30, 1803, a. 55.

ISAAC BACHUS, A.M., b. Norwich, Ct., Jan. 9, 1724, son of Samuel and Elizabeth (Tracy) Bachus; Brown U., A.M., (Hon.), 1797; Trustee, Brown U., 1765-1799; Ord. Middleborough, (New Light Chh. at Titicut), Apr. 13, 1748; sett. Middleborough, (New Light Chh.), 1747-1756; inst. Middleborough, (1st Bapt. Chh. at Titicut), July 23, 1756; sett. Middleborough, (1st Bapt. Chh.), 1756-1806; agent for the Bapt. churches of Mass., 1772; membr. Cont. Congress at Phila., 1774; membr. Const. Convent. at Boston, 1788; defender of religious liberty; historian of the Bapt. Churches; Bapt.; d. Middleborough, Nov. 20, 1806, a. 83.

SIMON BACHUS, A.M., b. Norwich, Ct., Feb. 11, 1700/1, son of Joseph and Elizabeth (Huntington) Bachus; Y. C., 1724, A.B., A.M.; Ord. Newington, Ct., (2nd Chh. in Wethersfield), Jan. 25, 1727; sett. Newington, Ct., 1726-1745; Chaplain at Louisburg, Cape Breton, 1745; d. Cape Breton, Feb. 2, 1744/5, a. 45.

SIMON BACHUS, JR., A.M., b. Norwich, Ct., Feb. 13, 1737/8, son of Rev. Simon and Eunice (Edwards) Bachus; Y. C., 1759, A.B., A.M.; Ord. Granby, Oct. 28, 1762; sett. Granby, 1762-1784; dism. Mar. 3, 1784; inst. North Bristol, Ct., Oct. 13, 1790; sett. North

Bristol, Ct., 1790-1801; dism. Apr. 14, 1801; d. Stratford, Ct., Aug. 7, 1823, a. 85.

JACOB BACON, A.M., b. Wrentham, Sept. 9, 1706, son of Thomas and Hannah (Fales) Bacon; H. C., 1731, A.B., A.M.; sett. Union, Ct., 1735-1736; Ord. Keene, N. H., (Upper Ashuelot), Oct. 18, 1738; sett. Keene, N. H., 1737-1747; left. Apr. 1747, when the town was threatened by the Indians; inst. Plymouth, (3rd Chh.), 1749; sett. Plymouth, 1749-1776; sett. Carver; d. Rowley, Aug. 14, 1787, a. 81.

JOHN BACON, A.M., b. Canterbury, Ct., Apr. 9, 1738, son of Dea. John and Ruth (Spaulding) Bacon; Princeton, 1765, A.B., A.M.; A.M., (Hon.), H. C., 1771; preached at Lewes and in Somerset Co., Del.; Ord. Boston (Old South Chh.), Sept. 25, 1771; sett. Boston, 1771-1775; dism. Feb. 8, 1775; magistrate in civil life at Stockbridge; Rep. Mass. Legislature, 12 terms; Judge Ct. of Common Pleas, 1779-1807; presiding judge, 1807-1811; memb. Mass. Senate, 10 terms; Pres. Mass. Senate; Membr. of Congress, 1801-1803; Fellow, Am. Acad. Arts and Sciences; his son, Ezekiel Bacon was Treasurer of the U. S.; d. Stockbridge, Oct. 25, 1820.

MOSES BADGER, A.M., b. Haverhill, July 11, 1743, son of Joseph and Hannah (Moody) Badger; H. C., 1761, A.B., A.M.; sett. Amesbury (King George III's Chap.), 1768-1778; ordered away by the govt. for Tory principles; sett. Portsmouth, N. H. and Providence, R. I.; Epis.; d. Providence, R. I., Sept. 19, 1792.

STEPHEN BADGER, A.M., b. Charlestown, Apr. 26, 1726, son of Stephen, Jr. and Mary (Noseitor) Badger; H. C., 1747, A.B., A.M.; Librarian, H. C., 1751-1753; Ord. Natick, Mar. 27, 1753; sett. Natick, 1753-1799; Indian missionary and minister; wrote much concerning the Indians; was the "Parson Lothrop," in Mrs. Stowe's "Old Town Folks;" liberal; d. Natick, Aug. 28, 1808, a. 82.

ABNER BAILEY, A.M., b. Newbury, Jan. 15, 1715/6, son of Joshua, Jr. and Sarah (Coffin) Bailey; H. C., 1736, A.B., A.M.; Ord. Salem-New, N. H., Jan. 30, 1740; sett. Salem-New, N. H., 1740-1798; d. Salem-New, N. H., Mar. 10, 1798, a. 82.

ENOCH BAILEY, A.M., b. Newbury, Sept. 20, 1719, son of Joshua, Jr. and Sarah (Coffin) Bailey; H. C., 1742, A.B., A.M.; sett. Ipswich Farms. 1746; Chaplain, French and Indian Wars; d. Albany, N. Y., Aug. 1757, a. 38.

JACOB BAILEY, A.M., b. Rowley, Apr. 16, 1731, son of Dea. David and Mary (Hodgkins) Bailey; H. C., 1755, A.B., A.M.; Ord. by Bishop of Peterborough, Eng., Mar. 16, 1760; missionary, S.P.G.F.P.; sett. Pownalborough, Me., (St. John's Epis. Chh.), 1760-1779; removed to Halifax, N. S., June 1779; sett. Annapolis, N. S., 1782-1808; Epis.; d. Annapolis, N. S., Mar. 22, 1818.

JAMES BAILEY, A.M., b. Newbury, Sept. 12, 1650, son of John, Jr. and Eleanor (Emery) Bailey; H. C., 1669, A.B., A.M.; Ord.

Danvers, Oct. 28, 1671, as the first minister; sett. Danvers, 1671-1680; sett. Killingworth, Ct., 1682-1691; physician; d. Roxbury, June 18, 1707, a. 56.

JAMES BAILEY, JR., A.M., b. Roxbury, Mar. 22, 1697/8, son of Lieut. James and Elizabeth (Ruggles) Bailey; H. C., 1719, A.B., A.M.; Ord. South Weymouth, Sept. 26, 1723; sett. South Weymouth, 1723-1766; d. South Weymouth, Aug. 22, 1766, a. 69.

JOHN BAILEY, b. Blackburn, Lanc., Eng., Feb. 24, 1644; educ. by Dr. Harrison; sett. Chester, Eng., 1666-1670; sett. Abbey Chh., Limerick, Ire., 1670-1684; came to N. E., 1684; sett. Boston, (asst. min. Old South Chh.), 1684-1686; Ord Watertown, Oct. 6, 1686; sett. Watertown, 1686-1692; inst. Boston (1st Chh.), July 17, 1693; sett. Boston, (1st Chh.), 1693-1697; Artillery Election Sermon, 1692; his portrait is owned by the Mass. Hist. Soc.; d. Boston, Dec. 12, 1697, a. 53.

JOSIAH BAILEY, A.M., b. Newbury, Jan. 26, 1733/4, son of Edmund and Mary (Parkhurst) Bailey; H. C., 1752, A.B., A.M.; Ord. Hampton Falls, N. H., Oct. 19, 1757; sett. Hampton Falls, N. H., 1757-1762; d. Hampton Falls, N. H., Sept. 12, 1762, a. 28.

THOMAS BAILEY, younger brother of Rev. John Bailey, b. Eng., 1653; Ord. Watertown, Nov. 2, 1687; sett. Watertown, 1687-1689; d. Watertown, Jan. 31, 1688/9, a. 35.

DANIEL BAKER, A.M., b. Dedham, Apr. 18, 1686, son of John and Abigail Baker; H. C., 1706, A.B., A.M.; Ord. Sherborn, 1712; sett. Sherborn, 1710-1731; d. Sherborn, May 14, 1731, a. 46.

JAMES BAKER, A.M., b. Dorchester, Sept. 5, 1739, son of James and Priscilla Baker; H. C., 1760, A.B., A.M.; clergyman, physician, apothecary, chocolate manufacturer at Dorchester; founder of the firm of Walter Baker & Co., 1780; d. Dorchester, Jan. 2, 1825.

JOHN BAKER, lay preacher; admitted, First Chh., Boston, Mar. 26, 1642; sett. York and Saco, Me.; sett. as preacher at Dover, N. H., 1647-1650; Lieut. and Deputy to the General Court; executed at London, England.

NICHOLAS BAKER, A.M., b. Hingham, Norfolk, Eng., ca. 1610; St. John's Coll., Camb., A.B., 1631/2; A.M., 1635; came to N. E., 1635; lived at Hingham, 1635-1644; at Hull, 1644; Deputy to the Gen. Ct., 1636, 1638; Ord. Scituate, (1st Chh.), 1660; sett. Scituate, 1660-1678; d. Scituate, Aug. 22, 1678, a. 67.

THOMAS BAKER, Ord. Newport, R. I., (2nd Bapt. Chh.), 1655; sett. Newport, R. I., (2nd Bapt. Chh.), 1655-1656; removed to North Kingston, R. I.; sett. North Kingston, R. I., 1666-1710; Bapt.; d. North Kingston, R. I., ca. 1710.

BENJAMIN BALCH, A.M., b. Dedham, Feb. 12, 1743, son of Thomas and Mary (Sumner) Balch; H. C., 1763, A.B., A.M.; Ord. Blackstone, (Chestnut Hill Chh., Second Parish in Mendon), Sept. 14, 1768; sett. Blackstone, 1768-1773; left, Mar. 27, 1773; Lieut. in Rev.

War at Lexington, Apr. 19, 1775; Chaplain in the Army and Navy, Rev. War; sett. Barrington, N. H., 1784-1815; d. Barrington, N. H., May 4, 1815, a. 72.

THOMAS BALCH, A.M., b. Charlestown, Oct. 17, 1711, son of Benjamin and Mary (Prentice) Balch; H. C., 1733, A.B., A.M.; A.M., (Hon.), Y. C., 1741; Ord. Norwood, June 30, 1736; sett. Norwood, 1736-1774; Artillery Election Sermon, 1763; d. Norwood, Jan. 8, 1774, a. 62.

WILLIAM BALCH, A.M., b. Beverly, Sept. 30, 1704, son of Freeborn and Elizabeth (Fairfield) Balch; H. C., 1724, A.B., A.M.; Ord. Groveland, (2nd Chh. in Bradford), June 7, 1727; sett. Groveland, 1727-1792; Arminian in theology; Election Sermon, 1749; Convention Sermon, 1760; d. Groveland, Jan. 12, 1792.

EBENEZER BALDWIN, A.M., b. Bozrah, Ct., July 3, 1745, son of Capt. Ebenezer and Bethia (Barker) Baldwin; Y. C., 1763, A.B., A.M.; Ord. Danbury, Ct., Sept. 19, 1770; sett. Danbury, Ct., 1769-1776; Chaplain, 1776; d. in service at New York City, Oct. 1, 1776, a. 32.

MOSES BALDWIN, A.B., b. Newark, N. J., Nov. 5, 1732, son of John and Lydia (Harrison) Baldwin; Princeton, 1757, A.B. (mem. of the first class to be grad.); Ord. Palmer, June 17, 1761; sett. Palmer, 1761-1811; dism. June 19, 1811; Presb.; d. Palmer, Nov. 2, 1813, a. 81.

SAMUEL BALDWIN, A.M., b. Sudbury, Aug. 27, 1731, son of Col. David and Abigail (Jennison) Baldwin; H. C., 1752, A.B., A.M.; Ord. Hanover, Dec. 1, 1756; sett. Hanover, 1756-1780; dism. Mar. 8, 1780; d. Hanover, Dec. 1, 1784.

JOHN BALLANTINE, A.M., b. Boston, Oct. 30, 1716, son of Col. John and Mary (Winthrop) Ballantine; H. C., 1735, A.B., A.M.; Ord. Westfield, June 17, 1741; sett. Westfield, 1741-1776; d. Westfield, Feb. 12, 1776, a. 60.

WILLIAM GAY BALLANTINE, A.B., b. Westfield, ca. 1750, son of Rev. John and Mary (Gay) Ballantine; H. C., 1771, A.B.; Ord. Washington, June 15, 1774; sett. Washington, 1774-1820; d. Washington, Nov. 30, 1820.

ABNER BALLOU, b. Cumberland, R. I., Oct. 28, 1725, son of Obadiah and Damaris (Bartlett) Ballou; Ord. Cumberland, R. I., 1772; sett. Cumberland, R. I., 1775-1806; Bapt.; d. Cumberland, R. I., Jan. 4, 1806, a. 80.

BENJAMIN BALLOU, b. Smithfield, R. I., Nov. 8, 1747, son of Rev. Maturin and Lydia (Harris) Ballou; prob. not ordained; sett. Scituate, R. I. and Smithfield, R. I.; sett. Guilford, Vt., before 1771; sett. Monroe; Bapt. and Universalist; d. Monroe, Feb. 16, 1834, a. 86.

MATURIN BALLOU, b. Providence, R. I., Oct. 30, 1722, son of Peter and Rebecca (Esten) Ballou; sett. Providence, R. I., 1752-1753; sett. Pawtucket, R. I., 1754-1759; sett. Scituate, R. I., 1759-

1768; Ord. Richmond, N. H., (1st Chh., Bapt.), Sept. 27, 1770; sett. Richmond, N. H., 1770-1790; dism. Mar. 18, 1790; father of Rev. Hosea Ballou, the founder of the Universalist Chh. in America; Bapt.; d. Richmond, N. H., after Mar. 16, 1804.

JONATHAN BARBER, A.M., b. West Springfield, Jan. 31, 1712/3, son of Thomas and Sarah (Ball) Barber; Y. C., 1730, A.B., A.M.; Ord. Orient, L. I., N. Y., Nov. 10, 1757; sett. Orient, L. I., N. Y., 1735-1740; 1757; inst. Groton, Ct., (1st Chh.), Nov. 3, 1758; sett. Groton, Ct., 1758-1768; dism. Dec. 1768; d. Groton, Ct., Oct. 8, 1783, a. 71.

WILLIAM BARCLAY, sett. Quincy, (Christ Chh.), 1702; Epis.

NEHEMIAH BARKER, A.M., b. Marshfield, 1720, son of John, Jr. and Bethiah (Ford) Barker; Y. C., 1742, A.B., A.M.; Ord. South Killingly, Ct., (3rd or Breakneck Hill Chh.), 1746; sett. South Killingly, Ct., 1746-1755; sett. Southold, L. I., N. Y., (Mattituck Chh.), 1756-1772; d. Southold, L. I., N. Y., Mar. 10, 1772, a. 52.

GEORGE BARLOW, sett. Exeter, N. H., 1637; freeman, 1648; sett. Saco, Me., 1652; lay preacher; in 1653, he was forbidden to preach by the General Court, to be fined ten pounds for each offense; d. Scarborough, Me., before 1655.

EDWARD BARNARD, A.M., b. Andover, June 15, 1720, son of Rev. John and Sarah (Martyn) Barnard; H. C., 1736, A.B., A.M.; Ord. Haverhill, Apr. 16, 1743; sett. Haverhill, 1743-1774; Arminian in theology; Election Sermon, 1766; Convention Sermon, 1773; d. Haverhill, Jan. 26, 1774, a. 53.

JEREMIAH BARNARD, A.M., b. Bolton, Feb. 28, 1750; H. C., 1773, A.B., A.M.; sett Westmoreland, N. H., Apr. 1776-Nov. 1777; Ord. Amherst, N. H., Mar. 3, 1780; sett. Amherst, N. H., 1780-1835; d. Amherst, N. H., Jan. 15, 1835, a. 84.

JOHN BARNARD, A. M., b. Boston, Nov. 6, 1681, son of John and Esther (Travis) Barnard; H. C., 1700, A.B., A.M.; sett. Boston, (asst. min., Brattle St. Chh.), 1705; Chaplain, Annapolis, Canada, 1707; Chaplain, Ship "Lusitania," 1709; visited Eng. 1709-10; Ord. Marblehead, (1st Chh.), July 18, 1716; sett. Marblehead, 1715-1770; Artillery Election Sermon, 1718; Election Sermon, 1734; Convention Sermon, 1738; Dudleian Lecture, 1756; d. Marblehead, Jan. 24, 1770, a 89, s.p.

JOHN BARNARD, A.M., b. Andover, Feb. 26, 1689/90, son of Rev. Thomas and Elizabeth (Price) Barnard; H. C., 1709, A.B., A.M.; taught school at Boston, 1713-1718/19; Ord. Andover, (1st Chh.), Apr. 8, 1719; sett. Andover, 1718-1757; Election Sermon, 1746; Convention Sermon, 1749; d. Andover, June 14, 1757, a. 67.

THOMAS BARNARD, A.M., b. Hartford, Ct., 1658, son of Francis and Hannah (Marvin) Barnard of Hadley; H. C., 1679, A.B.,

A.M.; teacher at Roxbury, 1680-1682; Ord. Andover, Mar. 1682; sett. Andover, 1682-1718; d. Andover, Oct. 12, 1718, a. 60.

THOMAS BARNARD, A.M., b. Andover, Aug. 17, 1716, son of Rev. John and Sarah (Martyn) Barnard; H. C., 1732, A.B., A.M.; Ord. West Newbury, (1st Chh.), Jan. 31, 1738/9; sett. West Newbury, 1739-1752; dism. Jan. 12, 1751/2; inst. Salem, (1st Chh.), Sept. 18, 1755; sett. Salem, 1755-1776; Arminian in theology; Rep. Gen. Ct., 1755; Artillery Election Sermon, 1758; Election Sermon, 1763; Dudleian Lecture, 1768; d. Salem, Aug. 15, 1776, a. 60.

THOMAS BARNARD, D.D., b. Newbury, Feb. 5, 1748, son of Rev. Thomas and Mary Barnard; H. C., 1766, A.B., A.M.; S.T.D., U. of Edinburgh, 1794; S.T.D., Brown U., 1794; Ord. Salem, (North Chh.), June 13, 1773; sett. Salem, 1773-1814; Artillery Election Sermon, 1789; Convention Sermon, 1793; Dudleian Lecture, 1795; liberal; Unitarian; Fellow, Am. Acad.; d. Salem, Oct. 1, 1814, a. 67.

DAVID BARNES, D.D., b. Marlborough, Mar. 24, 1731, son of Daniel and Zeruiah (Eager) Barnes; H. C., 1752, A.B., A.M.; S.T.D., 1799; Ord. Norwell, (2nd Chh. in Scituate), Dec. 4, 1754; sett. Norwell, 1754-1811; Dudleian Lecture, 1780; Unitarian; d. Norwell, Apr. 26, 1811, a. 80.

JONATHAN BARNES, A.M., b. Marlborough, Nov. 6, 1749, son of Jonathan and Rachel Barnes; H. C., 1770, A.B., A.M.; Ord. Hillsborough, N. H., Nov. 25, 1772, as the first minister; sett. Hillsborough, N. H., 1772-1803; struck by lightning, 1803; dism. Oct. 20, 1803; Arminian; d. Hillsborough, N. H., Aug. 3, 1805, a. 55.

THOMAS BARNES, came to Swansea as early as 1669; Ord. Swansea, (2nd Bapt. Chh.), 1693; sett. Swansea, 1693-1706; Bapt.; d. Swansea, June 8, 1706.

THOMAS BARNETT, b. Eng.; ejected for non-conformity, 1662; sett. New London, Ct., 1685-1686; perhaps d. soon.

JACOB BARNEY, b. England, son of Jacob and Elizabeth Barney; founder of Baptist churches at Charlestown, Swansea, and at Boston, 1668; dwelt at Salem, removed to Bristol, R. I., and Rehoboth, ca. 1673; Freeman at Salem, May 14, 1634; deputy, 1635, 1647; opposed the sentence of the Gen. Ct. against those who petitioned for freer franchise; Bapt.; d. Rehoboth; will dated July 30, 1690; probated Jan. 10, 1690/1.

CALEB BARNUM, A.M., b. Danbury, Ct., June 30, 1737, son of Thomas and Deborah Barnum; Princeton, 1757, A.B.; A. M., 1768; A.M., (Hon.), H. C., 1768; Ord. Franklin, June 4, 1760; sett. Franklin, 1760-1768; dism. Mar. 6, 1768; inst. Taunton, (1st Chh.), Feb. 2, 1769; sett. Taunton, 1768-1776; Chaplain, Am. Rev., 1775-1776; ill at Ticonderoga and died on his way home; d. Pittsfield, Aug. 23, 1776, a. 39.

SAMUEL BARRETT, JR., A.M., b. Boston, Dec. 1, 1700, son of Samuel and Sarah (Manning) Barrett; H. C., 1721, A.B., A.M.;

Ord. Hopkinton, Sept. 2, 1724; sett. Hopkinton, 1724-1772; d. Hopkinton, Dec. 11, 1772, a. 72.

JEREMIAH BARSTOW, b. July 5, 1727; inst. Sutton, (2nd Bapt. Chh.), May 26, 1768; sett. Sutton, 1768-1772; dism. Oct. 1, 1772; Bapt.; d. Thompson, Ct., June 4, 1795.

ANDREW BARTHOLOMEW, A.M., b. Branford, Ct., Nov. 7, 1714, son of Andrew and Hannah (Frisbie) Bartholomew; Y. C., 1731, A.B., A.M.; Ord. Harwinton, Ct., Oct. 4, 1738; sett. Harwinton, Ct., 1737-1774; dism. Jan. 26, 1774; d. Harwinton, Ct., Mar. 6, 1776.

MOSES BARTLETT, A.M., b. Madison, Ct., Feb. 8, 1707/8, son of William and Hannah (Evarts) Bartlett; Y. C., 1730, A.B., A.M.; Ord. Portland, Ct., (3rd Chh. of Middletown), June 6, 1733; sett. Portland Ct., 1733-1766; d. Portland, Ct., Dec. 27, 1766, a. 59.

NATHANIEL BARTLETT, A.M., b. Guilford, Ct., Apr. 22, 1727, son of Daniel and Ann (Collins) Bartlett; Y. C., 1749, A.B., A.M.; Ord. Redding, Ct., May 23, 1753; sett. Redding, Ct., 1753-1810; d. Redding, Ct., Jan. 11, 1810, a. 83.

AARON BASCOM, A.M., b. Warren (Western), Dec. 1, 1746, son of Lieut. Samuel and Mary Bascom; H. C., 1768, A.B., A.M.; Ord. Chester, Dec. 20, 1769; sett. Chester, 1769-1814; d. Chester, May 19, 1814, a. 68.

JONATHAN BASCOM, A.B., b. Lebanon, Ct., Sept. 14, 1740, son of Ens. Daniel and Elizabeth (French) Bascom; Y. C., 1764, A.B.; Ord. Orleans, Oct. 14, 1772; sett. Orleans, 1772-1807; d. Orleans, Mar. 18, 1807, a. 67.

BENJAMIN BASS, A.M., b. Braintree, Dec. 19, 1694, son of Joseph and Mary (Belcher) Bass; H. C., 1715, A.B., A.M.; Ord. Hanover, Dec. 11, 1728; sett. Hanover, 1728-1756; d. Hanover, May 23, 1756, a. 63.

BISHOP EDWARD BASS, D.D., b. Dorchester, Nov. 23, 1726, son of Joseph and Elizabeth (Breck) Bass; H. C., 1744, A.B., A.M.; S.T.D., U. of Penna., 1789; Ord. Fulham, Eng., May 24, 1752; sett. Newbury, (Queen Anne's Chapel), 1752-1766; sett. Newburyport, (St. Paul's Chh.), 1751-1803; Episcopal Bishop of Mass., N. H., and R. I., May 7, 1797-1803; d. Newburyport, Sept. 10, 1803, a. 77, s. p.

JOHN BASS, A.M., b. Braintree, Mar. 26, 1717, son of John and Hannah Bass; H. C., 1737, A.B., A.M.; Ord. Ashford, Ct., Sept. 7, 1743; sett. Ashford, Ct., 1743-1751; dism. June 5, 1751; sett, Providence, R. I., (1st Cong. Chh.), 1752-1758; physician; d. Providence, R. I., Oct. 24, 1762.

JEREMIAH BASSETT, b. Bridgewater, 1678, son of Joseph and Mary (Lapham) Bassett; removed to Norton, 1713, where he became the first schoolmaster; sett. as minister at Taunton, (1st Bapt. Chh.), 1744-1768; Bapt.; d. Taunton, July 29, 1768, a. 90.

JOSEPH BAXTER, A.M., b. Braintree, June 4, 1676, son of Lieut. John and Hannah (White) Baxter; H. C., 1693, A.B., A.M.; Ord. Medfield, Apr. 21, 1697; sett. Medfield, 1694-1745; Artillery Election Sermon, 1716; Election Sermon, 1727; d. Medfield, May 2, 1745, a. 69.

BENJAMIN BEACH; minister of a Separatist Chh. at Prospect, Ct., 1770-1780.

JOHN BEACH, A.M., b. Stratford, Ct., Oct. 6, 1700, son of Isaac and Hannah (Birdseye) Beach; Y. C., 1721, A.B., A.M.; Ord. Newtown, Ct., (Cong. Chh.), Jan. 25, 1725; sett. Newtown, Ct., (Cong. Chh.), 1724-1732; dism. Feb. 2, 1731/2; Ord. London, Eng., (Epis.), 1732; sett. Newtown, Ct., (Epis. Chh.), 1732-1782; sett. Redding, Ct., (Epis. Chh.), 1732-1782; Cong.; Epis.; d. Newtown, Ct., Mar. 19, 1782, a. 82.

JOSEPH BEAN, A.M., b. Boston, Apr. 16, 1716 son of Joseph and Hannah (Needham) Bean; H. C., 1748, A.B., A.M.; Ord. Wrentham, Dec. 5, 1750; sett. Wrentham, 1750-1784; Century Sermon, 1773; d. Wrentham, Dec. 12, 1784, a. 68.

GEORGE BECKWITH, A.M., b. Lyme, Ct., 1703, son of Matthew Beckwith, Jr.; Y. C., 1728, A.B., A.M.; Fellow, 1763-1777; Ord. Lyme, Ct., (Third, North or Hamburg parish), Jan. 22, 1729/30; sett. Lyme, Ct., 1730-1794; Chaplain at Crown Point, 1755, 1758; Ct. Election Sermon, 1756; d. Lyme, Ct., Dec. 26, 1794, a. 92.

GEORGE BECKWITH, JR., A.M., b. Lyme, Ct., 1747, son of Rev. George and Sarah (Brown) Beckwith; Y. C., 1765, A.B., A.M.; sett. Wyoming, Pa., 1769-1770; Ord. Litchfield South Farms, (Morris, Ct.), Oct. 22, 1772; sett. Morris, Ct., 1772-1781; physician; d. Triangle, N. Y., Oct. 1824, a. 77.

JAMES BECKWITH, Ord. Montville, Ct., (Chesterfield Chh.), Oct. 1768; sett. Montville, Ct., 1768-1772.

JAMES BEEBE, A.M., b. Danbury, Ct., 1717 or 1718, son of Capt. James Beebe; Y. C., 1745, A.B., A.M.; Ord. Trumbull, Ct., (North Stratford), May 6, 1747; sett. Trumbull, Ct., 1747-1785; d. Trumbull, Ct., Sept. 8, 1785, a. 68.

JOSEPH BELCHER, A.M., b. Milton, May 14, 1669, son of Quartermaster Joseph and Rebecca (Gill) Belcher; H. C., 1690, A.B., A.M.; Ord. Dedham, Nov. 29, 1693; sett. Dedham, 1693-1721; Artillery Election Sermon, 1698; Election Sermon, 1701; his portrait in oils hangs in the First Church, Dedham; d. Roxbury, Apr. 27, 1723, a. 53.

JOSEPH BELCHER, A.M., b. Braintree, Aug. 19, 1704, son of Dea. Gregory and Elizabeth (Ruggles) Belcher; H. C., 1723, A.B., A.M.; called to Walpole, May 17, 1728; dism. May 5, 1729; Ord. Easton, Oct. 6, 1731; sett. Easton, 1731-1744; dism. Apr. 16, 1744; d. 1773.

SAMUEL BELCHER, A.B., b. Ipswich, 1639, son of Jeremy

Belcher; H. C., 1659, A.B.; sett. Isles of Shoals, N. H., 1660-1692; Ord. West Newbury, (First Chh.), Nov. 10, 1698; sett. West Newbury, 1695-1711; Election Sermon, 1707; d. Ipswich, Mar. 10, 1714/5, a. 74.

JOSHUA BELDEN, A.M., b. Wethersfield, Ct., July 19, 1724, son of Silas and Abigail (Robbins) Belden; Y. C., 1743, A.B., A.M.; Ord. Newington, Ct., (2nd Parish in Wethersfield), Nov. 11, 1747; sett. Newington, Ct., 1747-1803; retired 1803; d. Newington, Ct., July 23, 1813, a. 89.

JOSEPH BELLAMY, D.D., b. New Cheshire, Ct., Feb. 20, 1718/9, son of Matthew and Sarah (Wood) Bellamy; Y. C., 1735, A.B., A.M.; D.D., U. of Aberdeen, 1768; Ord. Bethlehem, Ct., (Woodbury), Apr. 2, 1740; sett. Bethlehem, Ct., 1740-1790; much of this time he travelled as an itinerant missionary; Ct. Election Sermon, 1762; d. Bethlehem, Ct., Mar. 6, 1790, a. 72.

JEREMY BELKNAP, D.D., b. Boston, June 4, 1744, son of Joseph and Sarah (Byles) Belknap; H. C., 1762, A. B., A.M.; S.T.D., 1792; Ord. Dover, N. H., Feb 18, 1767; sett Dover, N. H., 1767-1786; dism. Sept. 11, 1786; inst. Boston, (Federal St. Chh., now the Arlington St. Chh., Unitarian), Apr. 4, 1787; sett. Boston, 1787-1798; Clerk of the Convention of Congregational Ministers, 1769-1774; published a History of N. H.; N. H. Election Sermon, 1785; Dudleian Lecture, 1790; Convention Sermon, 1796; Founder, Mass. Hist. Soc.; member Am. Acad. Arts & Sciences; member Am. Phil. Soc.; d. Boston, June 20, 1798, a. 54.

ABNER BENEDICT, A.M., b. North Salem, N. Y., Nov. 9, 1740, son of Dea. Peter and Agnes (Tyler) Benedict; Y. C., 1769, A.B., A.M.; Ord. Middlefield, Ct., Nov. 28, 1771; sett. Middlefield, Ct., 1771-1785; inst. New Lebanon Springs, N. Y., June 8, 1786; sett. New Lebanon Springs, N. Y., 1786-1791; sett. West Chester, N. Y., (Presb. Chh.), 1792-1801; sett. North Stamford, N. Y., (Cong. Chh.), 1794-1795; supplied, 1796-1818; Chaplain, 1776; d. Roxbury, N. Y., Nov. 19, 1818, a. 78.

JOEL BENEDICT, D.D., b. North Salem, N. Y., Jan. 8, 1745, son of Dea. Peter and Agnes (Tyler) Benedict; Princeton, 1765, A.B.; A.M., 1768; S.T.D., Union Coll., 1808; S.T.D., Dart. Coll., 1814; sett. Newcastle, Me., 1770; Ord. Lisbon, Ct., (Newent), Feb. 21, 1771; sett. Lisbon, Ct., 1771-1782; dism. Apr. 30, 1782; inst. Plainfield, Ct., Dec. 21, 1784; sett. Plainfield, Ct., 1784-1816; d. Plainfield, Ct., Feb. 13, 1816.

NOAH BENEDICT, A.M., b. Danbury, Ct., May 25, 1737, son of Capt. Daniel and Sarah (Hickok) Benedict; Princeton, 1757, A.B.; A.M., (Hon.), Y. C., 1760; Fellow, Y. C., 1801-1812; Ord. Woodbury, Ct., (First Chh.), Oct. 22, 1760; sett. Woodbury, Ct., 1760-1813; Chaplain, 13th Ct. Regt., 1795-1812; d. Woodbury, Ct., Apr. 20, 1813, a. 76.

BISHOP GEORGE BERKELEY, D.D., b. Kilkrin, Ireland, Mar. 12, 1684, son of William Berkeley; Trinity Coll., Dublin, A.B.; Fellow, 1707-1724; D.D., 1717; Chaplain to the Lord Lieut. of Ireland, 1721; Dean of Derry, 1724; resided at Newport, R. I., 1729-1731; Bishop of Cloyne, 1734-1752; eminent philosopher; Epis.; d. Oxford, Eng., Jan. 14, 1753.

RICHARD BERNARD, A.B., b. Epworth, Lincolnshire, England, 1567, son of John Bernard; Christ Coll., Camb., 1594/5, A. B.; Vicar of Worksop, Nottinghamshire, England, 1601-1613/4; Rector at Batcombe, Somersetshire, 1613/4-1624; sett. Weymouth, Mass. Bay Colony, 1624-1635; returned to England, 1635; Rector at Batcombe, Somersetshire, 1635-1641; conformable Puritan opposed to total separation of church and state; d. Batcombe, Somersetshire, England, March, 1641.

DAVID BETHUNE, sett. Newport, R. I., (Trinity Chh.), Oct. 1700-1701; Epis.

ADONIJAH BIDWELL, A.M., b. Hartford, Ct., Oct. 18, 1716, son of Thomas and Prudence (Scott) Bidwell; Y. C., 1740, A.B., A.M.; Ord. Oct. 5, 1744; Naval Chaplain, 1744; under Sir William Pepperell, 1745, at the capture of Cape Breton; teacher, 1746-1749; inst. Monterey, (Tyringham), Oct. 3, 1750; sett. Monterey, 1750-1784; d. Monterey, June 2, 1784.

JACOB BIGELOW, A.M., b. Waltham, Feb. 19, 1742/3, son of Jacob and Susanna (Mead) Bigelow; H. C., 1766, A.B., A.M.; Ord. Sudbury, Nov. 11, 1772; sett. Sudbury, 1772-1814; retired, June 1, 1814; d. Sudbury, Sept. 12, 1816, a. 73.

SAMUEL BIGELOW, bapt. Watertown, May 28, 1738, (son of Ebenezer and Hannah (Brown) Bigelow): Ord. New Salem, May 21, 1772; sett. New Salem, (Bapt. Chh.), 1772-1790; Bapt.

SILAS BIGELOW, A.M., b. Shrewsbury, Oct. 10, 1739, son of Samuel, Jr. and Jedidah (Hathorn) Bigelow; H. C., 1765, A.B., A.M.; Ord. Paxton, Oct. 21, 1767; sett. Paxton, 1767-1769; d. Paxton, Nov. 16, 1769, a. 30.

EDWARD BILLINGS, A.M., b. Sunderland, Aug. 10, 1707, son of Ebenezer and Hannah (Church) Billings; H. C., 1731, A.B., A.M.; Ord. Belchertown, Apr. 1739; sett. Belchertown, 1739-1752; sett. Greenfield, 1754-1757; d. Greenfield, 1760.

RICHARD BILLINGS, A.M., b. Dorchester, Sept. 21, 1675, son of Capt. Ebenezer and Hannah (Wales) Billings; H. C., 1698, A.B., A.M.; Ord. Little Compton, R.I., Nov. 30, 1704; sett. Little Compton, R. I., as first min., 1704-1748; preached also to the Indians; physician; d. Little Compton, R. I., Nov. 20, 1748.

WILLIAM BILLINGS, A.M., b. Preston, Ct., Feb. 15, 1696/7, son of Capt. William and Hannah (Sterry) Billings; Y. C., 1720, A.B., A.M.; Ord. Hampton, Ct., (2nd Chh., Windham), June 5, 1723 as

THE REVEREND JOHN COTTON (?) (1585-1652)
*Reproduced from the portrait owned by
the Connecticut Historical Society*

King's Chapel, Boston
1686

the first minister; sett. Hampton, Ct., 1723-1733; d. Hampton, Ct., May 20, 1733.

JONATHAN BIRD, A.M., b. Avon, Ct., Mar. 6, 1746/7, son of Jonathan and Hannah (Thompson) Bird; Y. C., 1768, A.B., A.M.; sett. Berlin, Ct., 1775-1780; sett. Canaan, Ct., 1789-1790; sett. Conway, Mass; physician and preacher; not ordained; d. Hebron, Ct., Oct. 22, 1813, a. 67.

SAMUEL BIRD, b. Dorchester, Mar. 27, 1724, son of Benjamin and Johannah (Harris) Bird; H. C., class of 1744, but did not grad.; Ord. Dunstable, (New Light Chh.), Aug. 31, 1747; sett. Dunstable, 1747-1751; inst. New Haven, Ct., (White Haven Chh.), Oct. 13, 1751; sett. New Haven, 1751-1768; dism. Jan. 19, 1768, because of ill health; Chaplain, French and Indian War, 1755; d. New Haven, Ct., May 3, 1784, a. 60.

NATHAN BIRDSEYE, A.M., b. Stratford, Ct., Aug. 19, 1714, son of Joseph and Sarah (Thompson) Birdseye; Y. C., 1736, A.B., A.M.; Ord. West Haven, Ct., Oct. 12, 1742; sett. West Haven, Ct., 1742-1758; dism. June 1758; farmer; d. Stratford, Ct., Jan. 22, 1818, a. 103 yrs.

JOHN BISHOP, A.M., (son of William Bishop of Holway, Dorset, b. 1612; A.B., Balliol Coll., Oxford, 1632; A.M., 1635; Rector of Batcombe, Dorset, 1636?); sett. Taunton, 1640; went on foot from Boston to Stamford, Ct., 1644; sett. Stamford, Ct., 1644-1694; d. Stamford, Ct., (will made Nov. 16), 1694.

HEZEKIAH BISSELL, A.M., b. East Windsor, Ct., Jan. 30, 1710/11, son of Sergt. David and Ruth (Warner) Bissell; Y. C., 1733, A.B., A.M.; Ord. Bloomfield, Ct., (Wintonbury), Feb. 15, 1737/8; sett. Bloomfield, Ct., as first minister, 1737-1783; d. Wintonbury, Ct., Jan. 28, 1783, a. 72.

GEORGE BISSET, educated in England; came from England to Newport, 1767; ass't. min. and schoolmaster; inst. Newport, R. I., (Trinity Chh.), Oct. 28, 1771; sett. Newport, R. I., (Trinity Chh.), 1767-1779; left, Oct. 25, 1779; resided, N. Y. City, 1779-1784; resided, London, Eng., 1784-1786; sett. St. John's, N. B., 1786-1788; Epis.; d. St. John's, N. B., Mar. 3, 1788.

WILLIAM BLACKSTONE, A.M., bapt. Horncastle, Lincolnshire, Eng., Mar. 5, 1595/6; son of John and Agnes (Hawley) Blaxton; Emmanuel Coll., Camb., A.B., 1617/8; A.M., 1621; Ord. by the Bishop of Peterborough, May 23, 1619; came to N. E., 1623; sett. Weymouth, 1623-1625; lived as a literary hermit on the site of the present city of Boston, 1625; afterwards, for 25 years, near what is now known as the Blackstone River; left a large library; Epis.; d. Pawtucket, R. I., May 26, 1675. [buried Rehoboth, Mass., May 28, 1675].

CHRISTOPHER BLACKWOOD, A.M., b. Yorkshire, England, ca, 1608, son of William Blackwood; Pembroke Coll., Camb., 1624/5, A.B., A.M.; Ord. London, Eng., June 8, 1628; Vicar of

Stockbury, Kent., 1631; came to N. E., 1640; sett. Scituate, 1641-1642, as the successor of Rev. John Lothrop; returned to England, 1642; d. Dublin, Ireland, ca. 1670, where his will was probated.

SAMEL BLAIR, D.D., b. Fogg's Manor, Chester Co., Pa., 1741, son of Rev. Samuel Blair; Princeton, 1760, A.B., A.M.; Tutor, 1761-1764; A.M., (Hon.), H. C., 1767; S.T.D., U. of Penna., 1790; inst. Boston, (Old South Chh.), Nov. 26, 1766; sett. Boston, 1766-1769; dism. Oct. 10, 1769; membr. Am. Phil. Soc.; Chaplain, Continental Congress, 2 yrs.; d. Germantown, Pa., Sept., 1818, a. 78.

JAMES BLAKE, A.B., b. Dorchester, Dec. 10, 1750, son of Samuel and Patience (White) Blake; H. C., 1769, A.B.; supplied at Weymouth, (First Chh.), 1769-1771; "a young man of rare excellence and promise"; d. Dorchester, Nov. 17, 1771, a 21.

ADAM BLAKEMAN, b. Staffordshire, Eng., 1599; matric. Christ Church Coll., Oxford, May 28, 1617, a. 19 yrs.; preached in Leicestershire and Derbyshire; came to N. E., 1638; sett. Stratford, Ct., June 1640-1665, as the first minister; d. Stratford, Ct., Sept. 7, 1665.

BENJAMIN BLAKEMAN, A.B., b. Stratford, Ct., ca. 1643, son of Rev. Adam and Jane Blakeman; H. C., 1663, A.B.; Ord. Malden, 1674; sett. Malden, (colleague), 1674-1679; Scarborough, Me., Rep. Gen. Ct., 1682; Saco, Me., Rep. Gen. Ct., 1683; d. Boston, 1688-1700.

RICHARD BLINMAN, A.B., bapt. Chepstowe, Co. Monmouth, Wales, Feb. 2, 1608; son of William and Jane (Morgan) Blinman; matric. New Inn Hall, Oxford, Apr. 24, 1635; A.B., 1635/6; came to N. E., 1640; sett. Marshfield, 1641-1642, as the first minister; sett. Gloucester, 1642-1648, as the first minister; sett. New London, Ct., 1650-1657; sett. New Haven, Ct., 1657-1658; sett. Newfoundland, 1659; returned to Bristol, Eng., where he died between Apr. 13 and July 26, 1687.

DANIEL BLISS, A.M., b. Springfield, June 21, 1715, son of Thomas and Hannah (Cadwell) Bliss; Y. C., 1732, A.B., A.M.; A.M., (Hon.), H. C., 1738; Ord. Concord, Mar. 7, 1739; sett. Concord, 1738-1764; d. Concord, May 11, 1764, a. 50.

JOHN BLISS, A.M., b. Norwich, Ct., Oct. 23, 1690, son of Samuel and Ann (Elderkin) Bliss; Y. C., 1710, A.B., A.M.; Ord. Hebron, Ct., (Cong. Chh.), Nov. 19, 1717, as the first minister; sett. Hebron, Ct., (Cong. Chh.), 1714-1734; sett. Hebron, Ct., (Epis. Chh.), 1735-1742; Epis.; d. Hebron, Ct., Feb. 1, 1741/2, a. 51.

JOHN BLISS, A.M., b. Longmeadow, June 6, 1736, son of Ebenezer and Joanna (Lamb) Bliss; Y. C., 1761, A.B., A.M.; Ord. Ellington, Ct., Oct. 9, 1765; sett. Ellington, Ct., 1765-1780; dism. Dec. 1780; d. Ellington, Ct., Feb. 12, 1790, a. 54.

ABRAHAM BLOSS, (possibly b. Barnstable, Feb. 27, 1680/1, son of Joseph and Hannah (Hull) Bloss), Ord. Upton, (First Bapt. Chh.), 1751; sett. North Attleborough, (Bapt. Chh.), 1767-1769;

Bapt.; (name spelled Bloise and Boise); d. North Attleborough, Sept. 16, 1769.

THOMAS BLOWERS, A.M., b. Cambridge, Aug. 1, 1677, son of Pyam and Elizabeth (Belcher) Blowers; H. C., 1695, A.B., A.M.; Ord. Beverly, Oct. 29, 1701; sett. Beverly, 1701-1729; Artillery Election Sermon, 1717; d. Beverly, June 17, 1729, a. 52.

JOHN BLUNT, A.M., b. Andover, 1706/7, son of William and Sarah (Foster) Blunt; H. C., 1727, A.B., A.M.; Ord. Newcastle, N. H., Dec. 20, 1732; sett. Newcastle, N. H., 1732-1747; d. Newcastle, N. H., Aug. 7, 1748, a. 42.

JOHN BLUNT, Ord. Sturbridge, (Separatist Chh.), Sept. 28, 1748; sett. Sturbridge, 1747-1749; sett. Sturbridge, (Bapt. Chh.), 1750-1755; an unlettered but sincere and able preacher; Bapt.; killed at the battle of Lake George, Sept. 8, 1755.

ANDREW BOARDMAN, A.M., bapt. Cambridge, Feb. 20, 1720/1, son of Capt. Moses and Abigail (Hastings) Boardman; H. C., 1737, A.B., A.M.; Ord. Chilmark, Sept. 1746; sett. Chilmark, 1746-1776; d. Chilmark, Nov. 19, 1776, of small pox.

BENJAMIN BOARDMAN, A.M., b. Glastonbury, Ct., Aug. 3, 1731, son of Edward and Dorothy (Smith) Boardman; Y. C., 1758, A.B., A.M.; Tutor, Y. C., 1760-1761; Ord. Haddam, Ct., Jan. 5, 1762; sett. Haddam, Ct., 1762-1783; dism. Sept. 1783; inst. Hartford, Ct., (South Chh.), May 5, 1784; sett. Hartford, Ct., 1784-1789; Chaplain, Rev. War, 1775-1776; d. Hartford, Ct., Feb. 12, 1802, a. 70.

DANIEL BOARDMAN, A.M., b. Wethersfield, Ct., July 12, 1687, son of Daniel and Hannah (Wright) Boardman; Y. C., 1709, A.B., A.M.; Ord. New Milford, Ct., Nov. 21, 1716; sett. New Milford, Ct., 1712-1744; d. New Milford, Ct., Sept. 25, 1744, a. 57.

DANIEL BONDET, b. of a noble French family, his mother being dau. of Philippe de Nautonnier, Sieur de Castelfranc; Professor at Saumur, France; sett. Oxford, (Huguenot Chh.), 1686-1696; sett. New Rochelle, N. Y., (French Protestant Chh.), 1697-1722; preached in three languages: English, French and the Indian tongue; d. New Rochelle, N. Y., 1722.

DAVID de BONREPOS, sett. Boston, (Huguenot Chh.), 1687-1689; sett. New Rochelle, N. Y., (French Protestant Chh.), 1689-1696; sett. New Paltz, N. Y., 1696-1700; sett. Fresh Kill, Staten Island, 1696-1717; d. Staten Island, N. Y., 1734.

AARON JORDON BOOGE, A.M., b. West Avon, Ct., May 6, 1752, son of Rev. Ebenezer and Damaris (Cook) Booge; Y. C., 1774, A.B., A.M.; Ord. East Granby, Ct., (Turkey Hills Parish), Nov. 27, 1776, as the first minister; sett. East Granby, Ct., 1776 (Spring)-1785; dism. Dec. 8, 1785; inst. West Granville, Mass., Nov. 17, 1786; sett. West Granville, 1786-1793; dism. July 1793; sett. Stephentown, N. Y., (Presb. Chh.), Nov. 1800-Jan. 1809; Chaplain, U.S.A., 1812-1818; d. New Lebanon, N. Y., Jan. 22, 1826, a. 75.

EBENEZER BOOGE, A.M., b. East Haddam, Ct., May 9, 1716, son of John and Rebecca (Walkley) Booge; Y. C., 1748, A.B., A.M.; Ord. West Avon, Ct., (5th Chh. in Farmington), Nov. 27, 1751, as the first minister; sett. West Avon, Ct., 1751-1767; d. Northington, Ct., Feb. 2, 1767, a. 51.

ROBERT BOOTHE, b. England ca. 1602; at Exeter, N. H., 1645; lay preacher at Biddeford, Me., July 5, 1653-1659; magistrate, selectman, town clerk; sett Wells, Cape Porpus and Saco, Me.; d. Saco, Me., Oct. 26, 1672.

JOEL BORDWELL, A.M., b. Deerfield, Oct. 10, 1732, son of Samuel and Martha (Allen) Bordwell; Y. C., 1756, A.B., A.M.; Ord. Kent, Ct., Oct. 8, 1758; sett. Kent, Ct., 1758-1811; d. Kent, Ct., Dec. 6, 1811, a. 80.

WILLIAM BOSSON, A.M.; H. C., 1723, A.B., A.M.: lived at Roxbury; Chaplain at Castle William for many years; d. 1748.

EPHRIAM BOSTWICK, A.M., b. Stratford, Ct., 1706, son of Zechariah and Elizabeth Bostwick; Y. C.. 1729, A.B., A.M.; Ord. Greenwich, Ct., (First Chh.), Oct. 8, 1735; sett. Greenwich, Ct., 1730-1746; d. Stamford, Ct., Mar. 1755.

GIDEON BOSTWICK, A.M., b. New Milford, Ct., Sept. 21, 1742, son of Capt. Nathaniel and Esther (Hitchcock) Bostwick; Y. C., 1762, A.B., A.M.; teacher at Great Barrington, 1763; Ord. London, Eng., Mar. 11, 1770; sett. Great Barrington, (St. James' Chh.), as Rector, June 1770-1793; sett. Lanesborough, (St. Luke's Chh.), 1770-1793; Royalist; Epis.; d. New Milford, Ct., June 13, 1793, a. 50.

EPHRIAM BOUND, b. ca. 1719, son of James Bound, an Englishman, who with six others formed the Second Baptist Chh. in Boston; Ord. Warwick, R. I., Sept. 7, 1743; sett. Boston, (2nd Bapt. Chh.), 1743-1765; d. Boston, June 18, 1765, a. 46.

HON. EZRA BOURNE, b. Sandwich, Aug. 6, 1676, son of Shearjashub, Esq. and Bathsheba (Skiff) Bourne; Indian missionary at Mashpee; probably not ordained; Judge and Chief Justice, Court of Common Pleas, Barnstable Co.; d. Mashpee, Sept. 1764, a. 88.

JOSEPH BOURNE, A.M., b. Sandwich, May 10, 1701, son of Hon. Ezra and Martha (Prince) Bourne; H. C., 1722, A.B., A.M.; Ord. Mashpee, (Indian Chh.), Nov. 26, 1729; sett. Mashpee, 1729-1742; d. 1767, a. 66, s. p.

RICHARD BOURNE, b. Devonshire, Eng., ca. 1610, son of William and Ursula (Day) Bourne; was in Scituate, N. E., 1630; Sandwich, 1641, where he was Dep. Gen. Ct. and membr. of the Council of War, 1675; he obtained a deed of the township of Mashpee, which he reserved for the sole use of the Indians; Ord. over the Indian Chh. at Mashpee, as the first minister, by Eliot and Cotton, 1670; sett. Mashpee, 1670-1682; d. Mashpee, 1682.

SHEARJASHUB BOURNE, A.M., b. Sandwich, Dec. 21, 1699, son of Melatiah, Esq. and Desire (Chipman) Bourne; H. C., 1720,

A.B., A.M.; Ord. Scituate, (1st Chh.), Dec. 3, 1724; sett. Scituate, 1724-1761; dism. Aug. 6, 1761; d. Roxbury, Aug. 14, 1768, a. 69.

PETER BOURS, A.M., b. Newport, R. I., 1726, son of the Hon. Peter, Esq. and Ann (Fairchild) Bours; H. C., 1747, A.B., A.M.; sett. Marblehead, (St. Michael's Chh.), 1753-1762; Epis.; d. Marblehead, Feb. 24, 1762, a. 36.

PENUEL BOWEN, A.M., b. Woodstock, Ct., June 28, 1742, son of Penuel and Frances (Davis) Bowen; H. C., 1762, A.B., A.M.; Ord. Boston, (New South Chh.), Apr. 30, 1766; sett. Boston, 1766-1772; left May 19, 1772; then became an Epis.; Rector, St. John's Chh., Colleton, John's Island, S. C., 1787; d. Colleton, S. C., Oct. 26, 1788.

BENJAMIN BOWERS, A.M., b. Chelmsford, 1713, son of Capt. Jonathan and Hannah (Barrett) Bowers; H. C., 1733, A.B., A.M.; Ord. Haddam, Ct., Sept. 14, 1740; sett. Haddam, Ct., (Chh. at Haddam Neck), 1740-1761; d. Haddam, Ct., May 16, 1761.

JOHN BOWERS, A.B., b. Eng.; son of George and Barbara Bowers; H. C., 1649, A.B.; taught school at Plymouth, 1652-1653; taught school at New Haven, Ct., 1653-1660; preached at Branford, Ct., 1667-1672/3; Ord. Derby, Ct., Nov. 18, 1673, as the first minister; sett. Derby, Ct., 1673-1687; d. Derby, Ct., June 14, 1687.

NATHANIEL BOWERS, son of Rev. John and Bridget (Thompson) Bowers of Derby, Ct.; sett. Rye, N. Y., 1688-1700; called to Greenwich, Ct., July 23, 1700; sett. Greenwich, Ct., 1700-1708; sett. Newark, N. J.

NICHOLAS BOWES, A.M., b. Nov. 4, 1706, son of Nicholas and Martha (Remington) Bowes; H. C., 1725, A.B., A.M.; Ord. Bedford, July 15, 1730; sett. Bedford, 1730-1754; dism. Aug. 22, 1754; in 1745, he refused to admit Rev. George Whitefield to his pulpit; taught school at Bedford, 1755; Chaplain at Fort Edward, 1755; d. at Brookfield on his way home, 1755.

JONATHAN BOWMAN, A.M., b. Lexington, Feb. 23, 1703/4, son of Hon. Joseph and Phebe Bowman; H. C., 1724, A.B., A.M.; Ord. Dorchester, Nov. 5, 1729; sett. Dorchester, 1729-1773; resigned Dec. 14, 1773; liberal; d. Dorchester, May 30, 1775, a. 71.

JOSEPH BOWMAN, A.M., b. Westborough, Jan. 21, 1734/5, son of Joseph and Thankful (Forbush) Bowman; H. C., 1761, A.B.; A.M., 1763; A.M., (Hon.), Dart. Coll., 1802; Ord. Boston, (Old South Chh.), Aug. 31, 1762, as a missionary to the Indians; inst. Oxford, Nov. 14, 1764; sett. Oxford, 1764-1782; dism. Aug. 28, 1782; Chaplain, Regt. of Col. Ebenezer Learned, Rev. War, 1775; inst. Barnard, Vt., Sept. 22, 1784; sett. Barnard, Vt., 1784-1806; Trustee, Dart. Coll., 1801-1806; d. Barnard, Vt., Apr. 27, 1806, a. 73.

ALEXANDER BOYD, A.B., U. of Glasgow; came to N. E., before 1748; sett. Georgetown, Me., 1748-1753; Ord. Newburyport,

Mass., for the ministry at Newcastle, Me., Sept. 19, 1754; sett. Newcastle, Me., 1753-1758; dism. 1758; Presb.

SAMUEL BRACKENBURY, A.M., b. Malden, Feb. 10, 1645/6, son of William and Alice Brackenbury; H. C., 1664, A.B., A.M.; asst. min., Rowley, 1669-1671; physician; prob. not ordained; d. 1678, a. 31.

JOSHUA BRACKETT, M.D., b. Greenland, N. H., May 1733; H. C., 1752, A.B., A.M.; M.D., (Hon.), H. C., 1792; entered the ministry but did not remain in that profession long; became a skillful and successful physician; sett. Portsmouth, N. H.; honorary member, Mass. Medical Soc., 1783; President, N. H. Medical Society, 1793; d. Portsmouth, N. H., July 17, 1802.

BENJAMIN BRADSTREET, A.M., b. Newbury, ca. 1705, son of Dr. Humphrey and Sarah (Pierce) Bradstreet; H. C., 1725, A.B., A.M.; Ord. Gloucester, (Annisquam Parish), Sept. 18, 1728; sett. Gloucester, 1728-1762; d. Gloucester, May 2, 1762.

DUDLEY BRADSTREET, JR., A.M., b. Andover, Apr. 27, 1678, son of Col. Dudley and Ann (Wood) (Price) Bradstreet; H. C., 1698, A.B., A.M.; Ord. Groton, Dec. 6, 1706; sett. Groton, 1706-1712; Ord. priest at London, Apr. 18, 1714; Epis.; d. London, May 16, 1714, of small pox.

SIMON BRADSTREET, A.M., b. Ipswich, Sept. 28, 1640, son of Gov. Simon and Anne (Dudley) Bradstreet; H. C., 1660, A.B., A.M.; Ord. New London, Ct., Oct. 5, 1670, as the first minister; sett. New London, Ct., 1666-1683; d. New London, Ct., between Sept. 6 and Nov. 19, 1683, a. 43.

SIMON BRADSTREET, JR., A.M., b. New London, Ct., Mar. 7, 1670/1, son of Rev. Simon and Lucy (Woodbridge) Bradstreet; H. C., 1693, A.B., A.M.; Overseer, H. C.; Ord. Charlestown, Oct. 26, 1698; sett. Charlestown, 1697-1741; d. Charlestown, Dec. 31, 1741, a. 70.

SIMON BRADSTREET, 3rd., A.M., bapt. Charlestown, June 26, 1709, son of Rev. Simon, Jr. and Mary (Long) Bradstreet; H. C., 1728, A.B., A.M.; Ord. Marblehead, (2nd Chh.), Jan. 4, 1738; sett. Marblehead, 1738-1771; d. Marblehead, Oct. 5, 1771.

CHILEAB BRAINARD, A.M., b. Haddam, Ct., Oct. 10, 1708, son of William and Sarah (Bidwell) Brainard; Y. C., 1731, A.B., A.M.; Ord. Eastbury, Ct., (2nd Chh. in Glastonbury), Jan. 14, 1735/6, as the first minister; sett. Eastbury, Ct., 1735-1738; d. Glastonbury, Jan. 1, 1738/9, a. 30.

NEHEMIAH BRAINARD, A.M., b Haddam, Ct., Feb. 20, 1712, son of Hon. Hezekiah and Dorothy (Hobart) Brainard; Y. C., 1732, A.B., A.M.; Ord. Eastbury, Ct., (2nd Chh. in Glastonbury), Jan. 23, 1740; sett. Eastbury, Ct., 1739-1742; d. Glastonbury, Ct., Nov. 9, 1742, a. 31.

WILLIAM BRATTLE, S.T.B., F.R.S., b. Boston, Nov. 22,

1662, son of Thomas and Elizabeth (Tyng) Brattle; H. C., 1680, A.B., A.M.; S.T.B., 1692, being the first time this degree was conferred; F.R.S., London, 1713; membr. Corp., H. C., 1703; Tutor, Fellow, H. C., 1703-1717; Treas., H. C., 1713-1715; Ord. Cambridge, Nov. 25, 1696; sett. Cambridge, 1696-1717; published a book of logic used as a text-book at H. C.; d. Cambridge, Feb. 15, 1716/17, a. 55.

THOMAS WELLS BRAY, A.M., b. Branford, Ct., Sept. 22, 1738, son of John and Lydia (Hoardley) Bray; Y. C., 1765, A.B., A.M.; Ord. North Guilford, Ct., Dec. 3, 1766; sett. North Guilford, Ct., 1766-1808; Chaplain, Rev. army; d. North Guilford, Ct., Apr. 23, 1808, a. 70.

ROBERT BRECK, A.M., b. Dorchester, Dec. 7, 1682, son of Capt. John and Susanna Breck; H. C., 1700, A.B., A.M.; Ord. Marlborough, Oct. 25, 1704; sett. Marlborough, 1704-1731; Election Sermon, 1728; d. Marlborough, Jan. 6, 1730/1, a. 49.

ROBERT BRECK, JR., A.M., b. Marlborough, July 25, 1713, son of Rev. Robert and Elizabeth (Wainwright) Breck; H. C., 1730, A.B., A.M.; Ord. Springfield, July 26, 1736; sett. Springfield, 1734-1784; an Arminian in theology; Convention Sermon, 1771; d Springfield, Apr. 23, 1784, a. 71.

SILAS BRETT, b. Bridgewater, Feb. 28, 1715/6, son of Seth and Sarah (Alden) Brett; Ord. Fall River, (Freetown), Dec. 2, 1747; sett. Fall River, 1747-1776; resigned Feb. 24, 1776; d. Easton, Apr. 17, 1791.

DANIEL BREWER, A.M., b. Roxbury, Feb. 7, 1669, son of Daniel and Hannah (Morrill) Brewer; H. C., 1687, A.B., A.M.; Ord. Springfield, May 16, 1694; sett. Springfield, 1694-1733; d. Springfield, Nov. 5, 1733, a. 66.

DANIEL BREWER, A.M., b. Springfield, Feb. 23, 1742/3, son of Charles and Anne (Breck) Brewer; Y. C., 1765, A.B., A.M.; Ord. Guilford, Ct., (4th Chh.), Sept. 18, 1771; sett. Guilford, 1771-1775; dism. Mar. 8, 1775; became a Sandemanian; elder in Sandemanian churches at Taunton, Mass. and Newtown, Ct.; d. Taunton, Dec. 3, 1825, a. 83.

NATHANIEL BREWSTER, Th.B., b. ca. 1620, probably son of Francis and Lucy Brewster, who sett. at New Haven having come from London to N. E.; H. C., 1642, A.B.; Th.B., U. of Dublin, Ireland; minister at Netisheard and Irsted, Norfolk; then resided in Dublin about a year; sett. at Alby and Twaite, Norfolk, 1658-1662; ejected, 1662; returned to N. E., Aug. 1662; preached at the First Church in Boston, 1663; sett. Brookhaven, L. I., N. Y., 1665-1690; d. Brookhaven, L. I., N. Y., Dec. 18, 1690.

WILLIAM BREWSTER, b. Scrooby, Nottinghamshire, Eng., 1566/7, son of William and Prudence Brewster; matric. at Peterhouse, Camb., 1580, but did not grad.; served under William Davidson, ambassador and Secretary of State to Queen Elizabeth, 1584-1587; postmaster at Scrooby, 1587-1602; with the Pilgrims in Holland, 1608-1620; came in the "Mayflower," 1620, to Plymouth; sett. Plymouth (Ruling Elder), 1620-1629, as the first minister; sett. Duxbury, 1632-1637, as the first minister; Deputy to the Gen. Ct., 1636; Chaplain, Plymouth Military Co.; d. Plymouth, Apr. 16, 1644.

JOSEPH BRIANT, perhaps an Indian; minister at Mashpee (Indian Chh.); d. Mashpee, Apr. 25, 1759.

LEMUEL BRIANT, A.M., bapt. Scituate, Feb. 25, 1721/2, son of Thomas, Esq. and Mary (Ewell) Briant; H. C., 1739, A.B., A.M.; Ord. Quincy, (First Chh. in Braintree), Dec. 4, 1745; sett. Quincy, 1745-1753; dism. Oct. 22, 1753; "was a Unitarian" according to President John Adams; d. Hingham, Oct. 1, 1754, a. 32.

SOLOMON BRIANT, b. 1695; said to have been an Indian; sett. Mashpee, (Indian Chh.), as a missionary, 1742-1745; d. Mashpee, May 8, 1775, a. 80.

CHRISTOPHER BRIDGE, A.M., b. Tillington, Essex, Eng., 1671, son of Rev. Robert Bridge; St. John's Coll., Camb., A.B., 1692/3; A.M.; inst. Boston, (King's Chapel), Mar. 5, 1699; sett. Boston, (King's Chapel), as Queen's Lecturer, 1699-1706; sett. Kingston, R. I., (Narrangansett Chh.), 1706-1709; sett. Rye, N. Y., Jan. 1709/10-1719; Epis.; d. Rye, N. Y., May 22, 1719, a. 48.

EBENEZER BRIDGE, A.M., b. Boston, Mar. 4, 1715/6, son of Ebenezer and Mary (Roberts) Bridge; H. C., 1736, A.B., A.M.; Ord. Chelmsford, May 20, 1741; sett. Chelmsford, 1741-1792; Artillery Election Sermon, 1752; Election Sermon, 1767; Convention Sermon, 1780; d. Chelmsford, Oct. 1, 1792, a. 78.

JOSIAH BRIDGE, A.M., b. Lexington, Dec. 28, 1739, son of Dea. John and Sarah (Tidd) Bridge; H. C., 1758, A.B., A.M.; Ord. Wayland, Nov. 4, 1761; sett. Wayland, 1761-1801; an Arminian in theology; Election Sermon, 1789; Convention Sermon, 1792; Dudleian Lecture, 1797; d. Wayland, June 19, 1801, a. 62.

MATTHEW BRIDGE, A.M., b. Lexington, July 18, 1721, son of Matthew and Abigail (Bowman) Bridge; H. C., 1741, A.B., A.M.; Ord. Framingham, Feb. 19, 1745/6; sett. Framingham, 1745-1775; Chaplain in the Rev. War; died in service; d. Framingham, Sept. 2, 1775, a. 55.

THOMAS BRIDGE, A.M., b. Hackney, Eng., 1656; Oxford U.; came to America, 1682; A.M., (Hon.), H. C., 1712; merchant and preacher at Jamaica, New Providence, Bermuda and West Jersey; came to Boston, Mar. 17, 1704; Ord Boston, (1st Chh.), May 10, 1705; sett. Boston, 1705-1715; Artillery Election Sermon, 1705; d. Boston, Sept. 26, 1715, a. 58.

JAMES BRIDGHAM, A.M., b. Boston, Mar. 21, 1706, son of James and Mercy (Stoddard) Bridgham; H. C., 1726, A.B., A.M.; Ord. Brimfield, June 9, 1736; sett. Brimfield, 1736-1776; d. Brimfield, Sept. 16, 1776, a. 69.

ZECHARIAH BRIGDEN, A.M., bapt. Charlestown, Aug. 2, 1639, son of Thomas and Thomasine Brigden; H. C., 1657, A.B., A.M; Tutor and Fellow; sett. Stonington, Ct., 1660-1662, before the church was organized; d. Stonington, Ct., Apr. 24, 1662, a. 23.

EPHRAIM BRIGGS, A.M., b. Mansfield, Apr. 19, 1736, son of Dea. Richard and Abigail (Andros) Briggs; H. C., 1764, A.B., A.M.; Ord. Halifax, Apr. 29, 1767; sett. Halifax, 1767-1799; d. Halifax, Dec. 2, 1799.

JAMES BRIGGS, A.M., b. Norton, Jan. 17, 1745/6, son of Dea. James and Damaris (White) Briggs; Y. C., 1775, A.B.; A.M., 1784; Ord. Cummington, July 7, 1779; sett. Cummington, 1771-1825; d. Cummington, Dec. 7, 1825, a. 80.

BENJAMIN BRIGHAM, A.M., b. Marlborough, Mar. 11, 1742, son of Benjamin and Hannah Brigham; H. C., 1764, A.B., A.M.; Ord. Fitzwilliam, N. H., Mar. 27, 1771; sett. Fitzwilliam, N. H., 1771-1799; d. Fitzwilliam, N. H., June 11, 1799, a. 57.

FRANCIS BRIGHT, A.B., b. ca. 1603, son of Edward Bright, of London, Eng.; matric. New Inn Hall, Oxford, Feb. 18, 1624/5; A.B., New Inn Hall, Oxford, Feb. 23, 1624/5; sett. Rayleigh, Essex, Eng.; was at Salem, Mass., 1629; sett. Charlestown, but returned to England, 1630; conformist.

DANIEL BRINSMADE, A.M., b. Stratford, Ct., July 31, 1718, son of Lieut. Daniel and Mary Brinsmade; Y. C., 1745, A.B., A.M.; Ord. Washington, Ct., (Judea Parish), Mar. 1, 1748/9; sett. Washington, Ct., 1749-1793; d. Washington, Ct., Apr. 23, 1793, a. 74.

WILLIAM BRINSMEAD, JR., b. Dorchester, son of William Brinsmead; H. C., 1644-1647, but did not grad.; preached at Plymouth, 1660-1665; Ord. Marlborough, Oct. 3, 1666, as the first minister; sett. Marlborough, 1666-1701; Election Sermon, 1681; d. Marlborough, July 3, 1701.

WILLIAM BRINTNALL, A.M., son of Capt. Thomas and Hannah (Willard) Brintnall; Y. C., 1721, A.B., A.M.; A. M., H. C., 1724; preached as a candidate at Rutland, 1721; schoolmaster at Sudbury, 1722-1726; was in command of troops at Rutland, Aug. 1725; was in Sudbury, till 1734; at Rutland, 1734-1737; removed to Framingham, 1737; d. 1745.

JOHN BROCK, A.M., b. Stradbrook, Suffolk, Eng., 1620, son of Henry and Elizabeth Brock, who came to Dedham, 1637; H. C., 1646, A.B., A.M.; preached at Rowley, 1648-1650; preached at the Isles of Shoals, N. H., 1650-1662; Ord. Wakefield, (1st Chh. in Reading), Nov. 13, 1662; sett. Wakefield, 1662-1688; d. Wakefield, (Reading), June 18, 1688, a. 68.

THOMAS BROCKWAY, A.M., b. Lyme, Ct., Jan. 20, 1744/5, son of William and Hannah (Clark) Brockway; Y. C., 1768, A.B., A.M.; Ord. Columbia, Ct., (2nd Chh. in Lebanon), June 24, 1772;

sett. Columbia, Ct., 1772-1807; Rev. Soldier, 1776; Chaplain, Col. Samuel Selden's Regt., 1776; d. Lyme, Ct., July 4, 1807, a. 63.

CHARLES BROCKWELL, A.M., b. Hertfordshire, Eng., 1696; admitted sizar, St. Catherine's Hall, Camb., 1716/7; A.B., A.M.; supply at Scituate, (St. Andrew's Chh.), 1726-1730; sett. Salem, (St. Peter's Chh.), Oct. 8, 1738-Nov. 27, 1746; inst. Boston, (King's Chapel), as King's Lecturer, 1747; sett. Boston, 1747-1755; Epis.; d. Boston, Aug. 20, 1755, a. 59.

EDWARD BROOKS, A.M., b. Medford, Oct. 31, 1733, son of Samuel and Mary (Boutwell) Brooks; H. C., 1757, A.B., A.M.; Librarian, H. C., 1758-1760; Ord. North Yarmouth, Me., July 4, 1764; sett. North Yarmouth, Me., 1764-1769; dism. Mar. 1769; Chaplain of the Frigate "Hancock," 1777; d. Medford, May 6, 1781, a. 48. (Bond says b. Nov. 4).

THOMAS BROOKS, A.M., b. Eng., ca. 1719; came to N. E., 1745; Y. C., 1755, A.B., A.M.; Ord. Brookfield, Ct., (formerly Newbury, Ct.), Sept. 28, 1757; sett. Brookfield, Ct., 1757-1796; dism. Dec. 27, 1796; first minister of Brookfield, for whom the town was named; d. Brookfield, Ct., Sept. 12, 1799, a. 80.

AARON BROWN, A.M., b. Windsor, Ct., May 3, 1725, son of Dea. Cornelius and Abigail (Barber) Brown; Y. C., 1749, A.B., A.M.; Ord. Putnam, Ct., (Killingly, 1st Chh.), Jan. 9, 1754; sett. Putnam, Ct., 1753-1775; d. Ashford, Ct., Sept. 12, 1775, a. 51.

ARTHUR BROWNE, A.M., b. Drogheda, Ireland, 1699, son of Rev. Archdeacon John Brown; Trinity Coll., Dublin, A.B., A.M., 1729; missionary for the Venerable Society for the Propagation of the Gospel in Foreign Parts; Ord. by the Bishop of London, 1729; sett. Providence, R. I., (King's Chapel), 1730-1736; left Feb. 1736; inst. Portsmouth, N. H., (Queen's Chapel), 1736; sett. Portsmouth, N. H., 1736-1772; Epis.; d. Cambridge, June 10, 1773, a. 73.

CHAD BROWN, came to Boston, 1638, and to Providence, R. I., 1638; Ord. Providence, R. I., (1st Bapt. Chh.), 1642; sett. Providence, R. I., 1642-1650; Bapt.; d. Providence, R. I., before Sept. 2, 1650.

COTTON BROWN, A.M., b. Haverhill, Jan. 21, 1726/7, son of Rev. John and Johanna (Cotton) Brown; H. C., 1743, A.B., A.M.; Ord. Brookline, Oct. 26, 1748; sett. Brookline, 1748-1751; d. Brookline, Apr. 13, 1751, a. 25.

DANIEL BROWNE, A.M., b. New Haven, Ct., Apr. 26, 1698, son of Eleazer and Sarah (Bulkley) Brown; Y. C., 1718, A.B., A.M.; Tutor. Y. C., 1718-1722; taught school, 1715-1718; Ord. London, Eng., Mar. 31, 1723, by the Bishop of Norwich; Epis.; d. London, Eng., Apr. 13, 1723, s. p.

EDMUND BROWNE, bapt. Lavenham, Suffolk, England, Oct. 28, 1606, son of Edmund Browne of that place; matric., sizar at Emmanuel Coll., Camb., 1624; came to N. E., 1638; sett. Plymouth, 1638; Ord. Sudbury, Aug. 1640, as the first minister; sett. Sudbury, (Wayland), 1640-1678; Artillery Election Sermon, 1666; benefactor of H. C.; d. Sudbury, June 22, 1678.

ELEAZER BROWN, 3rd., b. Stonington, Ct., June 1, 1728, son of Eleazer, Jr. and Temperance (Holmes) Brown; Ord. Stonington, Ct., (1st Bapt. Chh. of North Stonington), June 24, 1770; sett. Stonington, Ct., 1768-1795; Bapt.; d. Stoningon, Ct., July 11, 1795.

ELIJAH BROWN, A.M., b. Waltham, May 31, 1744, son of Ebenezer and Abigail (Adams) Brown; H. C., 1765, A.B., A.M.; Ord. Sherborn, Nov. 28, 1770; sett. Sherborn, 1770-1816; d. Sherborn, Oct. 24, 1816, a. 72, s. p.

JAMES BROWN, (b. prob. at Southampton, Eng., ca. 1618, son of Joseph Brown); came in the "James," 1635, aged 17 yrs.; preached at Portsmouth, N. H., 1654-1656; resided at Newbury, 1656-1674.

JAMES BROWN, b. Providence, R. I., 1666, son of John and Mary (Holmes) Brown, and grandson of Rev. Chad Brown; Ord. Providence, R. I., (1st Bapt. Chh.), 1726; sett. Providence, R. I., 1726-1732; membr. Town Council, 1705-1727; Town Treasurer, 1714-1718; Bapt.; d. Providence, R. I., Oct. 28, 1732.

JOHN BROWN, A.M., b. Brighton, Nov. 1, 1696, son of Ichabod and Martha Brown; H. C., 1714, A.B., A.M.; Ord. Haverhill, May 13, 1719; sett. Haverhill, 1719-1742; d. Haverhill, Dec. 2, 1742.

JOHN BROWN, JR., A.M., b. Haverhill, Mar. 9, 1723/4, son of Rev. John and Johanna (Cotton) Brown; H. C., 1741, A.B., A.M.; Ord. Cohasset, Sept. 2, 1747; sett. Cohasset, 1747-1791; Artillery Election Sermon, 1766; Chaplain in the army, 1759; Unitarian according to President John Adams, 1815; d. Cohasset, Aug. 22, 1791, a. 67.

JOSEPH BROWN, A.M., b. Lexington, Apr. 14, 1741, son of Dea. James and Jane (Bowman) Brown; H. C., 1763, A.B., A.M.; Ord. Winchendon, May 24, 1769; sett. Winchendon, 1769-1799; dism. Sept. 3, 1799; sett. Springfield, Vt.; d. 1811.

JOSIAH BROWN, A.M., bapt. Lexington, Aug. 21, 1715, son of Dea. Joseph and Ruhamah (Wellington) Brown; H. C., 1735, A.B., A.M.; preached at Lancaster, 1747; sometime minister at Athol and Sterling; d. Sterling, Feb. 6, 1773, a. 57.

MARMADUKE BROWNE, A.B., b. Providence, R. I., 1731, son of Rev. Arthur and Mary (Cox) Browne; Trinity Coll., Dublin, 1754, A.B.; Ord. Dea. by Bishop of London; sett. Portsmouth, N. H., (Queen's Chapel, asst. min.), 1755-1760; inst. Newport, R. I., (Trinity Chh.), Dec. 11, 1760; sett. Newport, R. I., 1760-1771; Epis.; d. Newport, R. I., Mar. 19, 1771.

NATHANIEL BROWN, JR., b. Ledyard, Ct.; Ord. Groton, Ct., (Separatist Chh.), Nov. 14, 1751; sett. North Groton, Ct., (Separatist Chh.), 1751-1755.

RICHARD BROWN, JR., A.B., b. Newbury, Sept. 12, 1675, son of Richard and Mary (Jaques) Brown; H. C., 1697, A.B.; taught school at Newbury; sett. Haverhill, 1709-1711; Ord. Wakefield, (1st Chh. in Reading), June 25, 1712; sett. Wakefield, 1712-1732; d. Wakefield, (Reading), Oct. 20, 1732, a. 57.

SAMUEL BROWNE, A.B., b. Newbury, Sept. 4, 1687, son of Joshua and Sarah (Sawyer) Browne; H. C., 1709, A.B.; Ord. Abington, Nov. 17, 1714; sett. Abington, 1712-1749; d. Abington, Sept. 19, 1749, a. 62.

SIMEON BROWN, b. Stonington, Ct., Jan. 31, 1723, son of James and Elizabeth (Randall) Brown; deacon at Westerly, R. I., 1750-1765; Ord. Stonington, Ct., (2nd Bapt. Chh of North Stonington), 1764; sett. Stonington, Ct., 1764-1813; Bapt.; d. North Stonington, Ct., Nov. 24, 1815.

THOMAS BROWNE, A.M., b. Haverhill, 1733, son of Rev. John and Johanna (Cotton) Brown; H. C., 1752, A.B., A.M.; Ord. Marshfield, (1st Chh.), Sept. 5, 1759; sett. Marshfield, 1759-1763; dism. Nov. 1, 1763; inst. Westbrook, Me., (Stroudwater Parish, or 4th Parish in Falmouth), Aug. 21, 1765; sett. Westbrook, Me., 1765-1797; d. Westbrook, Me., Oct. 18, 1797.

TIMOTHY BROWN, A.M., b. Concord, Aug. 17, 1712, son of Thomas and Hannah (Potter) Brown; H. C., 1729, A.B., A.M.; preached at Spruce Creek, Kittery, Me., 1743; Ord. Little Compton, R. I., May 2, 1753; sett. Little Compton, R. I., 1753-1763; d. Apr. 10, 1763.

DAVID BROWNSON, A.B., b. New Milford, Ct., Oct. 23, 1739, son of Josiah and Prudence (Hurlburt) Brownson; Y. C., 1762, A.B.; Ord. Oxford, Ct., Apr. 25, 1764; sett. Oxford, Ct., 1764-1779; d. Oxford, Ct., Nov. 12, 1806, a. 67.

DANIEL BUCK, A.B., b. Wethersfield, Ct., Sept. 13, 1695, son of David and Elizabeth (Hubbard) Buck; Y. C., 1718, A.B.; sett. Southington, Ct., 1724-1726; d. Southington, Ct., Apr. 1726.

DANIEL BUCKINGHAM, A.M., b. Milford, Ct., Oct. 27, 1712, son of Gideon and Sarah (Hunt) Buckingham; Y. C., 1735, A.B., A.M.; Ord. Green Farms, Ct., (2nd Chh. in Fairfield), Mar. 17, 1741/2; sett. Green Farms, Ct., 1742-1766; d. Green Farms, Ct., May 23, 1766, a. 54, s. p.

STEPHEN BUCKINGHAM, A.M., b. Saybrook, Ct., Sept. 4, 1675, son of Rev. Thomas and Hester (Hosmer) Buckingham; H. C., 1693, A.B.; A.M., Y. C., 1702; Trustee, Y. C., 1716; Ord. Norwalk, Ct., Nov. 17, 1697; sett. Norwalk, Ct., 1695-1727; resigned Feb. 24, 1726/7; Ct. Election Sermon, 1711; d. Norwalk, Ct., Feb. 3, 1746/7, s. p.

THOMAS BUCKINGHAM, bapt. Milford, Ct., Nov. 8, 1646, son of Thomas and Hannah Buckingham; Ord. Old Saybrook, Ct., 1670, summer; sett. Old Saybrook, Ct., 1665-1709; Founder and Trustee of Y. C.; d. Saybrook, Ct., Apr. 1, 1709, a. 63.

THOMAS BUCKINGHAM, A.M., b. Milford, Ct., Mar. 1, 1671, son of Elder Daniel and Alice (Newton) Buckingham; H. C., 1690, A.B.; A.M., 1725; Trustee, Y. C., 1715-1731; Ord. Hartford, Ct., (2nd Chh.), 1694; sett. Hartford, Ct., 1694-1731; Chaplain at Port Royal, 1710; Chaplain at Crown Point, 1711; Ct. Election Sermon, 1728; d. Hartford, Ct., Nov. 19, 1731, a. 61.

JOSEPH BUCKMINSTER, A.M., b. Framingham, Mar. 1, 1719/20, son of Col. Joseph, Jr. and Sarah (Lawson) Buckminster; H. C., 1739, A.B., A.M.; Ord. Rutland, Sept. 15, 1752; sett. Rutland, 1752-1792; d. Rutland, Nov. 3, 1792, a. 73.

JOSEPH BUCKMINSTER, D.D., b. Rutland, Oct. 3, 1751, son of Rev. Joseph and Lucy (Williams) Buckminster; Y. C., 1770, A.B., A.M.; D.D., Princeton, 1803; Tutor, Y. C., 1770-1773; began preaching 1775; sett. North Church, Portsmouth, N. H., 1778-1812; N. H. Election Sermon, 1787; d. Reedsborough, Vt., June 9, 1812.

NATHAN BUCKNAM, A.M., b. Malden, Nov. 2, 1703, son of Josse and Hannah (Peabody) Bucknam; H. C., 1721, A.B., A.M.; Ord. East Medway, (1st Chh. in Medway, now in Millis), Dec. 23, 1724; sett. Millis, 1724-1795; more than 70 years; d. Medway, Feb. 6, 1795, a. 92.

SAMUEL BUELL, D.D., b. Coventry, Ct., Aug. 20, 1716, son of Capt. Peter and Hannah (Welles) Buell; Y. C., 1741, A.B., A.M.; S.T.D., Dart. Coll., 1791; Ord. New Fairfield, Ct., Nov. 9, 1742; itinerant preacher, 1742-1745; inst. East Hampton, L. I., N. Y., Sept. 19, 1746; sett. East Hampton, L. I., N. Y., 1746-1798; d. East Hampton, L. I., N. Y., July 19, 1798, a. 82.

EDWARD BULKLEY, bapt. Odell, Bedfordshire, Eng., June 12, 1614, son of Rev. Peter, B.D. and Jane (Allen) Bulkley; matric. St. Catherine's Hall, Camb., 1629; came to Boston, 1635; H. C., but did not grad.; Ord. Marshfield, 1642/3; sett. Marshfield, 1642-1656; sett. Concord, 1659-1694; Artillery Election Sermon, 1679; Election Sermon, 1680, d. Chelmsford, Jan. 2, 1695/6, a. 82.

GERSHOM BULKLEY, A.M., J.P., b. Cambridge, Jan. 1635/6, son of Rev. Peter, B.D. and Grace (Chetwood) Bulkley; H. C., 1655, A.B., A.M.; Fellow, H. C.; sett. New London, Ct., 1660-1666; Ord. Wethersfield, Ct., Oct. 29, 1669; sett. Wethersfield, Ct., 1666-1677; dism. 1677; Surgeon and Chaplain, King Philip's War, 1675-1677; wounded at Princeton, Mass., Mar., 1676; practiced surgery and medicine, 1677; Deputy, Gen. Assembly of Ct., 1679; J. P.; Ct. Election Sermon, 1680; d. Glastonbury, Ct., Dec. 2, 1713, a. 78.

JOHN BULKLEY, A.M., b. Wethersfield, Ct., 1679, son of Rev. Gershom and Sarah (Chauncy) Bulkley; H. C., 1699, A.B., A.M.; Ord. Colchester, Ct., Dec. 20, 1703, as the first minister; sett. Colchester, Ct., 1703-1731; physician; Ct. Election Sermon, 1713; d. Colchester, Ct., June 9, 1731.

PETER BULKLEY, B.D., b. Odell, Bedfordshire, Eng., Jan.

45

31, 1582/3, son of Rev. Edward, D.D. and Olive (Irby) Bulkley; St. John's Coll., Camb., A.B., 1604/5; A.M., 1608; B.D.; Fellow, St. John's Coll., 1605; excellent Latin scholar; Ord. by the Bishop of Ely, June 1608; Canon of Litchfield, 1609; University preacher, 1610; instituted at Odell, Bedfordshire, Jan. 12, 1609/10; Rector of Odell, as successor to his father, 1610-1635; came to N. E., 1635; Ord. Cambridge, Apr. 1637, for service at Concord; sett. Concord, 1636-1659, as the first minister; left a large portion of his library to Harvard College; published a book, 1646; d. Concord, Mar. 9, 1658/9, a. 77.

HON. PETER BULKLEY, A.M., b. Concord, Jan. 3, 1640/1, son of Rev. Edward and Lucian Bulkley; H. C., 1660, A.B., A.M.; Fellow, 1663; sett. Stratford, Ct., 1666; sett. Braintree, 1669-1670; deputy, 1673-1676; speaker, 1676; assistant, 1677-1686; captain, 1677; major, 1680; marshal, 1686; judge of the superior court, 1687; d. Concord, May 25, 1688.

NEHEMIAH BULL, A.M., b. Farmington, Ct., 1701, son of John and Esther (Royce) Bull; Y. C., 1723, A.B., A.M.; Ord. Westfield, Oct. 26, 1726; sett. Westfield, 1725-1740; d. Westfield, Apr. 12, 1740, a. 39.

JOSEPH BULLEN, A.M., b. Sutton, 1753, son of Joseph Bullen; Y. C., 1772, A.B.; A.M., 1780; Ord. Westminster, Vt., July 6, 1774; sett. Westminster, Vt., 1774-1785; dism. Sept. 26, 1785; removed to Athens, Vt., 1788; served in Vt. legislature from Athens; preached at Athens, Vt., 1788-1791; due to his efforts a Cong. Chh. was established there in 1797; became an Indian missionary, Mar. 21, 1799, and sett. at Pontotoc, Miss., 1799-1811, in this work; d. Natchez, Miss., Mar. 26, 1825, a. 72.

BENJAMIN BUNKER, A.M., bapt. Charlestown, Sept. 20, 1635, son of George and Judith Bunker (for whom Bunker Hill was named); H. C., 1658, A.B., A.M.; Ord. Malden, Dec. 9, 1663; sett. Malden, 1663-1670 (colleague); d. Malden, Feb. 2, 1669/70, a. ca. 35.

GEORGE BURDETT, A.M., b. ca. 1602; scholar at Trinity Coll., Dublin, Apr. 24, 1619; A.B., Trinity Coll., Dublin; admitted to Sidney Sussex Coll., Camb., 1623/4; A.M.; an Anglican clergyman at Brightwell, Havering and Great Yarmouth, Norfolk, Eng., 1625-1632; Curate at Saffron-Walden, 1632; Lecturer at Norwich, (called A.M.); suspended, 1635; came to N. E.; admitted Freeman of Massachusetts Bay Colony, Sept. 2, 1635; sett. Salem, 1635-1637; sett. Dover, N. H., 1637-1638; sett. York, Me., 1638-1640; constantly in trouble; banished for disturbing the peace, 1639; departed for England, 1640; said to have joined the Royalist Army; later was Chancellor of Leighlin, 1666; Dean of Leighlin, 1668; Epis.; d. 1671.

THOMAS BURLINGAME, b. Cranston, R. I., May 29, 1668, son of Thomas and Martha (Lippitt) Burlingame; Ord. Providence, R. I., (1st Bapt. Chh.), 1733; sett. Providence and Cranston, R. I., 1733-1740; Bapt.; d. Cranston, R. I., Jan. 7, 1740.

JACOB BURNAP, D.D., b. Reading, Oct. 20, 1748, son of Isaac and Sarah (Emerson) Burnap; H. C., 1770, A.B., A.M.; S.T.D., 1814; Ord. Merrimack, N. H., Oct. 14, 1772, as the first minister; sett. Merrimack, N. H., 1772-1821; N. H. Election Sermon, 1801; d. Merrimack, N. H., Dec. 26, 1821, a. 73.

WILLIAM BURNHAM, A.M., b. Wethersfield, Ct., 1684, son of William and Elizabeth Burnham; H. C., 1702, A.B., A.M.; Ord. Kensington, Ct., (2nd Chh. in Farmington), Dec. 10, 1712; sett. Kensington, Ct., 1712-1750; Ct. Election Sermon, 1722; d. Kensington, Ct., Sept. 23, 1750, a. 66.

ROBERT BURNS, Ord. Palmer, Nov. 1753; sett. Palmer, 1753-1756; Presb.

ISAAC BURR, A.M., b. Hartford, Ct., July 4, 1697, son of Thomas and Sarah Burr; Y. C., 1717, A.B., A.M.; Ord. Worcester, Oct. 13, 1725; sett. Worcester, 1724-1745; dism. Mar. 1745; sett. Windsor, Ct., 1747-1751; uncle of Vice-President Aaron Burr; d. Windsor, Ct., 1751, a. 54.

JONATHAN BURR, A.M., bapt. Redgrave, Suffolk, Eng., Apr 12, 1604, son of John Burr; Corpus Christi Coll., Camb., A. B., 1623/4; A.M.; sett. Horningsheath; Rector of Rickinghall Superior, Suffolk, Eng., 1630, till silenced by Archbishop Laud in 1639; came to N. E., 1639; Ord. Dorchester, Feb. 1640; sett. Dorchester, 1640-1641; d. Dorchester, Aug. 9, 1641, a. 37.

EDEN BURROUGHS, D.D., b. Stratford, Ct., Jan. 19, 1737/8, son of Stephen and Ruth (Nichols) Burroughs; Y. C., 1757, A.B., A.M.; A.M., Dart. Coll., 1773; S.T.D., Dart. Coll., 1806; Trustee, Dart. Coll., 1773-1813; Ord. South Killingly, Ct., Jan. 23, 1760; sett. South Killingly, Ct., (2nd Chh. in Killingly), 1760-1763; sett. South Killingly, Ct., (3rd Chh.), 1763-1771; inst. Hanover Center, N. H., Sept. 1, 1772; sett. Hanover Center, N. H., 1772-1809; sett. Hartford, Vt., 1809-1813; d. Hartford, Vt., May 22, 1813, a. 75.

GEORGE BURROUGHS, A.B., b. ca. 1650, son of Nathaniel and Rebecca Burroughs, of Limehouse, Stepney, Middlesex, Eng.; H. C., 1670, A.B.; sett. Portland, Me., (1st Parish in Falmouth), 1674-1676; driven out by the Indians; prob. preached at Salisbury, 1676-1680; Ord. Danvers, Nov. 25, 1680; sett. Danvers, 1680-1683; sett. Portland, Me., 1683-1690; town sacked again in 1690, by the Indians; sett. Danvers again, 1690-1692; executed for witchcraft on Gallows Hill, Salem, Aug. 19, 1692, a. 42.

PELEG BURROUGHS, of Newport, R. I.; Ord. Tiverton, R. I., (Chh. of Tiverton and Little Compton, R. I. and Dartmouth, Mass.), Apr. 13, 1780; sett. Tiverton, R. I., 1775-1800; Bapt.; d. Tiverton, R. I., Aug. 1800.

SILAS BURROWS, b. Groton, Ct., 1741, son of Amos and Mary (Rathbone) Burrows; Ord. Groton, Ct., (2nd Bapt. Chh. in Groton), 1765; sett. Groton, Ct., 1765-1818; Bapt.; d. Groton, Ct., 1818.

JOHN BURT, A.M., b. Boston, Dec. 29, 1716, son of John and Abigail (Cheever) Burt; H. C., 1736, A.B., A.M.; Ord. Bristol, R. I., May 13, 1741; sett. Bristol, R.I., 1740-1775; d. Bristol, R. I., Oct. 7, 1775, a. 59.

JOHN BUSS, b. ca. 1640; inst. Wells, Me., Sept. 2, 1672; sett. Wells, Me., 1672-1682; later a preacher and physician at Durham, N. H.; d. Wells, Me., Mar. 1736, a. 96.

AMOS BUTLER, A.M., b. Hartford, Ct., 1747; Y. C., 1767, A.B., A.M.; Ord. Williamsburg, July 14, 1773; sett. Williamsburg, 1773-1777; d. Williamsburg, Oct. 13, 1777, a. 30.

BENJAMIN BUTLER, A.M., b. Windham, Ct., Apr. 19, 1729, son of Malachi and Jemima (Daggett) Butler; H. C., 1752, A.B., A.M.; Ord. Nottingham, N. H., 1758; sett. Nottingham, N. H., 1758-1770; dism. Aug. 1, 1770; magistrate; d. Nottingham, N. H., Dec. 26, 1804, a. 75.

HENRY BUTLER, A.M., b. Kent, Eng., ca. 1624; came to N. E., 1642; H. C., 1651, A.B., A.M.; taught school at Dorchester; preached for 11 or 12 years at Milton; returned to England, where he was minister at Yeovil, Somersetshire; d. Apr. 24, 1696, a. 72.

ZEBULON BUTLER, A.M., b. Edgartown, Apr. 27, 1749, son of Elijah and Thankful (Smith) Butler; H. C., 1770, A.B., A.M.; Ord. Falmouth, Oct. 18, 1775; sett. Falmouth, 1775-1778; manufacturer of snuff at Nantucket; d. ca. 1791.

MATHER BYLES, D.D., b. Boston, Mar. 15, 1706, son of Josiah and Elizabeth Byles; H. C., 1725, A.B., A.M.; S.T.D., U. of Aberdeen, 1765; Ord. Boston, (Hollis St. Chh.), Dec. 20, 1732 as the first minister; sett. Boston, 1732-1776; Artillery Election Sermon, 1740; Tory and wit; d. Boston, July 5, 1788, a. 82.

MATHER BYLES, JR., D.D., b. Boston, Jan. 12, 1734, son of Rev. Dr. Mather anad Anna (Gale) Byles; H. C., 1751, A.B., A.M.; Librarian, H. C., 1755-1757; A.M., (Hon.), Y. C., 1757; S.T.D., Oxford, 1770; Ord. New London, Ct., (Cong. Chh.), Nov. 18, 1757; sett. New London, Ct., 1757-1768; became an Epis.; inst. Boston, (Christ Chh.), as Rector, Sept. 1768; sett. Boston, (Christ Chh.), 1768-1775; left Apr. 1775; Tory; sett. Portsmouth, N. H., 1775-1776; banished 1778; Rector and Chaplain, St. John's, New Brunswick; d. St. John's, N. B., Mar. 12, 1814.

MARSTON CABOT, A.M., b. Boston, Feb. 20, 1705/6, son of George and Abigail (Marston) Cabot; H. C., 1724, A.B., A.M.; Ord. Thompson, Ct., Dec. 4, 1729 (or Feb. 25, 1730); sett. Thompson, Ct., 1729-1756; d. Thompson, Ct., Apr. 8, 1756.

ELISHA CALLENDER, A.M., b. Boston, Apr. 27, 1692, son of Rev. Ellis and Mary Callender; H. C., 1710, A.B., A.M.; Ord. Boston, (1st Bapt. Chh.), May 21, 1718; sett. Boston, 1718-1738; Bapt.; d. Boston, Mar. 31, 1738.

ELLIS CALLENDER, b. 1651; Ord. Boston, (1st Bapt. Chh.),

THE REVEREND COTTON MATHER (1633-1728)
By Peter Pelham (1634-1751)
*Reproduced from the portrait owned by
the American Antiquarian Society*

Interior of the Second Meeting House of the First Parish in Hingham as it appears today. The church was built in 1681; the pulpit installed in 1755.

1708; sett. Boston, 1708-1726; came to Boston, 1669; freeman, 1690; had been a lay preacher for 30 years before his ordination; Bapt.; d. Boston, May 18, 1738, a. 87.

JOHN CALLENDER, A.M., b. Boston, 1706, son of John Callender, Esq.; H. C., 1723, A.B., A.M.; preached at Swansea, (1st Bapt. Chh.), 1728-1730; Ord. Newport, R. I., (1st Bapt. Chh.), Oct. 13, 1731; sett. Newport, R. I., 1731-1748; wrote a History of R. I.; Bapt.; d. Newport, R. I., Jan. 26, 1748, a. 42.

ICHABOD CAMP, A.M., b. Durham, Ct., Feb. 15, 1725/6, son of John Camp; Y. C., 1743, A.B., A.M.; Ord. London, Eng., Mar. 25, 1751; sett. Middletown, Ct., (Epis. Chh.) and Wallingford, Ct., (Epis. Chh.), 1752-1760; sett. Louisburg, Va., 1760; sett. Amherst, Vt., 1762-1786; Epis.; d. Kaskaskia, Ill., Apr. 20, 1786.

SAMUEL CAMP, A.M., b. Canaan, Ct., 1744, son of Dea. Hezekiah anad Lydia (Clark) Camp; Y. C., 1764, A.B., A.M.; Ord. Ridgebury, Ct., Jan. 18, 1769, as the first minister; sett. Ridgebury, Ct., 1769-1804; dism. Nov. 1804; d. Ridgebury, Ct., Mar. 10, 1813, a. 68.

ARCHIBALD CAMPBELL, A.M., b. Oxford, Aug. 17, 1736, son of Rev. John and Esther (Fairchild) Campbell; H. C., 1761, A.B., A.M.; Ord. Easton, (1st Chh.), Aug. 17, 1763; sett. Easton, 1763-1782; dism. Aug. 11, 1782; inst. Charlton, (1st Chh.), Jan. 8, 1783; sett. Charlton, 1783-1793; dism. Apr. 9, 1793; sett. Alstead, N. H., 1799-1800; d. Stockbridge, Vt., July 15, 1818, a. 81.

JOHN CAMPBELL, A.B., b. in the North of Scotland, 1691; Edinburgh, A.B., 1716; came to N. E., 1717; Ord. Oxford, Mar. 1, 1721; sett. Oxford, 1721-1761; was not sympathetic to the preaching of Whitefield; d. Oxford, May 25, 1761.

OTHNIEL CAMPBELL, A.M., b. Taunton, Feb. 8, 1695/6, son of Ebenezer and Hannah (Pratt) Campbell; H. C., 1728, A.B., A.M.; Ord. Carver, 1734; sett. Carver, 1733-1746; inst. Tiverton, R. I., Oct. 1, 1746; sett. Tiverton, R. I., 1746-1778; d. Tiverton, R. I., Oct. 15, 1778.

HENRY CANER, D.D., b. England, 1700, son of Henry and Abigail Caner; Y. C., 1724, A.B., A.M.; A.M., Oxford, 1736; S.T.D., Oxford, 1766; Ord. England, 1727; sett. Fairfield, Ct., (Epis. Chh.), Norwalk, Ct., (Epis. Chh.), and Stratford, Ct., (Christ Chh., Epis.), 1727-1746; inst. Boston, (King's Chapel), Apr. 11, 1747, as Rector; sett. Boston, 1747-1776; left Mar. 10, 1776; Tory; Epis.; d. Long Ashton, Eng., Dec. 1792, a. 92.

RICHARD CANER, A.M., b. Boston, June 4, 1717, son of Henry and Abigail Caner; Y. C., 1736, A.B., A.M.; Ord. London, Eng., Oct. 1741; sett. Norwalk, Ct., (Epis. Chh.), June 1742-1745; sett. Staten Island, N. Y., (St. Andrew's Chh.), 1745; Epis.; d. New York City, Dec. 14, 1745, a. 28, of small pox.

THOMAS CANFIELD, A.M., b. Milford, Ct., Aug. 6, 1720,

son of Thomas and Mary (Camp) Canfield; Y. C., 1739, A.B., A.M.; Ord. Roxbury, Ct., Aug. 22, 1744; sett. Roxbury, Ct., 1743-1794; d. Roxbury, Ct., Jan. 16, 1794, a. 74.

JOSEPH CAPEN, A.M., b. Dorchester, Dec. 20, 1658, son of Capt. John and Mary (Bass) Capen; H. C., 1677, A.B., A.M.; Ord. Topsfield, June 11, 1684; sett. Topsfield, 1681-1725; d. Topsfield, June 30, 1725, a. 66.

JOHN CARNES, A.M., b. Boston, July 11, 1723, son of John and Sarah (Baker) Carnes; H. C., 1742, A.B., A.M.; Ord. Stoneham, Dec. 17, 1746; sett. Stoneham, 1746-1757; inst. Rehoboth, (1st Chh., Seekonk), Apr. 19, 1759; sett. Rehoboth, 1759-1764; dism. Dec. 4, 1764; Chaplain, Am. Rev., 1776-1781; d. Lynn, Oct. 20, 1802, a. 78.

ABRAHAM CARPENTER, b. Rehoboth, Sept. 23, 1739, son of Abiel and Prudence Carpenter; Ord. Plainfield, N. H., 1773, as the first minister; sett. Plainfield, 1773-1790; sett. Rutland, Vt., ca. 1790; nephew of Col. Ethan Allen of Vt.; soldier in the French and Indian Wars; d. Rutland, Vt., Aug. 21, 1797, a. 57.

EZRA CARPENTER, A.M., b. Rehoboth, Mar. 20, 1698/9, son of Nathaniel and Mary (Preston) Carpenter; H. C., 1720, A.B., A.M.; Ord. Hull, Nov. 24, 1725; sett. Hull, 1723-1746; dism. Nov. 24, 1746; inst. Keene, N. H., Oct. 4, 1753, as minister of the churches at Keene and Swanzey; sett. Keene, N. H., 1753-1760; sett. Swanzey, N. H., 1753-1769; dism. Mar. 16, 1769; Chaplain at Crown Point, 1757; d. Walpole, N. H., Aug. 26, 1785, a. 86.

WILLIAM CARPENTER, b. Rehoboth, June 26, 1711, son of Obadiah and Deliverance (Preston) Carpenter; Ord. Norton, (Separatist Chh.), Sept. 7, 1748; sett. Norton, (Sept. Chh.), 1748-1761; inst. Norton, (Bapt. Chh.), Apr. 1, 1761; sett. Norton and Taunton, (combined Bapt. Chhs.), 1761-1768; Bapt.; d. Norton, Aug. 23, 1768.

ESECK CARR, b. Little Compton, R. I., Mar. 25, 1733, son of Robert and Elizabeth (Cuthbert) Carr; sett. Easton, (Bapt. Chh.), 1766-1794; Bapt.; d. Easton, Feb. 19, 1794.

SAMUEL CARTER, A.B., b. Watertown, Aug. 8, 1640, son of Rev. Thomas and Mary (Parkhurst) Carter; H. C., 1660, A.B.; supplied at Lancaster, 1680-1688; supplied at Groton, 1691-1692; Selectman, Woburn, 1679, 1681, 1682, 1683; Town Clerk, 1690 at Woburn; teacher of the grammar school at Lancaster, 1685-1686; Ord. Groton, 1693; d. Groton, 1693, a. 53.

THOMAS CARTER, A.M., b. Hinderclay, Suffolk, Eng., bapt. July 3, 1608, son of James Carter; St. John's Coll., Camb., A. B., 1629/30; A.M., 1633; came to N. E., 1637; served as minister at Dedham and Watertown; Ord. Woburn, Nov. 22, 1642, as the first minister; sett. Woburn, 1642-1684; d. Woburn, Sept. 5, 1684.

THOMAS CARY, A.M., b. Charlestown, Oct. 7, 1745, son of Capt. Samuel, Esq. and Margaret (Graves) Cary; H. C., 1761,

A.B., A.M.; Ord. Newburyport, (1st Chh.), May 11, 1768; sett. Newburyport, 1768-1808; d. Newburyport, Nov. 24, 1808.

BENJAMIN CARYL, A.M., b. Hopkinton, Apr. 22, 1732, son of Benjamin and Mary (Knowlton) Caryl; H. C., 1761, A.B., A.M.; Ord. Dover, Nov. 10, 1762; sett. Dover, 1762-1811, as the first minister; d. Dover, Nov. 13, 1811, a. 79.

BENAJAH CASE, A.M., J.P., b. Simsbury, Ct., son of Joseph and Ann (Eno) Case; Y. C., 1733, A.B., A.M.; Ord. New Fairfield, Ct., Nov. 9, 1742; sett. New Fairfield, Ct., 1742-1753; dism. Jan. 2, 1753; d. New Fairfield, Ct., Feb. 1762.

ISAAC CHALKER, A.M., b. Saybrook, Ct., Sept. 12, 1707, son of Lieut. Abraham and Deborah (Barber) Chalker; Y. C., 1728, A.B., A.M.; Ord. Cornwall, Montgomery Co., N. J., 1734; sett. Cornwall, N. J., 1734-1743; inst. Buckingham, Ct., (2nd Chh. in Glastonbury), Oct. 1744; sett. Buckingham, Ct., 1743-1765; d. Buckingham, Ct., May 28, 1765, a. 58.

THEOPHILUS CHAMBERLAIN, A.B., b. Northfield, Oct. 20, 1737, son of Ephraim and Anna (Merriman) Chamberlain; Y. C., 1765, A.B.; Ord. Lebanon, Ct., Apr. 24, 1765; Indian missionary, N. Y., 1765-1767; taught school in Boston, 1768; became a Sandemanian; re-ordained, Boston, Feb. 1769; sett. Danbury, Ct., (Sandemanian Chh.), 1769-1772; loyalist; soldier in Capt. John Burk's Co. of Rangers, 1757; captured and taken via Ticonderoga to Canada; Deputy Surveyor General of Province of Canada; d. Preston, N. S., July 20, 1824, a. 87.

JUDAH CHAMPION, A.M., b. East Haddam, Ct., Aug. 20, 1729, son of Col. Henry and Mehitable (Rowley) Champion; Y. C., 1751, A.B., A.M.; Ord. Litchfield, Ct., July 4, 1753; sett. Litchfield, Ct., 1753-1810; Ct. Election Sermon, 1776; d. Litchfield, Ct., Oct. 8, 1810, a. 82.

JOSEPH CHAMPNEY, A.M., b. Cambridge, Sept. 19, 1704, son of Joseph and Sarah Champney; H. C., 1721, A.B., A.M.; Librarian, H. C., 1728-1729; Ord. Beverly, Dec. 10, 1729; sett. Beverly, 1729-1773; d. Beverly, Feb. 23, 1773.

JAMES CHANDLER, A.M., b. Andover, June 10, 1706, son of Thomas and Mary (Stevens) Chandler; H. C., 1728, A.B., A.M.; Ord. Georgetown, Oct. 18, 1732; sett. Georgetown, 1732-1788; Artillery Election Sermon, 1774; d. Georgetown, Apr. 19, 1789, a. 83.

JOHN CHANDLER, A.M., b. Andover, Dec. 14, 1723, son of Thomas and Mary (Stevens) Chandler; H. C., 1743, A.B., A.M.; Ord. Billerica, Oct. 21, 1747; sett. Billerica, 1747-1760; dism. June 5, 1760; d. Billerica, Nov. 10, 1762, a. 39.

SAMUEL CHANDLER, A.M., bapt. Andover, July 5, 1713, son of Josiah and Sarah (Ingalls) Chandler; H. C., 1735, A.B., A.M.; Ord. York, Me., (2nd Parish at Scotland), Jan. 20, 1742; sett. York, Me., 1742-1751; inst. Gloucester, (1st Chh.), Nov. 13, 1751; sett.

Gloucester, 1751-1775; Chaplain under Col. Plaisted at Crown Point, 1755; Thanksgiving Sermon, 1759; d. Gloucester, Mar. 16, 1775, a. 62.

EBENEZER CHAPLIN, A.M., b. Hampton, Ct., Sept. 16, 1733, son of Benjamin and Jamison (Alden) Chaplin; Y. C., 1763, A.B.; A.M., 1767; Ord. Millbury, Nov. 14, 1763; sett. Millbury, 1764-1792; dism. Mar. 22, 1792; d. Hardwick, Dec. 13, 1822, a. 90.

BENJAMIN CHAPMAN, A.M., b. 1725, of parentage unknown; Princeton, 1754, A.B., A.M.; A.M., (Hon.), Y. C., 1761; Ord. Southington, Ct., (3rd Chh. in Farmington), Mar. 17, 1756; sett. Southington, Ct., 1756-1774; dism. Sept. 28, 1774; d. Southington, Ct., June 22, 1786, a. 61.

DANIEL CHAPMAN, A.M., b. Saybrook, Ct., Mar. 14, 1688/9, son of Dea. Nathaniel and Mary (Collins) Chapman; Y. C., 1707, A.B., A.M.; Ord. Green Farms, Ct., (West Farms or 2nd Parish in Fairfield), Oct. 26, 1715; sett. Green Farms, Ct., 1712-1741; d. Green Farms, Ct., Nov. 28, 1741, a. 52.

ELIPHAZ CHAPMAN, b. Newmarket, N. H., Mar. 7, 1750, son of Samuel and —— (York) Chapman; sett. Georgetown, (Separatist Chh.), 1770-1772; sett. Madbury, N. H.; Ord. Methuen, (2nd Chh.), Nov. 1772; sett. Methuen, 1772-1777; went to Bethel, Vt., Feb. 1791; became a farmer; d. Newry, Me., Jan. 20, 1814.

HEZEKIAH CHAPMAN, A.M., b. Saybrook, Ct., Aug. 31, 1746, son of Dea. Caleb and Thankful (Lord) Chapman; Y. C., 1766, A.B., A.M.; Ord. Uxbridge, Jan. 27, 1774; sett. Uxbridge, 1773-1781; dism. Apr. 5, 1781; after leaving Uxbridge he became a lawyer in western N. Y.; d. 1794.

JOSIAH CHASE, A.M., b. Newbury, Nov. 30, 1713, son of Dea. Thomas and Sarah (Stevens) Chase; H. C., 1738, A.B., A.M.; Ord. Kittery, Me., (2nd or Spruce Creek Parish Chh.), Sept. 19, 1750; sett. Kittery, Me., 1750-1778; d. by being frozen to death on his way home from a wedding, Dec. 10, 1778, having missed his path and having fallen into Spruce Creek.

RICHARD CHASE, b. Yarmouth, Mar. 3, 1714/5, son of Thomas and Sarah (Gowell) Chase; Ord. Harwich, (2nd Separatist Chh.), Dec. 11, 1751; sett. Harwich, 1751-1756; inst. Harwich, (1st Bapt. Chh.), Sept. 9, 1756; sett. Harwich, (Bapt. Chh.), 1756-1787; dism. Jan. 7, 1787; Bapt.; d. Jan. 1794, a. 80.

STEPHEN CHASE, A.B., b. Newbury, Oct. 26, 1705, son of Joseph and Abigail (Thurston) Chase; H. C., 1728, A.B.; Ord. Lynnfield, Nov. 24, 1731; sett. Lynnfield, 1731-1747; inst. Newcastle, N. H., Dec. 5, 1750; sett. Newcastle, N. H., 1750-1778; d. Newcastle, N. H., Jan. 1, 1778, a. 73.

BARNABAS CHAUNCY, A.M., b. England, 1637, son of President Charles and Catharine (Eyre) Chauncy; H. C., 1657, A.B., A.M.; sett. Saco, Me., 1665-1666; d. 1675.

PRESIDENT CHARLES CHAUNCY, B.D., b. Yardley-bùry, Hertfordshire, Eng., 1589, and bapt., Nov. 5, 1592, son of George Chauncy; Trinity Coll., Camb., A.B., 1613/4; A.M., 1617; B.D., 1624; Fellow of Trinity Coll.; Prof. of Hebrew and Greek at Trinity Coll.; Vicar of St. Michael's, Camb., 1626; Vicar of Ware, Hertfordshire, Eng., 1627-1633; Vicar at Marston-St. Laurence, Northants, Eng., 1633-1637; brought before the Court of High Commission in 1630, and again in 1635, when he was suspended from the ministry and imprisoned; came to Plymouth, Mass., Jan. 1, 1637/8; asst. min., Plymouth, under Mr. Rayner, 1638-1640; sett. Scituate, 1641-1654; inst. Second President of Harvard Coll., Nov. 2, 1654; served as Pres., 1654-1671; physician; had six sons all educated as preachers and physicians; Election Sermon, 1656; d. Cambridge, Feb. 19, 1671, a. 82.

CHARLES CHAUNCY, A.M., b. Stratford, Ct., Sept. 3, 1668, son of Rev. Israel and Mary (Nichols) Chauncy; H. C., 1686, A.B., A.M.; Ord. Stratfield, Ct., (now Bridgeport), June 13, 1695, as the first minister; sett. Stratfield, Ct., 1690-1714; Chaplain, Ct. forces, 1690-1691; Ct. Election Sermon, 1702; physician; d. Stratfield, Ct., Dec. 31, 1714, a. 46.

CHARLES CHAUNCY, D.D., b. Boston, Jan. 1, 1705, son of Charles and Sarah (Walley) Chauncy; H. C., 1721, A.B., A.M.; S.T.D., U. of Edinburgh, 1742; Ord. Boston, (1st Chh.), Oct. 25, 1727; sett. Boston, 1727-1787; founder of the Am. Acad. of Arts and Sciences; defender of liberal Congregationalism; Artillery Election Sermon, 1734; Election Sermon, 1747; Convention Sermon, 1744, 1765; Dudleian Lecture, 1762; d. Boston, Feb. 10, 1787, a. 82.

ISAAC CHAUNCY, M.D., b. Ware, Eng., Aug. 23, 1632, son of President Charles and Catharine (Eyre) Chauncy; H. C., 1651, A.B., A.M.; M.D.; sett. London, Eng., (Berry St. Chh.); physician; d. London, Eng., Feb. 28, 1712, a. 80.

ISAAC CHAUNCY, A.M., b. Stratford, Ct., Oct. 5, 1670, son of Rev. Israel and Mary (Nichols) Chauncy; H. C., 1693, A.B., A.M.; Ord. Hadley, Sept. 9, 1696; sett. Hadley, 1695-1745; d. Hadley, May 2, 1745, a. 74.

ISRAEL CHAUNCY, A.M., b. Scituate, 1644, son of President Charles and Catharine (Eyre) Chauncy; H. C., 1661, A.B., A.M.; Founder and Trustee, Y. C.; Ord. Stratford, Ct., Dec. 1666; sett. Stratford, Ct., 1665-1703; Chaplain, King Philip's War, 1675/6; chosen Pres. of Y. C., but declined; d. Stratford, Ct., Mar. 14, 1702/3, a. 59.

NATHANIEL CHAUNCY, A.M., b. Plymouth, 1639, son of President Charles anad Catharine (Eyre) Chauncy; H. C., 1661, A.B., A.M.; Tutor and Fellow, H. C., 1663-1666; sett. Windsor, Ct., 1667-1680; sett. Hatfield, 1682-1685; physician; d. Hatfield, Nov. 4, 1685, a. ca. 46.

NATHANIEL CHAUNCY, A.M., b. Hatfield, Sept. 21, 1681,

son of Rev. Nathaniel and Abigail (Ford) Chauncy; Y. C., 1702, A.B., A.M.; Fellow, Y. C., 1746-1752; Ord. Durham, Ct., Feb. 7, 1711; sett. Durham, Ct., 1706-1756, as first minister; Ct. Election Sermon, 1719; d. Durham, Ct., Feb. 1, 1756.

JOHN CHECKLEY, A.M., b. Boston, 1680, son of John Checkley; U. of Oxford, 1735, A.M.; Ord. by the Bishop of Exeter, 1739; missionary for the Venerable Society for the Propagation of the Gospel in Foreign Parts; sett. Providence, R. I., (King's Chapel), 1739-1754; also preached at Warwick, R. I., and at Attleborough; Epis.; d. Providence, R. I., Feb. 15, 1753/4, a. 73.

SAMUEL CHECKLEY, A.M., b. Boston, Feb. 11, 1695/6, son of Samuel and Mary (Scottow) Checkley; H. C., 1715, A.B., A.M.; Ord. Boston, (New North Chh.), Apr. 15, 1719; sett. Boston, 1719-1769, as the first minister of this church; Artillery Election Sermon, 1720; Election Sermon, 1755; d. Boston, Dec. 1, 1769, a. 73.

SAMUEL CHECKLEY, JR., A.M., b. Boston, Dec. 27, 1723, son of Rev. Samuel and Elizabeth (Rolfe) Checkley; H. C., 1743, A.B., A.M.; Ord. Boston, (2nd Chh.), Sept. 3, 1747; sett. Boston, 1747-1768; Artillery Election Sermon, 1757; d. Boston, Mar. 19, 1768, a. 44.

AMES CHEEVER, A.M., b. Marblehead, Oct. 24, 1686, son of Rev. Samuel and Ruth (Angier) Cheever; H. C., 1707, A.B., A.M.; supplied at Dunstable, 1713-1715; Ord. Manchester, Oct. 4, 1716; sett. Manchester, 1716-1743; dism. Feb. 27, 1743; d. Manchester, Jan. 15, 1756, a. 70.

AMES CHEEVER, b. Manchester, June 24, 1723, son of Rev. Ames and Anna (Gerrish) Cheever; preached occasionally; d. Manchester, Mar. 4, 1802.

EDWARD CHEEVER, A.M., b. Lynn, May 2, 1717, son of Thomas and Mary (Baker) Cheever; H. C., 1737, A.B., A.M.; Ord. Saugus, Dec. 5, 1739; sett. Saugus, 1738-1748; inst. Eastham, 1751; sett. Eastham, 1751-1794; d. Eastham, Aug. 17, 1794, a. 78.

ISRAEL CHEEVER, A.M., b. Concord, Sept. 27, 1722, son of Daniel and Ruth (Meads) Cheever; H. C., 1749, A.B.; A.M., 1753; Ord. New Bedford, 1753; sett. New Bedford, 1753-1759; d. Liverpool, N. S., June 1812, a. 90.

SAMUEL CHEEVER, A.B., b. New Haven, Ct., Sept. 22, 1639, son of Ezekiel and Mary Cheever, (Ezekiel was the famous school master of Boston); H. C., 1659, A.B.; Ord. Marblehead, Aug. 13, 1684; sett. Marblehead, 1668-1724; for 48 years he was never absent from his duties for a single Sunday; Artillery Election Sermon, 1684; Election Sermon, 1712; d. Marblehead, May 29, 1724, a. 85.

THOMAS CHEEVER, A.M., b. Ipswich, Aug. 23, 1658, son of Ezekiel and Ellen (Lothrop) Cheever; H. C., 1677, A.B., A.M.; Ord. Malden, July 27, 1681; sett. Malden, 1679-1686, as colleague; dism. May 20, 1686; taught school, 1686-1715; re-ord. Chelsea,

(Church of Christ in Rumney Marsh, Revere), Oct. 19, 1715; sett. Chelsea, 1715-1749; he was the first minister of the First Church in Chelsea; d. Chelsea, Dec. 27, 1749.

THOMAS CHENEY, A.M., b. Roxbury, ca. 1692, son of Thomas and Hannah (Woodie) Cheney; H. C., 1711, A. B., A.M.; Ord. Brookfield, Oct. 16, 1717; sett. Brookfield, 1716-1747; called by the parish before the church was organized, Apr. 5, 1716; d. Brookfield, Dec. 11, 1747, a. 57.

JABEZ CHICKERING, A.M., b. Dover, Nov. 4, 1753, son of Joseph and Rebecca (Newell) Chickering; H. C., 1774, A.B., A.M.; Ord. Norwood, July 3, 1776; sett. Norwood, 1776-1812; d. Norwood, Mar. 12, 1812, a. 59.

JOHN CHIPMAN, A.M., b. Barnstable, Feb. 16, 1691, son of Samuel and Sarah (Cobb) Chipman; H. C., 1711, A.B., A.M.; Ord. Beverly, (2nd Chh.), Dec. 28, 1715; sett. Beverly, 1715-1775; d. Beverly, Mar. 23, 1775.

BENJAMIN CHOATE, A.M., b. Ipswich, 1680, son of John and Anne Choate; H. C., 1703, A.B., A.M.; minister at Kingston, N. H., 1707-1717; d. Kingston, N. H., Nov. 26, 1753, a. 73.

AARON CHURCH, A.M., b. Springfield, Feb. 21, 1745/6, son of Dea. Jonathan and Miriam (Church) Church; Y. C., 1765, A.B., A.M.; Ord. East Hartland, Ct., Oct. 20, 1773; sett. East Hartland, Ct., 1773-1815; d. East Hartland, Ct., Apr. 19, 1823, a. 78.

SELDEN CHURCH, A.M., b. East Haddam, Ct., Sept. 2, 1744, son of John and Lydia (Chapman) Church; Y. C., 1765, A.B., A.M.; A.M., (Hon.), Dart. Coll., 1791; Ord. Campton, N. H., June 2, 1774, as first minister; sett. Campton, N. H., 1774-1792; removed to Austerlitz, N. Y.; d. Austerlitz, N. Y., July 14, 1802, a. 57.

NATHANIEL CLAP, A.M., b. Dorchester, Jan. 20, 1668/9, son of Nathaniel and Elizabeth (Smith) Clap; H. C., 1690, A.B., A.M.; Ord. Newport, R. I., (1st Cong. Chh.), Nov. 3, 1720; sett. Newport, R. I., 1695/6-1745; d. Newport, R. I., Oct. 30, 1745.

NOAH CLAP, A.M., b. Dorchester, Jan. 25, 1718, son of Dea. Jonathan and Sarah (Capen) Clap; H. C., 1735, A.B., A.M.; studied theology and preached for a time, but gave up the ministry on account of poor health; taught school at Dorchester 20 yrs.; Selectman; Town Treasurer and Town Clerk many years; d. Dorchester, Apr. 10, 1799.

PRESIDENT THOMAS CLAP, A.M., b. Scituate, June 26, 1703, son of Dea. Stephen and Temperance Clap; H. C., 1722, A.B, A.M.; Ord. Windham, Ct., Aug. 3, 1726; sett. Windham, Ct., 1725-1739; dism. Dec. 10, 1739; inst. President, Y. C., Apr. 2, 1740; served as Pres., 1740-1764; resigned Sept. 10, 1764; d. New Haven, Ct., Jan. 7, 1767.

HON. COL. THOMAS CLAP, A.M., b. Scituate, Nov. 11, 1705, son of Lieut. John and Hannah (Gill) Clap, and cousin of Pres. Clap of Y. C.; H. C., 1725, A.B., A.M.; Ord. Taunton, Feb. 26, 1729;

sett. Taunton, 1729-1739; man of independent means; returned to Scituate where he was Chief Justice and a Colonel in the militia; Rep. Gen. Ct., 14 yrs.; d. Scituate, May 31, 1774, a. 69.

SUPPLY CLAP, A.M., b. Dorchester, June 1, 1711, son of Dea. Samuel and Mary (Paul) Clap; H. C., 1731, A.B., A.M.; teacher at Dorchester, 1731-1734; Ord. Burlington, Oct. 28, 1735; sett. Burlington, 1735-1748; d. Burlington, Jan. 8, 1747/8.

EPHRAIM CLARK, b. 1722; Ord. Stonington, Ct.; inst. South Portland, Me., (2nd Parish in Falmouth, at Cape Elizabeth), May 21, 1756; sett. South Portland, Me., 1756-1797; said to have been an unlearned man; d. Cape Elizabeth, Me., Dec. 11, 1797, a. 75.

JAMES CLARKE, b. Newport, R. I., 1649, son of Capt. Jeremiah and Frances (Latham) Clarke; Ord. Newport, R. I., (2nd Bapt. Chh.), 1701; sett. Newport, R. I., 1700-1736; Bapt.; d. Newport, R. I., Dec. 1, 1736, a. 87.

DR. JOHN CLARKE, b. Westhorpe, Suffolk, Eng., Oct. 8, 1609, son of Thomas and Rose (Kerrick) Clarke; (perhaps A. B., Corpus Christi Coll., Camb., 1626/7; A.M., 1630); came to Boston, Nov. 1637, where he practiced medicine; came to Newport, R. I., May 1639; Ord. Newport, R. I., (1st Bapt. Chh., as first minister of the second Bapt. Chh. in America), 1644; sett. Newport, R. I., 1641-1676; physician; Ass't. and Treas. of R. I. Colony, 1649; agent for R. I. in Eng., 1651-1663; Deputy-Gov. of R. I., 1669-1672; Bapt.; d. Newport, R. I., Apr. 20, 1676, a. 66.

JOHN CLARK, A.M., b. Newbury, Jan. 24, 1670, son of Nathaniel and Elizabeth (Somerby) Clark; H. C., 1690, A.B., A.M.; Ord. Exeter, N. H., (present 1st Chh., a reorganization of the old 1st Chh.), Sept. 11, 1698; sett. Exeter, N. H., 1698-1705; d. Exeter, N. H., July 25, 1705, a. 35.

JONAS CLARKE, A.M., b. Newton, Dec. 25, 1730, son of Thomas and Mary (Bowen) Clarke; H. C., 1752, A.B., A.M.; Ord. Lexington, Nov. 5, 1755; sett. Lexington, 1755-1805; Artillery Election Sermon, 1768; witnessed the Battle of Lexington; Election Sermon, 1781; d. Lexington, Nov. 15, 1805.

JOSEPH CLARKE, b. Westerly, R. I., Apr. 4, 1670, son of Joseph and Bethia (Hubbard) Clarke; Ord. Westerly, R. I., Aug. 21, 1712; sett. Westerly, R. I., 1712-1719; Bapt.; d. Westerly, R. I., June 5, 1719, a. 49.

JOSHUA CLARKE, b. Westerly, R. I., Apr. 26, 1717, son of Rev. Thomas and Elizabeth (Babcock) Clarke; Ord. Hopkinton, R. I., May 1768; sett. Hopkinton, R. I., (Seventh Day Bapt. Chh.), 1773-1793; member, R. I. Legislature; Trustee, Brown U.; soldier in the Colonial and Rev. Wars; Bapt.; d. Westerly, R. I., Mar. 8, 1793, a. 76.

JOSIAS CLARKE, A.B., b. Tarvin, Cheshire, Eng., 1622, son of Rev. Sabaoth Clarke; matric. at New Inn Hall, Oxford, Apr. 9,

1641, a. 19; Queens' Coll., Oxford, 1644/5, A.B.; Rector of Tattershall, Cheshire, 1658; Chaplain of the Fort at New York; sett. Boston, (asst. min., King's Chapel), 1686-1687; returned to England, Apr. 7, 1687; Vicar of Broxbourne, Herts., 1689-1694; Epis.

MATTHEW CLARK, b. Ireland, ca. 1659; officer in the army in Ireland; active in the defence of Londonderry, Ireland, during the siege of 1689; inst. Derry, (Londonderry), N. H., 1729; sett. Derry, N.H., 1729-1735; Presb.; d. Derry, N. H., Jan. 25, 1735, a. 76.

PETER CLARK, A.M., b. Watertown, Mar. 12, 1693/4, son of Uriah and Mary Clark; H. C., 1712, A.B., A.M.; Ord. Danvers, June 5, 1717; sett. Danvers, 1716-1768; carried on controversy over "original sin;" Artillery Election Sermon, 1736; Election Sermon, 1739; Convention Sermon, 1745; Dudleian Lecture, 1763; d. Danvers, June 10, 1768, a. 76.

RICHARD SAMUEL CLARKE, A.M., b. West Haven, Ct., 1738, son of Samuel Clark; Y. C., 1762; A.B., 1765; A.M., 1765; A.B., Columbia, 1762; A.M., Columbia, 1766; Ord. in Eng., Feb. 1767; sett. New Milford, Ct., (Epis. Chh.), June 1767-1786; sett. Gagetown, New Brunswick, May 1786-1811; sett. St. Stephen, N. B., 1811-1824; Epis.; d. St. Stephen, N. B., Oct. 6, 1824, a. 87.

SAMUEL CLARKE, A.M., Princeton, 1751, A.B., A.M.; A.M., (Hon.), Y. C., 1757; Ord. Kensington, Ct., (2nd Chh. in Farmington), July 1756; sett. Kensington, Ct., 1756-1776; d. 1776.

SETH CLARK, b. Northampton, Apr. 1723, son of Noah and Eunice (Dickenson) Clark; Ord. Wilbraham, (Bapt. Chh.), June 13, 1770; sett. Wilbraham, 1770-1813; Bapt.; d. Wilbraham, Sept. 1813, a. 90.

THOMAS CLARK, A.M., b. Boston, Mar. 2, 1652/3, son of Elder Jonas and Elizabeth Clark; H. C., 1670, A.B., A.M.; Ord. Chelmsford, Mar. or Apr. 1678/9; sett. Chelmsford, 1677-1704; Chaplain, King Philip's War; in the Great Swamp Fight, 1675; d. Chelmsford, Dec. 7, 1704, a. 52.

THOMAS CLARKE, b. Westerly, R. I., Mar. 17, 1686, son of Joseph and Bethia (Hubbard) Clarke; Ord. Westerly, R. I., Aug. 26, 1735; sett. Westerly, R. I., (Seventh Day Bapt. Chh. at Hopkinton, R. I.), 1735-1767; Bapt.; d. Hopkinton, R. I., Nov. 26, 1767.

WARD CLARK, A.M., b. Exeter, N. H., Dec. 12, 1703, son of Rev. John and Elizabeth (Woodbridge) Clark; H. C., 1723, A.B., A.M.; Ord. Kingston, N. H., Sept. 29, 1725; sett. Kingston, N. H., 1725-1737; d. Kingston, N. H., May 6, 1737, a. 33.

WILLIAM CLARK, A.M., b. Danvers, Aug. 2, 1740, son of Rev. Peter and Deborah (Hobart) Clark; H. C., 1759, A.B., A.M.; Ord. London, Eng., Dec. 21, 1768; sett. Quincy, (Christ Chh. in Braintree), 1767; sett. Dedham, (St. Paul's Chh.), 1767-1776, as Rector; sett. Canton, (English Chh.), 1767-1776; refugee; fled to Eng.; sett.

Nova Scotia, 1786-1795; came back to N. E., 1795, where he remained until his death; Epis.; d. Quincy, Nov. 4, 1815, a. 76.

AARON CLEAVELAND, A.M., b. Cambridge, Oct. 29, 1715, son of Aaron and Abigail (Waters) Cleaveland; H. C., 1735, A.B., A.M.; Ord. Haddam, Ct., (Cong. Chh.), July 1739; sett. Haddam, Ct., 1739-1746; inst. Malden, (South Chh., Cong., now Everett), June 1747; sett. Malden, (South Chh.), 1747-1750; dism. Oct. 1750; became a clergyman of the Established Chh.; Ord. in Eng., by the Bishop of London, 1754; sett. Norwich, Ct., (Epis. Chh.), 1754; sett. Groton, Ct., (Epis. Chh.), 1754; sett. Halifax, N. S., 1755; sett. Newcastle, Del., 1757; Epis.; d. at the home of Benjamin Franklin, his friend, Philadelphia, Pa., Aug. 11, 1757, a. 41.

EBENEZER CLEAVELAND, A.M., b. Canterbury, Ct., Dec. 25, 1725, son of Josiah and Abigail (Paine) Cleaveland; Y. C.; left before graduation, but was given his A.B., as of 1749; A.B., 1775; A.M., 1775; A.M., (Hon.), Dart. Coll., 1775; Ord. Rockport, (5th Parish of Gloucester), Dec. 1755; sett. Rockport, 1755-1780; dism. June 25, 1780; but preached often, 1780-1805; Chaplain in French and Indian Wars, 1756-1760; was at Ticonderoga and Lake George, 1758; Chaplain in the Am. Rev., 1775; d. Rockport, July 4, 1805, a. 80.

JOHN CLEAVELAND, A.M., b. Canterbury, Ct., Apr. 11, 1722, son of Josiah and Abigail (Paine) Cleaveland; Y. C., but left before graduation, but was granted his A.B., as of 1745; A.B., 1763; A.M., 1763; A.M., (Hon.), Dart. Coll., 1782; Ord. Essex, (2nd or Separatist Chh.), Feb. 25, 1747; sett. Essex, (2nd Chh.), 1746-1774; sett. Essex, (1st and 2nd Chhs. united), 1774-1799; Chaplain at Ticonderoga, 1758; at Louisburg, 1759; during the Am. Rev., 1775-1776; d. Essex, Apr. 22, 1799, a. 77.

THOMAS COBBETT, A.M., b. Newbury, Buckinghamshire, Eng., 1608, son of Thomas Cobbett; matric., Trinity Coll., Oxford, Oct. 12, 1627, a. 19; A.B., Trinity Coll., Oxford, 1627/8; A.M., St. Mary's Hall, Oxford, 1632; sett. Lincolnshire, where he was silenced for non-conformity; came to N. E., 1637; sett. Lynn, 1637-1655; sett. Ipswich, 1655-1685; Election Sermons, 1649, 1666; d. Ipswich, Nov. 5, 1685, a. 77.

ELIJAH CODDING, Ord. Wales, Nov. 11, 1775; sett. Wales, 1773-1826; Bapt.

ENOCH COFFIN, A.M., b. Newbury, Feb. 7, 1695/6, son of Hon. Nathaniel and Sarah (Dole) Coffin; H. C., 1714, A.B., A.M.; sett. Dunstable, Dec. 1, 1718-June 1720; sett. Concord, N. H., May 15, 1726-Aug. 1728; d. Concord, N. H., Aug. 17, 1728, a. 32.

PAUL COFFIN, D.D., b. Newbury, Jan. 16, 1737/8, son of Col. Joseph, Esq. and Margaret (Morse) Coffin; H. C., 1759, A.B., A.M.; S.T.D., 1812; Ord. Buxton, Me., Mar. 16, 1763; sett. Buxton, Me., 1761-1818; Election Sermon, 1799; Arminian; d. Buxton, Me., June 6, 1821, a. 84.

PETER COFFIN, A.M., b. Exeter, N. H., Dec. 8, 1713, son of Capt. Eliphalet and Judith (Coffin) Coffin; H. C., 1733, A.B., A.M.; Ord. East Kingston, N. H., Nov. 14, 1739, or Jan. 20, 1739/40; sett. East Kingston, N. H., 1739-1772; d. East Kingston, N. H., Dec. 19, 1777, a. 64.

JAMES COGSWELL, D.D., b. Saybrook, Ct., Jan. 6, 1719/20, son of Samuel and Ann (Mason) Cogswell; Y. C., 1742, A.B., A.M.; S.T.D., 1790; Ord. Canterbury, Ct., Dec. 28, 1744; sett. Canterbury, Ct., 1744-1771; dism. Nov. 5, 1771; inst. Scotland, Ct., (Windham), Feb. 19, 1772; sett. Scotland, Ct., 1772-1804; Ct. Election Sermon, 1771; d. Hartford, Ct., Jan. 2, 1807, a. 87.

JOSEPH COIT, A.M., b. New London, Ct., Apr. 4, 1673, son of Dea. Joseph and Martha (Harris) Coit; H. C., 1697, A.B.; Y. C., 1700, A.M.; Ord. Plainfield, Ct., Jan. 3, 1704/5, as the first minister; sett. Plainfield, Ct., 1699-1748; dism. Mar. 6, 1747/8; d. Plainfie'd, Ct., July 1, 1750, a. 77.

EZEKIEL COLE, b. 1723; Ord. Sutton, (Separatist Chh.), Jan. 31, 1751; sett. Sutton, 1751-1799; d. Sutton, Oct. 23, 1799, a. 76.

DANIEL COLLINS, A.M., b. Guilford, Ct., Jan. 30, 1738/9, son of Capt. Daniel and Lois (Cornwell) Collins; Y. C., 1760, A.B., A.M.; Ord. Lanesborough, Apr. 17, 1764; sett. Lanesborough, 1764-1822; Trustee, Williams Coll., 1793-1808; loyalist; d. Lanesborough, Aug. 26, 1822, a. 84.

NATHANIEL COLLINS, A.M., b. Cambridge, Mar. 7, 1641/2, son of Dea. Edward and Martha Collins; H. C., 1660, A.B., A.M.; Ord. Middletown Ct., Nov. 4, 1668, (when the chh. was gathered); sett. Middletown, Ct., 1664-1684; d. Middletown, Ct., Dec. 28, 1684.

NATHANIEL COLLINS, A.B., b. Middletown, Ct., June 13, 1677, son of Rev. Nathaniel and Mary (Whiting) Collins; H. C., 1697, A.B.; Ord. Enfield, Ct., June 3, 1699, as the first minister; sett. Enfield, Ct., 1697-1724; dism. Mar. 1724; Rep. Gen. Ct. of Mass., 1726-1728; 1734-1736; d. Glastonbury, Ct., Dec. 31, 1756.

NATHANIEL COLLINS, b. Enfield, Ct., Aug. 17, 1709, son of Rev. Nathaniel and Alice (Adams) Collins; minister at Westfield, Mass., (Separatist Chh.); Ord. Enfield, Ct., (Separatist Chh.), Aug. 20, 1762; sett. Enfield, Ct., (Separatist Chh.), 1762-1787; d. Enfield, Ct., Dec. 5, 1787.

TIMOTHY COLLINS, A.M., J.P., b. Guilford, Ct., Apr. 13, 1699, son of John, Jr. and Ann (Leete) Collins; Y. C., 1717, A.B., A.M.; Ord. Litchfield, Ct., June 20, 1723; sett. Litchfield, Ct., 1720-1752; dism. Oct. 14, 1752; Justice of the Peace, 1753; physician; magistrate; surgeon, 1755, on the expedition to Crown Point; d. Litchfield, Ct., Feb. 7, 1777, a. 78.

BENJAMIN COLMAN, D.D., b. Boston, Oct. 19, 1673, son of William and Elizabeth Colman; H. C., 1692, A.B., A.M.; S.T.D.,

U. of Glasgow, 1731; chosen President of H. C., but did not accept; Fellow, H. C., 1717-1728; Ord. London, Eng., by the Presbytery, Aug. 4, 1699; sett. Boston, (Brattle St. Chh.), 1699-1747; Commissioner of the Soc. for the Propagation of the Gospel in N. E. and for Parts Adjacent; Artillery Election Sermons, 1702, 1738; Election Sermons, 1718, 1723; d. Boston, Aug. 29, 1747, a. 73.

BENJAMIN COLTON, A.M., b. Longmeadow, 1690, son of Ephraim and Esther (Marshfield) Colton; Y. C., 1710, A.B., A.M.; Ord. West Hartford, Ct., (4th Chh. in Hartford), Feb. 24, 1713/4; sett. West Hartford, Ct., 1713-1759; Ct. Election Sermon, 1737; d. West Hartford, Ct., Mar. 1, 1759.

ELI COLTON, A.M., b. West Hartford, Ct., Aug. 8, 1716, son of Rev. Benjamin and Ruth (Taylor) Colton; Y. C., 1737, A.B., A.M.; Ord. Stafford, Ct., (1st Chh.), Sept. 14, 1744; sett. Stafford, Ct., 1744-1756; d. Stafford, Ct., June 8, 1756, a. 40.

GEORGE COLTON, A.M., b. West Hartford, Ct., July 11, 1736, son of Rev. Benjamin and Elizabeth (Pitkin) Colton; Y. C., 1756, A.B., A.M.; Ord. Bolton, Ct., (1st Chh.), Nov. 9, 1763; sett. Bolton, Ct., 1763-1812; d. Bolton, Ct., June 27, 1812, a. 76.

JONATHAN COLTON, A.M., b. Longmeadow, Mar. 11, 1726, son of Capt. George and Mercy (Hitchcock) Colton; Y. C., 1745, A.B., A.M.; Ord. London, Eng., Mar. 1752; sett. Hebron, Ct., (Epis. Chh.), 1748-1751; Epis.; d. at sea, Mar. 7, 1752, a. 27.

JAMES COLVIN, b. Providence, R. I., Nov. 24, 1695, son of John and Dorothy Colvin; Ord. Scituate, R. I., (Bapt. Chh.), 1738; sett. Scituate, R. I., 1738-1755; Bapt.; d. Coventry, R. 1., Mar. 5, 1755.

JOHN COMER, b. Boston, Aug. 1, 1704, son of John and Mary (Pittom) Comer; H. C. and Y. C., but was not grad.; sett. Swansea, 1725-1726; Ord. Newport, R. I., (1st Bapt. Chh.), May 19, 1726; sett. Newport, R. I., (1st Bapt. Chh.), 1726-1729; supply, Newport, R. I., (2nd Bapt. Chh.), 1729-1731; inst. Rehoboth, (1st Bapt. Chh.), Jan. 20, 1732; sett. Rehoboth, 1732-1734; Bapt.; d. Rehoboth. May 23, 1734, a. 30.

SYLVANUS CONANT, A.M., b. Bridgewater, Nov. 17, 1720, son of Lot and Deborah (Lovell) Conant; H. C., 1740, A.B., A.M.; Ord. Middleborough, (2nd Parish of the 1st Chh.), Mar. 28, 1745; sett. Middleborough, (2nd Parish), 1744-1748; sett. Middleborough, (1st and 2nd Parish and 1st Chh.), 1748-1777; Chaplain at Crown Point, 1755; d. Middleborough, Dec. 8, 1777, of small pox.

WILLIAM CONANT, A.M., b. Bridgewater, June 29, 1742, son of David and Sarah (Hayward) Conant; Y. C., 1770, A.B., A.M.; A.M., (Hon.), Dart. Coll., 1780; Ord. Lyme, N. H., Dec. 22, 1773, as the first minister; sett. Lyme, N. H., 1773-1810; d. Lyme, N. H., Mar. 8, 1810, a. 67.

JEREMIAH CONDY, JR., A.M., b. Boston, Feb. 9, 1708, son of Jeremiah and Susanna (Hiller) Condy; H. C., 1726, A.B., A.M.; taught school in Boston, 1729; was in England, 1730-1738; Ord. Boston, (1st Bapt. Chh.), Feb. 14, 1738/9; sett. Boston, 1738-1764; resign., Aug. 1764; reputed to have been an Arminian in theology; Bapt.; d. Boston, 1768, a. 59.

BENJAMIN CONKLIN, A.B., b. Southold, L. I., N. Y., 1732; Princeton, 1755, A.B.; Ord. Leicester. Nov. 23, 1763; sett. Leicester, 1763-1794; d. Leicester, Jan. 30, 1798, a. 67.

JOHN COOKE, b. England, son of Francis Cooke of the Mayflower, 1620; deacon at Plymouth; removed to Dartmouth; sett. Dartmouth, (Bapt. Chh.), 1676-1695, as the first minister; Rep. Gen. Ct. 1673; chief magistrate at Dartmouth; Bapt.; d. Dartmouth, Nov. 23, 1695.

JOSIAS COOK, b. Mendon, 1691, son of Nicholas and Johanna (Rockett) Cook; sett. Cumberland, R. I., 1749-1774, as the first minister; Bapt.; d. Cumberland, R. I., Apr. 28, 1774, a. 83.

NATHANIEL COOK, b. Bellingham, Sept. 15, 1718, son of Dea. Nicholas, Jr. and Mehitable (Staples) Cook; Ord. Cumberland, R. I., 1752; sett. Cumberland, R. I., 1752-1773; Bapt.; d. Cumberland, R. I., Apr. 17, 1773.

SAMUEL COOKE, A.M., b. Guilford, Ct., Nov. 22, 1687, son of Thomas, Jr. and Sarah (Mason) Cooke; Y. C., 1705, A.B., A.M.; Fellow; Ord. Stratfield, Ct., Feb. 14, 1715/6; sett. Stratfield, Ct., 1715-1747; d. Stratfield, Ct., Dec. 2, 1747, a. 60.

SAMUEL COOKE, A.M., b. Hadley, Jan. 10, 1709, son of Lieut. Samuel and Ann (Marsh) Cooke; H. C., 1735, A.B., A.M.; Ord. Arlington, Sept. 12, 1739; sett. Arlington, 1739-1783; Artillery Election Sermon, 1753; Dudleian Lecture, 1767; Election Sermon, 1770; Convention Sermon, 1776; d. Arlington, Jan. 4, 1783, a. 74.

WILLIAM COOKE, A.M., b. Hadley, June 20, 1696, son of Westwood and Sarah (Coleman) Cooke; H. C., 1716, A.B., A.M.; Librarian, H. C., 1720-1721; Ord. Wayland, Mar. 20, 1723; sett. Wayland, 1723-1760; d. Wayland, June 17, 1760, a. 64.

SAMUEL COOLIDGE, A.M., b. Watertown, Aug. 16, 1703, son of Lieut. Richard and Susanna Coolidge; H. C., 1724, A.B., A.M.; Librarian, H. C., 1734-1735; Chaplain at Castle Island; Schoolmaster at Watertown, 1725, 1751; d. Jan. 1767, unm.

MR. COOLEY, sett. Lyme, Ct., (1st Bapt. Chh.), ca. 1752; Bapt.

SAMUEL COOPER, D.D., b. Boston, Mar. 28, 1725, son of Rev. William and Judith (Sewall) Cooper; H. C., 1743, A.B., A.M.; A.M., (Hon.), Y. C., 1750; S.T.D., U. of Edinburgh, 1767; Fellow, H. C., 1767-1783; Ord. Boston (Brattle St. Chh.), May 22, 1746; sett. Boston, 1744-1783; V. P., Am. Acad. Arts and Sciences, 1780; member Corp. H. C., 1767-1783; Artillery Election Sermon, 1751;

Election Sermon, 1756; Convention Sermon, 1770; Dudleian Lecture, 1773; d. Boston, Dec. 23, 1783, a. 58.

WILLIAM COOPER, A.M., b. Boston, Mar. 20, 1694, son of Thomas and Mehitable (Minot) Cooper; H. C., 1712, A.B., A.M.; Ord. Boston, (Brattle St. Chh.), May 23, 1716; sett. Boston, 1715-1743; chosen President of H. C., but did not accept; Artillery Election Sermon, 1722; Election Sermon, 1740; d. Boston, Dec. 13, 1743, a. 50.

RENE COSSIT, A.M., b. Granby, Ct., Dec. 29, 1744, son of Rene and Phoebe (Hillyer) Cossit; Brown U., 1771, A.B., A.M.; Ord. by the Bishop of London, 1773; inst. Claremont, N. H., (Union Chh. at West Claremont, Epis.), Nov. 1773; sett. Claremont, N. H., 1773-1785; missionary at Sydney, Cape Breton Island, 1785-1815; Epis.; d. Yarmouth, N. S., 1815.

JOHN COTTON, B.D., b. Derby, England, Dec. 4, 1585, son of Roland, Esq. and Mary (Hulbert) Cotton; Trinity Coll., Camb., A.B., 1602/3; A.M., Emmanuel Coll., Camb., 1606; B. D., Emmanuel Coll., Camb., 1613; Fellow, 1606, Head Lecturer, Dean and Catechist of Emmanuel Coll., Camb.; Ord. Lincoln, Eng., July 13, 1610; Vicar of St. Botolph's Chh., Boston, Lincolnshire, Eng., 1612-1633; came to N. E., 1633; Ord. Boston, (1st Chh.), Oct. 10, 1633; sett. Boston, 1633-1652; Election Sermon, 1634; Artillery Election Sermon, 1651; his portrait is owned by the Conn. Hist. Soc.; d. Boston, Dec. 23, 1652, a. 67.

JOHN COTTON, JR., A.M., b. Boston, Mar. 15, 1639/40, son of Rev. John and Sarah (Hawkred) (Story) Cotton; H. C., 1657, A.B., A.M.; sett. Wethersfield, Ct., 1659-1663; missionary to the Indians at Edgartown, Martha's Vineyard, 1664-1667; Ord. Plymouth, June 30, 1669; sett. Plymouth, 1669-1697; dism. Oct. 5, 1697; inst. Charleston, S. C., Mar. 15, 1699; buried at Plymouth, Mass.; d. Charleston, S. C., Sept. 18, 1699, a. 59.

JOHN COTTON, A.M., b. Hampton, N. H., May 8, 1658, son of Rev. Seaborn and Dorothy (Bradstreet) Cotton; H. C., 1678, A.B., A.M.; Librarian, H. C., 1681-1690; Fellow, H. C., 1681-1690; Ord. Hampton, N. H., Nov. 19, 1696; sett. Hampton, N. H., 1696-1710; d. Hampton, N. H., Mar. 27, 1710, a. 51.

JOHN COTTON, A.M., b. Guilford, Ct., Aug. 3, 1661, son of Rev. John, Jr. and Jane (Rossiter) Cotton; H. C., 1681, A.B., A.M.; sett. Exeter, N. H., 1684-1690; Ord. Yarmouth, 1693; sett. Yarmouth, 1691-1705; d. Yarmouth, Feb. 21, 1705/6, a. 44.

JOHN COTTON, A.M., b. July 15, 1693, son of Rev. Roland and Elizabeth (Saltonstall) Cotton; H. C., 1710, A.B., A.M.; Ord. Newton, Nov. 3, 1714; sett. Newton, 1714-1757; Election Sermon, 1753; his portrait is owned by John Eliot Thayer of Lancaster, Mass; d. Newton, May 17, 1757, a. 64.

JOHN COTTON, A.M., b. Plymouth, Apr. 1712, son of Rev. Josiah and Hannah (Sturtevant) Cotton; H. C., 1730, A.B., A.M.;

Ord. Halifax, 1735; sett. Halifax, 1735-1756; author of a "History of Plymouth Church;" Registrar of Deeds, Plymouth Co.; d. Plymouth, Dec. 4, 1789.

JOSIAH COTTON, A.M., b. Plymouth, Jan. 8, 1679/80, son of Rev. John and Jane (Rossiter) Cotton; H. C., 1698, A.B., A.M.; school teacher at Marblehead, 1698-1704; preached at Yarmouth, 1704; Indian missionary, 1707-1744; compiled a dictionary of the Indian language; taught school at Plymouth, 1705-1711, et seq.; Clerk of the Inferior Court, and Registrar of Deeds, 1713; Justice of the Peace; Registrar of Probate; Notary Public; Registrar of Deeds; Special Justice, Ct. of Common Pleas until 1739; Justice of the Inferior Court, 1715-1747; Rep., 1721, 1723, 1727; d. Plymouth, Aug. 16 (27), 1756.

JOSIAH COTTON, A.M., b. Sandwich, June 5, 1703, son of Rev. Roland and Elizabeth (Saltonstall) Cotton; H. C., 1722, A.B., A.M.; Ord. Providence, R. I., (1st Cong. Chh.), Oct. 23, 1728; sett. Providence, R. I., 1728-1747; inst. Woburn, (3rd Chh.), July 15, 1747; sett. Woburn, 1747-1756; inst. Sandown, N. H., Nov. 27, 1759; sett. Sandown, N. H., 1759-1780; d. Sandown, N. H., May 27, 1780, a. 76.

JOSIAH COTTON, A.M., b. Halifax, 1747, son of Rev. John and Hannah (Sturtevant) Cotton; Y. C., 1771, A.B., A.M.; Ord. Wareham, Nov. 1, 1774; sett. Wareham, 1774-1779; dism. May 31, 1779; magistrate and clerk of the County Court; d. Plymouth, Apr. 19, 1819, a. 71.

NATHANIEL COTTON, A.M., b. Sandwich, June 17, 1698, son of Rev. Roland and Elizabeth (Saltonstall) Cotton; H. C., 1717, A.B., A.M.; Ord. Bristol, R. I., (Cong. Chh.), Aug. 20, 1721; sett. Bristol, R. I., 1721-1729; d. Bristol, R. I., July 3, 1729, a. 31.

ROLAND COTTON, A.M., b. Plymouth, Dec. 27, 1667, son of Rev. John and Jane (Rossiter) Cotton: H. C. 1685 A.B. A.M.; Ord. Sandwich, Nov. 24, 1694; sett. Sandwich, 1691-1722; Artillery Election Sermon, 1706; Election Sermon, 1717; d. Sandwich, Mar. 22, 1721/2.

SAMUEL COTTON, A.M., b. Newton, Jan. 24, 1737/8, son of Rev. John and Mary (Gibbs) Cotton; H. C., 1759, A.B., A.M.; Ord. Litchfield, N. H., Jan. 2, 1765; sett. Litchfield, 1765-1781; also preached at Francestown, N. H., 1773-1781; d. Claremont, N. H., Nov. 25, 1819, a. 81.

SEABORN COTTON, A.M., b. at sea enroute to N. E., Aug. 12, 1633, son of Rev. John and Sarah (Hawkred) (Story) Cotton; H. C., 1651, A.B., A.M.; sett. Wethersfield, Ct., and Windsor, Ct., 1655; Ord. Hampton. N. H., May 4, 1659; sett. Hampton, N. H., 1657-1686; Artillery Election Sermon, 1673; d. Hampton, N. H., Apr. 19, 1686, a. 52.

THEOPHILUS COTTON, A.M., b. Plymouth, May 5, 1682, son of Rev. John and Joanna (Rossiter) Cotton; H. C., 1701, A.B.,

A.M.; Ord. Hampton Falls, N. H., Jan. 2, 1712; sett. Hampton Falls, N..H., 1712-1726; d. Hampton Falls, N. H., Aug. 16, 1726, a. 44, s. p.

WARD COTTON, AM., b. Sandwich, Sept. 8, 1711, son of Rev. Roland and Elizabeth (Saltonstall) Cotton; H. C., 1729, A.B., A.M.; Ord. Hampton, N. H., June 19, 1734; sett. Hampton, N. H., 1734-1765; dism. Nov. 12, 1765; d. Plymouth, Nov. 27, 1768, a. 57.

THOMAS CRAIGHEAD, A.M., b. Donoughmore, County Donegal, Ireland, son of Rev. Robert and Agnes (Hart) Craighead; studied medicine; Edinburgh U., July 28, 1691, A.M.; Ord. Donegal, Ireland, 1698; minister of the Presbyterian churches of Donegal and Ballyshannon, County Donegal, Ireland, 1698-1714; arrived at Boston, N. E., Oct. 1714, in the ship "Thomas and Jane;" sett. Freetown, Jan. 1715-1723; sett. White Clay Creek, Del., 1724-1731; sett. Pequea, Lancaster Co., Pa., 1733-1736; sett. Hopewell, now Newville, Pa., 1737-1739; Moderator, Presbyt. synod, 1726; d. Newville, Pa., Apr. 1739.

JOSEPH CRANDAL, b. Westerly, R. I., son of Elder John and Hannah Crandal; Ord. Newport, R. I., (3rd Bapt. or Seventh Day Bapt. Chh.), May 8, 1715; sett. Newport, R. I., 1715-1737; Bapt.; d. Newport, R. I., Sept. 13, 1737.

BENJAMIN CROCKER, A.M., b. Barnstable, Sept. 26, 1692, son of Josiah and Melatiah (Hinckley) Crocker; H. C., 1713, A.B., A.M.; taught grammar school at Inswich for many years; preached at Gorham, Me., Feb. 16, 1742/3 to Sept. 12, 1743; supplied at Ipswich, 1752-1753; sett. Harwich, (South Parish), 1754-1765; Rep. Gen. Ct., from Ipswich, 1726, 1734, 1746; d. 1766, a. 75.

JOSEPH CROCKER, A.M., b. Barnstable, 1714, son of Thomas and Hannah Crocker; H. C., 1734, A.B., A.M.; Ord. Orleans, Sept. 12, 1739; sett. Orleans, 1739-1772; d. Orleans, Mar. 2, 1772, a. 58.

JOSIAH CROCKER, A.M., b. Yarmouth, Oct. 30, 1719, son of Capt. Josiah and Desire (Thacher) Crocker; H. C., 1738, A.B., A.M.; Ord. Taunton, May 19, 1742; sett. Taunton, 1742-1765; dism. Nov. 1, 1765; d. Taunton, Aug. 28, 1774, a. 55.

JOSIAH CROCKER, A.M., b. Orleans, Mar. 15, 1740/1, son of Rev. Joseph and Reliance (Allen) Crocker; H. C., 1760, A.B., A.M.; called to Dennis, Dec. 7, 1763; sett. Dennis, 1763-1764; d. Dennis, June 20, 1764.

THOMAS CROSBY, A.B., bapt. Holme-on-Spaulding-Moor, Yorkshire, Eng., Feb. 26, 1634/5, son of Simon and Ann (Brigham) Crosby; H. C., 1653, A.B.; sett. Eastham, 1655-1670; perhaps not ordained; merchant at Harwich; d. Boston, June 13, 1702, a. 67.

PARSON CROSBY, sett. Thompson, Ct., (2nd Bapt. Chh.), 1773; Bapt.

ANDREW CROSWELL, A.M., b. Charlestown, Jan. 30, 1708/9, son of Caleb and Abigail (Stimpson) Croswell; H. C., 1728, A.B., A.M.; Ord. Ledyard, Ct., (2nd Chh. in Groton), Oct. 14, 1736;

sett. Ledyard, Ct., 1736-1746; dism. Aug. 21, 1746; inst. Boston, (School St. or 11th Cong. Chh.,), Oct. 6, 1748; sett. Boston, 1743-1785; published many sermons; d. Boston, Apr. 12, 1785, a. 77.

ALEXANDER CUMMING, A.M., b. Freehold, N. J., 1726, son of Robert Cumming; educated by his uncle, Rev. Dr. Samuel Blair; A. M., (Hon.), Princeton, 1760; A.M., (Hon.), H. C., 1761; Ord. New York City, (1st Presb. Chh.), Oct. 1750; sett. New York City, 1750-1753; inst. Boston, (Old South Chh.), Feb. 25, 1761; sett. Boston, 1761-1763; d. Boston, Aug. 25, 1763, a. 37.

HENRY CUMMINGS, D.D., b. Hollis, N. H., Sept. 16, 1739, son of Ensign Jerahmael and Hannah (Farewell) Cummings; H. C., 1760, A.B., A.M.; S.T.D., 1800; Ord. Billerica, Jan. 26, 1763; sett. Billerica, 1763-1823; Election Sermon, 1783; Dudleian Lecture, 1791; Convention Sermon, 1795; an Arminian in theology; later a Unitarian; delegate to the Mass. Constitutional Convention, 1780; d. Baltimore, Md., Sept. 5, 1823.

JOSEPH CURRIER, A.M., b. Amesbury, Mar. 18, 1742/3, son of Abner and Mary (Harvey) Currier; H. C., 1765, A.B., A.M.; Ord. Goffstown, N. H., Oct. 30, 1771; sett. Goffstown, N. H., 1771-1774; d. Corinth, Vt., July 24, 1829, a. 86.

CALEB CURTISS, b. Wallingford, Ct., Feb. 3, 1727, son of Joseph and Martha (Collins) Curtiss; Ord. Charlton, Oct. 15, 1761; sett. Charlton, 1761-1776; dism. Oct. 29, 1776; later sett. Dudley; Rep. Gen. Ct., 1775; d. Charlton, Mar. 21, 1802.

JEREMIAH CURTIS, A.M., bapt. Stratfield, Ct., (now Bridgeport), May 26, 1706, son of Zechariah and Hannah (Porter) Curtis; Y. C., 1724, A.B., A.M.; Ord. Southington, Ct., (3rd Chh. in Farmington), Nov. 13, 1726; sett. Southington, Ct., 1726-1755; dism. Nov. 1755; d. Southington, Ct., Mar. 21, 1795, a. 89.

PHILIP CURTIS, A.M., b. Roxbury, Oct. 4, 1717, son of Samuel and Hannah (Gore) Curtis; H. C., 1738, A.B., A.M.; Ord. Sharon, Jan. 5, 1742/3; sett. Sharon, 1741-1797; d. Sharon, Nov. 22, 1797, a. 81.

GEORGE CURWIN, A.M., b. Salem, May 21, 1683, son of Hon. Jonathan and Elizabeth (Gibbs) Curwin; H. C., 1701, A.B., A.M.; Ord. Salem, May 19, 1714; sett. Salem, 1714-1717; d. Salem, Nov. 23, 1717, a. 35.

CALEB CUSHING, A.M., b. Scituate, Jan. 6, 1672/3, son of Hon. John and Sarah (Hawke) Cushing; H. C., 1692, A.B., A.M.; Ord. Salisbury, Nov. 9, 1698; sett. Salisbury, 1698-1752; his home was used as a garrison, 1702; d. Salisbury, Jan. 25, 1752, a. 80.

JACOB CUSHING, D.D., b. Shrewsbury, Feb. 17, 1729/30, son of Rev. Job and Mary (Prentice) Cushing; H. C., 1748, A.B., A.M.; S.T.D., 1807; Ord. Waltham, Nov. 22, 1752; sett. Waltham, 1752-1809; Convention Sermon, 1789; Dudleian Lecture, 1792; d. Waltham, Jan. 18, 1809, a. 79.

JAMES CUSHING, A.M., b. Salisbury, Nov. 20, 1705, son of the Rev. Caleb and Elizabeth (Cotton) Cushing; H. C., 1725, A.B., A.M.; Ord. Haverhill, (2nd or North Parish now Plaistow), Dec. 2, 1730; sett. Haverhill, 1730-1764; part of his parish became Plaistow, N. H., in 1741, when the state line was changed; d. Plaistow, N. H., May 13, 1764, a. 58.

JEREMIAH CUSHING, A.B., b. Hingham, July 3, 1654, son of Daniel, Esq. and Lydia (Gilman) Cushing; H. C., 1676, A.B.; sett. Hingham, 1681; sett. Haverhill, 1682-1683; Ord. Scituate, May 27, 1691; sett. Scituate, 1691-1705; d. Scituate, Mar. 22, 1705/6, a. 51.

JOB CUSHING, A.M., b. Hingham, July 19, 1694, son of Capt. Matthew and Jael (Jacob) Cushing; H. C., 1714, A.B., A.M.; Ord. Shrewsbury, Dec. 4, 1723; sett. Shrewsbury, 1723-1760; d. Shrewsbury, Aug. 6, 1760, a. 67.

JOHN CUSHING, A.M., b. Salisbury, Apr. 10, 1709, son of Rev. Caleb and Elizabeth (Cotton) Cushing; H. C., 1729, A.B., A.M.; Ord. West Boxford, Dec. 29, 1736; sett. West Boxford, 1736-1772; d. West Boxford, Jan. 25, 1772.

JOHN CUSHING, D.D., b. Shrewsbury, Aug. 22, 1744, son of Rev. Job and Mary (Prentice) Cushing; H. C., 1764, A.B.; A. M., 1769; S.T.D., 1822; Ord. Ashburnham, Nov. 2, 1768; sett. Ashburnham, 1768-1822; d. Ashburnham, Apr. 27, 1823.

JONATHAN CUSHING, A.M., b. Hingham, Dec. 20, 1689, son of Peter and Hannah (Hawke) Cushing; H. C., 1712, A.B., A.M.; Ord. Dover, N. H., Sept. 18, 1717; sett. Dover, N. H., 1717-1769; d. Dover, N. H., Mar. 25, 1769, a. 79.

ISAAC CUSHMAN, b. Plymouth, Feb. 8, 1647/8, son of Elder Thomas and Mary (Allerton) Cushman; Ord. Plympton, Oct. 27, 1698, as the first minister; sett. Plympton, 1698-1732; d. Plympton, Oct. 21, 1732, a. 84.

ROBERT CUSHMAN, b. (perhaps at Canterbury) England, 1580; a leader and financial agent of the Mayflower Pilgrims; came to N. E. in the "Fortune," 1621, but returned to England one month later; he preached at Plymouth, Dec. 9, 1621; d. England, 1625/6.

MANASSEH CUTLER, LL.D., b. Killingly, Ct., May 3, 1742, son of Hezekiah and Susanna (Clark) Cutler; Y. C., 1765, A.B.; A.M., 1768; LL.D., 1791; A.M., (Hon.), H. C., 1768; Ord. Hamilton, Sept. 11, 1771; sett. Hamilton, 1771-1823; Fellow, Am. Acad. Arts and Sciences; Am. Phil. Soc.; Am. Antiquarian Soc.; Mass. Hist. Soc.; Member of Congress; d. Hamilton, July 25, 1823.

ROBERT CUTLER, A.M., b. Cambridge, Apr. 3, 1721, son of James and Alice Cutler; H. C., 1741, A.B., A.M.; Ord. Epping, N. H., Dec. 9, 1747; sett. Epping, N. H., 1747-1755; dism. Dec. 9, 1755; inst. Greenwich, Feb. 13, 1760; sett. Greenwich, 1760-1786; d. Greenwich, Feb. 7, 1786, a. 64.

TIMOTHY CUTLER, D.D., b. Charlestown, May 31, 1684,

son of Major John and Martha (Wiswall) Cutler; H. C., 1701, A.B., A.M.; Rector (or President), Y. C., 1719-1722; S.T.D., Oxford, 1723; S.T.D., Camb., 1723; Ord. Stratford, Ct., (Cong. Chh.), Jan. 11, 1709/10; sett. Stratford, Ct., 1710-1719; inst. Boston, (Christ Chh., Epis), Dec. 29, 1723, as the first minister; sett. Boston, 1723-1765; Epis.; Ct. Election Sermon, 1717; d. Boston, Aug. 7, 1765, a. 81.

AMMI RUHAMMAH CUTTER, A.M., bapt. West Cambridge, May 6, 1705, son of William and Rebecca (Rolfe) Cutter; H. C., 1725, A.B., A.M.; Ord. North Yarmouth, Me., Nov. 18, 1730; sett. North Yarmouth, Me., 1730-1735; Arminian; was dism. from the ministry because of his liberal views, Dec. 12, 1735; physician; Capt. of a military co.; d. Louisburg, Canada, Mar. 1746.

ELIHU DAGGETT, b. Attleborough, Aug. 6, 1710, son of Capt. Mayhew and Joanna (Biven) Daggett; Ord. Attleborough, (Separatist Chh.), July 3, 1765; sett. Attleborough, 1765-1769; d. Attleborough, Aug. 29, 1769, a. 60.

NAPHTALI DAGGETT, D.D., b. Attleborough, Sept. 8, 1727, son of Ebenezer anad Mary (Blackinton) Daggett. Y. C., 1748, A.B., A.M.; A.M., (Hon.), H. C., 1771; S.T.D., Princeton, 1774; Ord. Smithtown, L.I., N. Y., (Presb. Chh.), Sept. 18, 1751; sett. Smithtown, N. Y., 1751-1755; inst. Y. C., Prof. of Divinity, Mar. 4, 1756; sett. Y. C., 1755-1780; President, pro tem., Y. C., Oct. 1766-Mar. 1777; d. New Haven, Ct., Nov. 25, 1780, a. 54.

PIERRE DAILLE, b. ca. 1648; professor at Saumur, France; exiled; came to N. Y., 1683; sett. New Paltz, N. Y., 1683-1696; sett. Boston, (French Huguenot Chh.), 1696-1715; d. Boston, May 20, 1715, a. ca. 66.

TIMOTHY DALTON, A.B., b. England, ca. 1588; matric., St. John's Coll., Camb., 1610; St. John's Coll., Camb., 1613/4, A.B.; Ord. June 19, 1614; Vicar of Woolverstone, Suffolk, 1615-1636; suspended by Bishop Wren, April 1636; Rector of Flowton, 1616-1624; came to N. E., 1636; sett. Watertown and Dedham; inst. Hampton, N. H., 1639; sett. Hampton, N. H., 1639-1661; d. Hampton, N. H., Dec. 28, 1661.

GEORGE DAMAN, A.M., b. Dedham, July 7, 1736, son of John and Elizabeth (Metcalf) Daman; H. C., 1756, A.B., A.M.; Ord. Tisbury, Oct. 1, 1760; sett. Tisbury, 1760-1781; dism. Mar. 28, 1781; d. Woodstock, Vt., Dec. 1796, a. 60.

JAMES DANA, D.D., b. Cambridge, 1735, son of Caleb and Phoebe (Chandler) Dana; H. C., 1753, A.B., A.M.; D.D., U. of Edinburgh, 1768; Ord. Wallingford, Ct., Oct. 11, 1758; sett. Wallingford, Ct., 1758-1789; inst. New Haven, Ct., (1st Chh.), Apr. 29, 1789; sett. New Haven, Ct., 1789-1805; dism. Dec. 1805; Ct. Election Sermon, 1779; d. New Haven, Ct., Aug. 18, 1812.

JOSEPH DANA, D.D., b. Pomfret, Ct., Nov. 2, 1742, son of Dea. Joseph and Mary (Fulham) Dana; Y. C., 1760, A.B., A.M.;

S.T.D., H. C., 1801; supply, Boston, (Old South Chh.), 1763; Ord. Ipswich, (2nd Chh.), Nov. 7, 1765; sett. Ipswich, 1764-1827; Convention Sermon, 1801; d. Ipswich, Nov. 16, 1827, a. 85.

JOSIAH DANA, A.M., b. Pomfret, Ct., Aug. 22, 1742, son of Samuel and Mary (Sumner) Dana; H. C., 1763, A.M.; A.M., (Hon.), Y. C., 1766; A.M., Brown, 1790; A.M., Dart. Coll., 1794; Ord. Barre, Oct. 7, 1767; sett. Barre, 1767-1801; d. Barre, Oct. 1, 1801.

SAMUEL DANA, A.M., b. Brighton, Jan. 14, 1738/9, son of William and Mary (Green) Dana; H. C., 1755, A.B., A.M.; Ord. Groton, June 3, 1761; sett. Groton, 1760-1775; dism. May 1775; removed to Amherst, N. H.; Registrar of Probate, 1784-1787; Judge of Probate, 1787-1792; N. H. State Senator, 1793; d. Amherst, N. H., Apr. 1, 1798, a. 59.

FRANCIS DANE, bapt. Bishops-Stortford, Eng., Nov. 20, 1615, son of Dr. John and Frances Dane; matric. sizar, King's Coll., Camb., 1633; came to N. E., 1636; Ord. Andover, 1648; sett. Andover, 1648-1697; liberal; d. Andover, Feb. 17, 1696/7, a. 82.

JOHN DANFORTH, A.M., b. Roxbury, Nov. 8, 1660, son of Rev. Samuel and Mary (Wilson) Danforth; H. C., 1677, A.B., A.M.; Fellow, H. C., 1697-1707; Ord. Dorchester, June 8, 1682; sett. Dorchester, 1682-1730; Artillery Election Sermon, 1693; Election Sermon, 1697; d. Dorchester, May 26, 1730, a. 70.

SAMUEL DANFORTH, A.M., b. Framlingham, Suffolk, Eng., Sept. 1626, son of Nicholas and Elizabeth Danforth; came to N. E., 1634; H. C., 1642, A.B., A.M.; Fellow, 1650-1654; Ord. Roxbury, Sept. 24, 1650; sett. Roxbury, 1650-1674; Astronomer; Artillery Election Sermon, 1667; Election Sermon, 1670; d. Roxbury, Nov. 19, 1674, a. 48.

SAMUEL DANFORTH, JR., A.M., b. Roxbury, Dec. 10, 1666, son of Rev. Samuel and Mary (Wilson) Danforth; H. C., 1683, A.B., A.M.; Ord. Taunton, Sept. 21, 1687; sett. Taunton, 1687-1727; student of law, theology, medicine and astronomy; physician; Indian commissioner; Artillery Election Sermon, 1708; Election Sermon, 1714; d. Taunton, Nov. 14, 1727, a. 60.

ZADOCK DARROW, b. Waterford, Ct., Dec. 25, 1728, son of Ebenezer and —— (Rogers) Darrow; Ord. Waterford, Ct., (1st Bapt. Chh. of Waterford, New London, Ct.), 1769; sett. Waterford, 1767-1827; Seventh Day Bapt.; d. Waterford, Ct., Feb. 16, 1827, a. 99.

ADDINGTON DAVENPORT, JR., A.M., b. Boston, May 16, 1701, son of Addington and Elizabeth (Wainwright) Davenport; H. C., 1719, A.B., A.M.; A.M., Oxford, 1732; sett. Scituate, (St. Andrew's Chh.), 1730-1737; inst. Boston, (King's Lecturer at King's Chapel), Apr. 15, 1737; sett. Boston, (King's Chapel), 1737-1740;

inst. Boston, (Trinity Chh.), May 8, 1740; sett. Boston, (Trinity Chh.), 1740-1746; Epis.; d. Boston, Sept. 8, 1746.

EBENEZER DAVENPORT, sett. Greenwich, Ct., (1st Chh.), 1763-1769.

JAMES DAVENPORT, A.B., b. Stamford, Ct., 1716, son of Rev. John and Elizabeth (Morris) (Maltby) Davenport; Y. C., 1732, A.B.; lic. to preach, Oct. 8, 1735; Ord. Southold, L. I., N. Y., 1738; itinerant preacher in N. Y., N. J., and Ct.; sett. Southold, L. I., 1738-1743; founded Separatist Chh., in New London, Ct., Mar. 6, 1743; sett. New London, Ct., (Separatist Chh.), 1743-1744; sett. Hopewell, N. J.; d. Hopewell, N. J., 1757.

JOHN DAVENPORT, B.D., bapt. Coventry, Warwickshire, Eng., Apr. 9, 1597, son of Hon. Henry and Winifred (Barnabit) Davenport; Brazenose Coll., Oxford, A.B.; Merton Coll., Oxford, 1616, A.M.; Magdalen Hall, Oxford, 1625, B.D.; Curate of St. Lawrence Jewry, London, 1619-1624; Vicar of St. Stephen's Chh., Coleman St., London, 1625-1633; resigned, Aug. 5, 1633; sett. Amsterdam, Holland, 1633-1635; came to Boston, June 26, 1637; Ord. New Haven, Ct., Aug. 22, 1639, as the first minister of the 1st Chh.; sett. New Haven, Ct., 1638-1667; inst. Boston, (1st Chh.), Dec. 9, 1668; sett. Boston, 1668-1670; Overseer, H. C.; Election Sermon, 1669; his portrait is owned by Yale University; d. Boston, Mar. 15, 1669/70, a. 72.

JOHN DAVENPORT, A.M., b. Boston, Feb. 22, 1668/9, son of Rev. John and Abigail (Pierson) Davenport; H. C., 1687, A.B., A.M.; Trustee, Y. C., 14 yrs.; Ord. Stamford, Ct., 1694; sett. Stamford, Ct., 1692-1731; Ct. Election Sermons, 1703, 1729; d. Stamford, Ct., Feb. 5, 1730/1, a. 61.

EBENEZER DAVID, A.B., came from Phila., Pa.· Brown U., 1772, A.B.; Ord. Newport, R. I., (3rd or Sabbatarian Bapt. Chh.), 1775; sett. Newport, R. I., (3rd Bapt. Chh.), 1775-1778; Chaplain, 9th Cont. Regt. of Infantry, 1776; Chaplain, 2nd R. I. Regt., 1777-1778; Bapt.; d. Mar. 19, 1778.

WILLIAM DAVIDSON, A.M., b. Ireland, 1714; Edinburgh U., 1733, A.B., A.M.; Ord. Derry, N. H., (1st Chh.), 1740; sett. Derry, N. H., 1740-1791; Presb.; d. Derry, N. H., Feb. 15, 1791, a 77.

THOMAS DAVIES, A.M., b. Kington, Herefordshire, England, Dec. 21, 1736, son of John, Jr. and Elizabeth (Brown) Davies; Y. C., 1758, A.B.; A.M., 1763; Ord. England, Aug. 24, 1761, by the Archbishop of Canterbury; Missionary of the Venerable Society for the Propagation of the Gospel in Foreign Parts; sett. New Milford, Ct., 1761-1766; also minister at the following places in Ct.: Roxbury, Sharon, New Preston, New Fairfield, Litchfield (St. Michael's Parish), Washington, (St. John's Chh.), Kent, Cornwall, Salisbury, Woodbury, (all in Ct.), and at Great Barrington, Mass.; Epis.; d. New Milford, Ct., May 12, 1766, a. 30.

AARON DAVIS, Ord. Dartmouth, (1st Bapt. Chh.), 1698; sett. Dartmouth, 1698-1720; this church was in Dartmouth, Mass., Little Compton, R. I., and Tiverton, R. I.; Bapt.; d. Dartmouth, ca. 1720.

JOHN DAVIS, A.M., son of William Davis of New Haven, Ct.; H. C., 1651, A.B., A.M.; sett. Hartford, Ct., 1655-1657; preacher and teacher; d. en route to England, Nov. 1657.

JOHN DAVIS, A.M., b. Welsh Tract, Newcastle Co., Del., 1737, son of Rev. David and Rachel (Thomas) Davis; U. of Pa., 1763, A.B., A.M.; Brown U., 1769, A.M.; Tutor, U. of Pa., 1762-1764; Fellow, Brown U., 1768-1772; preached at Welsh Tract, 1769-1770; Ord. Boston, (2nd Bapt. Chh.), Sept. 9, 1770; sett. Boston, 1770-1772; dism. July 19, 1772; champion of the religious rights of the Baptists in Mass.; Member Am. Phil. Soc., 1770; Bapt.; d. near Wheeling, W. Va., Dec. 13, 1772.

JOSEPH DAVIS, A.M., b. Concord, July 16, 1720, son of Lieut. Simon and Dorothy (Heald) Davis; H. C., 1740, A.B., A.M.; Ord. Holden, Dec. 22, 1742; sett. Holden, 1742-1773; dism. Jan. 1773; sett. Westmoreland, N. H.; d. Holden, Mar. 4, 1799, a. 78.

NATHAN DAVIS, A.M., b. Cambridge, Nov. 30, 1747, son of Samuel and Sarah Davis of Acton; H. C., 1759, A.B., A.M.; Ord. Dracut, Nov. 20, 1765; sett. Dracut, 1765-1781; dism. Jan. 1781; d. Boston, Mar. 4, 1803.

HENRY DAWSON, came from London, Eng., to Newport, R. I., 1767; Ord. Newport, R. I., (Independent Bapt. Chh.), Apr. 14, 1771; Bapt.

JEREMIAH DAY, A.M., b. Colchester, Ct., Jan. 25, 1736/7, son of Thomas and Mary (Welles) Day; Y. C., 1756, A.B., A.M.; Ord. Washington, Ct., (New Preston Parish), Jan. 31, 1770; sett. Washington, Ct., 1769-1806; d. New Preston, Ct., Sept. 12, 1806, a. 70.

BARZILLAI DEAN, A.M., b. Groton, Ct., Dec. 28, 1714, son of John and Lydia (Thacher) Dean; Y. C., 1737, A.B., A.M.; sett. Hebron, Ct., (Epis. Chh.), 1745; Ord. London, Eng., Nov. 21, 1745; Epis.; d. at sea en route from England to Ct., 1746.

JAMES DEAN, A.M., b. Groton, Ct., Aug. 20, 1748, son of John and Sarah (Douglass) Dean; Dart. Coll., 1773, A.B., A.M.; Ord. missionary to the Indians; Major, Rev. army; Preceptor, Moor's School, 1772-1773; farmer; d. Westmoreland, N. Y., Sept. 10, 1823.

SAMUEL DEANE, D.D., b. Dedham, July 10, 1733, son of Samuel and Rachel (Dwight) Deane; H. C., 1760, A.B., A.M.; S.T.D., Brown U., 1790; Tutor, H. C., 1763-1764; Librarian, H. C., 1760-1762; Vice-President and Trustee, Bowdoin Coll., 1794-1813; Ord. Portland, Me., (1st Parish in Falmouth and Portland), Oct. 17, 1764; sett. Portland, Me., 1764-1814; Fellow, Am. Acad. Arts and Sciences; Election Sermon, 1794; Unitarian; d. Portland, Me., Nov. 12, 1814.

SETH DEAN, A.M., b. Plainfield, Ct., Aug. 7, 1715, son of William and Sarah (Olcott) Dean; Y. C., 1738, A.B.; A.M., 1742; Ord. Rindge, N. H., Nov. 6, 1765; sett. Rindge, N. H., 1765-1780; dism. Sept. 1780; d. East Putnam, Ct., Apr. 25, 1782, a. 66.

DAVID DEMING, A.M., b. Wethersfield, Ct., July 20, 1681, son of David and Mary Deming; H. C., 1700, A.B., A.M.; sett. Cromwell, Ct., 1703-1711; sett. Needham, Mass., 1712-1714; Ord. Medway, (1st Chh., now in Millis), Nov. 23, 1715; sett. Medway (Millis) 1714-1722; dism. Oct. 16, 1722; sett. Lyme, Ct., 1723-1730; sett. North Lyme, Ct., 1736; d. North Lyme, Ct., Feb. 11, 1745/6, a. 65.

JOHN DENNIS, A.M., b. Ipswich, Nov. 3, 1708, son of John and Lydia (White) Dennis; H. C., 1730, A.B., A.M.; Ord. at Northfield, Mass., Dec. 4, 1754, for Charlestown, N. H.; sett. Charlestown, N. H., 1754-1756; dism. Mar. 31, 1756; sett. Harwich, 1756-1760; d. Ipswich, Sept. 2, 1773, a. 64.

JOSIAH DENNIS, A.M., b. Ipswich, 1694; H. C., 1723, A.B., A.M.; Ord. Dennis, June 23, 1727; sett. Dennis, 1725-1763, being the first minister of the church and town which was named for him; d. Dennis, Aug. 31, 1763, a. 69.

JOHN DENISON, A.M., b. Ipswich, 1666, son of John and Martha (Symonds) Denison; H.C., 1684, A.B., A.M.; preached at Lancaster; Ord. Ipswich, 1686; sett. Ipswich, 1686-1689; colleague of Rev. William Hubbard, the historian; d. Essex, Sept. 14, 1689, a. 23.

JOHN DENISON, A.M., b. Ipswich, son of Rev. John and Elizabeth (Saltonstall) Denison; H. C., 1710, A.B., A.M.; Librarian, H.C., 1713-1714; preached a year but was not ordained; lawyer and colonel; d. Ipswich, Nov. 25, 1724.

JOSEPH DENISON, A.M., b. Windham, Ct., Nov. 2, 1738, son of Nathan and Ann (Cary) Denison; Y. C., 1763, A.B., AM.; Ord. Middlefield, Ct., Feb. 28, 1765; sett. Middlefield, Ct., 1764-1770; d. Middlefield, Ct., Feb. 12, 1770, a. 31.

THOMAS DENISON, b. Montville, Ct., Oct. 20. 1709, son of Capt. Robert and Joanna (Stanton) Denison; Ord. Franklin, Ct., (Separatist Chh. at Norwich Farms), Oct. 29, 1747; sett. Franklin, Ct., 1747-1759; Cong.; Sept.; Bapt.; d. Pomfret, Ct., Oct. 24, 1787.

WILLIAM DENISON, A.M., b. Roxbury, Sept. 18, 1664, son of Edward and Elizabeth (Denison) Denison; H. C., 1681, A.B., A.M.; preached but was never ordained; Rep. Gen. Ct., 20 yrs.; d. Roxbury, Mar. 22, 1717/8, a. 53.

RICHARD DENTON, A.B., b. Yorkshire, Eng., 1603; A.B. at St. Catherine's Hall, Camb., 1623/4; Ord. by the Bishop of Peterborough, June 8, 1623; Curate at Coley Chapel, Halifax, Yorkshire, 1631; sett. Stamford, Ct., 1641-1644; removed, 1644; sett. Hempstead, L. I., N. Y., 1644-1659; returned to England, 1659; d. Essex, England, 1662/3.

EBENEZER DEVOTION, A.B., b. Brookline, bapt. Roxbury, Oct. 19, 1684, son of John and Hannah (Pond) Devotion; H. C., 1707, A.B.; Ord. Suffield, Ct., June 28, 1710; sett. Suffield, Ct., 1709-1741; d. Suffield, Ct., Apr. 11, 1741, a. 57.

EBENEZER DEVOTION, A.M., b. Suffield, Ct., May 8, 1714, son of Rev. Ebenezer and Hannah (Breck) Devotion; Y. C., 1732, A.B., A.M.; Ord. Scotland, Ct., (Windham, 3rd Chh.), Oct. 22, 1735; sett. Scotland, Ct., 1735-1771; Ct. Election Sermon, 1753; Rep. Gen. Assembly, Ct., 1760, 1770, 1771; d. Windham, Ct., (Scotland), July 16, 1771, a. 57.

JOHN DEVOTION, A.M., bapt. Suffield, Ct., July 12, 1730, son of Rev. Ebenezer and Naomi (Taylor) Devotion; Y. C., 1754, A.B., A.M.; Ord. Westbrook, Ct., (3rd Chh., Saybrook), Dec. 26, 1757; sett. Westbrook, Ct., 1757-1802; Ct. Election Sermon, 1777; d. Saybrook, Ct., Sept. 6, 1802, a. 72.

JEDEDIAH DEWEY, 3rd., b. Westfield, Apr. 11, 1714, son of Sergt. Jedediah, Jr. and Rebecca (Williams) Dewey; Ord. Westfield, (Separatist Chh.), Mar. 7, 1754; sett. Westfield, 1748-1763; removed to Bennington, Vt., 1763; sett. Bennington, Vt., (1st Chh. in Vt.), 1763-1778; d. Bennington, Vt., Dec. 1, 1778, a. 64.

GREGORY DEXTER, b. Olney, Northants., Eng., 1610; came to Providence, R. I., 1643; Ord. Providence, R. I., (1st Bapt. Chh.), 1654; sett. Providence, R. I., 1654-1700; Deputy, Gen. Ct., R. I., 1654-1655; President, R. I. Colony, 1653-1654; commissioner, 1651-1654; preacher and printer; Bapt.; d. Providence, R. I., 1700, a. 91.

SAMUEL DEXTER, A.M., b. Malden, Oct. 23, 1700, son of Dea. Capt. John and Winnefred (Sprague) Dexter; H. C., 1720, A.B., A.M.; Ord. Dedham, May 6, 1724; sett. Dedham, 1724-1755; publ. Century Discourse, 1738; his diary has been published; d. Dedham, Jan. 29, 1755, a. 55.

EBENEZER DIBBLEE, D.D., b. Danbury, Ct., 1715, son of Wakefield Dibblee; Y. C., 1734, A.B., A.M.; S.T.D., Columbia, 1793; Ord. London, Eng., Sept. 1748; sett. Stamford, Ct., (Epis. Chh.), 1748-1799; sett. Greenwich, Ct., (Epis. Chh.), 1748-1799; Epis.; d. Stamford, May 9, 1799, a. 84.

MOSES DICKENSON, A.M., b. Springfield, Dec. 12, 1695, son of Hezekiah and Abigail (Blakeman) Dickenson; Y. C., 1717, A.B., A.M.; Fellow; Ord. Hopewell, N. J., (Presb. Chh.), 1719; sett. Hopewell, N. J., and Maidenhead, N. J., (Presb. Chhs.), 1719-1727; inst. Norwalk, Ct., (1st Chh.), Nov. 1, 1727; sett. Norwalk, Ct., 1727-1778; Ct. Election Sermon, 1755; d. Norwalk, Ct., May 1, 1778, a. 82.

JAMES DIMAN, A.M., b. Bristol, R. I., Nov. 29, 1707, son of Thomas and Hannah (Finney) Diman; H. C., 1730, A.B., A.M.; Librarian, H.C., 1735-1737; Ord. Salem, (2nd Chh.), May 11, 1737; sett. Salem, 1737-1788; d. Salem, Oct. 8, 1788, a. 81.

THOMAS DIMMOCK, freeman and deputy, Barnstable, 1639; Lieut., 1643; Ord. Barnstable, Aug. 7, 1650; sett. Barnstable, 1650-1658; his nunc. will was probated, June 4, 1658.

RICHARD DINGLEY, came from Eng. to Boston; sett. Newport., R. I., 1685; Ord. Newport, R. I., (1st Bapt. Chh.), 1690; sett. Newport, R. I., 1689-1694; removed to South Carolina, 1694; Bapt.

SAMUEL DIX, A.M., b. Reading, Mar. 23, 1736, son of Samuel and Hannah (Batchelder) Dix; H. C., 1758, A.B., A.M.; Ord. Townsend, Mar. 4, 1761; sett. Townsend, 1761-1797; d. Townsend, Nov. 12, 1797.

EZEKIEL DODGE, A.M., b. Manchester, Apr. 21, 1723, son of Jabez and Margaret (Knowlton) Dodge; H. C., 1749, A.B., A.M.; Ord. Abington, May 23, 1750; sett. Abington, 1750-1770; d. Abington, June 5, 1770, a. 48.

JONATHAN DODSON, b. Scituate, 1659, son of Anthony and Mary (Williams) Dodson; appointed at Freetown, June 2, 1713; sett. Freetown, 1713-1717.

BENJAMIN DOOLITTLE, A.M., b. Wallingford, Ct., July 10, 1695, son of John and Mary (Peck) Doolittle; Y. C., 1716, A.B., A.M.; Ord. Northfield, Sept. 2, 1718; sett. Northfield, 1717-1748; physician; Arminian; d. Northfield, Jan. 9, 1748, a. 54.

JONATHAN DORBY, A.M., b. Boston, Sept. 14, 1726, son of Capt. Eleazer and Mary (Cushing) Dorby; H. C., 1747, A.B., A.M.; A.M., (Hon.), Y. C., 1753; Ord. Norwell, (2nd or South Chh. in Scituate), Nov. 13, 1751; sett. Norwell, 1751-1754; d. Hingham, Apr. 22, 1754.

EDWARD DORR, A.M., b. Lyme, Ct., Nov. 2, 1722, son of Edmund and Mary (Griswold) Dorr; Y. C., 1742, A.B., A.M.; Ord. Hartford, Ct., (1st Chh.), Apr. 27, 1748; sett. Hartford, Ct., 1747-1772; Ct. Election Sermon, 1765; d. Hartford, Ct., Oct. 20, 1772, a. 50.

JOSEPH DORR, A.M., b. Roxbury, 1689/90, son of Edward and Elizabeth (Hawley) Dorr; H. C., 1711, A.B., A.M.; Ord. Mendon, Feb. 24, 1716; sett. Mendon, 1716-1768; organized the Mendon Assn. of ministers at his home, and was for many years its moderator; d. Mendon, Mar. 9, 1768, a. 79.

SAMUEL DORRANCE, A.M., b. Ireland, 1685; U. of Glasgow, 1709, A.B., A.M.; sett. Dunbarton, Ireland, 1711-1720; Ord. Voluntown, Ct., Dec. 23, 1723, as the first minister; sett. Voluntown, Ct., 1723-1770; dism. Dec. 12, 1770; Presb.; d. Voluntown, Ct., Nov. 12, 1775, a. 90.

FRANCIS DOUGHTY, b. England, 1602, son of Francis Doughty, Gent. of Hempstead, Oldsbury Parish, Gloucestershire; was a preacher residing at Taunton, 1637; planter at Dorchester, 1639; received a grant at "Maspeth," near Newtown, L. I., N. Y.; said to be the first Puritan preacher in the English language in New York City,

1642; administered the Lord's Supper there, 1644; and preached there, 1643-1648; departed for Virginia, 1648, where he sett. on the Eastern shore of Chesapeake Bay; minister in Va., 1656-1658.

NATHANIEL DRAPER, A.B., b. Roxbury, Oct. 10, 1706, son of Nathaniel and Abigail (Lyon) Draper; Y. C., 1745, A.B.; Ord. Cambridge, (Separatist Chh.), Apr. 24, 1751; sett. Cambridge, 1751-1753; Bapt.; d. Roxbury, Mar. 28, 1767.

SAMUEL DROWN, b. Bristol, R. I., July 31, 1721, son of Solomon and Hester Drown; Ord. Portsmouth, N. H., (Independent Chh.), Nov. 2, 1761, as the first minister; sett. Portsmouth, N. H., 1761-1770; d. Portsmouth, N. H., Jan. 17, 1770, a. 48.

SAMUEL DUDLEY, bapt. All Saints, Northampton, England, Nov. 30, 1608, son of Gov. Thomas and Dorothy (Yorke) Dudley; matric., Emmanuel Coll., Camb., 1626; came to N. E. in the "Arabella," 1630; lived at Cambridge, Ipswich and Salisbury as a planter and farmer; called to Exeter, N. H., May 30, 1650; sett. Exeter, N. H., as minister, 1650-1683; Rep. at Salisbury, 1644; d. Exeter, N. H., Feb. 10, 1682/3, a. 77.

SHUBAEL DUMMER, A.B., b. Newbury, Feb. 17, 1636, son of Richard and Mary Dummer of Bishopstoke, Hampshire, Eng. and Roxbury, Mass.; H. C., 1656, A.B; Ord. York, Me., Dec. 3, 1673; sett. York, Me., 1662-1692; killed by the Indians at York, Me., Jan. 25, 1691/2.

ASA DUNBAR, A.M., b. Bridgewater, May 26, 1745, son of Samuel and Mary (Hayward) Dunbar; H. C., 1767, A.B., A.M.; Ord. Salem, (1st Chh.), July 22, 1772; sett. Salem, 1772-1779; dism. Apr. 23, 1779; practiced law at Keene, N. H., 1783-1787; he was grandfather of Henry D. Thoreau of Concord; d. Keene, N. H., June 22, 1787.

SAMUEL DUNBAR, A.M., b. Boston, Oct. 2, 1704, son of John and Margaret (Holmes) Dunbar; H. C., 1723, A.B., A.M.; taught school in Boston, 1724; Ord. Canton, Nov. 15, 1727; sett. Canton, 1727-1783; Artillery Election Sermon, 1748; Election Sermon, 1760; Convention Sermon, 1769; Chaplain at Crown Point, 1755; d. Canton, June 15, 1783, a. 79.

JONATHAN DUNHAM, b. Plymouth, 1632, son of Dea. John and Abigail (Barlow) Dunham; not a coll. grad.; missionary to the Indians at Saco, Me., 1659; sett. Falmouth, Me., as a lay preacher, 1679-1684; Ord. Edgartown, Oct. 11, 1694; sett. Edgartown, 1684-1717; d. Edgartown, Dec. 18, 1717, a. ca. 85.

ROBERT DUNLAP, A.M., b. Barilla, Co. Antrim, Ulster, Ireland, Aug. 1715; U. of Edinburgh, A.B., A.M., 1734; came to N. E., 1736; preached at various places in Mass. and Me.; Ord. Boston, (in the French Huguenot Chapel, for the ministry at Brunswick, Me.), Aug. (or Sept.), 1747; sett. Brunswick, Me., (1st Parish), 1746-1760; dism. Oct. 29, 1760; Presb.; d. Brunswick, Me., June 26, 1776.

BENJAMIN DUNNING, A.M., b. Newtown, Ct., June 30, 1740, son of Benjamin and Sarah (Burritt) Dunning; Y. C., 1759, A.B.; A.M., 1763; Ord. Marlborough, Ct., Sept. 1762; sett. Marlborough, Ct., 1762-1773; dism. May 25, 1773; inst. Centerbrook, Ct., May 24, 1775; sett. Centerbrook, Ct., 1775-1785; d. Centerbrook, Ct., May 12, 1785, a. 45.

PRESIDENT HENRY DUNSTER, A.M., bapt. Baleholt, Lancashire, England, Nov. 26, 1609, son of Henry Dunster; Magdalene Coll., Camb., A. B., 1630/1; A.M., 1634; taught school at Bury, Lancashire, for some years; Curate of Bury, 1634; arrived at Boston, 1640; came to N. E. to escape persecution for non-conformity; First President, Harvard College, inst., Aug. 27, 1640; sett. H. C., as Prest., 1640-1654; sett. Scituate, (1st Chh.), 1654-1659; physician, teacher and preacher; though a Congregationalist, he held Bapt. views; d. Scituate, Feb. 27, 1658/9.

ISAIAH DUNSTER, A.M., b. Cambridge, Oct. 21, 1720, son of Henry and Martha (Russell) Dunster; H. C., 1741, A.B., A.M.; Ord. Brewster, Nov. 2, 1748; sett. Brewster, 1748-1791; d. Brewster, Jan. 18, 1791, a. 72.

DANIEL DWIGHT, A.M., b. Dedham, Oct. 28, 1707, son of Michael and Rachel (Avery) Dwight; H. C., 1726, A.B., A.M.; sett. Hanover, 1727; preacher and merchant; d. Dedham, July 4, 1747, a. 39.

JOSIAH DWIGHT, A.M., b. Dedham, Feb. 8, 1670/1, son of Capt. Timothy and Ann (Flint) Dwight; H. C., 1687, A.B.; A.M., 1720; Ord. Woodstock, Ct., 1695; sett. Woodstock, Ct., 1690-1726; dism. Sept. 3, 1726; inst. Westwood, (3rd Parish in Dedham), June 4, 1735; sett. Westwood, 1735-1743; dism. May 20, 1743; d. Thompson, Ct., Aug. 8, 1748, a. 77.

PRESIDENT TIMOTHY DWIGHT, D.D., LL.D., b. Northampton, May 14, 1752, son of Major Timothy Dwight; Y. C., 1769; A.B., A.M.; D.D., Princeton, 1787; LL.D., H. C., 1810; Tutor, Y.C., 1771-1777; Prof. of Divinity, Y. C., 1795-1817; President, Y. C., Sept. 8, 1795-1817; Ord. Greenfield Hill., Ct. (Fairfield), Nov. 5, 1783; supply, Westfield, Mass., 1778-1779; Deerfield, 1780; Granby, 1781; sett. Greenfield Hill, Ct., 1783-1795; Chaplain, Gen. Parsons' Brigade, Rev. War, 1777-1778; Rep. Mass. Legislature, 1782-1783; Ct. Election Sermon, 1791; d. New Haven, Ct., Feb. 11, 1817, a. 65.

THOMAS EAGER. A.M., (b. Dublin, Ireland. 1670. son of William Eager; matric., Trinity Coll., Dublin. May 22, 1688, aged 18 yrs.; A.B., Trinity Coll., Dublin. 1692; A.M., 1695); sett. Quincy, (Christ Chh. in Braintree), 1711-1713; Epis.

JONATHAN EAMES, A.M., b. Wilmington, Nov. 9, 1730, son of Daniel and Abigail (Nourse) Eames; H. C., 1752, A.B., A.M.; Ord. Newtown, N. H., (Cong. Chh.), Jan. 17, 1759; sett. Newtown, N. H., 1759-1791; d. Wentworth, N. H., Sept. 3, 1800, a. 69.

ELISHA EATON, A.M., b. Plymouth, 1701, son of Benjamin,

Jr. and Mary (Coombs) Eaton; H. C., 1729, A.B., A.M.; Ord. Randolph, June 2, 1731; sett. Randolph, 1731-1750; dism. Jan. 7, 1750; sett. Harpswell, Me., (1st Parish), 1753-1764; d. Harpswell, Me., Apr. 22, 1764, a. 62.

JOSHUA EATON, A.B., b. Waltham, Dec. 15, 1714, son of Joshua and Lydia (Livermore) Eaton; H. C., 1735, A.B.; Ord. Spencer, Nov. 7, 1744; sett. Spencer, 1744-1772; practiced law, 1737-1742; first lawyer to settle in Worcester; d. Spencer, Apr. 2, 1772, a. 58.

NATHANIEL EATON, PH.D., M.D., b. Great Budworth, Cheshire, Eng., 1609, son of Rev. Richard Eaton, Rector of Budworth; matric. Trinity Coll., Cambridge, 1629/30; Ph.D., U. of Padua, Italy, 1647; M.D., Padua, 1647; sett. Leyden, Holland, 1632-1637; came to N. E., 1637; first master of the school at Cambridge, Mass., which later became Harvard College, 1638-1639; he returned to Eng., where he was Vicar of Bishop's Castle, Salop, 1661; Rector of Bideford, Devon, 1668; d. a prisoner for debt, 1674.

SAMUEL EATON, A.M., b. Great Budworth, Cheshire, Eng., 1597, son of Rev. Richard Eaton, Vicar of Budworth; Magdalene Coll., Camb., A.B., 1625/6; A.M., 1628; Ord. by the Bishop of Peterborough, Dec. 19, 1625; came to N. E., 1637; inst. New Haven, Ct., 1639; sett. New Haven, Ct., 1639-1640; returned to Eng.; sett. Duckenfield, Stockport, Cheshire, 1640-1662; silenced 1662; brother of Gov. Theophilus Eaton of the New Haven Colony; d. Denton, Lancashire, Eng., Jan. 9, 1664/5, a. 68.

SAMUEL EATON, A.M., b. Randolph, Apr. 3, 1736, son of Rev. Elisha and Catharine (Belcher) (Clough) Eaton; H. C., 1763, A.B., A.M.; Ord. Harpswell, Me., (1st Parish), Oct. 24, 1764; sett. Harpswell, 1761-1822; Pres. Bd. of Overseers of Bowdoin College; d. Harpswell, Me., Nov. 5, 1822.

PRESIDENT JONATHAN EDWARDS, A.M., b. East Windsor, Ct., Oct. 5, 1703, son of Rev. Timothy and Esther (Stoddard) Edwards; Y. C., 1720, A.B., A.M.; Tutor, 1724-1726; Ord. Northampton, Feb. 15, 1726/7, as colleague with his grandfather, Rev. Solomon Stoddard; sett. Northampton, 1727-1750; dism. June 22, 1750; sett. Stockbridge, 1750-1758; preacher to the Indians; inst. Princeton U., as President, Jan. 1758; one of the leading intellects America has produced; most celebrated Calvinist in America; d. Princeton, N. J., Mar. 22, 1758, a. 55.

PRESIDENT JONATHAN EDWARDS, D.D., b. Northampton, May 26, 1745, son of Rev. Jonathan and Sarah (Pierpont) Edwards; Princeton, 1765, A.B.; Tutor, 1767-1769; D.D., Princeton; Ord. New Haven, Ct., (White Haven Chh.), Jan. 5, 1769; sett. New Haven, Ct., 1769-1795; dism. May 1795; inst. Colebrook, Ct., 1796; sett. Colebrook, Ct., 1796-1799; dism. July 1799; inst. Union Coll., as President, 1799-1801; Ct. Election Sermon, 1794; d. Schenectady, N. Y., Aug. 1, 1801.

TIMOTHY EDWARDS, A.M., b. Hartford, Ct., May 14, 1669, son of Richard and Elizabeth (Tuttle) Edwards; H. C., 1691, A.B., A.M.; Ord. South Windsor, Ct., (2nd Chh.), May 28, 1698; sett. Windsor Farms, Ct., 1694-1758; Chaplain, 1711; Ct. Election Sermons, 1708, 1732; d. Windsor, Ct., Jan. 27, 1758.

EDWARD EELLS, A.M., b. Scituate, 1712, son of Rev. Nathaniel and Hannah (North) Eells; H. C., 1733, A.B., A.M.; Ord. Cromwell, Ct., (2nd Chh. in Middletown), Sept. 6, 1738; sett. Cromwell, Ct., 1738-1776; Ct. Election Sermon, 1767; d. Middletown, Ct., Oct. 12, 1776, a. 64.

JAMES EELLS, A.M., b. Upper Middletown, Ct., Mar. 11, 1742/3, son of Rev. Edward and Martha (Pitkin) Eells; Y. C., 1763, A.B., A.M.; Ord. Buckingham, Ct., (Eastbury), Aug. 23, 1769; sett. Buckingham, 1769-1805; d. Eastbury, Ct., Jan. 20, 1805, a. 62.

JOHN EELLS, A.M., bapt. Guilford, Ct., Apr. 11, 1703, son of Samuel, Jr. and Hannah (Wetherell) Eells; Y. C., 1724, A.B., A.M.; Ord. New Canaan, Ct., June 20, 1733; sett. New Canaan, Ct., 1732-1741; d. New Canaan, Ct., Oct. 15, 1785, a. 83.

JOHN EELLS, A.M., bapt. Stonington, Ct., Mar. 13, 1736/7, son of Rev. Nathaniel and Mercy (Cushing) Eells; Y. C., 1755, A.B., A.M.; Ord. Glastonbury, Ct., (1st Chh.), June 27, 1759; sett. Glastonbury, Ct., 1759-1791; d. Glastonbury, Ct., May 17, 1791, a. 55.

NATHANIEL EELLS, A.M., b. Milford, Ct., Nov. 26, 1677, son of Major Samuel, Esq. and Anna (Lenthal) Eells; H. C., 1699, A.B.; A.M., 1743; Ord. Norwell, (South or 2nd Chh. in Scituate), June 14, 1704; sett. Norwell, 1704-1750; Election Sermon, 1743; he married the aunt of Lord North, Prime Minister of England during the Revolutionary War; d. Scituate, Aug. 25, 1750, a. 73.

NATHANIEL EELLS, A.M., b. Scituate, 1710, son of Rev. Nathaniel and Hannah (North) Eells; H. C., 1728, A.B., A.M.; Ord. East Stonington, Ct., July 14, 1733; sett. East Stonington, Ct., 1733-1781; Ct. Election Sermon, 1748; d. East Stonington, Ct., 1786.

SAMUEL EELLS, A.M., b. Cromwell, Ct., Jan. 13, 1744/5, son of Rev. Edward and Martha (Pitkin) Eells; Y. C., 1765, A.B., A.M.; Ord. Branford, Ct., (North or 2nd Parish), Mar. 29, 1769; sett. North Branford, Ct., 1769-1808; Capt., Rev. War, 1776; d. North Branford, Ct., Apr. 22, 1808, a. 64.

JOSHUA ELDERKIN, A.M., b. Norwich, Ct., Oct. 30, 1720, son of John and Susanna (Baker) Elderkin; Y. C., 1748, A.B., A.M.; Ord. Haddam, Ct., Sept. 1749; sett. Haddam, Ct., 1749-1753; dism. Apr. 18, 1753; physician; d. Canterbury, Ct., Feb. 11, 1801, a. 81.

ENOCH ELDREDGE, Ord. Barnstable, (Bapt. Chh.), Dec. 4, 1788; sett. Barnstable, (Bapt. Chh.), 1771-1794; Bapt.

ANDREW ELIOT, JR., D.D., b. Boston, Dec. 25, 1719, son of Andrew and Mary (Herrick) Eliot; H. C., 1737, A.B., A.M.; S.T.D., U. of Edinburgh, 1767; Fellow, H. C., 1765-1778; Member of the Corp., H. C., 1765; called to the Presidency, but declined, 1769; Ord. Boston. (New North Chh.), Apr. 14, 1742; sett. Boston, 1741-1772; Artillery Election Sermon, 1750; Convention Sermon, 1767; Election Sermon, 1765; Dudleian Lecture, 1771; d. Boston. Sept. 13, 1778, a. 59.

ANDREW ELIOT, A.M., b. Boston, Jan. 11, 1743, son of Rev. Dr. Andrew and Elizabeth (Langdon) Eliot; H. C., 1762, A.B., A.M.; Tutor, H. C., 1767-1774; Librarian, H. C., 1763-1767; Fellow, H. C., 1772-1774; A.M., (Hon.), Y. C., 1774; taught school at Boston, 1765; Ord. Fairfield, Ct., 1774; sett. Fairfield, Ct., 1774-1805; member Mass. Hist. Soc.; d. Fairfield, Ct., Oct. 26, 1805, a. 62.

BENJAMIN ELIOT, A.M., b. Roxbury, Jan. 29, 1646/7, son of Rev. John and Hannah (Mountford) Eliot; H. C., 1665, A.B., A.M.; sett. in Roxbury where he was an asst. to his father; towards the end of his life he appears to have been mentally deranged; d. Roxbury, Oct. 15, 1687, a. 40, unm.

JACOB ELIOT, A.M., b. Boston, Nov. 14, 1700, son of Joseph and Silence Eliot; H. C., 1720, A.B., A.M.; Ord. Lebanon, Ct., (3rd Chh.), Nov. 26, 1729, as the first minister; sett. Lebanon, Ct., 1728-1766; d. Lebanon, Ct., Apr. 12, 1766.

JARED ELIOT, A.M., F.R.S., b. Guilford, Ct., Nov. 7, 1685, son of Rev. Joseph and Mary (Wyllys) Eliot; Y. C., 1706, A.B., A.M.; A.M., (Hon.), H. C., 1709; Ord. Killingworth, Ct., Oct. 26, 1709; sett. Killingworth, Ct., 1707-1763; Fellow Royal Soc., 1756/7; physician; Ct. Election Sermon, 1738; d. Killingworth, Ct., Apr. 22, 1763, a. 78.

JOHN ELIOT, A.B., "the Apostle to the Indians," bapt. Widford, Herts., Eng., Aug. 5, 1604, son of Bennett and Lettice (Aggar) Eliot; Jesus Coll., Camb., A.B., 1622; resided for a time at Nazing, Essex; was asst. at Mr. Thomas Hooker's School, at Little Baddow, Essex, 1629; came to N. E., in the "Lyon," Nov. 2, 1631; Ord. Roxbury, Nov. 5, 1632; sett. Roxbury, 1631-1690; worked among the Indians at Natick and other places, 1650-1690; translated the Bible and other books into the Indian tongue; Election Sermon, 1659; d. Roxbury, May 20, 1690, a. 86.

JOHN ELIOT, JR., A.M., b. Roxbury, Aug. 3, 1636, son of Rev. John and Hannah (Mountford) Eliot; H. C., 1656, A.B., A.M.; Indian missionary, 1657-1663; Ord. Newton, July 20, 1664, as the first minister; sett. Newton, 1664-1668; d. Newton, Oct. 13, 1668, a. 32.

JOSEPH ELIOT, A.M., b. Roxbury, Dec. 20, 1638, son of Rev. John and Hannah (Mountford) Eliot; H. C., 1658, A.B., A.M.; Indian missonary, 1658-1662; sett. Northampton, Mass., 1662-1664; Ord. Guilford, Ct., 1664; sett. Guilford, Ct., 1664-1694; d. Guilford, Ct., May 24, 1694, a. 55.

EPHRAIM ELLIS, b. Rochester, 1717, son of Malachi and Susanna (Dennis) Ellis; preached to the Indians at Sandwich; d. Sandwich, June 4, 1784, a. 67.

JOHN ELLIS, A.M., b. Cambridge, Mar. 2, 1726/7, son of John and Hannah (Lillie) Ellis; H. C., 1750, A.B., A.M.; A.M., (Hon.), Y. C., 1753; Ord. Franklin, Ct., (3rd Chh. in Norwich), Sept. 5, 1753; sett. Franklin, Ct., 1753-1782; Chaplain, Am. Rev.; inst. Rehoboth, (1st Cong. Chh.), Mar. 30, 1785; sett. Rehoboth, 1785-1796; d. Franklin, Ct., Oct. 19, 1805, a. 78.

JONATHAN ELLIS, A.B., b. Sandwich, May 1, 1717, son of John and Sarah Ellis; H. C., 1737, A.B.; Ord. Plymouth, (2nd Chh. at Manomet), Nov. 8, 1738; sett. Plymouth, 1738-1749; dism. Oct. 31, 1749; inst. Little Compton, R. I., Nov. 29, 1749; sett. Little Compton, R. I., 1749-1785; d. Little Compton, R. I., Sept. 7, 1785.

DANIEL ELMER, A.M., b. East Windsor, Ct., ca. 1690, son of Samuel Elmer; Y. C., 1713, A.B., A.M.; sett. Brookfield, 1714-1715; sett. New Haven, Ct., 1716-1717; sett. Westborough, 1717-1724; removed Aug. 1724; Ord. Fairfield, N. J., (Church of Christ), 1728; sett. Fairfield, N. J., 1727-1755; d. Fairfield, N. J., Jan. 14, 1755, a. 65.

RICHARD ELVINS, bapt. Salem, Nov. 2, 1718, son of Richard and Sarah (Beadle) Elvins; was a baker at Salem who was converted by Whitefield; Ord. Dunstan, Me., (Blue Point or 2nd Parish of Scarborough), Nov. 7, 1744; sett. Dunstan, 1744-1776; d. Dunstan, Me., Aug. 12, 1776.

DAVID ELY, D.D., b. Lyme, Ct., July 7, 1749, son of Richard and Phoebe (Hubbard) Ely; Y. C., 1769, A.B., A.M.; A.M., Dart. Coll., 1782; D.D., Y. C., 1808; Fellow, Y. C., 1788-1816; Secretary, Y. C., 1793-1815; Ord. Huntington, Ct., Oct. 27, 1773; sett. Huntington, Ct., 1773-1816; d. Huntington, Ct., Feb. 16, 1816, a. 67.

RICHARD ELY, A.M., b. Lyme, Ct., Sept. 30, 1733, son of Dea. Richard, Jr. and Phoebe (Hubbard) Ely; Y. C., 1754, A.B., A.M.; Ord. North Madison, Ct., (5th Chh. in Guilford), June 8, 1757; sett. North Madison, Ct., 1757-1785; dism. Aug. 30, 1785; inst. Centerbrook, Ct., Jan. 18, 1786; sett. Centerbrook, Ct., 1786-1814; d. Chester, Ct., Aug. 23, 1814, a. 81.

MR. ELY, Ord. Somers, Ct., (Separatist Chh.), 1769; sett. Somers, Ct., 1769-1774; afterwards took a prominent part in Shays' Rebellion in western Massachusetts; d. in prison.

JOHN EMBLEN, b. 1633; came from England to Boston, 1684; isnt. Boston, (1st Bapt. Chh.), 1684; sett. Boston, 1684-1702; Bapt.; d. Boston, Dec. 9, 1702, a. 69.

DANIEL EMERSON, A.M., b. Reading, May 20, 1716, son of Peter and Annah (Brown) Emerson; H. C., 1739, A.B., A.M.; Ord. Hollis, N. H., Apr. 20, 1743; sett. Hollis, N. H., 1743-1793; emeritus, 1793-1801; d. Hollis, N. H., Sept. 30, 1801, a. 85.

EZEKIEL EMERSON, A.B., b. Uxbridge, Feb. 14, 1735/6, son of John and Mary Emerson; Princeton, 1763, A.B.; Ord. Georgetown, Me., July 3, 1765; sett. Georgetown, Me., 1765-1810; d. Georgetown, Me., Nov. 9, 1815, a. 79.

JOHN EMERSON, A.M., b. England, Feb. 26, 1625, son of Thomas and Elizabeth (Brewster) Emerson, of Ipswich; H. C., 1656, A.B., A.M.; Ord. Gloucester, Oct. 6, 1663; sett. Gloucester, 1661-1700; Chaplain, Canadian campaign, 1690; d. Gloucester, Dec. 2, 1700, a. 75.

JOHN EMERSON, A.M., b. Ipswich, ca. 1654, son of Nathaniel Emerson; H. C., 1675, A.B., A.M.; teacher at Newbury, 1680-1681; minister at Berwick, Me., 1683-1689; Chaplain under Major Savage, Sept. 7, 1689 to Nov. 23, 1689; later schoolmaster at Charlestown, 1691-1699, and at Salem, 1699-1712; d. Salem, Mar. 10, 1712.

JOHN EMERSON, JR., A.M., b. Gloucester, May 14, 1670, son of Rev. John and Ruth (Symonds) Emerson; H. C., 1689, A.B., A.M.; sett. Manchester, Mass., 1695-1697; sett. Salem, 1697-1699; sett. Ipswich, 1703; Ord. Newcastle, N. H., Nov. 8, 1704, as the first minister; sett. Newcastle, N. H., 1703-1712; inst. Portsmouth, N. H., (South or 2nd Chh.), Mar. 23, 1715, as the first minister; sett. Portsmouth, N. H., 1712-1732; d. Portsmouth, N. H., Jan. 21, 1731/2, a 62.

JOHN EMERSON, A.M., b. Charlesown, Feb. 27, 1706/7, son of Edward and Rebecca (Waldo) Emerson; H. C., 1726, A.B., A.M.; Ord. Topsfield, Nov. 27, 1728; sett. Topsfield, 1728-1774; d. Topsfield, July 11, 1774.

JOHN EMERSON, A.M., b. Malden, Nov. 25, 1745, son of Rev. Joseph and Mary (Moody) Emerson; H. C., 1764, A.B., A.M.; Ord. Conway, Dec. 21, 1769, as the first minister; sett. Conway, 1769-1826; d. Conway, June 26, 1826, a. 81.

JOSEPH EMERSON, b. Bishop's Stortford, Hertfordshire, England, June 25, 1620, son of Thomas and Elizabeth (Brewster) Emerson; sett. Wells, Me., 1664-1666; sett. Milton, 1666-1669; dism. Aug. 9, 1669; Ord. Mendon, Dec. 1, 1669, as the first minister; sett. Mendon, 1669-1675; retired to Concord at the outbreak of King Philip's War; d. Concord, Jan. 3, 1679/80.

JOSEPH EMERSON, A.M., b. Chelmsford, Apr. 20, 1700, son of Dea. Edward and Rebecca (Waldo) Emerson; H. C., 1717, A.B., A.M.; Ord. Malden, Oct. 31, 1721; sett. Malden, 1721-1767; d. Malden, July 13, 1767.

JOSEPH EMERSON, A.M., b. Malden, Aug. 25, 1724, son of Rev. Joseph and Mary (Moody) Emerson; H. C., 1743, A.B., A.M.; Ord. Pepperell, Feb. 25, 1746/7; sett. Pepperell, 1746-1775; d. as Chaplain to troops at Cambridge, Am. Rev. War, at Pepperell, Oct. 29, 1775.

WILLIAM EMERSON, A.M., b. Malden, May 21, 1743, son of Rev. Joseph and Mary (Moody) Emerson; H. C., 1761, A.B.,

A.M.; Ord. Concord, Jan. 1, 1766; sett. Concord, 1766-1776; Chaplain, Am. Rev. at Ticonderoga; father of Rev. William Emerson of the 1st Chh. in Boston, and grandfather, through the latter, of Rev. Ralph Waldo Emerson, the Yankee philosopher, of the 2nd Chh. in Boston, and of Concord; d. Rutland, Vt., Oct. 20, 1776, a. 33.

JACOB EMERY, A.M., b. Andover, Dec. 11, 1737, son of Joseph and Abigail (Merrill) Emery; H. C., 1761, A.B., A.M.; Ord. Pembroke, N. H., (Cong. Chh.), Aug. 3, 1768; sett. Pembroke, N. H., 1768-1775; dism. Mar. 23, 1775; member N. H. House of Rep., 1776-1777; d. Pembroke, N. H., Mar. 16, 1777, a. 39.

SAMUEL EMERY, A.M., b. Newbury, Dec. 20, 1670, son of John, Jr. and Mary (Webster) Emery; H. C., 1691, A.B., A.M.; Ord. Wells, Me., Oct. 29, 1701; sett. Wells, Me., 1698-1724; Chaplain of the garrison at Wells, 1698-1701; d. Biddeford, Me., Dec. 1, 1724.

STEPHEN EMERY, A.M., b. Exeter, N. H., Aug. 3, 1707, son of Rev. Samuel and Tabitha (Littlefield) Emery; H. C., 1730, A.B., A.M.; Ord. Nottingham, N. H., Nov. 3, 1742, as the first minister; sett. Nottingham, N. H., 1742-1749; inst. Chatham, May 17, 1749; sett. Chatham, 1749-1782; d. Chatham, May 18, 1782, a. 74.

NATHANIEL EMMONS, D.D., b. East Haddam, Ct., Apr. 20, 1745, son of Dea. Samuel, Jr. and Ruth (Cone) Emmons; Y. C., 1767, A.B.; A.M., 1772; A.M., Dart. Coll., 1786; S.T.D., Dart. Coll., 1798; Ord. Franklin, Apr. 21, 1773; sett. Franklin, 1769-1840; retired from active work, May 28, 1827; strong Calvinist; Election Sermon, 1798; Convention Sermon, 1804; d. Franklin, Sept. 23, 1840, a. 96.

SAMUEL EPPES, A.M., b. Ipswich, Feb. 24, 1647, son of Capt. Daniel and Elizabeth (Symonds) Eppes; H. C., 1669, A.B., A.M.; minister at Falmouth, Me., (now Portland), 1671; living in Boston, 1673; d. London, England, Apr. 1685, a. 38, of small-pox, prob. unm.

BENJAMIN ESTABROOK, A.M., b. Concord, Feb. 24, 1670/1, son of Rev. Joseph and Mary (Mason) Estabrook; H. C., 1690, A.B., A.M.; Ord. Lexington, Oct. 21, 1696; sett. Lexington, 1692-1697; d. Lexington, July 22, 1697, a. 26.

HOBART ESTABROOK, A.M., b. Canterbury, Ct., Dec. 17, 1716, son of Rev. Samuel and Rebecca (Hobart) Estabrook; Y. C., 1736, A.B., A.M.; Ord. East Haddam, Ct., Nov. 20, 1745; sett. Millington, Ct., 1745-1766; d. East Haddam, Ct., Jan. 28, 1766, a. 49.

JOSEPH ESTABROOK, A.M., b. Enfield, Middlesex, Eng., ca. 1640, of a long line of English ministers; came to N. E., 1660; H. C., 1664, A.B., A.M.; Ord. Concord, 1667; sett. Concord, 1667-1711; Election Sermon, 1705; d. Concord, Sept. 16, 1711, a. 71.

SAMUEL ESTABROOK, A.B., b. Concord, June 7, 1674, son of Rev. Joseph aand Mary (Mason) Estabrook; H. C., 1696, A.B.; asst. to his father at Concord, 1706-1710; Ord. Canterbury, Ct., June 13, 1711, as the first minister; sett. Canterbury, Ct., 1711-1727; Ct. Election Sermon, 1718; d. Canterbury, Ct., June 26, 1727.

JOHN EVELETH, A.B., b. Gloucester, Feb. 18, 1669/70, son of Joseph and Mary (Bragge) Eveleth; H. C., 1689, A.B.; Ord. Manchester, Oct. 1, 1693; sett. Manchester, 1689-1695; inst. Stow, Dec. 1, 1702; sett. Stow, 1700-1717; sett. Enfield, 1718; sett. Kennebunkport, Me., (Arundel Parish), 1719-1729; dism. Aug. 1729; sett. Kittery, Me., 1729-1734; d. Kittery, Me., Aug. 1, 1734, a. 65.

DANIEL EVERETT, (Averitt), b. Providence, R. I.; Ord. Richmond, R. I., (Bapt. Chh. at South Kingston, only minister), May 25, 1732; sett. Richmond, R. I., (South Kingston), 1725-1750; Bapt.; d. South Kingston, R. I., ca. 1750.

MOSES EVERETT, A.M., b. Dedham, July 15, 1750, son of Dea. Ebenezer and Joanna (Stevens) Everett; H. C., 1771, A.B., A.M.; Ord. Dorchester, Sept. 28, 1774; sett. Dorchester, 1774-1793; resigned Jan. 14, 1793, because of poor health; Rep. Mass. Legislature; appointed Special Justice, Court of Common Pleas, 1808; uncle of Rev. Edward Everett, and grand-uncle of Rev. Edward Everett Hale, D.D.; d. Mar. 25, 1813, a. 63.

NATHANIEL EWER, b. prob. on Cape Cod, 1722; Ord. Barnstable, (Separatist Chh.), May 10, 1750; sett. Barnstable, 1750-1760; inst. Newmarket Plains, N. H., Dec. 1773; sett. Newmarket, N. H., 1773-1797; dism. July 1797; New Light preacher; d. Newmarket, N. H., Apr. 1806, a. 84.

WILLIAM EWING, b. Scotland, 1728; Ord. Sturbridge, (2nd Bapt. Chh.), Sept. 27, 1768; sett. Sturbridge, 1750-1775; sett. Wales; Halifax, Vt.; Shutesbury; Rowley, 1785-1789; Weston; Bapt.

NICHOLAS EYRES, (Avers), b. Chipmanslade, Wilts., Eng., Aug. 22, 1691; came to N. Y., 1711; Ord. New York City, (1st Bapt. Chh.), Sept. 1724; sett. New York, N. Y., 1724-1731; resigned Oct. 1731; inst. Newport, R. I., (2nd Bapt. Chh.), Oct. 1731; sett. Newport, R. I., 1731-1759; Bapt.; d. Newport, R. I., Feb. 13, 1759.

JOHN FAIRFIELD, A.M., b. Boston, Dec. 26, 1737, son of William and Elizabeth (White) Fairfield; H. C., 1757, A.B; A.M., 1761; Ord. Saco, Me., (Pepperellborough), Oct. 27, 1762; sett. Saco, Me., 1762-1798; dism. Apr. 2, 1798; Arminian; d. Biddeford, Me., Dec. 16, 1819, a. 83.

DANIEL FARRAND, A.B., b. Milford, Ct., 1722; Princeton, 1750, A.B.; A.B., Y. C., 1777; Ord. Canaan, Ct., (South Parish) Aug. 12, 1752; sett. South Canaan, Ct., 1752-1803; d. Canaan, Ct., May 28, 1803, a. 81.

GEORGE FARRAR, A.M., b. Lincoln, Nov. 23, 1730, son of George, Jr. and Mary Farrar; H. C., 1751, A.B., A.M.; Ord. Easton, (1st Chh.), Mar. 26, 1755; sett. Easton, 1755-1756; d. Lincoln, Sept. 17, 1756, a. 26.

JOSEPH FARRAR, A.M., b. Lincoln, June 30, 1744, son of George and Mary (Barrett) Farrar; H. C., 1767, A.B., A.M.; Ord. Dublin, N. H., June 10, 1772, as the first minister; sett. Dublin, N. H.,

1772-1776; dism. June 7, 1776; inst. Dummerston, Vt., Aug. 24, 1779; sett. Dummerston, Vt., 1779-1783; d. Petersham, Apr. 5, 1816, a. 71.

STEPHEN FARRAR, A.M., b. Lincoln, Sept. 8, 1738, son of Dea. Samuel and Lydia (Barrett) Farrar; H. C., 1755, A.B., A.M.; Ord. New Ipswich, N. H., Oct. 22, 1760; sett. New Ipswich, N. H., 1758-1809; d. New Ipswich, N. H., June 23, 1809, a. 70.

SAMUEL FAYERWEATHER, A.M., b. Boston, Feb. 3, 1724, son of Thomas and Hannah (Waldo) Fayerweather; H. C., 1743, A.B., A.M.; A.M., Y. C., (Hon.), 1753; Camb. U., 1756; Oxford U., 1756; Columbia U., 1758; Ord. Newport, R. I., (2nd Cong. Chh.), 1754; sett. Newport, R. I., 1754-1756; Ord. Eng., Mar. 25, 1756, by the Bishop of Carlisle; sett. Winyaw, S. C., (Prince George's Parish), 1757-1760; sett. Narragansett, R. I., (Epis. Chh.), 1760-1774; d. Kingston, R. I., 1781.

BENJAMIN FESSENDEN, A.M., b. Cambridge, Jan. 7, 1701, son of Nicholas and Margaret (Cheney) Fessenden; H. C., 1718, A.B., A.M.; Ord. Sandwich, Sept. 12, 1722; sett. Sandwich, 1722-1746; "not only as a divine was he useful, but as a discreet and successful physician;" (G.S.) : d. Sandwich, Aug. 7, 1746.

THOMAS FESSENDEN, A.M., bapt. Lexington, July 15, 1739, son of William and Martha (Brown) Fessenden; H. C., 1758, A.B., A.M.; Ord. Walpole, N. H., Jan. 7, 1767; sett. Walpole, N. H., 1767-1818; his home and library were burned, Nov. 23, 1771; d. Walpole, N. H., May 9, 1813, a. 73.

WILLIAM FESSENDEN, A.M., b. Cambridge, Nov. 3, 1747, son of William and Mary (Palmer) Fessenden; H. C., 1768, A.B., A.M.; Ord. Fryeburg, Me., Oct. 11, 1775; sett. Fryeburg, Me., 1775-1805; d. Fryeburg, Me., May 5, 1805.

GILES FIRMIN, b. Suffolk, England, ca. 1615, son of Dea. Giles Firmin, who sett. at Boston, Mass.; matric. Emmanuel Coll., Camb., Dec. 15, 1629; arrived at Boston, May 26, 1632; returned to England to study medicine, 1633; ret. to N. E., 1637; took notes of the Antinomian Controversy; ret. to England where he preached at Shalford, Essex, 1648-1660; physician at Redgwell, Essex, 1670; preached there from 1672, until his death, Apr. 1697.

ELISHA FISH, A.M., b. Groton, Ct., 1719, son of Moses Fish; H. C., 1750, A.B., A.M.; Ord. Upton, June 5, 1751; sett. Upton, 1750-1795; d. Upton, Aug. 6 1795 a. 76.

JOSEPH FISH, A.M., b. Duxbury, Jan. 28, 1705/6, son of Thomas and Margaret (Woodworth) Fish; H. C., 1728, A.B., A.M.; Ord. North Stonington, Ct., Dec. 27, 1732; sett. North Stonington, Ct., 1731-1781; Ct. Election Sermon, 1760; d. North Stonington, Ct., May 22, 1781, a. 75.

NATHANIEL FISHER, A.M., b. Dedham, Apr. 5, 1686/7, son of Daniel and Mary (Fuller) Fisher; H. C., 1706, A.B., A.M.;

Ord. Dighton, 1710; sett. Dighton, 1710-1777; d. Dighton, Aug. 30, 1777, a. 91.

DANIEL FISK, b. Swansea, Mass., May 10, 1710, son of Samuel and Mehitable (Wheaton) Fisk; Ord. East Greenwich, R. I., (Bapt. Chh.), June 1743; sett. East Greenwich, R. I., 1743-1747; sett. Groton, Ct., autumn 1747-1756; Bapt.; d. Swansea, 1764.

JOHN FISKE, A.B., bapt. St. James, South Elmham, Suffolk, Eng., Mar. 20, 1607/8, son of John and Anne (Lawter) Fiske; Peterhouse Coll., Camb., A.B., 1628/9; came to N. E., 1637; sett. as preacher and school-master at Salem, 1637-1640; adm. freeman, Salem, Nov. 2, 1637; Ord. Wenham, Oct. 8, 1644, as the first minister; sett. Wenham, 1641-1655; sett. Chelmsford, 1655-1676, as the first minister; physician; d. Chelmsford, Jan. 14, 1676/7, a. 76.

JOHN FISKE, A.M., b. Braintree, Nov. 26, 1684, son of Rev. Moses and Sarah (Symmes) Fiske; H. C., 1702, A.B., A.M.; Ord. Killingly, Ct., (1st Chh. at Putnam), Oct. 19, 1715; sett. Putnam, Ct., 1712-1741; dism. Aug. 5, 1741; d. Killingly, Ct., May 18, 1773.

MOSES FISKE, A.M., b. Wenham, Apr. 12, 1642, son of Rev. John and Ann (Gipps) Fiske; H. C., 1662, A.B., A.M.; sett Westfield, 1668-1671; Ord. Braintree, (1st Chh., now in Quincy), Sept. 11, 1672; sett. Quincy, 1672-1708; Artillery Election Sermon, 1694; d. Braintree, (Quincy), Aug. 10, 1708, a. 66.

NATHAN FISKE, D.D., b. Weston, Sept. 9, 1733, son of Nathan and Anna (Warren) Fiske; H. C., 1754, A.B., A.M.; S.T.D., 1792; Ord. Brookfield, May 28, 1758; sett. Brookfield, 1758-1799; Hist. Sermon, Brookfield, 1775; Convention Sermon, 1788; Dudleian Lecture, 1796; d. Brookfield, Nov. 24, 1799, a. 66.

PHINEHAS FISKE, A.M., b. Wenham, Dec. 2, 1682, son of Dr. John and Hannah (Baldwin) Fiske; Y. C., 1704, A.B., A.M.; Tutor, Y. C., 1706-1713; Ord. Haddam, Ct., Sept. 15, 1714; sett. Haddam, Ct., 1714-1738; Ct. Election Sermon, 1726; d. Haddam, Ct., Oct. 17, 1738, a. 55.

SAMUEL FISKE, Ord. Scituate, R. I., (Bapt. Chh.), Aug. 1727; sett. Scituate, R. I., 1727-1744; Bapt.; d. 1744.

SAMUEL FISKE, A.M., b. Braintree, Apr. 6, 1689, son of Rev. Moses and Sarah (Symmes) Fiske; H. C., 1708, A.B., AM.; Ord. Salem, (1st Chh.), Oct. 8, 1718; sett. Salem, (1st Chh.), 1718-1735; sett. Salem, (3rd Chh.), 1735-1745; dism. Aug. 12, 1745; Election Sermon, 1731; d. Salem, Apr. 3, 1770, a. 81.

ELIJAH FITCH, A.M., b. Windham, Ct., Jan. 8, 1746, son of Capt. John and Alice (Fitch) Fitch; Y. C., 1765, A.B.; A.M., 1769; A.M., (Hon.), H. C., 1770; Ord. Hopkinton, Jan. 15, 1772; sett. Hopkinton, 1771-1788; author of "Beauties of Religion;" d. Hopkinton, Dec. 16, 1788, a. 43.

EPHRAIM FITCH, A.B., bapt. Norwich, Ct., Mar. 16, 1736, son of Joshua and Mary (Trumbull) Fitch; Y. C., 1756, A.B; studied for the ministry; sett. Edgremont, about 1761; Rep. to the Gen. Ct., 1767, 1778, 1781, 1788-1791; Justice of the Peace, 1781; Justice of Quorum, 1784; Delegate to the Constitutional Convention, 1779-1780; removed to Oxford, Chenengo County, N. Y., ca. 1792; d. Oxford, N. Y., ca. 1816.

JABEZ FITCH, A.M., b. Norwich, Ct., Apr. 1672, son of Rev. James and Priscilla (Mason) Fitch; H. C., 1694, A.B., A.M.; Tutor, H. C., 1697-1703; Fellow, H.C., 1700-1703; Ord. Ipswich, Oct. 27, 1703; sett. Ipswich, 1702-1723; dism. Dec. 13, 1723; inst. Portsmouth, N. H., (North Chh.), Apr. 14, 1725; sett. Portsmouth, N. H., 1724-1746; d. Portsmouth, N. H., Nov. 22, 1746, a. 74.

JAMES FITCH, b. Bocking, Essex, Eng., Dec. 24, 1622, son of Thomas and Ann (Pew) Fitch; educated by Rev. Thomas Hooker; came to N. E., 1638; Ord. Old Saybrook, Ct., 1646, as first minister; sett. Old Saybrook, Ct., 1646-1660; sett. Norwich, Ct., 1660-1702; Chaplain, King Philip's War; Ct. Election Sermon, 1674; d. Lebanon, Ct., Nov. 18, 1702, a. 80.

EDWARD FITZGERALD, minister of a Presby. Scotch-Irish Chh. in Worcester, ca. 1718-1725; Presby.

EBENEZER FLAGG, A.M., b. Woburn, Oct. 18, 1704, son of Ebenezer and Elizabeth (Carter) Flagg; H. C., 1725, A.B., A.M.; school-master at Woburn; Ord. Chester, N. H., Sept. 22, 1736; sett. Chester, N. H., 1736-1796; d. Chester, N. H., Nov. 14, 1796, a. 92.

ELIJAH FLETCHER, A.M., b. Westford, June 8, 1747, son of Timothy, Jr. and Bridget (Richardson) Fletcher; H. C., 1769, A.B., A.M.; Ord. Hopkinton, N. H., Jan. 27, 1773; sett. Hopkinton, N. H., 1773-1786; d. Hopkinton, N. H., Apr. 8, 1786, a. 39.

SETH FLETCHER, son of Rev. William Fletcher; was first instigated to preach by Rev. John Brock of Reading; and afterwards was encouraged by Wheelwright and Dalton of Hampton, N. H., where he was teaching, 1652-1654; sett. as preacher at Durham, N. H., 1656-1657, and at Wells, Me., 1657-1660; preached at Saco, Me., 1661-1675; sett. Southampton, L. I., N. Y., 1677, and later at Elizabeth, N. J.; d. Elizabeth, N. J., 1682 (administration granted, Sept. 18, 1682).

WILLIAM FLETCHER, A.B., (b. Leicestershire, England; matriculated sizar, Queens' Coll., Camb., 1625/6; Ord. Peterborough, Sept. 19, 1624; Rector of Aston, Yorkshire, 1631-1651); minister at Oyster River, N. H., 1656; returned to England; ejected, 1662; returned to N. E.; buried Saco, Me., Jan. 30, 1667/8.

HENRY FLYNT, A.M., b. Matlock, Derbyshire, Eng., ca. 1613, son of Henry Flynt; Jesus Coll., Camb., A.B., 1634/5; A.M., 1638; came to N. E., 1635; adm. 1st. Chh. Boston, Nov. 15, 1635; Ord. Braintree, (1st Chh., now in Quincy), Mar. 17, 1639/40; sett. Quincy, 1640-1668; Freeman, May 25, 1636; Artillery Election Sermon, 1657; d. Braintree, (Quincy), Apr. 27, 1668.

HENRY FLYNT, A.M., b. Dorchester, May 5, 1675, son of Rev. Josiah and Esther (Willet) Flynt; H. C., 1693, A.B., A.M.; Tutor, H. C., 1699-1754; Fellow, H. C., 1700-1760; sett. Norwich, Ct., 1696-1699; became Tutor at H. C., Aug. 7, 1699; resigned, Sept. 25, 1754; Secretary to the Board of Overseers, H. C., to 1758; d. Cambridge, Feb. 13, 1760, a. 85.

JOSIAH FLYNT, A.M., b. Braintree, Aug. 24, 1645, son of Rev. Henry and Margery (Hoar) Flynt; H. C., 1664, A.B., A.M.; Ord. Dorchester, Dec. 27, 1671; sett. Dorchester, 1671-1680; Artillery Election Sermon, 1677; d. Dorchester, Sept. 16, 1680, a. 35.

PEREZ FOBES, LL.D., b. Bridgewater, Sept. 21, 1742, son of Josiah and Freelove (Edson) Fobes; H. C., 1762, A.B.; A.M., 1786; LL.D., Brown, 1792; Ord. Raynham, Nov. 19, 1766; sett. Raynham, 1766-1786; Vice-President and Prof. of Natural Philosophy, Brown U., 1786-1798; Fellow, Brown U., 1795-1812; Fellow, Am. Acad. Arts and Sciences; Chaplain, Am. Rev., 1777; Election Sermon, 1795; wrote a Hist. of Raynham, 1794; d. Raynham, Feb. 23, 1812, a. 70.

DANIEL FOGG, JR., A.M., b. Hampton, N. H., Aug. 18, 1743, son of Daniel and Anna (Elkins) Fogg; H. C., 1764, A.B., A.M.; Ord. London, Eng., Aug. 24, 1770; sett. Boston, (King's Chapel), 1770-1771, as asst. min.; missionary at Bath, N. C., 1771-1772; Rector, Brooklyn, Ct., (Epis. Chh. at Pomfret), 1772-1815; Epis.; d. Pomfret, Ct., June 29, 1815.

JEREMIAH FOGG, A.M., b. Hampton, N. H., May 29, 1712, son of Seth and Sarah (Shaw) Fogg; H. C., 1730, A.B., A.M.; Ord. Kensington, N. H., Nov. 20, 1737, as the first minister; sett. Kensington, N. H., 1737-1789; was a Unitarian; he wrote, "Christ was no more than a mere man,—that he suffered and died only for himself—and that we are justified by works, meaning before God;" for this he was called before a Council, Jan. 20, 1789; d. Kensington, N. H., Dec. 1, 1789, a. 77.

PETER FOLGER, b. England, 1617/8, son of John Folger of Martha's Vineyard; came to N. E. with his father from Norwich, Eng., 1635; was in the service of the missionary corporation as assistant to Rev. Thomas Mayhew, Jr., and was left in charge of Mayhew's mission when the latter sailed for England in 1657; missionary to the Indians at Edgartown, Martha's Vineyard, 1656-1661; sett. Nantucket, 1663; grandfather of Benjamin Franklin; was learned in the Indian tongue and served as an interpreter; author of "A Looking Glass for the Times," 1675; d. Nantucket Island, 1690.

JOHN FOOT, A.M., b. North Branford, Ct., Apr. 2, 1742, son of Capt. John and Abigail (Frisbie) Foot; Y. C., 1765, A.B., A.M.; Ord. Cheshire, Ct., Mar. 12, 1767; sett. Cheshire, Ct., 1767-1813; d. Cheshire, Ct., Aug. 30, 1813, a. 72.

ELI FORBES, D.D., b. Westborough, Oct. 26, 1726, son of Dea. Jonathan and Hannah (Hayward) Forbes; H. C., 1751, A.B.;

A.M., 1754; S.T.D., 1804; Ord. North Brookfield, June 3, 1752; sett. North Brookfield, 1752-1775; dism. Mar. 1775; inst. Gloucester, (1st Chh.), June 5, 1776; sett. Gloucester, 1776-1804; Artillery Election Sermon, 1771; Convention Sermon, 1799; moderate Calvinist; Chaplain under Col. Timothy Ruggles, 1758-1759; d. Gloucester, Dec. 15, 1804, a. 78.

ABEL FORWARD, JR., A.M., b. Windsor, Ct., 1748, son of Lieut. Abel and Hannah (Phelps) Forward; Y. C., 1768, A.B., A.M.; Ord. Southwick, Oct. 27, 1773; sett. Southwick, 1773-1786; d. Southwick, Jan. 15, 1786, a. 38.

JUSTUS FORWARD, A.M., b. Suffield, Ct., May 11, 1730, son of Ensign Joseph and Mary (Lawton) Forward; Y. C., 1754, A.B., A.M.; Ord. Belchertown, Feb. 25, 1756; sett. Belchertown, 1756-1814; when he went to Belchertown the population was 300; at the end of his ministry it was 2,400; d. Belchertown, Mar. 8, 1814, a. 84.

ABIEL FOSTER, A.M., b. Andover, Aug. 8, 1735, son of Capt. Asa and Elizabeth (Abbot) Foster; H. C., 1756, A.B., A.M.; Ord. Canterbury, N. H., Jan. 21, 1761, as the first minister; sett. Canterbury, N. H., 1761-1779; memb. N. H. Senate; Pres. N. H. Senate; Chief Justice of the Court of Common Pleas for the Co. of Rockingham, N. H., 1789-1795; Delegate to the Continental Congress, 1783-1784; memb. Congress, 1789-1791; 1795-1803; d. Canterbury, N. H., Feb. 6, 1806, a. 70.

BENJAMIN FOSTER, D.D., b. Danvers, June 12, 1750, son of Gideon and Lydia (Goldthwaite) Foster; Y. C., 1774, A.B.; A.M., 1781; A.B., Brown, 1775; A.M., Brown U., 1786; D.D., Brown, 1792; Ord. Leicester, (Greenville Bapt. Chh.), Oct. 23, 1776; sett. Leicester, 1772-1782; sett. Danvers, (Bapt. Chh.), 1784; inst. Newport, R. I., 1785-1787; sett. New York City, (1st Bapt. Chh.), 1788-1798; Bapt.; d. of yellow fever, New York City, Aug. 26, 1798, contracted while ministering to the sick.

DAN FOSTER, A.M., b. Harvard, 1748, son of Rev. Isaac and Elizabeth (Emerson) Foster; A.M., (Hon.), Y. C., 1774; A. M., (Hon.), Dart. Coll., 1774; Ord. Windsor, Ct., (3rd or Poquonock Society), June 12, 1771; sett. Windsor, Ct., 1771-1783; dism. Oct. 23, 1783; sett. Weathersfield, Vt., 1787-1799; sett. Charlestown, N. H., 1804-1809; d. Charlestown, N. H., Mar. 1810, a. 62.

EMERSON FOSTER, A.M., b. Suffield, Ct., 1747, son of Isaac and Elizabeth (Emerson) Foster; Dart. Coll., 1773, A.B., A.M.; preached at Granby, Ct., (Turkey Hills Parish), 1774-1775, Ord. Killingly, Ct., Jan. 21, 1778; sett. Killingly, Ct., 1778-1779; dism. July 27, 1779; sett. New London, Ct., 1780-1782; inst. Orange, Mass., Dec. 12, 1782; sett. Orange, 1782-1790; sett. Clarendon, Vt., Pomfret, Vt. and Orient, L. I., N. Y., 1800-1805; Unitarian-Universalist; d. Brooklyn N. Y., 1814, a. 67.

JACOB FOSTER, A.M., b. Holliston, Mar. 10, 1732, son of

Capt. Jacob and Mary (Suffield) Foster; H. C., 1754, A.B., A.M.; Ord. South Berwick, Me., (1st Parish in Berwick), Sept. 1, 1756; sett. South Berwick, Me., 1756-1777; Chaplain, Rev. army, 1775-1776; inst. Nelson, N. H., (then Packersfield), 1781; sett, Nelson, N. H., 1781-1791; sett. Rye, N. H.; d. Rye, N. H., Dec. 3, 1798, a. 66.

ISAAC FOSTER, A.M., b. Charlestown, 1652, son of Capt. Willim and Ann (Brackenbury) Foster; H. C., 1671, A.B., A.M.; Fellow and Tutor, H. C., 1678; Ord. Hartford, Ct., (1st Chh.), 1679; sett. Hartford, Ct., 1679-1682; d. Hartford, Ct., Aug. 20, 1682, a. 30.

ISAAC FOSTER, A.M., b. Rowley, Feb. 19, 1725, son of Daniel and Hannah (Clarke) Foster; A.M., (Hon.), Y. C., 1770; Ord. West Stafford Ct., (2nd Chh. in Stafford), Oct. 31, 1764; sett. West Stafford, Ct., 1764-1807; Universalist, 1780-1807; d. West Stafford, Ct., 1807.

JOHN FOWLE, A.M., b. Charlestown, July 31, 1714, son of John and Mary (Burrell) Fowle; H. C., 1732, A.B., A.M.; Ord. Cohasset, Dec. 31, 1741; sett. Cohasset, 1741-1746; dism. 1746, because of mental derangement; d. Cohasset, Apr. 21, 1764.

JOHN FOWLE, A.M., b. Woburn, Feb. 1, 1726/7, son of Maj. John and Mary (Converse) Fowle; H. C., 1747, A.B., A.M.; sett. Norwalk, Ct., (Epis. Chh.), 1751-1756; Epis.; taught school at Woburn, 1758-1770; d. Boston, Oct. 15, 1786, a. 61.

AMOS FOWLER, A.M., b. North Guilford, Ct., Feb. 8, 1727/8, son of Daniel and Grace Fowler; Y. C., 1753, A.B., A.M.; Ord. Guilford, Ct., June 8, 1757; sett. Guilford, Ct., 1757-1800; d. Guilford, Ct., Feb. 10, 1800, a. 72.

JOSEPH FOWLER, A.M., b. Lebanon, Ct., 1722, son of Sergt. Jonathan and Hannah (Clark) Fowler; Y. C., 1743, A.B., A.M.; Ord. East Haddam, Ct., May 15, 1751; sett. East Haddam, Ct., 1751-1771; d. East Haddam, Ct., June 10, 1771, a. 49.

JABEZ FOX, A.M., b. Concord, 1647, son of Thomas and Rebecca Fox; H. C., 1665, A.B., A.M.; Ord. Woburn, Sept. 5, 1679; sett. Woburn, 1678-1703; d. Boston, Feb. 28, 1702/3, a. 56, of small pox.

JOHN FOX, A.M., b. Cambridge, May 10, 1678, son of Rev. Jabez and Judith (Rayner) Fox; H. C., 1698, A.B., A.M.; Ord. Woburn, Nov. 17, 1703; sett. Woburn, 1703-1756; d. Woburn, Dec. 12, 1756, a. 77.

SAMUEL FOXCROFT, A.M., b. Boston, 1735, son of Rev. Thomas and Anna (Coney) Foxcroft; H. C., 1754, A.B., A.M.; teacher at Princeton U.; Ord. New Gloucester, Me., Jan. 16, 1765; sett. New Gloucester, Me., 1765-1793; dism. Jan. 1793; d. New Gloucester, Me., Mar. 9, 1807, a. 72.

THOMAS FOXCROFT, A.M., b. Cambridge, Feb. 26, 1696/7, son of Col. Francis (Warden of King's Chapel, Boston) and Elizabeth

(Danforth) Foxcroft; H. C., 1714, A.B., A.M.; Ord. Boston, (1st Chh.), Nov. 20, 1717; sett. Boston, 1717-1769; Artillery Election Sermon, 1723; Dudleian Lecture, 1761; d. Boston, June 18, 1769, a. 72.

JONATHAN FRENCH, A.M., b. Braintree, Jan. 30, 1740, son of Dea. Moses and Esther (Thayer) French; H. C., 1771, A.B., A.M.; Ord. Andover, Sept. 23, 1772; sett. Andover, 1772-1809; soldier, French and Indian War, 1757; sergt. at Castle William, Boston Harbor, 1757-1767; Election Sermon, 1796; d. Andover, July 28, 1809, a. 70.

THOMAS FRINK, A.M., b. Sudbury, Jan. 1, 1705, son of Lieut. Thomas and Sarah (Noyes) Frink; H. C., 1722, A.B., A.M.; Ord. Rutland, Nov. 1, 1727; sett. Rutland, 1723-1740; resigned Sept. 8, 1740; inst. Plymouth, (3rd Chh.), Nov. 3, 1743; sett. Plymouth, 1743-1748; inst. Barre, Oct. 1753; sett. Barre, 1753-1766; dism. July 16, 1766; Election Sermon, 1758; d. Rutland, Aug. 21, 1777, a. 73.

LEVI FRISBIE, A.M., b. Branford, Ct., Mar. 31, 1748, son of Elisha and Rachel (Levi) Frisbie; Y. C., (1767-1770); Dartmouth, 1771, A.B., A.M.; Ord. Indian missionary at Dart. Coll., May 21, 1772; inst. Ipswich, (1st Chh.), Feb. 7, 1776; sett. Ipswich, 1776-1806; d. Ipswich, Feb. 21, 1806.

AMARIAH FROST, A.M., b. Framingham, Oct. 4, 1720, son of Samuel and Elizabeth (Rice) Frost; H. C., 1740, A.B., A.M.; Ord. Milford, Dec. 21, 1742; sett. Milford, 1742-1792; d. Milford, Mar. 14, 1792.

STEPHEN FROST, A.M., bapt. Cambridge, Jan. 18, 1719, son of Edmund and Hannah (Cooper) Frost; H. C., 1739, A.B., A.M.; was master of the Lancaster Grammar School, 1740-1744; preached occasionally at Lancaster, 1744-1747; he was admitted to the First Church in Lancaster, Apr. 29, 1744; d. Aug. 9, 1749.

EBENEZER FROTHINGHAM, bapt. Charlestown, June 9, 1717, son of Dea. Samuel and Hannah (Hunting) Frothingham; Ord. Wethersfield, Ct., Oct. 28, 1747; sett. Middletown Ct., (Separatist Chh.), 1747-1792; d. Middletown, Ct., Nov. 30, 1798, a. 81.

DANIEL FULLER, A.M., b. Dedham, Apr. 20, 1699, son of Thomas Fuller, Jr.; Y. C., 1721, A.B., A.M.; Ord. Willington, Ct., Sept. 20, 1728; sett. Willington, Ct., 1728-1758; d. Willington, Ct., Dec. 6, 1758, a. 60, of small pox.

DANIEL FULLER, A.M., b. Sept. 1, 1740, son of Benjamin and Mary (Fuller) Fuller; H. C., 1764, A.B., A.M.; Ord. Gloucester, (2nd Chh.), Jan. 10, 1770; sett. Gloucester, 1770-1821; d. Dorchester, May 23, 1829.

JOHN FULLER, b. Lebanon, Ct., 1722; not a grad.; Ord. Lyme, Ct., (Separatist Chh.), Dec. 25, 1746; re-ord. Norwich, Ct., (Bean Hill), Aug. 17, 1759; sett. Norwich, Ct., 1759-1762; inst. Plainfield, Ct., Feb. 3, 1769; sett. Plainfield, Ct., 1769-1777; New Light preacher; d. Plainfield, Ct., Oct. 3, 1777, a. 55.

SAMUEL FULLER, b. Plymouth, 1624, son of Dea. Samuel and Bridget (Lee) Fuller, of the Mayflower, 1620; Ord. Middleborough, Dec. 26, 1694; sett. Middleborough, 1678-1695; deacon at Plymouth; d. Middleborough, Aug. 17, 1695.

TIMOTHY FULLER, A.M., b. Middleton, May 18, 1739, son of Jacob and Abigail (Holton) Fuller; H. C., 1760, A.B., A.M.; Ord. Princeton, Sept. 9, 1767; sett. Princeton, 1767-1776; sett. Chilmark, (as a supply), 1776-1782; sett. Merrimac, N. H.; d. Merrimac, N. H., July 3, 1805.

WILLIAM GAGER, A.M., b. New London, Ct., Dec. 29, 1704, son of Samuel and Rebecca (Lay) Gager; Y. C., 1721, A.B., A.M.; Ord. Columbia, Ct., (2nd Chh. in Lebanon), May 27, 1725; sett. Columbia, Ct., 1725-1739; dism. May 1739; d. Lebanon, Ct., 1769.

ANDREW GARDNER, A.M., b. Brookline, Nov. 15, 1674, son of Capt. Andrew and Sarah (Mason) Gardner; H. C., 1696, A.B., A.M.; Chaplain, 1704; sett. Lancaster, May 1701, where he was soon to be ordained when he was accidentally killed while doing sentry duty in the Indian wars, Oct. 26, 1704, a. 30.

ANDREW GARDNER, JR., A.M., b. Brookline; H. C., 1712, A.B., A.M.; Ord. Worcester, 1719, as the first minister; sett. Worcester, 1719-1722; dism. Oct. 31, 1722; inst. Lunenburg, May 15, 1728; sett. Lunenburg, 1728-1732; dism. Nov. 3, 1732; sett. Winchester, N. H.; sett. Charlestown, N. H., 1746-1755; preacher, physician, surgeon and chaplain at Fort Dummer, 1748; at Great Meadows Fort, Putney, Vt., 1755-1757; sett. Rockingham, Vt., 1760-1771; sett. Bath, N. H., 1771-1773; d. Bath, N. H., 1773.

BENJAMIN GARDNER, b. West Greenwich, R. I., 1715, son of Joseph and Hannah (Briggs) Gardner; Ord. West Greenwich, R. I., (Bapt. Chh.); came to Pownal, Vt., 1764, and preached there; inst. Pownal, Vt., (1st Chh.—Bapt.), 1772; sett. Pownal, Vt., 1772-1774; dism. 1774; Bapt.; d. Pownal, Vt., Dec. 10, 1793, a. 78.

FRANCIS GARDNER, A.M., b. Stow, Feb. 17, 1735/6, son of Rev. John and Mary (Baxter) Gardner; H. C., 1755, A.B., A.M.; Ord. Leominster, Dec. 22, 1762; sett. Leominster, 1762-1814; d. Watertown, June 2, 1814.

JAMES GARDNER, b. Scotland; Ord. Marshfield, (1st Chh.), Mar. 14, 1707; sett. Marshfield, 1707-1739; d. Marshfield, Sept. 6, 1739.

JOHN GARDNER, A.M., b. Charlestown, July 22, 1696, son of John and Elizabeth (Lane) Gardner; H. C., 1715, A.B., A.M.; Ord. Stow, Nov. 26, 1718; sett. Stow, 1718-1775; d. Stow, Jan. 10, 1775, a. 80.

JOSEPH GARDNER, A.M., b. Boston, May 8, 1713, son of Samuel and Eliza Gardner; H. C., 1732, A.B., A.M.; Ord. Newport,

R. I.; sett. Newport, R. I., (1st Cong. Chh.), 1740-1743; d. Apr. 4, 1806.

JOSHUA GARDNER, A.M., b. 1688 (probably at Roxbury, son of Joshua and Mary (Weld) Gardner); H. C., 1707, A.B., A.M.; Ord. Haverhill, (1st Chh.), Jan. 11, 1710/11; sett. Haverhill, 1710-1715; d. Haverhill, Mar. 21, 1715/6.

BUNKER GAY, A.M., b. Dedham, July 31, 1735, son of Lusher and Mary (Ellis) Gay; H. C., 1760, A.B., A.M.; Ord. Hinsdale, N. H., Aug. 17, 1763, as the first minister; sett. Hinsdale, N. H., 1763-1815; d. Hinsdale, N. H., Oct. 19, 1815, a. 80.

EBENEZER GAY, D.D., b. Dedham, Aug. 15, 1696, son of Nathaniel and Lydia (Lusher) Gay; H. C., 1714, A.B., A.M.; S.T.D., 1785; Ord. Hingham, June 11, 1718; sett. Hingham, 1717-1787; Artillery Election Sermon, 1728; Election Sermon, 1745; Convention Sermon, 1746; Dudleian Lecture, 1759; liberal; Unitarian; opposed to creeds; d. Hingham, Mar. 18, 1787, a. 91.

EBENEZER GAY, D.D., b. Dedham, May 4, 1718, son of Lusher and Mary (Ellis) Gay; H. C., 1737, A.B., A.M.; S.T.D., 1792; Ord. Suffield, Ct., (1st Chh.), Jan. 13, 1742; sett. Suffield, Ct., 1742-1796; d. Suffield, Ct., Mar. 7, 1796.

WILLIAM GAYLORD, A.M., b. West Hartford, Ct., Nov. 29, 1709, son of Dea. William and Hope (Butler) Gaylord; Y. C., 1730, A.B., A.M.; Ord. Wilton, Ct., Feb. 14, 1732/3; sett. Wilton, Ct., 1732-1767; d. Wilton, Ct., Jan. 2, 1767 a. 58.

JOSHUA GEE, A.M., b. Boston, June 29, 1698, son of Joshua and Elizabeth (Thacher) Gee; H. C., 1717, A.B., A.M.; Librarian, H. C., 1721-1722; Ord. Boston, (2nd Chh.), Dec. 18, 1723; sett. Boston, 1723-1748; d. Boston, May 22, 1748, a. 50.

JOSEPH GERRISH, A.B., b. Newbury, Mar. 23, 1650, son of Capt. William and Joanna (Goodale) Gerrish; H. C., 1669, A.B.; Ord. Wenham, Jan. 13, 1674/5; sett. Wenham, 1673-1720; d. Wenham, Jan. 6, 1719/20, a. 69.

HENRY GIBBS, A.M., b. Boston, Oct. 8, 1668, son of Robert and Elizabeth (Sheafe) Gibbs; H. C., 1685, A.B., A.M.; Fellow, H. C., 1700-1707; Ord. Watertown, Oct. 6, 1697; sett. Watertown, 1690-1723; Artillery Election Sermon, 1704; attended witchcraft persecutions; was horrified by them; because of his wisdom there were none in Watertown; d. Watertown, Oct. 21, 1723, a. 56.

WILLIAM GIBBS, A.M., b. Boston, 1715, son of John and Mary Gibbs; H. C., 1734, A.B., A.M.; sett. St. Andrew's Parish, Simsbury, Ct., 1747-1777; Epis.; d. Simsbury, Ct., Apr. 7, 1777, s. p.

RICHARD GIBSON, A.B., b. Yorkshire, Eng.; matric. Emmanuel Coll., Camb., 1627; A.B., Magdalen Coll., Oxford; was brought as an Anglican minister by Robert Trelawny, Esq., to his colony at Richmond Island, Maine; sett. Casco, Me., (Epis. Chh. at Richmond Island), 1636-1638; sett. Saco, Me. and Appledore, Me., (Isles of

Shoals), 1638-1639; sett. Portsmouth, N. H., (Epis. Chapel), 1640-1642; the people of Portsmouth, in 1640, founded and built "the parsonage house, chappell, with the appurtences, at their own proper costs and charges," and "made choyse of Mr. Richard Gibson to be the first parson of the said parsonage;" left 1642; Winthrop, who was opposed to him on the ground of his religion, charges that he provoked the people of the Isles of Shoals to revolt against the government; returned to England, 1643; Epis.; d. soon after Oct. 21, 1645.

WILLIAM GIBSON, b. London, England, 1638, son of Roger Gibson; came from London to N. E., Oct. 1675; ordained before he came to Newport; Ord. Newport, R. I., (3rd or Sabbatarian Bapt. Chh.), 1704; sett. Newport, R. I., (3rd Bapt. Chh.), 1704-1717; Bapt.; d. Newport, R. I., Mar. 12, 1717, a. 79.

THOMAS GILBERT, b. Scotland, 1610; minister at Chedlic and Edling in England; came to N. E., 1661; Ord. Topsfield, Nov. 4, 1663, as the first minister; sett. Topsfield, 1663-1671; dism. 1671; in 1666, he was accused of sedition; in 1670, of intemperance; d. Charlestown, Oct. 28, 1673, a. 63.

ALEXANDER GILLET, A.M., b. East Granby, (Turkey Hills), Ct., Aug. 14, 1749, son of Capt. Zaccheus and Ruth (Phelps) Gillet; Y. C., 1770, A.B., A.M.; Ord. Wolcott, Ct., (Farmingbury), Dec. 29, 1773; sett. Wolcott, Ct., 1773-1791; dism. Nov. 10, 1791; inst. Torrington, Ct., May 22, 1792; sett. Torrington, Ct., 1792-1826; d. Torrington, Ct., Jan. 19, 1826, a. 77.

NICHOLAS GILMAN, A.M., b. Exeter, N. H., Jan. 8, 1707/8, son of Judge Nicholas and Sarah (Clark) Gilman; H. C., 1724, A.B., A.M.; preached at Portsmouth Plains, N. H., 1728; at Hampton, N. H., 1732-1733; at Drinkwater, N. H., 1734-1735; Ord. Durham, N. H., Mar. 3, 1742; sett. Durham, N. H., 1742-1748; d. Durham, N. H., Apr. 13, 1748, a. 41.

TRISTRAM GILMAN, A.M., b. Durham, N. H., Nov. 24, 1735, son of Rev. Nicholas and Mary (Thyng) Gilman; H. C., 1757, A.B.; A.M., 1761; Ord. North Yarmouth, Me., Dec. 8, 1769; sett. North Yarmouth, Me., 1769-1809; Trustee, Bowdoin Coll.; first President, Maine Missionary Society; d. North Yarmouth, Me., Apr. 1, 1809, a. 74.

CHARLES GLEASON, A.M., b. Brookline, Dec. 29, 1718, son of William and Thankful (Trowbridge) Gleason; H. C., 1738, A.B., A.M.; Ord. Dudley, Oct. 31, 1744; sett. Dudley, 1744-1790; d. Dudley, May 7, 1790, a. 72.

PELATIAH GLOVER, b. Dorchester, 1637, son of Hon. John and Ann Glover; H. C., 1650-1654, but did not grad.; Ord. Springfield, June 18, 1661; sett. Springfield, 1661-1692; d. Springfield, Mar. 29, 1692, a. 55.

DAVID GODDARD, A.M., b. Watertown, Sept. 26, 1706, son of Capt. Edward, J. P. and Susanna (Stone) Goddard; H. C.,

1731, A.B., A.M.; Ord. Leicester, June 30, 1736; sett. Leicester, 1736-1754; d. Framingham, Jan. 19, 1754, a. 48.

EDWARD GODDARD, A.B., b. Shrewsbury, Mar. 12, 1745, son of Edward and Hepzibah (Hapgood) Goddard; H. C., 1764, A.B.; Ord. Swanzey, N. H., Sept. 27, 1769; sett. Swanzey, N. H., 1769-1798; dism. July 5, 1798; d. Swanzey, N. H., Oct. 13, 1811, a. 66.

WILLIAM GODDARD, A.M., b. Leicester, Apr. 27, 1740, son of Rev. David and Mercy (Stone) Goddard; H. C., 1761, A.B.; A.M., 1765; Ord. Westmoreland, N. H., Nov. 7, 1764, as the first minister; sett. Westmoreland, N. H., 1764-1775; dism. 1775, because of ill health; remov. to Orange, 1778; to Petersham, 1779; d. Petersham, June 16, 1788, a. 48.

ENOCH GOFF, b. Rehoboth, Nov. 3, 1741, son of Robert and Hannah (Horton) Goff; Ord. Dighton, (West Bapt. Chh.), Dec. 2, 1772; sett. Dighton, 1772-1810; d. Dighton, Mar. 17, 1810.

HEZEKIAH GOLD, A.M., b. Hartford, Ct., 1694, son of Deputy-Gov. Nathan and Hannah (Talcott) Gold; H. C., 1719, A.B., A.M.; Ord. Stratford, Ct., (1st Chh.), June 1722; sett. Stratford, 1722-1752; d. 1761.

HEZEKIAH GOLD, JR., A.M., b. Stratford, Ct., Jan. 18, 1731, son of Rev. Hezekiah and Mary (Ruggles) Gold; Y. C., 1751, A.B., A.M.; Ord. Cornwall, Ct., Aug. 27, 1755; sett. Cornwall, Ct., 1755-1786; dism. May 6, 1786; Rep. Gen. Assembly of Ct., 1787; d. Cornwall, Ct., May 31, 1790, a. 60.

JESSE GOODELL, A.M., b. Pomfret, Ct., Dec. 8, 1736, son of Edward and Lydia (Eaton) Goodell; Y. C., 1761, A.B., A.M.; Ord. Westminster, Vt., June 11, 1767; sett. Westminster, Vt., 1767-1769; left Dec. 1769; d. June 14, 1776.

JOSIAH GOODHUE, A.B., b. Stratham, N. H., 1729, son of Dea. Samuel and Abigail (Bartlett) Goodhue; H. C., 1755, A.B.; Ord. Dunstable, June 8, 1757; sett. Dunstable, 1757-1774; dism. Sept. 28, 1774; inst. Putney, Vt., Oct. 17, 1776; sett. Putney, Vt., 1776-1797; d. Putney, Vt., Nov. 16, 1797.

ELIZUR GOODRICH, D.D., b. South Wethersfield, (Rocky Hill), Ct., Oct. 26, 1734, son of Dea. David and Hepzibah (Boardman) Goodrich; Y. C., 1752, A.B., A.M.; S.T.D., Princeton, 1783; Tutor, Y. C., 1755-1756: Membr. Corp. Y. C., 1776-1797; Ord. Durham, Ct., Nov. 24, 1756; sett. Durham, Ct., 1756-1797; Ct. Election Sermon, 1787; d. Norfolk, Ct., Nov. 22, 1797, a. 64.

SEWALL GOODRIDGE, A.M., b. Lunenburg, July 7, 1743, son of Benjamin and Sarah Goodridge; H. C., 1764, A.B., A.M.; Ord. Lyndeborough, N. H., Sept. 7, 1768; sett. Lyndeborough, N. H., 1768-1809; d. Lyndeborough, N. H., Mar. 14, 1809, a. 65.

JOHN GOODSELL, A.M., b. East Haven, Ct., Dec. 21, 1706, son of Thomas and Sarah (Hemingway) Goodsell; Y. C., 1724, A.B.,

A.M.; Ord. Greenfield, Ct., May 18, 1726; sett. Greenfield, Ct., 1726-1756; dism. Apr. 20, 1756; d. Greenfield, Ct., Dec. 26, 1763, a. 57.

DANIEL GOOKIN, JR., A.M., b. Cambridge, July 12, 1650, son of Maj.-Gen. Daniel and Mary (Dolling) Gookin; H. C., 1669, A.B., A.M.; Fellow, H. C., 1673-1681; Librarian, H. C., 1674-1681; Ord. Sherborn, Mar. 26, 1685; sett. Sherborn, 1680-1718; preached to the Indians at Natick, 1685-1718; d. Sherborn, Jan. 8, 1717/8, a. 68.

NATHANIEL GOOKIN, A.M., b. Cambridge, Oct. 22, 1656, son of Maj.-Gen. Daniel and Mary (Dolling) Gookin; H. C., 1675, A.B., A.M.; Tutor and Fellow, H. C., 1690-1692; Ord. Cambridge, Nov. 15, 1682; sett. Cambridge, 1682-1692; d. Cambridge, Aug. 15, 1692, a. 35.

NATHANIEL GOOKIN, A.M., b. Cambridge, Apr. 15, 1687, son of Rev. Nathaniel and Hannah (Savage) Gookin; H. C., 1703, A.B., A.M.; Librarian, H. C., 1707-1709; Ord. Hampton, N. H., Nov. 14, 1710; sett. Hampton, N. H., 1710-1734; d. Hampton, N. H., Aug. 25, 1734, a. 47.

NATHANIEL GOOKIN, A.M., b. Hampton, N. H., Feb. 18, 1713, son of Rev. Nathaniel and Dorothy (Cotton) Gookin; H. C., 1731, A.B., A.M.; Ord. North Hampton, N. H., Oct. 31, 1739, as the first minister; sett. North Hampton, N. H., 1739-1766; d. North Hampton, N. H., Oct. 22, 1766, a. 53.

WILLIAM GORDON, D.D., b. Hitchen, England, 1727; A.M., (Hon.), H. C., 1772; A.M., (Hon.), Y. C., 1773; S.T.D., (Hon.), Princeton, 1777; Ord. Jamaica Plain, July 6, 1772; sett. Jamaica Plain, 1772-1786; resigned, Mar. 17, 1786; returned to Eng.; published a history of the Am. Rev.; Chaplain to the Provincial Congress, 1775; Election Sermon, 1775; Dudleian Lecture, 1781; d. England, Oct. 19, 1807, a. 80.

JOHN GORTON, b. Cranston, R. I., Apr. 22, 1723, son of Samuel and Elizabeth (Greene) Gorton; Ord. East Greenwich, R. I., Sept. 6, 1753; sett. East Greenwich, R. I., 1753-1792; Bapt.; d. East Greenwich, R. I., June 6, 1792.

SAMUEL GORTON, bapt. Manchester, Lancashire, England, Feb. 12, 1592/3, son of Thomas Gorton; came to N. E. from London, 1637; sett. Boston and Plymouth; came to R. I., June 1638; sett. Pawtuxet and Warwick, R. I.; imprisoned at Charlestown, Mass.; preached at Warwick, R. I., 1641-1677; Deputy to Gen. Ct., R. I., 1651, et seq.; commissioner to the Narragansett Indians, 1651-1663; Gortonist; d. Warwick, R. I., Dec. 10, 1677.

STEPHEN GORTON, b. Warwick, R. I., Mar. 21, 1703/4, son of Benjamin and Ann (Lancaster) Gorton; Ord. Waterford, Ct., (2nd Bapt. Chh. in Ct., at New London), Mar. 28, 1726; sett. Waterford, Ct., 1726-1774; Bapt.; d. Southington, Ct., 1779, a. ca. 76.

THOMAS GOSS, A.M., b. Brookfield, July 6, 1716, son of Capt. Philip and Judith (Hayward) Goss; H. C., 1737, A.B., A.M.;

Ord. Bolton, Nov. 4, 1741; sett. Bolton, 1741-1771; dism. Aug. 13, 1771, by the church because he held too high views of the powers of the clergy; sett. Bolton, (2nd Chh., which met in his home), 1771-1780; d. Bolton, Jan. 17, 1780, a. 63.

EBENEZER GOULD, A.M., b. Guilford, Ct., 1701, son of Benjamin and Elizabeth Gould; Y. C., 1723, A.B., A.M.; Ord. Greenwich, Ct., 1728; sett. Greenwich, Ct., 1728-1739; inst. Southold, L. I., N. Y., Sept. 1740; sett. Southold, L. I., N. Y., 1740-1747; inst. Middletown, Ct., (4th Chh. at Middlefield), Oct. 10, 1747; sett. Middletown, Ct., 1747-1756; d. Granville, Mass., 1778/9.

THOMAS GOULD, b. ca. 1607; inhabitant at Charlestown, June 7, 1640; Noodles Island; excommunicated from the First Church in Charlestown, July 30, 1665; sett. Boston, (1st Bapt. Chh.), 1665-1675, as the first minister; Bapt.; d. Boston, Oct. 27, 1675.

JOHN GRAHAM, A.M., b. Edinburgh, Scotland, 1694; Glasgow U., 1714; A.M., (Hon.), Y. C., 1737; came to Londonderry, N. H., 1718; Ord. Stafford, Ct., May 25, 1723, as the first minister; sett. Stafford, Ct., 1723-1731; inst. Southbury, Ct., (South Chh. at Woodbury), Jan. 17, 1733, as the first minister; sett. Southbury, Ct., 1733-1774; physician; d. Southbury, Ct., Dec. 11, 1774, a. 80.

JOHN GRAHAM, JR., A.M., b. Exeter, N. H., Aug. 22, 1722, son of Rev. John and Love (Sanborn) Graham; Y. C., 1740, A.B.; A.M., 1759; Ord. West Suffield, Ct., (2nd Chh. in Suffield), Oct. 22, 1746, as the first minister; sett. West Suffield, Ct., 1746-1796; physician; Chaplain, 1762, in the expedition against Havana; d. West Suffield, Ct., Apr. 20, 1796, a. 74.

RICHARD CROUCH GRAHAM, A.B., b. Southbury, Ct., Mar. 11, 1739, son of Rev. John and Abigail (Chauncy) Graham; Y. C., 1760, A.B.; Ord. Pelham, July 6, 1763; sett. Pelham, 1760-1771; d. Pelham, Feb. 25, 1771, a. 32.

OLIVER GRANT, Ord. Mansfield, Ct., (Separatist Chh.), ca. 1743.

JOHN GRAVES, Vicar of Clapham in Yorkshire in the diocese of Chester; sett. Providence, R. I., (King's Chapel, now St. John's Cathedral), 1755-1776; Epis.; brother of Rev. Matthew Graves of New London.

MATTHEW GRAVES, came from England; said to have been a brother of Rev. John Graves of Providence; inst. New London, Ct., (St. John's Epis. Chh.), Apr. 26, 1748; sett. New London, Ct., 1748-1778; sett. Hebron, Ct., 1752-1757; d. New York City, Apr. 5, 1780, unm.

STARLING GRAVES, A.M., b. East Haddam, Ct., son of Benjamin Graves; Y. C., 1765, A.B., A.M.; Ord. East Hartland, Ct., June 29, 1768, as the first minister; sett. East Hartland, Ct., 1768-1772; d. East Hartland, Ct., Sept. 1772.

ELLIS GRAY, A.M., b. Boston, Sept. 7, 1715, son of Edward

and Hannah (Ellis) Gray; H. C., 1734, A.B., A.M.; Ord. Boston, (New Brick Chh.), Sept. 27, 1738; sett. Boston, 1738-1752; Artillery Election Sermon, 1749; d. Boston, Jan. 17, 1752/3, a. 37.

JAMES GREATON, A.M., b. Roxbury, July 10, 1730, son of James and Catherine Greaton; Y. C., 1754, A.B., A.M.; A.M., (Hon.), H. C., 1760; inst. Boston, (Christ Chh.), May 30, 1760; sett. Boston, 1760-1767; left Aug. 31, 1767; sett. Huntington, L. I., N. Y., 1768-1773; Epis.; d. Huntington, L. I., N. Y., Apr. 17, 1773, a. 43.

ELISHA GREEN, b. Warwick, R. I., Aug. 5, 1698, son of James and Mary (Fones) Green; Ord. Cranston, R. I., July 30, 1764; sett. Cranston, R. I., 1764; Bapt.; d.

HENRY GREENE, bapt. Great Bromley, Essex, England, Jan. 20, 1618/9; matric., Emmanuel Coll., Camb., 1635; came to N. E., 1640; adm. freeman, Watertown, May 13, 1642; Ord. Wakefield, (1st Chh. in Reading), Nov. 5, 1645, as the first minister; sett. Wakefield, 1645-1648; d. Reading, Oct. 11, 1648.

JOHN GREEN, A.M., b. Malden, Mar. 20, 1699/1700, son of John and Isabell Green; H. C., 1719, A.B., A.M.; preached but was not ordained; merchant; d. after 1740.

JOSEPH GREEN, A.M., b. Cambridge, Nov. 24, 1675, son of John and Ruth (Michelson) Green; H. C., 1695, A.B., A.M.; Ord. Danvers, (Salem Village), Nov. 10, 1698; sett. Danvers, 1697-1715; d. Danvers, Nov. 26, 1715, a. 40. (G. S. says Dec. 6, 1715).

JOSEPH GREEN, A.M., bapt. Boston, June 22, 1701, son of Joseph and Mary (Beck) Green; H. C., 1720, A.B., A.M.; taught school in Boston, 1724; Ord. Barnstable, (East Chh.), May 12, 1725; sett. Barnstable, 1725-1770; d. Barnstable, Oct. 4, 1770.

JOSEPH GREEN, JR., A.M., b. Barnstable, Sept. 12, 1727, son of Rev. Joseph and Hannah (Russell) Green; H. C., 1746, A.B., A.M.; A.M., (Hon.), Y. C., 1752; Ord. Marshfield, (1st Chh.), Feb. 21, 1753; sett. Marshfield, 1753-1758; dism. Jan. 9, 1758; inst. Yarmouth, (West Chh.), Sept. 15, 1762; sett. Yarmouth, 1762-1768; d. Yarmouth, Nov. 5, 1768, a. 42.

NATHANAEL GREENE, b. Warwick, R. I., Nov. 4, 1707, son of Jabez and Mary (Barton) Greene; Quaker preacher at Warwick, R. I.; father of General Nathanael Greene; d. Warwick, R. I., Oct. 1768.

NATHANIEL GREEN, b. Stoneham, Apr. 16, 1721, son of Capt. Nathaniel and Elizabeth (Sprague) Green; Ord. Charlton, (Bapt. Chh.), Oct. 12, 1763; sett. Charlton, 1763-1791; Bapt.; d. Charlton, Mar. 20, 1791.

PERCIVAL GREEN, A.M., b. Cambridge, Mar. 29, 1659/60, son of John and Ruth (Michelson) Green; H. C., 1680, A.B., A.M.; sett. Wells, Me., 1683-1684; d. Cambridge, July 10, 1684, a. 25.

ROLAND GREEN, A.M., b. Malden, Sept. 10, 1737, son of

James and Deborah (Hartwell) Green; H. C., 1758, A.B., A.M.; Ord. Mansfield, Aug. 26, 1761; sett. Mansfield, 1761-1808; d. Mansfield, July 4, 1808, a. 71.

DR. THOMAS GREEN, b. Malden, 1699, son of Capt. Samuel and Elizabeth (Upham) Green; sett. Sutton, (1st Bapt. Chh.), 1737; sett. Leicester, (Greenville Bapt. Chh.), 1738-1773; physician; Bapt.; d. Leicester, Aug. 19, 1773, a. 74.

TIMOTHY GREENE, b. East Greenwich, R. I., July 14, 1725, son of John and Ann Nancy (Hill) Greene; Ord. Coventry, R. I., Sept. 1, 1763; sett. Coventry, R. I., 1763-1770; Bapt.; d. 1780.

DANIEL GREENLEAF, A.M., b. Newbury, Feb. 10, 1679/80, son of Capt. Stephen and Elizabeth (Gerrish) Greenleaf; H. C., 1699, A.B.; A.M., 1726; schoolmaster at Portsmouth, N. H., 1701-1703; sett. Isles of Shoals, N. H., 1705-1706; Ord. Yarmouth, 1708; sett. Yarmouth, 1708-1726; physician and apothecary; resided at Boston, 1727-1763; d. Boston, Aug. 27, 1763.

JOHN GREENWOOD, A.M., b. Rehoboth, May 20, 1697, son of Rev. Thomas and Elizabeth (Wiswall) Greenwood; H. C., 1717, A.B., A.M.; Ord. Rehoboth, 1721; sett. Rehoboth, (1st Chh.), 1720-1766; d. Rehoboth, Dec. 1, 1766.

THOMAS GREENWOOD, A.M., b. Weymouth, Jan. 22, 1670/1, son of Hon. Thomas, J. P. and Hannah (Ward) Greenwood; H. C., 1690, A.B., A.M.; Ord. Rehoboth, Oct. 24, 1694; sett. Rehoboth, 1693-1720; d. Rehoboth, Sept. 8, 1720.

BENJAMIN GRISWOLD, JR., A.B., b. Windsor, Ct., Dec. 15, 1727, son of Capt. Benjamin and Esther (Gaylord) Griswold; Y. C., 1749, A.B.; licensed to preach, Oct. 2, 1750; d. Windsor, Ct., Sept. 1, 1751, a. 24, s. p.

GEORGE GRISWOLD, A.M., b. Lyme, Ct., Aug. 13, 1692, son of Matthew, Jr. and Phebe (Hyde) Griswold; Y. C., 1717, A.B., A.M.; Ord. East Lyme, Ct., (2nd Chh. in Lyme at Niantic), Nov. 25, 1724; sett. East Lyme, Ct., 1719-1761; d. East Lyme, Ct., Oct. 14, 1761.

SYLVANUS GRISWOLD, A.M., b. Lyme, Ct., Feb. 3, 1732/3, son of Rev. George and Hannah (Lynde) Griswold; Y. C., 1757, A.B., A.M.;Ord. West Springfield, (2nd Cong. Chh.), Nov. 17, 1762; sett. West Springfield, 1762-1819; d. West Springfield, Dec. 4, 1819, a. 87.

DANIEL GROSVENOR, A.M., b. Pomfret, Ct., Apr. 20, 1750, son of Ebenezer, Jr. and Lucy (Cheney) Grosvenor; Y. C., 1769, A.B., A.M.; A.M., (Hon.), Dart. Coll., 1792; Ord. Grafton, Oct. 19, 1774; sett. Grafton, 1774-1788; dism. Jan. 1, 1788; inst. Paxton, Nov. 5, 1793; sett. Paxton, 1793-1802; dism. Nov. 17, 1802; soldier, Am. Rev.; d. Petersham, July 22, 1834, a. 84.

EBENEZER GROSVENOR, A.M., b. Pomfret, Ct., Mar. 6, 1738/9, son of Ebenezer, Jr. and Lucy (Cheney) Grosvenor; Y. C.,

1759, A.B., A.M.; A.M., (Hon.), H. C., 1763; Ord. Scituate, Apr. 20, 1763; sett. Scituate, 1763-1780; dism. Apr. 1780; inst. Harvard, June 19, 1782; sett. Harvard, 1782-1788; Arminian; d. Harvard, May 28, 1788, a. 49.

WILLIAM GROSVENOR, A.M., b. Roxbury, Jan. 8, 1672/3, son of John and Esther (Clarke) Grosvenor; H. C., 1693, A.B., A.M.; called to Brookfield, Oct. 24, 1705; sett. Brookfield, 1705-1708; dism. Aug. 25, 1708; sett. Charleston, S. C.; d. 1733.

EBENEZER GURLEY, A.M., b. Mansfield, Ct., May 25, 1747, son of Dea. Jonathan and Hannah (Baker) Gurley; Dart. Coll., 1772, A.B., A.M.; Ord. Guilford, Vt., Oct. 28, 1775; sett. Guilford, Vt., 1774-1776; d. Guilford, Vt., July 17, 1776 a. 29.

JOHN GURLEY A.B., b. North Mansfield, Ct., Feb. 8, 1749, son of Capt. Samuel and Hannah (Baker) Gurley; Y. C., 1773, A.B.; Ord. Lebanon, Ct., (Exeter Parish), May 31, 1775, as the first minister; sett. Lebanon, Ct., 1775-1812; d. Lebanon, Ct., Feb. 27, 1812, a. 63.

ROBERT GUTCH, bapt. Glastonbury, Co. Somerset, England, Apr. 5, 1617, son of John and Magdalen Gutch; came to Salem, 1637/8; adm. First Chh., Salem, 1641; freeman, Dec. 27, 1642; "preacher to the ffishermen" near Kennebec River, Me.; sett. Pemequid, Me., Apr. 14, 1657; at Bath, Me., 1660; drowned in the Kennebec River, Oct. 1667.

WILLIAM GUY, A.M., b. Nottinghamshire, England; admitted Corpus Christi Coll., Camb., 1690; matric., 1691; A. B., Corpus Christi Coll., Camb., 1694/5; Ord. Deacon, at York, England, Feb. 1694/5; Ord. Priest, at London, Jan. 18, 1711; missionary, V.S.P.G. F.P., 1711; assistant min., St. Philip's Chh., Charleston, S. C., 1711; sett. St. Helena, Port Royal Island, S. C., 1711-1715; sett. North Kingston, R. I., (Epis. Chh.), 1717-1718; rector, St. Andrew's Chh., near Charleston, S. C., 1719-1751; Epis.; d. St. Andrew's Parish, S. C., 1751.

JAMES HALE, A.M., b. Beverly, Oct. 14, 1685, son of Rev. John and Sarah (Noyes) Hale; H. C., 1703, A.B., A.M.; Tutor, Y. C., 1707-1709; Ord. Ashford, Ct., Nov. 26, 1718, as first minister; sett. Ashford, Ct., 1716-1742; d. Ashford, Ct., Nov. 22, 1742, a. 57.

JOHN HALE, A.M., b. Charlestown, June 3, 1636, son of Dea. Robert and Joanna Hale; H. C., 1657, A.B., A.M.; Ord. Beverly, Sept. 20, 1667, as the first minister; sett. Beverly, 1664-1700; Artillery Election Sermon, 1683; Election Sermon, 1684; Chaplain in the Expedition to Canada, 1690; preached against witches, 1692, until his wife was accused of being a witch; then he wrote ably against the witchcraft persecutions; d. Beverly, May 15, 1700, a. 63.

MOSES HALE, A.B., b. Newbury, July 10, 1678, son of John and Sarah (Symonds) Hale; H. C., 1699, A.B.; Ord. Newbury, (Byfield Parish), Nov. 17, 1706; sett. Newbury, 1702-1744; d. Newbury, Jan. 6, 1743/4, a. 65.

MOSES HALE, A.M., b. Boxford, Dec. 25, 1701, son of Joseph and Mary (Watson) Hale; H. C., 1722, A.B., A.M.; Ord. Chester, N. H., Oct. 20, 1731, as the first minister; sett. Chester, N. H., 1731-1734; dism. 1734, because most of the inhabitants were Presbyterian in faith, and during the year, 1734, a Presb. Chh. was formed; d. 1760, a. 58.

MOSES HALE, A.M., b. Newbury, Jan. 18, 1714/5, son of Joseph and Mary (Moody) Hale; H. C., 1734, A.B., A.M.; Ord. West Newbury, (1st Chh.), Feb. 20, 1751/2; sett. West Newbury, 1752-1779; d. West Newbury, Jan. 15, 1779, a. 64.

MOSES HALE, A.M., b. Rowley, Feb. 19, 1749, soon of Rev. Moses and Mehitable (Sumner) Hale; H. C., 1771, A.B., A.M.; Ord. West Boxford, Nov. 16, 1774; sett. West Boxford, 1774-1786; d. West Boxford, May 25, 1786.

AVERY HALL, A.M., b. Meriden, Ct., Dec. 2, 1737_1 son of Rev. Theophilus and Hannah (Avery) Hall; Y. C., 1759, A.B., A.M.; Ord. Rochester, N. H., Oct. 15, 1766; sett. Rochester, N. H., 1765-1775; dism. Apr. 10, 1775; removed to Wakefield; magistrate; J. P.; d. Wakefield, Aug. 5, 1820, a. 82.

DAVID HALL, D.D., b. Yarmouth, Aug. 5, 1704, son of Joseph and Hannah (Miller) Hall; H. C., 1724, A.B., A.M.; S.T.D., Dart. Coll., 1777; Ord. Sutton, Oct. 15, 1729; sett. Sutton, 1728-1789; d. Sutton, May 8, 1789, a. 85.

GERSHOM HALL, bapt. Yarmouth, Mar. 5, 1647/8, son of John Hall; sett. Chatham, Jan. 4, 1703-July 1, 1706; d. Yarmouth, Oct. 31, 1732.

LYMAN HALL, A.M., b. Wallingford, Ct., Apr. 12, 1724, son of John and Mary (Street) Hall; Y. C., 1747, A.B., A.M.; Ord. New Cheshire, Ct., Sept. 27, 1749; sett. New Cheshire, Ct., 1749-1751; dism. June 18, 1751; sett. in Georgia, 1758; delegate, Continental Congress, 1775; Signer of the Declaration of Independence; Governor of Georgia, 1783; first governor of the state; preacher; teacher; school-master; judge; d. Burke Co., S. C., Oct. 19, 1790, a. 67.

SAMUEL HALL, A.M., b. Wallingford, Ct., Oct. 5, 1695, son of Hon. John and Mary (Lyman) Hall; Y. C., 1716, A.B., A.M.; Tutor, Y. C., 1716-1718; Ord. Cheshire, Ct., Dec. 9, 1724; sett. Cheshire, Ct., 1722-1766; Ct. Election Sermon, 1746; d. Cheshire, Ct., Feb. 26, 1776, a. 80.

THEOPHILUS HALL, A.M., b. Wallingford, Ct., Apr. 1, 1707, son of Samuel and Love (Royce) Hall; Y. C., 1727, A.B., A.M.; Ord. Meriden, Ct., Oct. 29, 1729, as the first minister; sett. Meriden, Ct., 1728-1767; d. Meriden, Ct., Mar. 25, 1767, a. 60.

WILLARD HALL, A.M., b. Charlestown, Mar. 11, 1702/3, son of Stephen and Grace (Willis) Hall; H. C., 1722, A.B., A.M.;

Ord. Westford, Nov. 15, 1727; sett. Westford, 1727-1779; Tory; physician; J. P.; d. Westford, Mar. 19, 1779, a. 77.

JOHN HAMMETT, b. Newport, R. I., Oct. 10, 1705, son of John and Sarah (Carr) Hammett; Ord. Warwick, R. I., June 18, 1744; sett. Warwick, R. I., 1744-1752; Bapt.; d. Warwick, R. I., Dec. 28, 1752.

EBENEZER HANCOCK, A.M., b. Lexington, Dec. 7, 1710, son of Rev. John and Elizabeth (Clark) Hancock; H. C., 1728, A.B., A.M.; Ord. Lexington, Jan. 1734, as colleague with his father; sett. Lexington, 1734-1739; d. Lexington, Jan. 28, 1739/40, a. 30.

JOHN HANCOCK, A.M., b. Cambridge, Mar. 1, 1671, son of Dea. Nathaniel and Mary (Prentice) Hancock; H. C., 1689, A.B., A.M.; Ord. Lexington, Nov. 2, 1698; sett. Lexington, 1697-1752; Election Sermon, 1722; d. Lexington, Dec. 5, 1752, a. 81.

JOHN HANCOCK, JR., A.M., b. Lexington, June 1, 1702, son of Rev. John and Elizabeth (Clark) Hancock; H. C., 1719, A.B., A.M.; Librarian, H. C., 1723-1726; Ord. Quincy, (1st Chh. in Braintree), Nov. 2, 1726; sett. Quincy, 1726-1744; Artillery Election Sermon, 1730; his son was Gov. John Hancock, president of the Continental Congress, and the first Signer of the Declaration of Independence; d. Quincy, (Braintree), May 7, 1744, a. 41.

NATHANIEL HANCOCK, A.M., ESQ., b. Cambridge, Jan. 14, 1701/2, son of Nathaniel and Prudence (Russell) Hancock; H. C., 1721, A.B., A.M.; Ord. Tisbury, July 26, 1727; sett. Tisbury, 1725-1756; Judge of the King's Bench, 1761; d. Tisbury, Sept. 10, 1774, a. 73.

THOMAS HANFORD, b. Eng., son of Eglin Hanford, who m. (2), Dea. Richard Sealis of Scituate; came from England to Scituate, 1643; Ord. Norwalk, Ct., 1654, as the first minister; sett. Norwalk, Ct., 1654-1693; freeman, Plymouth Col., 1650; d. Norwalk, Ct., 1693.

JOHN HARDEN, b. Kent, England, prob. son of Stephen and Philip Harding; Ord. Newport, R. I., (2nd Bapt. Chh.), 1679; sett. Newport, R. I., 1679-1700; Bapt.; d. Newport, R. I., 1700.

ELISHA HARDING, A.M., b. Medfield, Apr. 11, 1711, son of Abraham and Mary (Partridge) Harding; H. C., 1745, A.B., A.M.; Ord. Brookfield, Sept. 13, 1749; sett. Brookfield, 1749-1755; dism. May 8, 1755; Chaplain to Col. Benjamin Bellows, at Rockingham, Vt., 1755-1771; sett. as minister at Rockingham, Vt., 1771-1773; d. Walpole, N. H., Dec. 8, 1784.

JOHN HARRIMAN, A.M., bapt. New Haven, Ct., Jan. 24, 1647/8, son of John and Elizabeth Harriman; H. C., 1667, A.B., A.M.; sett. New Haven, Ct., 1670-1674, as teacher and preacher; sett. Southampton, L. I., N. Y., 1675-1676, as preacher; sett. New Haven, Ct., 1676-1682, as preacher; sett. East Haven, Ct., 1683, as preacher; sett. New Haven, Ct., 1683-1687, as teacher; inst. Elizabeth, N. J.,

Sept. 30, 1687; sett. Elizabeth, N. J., 1687-1705; d. Elizabeth, N. J., Aug. 20, 1705.

BENJAMIN HERRINGTON, b. R. I.; Ord. North Kingston, R. I.; inst. Swansea, Aug. 15, 1742; sett. Swansea, 1742-1750; dism. May 3, 1750; went to Canterbury, Ct., where he preached to a few old people, and lived in obscurity to old age; Bapt.

TIMOTHY HARRINGTON, A.M., b. Cambridge, Jan. 30, 1715/6, son of Thomas and Abigail Harrington; H. C., 1737, A.B., A.M.; Ord. Swanzey, N. H., (Lower Ashuelot), Nov. 4, 1741; sett. Swanzey, N. H., 1741-1748; driven out by Indian depredations; dism. Oct. 12, 1748, by a special meeting at Rutland; inst. Lancaster, Nov. 6, 1748; sett. Lancaster, 1748-1795; published a Century Sermon, Lancaster, 1753; d. Lancaster, Dec. 18, 1795, a. 80.

HENRY HARRIS, A.M., b. Llangam, Monmouth, Eng., ca. 1689, son of Evan Harris, of Llangam, Gent.; matric. Jesus Coll., Oxford, Mar. 21, 1703/4, a. 15; A.B., 1707; A.M.; Fellow, Jesus Coll., Oxford, 1707-1729; inst. Boston, (King's Lecturer at King's Chapel, Apr. 1709; sett. Boston, 1709-1729; Epis.; d. Boston, Oct. 16, 1729.

JARED HARRISON, A.M., b. North Branford, Ct., May 31, 1716, son of Samuel and Elizabeth (Denison) Harrison; Y. C., 1736, A.B., A.M.; Ord. Chester, Ct., (4th Chh. in Saybrook), Sept. 15, 1742, as the first minister; sett. Chester, Ct., 1742-1751; d. North Branford, Ct., before Oct. 4, 1770.

THOMAS HARRISON, D.D., b. Hull, Yorkshire, England, ca. 1618, son of Robert Harrison, merchant; adm. pensioner, Sidney Sussex Coll., Camb., Apr. 12, 1634, (aged 16); A.B., Sidney Sussex Coll., Camb., 1637/8; came to Va., 1642, as chaplain to the Governor, Sir William Berkeley; minister of a Puritan Chh. at Nansemond, Va.; came to Boston, N. E., Oct. 20, 1648, for two years; returned to England; minister at St. Dunstan-in-the-East, London, 1651-1653; accompanied Henry Cromwell to Ireland; had a license to preach in Cheshire, England, 1672; generally styled Dr.; author of *Topica Sacra*; said to have d. at Dublin, 1682.

ASAHEL HART, A.M., b. Farmington, Ct., 1743, son of Nathaniel and Abigail (Hooker) Hart; Y. C., 1764, A.B., A.M.; Ord. East Canaan, Ct., Mar. 14, 1770, as the first minister; sett. East Canaan, Ct., 1770-1775; d. North Canaan, Ct., June 28, 1775, a. 33.

JOHN HART, A.M., b. Farmington, Ct., Apr. 12, 1682, son of Hon. Capt. Thomas and Ruth (Hawkins) Hart; Y. C., 1703, A.B., A.M.; Tutor, Y. C.; Ord. East Guilford, Ct., (2nd Chh. at Madison), Nov. 25, 1707; sett. East Guilford, Ct., 1705-1731; d. East Guilford, Ct., Mar. 4, 1730/1.

LEVI HART, D.D., b. Southington, Ct., Apr. 10, 1738, son of Dea. Thomas and Ann (Stanley) Hart; Y. C., 1760, A.B., A.M.; A.B., Dart. Coll., 1784; D.D., Princeton, 1800; member Corporation,

Dart. Coll., 1784-1788; member Corp., Y. C., 1791-1807; Ord. Griswold, Ct., (2nd Chh. in Preston), Nov. 4, 1762; sett. Griswold, Ct., 1762-1808; Ct. Election Sermon, 1786; d. Jewett City, Ct., (Griswold), Oct. 27, 1808, a. 70.

WILLIAM HART, A.M., b. East Guilford, Ct., May 9, 1713, son of Rev. John and Rebecca (Hubbard) Hart; Y. C., 1732, A.B., A.M.; Ord. Old Saybrook, Ct., (1st Chh.), Nov. 17, 1736; sett. Old Saybrook, Ct., 1736-1784; Arminian; d. Saybrook, Ct., July 11, 1784, a. 72.

JOHN HARVARD, A.M., bapt. Southwark, London, England, Nov. 29, 1607, son of Robert and Katharine (Rogers) Harvard; Emmanuel Coll., Camb., A.B., 1631/2; A.M., 1635; came to N. E., 1637; Ord. Charlestown, Nov. 6, 1637; sett. Charlestown, 1637-1638; bequeathed half of his estate and his library to Harvard College, which took his name; d. Charlestown, Sept. 14, 1638.

JOHN HARVEY, A.M., b. Ireland, 1680, son of Robert Harvey; adm. pensioner, Trinity Coll., Dublin, Apr. 3, 1697, aged 17; Trinity Coll., Dublin, A.B., 1701; A.M., 1704; Ord. Palmer, June 5, 1734, by the Londonderry Presbytery; sett. Palmer, 1730-1738; sett. Peterborough, N. H.; Presb.; d. Blanford.

DR. THOMAS HARWARD, A.M., b. 1700, prob. son of Dr. Thomas Harwood, of Littleton, Middlesex; University Coll., Oxford, A.B., 1721; A.M., 1724; incumbent at Guilford, Surrey, Eng.; inst. Boston, (King's Lecturer at King's Chapel), 1731; sett. Boston, 1731-1736; Licentiate of the Royal College of Physicians in London; Epis.; d. Boston, Apr. 15, 1736.

ISAAC HASEY, A.M., bapt. Cambridge, July 25, 1742, son of Abraham and Jemima (Felch) Hasey; H. C., 1762, A.B., A.M.; Ord. Lebanon, Me., June 23, 1765; sett. Lebanon, Me., 1765-1812; d. Lebanon, Me., Oct. 17, 1812.

JOHN HASTINGS, b. Suffield, Ct., 1743, son of Rev. Joseph Hastings; Ord. Suffield, Ct., (Bapt. Chh.), 1775; sett. Suffield, Ct., 1775-1811; Bapt.; d. Suffield, Ct., Mar. 17, 1811, a. 68.

JOSEPH HASTINGS, b. Northampton, Dec. 27, 1703, son of Benjamin and Mary (Parsons) Hastings; Ord. Suffield, Ct., (Separatist Chh.), Apr. 18, 1750; sett. Suffield, Ct., (Sept. Chh.), 1742-1763; sett. Suffield, Ct., (Bapt. Chh.), 1763-1785; Bapt.; d. Suffield, Ct., 1785, a. 82.

JOSEPH STACEY HASTINGS, A.M., b. Newton, Feb. 9, 1744/5, son of Samuel and Hepzibah Hastings; H. C., 1762, A.B., A.M.; Ord. North Hampton, N. H., Feb. 11, 1767; sett. North Hampton, N. H., 1767-1774; dism. July 3, 1774; embraced Sandemanianism; went to Nova Scotia, thence to Boston, where he kept a grocery store; d. on a journey to Vermont, June 30, 1807, a. 62.

GEORGE HATTON, A.M., adm. sizar St. Catharine's Coll., Camb., 1677; matric., Easter, 1677; inst. Boston, (asst. Rector at

King's Chapel), July 16, 1693; sett. Boston, 1693-1696; left July 27, 1696; during his three years at King's Chapel he was the only Anglican minister in America; in 1696, he went to the Bahama Islands.

SAMUEL HAUGH, bapt. Boston, Lincolnshire, Eng., Dec. 23, 1621, son of Hon. Atherton and Elizabeth (Bulkeley) Haugh; attended H. C., but did not grad.; Ord. Wakefield, (1st Chh. in Reading), Mar. 1650; sett. Wakefield, 1648-1662; d. Boston, Mar. 30, 1662.

ELIAS HAVEN, A.M., b. Framingham, Apr. 16, 1714, son of Elder Joseph and Martha (Walker) Haven; H. C., 1733, A.B., A.M.; Ord. Franklin, Nov. 8, 1738; sett. Franklin, 1738-1754; d. Franklin, Aug. 10, 1754, a. 40.

JASON HAVEN, A.M., b. Framingham, Mar. 2, 1732/3, son of Dea. Moses and Hannah (Walker) Haven; H. C., 1754, A.B., A.M.; Ord. Dedham, Feb. 5, 1756; sett. Dedham, 1756-1803; Artillery Election Sermon, 1761; Election Sermon, 1769; Dudleian Lecture, 1789; Convention Sermon, 1791; d. Dedham, May 17, 1803. a. 70.

JOSEPH HAVEN, A.M., b. Hopkinton, May 14, 1747, son of Dea. Joseph and Miriam (Bayley) Haven; H. C., 1774, A.B., A.M.; Ord. Rochester, N. H., Jan. 10, 1776; sett. Rochester, N. H., 1776-1825; d. Rochester, N. H., Jan. 27, 1825, a. 77.

SAMUEL HAVEN, D.D., b. Framingham, Aug. 4, 1727, son of Hon. Joseph, Esq. and Mehitable (Haven) Haven; H. C., 1749, A.B., A.M.; S.T.D., U. of Edinburgh, 1770; S.T.D., Dart. Coll., 1773; Ord. Portsmouth, N. H., (South Parish), May 6, 1752; sett. Portsmouth, N. H., 1752-1806; N. H. Election Sermon, 1786; Dudleian Lecture, 1798; d. Portsmouth, N. H., Mar. 3, 1806, a. 78.

THOMAS HAVEN, A.M., b. Wrentham, Aug. 30, 1744, son of Rev. Elias and Mary (Messenger) Haven; H. C., 1765, A.B., A.M.; Ord. Reading, (3rd Parish or Old South Chh.), Nov. 7, 1770; sett. Reading, 1770-1782; d. Reading, May 7, 1782, a. 38.

GIDEON HAWLEY, A.M., b. Bridgeport, Ct., Nov. 5, 1727, son of Gideon and Anna (Bennett) Hawley; Y. C., 1749, A.B., A.M.; A.M., (Hon.), H. C., 1763; Ord. missionary to the Indians, Old South Chh., Boston, July 31, 1754; Indian missionary at Sturbridge and other places, 1752-1758; inst. Mashpee, (Indian Chh.), Apr. 10, 1758; sett. Mashpee, 1758-1807; d. Mashpee, Oct. 3, 1807, a. 80.

JOSEPH HAWLEY, A.B., b. Roxbury, June 7, 1654, son of Thomas and Dorothy (Harbottle) (Lamb) Hawley: H. C., 1674, A.B.; teacher; preacher at Northampton; not ordained; surveyor; Lt., Capt.; Rep. Gen. Ct., 1683-1692; d. Northampton, May 19, 1711, a. 57.

RUFUS HAWLEY, A.M., b. Granby, Ct., Feb. 21, 1740/1, son of Timothy and Rachel (Forward) Hawley; Y. C., 1767, A.B.; A.M., 1772; Ord. West Avon, Ct., (Northington Parish), Dec. 7, 1769; sett. West Avon, Ct., 1769-1826; d. West Avon, Ct., Jan. 26, 1826, a. 85.

STEPHEN HAWLEY, A.M., b. New Milford, Ct., 1738, son of Stephen and Mary (De Forest) Hawley; Y. C., 1759, A.B., A.M.; Ord. Bethany, Ct., Oct. 12, 1763; sett. Bethany, Ct., 1763-1804; d. Woodbridge, Ct., June 17, 1804, a. 66.

THOMAS HAWLEY, A.B., b. Northampton, Sept. 29, 1689, son of Capt. Joseph and Lydia (Marshall) Hawley; H. C., 1709, A.B.; Ord. Ridgefield, Ct., 1713; sett. Ridgefield, Ct., 1713-1738; town clerk, 1714-1738; d. Ridgefield, Ct., Nov. 8, 1738, a. 49.

JOSEPH HAYNES, A.B., b. Hartford, Ct., 1641, son of Gov. John and Mabel (Harlakenden) Haynes; H. C., 1658, A.B.; sett. Wethersfield, Ct., 1663-1664; Ord. Hartford, Ct., (1st Chh.), 1664; sett. Hartford, Ct., 1664-1679; d. Hartford, Ct., May 24, 1679.

PELEG HEATH, A.M., b. Roxbury, July 26, 1700, son of Peleg and Hannah (Weld) Heath; Y. C., 1721, A.B., A.M.; A.M., (Hon.), H. C., 1724; Ord. Barrington, R. I., Nov. 13, 1728; sett. Barrington, R. I., 1728-1740; d. Barrington, R. I., Oct. 25, 1748, a. 49.

STEPHEN HEATON, A.M., b. North Haven, Ct., Nov. 30, 1710, son of Theophilus and Sarah (Earl) Heaton; Y. C., 1733, A.B., A.M.; Ord. Goshen, Ct., Nov. 1740; sett. Goshen, Ct., 1740-1753; dism. June 11, 1753; Rep. Gen. Assembly, Ct., 1758, 1759, 1768; d. Goshen, Ct., Dec. 29, 1788, a. 79.

LEMUEL HEDGE, A.M., bapt. Hardwick, July 7, 1734, son of Elisha and Martha (Johnson) Hedge; H. C., 1759, A.B., A.M.; A.B., (Hon.), Y. C., 1759; A.M., (Hon.), Y. C., 1762; Ord. Warwick, Dec. 3, 1760; sett. Warwick, 1760-1777; Tory; d. Warwick, Oct. 17, 1777, a. 44.

JONATHAN HELYER, A.M., b. Boston, Apr. 19, 1719, son of John and Elizabeth Helyer; H. C., 1738, A.B., A.M.; taught school in Boston, 1738-1741/2; Ord. Newport, R. I., (1st Cong. Chh.), Jan. 20, 1744; sett. Newport, R. I., 1744-1745; d. Newport, R. I., May 27, 1745.

JACOB HEMINGWAY, A.M., b. New Haven, Ct., Dec. 6, 1683, son of Samuel and Sarah (Cooper) Hemingway; Y. C., 1704, A.B., A.M.; Ord. East Haven, Ct., Oct. 8, 1711; sett. East Haven, Ct., 1704-1754; Ct. Election Sermon, 1740; moderator, Gen. Assembly, Ct., 1743; d. East Haven, Ct., Oct. 7, 1754, a. 71.

MOSES HEMENWAY, D.D., b. Framingham, 1735, son of Ralph and Sarah (Haven) Hemenway; H. C., 1755, A.B., A.M.; S.T.D., 1785; S.T.D., Dart. Coll., 1792; Ord. Wells, Me., Aug. 8, 1759; sett. Wells, Me., 1759-1811; Election Sermon, 1784; Convention Sermon, 1786; Dudleian Lecture, 1783; d. Wells, Me., Apr. 5, 1811, a. 76.

PHINEHAS HEMENWAY, A.M., b. Framingham, Apr. 26, 1706, son of Joshua and Rebecca Hemenway; H. C., 1730, A.B., A.M.; Ord. Townsend, Oct. 16, 1734; sett. Townsend, 1734-1760; d. Townsend, May 20, 1760.

NATHANIEL HENCHMAN, A.M., b. Boston, Nov. 2, 1699, son of Dea. Nathaniel and Ann (Green) Henchman; H. C., 1717, A.B., A.M.; Ord. Lynn, Dec. 1720; sett. Lynn, 1720-1761; liberal; d. Lynn, Dec. 23, 1761, a. 61.

EPHRAIM HEWETT, (Huit), matric. St. John's Coll., Camb., 1611; curate in Cheshire and at Knowle, Warwickshire, Eng.; sett. Wroxhall, near Kenilworth, Warwickshire, where he was silenced by Archbishop Laud, 1638; came to N. E., 1639; Ord. Windsor, Ct., Dec. 10, 1639; sett. Windsor, Ct., 1639-1644; d. Windsor, Ct., Sept. 4, 1644.

AUGUSTINE HIBBERD, A.M., b. Windham, Ct., Mar. 27, 1748, son of Dr. Joseph and Martha (Smith) Hibberd; Dart. Coll., 1772, A.B., A.M.; Ord. Claremont, N. H., Oct. 19, 1774; sett. Claremont, N. H., 1774-1785; dism. Dec. 28, 1785; Chaplain, Rev. Army; Crown officer, at Stanstead, Canada, 1785; d. Stanstead, Canada, Dec. 4, 1831, a. 83.

JEDEDIAH HIBBERD, Ord. Lebanon, N. H., (Bapt. Chh.), ca. 1771; sett. Lebanon, N. H., 1771-1784; sett. Cornish, N. H., (Bapt. Chh.), 1788; Bapt.

THOMAS HIBBERT, A.M., bapt. Rowley, Oct. 30, 1726, son of George and Sarah (Ellsworth) Hibbert; H. C., 1748, A.B., A.M.; sett. Kittery, Me., 1753-1754; Ord. Amesbury, (1st Chh.), Nov. 6, 1754; sett. Amesbury, 1754-1784; dism. 1785; became a Presb. and organized a Presb. Chh. in Amesbury, 1784; d. Amesbury, Sept. 1793, a. 66.

FRANCIS HIGGINSON, A.M., b. Claybrook, Leicestershire, Eng., Aug. 6, 1586, son of Rev. John and Elizabeth Higginson, his father being the Rector of Claybrook; Jesus Coll., Camb., A.B., 1609/10; A. M., St. John's Coll., Camb., 1613; Ord. York, Eng., Dec. 1614; curate at Scrayingham, Yorks; Rector at Barton-in-Fabis, Notts., 1615; Vicar of Claybrook, Leicestershire, 1615; Lecturer at St. Nicholas, Leicester, 1617-1620; suspended for Puritanical opinions; came to N. E., 1629; Ord. Salem, July 20, 1629; sett. Salem, 1629-1630; author of New England's Plantation; d. Salem, Aug. 6, 1630, a. 44.

JOHN HIGGINSON, b. Claybrook, Leicestershire, Eng., Aug. 6, 1616, son of Rev. Francis and Anna (Herbert) Higginson; came to N. E., 1629; educated by Rev. Thomas Hooker; Chaplain at the Fort at Old Saybrook, Ct., 1636-1639; teacher at Hartford, Ct., 1641-1643; sett. Guilford, Ct., 1643-1659; Ord. Salem (1st Chh.), Aug. 1660; sett. Salem, 1660-1708; Artillery Election Sermon, 1662; Election Sermon, 1663; d. Salem, Dec. 9, 1708, a. 92.

ABRAHAM HILL, A.M., b. Cambridge, Sept. 27, 1719, son of Abraham and Prudence (Hancock) Hill; H. C., 1737, A.B., A.M.; Ord. Shutesbury, Oct. 27, 1742; sett. Shutesbury, 1742-1778; dism. Feb. 27, 1778; Tory; d. Oxford, June 8, 1788, a. 69.

SAMUEL HILL, A.M., b. Malden, Oct. 17, 1714, son of Abraham and Abigail Hill; H. C., 1735, A.B., A.M.; Ord. Marshfield, (1st Chh.), July 16, 1740; sett. Marshfield, 1740-1752; dism. Mar. 20, 1752; inst. Rochester, N. H., Nov. 5, 1760; sett. Rochester, N. H., 1760-1764; d. Rochester, N. H., Apr. 19, 1764, a. 50.

JAMES HILLHOUSE, A.M., b. Free Hall, Ulster, Ireland, 1687/8, son of John and Rachel Hillhouse; Glasgow U., A.M., 1709; Ord. Ireland; came to N. E., 1719; inst. Montville, Ct., (2nd Chh. in New London, or North Cong. Parish), Oct. 3, 1722, as the first minister; sett. Montville, Ct., 1722-1740; d. Montville, Ct., Dec. 15, 1740, a. 53.

TIMOTHY HILLIARD, A.M., b. Kensington, N. H., 1746, son of Dea. Joseph Chase and Huldah (Moulton) Hilliard; H. C., 1764, A.B., A.M.; Tutor, H. C., 1768-1771; Chaplain at Castle William, Boston Harbor, 1768; Ord. Barnstable, (East Chh.), Apr. 10, 1771; sett. Barnstable, 1771-1783; dism. Apr. 30, 1783; inst. Cambridge, (1st Chh.), Oct. 27, 1783; sett. Cambridge, 1783-1790; Dudleian Lecture, 1788; Unitarian; d. Cambridge, May 9, 1790, a. 44.

EBENEZER HINDS, b. Bridgewater, July 29, 1719, son of John and Hannah (Shaw) Hinds; Ord. Lakeville, (Bapt. Chh.), Jan. 26, 1758; sett. Lakeville, 1753-1793; Chaplain, French and Indian Wars; Bapt.; d. Lakeville, Apr. 29, 1812.

THEODORE HINSDALE, A.M., b. Hartford, Ct., Nov. 25, 1738, son of Capt. John and Elizabeth (Cole) Hinsdale; Y. C., 1762, A.B., A.M.; Ord. North Windsor, Ct., Apr. 30, 1766, as the first minister; sett. North Windsor, Ct., 1766-1794; dism., Feb. 1794; farmer at Dalton, Ct.; d. Hinsdale, Ct., Dec. 28, 1818, a. 81.

THOMAS HISCOX, b. Newport, R. I., 1686, son of Rev. William and Rebecca Hiscox; Dea., 1716; Chh. clerk, 1716; Ord. Westerly, R. I., 1727; sett. Westerly, R. I., 1727-1773; colleague with Rev. Joseph Maxson, 1750-1773; freeman, 1709; town treas., 1712-1772; deputy, 1714-1741; Bapt.; d. Westerly, R. I., Nov. 26, 1773.

WILLIAM HISCOX, b. 1638; Ord. Newport, R. I., (Seventh Day Bapt. Chh. or 3rd Bapt. Chh. in Newport), Dec. 23, 1671, as the first minister; sett. Newport, R. I., 1671-1704; General Treas. of R. I., 1703-1704; Bapt.; d. Newport, R. I., May 24, 1704, a. 66.

CALEB HITCHCOCK, A.M., b. Springfield, 1720; H. C., 1743, A.B., A.M.; Ord. Union, Ct., June 21, 1749; sett. Union, Ct., 1749-1758; d. Brimfield, Dec. 6, 1767.

ENOS HITCHCOCK, D.D., b. Brookfield, Mar. 7, 1744/5, son of Peletiah and Sarah (Parsons) Hitchcok; H. C., 1767, A.B., A.M.; A.M., (Hon.), Y. C., 1781; D.D., Brown U., 1788; Fellow, Brown U., 1785-1803; Ord. Beverly, (2nd Chh.), 1771; sett. Beverly, 1771-1780; inst. Providence, R. I., (1st Cong. Chh.), Oct. 1, 1783; sett. Providence, R. I., 1783-1803; Chaplain in Rev. War at Valley Forge, 1778, 1780-1783; d. Providence, R. I., Feb. 26, 1803, a. 58.

GAD HITCHCOCK, D.D., b. Springfield, Feb. 12, 1718/9, son

of Ebenezer and Mary (Sheldon) Hitchcock; H. C., 1743, A.B., A.M.; S.T.D., 1787; Ord. Hanson, Oct. 1748; sett. Hanson, 1748-1803; Artillery Election Sermon, 1765; Election Sermon, 1774; Dudleian Lecture, 1779; Convention Sermon, 1787; Chaplain in the Rev. War; Member Constitutional Convention of Mass.; Unitarian; d. Hanson, Aug. 8, 1803, a. 83.

JACOB HIX, b. Rehoboth, Jan. 1, 1738, son of Rev. John and Hannah (Galusha) Hix; Ord. Rehoboth, (7th Bapt. Chh.), Jan. 20, 1773; sett. Rehoboth, 1773-1809; Bapt.; d. Rehoboth, Mar. 30, 1809.

JOHN HIX, b. Rehoboth, May 10, 1712, son of Ephraim and Sarah Hix; Ord. Rehoboth, (5th Bapt. Chh.), Nov. 10, 1762; sett. Rehoboth, 1762-1799; Bapt.; d. Rehoboth, Mar. 1799, a. 87.

PRESIDENT LEONARD HOAR, M.D., b. Gloucestershire, England, 1630, son of Charles and Joanna (Henchman) Hoar; H. C., 1650, A.B.; returned to Eng., 1653; A.M., U. of Cambridge, 1654; M.D., U. of Cambridge, 1671; Rector of Wanstead, Essex, England, 1653-1662; ejected 1662; sett. Boston, (Old South Chh.), 1672; inst. Harvard College, (Third President), Dec. 10, 1672; sett. H. C., 1672-1675; physician; d. Boston, Nov. 28, 1675, a. 45.

GERSHOM HOBART, A.M., b. Hingham, Dec. 1645, son of Rev. Peter and Rebecca (Ibrook) Hobart; H. C., 1667, A.B., A.M.; Ord. Groton, Nov. 26, 1679; sett. Groton, 1678-1690; 1693-1704; his house was used as a garrison house; one of his children was killed by the Indians, another carried away captive; d. Groton, Dec. 19, 1707, a. 62.

JEREMIAH HOBART, A.M., b. England, Apr. 6, 1631, son of Rev. Peter Hobart; H. C., 1650, A.B., A.M.; sett. Wells, Me., 1667; Ord. Topsfield, Oct. 2, 1672; sett. Topsfield, 1672-1680; dism. Sept. 21, 1680; inst., Hempstead, L. I., N. Y., Oct. 17, 1683; sett. Hempstead, L. I., 1683-1691; inst. Haddam, Ct., Nov. 14 1700, as the first minister; sett. Haddam, Ct., 1691-1715; d. Haddam, Ct., Nov. 6, 1715, a. 84.

JOSHUA HOBART, A.M., b. England, 1628, son of Rev. Peter Hobart; H. C., 1650, A.B., A.M.; preached at Beverly, 1650-1655; preached at Barbadoes; went to London; Ord. Southold, L. I., N. Y., Oct. 7, 1674; sett. Southold, 1674-1717; d. Southold, L. I., N. Y., Feb. 28, 1716/7.

NEHEMIAH HOBART, A.M., b. Hingham, Nov. 21, 1648, son of Rev. Peter and Rebecca (Ibrook) Hobart; H. C., 1667, A.B., A.M.; Fellow, H.C., 1681-1692; 1697-1712; Ord. Newton, Dec. 23, 1674; sett. Newton, 1672-1712; d. Newton, Aug. 25, 1712, a. 64.

NEHEMIAH HOBART, A.M., b. Hingham, Apr. 27, 1697, son of Dea. Lt. David and Sarah (Joyce) Hobart; H. C., 1714, A.B., A.M.; Ord. Cohasset, Dec. 13, 1721; sett. Cohasset, 1721-1740; Unitarian; Jacob Flint said of him, "He did not consider Jesus Christ equal with the Father, nor the Holy Spirit anything distinct from God's influence;" d. Cohasset, May 31, 1740, a. 43.

NOAH HOBART, A.M., b. Hingham, Jan. 2, 1705/6, son of Dea. Lt. David and Sarah (Joyce) Hobart; H. C., 1724, A.B.; A.M., 1729; Ord. Fairfield, Ct., (1st Chh.), Feb. 7, 1733; sett. Fairfield, Ct., 1733-1773; Ct. Election Sermon, 1750; d. Fairfield, Ct., Dec. 6, 1773, a. 67.

PETER HOBART, A.M., bapt. Hingham, Norfolk, England, Oct. 13, 1604, son of Edmund and Martha (Dewey) Hobart; Magdalene Coll., Camb., A.B., 1625/6; A.M., 1629; Ord. Norwich, England, Dec. 3, 1627; Curate at Haverhill, England; came to Charlestown from Hingham, England, June 1635; Ord. Hingham, Sept. 18, 1635, as the first minister; sett. Hingham, 1635-1679; Artillery Election Sermon, 1655; d. Hingham, Jan. 20, 1678/9.

JAMES HOBBS, A.M., b. Hampton, N. H., June 6, 1726, son of James and Lucy (Dow) Hobbs; H. C., 1748, A.B., A.M.; Ord. Pelham, N. H., Nov. 13, 1751, as the first minister; sett. Pelham, N. H., 1751-1765; Arminian; d. Pelham, N. H., June 20, 1765, a. 39.

WILLIAM HOBBY, A.M., b. Boston, Aug. 13, 1707, son of John and Ann Hobby; H. C., 1725, A.B., A.M.; Ord. Wakefield, (1st Chh. in Reading), Sept. 5, 1733; sett. Wakefield, 1733-1765; Artillery Election Sermon, 1737; d. Wakefield, (Reading), June 18, 1765, a. 58.

CHARLES HOLDEN, b. Warwick, R. I., Sept. 24, 1695, son of Lt. Charles and Catharine (Greene) Holden; Ord. Warwick, R. I., June 16, 1757; sett. Warwick, R. I., 1757-1785; Bapt.; d. Warwick, R. I., Jan. 20, 1785.

ISRAEL HOLLEY, Ord. Suffield, Ct., (Separatist Chh.), June 29, 1763; sett. Suffield, Ct., 1763-1784; sett. at Granby and Cornwall, Ct.

EZEKIEL HOLLIMAN, came from Tring, Herts., England, to Warwick, R. I., 1634; sett. Providence, R. I., (1st Bapt. Chh.), 1639-1659, as asst. to Roger Williams; freeman, 1655; magistrate, 1656; warden, 1658; commissioner, 1652-1659; Bapt.; d. Providence, R. I., Sept. 17, 1659.

JOHN HOLMES, b. England, prob. son of William and Elizabeth Holmes who sett. at Marshfield; studied under President Chauncy, 1658; sett. Duxbury, 1658-1675; condemned treatment of Quakers; d. Duxbury, 1675.

OBEDIAH HOLMES, bapt. Reddish, Manchester, Lancashire, England, Mar. 18, 1609/10, son of Robert Hulme; arrived in N. E., 1639; Ord. Newport, R. I., (1st Bapt. Chh.), 1652; sett. Newport, R. I., 1652-1682; commissioner, 1656-1658; Bapt.; d. Newport, R. I., Oct. 15, 1682.

STEPHEN HOLMES, A.M., b. Woodstock, Ct., 1731, son of Dea. David Holmes; Y. C., 1752, A.B.; A.M., 1756; Ord. Centerbrook, Ct., (2nd Chh. in Saybrook), Nov. 27, 1757; sett. Centerbrook, Ct., 1757-1773; d. Centerbrook, Ct., Sept. 13, 1773, a. 42.

WILLIAM HOMES, A.M., b. Ireland, 1663; A.M., U. of Edinburgh, 1692; came to N. E., 1686; returned to Ireland; Ord. Strabane, Ireland, Dec. 21, 1692; sett. Strabane, Ireland, 1692-1714; Ord. Chilmark, Sept. 15, 1715; sett. Chilmark, 1715-1746; d. Chilmark, June 20, 1746, a. 83.

NATHAN HOLT, A.M., b. Andover, Feb. 28, 1725, son of Nicholas and Dorcas (Abbot) Holt; H. C., 1757, A.B., A.M.; Ord. Peabody, Jan. 3, 1759; sett. Peabody, 1759-1792; d. Peabody, Aug. 2, 1792, a. 67.

PRESIDENT EDWARD HOLYOKE, A.M., b. Boston, (twin), June 26, 1689, son of Eliezur and Mary Holyoke; H. C., 1705, A.B., A.M.; Tutor, H. C., 1712-1716; Fellow, H. C., 1713-1716; Librarian, H. C., 1709-1712; Ord. Marblehead, (2nd Chh.), Apr. 25, 1716, as the first minister; sett. Marblehead, 1716-1737; resign. July 25, 1737; inst. Harvard College, (as President). Sept. 28, 1737; President, H. C., 1737-1769; Election Sermon, 1736; Convention Sermon, 1740; Dudleian Lecture, 1755; d. Cambridge, June 1, 1769, a. 80.

ELIEZUR HOLYOKE, A.M., b. Boston, May 11, 1731, son of Samuel and Elizabeth (Bridgham) Holyoke; H. C., 1750, A.B., A.M.; Librarian, H. C., 1757-1758; Ord. Boxford, (1st Chh.), Jan. 31, 1759; sett. Boxford, 1759-1793; d. Boxford, Mar. 31, 1806, a. 74.

JAMES HONEYMAN, b. Kinneff, Kincardinshire, Scotland, ca. 1675, son of Rev. James and Mary (Leask) Honeyman; Ord. before Mar. 22, 1702/3; Chaplain, British Navy, 1704; Missionary, Venerable Society for the Propagation of the Gospel in Foreign Parts, 1704; sett. Newport, R. I., (Trinity Chh.), 1704-1750; his portrait hangs at Trinity Chh.; Epis.; d. Newport, R. I., July 2, 1750.

WILLIAM HOOKE, A.M., Gent., b. Southampton, England, 1601; Trinity Coll., Oxford, A.B., 1620; A.M., 1623; Rector of Upper Clatford, Hants., 1627; Vicar at Axmouth, Devonshire, 1632; Ord. Taunton, Jan. 17, 1640/1, as the first minister; sett. Taunton, 1637-1644; sett. New Haven, Ct., 1644-1656; returned to England where he was minister at Exmouth, Devon, and domestic chaplain to Oliver Cromwell; minister at Savoy, Strand, London; silenced for nonconformity, May 24, 1662; married a sister of Gen. Walley, one of the regicides; d. London, England, Mar. 21, 1677/8, a. 77.

JOHN HOOKER, A.M., b. Kensington, Ct., Mar. 19, 1728/9, son of John and Mercy (Hart) Hooker; Y. C., 1751, A.B., A.M.; Ord. Northampton, Dec. 5, 1753; sett. Northampton, 1753-1777; d. Northampton, Feb. 6, 1777, a. 48, of small-pox.

NATHANIEL HOOKER, JR., A.M., b. Hartford, Ct., Dec. 15, 1737, son of Capt. Nathaniel and Eunice (Talcott) Hooker; Y. C., 1755, A.B., A.M.; Ord. West Hartford, Ct., (4th Chh. in Hartford),

Dec. 21, 1757; sett. West Hartford, Ct., 1757-1770; d. West Hartford, Ct., June 9, 1770, a. 33.

SAMUEL HOOKER, A.M., b. Cambridge, 1635, son of Rev. Thomas and Susan (Garbrand) Hooker; H. C., 1653, A.B., A.M.; Fellow, H. C., 1654; Ord. Farmington, Ct., July 1661; sett. Farmington, Ct., 1661-1697; Ct. Election Sermons, 1677, 1693; d. Farmington, Ct., Nov. 6, 1697, a. 62.

THOMAS HOOKER, A.M., b. Birstall, Leicestershire, Eng., July 7, 1586, son of Thomas Hooker; Emmanuel Coll., Camb., A.B., 1607/8; A.M., 1611; Fellow of the U., 1609-1618; Curate of Esher, Surrey, and lecturer at Chelmsford, Essex, 1620-1629; preached at Chelmsford, Essex, 1625-1629; silenced by Archbishop Laud, 1630; kept a private school at Little Baddow, Essex, where John Eliot was his asst., 1629-1631; in Holland, 1631-1633; came to N. E., 1633; Ord. Cambridge, Oct. 11, 1633, as the first minister; sett. Cambridge, 1633-1636; removed to Hartford, Ct., 1636; sett. Hartford, Ct., 1636-1647; d. Hartford, Ct., July 7, 1647, a. 61.

WILLIAM HOOPER, A.B., b. Scotland; A.B., Edinburgh, Mar. 26, 1723; Ord. Boston, (West Chh.), May 18, 1737; sett. Boston, (West Chh.), 1737-1746; dism. Nov. 19, 1746; inst. Boston, (Trinity Chh.), 1747-1767; Artillery Election Sermon, 1743; Epis.; his son William Hooper, (H. C., 1760), was a signer of the Declaration of Independence; d. Boston, Apr. 14, 1767.

DANIEL HOPKINS, D.D., b. Waterbury, Ct., Oct. 16, 1734, son of Capt. Timothy and Mary (Judd) Hopkins; Y. C., 1758, A.B., A.M.; S.T.D., Dart. Coll.; 1809; licensed to preach, 1759; Ord. Salem, (3rd Chh.), Nov. 18, 1778; sett. Salem, (3rd Chh.), 1775-1814; member of the Governor's Council, 1776-1778; member of the Third Provincial Congress of Mass., 1775; d. Salem, Dec. 14, 1814, a. 81.

REUBEN HOPKINS, b. Scituate, R. I., July 1, 1717, son of Thomas and Elizabeth Hopkins; Ord. Scituate, R. I., July 8, 1762; sett. Scituate, R. I., 1762-1792; Bapt.; d. Scituate, R. I., Jan. 8, 1792.

SAMUEL HOPKINS, A.B., b. Waterbury, Ct., Dec. 27, 1693, son of Lieut. John and Sarah (Strong) Hopkins; Y. C., 1718, A.B.; Ord. West Springfield, June 1, 1720; sett. West Springfield, 1720-1755; author of many works relating to the Indians; d. West Springfield, Oct. 5, 1755, a. 62.

SAMUEL HOPKINS, D.D., b. Waterbury, Ct., Sept. 17, 1721, son of Capt. Timothy and Mary (Judd) Hopkins; Y. C., 1741, A.B.; S.T. D., Brown U., 1790; Ord. Great Barrington, Dec. 28, 1743; sett. Great Barrington, 1743-1769; dism. Jan. 18, 1769; inst. Newport, R. I., (1st Cong. Chh.), Apr. 11, 1770; sett. Newport, R. I., 1770-1776; 1780-1803; sett. Canterbury, Ct., 1776-1780; founder of the Hopkinsian school of theology; author of a System of Divinity, 1793; he is the hero of Harriet Beecher Stowe's "Minister's Wooing;" d. Newport, R. I., Dec. 20, 1803, a. 83.

SAMUEL HOPKINS, D.D., b. West Springfield, Oct. 20, 1729, son of Rev. Samuel and Esther (Edwards) Hopkins; Y. C., 1749, A.B., A.M.; A.M., (Hon.), H. C., 1754; S.T.D., Y. C., 1802; Tutor, Y. C., 1751-1754; Ord. Hadley, Feb. 26, 1755; sett. Hadley, 1754-1809; d. Hadley, Mar. 8, 1811, a. 82.

EZRA HORTON, A.B., b. Southold, L. I., N. Y., Dec. 25, 1733; Princeton, 1754, A.B.; Ord. Union, Ct., June 14, 1759; sett. Union, Ct., 1759-1783; dism. Aug. 6, 1783; d. Union, Ct., Jan. 13, 1789.

STEPHEN HOSMER, A.B., bapt., Hartford, Ct., Aug. 8, 1679, son of Dea. Stephen and Hannah (Bushnell) Hosmer; H. C., 1699, A.B.; Ord. East Haddam, Ct., May 3, 1704, as the first minister; sett. East Haddam, Ct., 1704-1749; Ct. Election Sermon, 1720; d. East Haddam, Ct., June 16, 1749.

JOHN HOUSTON, A.M., b. Londonderry, N. H., Apr. 4, 1722; Princeton, 1753, A.B., A.M.; Ord. Bedford, N. H., Sept. 28, 1757; sett. Bedford, 1757-1778; dism. Oct. 1, 1778; moderator of the Presbytery of Palmer; Presb.; d. Bedford, N. H., Feb. 3, 1798, a. 75.

IVORY HOVEY, JR., A.M., b. Topsfield, July 3, 1714, son of Ivory and Anne Hovey; H. C., 1735, A.B.; A.M., 1739; Ord. Mattapoisett, (2nd Chh. in Rochester), Oct. 29, 1740; sett. Mattapoisett, 1740-1768; dism. Aug. 23, 1768; inst. Plymouth, (Manomet Chh.), Apr. 18, 1770; sett. Plymouth, 1770-1803; d. Plymouth, Nov. 4, 1803, a. 90.

JOHN HOVEY, A.M., b. Cambridge, June 12, 1707, son of John and Abial (Watson) Hovey; H. C., 1725, A.B., A.M.; Ord. Kennebunkport, Me., (Arundel), Sept. 16, 1741; sett. Kennebunkport, 1741-1768; dism. Aug. 16, 1768; d. Biddeford, Me., 1773, a. 66.

JOHN HOVEY, Ord. Mansfield, Ct., (Separatist Chh.), Feb. 1745/6; sett. Mansfield, Ct., 1746-1775; d. Mansfield, Ct., Oct. 28, 1775.

SAMUEL HOVEY, b. Bradford, Feb. 24, 1742/3, son of Samuel and Elizabeth (Perkins) Hovey; Ord. Mendon, (Milford Bapt. Chh.), May 31, 1749; Bapt.

NATHANIEL HOWARD, b. New London, Ct., 1721; Ord. New London, Ct., (Waterford Bapt. Chh.), 1748; sett. New London, Ct., 1748-1777; Bapt.; d. New London, Ct., (Waterford) Mar. 2, 1777.

SIMEON HOWARD, D.D., b. Bridgewater, Apr. 29, 1733, son of David and Bethia Howard; H. C., 1758, A.B., A.M.; S.T.D., U. of Edinburgh, 1785; Fellow, H. C., 1780-1784; Ord. Boston, (West Chh.), May 6, 1767; sett. Boston, 1767-1804; Artillery Election Sermon, 1773; Election Sermon, 1780; Dudleian Lecture, 1787; Convention Sermon, 1790; Fellow, Am. Acad.; his portrait in oils hangs in the First Chh. of Christ in Lancaster; d. Boston, Aug. 13, 1804, a. 71.

JOSEPH HOWE, A.M., b. Putnam, Ct., Jan. 14, 1746/7, son

of Rev. Perley and Damaris (Cady) Howe; Y. C., 1765, A.B., A.M.; A.M., (Hon.), H. C., 1775; Tutor, Y. C., 1769-1772; Ord. Boston, (New South Chh.), May 19, 1773; sett. Boston, 1772-1775; d. Hartford, Ct., Aug. 25, 1775, a. 28.

PERLEY HOWE, A.B., b. Killingly, Ct., ca. 1710, son of Capt. Sampson and Alice (Perley) Howe of Thompson, Ct.; H. C., 1731, A.B.; Ord. Dudley, June 12, 1735; sett. Dudley, 1735-1743; inst. Putnam, Ct., 1746; sett. Killingly, Ct., (1st Chh. at Putnam), 1746-1753; d. Killingly, Ct., (now Putnam), Mar. 10, 1753, a. 43.

JOHN HOWLAND, A.M., b. Barnstable, Apr. 13, 1720, son of John and Mary (Crocker) Howland; H. C., 1741, A.B. A.M.; Ord. Carver, 1746; sett. Carver, 1746-1804; d. Carver, Nov. 4, 1804, a. 84.

BELA HUBBARD, D.D., b. Guilford, Ct., Aug. 27, 1729, son of Lieut. Daniel and Diana (Ward) Hubbard; Y. C., 1758, A.B., A.M.; A.M., Columbia U., 1762; S.T.D., Y. C., 1804; Ord. Westminster, England, by the Bishop of Carlisle, Feb. 19, 1764; missionary of the Venerable Society P.G.F.P., at Guilford, Ct., and Killingworth, Ct., 1764-1767; sett. New Haven, Ct., (Trinity Chh.), 1767-1791; Epis.; d. New Haven, Ct., Dec. 6, 1812.

JOHN HUBBARD, A.M., b. New Haven, Ct., Jan. 24, 1726/7, son of Col. John and Elizabeth (Stevens) Hubbard; Y. C., 1744, A.B., A.M.; Ord. Meriden, Ct., June 22, 1769; sett. Meriden, Ct., 1769-1786; d. Meriden, Ct., Nov. 18, 1786, a. 60.

JOHN HUBBARD, A.M., b. Hatfield, Nov. 5, 1726, son of Dea. John and Hannah (Cowles) Hubbard; Y. C., 1747, A.B., A.M.; Ord. Northfield, May 30, 1750; sett. Northfield, 1750-1794; d. Northfield, Nov. 28, 1794, a. 68.

JONATHAN HUBBARD, A.M., b. Hatfield, (or Sunderland), Dec. 19, 1703, son of Dea. Isaac and Ann (Warner) Hubbard; Y. C., 1724, A.B., A.M.; sett. Eastbury, Ct., (now Buckingham), 1731-1733; Trenton, N. J., (Presb. Chh.); Ord. Sheffield, Oct. 22, 1735; sett. Sheffield, 1735-1764; dism. Dec. 1764; moderator of the council which dismissed Jonathan Edwards from his pulpit in Northampton; d. Sheffield, July 6, 1765, a. 62.

NATHANIEL HUBBARD, A.M., b. Boston, Oct. 13, 1680, son of John and Ann (Leverett) Hubbard; H. C., 1698, A.B., A.M.; preached at Hartford, Ct., 1703; Chaplain to the commission sent to confirm amity to the Five Nations, 1704; Justice and Councillor, 1737-1745; Rep. Gen. Ct.; deputy Judge of the Admiralty; Justice of the Mass. Supreme Ct., 1745-1748; d. Bristol, R. I., Jan. 10, 1748.

ROBERT HUBBARD, A.M., b. Middletown, Ct., Sept. 11, 1743, son of Robert and Elizabeth (Sill) Hubbard; Y. C., 1769, A.B., A.M.; Ord. Shelburne, Oct. 20, 1773, as the first minister; sett. Shelburne, 1773-1788; d. Middletown, Ct., Nov. 2, 1788, a. 45.

WILLIAM HUBBARD, A.M., b. England, ca. 1621, son of

THE REVEREND RICHARD MATHER (1596-1669)
*From an engraving of the portrait owned by
the American Antiquarian Society*

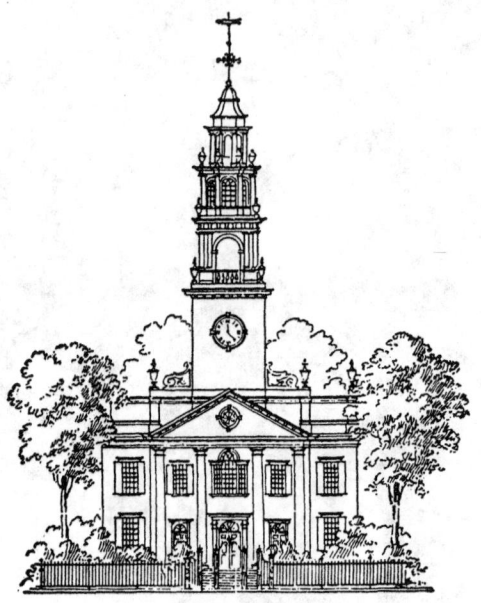

First Parish Church, Dorchester, 1630
Fifth Meeting House

William and Judith Hubbard, who came to Ipswich, N. E., 1635; H.C., 1642, A.B., A.M.; (first class at H. C.); Ord. Ipswich, Nov. 17, 1658; sett. Ipswich, 1642-1704; author of "Indian Wars," 1677; Election Sermon, 1676; d. Ipswich, Sept. 14, 1704, a. 83.

HUIT, see Hewett.

ISAAC HULL, sett. Boston, (1st Bapt. Chh.), 1675-1688; Bapt.

JOSEPH HULL, A.B., b. Crewkerne, Somersetshire, Eng., 1595, son of Thomas Hull; St. Mary's Hall, Oxford, 1614, A.B.; inst. Rector at Northleigh, Devon, Apr. 4, 1621; sett. Northleigh, Devon, 1621-1632; sailed from Weymouth, Dorset, for N. E., Mar. 20, 1635; Deputy from Hingham, 1638, 1639; inst. Weymouth, July 8, 1635, as the first minister; sett. Weymouth, 1635-1639; sett. Barnstable, 1639; sett. Yarmouth, (2nd Chh.), 1640-1646, as the only minister; returned to England, 1659, but did not remain long; sett. St. Buryan, Cornwall, Eng.; ejected 1662; returned to N. E., 1662; sett. Oyster River, N. H., (Durham), 1662; sett. Isles of Shoals, N. H., (and Appledore, Me.), 1662-1665; d. Isles of Shoals, N. H., Nov. 19, 1665.

DANIEL HUMPHREYS, A.M., b. Simsbury, Ct., ca. 1706, son of Dea. John and Sarah (Pettibone) Humphreys; Y. C., 1732, A.B., A.M.; Ord. Derby, Ct., (1st Chh.), Mar. 6, 1733/4; sett. Derby, Ct., 1733-1787; d. Derby, Ct., Sept. 2, 1787 a. 81.

JAMES HUMPHREY, A.M., b. Dorchester, Mar. 20, 1722, son of James and Susanna (Payson) Humphrey; H. C., 1744, A.B., A.M.; Ord. Athol, Nov. 7, 1750; sett. Athol, 1750-1782; dism. Feb. 13, 1782; d. Athol, May 8, 1796, a. 75.

NATHANIEL HUNN, A.M., b. Wethersfield, Ct., Sept. 10, 1708, son of Nathaniel, Jr. and Martha (Orvis) Hunn; Y. C., 1731, A.B., A.M.; Ord. Redding, Ct., Mar. 21, 1733; sett. Redding, Ct., 1733-1749; d. Boston, Aug. or Sept. 1749.

ZADOC HUNN, A.B., b. Wethersfield, Ct., Apr. 17, 1743, son of Gideon and Rebecca Hunn; Y. C., 1766, A.B.; Ord. Becket, June 5, 1771; sett. Becket, 1770-1788; dism. Oct. 1788; d. Canandaigua, N. Y., May 12, 1801, a. 58.

ASA HUNT, b. Braintree, July 1744; Ord. Middleborough, (3rd Calvinist Bapt. Chh.), Oct. 30, 1771; sett. Middleborough, 1771-1789; dism. Dec. 1789; Bapt.; d. Providence, R. I., Sept. 20, 1791.

JOHN HUNT, A.M., b. Northampton, Nov. 20, 1744, son of Capt. John and Esther (Wells) Hunt; H. C., 1764, A.B., A.M.; taught school at Northampton, 1765-1769; Ord. Boston, (Old South Chh.), Sept. 26, 1771; sett. Boston, 1771-1775; d. Northampton, Dec. 30, 1775, a. 31.

SAMUEL HUNT, A.M., b. Weymouth, Feb. 8, 1681/2, son of Capt. Ephraim and Joanna (Alcock) Hunt; H. C., 1700, A.B., A.M.; supply at Dunstable, 1706-1707; appointed by the General Court to be minister at Dartmouth, (New Bedford), June 8, 1708, as the first minister of the first church; sett. New Bedford, 1708-1730; Chaplain at Port Royal, 1707; d. New Bedford, Jan. 21, 1729/30, a. 48.

DAVID HUNTINGTON, A.M., b. Lebanon, Ct., Nov. 24, 1745, son of John and Mehitable (Metcalf) Huntington; Dart. Coll., 1773, A.B., A.M.; Y. C., 1773, A.B.; Ord. Salem, Ct., 1775; sett. Salem, Ct., 1775-1776; sett. Marlborough, Ct., 1776-1797; sett, Middletown, Ct., 1797-1803; d. Lyme, Ct., Apr. 13, 1812, a. 66.

ELIPHALET HUNTINGTON, A.M., b. Lebanon, Ct., Apr. 14, 1737, son of Dea. Daniel and Hannah (Metcalf) Huntington; Y. C., 1759, A.B.; A.M., 1763; Ord. South Killingly, Ct., Jan. 11, 1764; sett. South Killingly, Ct., 1764-1777; d. South Killingly, Ct., Feb. 8, 1777, a. 40, of small-pox.

ENOCH HUNTINGTON, A.M., b. Scotland Parish, Windham, Ct., Dec. 15, 1739, son of Nathaniel and Mehitable (Thurston) Huntington; Y. C., 1759, A.B., A.M.; Fellow, Y. C., 1780-1808; Secretary Y. C., 1788-1793; Ord. Middletown, Ct., (1st Chh.), Jan. 6, 1762; sett. Middletown, Ct., 1762-1809; d. Middletown, Ct., June 12, 1809, a. 69.

JONATHAN HUNTINGTON, A.B., b. Windham, Ct., June 17, 1733, son of Nathaniel and Mehitable (Thurston) Huntington; Princeton U., 1759, A.B.; Ord. Worthington, June 26, 1771; sett. Worthington, 1771-1781; d. Worthington, Mar. 11, 1781, a. 48.

JOHN HUNTINGTON, A.M., b. Norwich, Ct., Aug. 1736, son of John and Civil (Tracy) Huntington; Princeton U., 1759, A.B., A.M.; A.M., (Hon.), H. C., 1763; Ord. Salem, (3rd Chh.), Sept. 28, 1763; sett. Salem, 1763-1766; d. Salem, May 30, 1766, a. 30.

JOSEPH HUNTINGTON, D.D., b. Scotland Parish, Windham, Ct., May 5, 1735, son of Nathaniel and Mehitable (Thurston) Huntington; Y. C., 1762, A.B., A.M.; D.D., Dart. Coll., 1780; Trustee, Y. C., 1780-1788; Ord. South Coventry, Ct., (1st Chh.), June 29, 1763; sett. South Coventry, Ct., 1763-1794; Ct. Election Sermon, 1784; d. South Coventry, Ct., Dec. 25, 1794, a. 60.

NATHANIEL HUNTINGTON, A.M., b. Windham, Ct., Nov. 25, 1724, son of Nathaniel and Mehitable (Thurston) Huntington; Y. C., 1747, A.B., A.M.; Ord. Ellington, Ct., Nov. 15, 1749; sett. Ellington, Ct., 1749-1756; d. Ellington, Ct., Apr. 28, 1756, a. 32.

SIMON HUNTINGTON, A.M., b. Norwich, Ct., Sept. 12, 1719, son of Dea. Ebenezer and Sarah (Leffingwell) Huntington; Y. C., 1741, A.B., A.M.; licensed to preach; preached until his health failed; d. Norwich, Ct., Dec. 27, 1801.

AARON HUTCHINSON, A.M., b. Hebron, Ct., Mar. 1724; Y. C., 1747, A.B., A.M.; A.M., (Hon.), H. C., 1750; A.M., (Hon.), Dart. Coll., 1780; A.M., (Hon.), Princeton U., 1794; Ord. Grafton, June 6, 1750; sett. Grafton, 1750-1772; dism. Nov. 18, 1772; supply at Pomfret, Woodstock and Hartford, Vt., 1775-1780; d. Pomfret, Vt., Sept. 27, 1800.

EPHRAIM HYDE, A.M., b. Pomfret, Ct., May 3, 1739, son of Ephraim and Margaret (Griffin) Hyde; Y. C., 1759, A.B.; A.M., 1763; A.M., (Hon.), H. C., 1763; Ord. Rehoboth, (1st Chh.), May 14, 1766; sett. Rehoboth, 1766-1783; d. Rehoboth, Oct. 11, 1783, a. 45.

JEDEDIAH HYDE, b. Norwich, Ct., June 2, 1712, son of William and Anne (Bushnell) Hyde; Ord. Norwich, Ct., (Separatist Chh. at Bean Hill), Oct. 30, 1747; sett. Norwich,, 1747-1757; deposed, Sept. 22, 1757; d. Norwich, Ct., Sept. 26, 1761.

JONATHAN HYDE, b. Newton, 1709, son of Jonathan and Elizabeth (Williams) Hyde; Ord. Newton, (2nd Separatist Chh.), Jan. 17, 1751; sett. Newton-Brookline, 1751-1787; not a college graduate; d. Brookline, June 4, 1787, a. 78.

SAMUEL HYDE, b. Newton, Sept. 7, 1719, son of Jonathan and Hannah (Dana) Hyde; Ord. May 11, 1750; sett. Madbury, N. H., 1758-1770.

JONATHAN INGERSOLL, A.M., b. Westfield, 1714, son of Jonathan and Sarah (Miles) Ingersoll; Y. C., 1736, A.B., A.M.; Ord. Ridgefield, Ct., Aug. 8, 1739; sett. Ridgefield, Ct., 1739-1778; Chaplain, French War, 1758; Ct. Election Sermon, 1761; d. Ridgefield, Ct., Oct. 2, 1778, a. 65.

JESSE IVES, A.M., b. Meriden, Ct., Apr. 2, 1738, son of John and Hannah (Royce) Ives; Y. C., 1758, A.B., A.M.; Ord. Sprague, Ct., (Norwich, 8th Society), 1766; sett. Sprague, Ct., 1766-1770; inst., Monson, June 23, 1773; sett. Monson, 1773-1805; d. Monson, Dec. 31, 1805, a. 68.

SHADRACK IRELAND, bapt. Cambridge, Jan. 16, 1718, son of Abraham and Abigail (Greenland) Ireland; sett. Harvard, (Separatist Chh.), 1760-1780; forerunner of the Shakers at Harvard; d. Harvard, 1780.

EDWARD JACKSON, A.M., b. Newton, Apr. 3, 1700, son of Dea. Edward and Abigail Jackson; H. C., 1719, A.B., A.M.; Ord. Woburn, Aug. 1, 1729; sett. Woburn, 1729-1754; d. Woburn, Sept. 24, 1754.

JOSEPH JACKSON, A.M., b. Boston, Dec. 22, 1734, son of Joseph and Susanna (Gray) Jackson; H. C., 1753, A.B., A.M.; Tutor, H. C., 1758-1760; Ord. Brookline, Apr. 9, 1760; sett. Brookline, 1760-1796; d. Brookline, July 22, 1796.

WHITMAN JACOBS, b. Bristol, R. I.; sett. Thompson, Ct., (1st Bapt. Chh.), 1750-1770; inst. Royalston, Dec. 13, 1770; sett. Royalston, 1770-1786; sett. Guilford, Vt.; Bapt.; d. Royalston, Mar. 28, 1801.

JOHN JAMES, A.M., b. in Great Britain; bapt. Charlestown, Jan. or June, 1633, son of Rev. Thomas James; H. C., 1710, (Hon.), A.M.; sett. Haddam, Ct., 1683-1692; sett. Derby, Ct., 1693-1706; sett. Brookfield, 1712-1714; d. Wethersfield, Ct., Aug. 10, 1729.

THOMAS JAMES, A.M., bapt. Boston, Lincolnshire, England, Oct. 5, 1595, son of Rev. John James, B.D., Rector of Shirbeck, Lincolnshire; Emmanuel Coll., Camb., 1614/5, A.B.; A.M., 1618; Ord. by the Bishop of Peterborough, Mar. 17, 1616/7; minister in Lincolnshire, Eng.; came to N. E., 1631; Ord. Charlestown, Nov. 2, 1632, as the first minister; sett. Charlestown, 1632-1636; sett. New Haven, Ct., 1636-1642; missionary to Va., 1642-1643; returned to England, ca. 1643; sett. Needham Market, Suffolk, Eng., 1643-1662; "hired by the town, 1650;" ejected, ca. 1661; Presb.; preacher at West Creeting, 1680; non-conformist preacher till his death at Needham Market; d. Needham Market, Feb. 1682/3, a. 90. (Will made Feb. 5; proved Feb. 13).

THOMAS JAMES, b. England, 1620, son of Rev. Thomas and Elizabeth James; sett. East Hampton, Ct., 1650-1696; d. East Hampton, Ct., 1696.

RICHARD JAQUES, A.M., b. Newbury, Apr. 1, 1700, son of Sergt. Stephen and Deborah (Plummer) Jaques; H. C., 1720, A.B., A.M.; Ord. Gloucester, (2nd Chh.), Nov. 3, 1725; sett. Gloucester, 1725-1777; d. Gloucester, Apr. 12, 1777, a. 77.

BISHOP ABRAHAM JARVIS, D.D., b. Norwalk, Ct., May 5, 1739, son of Capt. Samuel and Naomi (Brush) Jarvis; Y. C., 1761, A.B., A.M.; S.T.D., 1797; Ord. at London, England, by the Bishop of Carlisle, Feb. 19, 1764; inst. Middletown, Ct., (Christ Chh., Epis.), Aug. 1, 1764; sett. Middletown Ct. 1764-1799; elected Bishop of Ct., Oct. 18, 1797; Epis.; d. New Haven, Ct., May 3, 1813, a. 74.

SAMUEL JEFFERDS, A.M., b. Salem, Apr. 6, 1704, son of Simon and Elizabeth Jefferds; H. C., 1722, A.B. A.M.; Ord. Wells, Me., Dec. 15, 1725; sett. Wells, Me., 1725-1752; d. Wells, Me., Feb. 1, 1752, a. 48.

EBENEZER JENCKES, b. Pawtucket, R. I., 1669, son of Hon. Joseph and Esther (Ballard) Jencks; Ord. Providence, R. I., (1st Bapt. Chh.), 1719; sett. Providence, R. I., 1719-1726; Bapt.; d. Providence, R. I., Aug. 14, 1726.

PHILIP JENKINS, b. North Kingston, R. I., Mar. 9, 1726/7, son of Jedediah and Hannah (Long) Jenkins; Ord. East Greenwich, R. I., (Bapt. Chh.), May 27, 1758; sett. East Greenwich, R. I., 1758-1794; Bapt.

THOMAS JENNER, b. Fordham, Essex, England, 1605, son of Thomas Jenner; matric. Christ's Coll., Camb., Feb. 16, 1623/4; came to N. E., 1635, with his father; sett. Roxbury, 1635; freeman, Sept. 8, 1636; Rep. Gen. Ct., 1640; minister at Weymouth, 1636-1640; minister at Saco. Me., 1640-1646; resigned Mar. 28, 1646; resided at Charlestown, 1646-1649; returned to England, 1650; inst. Coltis Hall., Norfolk, England, Apr. 17, 1651; sett. Coltis Hall, Norfolk, England, 1651-1657; his library was bought for H. C.; author of "Quakerism Anatomiz'd and Confuted," 1670; he has the distinction of being the first Puritan minister to settle in Maine; his will was proved at Dublin, Ireland, May 26, 1676.

ROBERT JENNEY, LL.D., b. Waneytown, Ireland, son of Archdeacon Robert Jenney; missionary, V.S.P.G.F.P., 1715; Chaplain on a Royal battleship; sett. New York City, (Trinity Chh.), 1715-1722; sett. Rye, N. Y., and Greenwich, Ct., 1722-1726; inducted, June 7, 1722; sett. Rye, N. Y., 1727-1728; sett. Hempstead, L. I., N. Y., 1728-1742; sett. Philadelphia, Pa., (Christ Chh.), 1742-1762; Epis.; d. Philadelphia, Pa., Jan. 1762.

WILLIAM JENNISON, A.M., b. Watertown, Feb. 9, 1706/7, son of Samuel and Mary (Stearns) Jennison; H. C., 1724, A.B., A.M.; Ord. Salem, (2nd or East Chh.), May 2, 1728; sett. Salem, 1728-1736; dism. Dec. 27, 1736; d. Watertown, Apr. 1, 1750, a. 43.

DAVID JEWETT, A.M., b. Rowley, Aug. 11, 1714, son of Joseph and Mary (Hibbert) Jewett; H. C., 1736, A.B., A.M.; Ord. Montville, Ct., (2nd Chh. in New London), Oct. 3, 1739; sett. Montville, Ct., 1739-1783; Chaplain in the Indian Wars, 1756; d. New London, Ct., June 6, 1783.

DAVID JEWETT, A.B., b. Boxford, Dec. 8, 1744, (Nov. 6, 1743, V.R.), son of Ezekiel and Martha (Thurson) Jewett; H. C., 1769, A.B.; Ord. Candia, N. H., Sept. 1, 1771; sett. Candia, N. H., 1771-1780; dism. 1780; inst. Winthrop, Me., Jan. 2, 1782; sett. Winthrop, Me., 1782-1783; d. Winthrop, Me., Feb. 28, 1783, a. 38.

JEDEDIAH JEWETT, A.M., bapt. Rowley, June 3, 1705, son of Jonathan and Mary (Wicom) Jewett; H. C., 1726, A.B., A.M.; Ord. Rowley, Nov. 19, 1729; sett. Rowley, 1729-1774; d. Rowley, May 8, 1774, a. 69.

DANIEL JOHNSON, A.M., b. Bridgewater, May 24, 1747, son of Daniel, Esq. and Betty (Latham) Johnson; H. C., 1767, A.B., A.M.; Ord. Harvard, Nov. 1, 1769; sett. Harvard, 1769-1777; shouldered a musket and went with the Harvard company to Cambridge on the Lexington alarm, Rev. War, 1775; Chaplain in the Rev.; d. Sept. 23, 1777.

DIODATE JOHNSON, A.M., b. New Haven, Ct., July 29, 1745, son of Rev. Stephen anad Elizabeth (Diodate) Johnson; Y. C., 1764, A.B., A.M.; Tutor, Y. C., 1765-1766; Ord. Millington, Ct., (Soc. at East Haddam), July 2, 1767; sett. Millington, Ct., 1767-1773; d. Lyme, Ct., Jan. 15, 1773, a. 27.

JACOB JOHNSON, A.M., b. Plainfield, Ct., 1721, son of Jacob and Rebecca Johnson; Y. C., 1740, A.B.; A.M., 1763; Ord. Ledyard, Ct., (2nd Chh. in Groton), June 10, 1748; sett. Ledyard, Ct., 1748-1772; dism. Oct. 1772; Indian missionary; sett. Wilkes-Barre, Pa., 1772-1797; d. Wilkes-Barre, Pa., Mar. 15, 1797, a. 76.

JAMES JOHNSON, A.B., b. Stratford, Ct., May 22, 1734, son of Joseph and Rachel (Mead) Johnson; Y. C., 1760, A.B.; Ord.

Easton, (North Fairfield), Ct., Dec. 14, 1763; sett. Easton, Ct., 1763-1810; d. Easton, Ct., Sept. 13, 1810, a. 77.

PRESIDENT SAMUEL JOHNSON, D.D., b. Guilford, Ct., Oct. 14, 1696, son of Dea. Samuel and Mary (Sage) Johnson; Y. C., 1714, A.B., A.M.; Tutor, Y. C., 1716-1719; A.M., U. of Oxford, 1723; A.M., U. of Camb., 1723; D.D., U. of Oxford, 1743; Ord. West Haven, Ct., (Cong. Chh. at Orange), Mar. 20, 1719/20; sett. West Haven, Ct., 1720-1722; became an Epis.; Ord. London, England, Mar. 31, 1723; sett. Stratford, Ct., (Christ Chh., Epis.), 1723-1754; 1764-1772; sett. Huntington, (Ripton), Ct., (Epis. Chh.), 1740-1754; first President, Columbia U., 1754-1763; Epis.; d. Stratford, Ct., Jan. 6, 1772, a. 76.

STEPHEN JOHNSON, A.M., b. Newark, N. J., May 17, 1724, son of Nathaniel and Sarah (Ogden) Johnson; Y. C., 1743, A.B., A.M.; Fellow, Y. C., 1773-1786; Ord. Lyme, Ct., (1st Chh. in Lyme), Dec. 10, 1746; sett. Old Lyme, Ct., 1746-1786; Chaplain, Am. Rev., 1775; Ct. Election Sermon, 1770; d. Old Lyme, Ct., Nov. 8, 1786, a. 62.

WILLIAM JOHNSON, A.M., b. Newbury, May 13, 1706, son of William and Martha (Pierce) Johnson; H. C., 1727, A.B., A.M.; Ord. West Newbury, (2nd Chh.), Sept. 15, 1731; sett. West Newbury, 1731-1772; d. West Newbury, Feb. 22, 1772.

WILLIAM JOHNSON, A.B., (prob. U. Edinburgh, A.B., 1704); minister for a short time of a Scotch-Presbyterian Chh. at Worcester, 1725-1736; inst. Windham, N. H., (Londonderry), Jan. 1747; sett. Windham, N. H., 1747-1752; dism. July 1752; removed to N. Y. state.

CORNELIUS JONES, A.M., b. Milford, Apr. 20, 1727, son of John, Jr. and Abigail (Holbrook) Jones; H. C., 1752, A.B., A.M.; Ord. Sandisfield, Feb. 24, 1756; sett. Sandisfield, 1756-1761; sett. Rowe, 1770-1781; he owned most of the present township of Rowe, where he began a church in 1770, and preached himself; d. Whitehall, N. Y., 1803.

EBENEZER JONES, Ord. Middleborough, (3rd Calvinist Bapt. Chh.), Oct. 28, 1761; sett. Middleborough, 1761-1763; Bapt.; d. Albany, N. Y., Sept. 1791.

ELIPHALET JONES, b. Concord, June 9, 1641, son of Rev. John and Susannah Jones; H. C., but did not grad.; sett. Greenwich, Ct., Feb. 2, 1669/70-1672; sett. Stamford, Ct., 1673; d. Huntington, L. I., N. Y., June 5, 1731.

ISAAC JONES, A.M., b. Enfield, 1717, son of Thomas and Mary (Meacham) Jones; Y. C., 1742, A.B., A.M.; Ord. Warren, Jan. 30, 1744/5; sett. Warren, 1744-1784; d. Warren, July 31, 1784, a. 67.

JABEZ JONES, sett. Colchester, Ct., (Separatist Chh.).

JOHN JONES, A.M., b. Northamptonshire, England, 1593; Queens' Coll., Camb., 1612/3, A.B.; A.M., 1616; Ord. Deacon at Peterborough, Dec. 19, 1613; Rector at Abbot's Ripton, Huntingtonshire, 1619-1630; came to N. E., 1635; Ord. Cambridge, Apr. 1637; sett. Concord, 1635-1644; sett. Fairfield, Ct., 1644-1665; d. Fairfield, Ct., between Jan. 17 and Feb. 9, 1664/5.

JOHN JONES, A.M., b. New Haven, Ct., Oct. 6, 1667, son of Lt. Gov. William and Hannah (Eaton) Jones; H. C., 1690, A.B., A.M.; sett. Lancaster, 1697-1700; sett. Greenwich, Ct., Sept. 13, 1709-May. 1711; prob. not ordained; drowned, New Haven, Ct., Jan. 28, 1718/9.

THOMAS JONES, A.M., b. Dorchester, Apr. 20, 1721, son of Ebenezer and Waitstill Jones; H. C., 1741, A.B., A.M.; teacher at Dorchester, 1741-1742; Ord. Burlington, Jan. 2, 1751; sett. Burlington, 1751-1774; d. Burlington, Mar. 13, 1774.

ROBERT JORDON, b. Worcester, England, 1613, son of Edward Jordon; matric. Balliol Coll., Oxford, June 15. 1632; came to N. E., 1639; followed Mr. Gibson as minister of the Episcopal Chh. at Casco Bay, Me., 1640-1648; married Sarah Winter, dau. of Gov. John Winter, of Lygonia in Maine, and by this marriage became sole proprietor of Robert Trelawny's large estate in New England; continued to preach occasionally at Spurwink, Me., (Casco Bay), 1648-1675; in 1675, he fled from the Indian menace to Portsmouth, N. H.; willed lands at Scarborough and Cape Elizabeth to his sons; Epis.; d. Newcastle, N. H., 1679.

JONATHAN JUDD, A.M., b. Waterbury, Ct., Oct. 4, 1719, son of Capt. William and Mary (Root) Judd; Y. C., 1741, A.B.; A.M., 1745; Ord. Southampton, June 8, 1743; sett. Southampton, 1743-1803; d. Southampton, July 28, 1803, a. 83.

REUBEN JUDD, A.B., b. Farmington, Ct., Sept. 16, 1716, son of Joseph and Sarah (Winchell) Judd; Y. C., 1741, A.B.; Ord. Washington, Ct., (Judea Parish), Sept. 1, 1742; sett. Washington, Ct., 1742-1747; dism. May 6, 1747; d. Fairfield, Ct., Feb.-Mar. 1753.

DAVID JUDSON, A.M., b. Stratford, Ct., Sept. 26, 1715, son of David and Phebe (Stiles) Judson; Y. C., 1738, A.B., A.M.; Ord. Newtown, Ct., Sept. 21, 1743; sett. Newtown, Ct., 1743-1776; d. Newtown, Ct., Sept. 24, 1776, a. 61.

EPHRAIM JUDSON, A.M., b. Woodbury, Ct., Dec. 11, 1737, son of Elnathan and Rebecca (Minor) Judson; Y. C., 1763, A.B., A.M.; Ord. Norwich, Ct., (2nd Chh.), Oct. 3, 1771; sett. Norwich, Ct., 1771-1778; dism. Dec. 15, 1778; inst. Taunton, 1780; sett. Taunton, 1780-1790; dism. Jan. 2, 1791; inst. Sheffield, May. 9, 1791; sett. Sheffield, 1791-1813; Chaplain, 1776; d. Sheffield, Feb. 23, 1813, a. 76.

JOHN KEEP, A.M., b. Longmeadow, Mar. 10, 1749, son of Samuel and Sarah (Bement) Keep; Y. C., 1769, A.B., A.M.; Ord.

Sheffield, June 10, 1772; sett. Sheffield, 1771-1784; d. Sheffield, Sept. 3, 1784, a. 36.

EPHRAIM KEITH, A.M., b. Bridgewater, Mar. 21, 1707, son of Joseph and Elizabeth Keith, and grandson of Rev. James Keith, first minister of Bridgewater; H. C., 1729, A.B., A.M.; sett. Hardwick, May 2, 1734-1735; sett. Petersham, 1736; returned to Bridgewater, where he was a farmer and Justice of the Peace, 1762; d. Bridgewater, Oct. 25, 1789.

GEORGE KEITH, A.M., b. Aberdeen, Scotland, 1638; U. of Aberdeen; Ord. as a minister of the Chh. of Scotland; became a Quaker, 1674; came to N. E., 1682 and again in 1688 and 1690; preached at Philadelphia, Pa., 1689, 1691-1700; became an Epis.; Ord. by the Bishop of London, as an Epis. priest, 1700; sett. as Epis. missionary in America, 1702-1704; Vicar of Edburton, Sussex, Eng., 1704-1715; Ep:s.; d. Edburton, Sussex, 1715.

JAMES KEITH, A.B., b. Scotland, 1643; educated at Aberdeen, Scotland; came to Boston, 1662; Ord. West Bridgewater, Feb. 18, 1663/4, as the first minister; sett. Bridgewater, 1663-1719; d. Bridgewater, July 23, 1719, a. 76.

ERASMUS KELLEY, A.M., b. Perkasie, Buck's County, Pa., July 24, 1748; A.B., U. of Pa., 1769; A.M., Brown U., 1772; A.M., U. of Pa., 1783; Ord. Newport, R. I., (1st Bapt. Chh.), Oct. 9, 1771; sett. Newport, R. I., 1771-1783; sett. Ct. and Pa., 1783-1784; Bapt.; d. Newport, R. I., Nov. 7, 1784.

WILLIAM KELLEY, A.B., b. Newbury, Oct. 31, 1744, son of John and Hannah (Somes) Kelley; H. C., 1767, A.B.; Ord. Warner, N. H., Feb. 2, 1772, as the first minister; sett. Warner, N. H., 1772-1801; dism. Mar. 11, 1801; d. Warner, N. H., May 18, 1813, a. 68.

EBENEZER KELLOGG, A.M., b. Norwalk, Ct., Apr. 5, 1737, son of Daniel and Eunice (Jarvis) Kellogg; Y. C., 1757, A.B., A.M.; Ord. Vernon, Ct., (2nd Chh. in Bolton), Nov. 24, 1762; sett. Vernon, Ct., 1762-1817; d. Vernon, Ct., Sept. 3, 1817 a. 81.

SAMUEL KENDALL, A.M., b. Woburn, June 30, 1708, son of Lieut. Samuel and Elizabeth (Pierce) Kendall; H. C., 1731, A.B., A.M.; Ord. New Salem, Dec. 15, 1742, as the first minister; sett. New Salem, 1742-1792; d. New Salem, Jan. 31, 1792, a. 85.

BENJAMIN KENT, A.M., b. 1708, son of Joseph and Rebecca (Chittenden) Kent; H. C., 1727, A.B., A.M.; Ord. Marlborough, Oct. 27, 1733; sett. Marlborough, 1733-1735: dism. Feb. 4, 1735; attorney at Boston, 1747-1785; d. Nova Scotia, 1788.

ELISHA KENT, A.M., b. Suffield, Ct., July 9, 1704, son of John and Abigail (Dudley) Kent; Y. C., 1729, A.B., A.M.; Ord. Newtown, Ct., Sept. 27, 1732; sett. Newtown, Ct., 1732-1743; dism. Feb. 25, 1742/3; sett. Philippi, N. Y., 1743-1776; d. Philippi, N. Y., July 17, 1776, a. 72.

JOSEPH KIDDER, A.M., b. Billerica, Nov. 18, 1741, son of Capt. Enoch, Jr. and Sarah (Hunt) Kidder; Y. C., 1764, A.B., A.M.; A.M., (Hon.), H. C., 1768; Ord. Dunstable, N. H., (now Nashua, N. H.), Mar. 18, 1767; sett. Dunstable, N. H. 1767-1818; d. Nashua, N. H., Sept. 6, 1818, a. 77.

SAMUEL KINGSBURY, A.M., b. Dedham, Dec. 28, 1736, son of Ebenezer and Abigail Kingsbury; H. C., 1759, A.B., A.M.; Ord. Edgartown, Nov. 25, 1761; sett. Edgartown, 1761-1778; d. Edgartown, Dec. 30, 1778, of small pox.

JOHN KINKEAD, Ord. Windham, N. H., Oct. 1760; sett. Windham, N. H., 1760-1765; dism. Apr. 1765; Presby.

AARON KINNE, A.M., b. Norwich, Ct., Sept. 24, 1744, son of Moses and Abigail (Read) Kinne; Y. C., 1765, A.B.; A.M., 1774; Ord. Groton, Ct., Oct. 19, 1769; sett. Groton, Ct., 1769-1798; dism. Nov. 15, 1798; sett. Winstead, Ct., 1800-1803; Rep. Gen. Ct. Mass., 1813-1815; d. Tallmadge, Ohio, July 14, 1824, a. 80.

DANIEL KIRTLAND, A.M., b. Saybrook, Ct., June 17, 1701, son of Lieut. John and Lydia (Pratt) Kirtland; Y. C., 1720, A.B., A.M.; Ord. Lisbon, Ct., (3rd Chh. in Norwich), Dec. 10, 1723; sett. Lisbon, Ct., 1723-1753; dism. Jan. 4, 1753; inst. South Groton, Ct., (1st Chh.), Dec. 17, 1754; sett. South Groton, Ct., 1754-1757; dism. Nov. 17, 1757; returned to Norwich, Ct.; d. Norwich, Ct., May 14, 1773, a. 72.

SAMUEL KIRKLAND, A.M., b. Norwich, Ct., Dec. 1, 1741, son of Rev. Daniel and Hannah (Perkins) Kirtland; Princeton, 1765, A.B.; A.M., Y. C., 1768; Ord. Lebanon, Ct., June 19, 1766; Indian missionary near Oneida Lake, N. Y., 1766-1808; Chaplain, Continental Army, 1775; d. Clinton, N. Y., Feb. 28, 1808.

JOSHUA KNAPP, A.B., b. Danbury, Ct., 1744; Y. C., 1770, A.B.; Ord. Winchester, Ct., Nov. 11, 1772, as the first minister; sett. Winchester, Ct., 1772-1789; dism. Oct. 21, 1789; inst. East Canaan, Ct., Oct. 14, 1790; sett. East Canaan, Ct., 1790-1795; d. Torrington, Ct., Mar. 25, 1816, a. 72.

EBENEZER KNEELAND, A.M., b. Middletown, Ct., son of Joseph and Lydia Kneeland; Y. C., 1761, A.B.; A.M., Columbia U., 1769; Ord. England, 1766; sett. Stratford, Ct., (Christ Chh.), 1767-1777; Epis.; d. Stratford, Ct., Apr. 17, 1777.

WILLIAM KNIGHT, A.M., son of William and Elizabeth (Stoughton) Knight, of St. Olave, Southwark, London (his mother was the widow of Rev. Thomas Stoughton, Emmanuel Coll., Camb., 1576/7); A.B., Emmanuel Coll., Camb., 1630/1; A.M., 1634; came to N. E., 1637; sett. Ipswich, where for some years he was a preacher; received a grant of 200 acres of land at Ipswich, 1639; Ord. Topsfield, July, 1641; visited England with his half-brother, Col. Israel Stoughton, 1643; sett. Topsfield, as first minister, 1641-1655; returned to England, 1655; presented by Oliver Cromwell to the living at St. Matthew's, Ipswich, England, July 11, 1655; Ord. priest by Bishop Brownrigg of Exeter, Aug. 8, 1659, having conformed; Curate of St. Mary-at-Elms, 1659-1694; buried at St. Mary-at-Elms, England, Jan. 6, 1694/5.

    HANSARD KNOLLYS, b. Cawkwell, Lincolnshire, England, ca. 1599, son of Rev. Richard Knollys, A.B. (Peterhouse Coll., Camb., 1585/6, minister at Cawkwell), matric., St. Catharine's Hall., Camb., Easter, 1629; Ord. by the Bishop of Peterborough, June 30, 1629; Vicar at Humberston, Linc., Eng., 1631-1634; master of the Gainsborough Grammar School; became a Separatist and renounced his orders, 1636; came to N. E., 1638; Ord. Dover, N. H., Oct. 1638; sett. as minister at Dover, N. H., (1st Chh.), 1638-1640; forced to retire; sett. Dover, L. I., N. Y.; returned to England, 1641; served in the army as chaplain under Cromwell, 1641; became a leader of the Baptists in England; served as the minister of a Baptist Chh. in London, 1645-1691; author of religious works; Anglican, Puritan and Baptist; buried at Bunhill Fields, London; d. London, England, Sept. 19, 1691, a. 92.

    JOHN KNOWLES, A.M., b. Lancashire, England; Magdalene Coll., Camb., A.B., 1623/4; A.M., 1627; Fellow, St. Catharine's Hall, Camb., 1627; Ord. at Peterborough, Oct. 3, 1627; lecturer at Colchester, 1635-1637; came to N. E., 1639; Ord. Watertown, Dec. 19, 1639; sett. Watertown, 1639-1651; in 1642, he went on a missionary journey to Va. with Mr. Tompson of Braintree; in 1651, he returned to England where he became lecturer at Bristol Cathedral, 1653-1658; silenced by the Act of Uniformity, 1662; Presby. minister in London, 1672; d. London, England, Apr. 10, 1685.

    THOMAS KNOWLTON, Ord. Plainfield, Ct., Sept. 11, 1742; sett. Gloucester, R.I., 1742-1763; Bapt.; d. Gloucester, R. I., ca. 1763.

    JAMES LABOURIE, sett. Oxford, (French Prot. Chh.), 1699-1704; sett. N. Y. City, (Huguenot Chh.), 1704-1734; Huguenot; d. New York City, 1734.

    JOSEPH LAMB, A.M., b. Stonington, Ct., 1690, son of John Lamb, Jr.; Y. C., 1717, A.B., A.M.; Ord. Mattituck, L. I., N. Y., Dec. 6, 1717; sett. Mattituck, L. I., 1717-1729; sett. Guilford, Ct., (4th Chh.), 1735-1741; sett. Barking Ridge, N. J., 1744-1749; d. Barking Ridge, N. J., July 28, 1749, a. 60.

    JOHN LAMBTON, A.B., prob. son of Robert Lambton of Northumberland; Peterhouse, Camb., A.B., 1701/2; Ord. Durham, England, Sept. 24, 1704; Rector of Middleton St. George, Durham, 1705-1712; Chaplain, British Navy, 1712; inst. Newbury (Queen Anne's Chapel), Nov. 14, 1713; sett. Newbury, 1712-1714; sett. Alnwick, Northumberland, 1718-1722; Epis.; will dated 1731/2.

    JOSEPH LAMSON, A.M., b. Stratford, Ct., Mar. 28, 1718, son of William and Elizabeth (Burch) Lamson; Y. C., 1741, A.B., A.M.; A.M., (Hon.), Columbia U., 1773; Ord. London, England,

1744/5; sett. Stratford, Norwalk and Fairfield, Ct., (Epis. Chhs.), 1747-1773; physician; Epis.; d. Fairfield, Ct., between June and Sept. 1773, a. 55.

THOMAS LANCASTER, A.M., b. Rowley, Jan. 24, 1742, son of Thomas and Dorothy (Northend) Lancaster; H. C., 1764, A.B., A.M.; Ord. Scarborough, Me., Nov. 8, 1775; sett. Scarborough, Me., (1st or Blue Point Parish), 1775-1831; d. Scarborough, Me., Jan. 12, 1831.

JOB LANE, A.M., b. Bedford, Feb. 14, 1741/2, son of Job and Sarah Lane; Y. C., 1764, A.B., A.M.; Tutor, Y. C., 1764-1768; licensed to preach; soldier French and Indian Wars; d. New Haven, Ct., Sept. 16, 1767, a. 25.

PRESIDENT SAMUEL LANGDON, D.D., b. Boston, Jan. 12, 1722/3, son of Samuel and Esther (Osgood) Langdon; H. C., 1740, A.B., A.M.; S.T.D., U. of Aberdeen, 1762; Chaplain of a Regt., 1745; was present at the taking of Louisburg; Ord. Portsmouth, N. H., (North Parish), Feb. 4, 1747; sett. Portsmouth, N. H., 1745-1774; dism. Oct. 9, 1774; became President of Harvard College, Oct. 14, 1774; served 1774-1780; resigned Aug. 30, 1780; inst. Hampton Falls, N. H., Jan. 18, 1781; sett. Hampton Falls, N. H., 1781-1797; President, Am. Acad. Arts and Sciences; held first doctorate conferred upon any clergyman of New Hampshire; Mass. Election Sermon, 1775; N. H. Election Sermon, 1788; Dudleian Lecture, 1775; Mass. Convention Sermon, 1777; d. Hampton, Falls, N. H., Nov. 29, 1797, a. 74.

SAMUEL LANKTON, A.M., b. Berlin, Ct., Oct. 23, 1723, son of Samuel and Elizabeth (Lee) Lankton; Y. C., 1747, A.B., A.M.; A.M., (Hon.), H. C., 1792; Ord. Scotland, Me., (2nd Parish in York), July 3, 1754; sett. Scotland, Me., 1754-1794; d. Scotland, Me., Dec. 19, 1794, a. 71.

THOMAS LARKHAM, A.M., (or Larcome), b. Lyme Regis, Dorset, England, Aug. 17, 1602; A.B., Trinity Hall, Camb., 1621/2; A.M., 1626; Ord. London, Eng., May 23, 1624; Vicar of Northam, Devon, Eng., 1620-1640; came to Dover, N. H., 1640, where he came into conflict with Rev. Hansard Knollys; sett. Dover, N. H., as minister, 1640-1642; returned to England, 1642; Vicar of Tavistock, Devon, 1648-1662; ejected 1662; became an apothecary at Tavistock, 1664-1669; buried at Tavistock, Devon, England, Dec. 23, 1669.

ELIJAH LATHROP, A.M., b. Barnstable, Nov. 18, 1724, son of Benjamin and Mercy (Baker) Lathrop; Y. C., 1749, A.B., A.M.; Ord. Hebron, Ct., (Gilead Society), Apr. 1, 1752, as the first minister; sett. Hebron, Ct., 1752-1797; d. Hebron, Ct., Aug. 3, 1797, a. 73.

JOHN LATHROP, D.D., b. Norwich, Ct., May 6, 1739, son of William and Mary (Kelly) Lathrop; Princeton, 1763, A.B., A.M.; A.M., (Hon.), H. C., 1768; S.T.D., U. of Edinburgh, 1785; Fellow, 1778-1816; Ord. Boston, (2nd Chh.), May 18, 1768; sett. Boston, 1768-1816; became joint minister of the Second Chh. and the Old

Brick Chh. in Boston; Artillery Election Sermon, 1774; Dudleian Lecture, 1793; Convention Sermon, 1800; Fellow, Am. Acad. Arts and Sciences; Unitarian; d. Boston, Jan. 4, 1816, a. 77.

JOSEPH LATHROP, D.D., b. Norwich, Ct., Oct. 20, 1731, son of Solomon and Martha (Perkins) Lathrop; Y. C., 1754, A.B., A.M.; S.T.D., Y. C., 1791; S.T.D., H. C., 1811; Ord West Springfield, Aug. 25, 1756; sett. West Springfield, 1756-1820; Fellow, Am. Acad. Arts and Sciences, 1792; liberal Calvinist; d. West Springfield, Dec. 31, 1820, a. 90.

JOHN LATIMER, A.B., b. Wethersfield, Ct., son of Jonathan and Mary Latimer; H. C., 1703, A.B.; sett. Chatham, Mar. 13, 1707-1709; d. Boston, 1713, will dated Nov. 27, 1713.

MICAH LAWRENCE, A.M., b. Lexington, Mar. 15, 1738/9, son of Jonathan and Elizabeth (Swain) Lawrence; H. C., 1759, A.B., A.M.; Ord. Winchester, N. H., Nov. 14, 1764; sett. Winchester, N. H., 1764-1777; dism. Feb. 19, 1777; d. Keene, N. H., Jan. 1794, a. 55.

WILLIAM LAWRENCE, A.M., b. Groton, May 7, 1723, son of Col. William and Susanna (Prescott) Lawrence; H. C., 1743, A.B., A.M.; Ord. Lincoln, Dec. 7, 1748; sett. Lincoln, 1748-1780; d. Lincoln, Apr. 11, 1780, a. 57.

DEODATE LAWSON, b. England, son of Rev. Thomas Lawson, of Denton, Norfolk, England; came to N. E., 1680; Ord. Norwell (2nd Chh. in Scituate), Nov. 1694; sett. Edgartown, 1681-1682; sett. Danvers, 1683-1688; sett. Norwell, 1694-1698; returned to England where he d.

JEREMIAH LEAMING, D.D., bapt. Durham, Ct., May 12, 1717, son of Jeremiah and Abigail (Turner) Leaming; Y. C., 1745, A.B., A.M.; A.M., Columbia U.. 1765; D.D., Columbia U., 1789; Ord. London, Eng., June 19, 1748; sett. Newport, R.I., (Trinity Chh.), as asst. min., 1747-1750; as minister, 1750-1754; sett. Norwalk, Ct., (Epis. Chh.), 1758-1776; sett. Stratford, Ct., (Epis. Chh.), 1784-1790; chosen Bishop of Ct. but declined; Epis.; d. New Haven, Ct., Sept. 15, 1804, a. 88.

MARK LEAVENWORTH, A.M., b. Huntington, Ct., 1711/2, son of Dr. Dea. Thomas Jr. and Mary Leavenworth; Y. C., 1737, A.B., A.M.; Ord. Waterbury, Ct., (1st Chh.), Mar. 1740; sett. Waterbury, Ct., 1740-1797; Chaplain, 1760, Col. Nathan Whiting's Regt. in Canada; Ct. Election Sermon, 1772; d. Waterbury, Ct., Aug. 20, 1797, a. 86.

DUDLEY LEAVITT, A.M., b. Stratham, N. H., 1720, son of Moses and Sarah Leavitt; H. C., 1739, A.B., A.M.; Ord. Salem, (3rd Chh.), Oct. 23, 1745; sett. Salem, 1745-1762; d. Salem, Feb. 7, 1762.

FREEGRACE LEAVITT, A.M., b. Suffield, Ct., Aug. 12, 1719, son of Lieut. Joshua and Hannah (Devotion) Leavitt; Y. C., 1745,

A.B., A.M.; Ord. Somers, Ct., July 6, 1748; sett. Somers, Ct., 1748-1761; d. Somers, Ct., Oct. 9, 1761, a. 42.

JONATHAN LEAVITT, A.M., b. Suffield, Ct., Jan. 11, 1730/1, son of Lieut. Joshua and Mary (Winchell) Leavitt; Y. C., 1758, A.B., A.M.; Ord. Walpole, N. H., May 27, 1761; sett. Walpole, N. H., 1761-1764; dism. June 19, 1764; inst. Charlemont, (1st Chh.), Oct. 1767; sett. Charlemont, 1767-1785, as the only minister of this church; dism. Apr. 15, 1785; d. Charlemont, Sept. 9, 1802, a. 71.

LEMUEL LE BARON, A.M., b. Plymouth, Sept. 1, 1747, son of Dr. Lazarus and Lydia (Bradford) Le Baron; Y. C., 1768, A.B., A.M.; Ord. Mattapoisett (2nd Chh. in Rochester), Jan. 29, 1772; sett. Mattapoisett, 1771-1836; d. Rochester, Nov. 26, 1836, a. 90.

BIEL LEDOYT, Ord. Woodstock, Ct., (Bapt. Chh.), May 26, 1768; sett. Woodstock, Ct., 1768-1790; sett. N. H., 1790-1806; returned and was sett. Woodstock, Ct., 1806-1813; Bapt.; d. Woodstock, Ct., Mar. 24, 1813.

ANDREW LEE, D.D., b. Lyme, Ct., May 7, 1745, son of Capt. John, Jr. and Abigail (Tully) Lee; Y. C., 1766, A.B., A.M.; member Corp. Y. C., 1807-1823; S.T.D., H. C., 1809; Ord. Hanover, Ct., (Lisbon), Oct. 28, 1768, as the first minister; sett. Hanover, Ct., 1768-1832; Chaplain, Col. Durkee's Fourth Ct. Regt., 1777; Ct. Election Sermon, 1795; d. Lisbon, Ct., Aug. 24, 1832, a. 88.

JASON LEE, b. Long Island, N. Y., 1740, son of Rev. Joseph Lee; Ord. Lyme, Ct., (2nd Bapt. Chh. of East Lyme), 1774; sett. Lyme, Ct., 1774-1810; Bapt.; d. Lyme, Ct., 1810, a. 70.

JONATHAN LEE, A.M., b. Coventry, Ct., July 10, 1718, son of David and Lydia (Strong) Lee; Y. C., 1742, A.B.; A.M., 1747; Ord. Salisbury, Ct., Nov. 23, 1744, as the first minister; sett. Salisbury, Ct., 1744-1788; Chaplain at Crown Point, 1756; Ct. Election Sermon, 1766; d. Salisbury, Ct., Oct. 8, 1788, a. 71.

JOSEPH LEE, JR., A.M., b. Concord, May 12, 1742, son of Joseh and Lucy Lee; H. C., 1765, A.B., A.M.; A.B., (Hon.), Y. C., 1765; Ord. Royalston, Oct. 10, 1768; sett. Royalston, 1768-1818; d. Royalston, Feb. 16, 1819, a. 77.

SAMUEL LEE, A.M., b. London, England, 1625, son of Samuel Lee; Wadham Coll., Oxford, A.B., 1644; A.M., 1648; Fellow, Wadham Coll., Oxford; Proctor of Oxford U., 1656; lecturer at Great St. Helen's Chh., London, 1656-1677; minister of the Holborn nonconformist Cong., London, 1677-1679; minister at Bignal, Oxfordshire, 1679; sett. Independent Chh., Newington Green, London; came to N. E.. 1686: Ord. Bristol, R. I., May 5, 1687; sett. Bristol, R. I., 1687-1691; d. in prison at St. Maloe, France, Dec. 1691.

JOHN LELAND, b. Grafton, May 14, 1754; began preaching at Grafton, June 20, 1774; licensed to preach, 1775; sett. Bellingham, 1775; missonary to Va., Oct. 1775-1791; Ord. Culpepper, Va., (as a

Presb.), Aug. 1776; Ord. Va., June 1787, (as a Bapt.) ; sett. Cheshire, Feb. 1792-1841; Bapt.; d. North Adams, Jan. 14, 1841.

ANDREW LE MERCIER, b. ca. 1692; educated at the U. of Geneva, France; came from Caen, Normandy, France, to N. E., 1715; sett. Boston, (French Prot. Chh.), 1715-1748; left Mar. 17, 1748; resided in Dorchester, 1722-1764; published in English, The Church History of Geneva, etc., 1732; Huguenot; d. Boston, Mar. 31, 1764, a. 72.

ROBERT LENTHALL, matriculated at Oriel Coll., Oxford, 1611; invited to become the minister at Weymouth, Mass., (1st Parish), before Mar. 13, 1638; sett. Weymouth, 1637-1639; freeman at R. I., Aug. 6, 1640; sett. Newport, R. I., (1st Cong. Chh.), 1640-1642; also taught school at Newport, R. I., Aug. 20, 1640-1642; returned to England, 1642; sett. Barnes, County Surrey, Eng., 1649-1658; will made at Barnes, Surrey, Eng., May 10, 1658; will proved, Sept. 3, 1658.

ABIEL LEONARD, D.D., b. Plymouth, Nov. 5, 1740, son of Rev. Nathaniel and Priscilla (Rogers) Leonard; H. C., 1759, A.B., A.M.; D.D., Princeton, 1777; Ord. Woodstock, Ct., (1st Chh.), June 23, 1763; sett. Woodstock, Ct., 1763-1777; Chaplain in Rev., 1775-1776; d. Woodstock, Ct., Aug. 14, 1777.

NATHANIEL LEONARD, A.M., b. Norton, Mar. 9, 1699/1700, son of George and Anna Leonard; H. C., 1719, A.B., A.M.; Ord. Plymouth, July 29, 1724; sett. Plymouth, 1724-1755; resigned 1755; d. Norton, June 11, 1761, a. 62.

GEORGE LESSLIE, A.M., b. Coleraine, Ireland, Nov. 25, 1727, son of Rev. James Lesslie; H. C., 1748, A.B., A.M.; Ord. Ipswich, (Linebrook Parish), Nov. 15, 1749; sett. Ipswich, 1748-1779; dism. Nov. 30, 1779; inst. Washington, N. H., July 12, 1780; sett. Washington, N. H., 1780-1800; d. Washington, N. H., Sept. i1, 1800, a. 72.

ELIPHALET LESTER, b. New London, Ct., May 1729, son of Daniel and Sarah (Brown) Lester; Ord. New London, Ct., (Waterford Bapt. Chh.) ; sett. Saybrook, Ct.; Bapt.

PRESIDENT JOHN LEVERETT, S.T.B., F.R.S., b. Boston, Aug. 25, 1662, son of Hudson and Sarah (Payton) Leverett; H. C., 1680, A.B., A.M.; S.T.B., 1692; F.R.S., 1713; Tutor and Fellow, H. C.; preached 1680-1684; Judge of the Superior Court; Judge of Probate; Member of the Corp., H. C., 1692; Rep. in the Legislature; Speaker, 1700; Member of the Governor's Council; President of Harvard College, 1707-1724; d. Boston, May 3, 1724, a. 61.

WILLIAM LEVERICH, A.M., (Leverick or Leveridge), b. Drawlington, Warwickshire, England, 1603, son of Saville Leverich; Emmanuel Coll., Camb., A.B., 1625/6; A.M., 1631; Ord. Peterborough, Nov. 1, 1627; Rector of Great Livermere, Suffolk, 1631; came to Salem in N. E. in the ship "James," Oct. 10, 1633; sett. Dover, N. H., 1633-1635; adm. First Chh. in Boston, Aug. 9, 1635; sett. Duxbury, 1637-1639; sett. Sandwich, 1639-1653, as the first minister; removed,

1653, to Oyster Bay, L. I., N. Y.; sett. Oyster Bay, L. I., 1653-1658; missionary to the Indians at Huntington, L. I., N. Y., 1658-1669; sett. Newton, L. I., N. Y., 1669-1677; called to Greenwich, Ct., May 23, 1673, where he is said to have been 1673-1677; d. Newton, L. I., N. Y., 1677.

ABNER LEWIS, b. Middleborough, Mar. 16, 1745; Ord. Freetown, June 26, 1776; sett. Freetown, 1776-1784; dism. Aug. 1784; Bapt.

DANIEL LEWIS, A.M., b. Hingham, Sept. 29, 1685, son of John and Hannah (Lincoln) Lewis; H. C., 1707, A.B., A.M.; Ord. Pembroke, Dec. 3, 1712; sett. Pembroke, 1712-1751; Election Sermon, 1748; d. Pembroke, June 29, 1753, a. 68.

ICHABOD LEWIS, A.M., b. Stratford, Ct., Apr. 4, 1744, son of Ichabod and Sarah (Beardslee) Lewis; Y. C., 1765, A.B., A.M.; licensed to preach, Oct. 29, 1766; supply at Southbury, Ct., 1767-1768; Ord. White Plains, N. Y., Oct. 11, 1769; sett. White Plains, N. Y., 1769-1776; left Nov. 1776; sett. Philippi, N. Y., June 17, 1777-1792; Chaplain, 1777; Presb.; d. South East, N. Y., Apr. 8, 1793, a. 49.

ISAAC LEWIS, D.D., b. Huntington, Ct., Jan. 21, 1745/6, son of Nathaniel and Ruth (Beardslee) Lewis; Y. C., 1765, A.B., A.M.; S.T.D., Y. C., 1792; member Corp. Y. C., 1816-1818; Ord. Wilton, Ct., Oct. 28, 1768; sett. Wilton, Ct., 1768-1786; dism. June 1786; inst. Greenwich, Ct., Oct. 18, 1786, (2nd Chh.); sett. Greenwich, Ct., 1786-1840; Chaplain, Col. Beardsley's Regt., 1776; Ct. Election Sermon, 1797; d. Greenwich, Ct., Aug. 27, 1840, a. 95.

ISAIAH LEWIS, A.M., b. Hingham, June 10, 1703, son of John and Hannah (Lincoln) Lewis; H. C., 1723, A.B., A.M.; Ord. Wellfleet, Sept. 23, 1730; sett. Wellfleet, 1730-1786; d. Wellfleet, Oct. 3, 1786, a. 83.

JUDAH LEWIS, A.M., b. Colchester, Ct., June 6, 1703, son of Thomas Lewis; Y. C., 1726, A.B., A.M.; Ord. West Chester, Ct., (West Chester or Colchester), Dec. 17, 1729; sett. West Chester, Ct., 1728-1739; d. Chester, Ct., Apr. 15, 1739, a. 36.

THOMAS LEWIS, A.B., b. Hingham, Sept. 30, 1707, son of Joseph and Sarah (Marsh) Lewis; H. C., 1728, A.B.; studied divinity; preached occasionally; d. Apr. 4, 1787.

THOMAS LEWIS, A.M., b. Waterbury, Ct., Aug. 6, 1716, son of Dea. Joseph and Sarah (Andrews) Lewis; Y. C., 1741, A.B., A.M.; Princeton, A.M., 1750; Ord. New Fairfield, Ct., (North Parish at Sherman), Mar. 28, 1744, as the first minister; sett. New Fairfield, Ct., 1744-1746; dism. Oct. 7, 1746; sett. Bethlehem, N. J., 1747-1754; sett. Hopewell, N. J., June 13, 1758-May 20, 1760; sett. Smithtown, L. I., N. Y., 1763-1769; sett. Mendham, N. J., 1769-1777; d. Mendham, N. J., Aug. 20, 1777, a. 61.

DANIEL LITTLE, A.M., b. Newbury, May 4, 1726, son of Enoch and Elizabeth (Worth) Little; A.M., (Hon.), H. C., 1766;

Ord. Kennebunk, Me., (2nd Parish in Wells), Mar. 27, 1751; sett. Kennebunk, Me., 1751-1800; colleague ordained, Aug. 1800; Fellow, Am. Acad. Arts and Sciences; d. Kennebunk, Me., Dec. 5, 1801.

EPHRAIM LITTLE, A.M., b. Marshfield, Sept. 27, 1676, son of Ephraim and Mary (Sturtevant) Little; H. C., 1695, A.B., A.M.; Ord. Plymouth, Oct. 4, 1699; sett. Plymouth, 1697-1723; d. Plymouth, Nov. 24, 1723.

EPHRAIM LITTLE, A.M., b. Marshfield, 1708, son of David, Esq. and Elizabeth (Southworth) Little; H. C., 1728, A.B., A.M.; Ord. Colchester, Ct., (1st Chh.), Sept. 20, 1732; sett. Colchester, Ct., 1732-1787; d. Colchester, Ct., 1787.

JONATHAN LIVERMORE, A.M., b. Northborough, Dec. 7, 1729, son of Dea. Jonathan and Abigail (Ball) Livermore; H. C., 1760, A.B., A.M.; Ord. Wilton, N. H., Dec. 14, 1763; sett. Wilton, N. H., 1763-1777; dism. Feb. 1777; d. Wilton, N. H., July 20, 1809, a. 80.

PRESIDENT SAMUEL LOCKE, D.D., b. Woburn, Nov. 23, 1731, son of Samuel and Rebecca (Richardson) Locke; H. C., 1755, A.B., A.M.; S.T.D., 1773; Ord. Sherborn, Nov. 7, 1759; sett. Sherborn, 1759-1770; dism. Feb. 2, 1770; inst. President, H. C., Mar. 21, 1770; served as President, 1770-1773; resigned Dec. 1, 1773; Artillery Election Sermon, 1762; Convention Sermon, 1772; d. Sherborn, Jan. 15, 1777, a. 45.

JAMES LOCKWOOD, A.M., b. Norwalk, Ct., Dec. 20, 1714, son of James and Lydia (Smith) Lockwood; Y. C., 1735, A.B., A.M.; Fellow, H. C., 1760-1772; Ord. Wethersfield, Ct., (1st Chh.), Feb. 28, 1738/9; sett. Wethersfield, Ct., 1739-1772; chosen President of Princeton 1758, and of Y. C. 1766, but declined both offers; Ct. Election Sermons, 1754, 1759; d. Wethersfield, Ct., July 20, 1772, a. 58.

SAMUEL LOCKWOOD, D.D., b. Norwalk, Ct., Nov. 30, 1721, son of James and Lydia (Smith) Lockwood; Y. C., 1745, A.B., A.M.; A.M., (Hon.), Princeton, 1761; Fellow, Y. C., 1777-1791; S.T.D., Y. C., 1789; Ord. Andover, Ct., Feb. 15, 1748/9; sett. Andover, Ct., 1748-1791; Ct. Election Sermon, 1774; d. New Lebanon, N. Y., June 18, 1791, a. 70.

JOHN LOCKYER, A.M., b. Beccles, Suffolk, England, son of William Lockyer of Colchester, England; Trinity Coll., Camb., A.B., 1697/8; A.M.; Ord. London, Eng., Oct. 27, 1701; sett. Newport, R. I., (Trinity Chh.), 1701-1704; Epis.; d. Boston, Apr. 20, 1704.

SOLOMON LOMBARD, A.M., b. Truro, Apr. 5, 1702, son of Jedediah, Jr. and Hannah (Lewis) Lombard; H. C., 1723, A.B.; A.M., 1727; Ord. Gorham, Me., Dec. 26, 1750; sett. Gorham, Me., 1750-1764; dism. Aug. 15, 1764; first Rep. Gen. Ct. from Gorham, Me., 1767; Justice, Court of Common Pleas, 1776-1781; d. Gorham, Me., 1781, a. 79.

BENJAMIN LORD, D.D., b. Saybrook, Ct., May 31, 1694,

The Old South Church in Boston (1669).
The Second Meeting House built in 1729.

Christ Church in Boston,
Episcopal, 1722.

son of Benjamin and Elizabeth (Pratt) Lord; Y. C., 1714, A.B.; A.M., 1719; S.T.D., 1774; Tutor, Y. C., 1715-1717; Trustee, Y. C., 1749-1772; Ord. Norwich, Ct., Nov. 20, 1717; sett. Norwich, Ct., 1716-1784; Ct. Election Sermon, 1751; d. Norwich, Ct., Mar. 31, 1784, a. 90.

HEZEKIAH LORD, A.M., b. Saybrook, Ct., Mar. 19, 1697/8, son of James and Elizabeth (Hill) Lord; Y. C., 1717, A.B., A.M.; Ord. Griswold, Ct., (2nd Chh. in Preston), Nov. 20, 1720; sett. Griswold, Ct., 1720-1761; d. Griswold, Ct., June 23, 1761, a. 63.

JOSEPH LORD, A.M., b. Charlestown, June 20, 1672, son of Thomas and Alice (Rand) Lord; H. C., 1691, A.B., A.M.; Ord. Dorchester, Oct. 22, 1695, for work at Dorchester, S. C.; there was no ordained minister "in all that country" near where he was going; sett. Dorchester, S. C., 1695-1716; inst. Chatham, June 15, 1720; sett. Chatham, 1718-1748; schoolmaster and physician; d. Chatham, June 6, 1748.

JOSEPH LORD, A.B., son of Rev. Joseph Lord; H. C., 1726, A.B.; practiced medicine in Sunderland, later at Athol; a preacher of good ability; was the first and only preacher employed at Templeton before Rev. Daniel Pond came in 1755; resided at Athol; afterwards removed to Vt. where he was judge of a county court; d. Westmoreland, N. H., 1788.

ISRAEL LORING, A.M., b. Hull, Apr. 6, 1682, son of Dea. John and Rachel (Sanders) Loring; H. C., 1701, A.B., A.M.; sett. Norwell, 1703-1705; Ord. Sudbury, Nov. 20, 1706; sett. Sudbury, 1705-1772; Election Sermon, 1737; Convention Sermon, 1742; moved to the West Precinct of Sudbury (now Sudbury proper), July 25, 1723; bapt. 1,400 children; minister at Sudbury for 66 years; d. Sudbury, Mar. 9, 1772.

NICHOLAS LORING, A.M., b. Hull, Sept. 1, 1711, son of Elder John and Jane (Baker) Loring; H. C., 1732, A.B., A.M.; Ord. North Yarmouth, Me., Nov. 10, 1736; sett. North Yarmouth, Me., 1736-1763; d. North Yarmouth, Me., July 31, 1763, a. 52.

JOHN LOTHROP, A.M., bapt. Etton, East Riding, Yorkshire, England, Dec. 20, 1584, son of Thomas Lothrop of Cherry Burton; Queens' Coll., Camb., A.B., 1606; A.M., 1609; Ord. Deacon, Dec. 20, 1607; curate at Bennington, Herts.; sett. Egerton, Kent, 1609-1622; sett. London, Eng., 1623-1634, (1st Cong. Chh. in the world, succeeding Rev. Henry Jacob as minister of the Independent Chh. at Southwark, London); silenced and imprisoned, 1632; arrived at Boston, N. E., on the ship "Griffin," Sept. 18, 1634; Ord. Scituate, Sept. 27, 1634, as the first minister; sett. Scituate, 1634-1639; sett. Barnstable, 1639-1653, as the first minister; author of "Queries respecting Baptism;" d. Barnstable, Nov. 8, 1653.

JOSEPH LOVETT, sett. Salem, Ct., (2nd Chh. in Colchester), 1719-1745.

JOHN LOWELL, A.M., b. Boston, Mar. 14, 1703/4, son of
Ebenezer and Elizabeth (Shaler) Lowell; H. C., 1721, A.B., A.M.;
Ord. Newburyport, (1st Religious Society), Jan. 19, 1725/6; sett.
Newburyport, 1725-1767; Convention Sermon, 1763; d. Newburyport,
May 15, 1767, a. 64.

HENRY LUCAS, A.B., prob. b. 1679, son of Henry Lucas of
Banbury, Oxon.; Trinity Coll., Oxford, A.B., 1699; Rector of Great
Wolston, Bucks., 1704; sett. Quincy, (Christ Chh. in Braintree), 1715;
inst. Newbury, (Queen Anne's Chapel), Sept. 17, 1715; sett. Newbury,
1715-1720; Epis.; d. Newbury, Aug. 23, 1720.

CAPTAIN SAMUEL LUTHER, b. 1636, son of Governor
John Luther of R. I.; Rep. Gen. Ct., before 1685; Captain of a Military
Co.; Ord. Swansea, July 22, 1685; sett. Swansea, 1685-1716; Bapt.; d.
Swansea, Dec. 20, 1716, a. 80.

JOHN LYFORD, A.M., Magdalen Coll., Oxford, A.B., 1597;
A.M., 1602; sometime minister at Leverlegkish near Laughgaid, Co.
Ardmagh, Ireland; came in the "Charity," to Plymouth, 1624;
preached at Plymouth, 1624; at Hull, 1625; at Cape Ann (Gloucester),
1625; at Salem, 1626-1629; went to Va., 1629; Epis.; d. Va. before
Oct. 10, 1634.

ISAAC LYMAN, A.M., b. Northampton, Feb. 25, 1724/5, son
of Capt. Moses and Mindwell (Sheldon) Lyman; Y. C., 1747, A.B.,
A.M.; Ord. York, Me., Dec. 20, 1749; sett. York, Me., 1749-1798;
colleague ordained, 1798; d. York, Me., Mar. 12, 1810, a. 85.

JONATHAN LYMAN, A.M., bapt. Durham, Ct., Apr. 21,
1717, son of Noah and Elizabeth Lyman; Y. C., 1742, A.B., A.M.;
Ord. Oxford, Ct., Jan. 9, 1745/6; sett. Oxford, Ct., 1745-1763; d.
Oxford, Ct., Oct. 19, 1763.

JOSEPH LYMAN, D.D., b. Lebanon, Ct., Apr. 3, 1749, son
of Jonathan and Bethia (Clark) Lyman; Y. C., 1767, A.B., A.M.;
Tutor, Y. C., 1770-1771; S.T.D., Williams, 1801; Ord. Hatfield, Mar.
4, 1772; sett. Hatfield, 1772-1828; President, American Board of Foreign Missions, 1823-1826; Trustee, Amherst Coll., 1825-1828; Convention Sermon, 1806; Election Sermon, 1787; d. Hatfield, Mar. 27,
1828, a. 79.

JAMES LYON, son of Matthew Lyon, of Warrington; matric.,
Oxford U., 1743; sett. Derby, Ct., and Waterbury, Ct., (Epis. Chhs.),
1743-1747; sett. L. I., N. Y.; Epis.; d. Setauket, L. I., N. Y., 1787.

JAMES LYON, A.M., b. Newark, N. J., July 1, 1735, son of
Zopher and Mary Lyon; Princeton, 1759, A.B., A.M.; Ord. Brunswick,
N. J., 1764; preached at Onslow, Nova Scotia, 1764; sett. Machias,
Me., 1771-1794; Presb.; d. Machias, Me., Oct. 12, 1794.

JOHN LYON, A.B., son of Rev. James Lyon of Derby, Ct.;
Y. C., 1761, A.B.; Ord. England, 1764; sett. Taunton, (St. Thomas'
Epis. Chh.), 1765-1769; minister of missionary chapels at Bridgewater and Middleborough as well as at Taunton; sett. Cedar Creek,

Lewes, Del., 1770-1773; sett. St. George's Parish, Accomac County, Va., 1773-1783; Epis.; d. Va., ca. 1796.

THADDEUS MACCARTY, A.M., b. Boston, July 18, 1721, son of Capt. Thaddeus and Mary (Greenough) Maccarty; H. C., 1739, A.B., A.M.; Ord. Kingston, Nov. 3, 1742; sett. Kingston, 1742-1745; dism. Nov. 3, 1745, because of his admiration for Whitefield which was not shared by his parish; inst. Worcester, June 10, 1747; sett. Worcester, 1747-1784; Artillery Election Sermon, 1755; Convention Sermon, 1782; President John Adams said of him, "though a Calvinist, not a bigot;" d. Worcester, July 20, 1784, a. 63.

DANIEL McCLALLEN, educated at Edinburgh, Scotland; Ord. Colrain, June 1, 1769; sett. Colrain, 1769-1773; Presb.; d. Colrain, Apr. 21, 1773.

WILLIAM McCLANACHAN, A.B., b. Ireland, 1714; U. of Edinburgh, 1730, A.B.; came to N. E. before 1734; inst. Georgetown, Me., Nov. 15, 1736; sett. Georgetown, Me., 1734-1738; inst. South Portland, Me., (2nd Chh., Presb., at Cape Elizabeth) Nov. 15, 1739; sett. South Portland, Me., 1739-1742; inst. Blandford, Oct. 5, 1744; sett. Blandford, 1744-1746; became a Chaplain in the army, 1745; Ord. Chelsea, (1st Chh. in Revere), Dec. 21, 1748; sett. Chelsea, 1747-1754; dism. Dec. 18, 1754; Ord. (Epis.), London, England, 1755; an Epis. missionary, 1754-1758; went to Philadelphia, Pa., 1758; Presb.; Cong.; Epis.

ALEXANDER McLEAN, A.M., b. Isle of Skye, Scotland; Aberdeen U., A.M.; Ord. Bristol, Me., Aug. 18, 1773; sett. Bristol, Me., 1772-1795; dism. 1795; physician; Presb.; d. Bristol, Me., 1805.

SAMUEL MACCLINTOCK, D.D., b. Medford, May 1, 1732, son of William Macclintock; Princeton, 1751, A.B., A.M.; A.M., (Hon.), H. C., 1761; S.T.D., Y. C., 1791; Ord. Greenland, N. H., Nov. 3, 1756; sett. Greenland, N. H., 1756-1803; N. H. Election Sermon, 1784; Chaplain, Rev. War; d. Greenland, N. H., Apr. 27, 1804, a. 71.

DAVID McCLURE, D.D., b. Newport, R. I., Nov. 18, 1748, son of Dea. John and Rachel (McClintock) McClure; Y. C., 1769, A.B., A.M.; A.M., Dart. Coll., 1773; Trustee, Dart. Coll., 1777-1800; S.T.D., Dart. Coll., 1800; Ord. Dart. Coll., N. H., May 20, 1772; inst. Hampton, N. H., Nov. 13, 1776; sett. North Hampton, N. H., 1776-1785; dism. Aug. 30, 1785; inst. South Windsor, Ct., June 11, 1786; sett. South Windsor, Ct., 1786-1820; d. South Windsor, Ct., June 25, 1820, a. 71.

ALEXANDER McDOWELL, A.B., b. Ireland; H. C., 1751, A.B.; Ord. Colrain, Sept. 28, 1753; sett. Colrain, 1753-1761; Presb.; d. 1762.

WILLIAM McGILCHRIST, A.M., b. 1707, son of James McGilchrist, of Inchianan, Scotland, Gent.; Balliol Coll., Oxford, A.B., 1732; A.M., 1735; Ord. 1733; sett. Charleston, S. C., 1741-

1745; sett. Salem, (St. Peter's Chh.), 1747-1780; Epis.; d. Salem, Apr. 19, 1780, a. 73.

DAVID McGREGORE, A.M., b. Londonderry, Ireland, Nov. 6, 1710, son of Rev. James and Marion (Cargil) McGregore; studied under his father; A.M., (Hon.), Princeton, 1764; Ord. Londonderry, N. H., (West Parish), Oct. 9, 1736, as the first minister; sett. Londonderry, N. H., 1737-1777; Presb.; d. Londonderry, N. H., May 30, 1777, a. 66.

JAMES McGREGORE, Gent., b. 1677; adm. a student at the U. of Glasgow, Jan. 18, 1697; came from Agadowey, Ireland, to New England, Oct. 14, 1718; removed to Londonderry, N. H., (then called Nutfield), Apr. 11, 1719; Ord. Derry, N. H., (1st Presb. Chh. in New England), 1719; sett. Londonderry, (now Derry), N. H., 1719-1729; Presb.; d. Derry, N. H., Mar. 5, 1729, a. 52.

JOHN McKINSTRY, A.M., b. Brode Parish, County Antrim, Ireland, 1677, son of Roger and Mary (Wilson) McKinstry; U. of Edinburgh, A.B., 1712; A.M.; arrived in Boston, 1718; Ord. Sutton, Nov. 9, 1720; sett. Sutton, 1720-1728; dism. Sept. 2, 1728; inst. Ellington, Ct., 1733; sett. Windsor, Ct., (Ellington Parish), 1733-1749, as the first minister; d. Ellington, Ct., Jan. 20, 1754.

JOHN McKINSTRY, A.M., b. Sutton, Dec. 31, 1723, son of Rev. John and Elizabeth (Fairfield) McKinstry; Y. C., 1746, A.B., A.M.; Ord. Chicopee, Sept. 27, 1752, as the first minister of that church; sett. Chicopee, 1751-1813, 61 years; d. Chicopee, Nov. 9, 1813, a. 90.

JAMES McSPARRAN, D.D., b. Dungiven, Co. Derry, Ireland; U. of Glasgow, A.M., 1709; D.D., U. of Oxford, 1731; Ord. London, England, Sept. 25, 1720; missionary at Bristol, Freetown, Swansea and Little Compton; sett. Kingston, R. I., (St. Paul's Chh., Narragansett), 1721-1757; Epis.; d. South Kingston, R. I., Dec. 1, 1757.

EBENEZER MACK, Ord. East Lyme, Ct., (Separatist Chh.), Jan. 12, 1749; sett. East Lyme, Ct., (2nd Sept. Chh.), 1749-1752; sett. East Lyme, Ct., (2nd Bapt. Chh.), 1752-1768; sett. Marlow, N. H.; Bapt.; d. Lyme, Ct., ca. 1795.

AMOS MAIN, A.M., b. York, Me., Jan. 19, 1708, son of Josiah Main; H. C., 1729, A.B., A.M.; Ord. Rochester, N. H., May 1737, as the first minister; sett. Rochester, N. H., 1737-1760; d. Rochester, N. H., Apr. 5, 1760, a. 52.

ALEXANDER MALCOLM, sett. as Rector at Marblehead, (St. Michael's Chh.), 1740-1749; Epis.

SAMUEL MANN, A.B., b. Cambridge, July 6, 1647, son of William and Mary (Jarrard) Mann; H. C., 1665, A.B.; teacher at Dedham, 1667-1672; 1676-1678; sett. Wrentham, 1670-1676; left Mar. 30, 1676, on account of King Philip's War; sett. Milton, 1678-

1680; Ord. **Wrentham, Apr. 13, 1692**; sett. Wrentham, 1680-1719; d. Wrentham, May 22, 1719, a. 72.

PRESIDENT JAMES MANNING, D.D., b. Elizabeth, N. J., Oct. 22, 1738, son of James and Christian Manning; Princeton, 1762, A.B., A.M.; D.D., U. of Pa., 1785; sett. Morristown, N. J., 1762-1763; Ord. Warren, R. I., Oct. 15, 1764; sett. Warren, R. I., (Bapt. Chh.), 1763-1770; inst. President, Brown U., Sept. 5, 1765; served as President, Brown U., 1765-1791; inst. Providence, R. I., (1st Bapt. Chh.), July 31, 1771; sett. Providence, R. I., (1st Bapt. Chh.), 1771-1791; member Cont. Congress, 1786; Bapt.; d. Providence, R. I., July 29, 1791, s. p.

JOSEPH MANNING, A.M., b. Cambridge, Jan. 26, 1730/1, son of William and Mary Manning; H. C., 1751, A.B., A.M.; Chaplain, Rev. Army; sett. Bath, Me.; d. Bath, Me., 1808.

RICHARD MANSFIELD, D.D., b. New Haven, Ct., Oct. 1, 1723, son of Deacon Jonathan and Susannah (Alling) Mansfield; Y. C., 1741, A.B., A.M.; S.T.D., 1792; Ord. London, England, Aug. 7, 1748, by the Archbishop of Canterbury; sett. Derby, Ct., (St. James' Epis. Chh.), 1749-1820; also Missionary V.S.P.G.F.P. at West Haven, Waterbury and Plymouth, Ct., 1749-1755; Epis.; d. Derby, Ct., Apr. 12, 1820, a. 96.

EDMUND MARCH, A.M., b. Newbury, 1703/4, son of Lieut. John and Mary (Angier) March; H. C., 1722, A.B., A.M.; Ord. Amesbury, July 3, 1728; sett. Amesbury, 1722-1743; d Amesbury, Mar. 6, 1791, a. 88.

JOHN MARRETT, A.M., b. Cambridge, Sept. 21, 1741, son of Amos and Mary (Dunster) Marrett; H. C., 1763, A.B., A.M.; Ord. Burlington, Dec. 21, 1774; sett. Burlington, 1774-1813; d. Burlington, Feb. 18, 1813.

BENJAMIN MARSH, b. Salem, Apr. 1, 1711, son of Benjamin and Hannah (King) Marsh; Ord. Sutton, (1st Bapt. Chh.), 1737; sett. Sutton, 1737-1775; Bapt.; d. Sutton, 1775.

CHRISTOPHER BRIDGE MARSH, A.M., b. Boston, Sept. 1743, son of Daniel and Martha (Bridge) Marsh; H. C., 1761, A.B., A.M.; Ord. Newburyport, (North Cong. Chh.), Oct. 19, 1768; sett. Newburyport, 1768-1773; d. Newburyport, Dec. 3, 1773.

CYRUS MARSH, A.M., b. Plainfield, Ct., Mar. 14, 1718/9, son of William, Jr. and Sarah (Button) Marsh; Y. C., 1739, A.B., A.M.; Ord. Kent, Ct., (1st Chh.), May 6, 1741, as the first minister; sett. Kent, Ct., 1741-1755; dism. Dec. 2, 1755: Rep. Gen. Assembly, 1761-1767; J. P., 1764; d. Kent, Ct., June 9, 1771, a. 52.

ELIHU MARSH, Ord. Windham, Ct., (Separatist Chh.), Oct. 7, 1747; Bapt.

ELISHA MARSH, A.M., b. Hadley, Mar. 27, 1713, son of Ebenezer and Mary (Parsons) Marsh; H. C., 1738, A.B., A.M.; A.M., (Hon.), Y. C., 1740; A.M., Dart. Coll., 1773; Ord. Westminster, Oct. 20, 1742; sett. Westminster, 1742-1757; lawyer at Walpole, N. H., 1770-1784; d. Lancaster, July 25, 1784.

JOHN MARSH, D.D., b. Haverhill, Nov. 2, 1742, son of Dea. David and Mary (Moody) Marsh; H. C., 1761, A.B., A.M.; A.M., (Hon.), Y. C., 1774; S.T.D., H. C., 1806; Tutor, H. C., 1771-1773; Fellow, Y. C., 1801-1820; Ord. Wethersfield, Ct., (1st Chh.), Jan. 1774; sett. Wethersfield, Ct., 1774-1821; Ct. Election Sermon, 1796; d. Wethersfield, Ct., Sept. 13, 1821.

JONATHAN MARSH, D.D., b. Hadley, Aug. 7, 1685, son of Jonathan and Dorcas (Dickinson) Marsh; H. C., 1705, A.B.; Trustee, Y. C., 1732-1745; S.T.D.; Ord. Windsor, Ct., (1st Chh.), June 1710; sett. Windsor, Ct., 1710-1747; Ct. Election Sermons, 1721, 1736; d. Windsor, Ct., Sept. 8, 1747.

JONATHAN MARSH, A.M., b. Windsor, Ct., Jan. 1, 1713/4, son of Rev. Dr. Jonathan and Margaret (Whiting) Marsh; Y. C., 1735, A.B., A.M.; Ord. New Hartford, Ct., Oct. 10, 1739; sett. New Hartford, Ct., 1739-1794; d. New Hartford, Ct., July 5, 1794, a. 80.

JOSEPH MARSH, A.M., b. Hadley, Jan. 16, 1685, son of Daniel and Hannah (Lewis) Marsh; H. C., 1705, A.B., A.M.; Ord. Quincy, (1st Chh. in Braintree), May 18, 1709; sett. Quincy, 1709-1726; d. Quincy, (Braintree), Mar. 8, 1725/6, a. 41.

THOMAS MARSH, Deacon, Mansfield, Ct., (1st Chh.); Ord. Mansfield, Ct., (Separatist Chh.), July 1, 1746.

JOHN RUTGERS MARSHALL, A.M., b. N. Y.; Columbia U., 1770, A.B.; A.M.; Ord. Woodbury, Ct., 1771; sett. Woodbury, Ct., (St. Paul's Chh.), 1771-1789; Epis.; d. Woodbury, Ct., Jan. 7, 1789.

JOSEPH MARSHALL, b. Windsor, Ct., Feb. 17, 1731, son of Samuel and Abigail Marshall; Ord. Canterbury, Ct., (Separatist Chh. in North Society), Apr. 18, 1759; sett. Canterbury, Ct., 1759-1768; dism. Aug. 29, 1768; sett. North Canaan, Ct., 16 years; sett. Green River, N. Y., 10 years; d. Starksborough, Vt., Feb. 20, 1813.

JOSIAH MARSHALL, A.B., b. Braintree, Nov. 28, 1700, son of John and Mary (Mills) Marshall; H. C., 1720, A.B.; Ord. Falmouth, Aug. 19, 1724; sett. Falmouth, 1724-1730; d. 1772.

DANIEL MARTIN, b. Swansea, Sept. 23, 1702, son of Dea. Melatiah and Deborah (Brooks) Martin; Ord. Rehoboth, (3rd Bapt. Chh.), Feb. 8, 1753; sett. Rehoboth, 1753-1781; house carpenter; Bapt.; d. Rehoboth, Nov. 18, 1781, a. 79.

EBENEZER MARTIN, A.M., b. Hampton, Ct., Mar. 31, 1732, son of Ebenezer and Jerusha (Durkee) Martin; Y. C., 1756, A.B.; A.M., 1781; Ord. Becket, Feb. 23, 1759, as the first minister; sett. Becket, 1759-1764; dism. Oct. 12, 1764; inst. Ashford, Ct., (Westford Parish), June 15, 1768; sett. Ashford, Ct., 1768-1777; sett. Austerlitz, N. Y., 1780-1787; d. Union, Broome Co., N. Y., Sept. 5, 1795, a. 64.

JOHN MARTYN, A.M., b. Boston, May 10, 1706, son of Capt.

Edward and Sarah Martyn; H. C., 1724, A.B.; A.M., 1743; Ord. Northborough, May 21, 1746; sett. Northborough, 1746-1767; d. Northborough, Apr. 30, 1767, a. 61.

JOHN MARTIN, sett. Thompson, Ct., (2nd Bapt. Chh.), 1773; Bapt.

MANASSEH MARTYN, b. Swansea, Feb. 2, 1681, son of John and Joanna (Esten) Martyn; Ord. Warwick, R. I., 1725; sett. Warwick, R. I., 1725-1754; Bapt.; d. Warwick, R. I., Mar. 20, 1754, a. 74.

RICHARD MARTYN, A.B., b. Portsmouth, N. H., Jan. 10, 1659/60, son of Richard Martyn; H. C., 1680, A.B.; schoolmaster at Wells, Me.; inst. Wells, Me., June 21, 1689; sett. Wells, Me., 1689-1690; d. Wells, Me., Dec. 6, 1690, a. 30.

ELIJAH MASON, A.M., b. Hartford. Ct.; Y. C., 1744, A.B.; A.M., 1748; Ord. Marlborough, Ct., May 21, 1749; sett. Marlborough, Ct., 1749-1761; inst. Chester, Ct., May 21, 1767; sett. Chester, Ct., 1767-1770; d. Chester, Ct., Jan. 13, 1770.

JOB MASON, b. Swansea, Feb. 28, 1695, son of Pelatiah and Hepzibah (Brooks) Mason: Ord. Swansea. (2nd Chh.). May 26, 1738; sett. Swansea, 1738-1775; Bapt.; d. Swansea, July 17, 1775.

JOSEPH MASON, b. Swansea, Mar. 6, 1663, son of Sampson and Mary (Butterworth) Mason; Ord. Swansea, (2nd Bapt. Chh.), July 1709; sett. Swansea, 1709-1738; Bapt.; d. Swansea, May 19, 1748, a. 85.

NATHAN MASON, b. Swansea, Nov. 12, 1726, son of Sampson and Experience (Lewis) Mason; Ord. Sackville, New Brunswick, Sept. 21, 1763; sett. Sackville, N. B., 1763-1771; inst. Cheshire, (2nd Bapt. Chh.), Sept. 21, 1771; sett. Cheshire, 1771-1804; Bapt.; d. Fort Ann, N. Y., Mar. 6, 1804.

RUSSELL MASON, b. Swansea, Apr. 22, 1714, son of Pelatiah and Hepzibah (Brooks) Mason; Ord. Swansea, (2nd Bapt. Chh.), Nov. 2, 1752; sett. Swansea, 1752-1799; Bapt.; d. Swansea, Jan. 11, 1799.

SAMPSON MASON, said to have served with Cromwell's Ironsides; came to N. E. before 1649; a founder of the 2nd Bapt. Chh. of Swansea, 1668; said to have been a minister there; Bapt.; bur. Rehoboth, Sept. 15, 1676.

ALLYN MATHER, A.M., b. Windsor, Ct., Mar. 21, 1747, son of Nathaniel and Elizabeth (Allyn) Mather; Y. C., 1771, A.B., A.M.; Ord. New Haven, Ct., (Fair Haven Chh.), Feb. 3, 1773; sett. New Haven, Ct., 1772-1784; d. Savannah, Ga., Nov. 12, 1784, a. 38.

AZARIAH MATHER, A.M., b. Windsor, Ct., Aug. 29, 1685, son of Rev. Samuel and Hannah (Treat) Mather; Y. C., 1705, A.B., A.M.; Tutor; Ord. Old Saybrook, Ct., (1st Chh.), Nov. 22, 1710; sett. Old Saybrook, Ct., 1709-1732; dism. June 1732; Ct. Election Sermon, 1725; d. Saybrook, Ct., Feb. 11, 1736/7, a. 52.

COTTON MATHER, D.D., F.R.S., b. Boston, Feb. 12, 1662/3, son of Rev. Dr. Increase and Maria (Cotton) Mather; H. C., 1678, A.B., A.M.; S.T.D., U. of Glasgow, 1710; Fellow, H. C., 1690-1703; Fellow Royal Society, 1717; Ord. Boston, (2nd Chh.), May 13, 1685; sett. Boston, 1683-1728; most distinguished of N. E. Puritan divines; author of Magnalia Christi Americana, 1702, and of 450 other works; Artillery Election Sermons, 1691, 1707; Election Sermons, 1689, 1690, 1696, 1700; Convention Sermons, 1690, 1721; d. Boston, Feb. 13, 1727/8, a. 65.

ELEAZER MATHER, A.B., b. Dorchester, May 13, 1637, son of Rev. Richard and Katharine (Hoult) Mather; H. C., 1656, A.B.; Ord. Northampton, June 18, 1661, as the first minister; sett. Northampton, 1658-1669; d. Northampton, July 24, 1669, a. 32.

PRESIDENT INCREASE MATHER, D.D., b. Dorchester, June 21, 1639, son of Rev. Richard and Katharine (Hoult) Mather; H. C., 1656, A.B.; A.M., Trinity Coll., Dublin, 1658; S.T.D., H. C., 1692, (first D.D. ever given at H. C.); Fellow, H. C., 1675-1685; Ord. Boston, (2nd Chh.), May 27, 1664; sett. Boston, 1661-1723; inst. sixth President of H. C., June 11, 1685; served as President, 1685-1701; voluminous writer; published 158 works; Artillery Election Sermons, 1665, 1710; Election Sermons, 1677, 1693, 1699, 1702; d. Boston, Aug. 23, 1723, a. 84.

MOSES MATHER, D.D., b. Lyme, Ct., Feb. 23, 1718/9, son of Timothy and Sarah (Noyes) Mather; Y. C., 1739, A.B., A.M.; Fellow, Y. C., 1777-1790; S.T.D., Princeton, 1791; Ord. Darien, Ct., (Middlesex), June 6, 1744, as the first minister; sett. Darien, Ct., 1744-1806; Ct. Election Sermon, 1781; d. Darien, Ct., Sept. 21, 1806, a. 88.

RICHARD MATHER, b. Lowton, Winwick, Lancashire, England, 1596, son of Thomas and Margaret Mather; Brazenose Coll., Oxford, matric. May 6, 1618; Ord. Toxteth, Co. Lancaster, 1618; sett. Toxteth and Prescott, Lancashire, 1618-1633; suspended 1633, for non-conformity; came to N. E. 1635; inst. Dorchester, Aug. 23, 1636; sett. Dorchester, 1636-1669; published the Bay Psalm Book and other works; Artillery Election Sermon, 1656; Election Sermons, 1660, 1664; his portrait is owned by the American Antiquarian Soc.; d. Dorchester, Apr. 22, 1669.

SAMUEL MATHER, A.M., b. Dublin, Ireland, May 13, 1626, son of Rev. Richard and Katharine (Hoult) Mather; came to N. E. 1635; H. C., 1643, A.B., A.M.; A.M., at Cambridge, Oxford and Dublin, First Fellow of H. C., 1650; asst. to Mr. Rogers at Rowley; sett. Boston, (1st Chh.), June 5, 1650, but was not ordained here; returned to England, 1650; minister at Leith, Scotland; Chaplain to the Lord Mayor of London, 1650; Chaplain, Magdalen Coll., Oxford, 1650-1653; Senior Fellow of Trinity Coll., Dublin, 1655; minister of St. Nicholas' Chh., Dublin, 1655; d. Dublin, Ireland, Oct. 29, 1671, a. 45.

SAMUEL MATHER, A.B., b. Dorchester, Sept. 5, 1651, son of Timothy and Elizabeth (Atherton) Mather; H. C., 1671, A.B.; Trustee, Y. C., 1701; sett. Deerfield, 1673-1675; sett. Branford, Ct., 1680; Ord. Windsor, Ct., 1684/5; sett. Windsor, Ct., 1682-1728; d. Windsor, Ct., Mar. 18, 1727/8, a. 77.

SAMUEL MATHER, D.D., b. Boston, Oct. 30, 1706, son of Rev. Dr. Cotton and Elizabeth (Clark) Mather; H. C., 1723, A.B., A.M.; S.T.D., 1773; A.M., (Hon.), Y. C., 1725; Glasgow, 1731; Fellow Am. Acad. Arts and Sciences; Ord. Boston, (2nd Chh.), June 21, 1732; sett. Boston, (2nd Chh.), 1732-1741; dism. Dec. 21, 1741; inst. Boston, (10th Cong. Society), July 19, 1742; sett. Boston, (10th Cong. Soc.), 1742-1785; Artillery Election Sermon, 1739; Convention Sermon, 1762; Dudleian Lecture, 1769; d. Boston, June 27, 1785, a. 79.

WARHAM MATHER, A.M., b. Northampton, Sept. 7, 1666, son of Rev. Eleazer and Esther (Warham) Mather; H. C., 1685, A.B., A.M.; sett. West Chester, N. Y., 1684; sett. Northfield, 1688-1690; sett. Killingworth, Ct., 1691-1693; sett. Farmington, Ct., 1704; not ordained; Justice of the Peace and of Quorum in Ct., 1710-1716; Justice of Probate, 1716-1727; d. New Haven, Ct., Aug. 12, 1745, a. 79.

MARMADUKE MATTHEWS, A.M., b. Swanzey, Glamorganshire, Wales, 1605, son of Marmaduke Matthews; matric., All Soul's Coll., Oxford, Feb. 20, 1623/4; A.B., 1624/5; A.M.; came to Boston, 1638; sett. Yarmouth, 1639-1643, as the first minister; sett. Hull, 1644-1649; Ord. Malden, 1651, as the first minister; sett. Malden, 1650-1652; returned to England where he became Vicar of St. John's Chh. in his native town of Swanzey; ejected 1662, for nonconformity; d. Swanzey, Wales, 1683.

DANIEL MAUDE, A.M., bapt. Halifax, Yorkshire, England, Oct. 9, 1586, son of Rev. Edward Maude, A.M., (Master of the Wakefield School, Yorkshire); A.B., Emmanuel Coll., Camb., 1606/7; A.M., 1610; came to N. E., 1635, with Rev. Richard Mather; appointed second school master of Boston, Aug. 12, 1636; served as school master, 1636-1643; admitted freeman, May 25, 1636; sett. as minister at Dover, N. H., 1643-1655; d. Dover, N. H., 1655, a. 70, s. p.

JOHN MAVERICK, A.M., bapt. Awliscombe, Devon, Oct. 27, 1578, son of Rev. Peter and Dorothy (Tucke) Maverick; Exeter Coll., Oxford, A.B., 1599; A.M., 1603; Ord. deacon at Exeter, July 26, 1597; inst. Beaworthy, Devon, Aug. 30, 1615, by the Bishop of Exeter; sett. Beaworthy, Devon, 1615-1629; Ord. Plymouth, England, Mar. 30, 1630, for service in N. E.; came on the "Mary and John," arriving at Dorchester, May 30, 1630; sett. Dorchester, 1630-1636; d. Boston, Feb. 3, 1635/6, a. 60.

JOHN MAXSON, b. Newport, R. I., 1639, son of Richard Maxson; freeman at Westerly, R. I., Oct. 19, 1668; Ord. Westerly, R. I., (1st Seventh Day Bapt. Chh. at Hopkinton, R. I.), Sept. 20,

1708; sett. Westerly, R. I., (Hopkinton), 1708-1720; Deputy, 1670-1705; Overseer of the Poor, 1687; Bapt.; d. Westerly, R. I., Dec. 17, 1720.

JOHN MAXSON, JR., b. Westerly, R. I., 1667, son of Rev. John and Mary (Mosher) Maxson; Ord. deacon, (Seventh Day Bapt. Chh.), Aug. 21, 1712; Ord. Westerly, R. I., (Seventh Day Bapt. Chh.), July 5, 1719; sett. Westerly, R. I., 1719-1748; freeman, 1716; Bapt.; d. Westerly, R. I., July 1748.

JOHN MAXSON, 3rd., b. Westerly, R. I., Apr. 21, 1701, son of Rev. John, Jr. and Judith (Clarke) Maxson; Ord. Newport, R. I., (Sabbatarian Bapt. Chh.), Nov. 24, 1754; sett. Newport, R. I., 1754-1778; Bapt.; d. Newport, R. I., 1778.

JOSEPH MAXSON, b. Westerly, R. I., 1672, son of Rev. John and Mary (Mosher) Maxson; Ord. Westerly, R. I., 1732, as an evangelist; sett. Westerly, R. I., 1739-1750; Bapt.; d. Westerly, R. I., Sept. 1750.

SAMUEL MAXWELL, b. Boston, Sept. 30, 1688, son of James and Dorcas (Stone) Maxwell; Ord. Swansea, (1st Chh.), Apr. 18, 1733; sett. Swansea, 1733-1739; dism. Apr. 15, 1739; became a Seventh Day Baptist; retracted and became a Congregational minister; inst. Rehoboth, (1st Chh.), Oct. 1745; sett. Rehoboth, 1745-1749; sett. Block Island, R. I., 1756-1758; d. Rehoboth, May 5, 1778.

ELEAZER MAY, A.M., b. Wethersfield, Ct., Mar. 11, 1733, son of Dea. Hezekiah and Anne (Stillman) May; Y. C., 1752, A.B., A.M.; Ord. Haddam, Ct., June 30, 1756; sett. Haddam, Ct., 1756-1803; d. Haddam, Ct., Apr. 14, 1803, a. 70.

EXPERIENCE MAYHEW, A.M., b. Martha's Vineyard, Jan. 27, 1673, son of Rev. John and Elizabeth (Hilliard) Mayhew; A. M., (Hon.), H. C., 1720; sett. Martha's Vineyard, Mar. 1694-1758; worked among the Indians; translated the Psalms, etc., into the Indian tongue, 1709; d. Martha's Vineyard, Nov. 29, 1758, a. 85.

JONATHAN MAYHEW, D.D., b. Martha's Vineyard, Oct. 8, 1720, son of Rev. Experience and Remember (Bourne) Mayhew; H. C., 1744, A.B., A.M.; S.T.D., U. of Aberdeen, 1749; Ord. Boston, (West Chh.), June 17, 1747; sett. Boston, 1747-1766; foremost preacher in N. E. in his day; Election Sermon, 1754; Dudleian Lecture, 1765; Unitarian; d. Boston, July 8, 1766, a. 46.

JOHN MAYHEW, b. Edgartown, 1652, son of Rev. Thomas, Jr. and Jane (Paine) Mayhew; sett. West Tisbury, 1673-1689; worked among the Indians; d. Tisbury, Feb. 22, 1688/9, a. 37.

JOSEPH MAYHEW, A.M., b. Chilmark, son of Rev. Experience and Remember (Bourne) Mayhew; H. C., 1730, A. B., A.M.; Tutor; sett. (acting minister), Nantucket, (1st Cong. Chh.), 1761-1766; d. 1782.

GOVERNOR THOMAS MAYHEW, SR., bapt. Tisbury, England, Apr. 1, 1593, son of Matthew and Alice (Barter) Mayhew;

came to Medford, 1635; agent for Matthew Craddock; acquired titles to the Vineyard, Nantucket and Elizabeth Islands; Governor of Martha's Vineyard; sett. Edgartown, 1658-1681; worked among the Indians; d. Edgartown, 1681, a. 90.

THOMAS MAYHEW, JR., b. England, 1620/1, son of Gov. Thomas Mayhew; came to N. E., 1631; Ord. Edgartown, 1642 (though this has been questioned); sett. Edgartown, 1642-1657, as the first minister; worked among the Indians; d. at sea en route for England, 1657, a. 37.

ZECHARIAH MAYHEW, bapt. Martha's Vineyard, May 17, 1718, son of Rev. Experience and Remember (Bourne) Mayhew; Ord. Martha's Vineyard, Dec. 10, 1767; sett. Chilmark. 1767-1806: worked among the Indians; d. Martha's Vineyard, Mar. 6, 1806, a. 89.

JOHN MAYO, b. Northamptonshire, England, 1598; matric. at Magdalen Hall, Oxford, 1615, ae. 17; came to New England, 1638; admitted freeman at Barnstable, Mar. 3, 1639/40; Ord. Barnstable, Apr. 15, 1640; sett. Barnstable, 1640-1646; sett. Eastham, 1646-1649, as the first minister; inst. Boston, (2nd Chh.), Nov. 9, 1655, as the first minister; sett. Boston, 1655-1673; left Boston, Apr. 15, 1673; returned to Barnstable; served in Lieut. Dymock's military Co., 1643; Artillery Election Sermon, 1658; called the "John Eliot" of the Cape; d. Yarmouth, May 3, 1676.

JOSEPH MEACHAM, A.M., b. Enfield, Ct., 1685, son of Isaac Meacham; H. C., 1710, A.B., A.M.; Ord. South Coventry, Ct., Oct. 1714; sett. South Coventry, Ct., 1714-1752; d. South Coventry, Ct., Dec. 16, 1752, a. 67.

ABRAHAM MEAD, A.B., b. Greenwich, Ct., June 15, 1721, son of Ebenezer and Hannah Mead; Y. C., 1739, A.B.; licensed to preach, Feb. 3, 1741/2; not ordained; d. East Hampton, L. I., N. Y., 1743, a. 22.

JAMES MEAD, teacher at Freetown, 1744; Ord. Middleborough, (New Light Chh.), Oct. 3, 1751; sett. Middleborough, 1751-1756; d. Middleborough, Oct. 2, 1756.

JAMES MELLEN, b. Framingham, Mar. 10, 1732/3, son of James and Abigail (Sanderson) Mellen; Ord. Wales, Sept. 11, 1765; sett. Wales, 1765-1769; Bapt.; d. Wales, Aug. 5, 1769.

JOHN MELLEN, A.M., b. Hopkinton, Mar. 14, 1722/3, son of Henry and Abigail Mellen; H. C., 1741, A.B., A.M.; Ord. Sterling, Dec. 19, 1744; sett. Sterling, 1744-1774; dism. Nov. 14, 1774; minister of the chh. which met at his home, 1774-1784; inst. Hanover, Feb. 11, 1784; sett. Hanover, 1784-1805; Convention Sermon, 1781; Arminian in theology; d. Reading, July 4, 1807, a. 85 .

BURRAGE MERRIAM, A.M., b. Wallingford, Ct., Oct. 27, 1739, son of John and Mary (Burrage) Merriam; Y. C., 1762, A.B., A.M.; Ord. Rocky Hill, Ct., (Stepney Parish), Feb. 27, 1765; sett.

Rocky Hill, Ct., 1765-1776; d. Stepney Parish, Rocky Hill, Ct., Nov. 30, 1776, a. 37.

JONAS MERRIAM, A.M., b. Lexington, Dec. 1730, son of Jonas and Abigail (Locke) Merriam; H. C., 1753, A.B.; A.M., 1757; Ord. Newton, Mar. 22, 1758; sett. Newton, 1757-1780; d. Newton, Aug. 13, 1780, a. 50.

MATTHEW MERRIAM, A.M., b. Wallingford, Ct., Jan. 25, 1738/9, son of Nathaniel and Elizabeth Merriam; Y. C., 1759, A.B., A.M.; A.M., (Hon.), H. C., 1765; Ord. Berwick, Me., (North or 2nd Parish), Sept. 25, 1765; sett. Berwick, Me., 1765-1797; d. Berwick, Me., Jan. 19, 1797, a. 58.

JONATHAN MERRICK, A.M., b. Springfield, Aug. 13, 1700, son of John and Mary (Day) Merrick; Y. C., 1725, A.B., A.M.; Fellow, Y. C., 1763-1769; Ord. North Branford, Ct., (2nd Chh. in Branford), 1729; sett. North Branford, Ct., 1727-1772; d. North Branford, Ct., June 27, 1772, a. 72.

NOAH MERRICK, A.M., b. West Springfield, Aug. 6, 1711, son of James and Sarah (Hitchcock) Merrick; Y. C., 1731, A.B., A.M.; Ord. Wilbraham, June 10, 1741; sett. Wilbraham, 1741-1776; d. Wilbraham, Dec. 22, 1776, a. 65.

GYLES MERRILL. A.M., b. Salisbury, Mar. 12, 1738/9, son of Dea. Moses, Jr. and Sarah (True) Merrill; H. C., 1759, A.B., A.M.; Ord. Plaistow, N. H., (formerly the 2nd Parish in Haverhill, Mass.), Mar. 6, 1765; sett. Plaistow, N. H., 1765-1801; d. Plaistow, N. H., Apr. 27, 1801, a. 62.

NATHANIEL MERRILL, A.M., b. Newbury, Mar. 1, 1712/3, son of Abel and Abigail (Stevens) Merrill; H. C., 1732, A.B., A.M.; Ord. Nottingham-West, N. H., (Hudson), Nov. 30, 1737, as the first minister; sett. Nottingham-West, N. H., 1737-1796; d. Nottingham-West, N. H., 1796, a. 83.

NATHANIEL MERRILL, A.B., b. Newbury, Mar. 17, 1743, son of Abel Merrill; H. C., 1767, A.B.; Ord. Boscawen, N. H., Oct. 19, 1768; sett. Boscawen, N. H., 1768-1774; became a Presbyterian and was dism. as such, Apr. 1, 1774; inst. Pelham, Mass., 1775; sett. Pelham, (1st Chh.), 1774-1781; Presb.; d. Oct. 1791.

JOHN MERRIMAN, b. Wallingford, Ct., Oct. 16. 1691, son of John and Elizabeth (Peck) Merriman; sett. Wallingford, Ct., (Bapt. Chh. at Southington), 1750-1784; Bapt.; d. Southington, Ct., Feb. 17, 1784.

NOAH MERWIN, A.M., b. Durham, Ct., May 9, 1752, son of Miles and Mary Merwin; Y. C., 1773, A.B., A.M.; Ord. Torrington, Ct., Oct. 30, 1776; sett. Torrington, Ct., 1776-1783; dism. Nov. 26, 1783; inst. Washington, Ct., Mar. 1785; sett. Washington, Ct., 1785-1795; d. Washington, Ct., Apr. 12, 1795, a. 43.

HENRY MESSENGER, A.M., b. Boston, Feb. 28, 1695, son of Thomas and Elizabeth (Mellows) Messenger; H. C., 1717, A.B.,

A.M.; Ord. Wrentham, Dec. 5, 1719; sett. Wrentham, 1719-1750; d. Wrentham, Mar. 30, 1750, a. 55.

JAMES MESSENGER, A.B., b. Wrentham, Dec. 14, 1737, son of Rev. Henry and Esther (Cheever) Messenger; H. C., 1762, A.B.; Ord. Ashford, Ct., Feb. 15, 1769; sett. Ashford, Ct., 1768-1782; d. Ashford, Ct., Jan. 6, 1782.

JOSEPH METCALF, A.M., b. Dedham, Apr. 2, 1682, son of Jonathan and Hannah (Kenrick) Metcalf; H. C., 1703, A.B., A.M.; Ord. Falmouth, 1707; sett. Falmouth, 1707-1723; d. Falmouth, Dec. 24, 1723.

THOMAS MIGHILL, A.M., b. Rowley, Oct. 29, 1639, son of Dea. Thomas and Ellen Mighill; H. C., 1663, A.B., A.M.; taught grammar school at Rowley, 1666-1668; preached at Milton, 1669-1677; Ord. Norwell, (2nd Chh. in Scituate), Oct. 15, 1684; sett. Norwell, 1680-1689; d. Norwell, Aug. 26, 1689, a. 49.

WILLIAM MILBURNE, lay minister at Saco, Me., 1685-1688; d. (prob.) Boston, Aug. 1699.

NATHANIEL MILLARD, (or Millerd), b. Rehoboth, Mar. 31, 1672, son of Robert and Elizabeth (Sabin) Millard; Ord. Rehoboth, (1st Bapt. Chh.), June 24, 1736; sett. Rehoboth, 1736-1741; Bapt.; d. Rehoboth, Mar. 16, 1740/1.

ALEXANDER MILLER, b. Ireland, 1711; came to N. E., 1719; Ord. Voluntown, Ct., (Separatist Chh.), Apr. 17, 1751; this Chh. united with the Plainfield Separatist Chh., 1758; sett. Voluntown and Plainfield, Ct., 1751-1798; d. Plainfield, Ct., Aug. 20, 1798, a. 87.

EBENEZER MILLER, D.D., b. Milton, June 20, 1703, son of Samuel and Rebecca (Belcher) Miller; H. C., 1722, A.B., A.M.; A.M., (Hon.), Oxford U., 1727; S.T.D., Oxford U., 1747; Ord. in England, 1727; inst. Quincy, (Christ Chh. in Braintree), Dec. 25, 1727; sett. Quincy, 1727-1763; preached at Canton, 1755-1763; Epis.; d. Quincy, Feb. 11, 1763.

JOHN MILLER, A.B., bapt. Ashford, Kent, England, Oct. 21, 1604, son of Martin and Lydia Miller; Gonville & Caius Coll., Camb., A.B., 1627/8; came to N. E., 1634; Ruling Elder, First Chh. in Roxbury, 1637-1639; sett. Rowley, (asst. min.), 1639-1641; sett. Yarmouth, 1647-1662; sett. Groton, 1662-1663, as the first minister; d. Groton, June 12, 1663.

JOHN MILLER, A.M., b. Milton, son of Samuel, Jr. and Rebecca (Minot) Miller; H. C., 1752, A.B., A.M.; Ord. Brunswick. Me., (1st Parish), Nov. 3, 1762; sett. Brunswick, Me., 1761-1788; d. Boston, Jan. 25, 1789.

THOMAS MILLET, b. Chertsey, England, 1605, son of Henry and Joice (Chapman) Myllet; came from Southwark, England, to Dorchester, in the "Elizabeth," 1635; freeman, 1637; resided at Dorchester; sett. Gloucester, (as successor to Rev. William Perkins), 1655-

1659; prob. not ordained; selectman at Gloucester, 1668; preacher at Brookfield, 1675-1676; d. 1675/6.

BENJAMIN MILLS, A.M., b. Thompson, Ct., Oct. 18, 1739, son of Josiah and Sarah (Davis) Mills; Y. C., 1762, A.B., A.M.; Ord. Chesterfield, Nov. 22, 1764; sett. Chesterfield, 1764-1774; dism. Dec. 21, 1774; Rep. Gen. Ct.; Member Prov. Congress; Chairman, Committee of Safety, 1776-1779; d. Chesterfield, Mar. 14, 1785, a. 46.

EBENEZER MILLS, A.B., b. Windsor, Ct., 1710, son of Peter and Joanna (Porter) Mills; Y. C., 1738, A.B.; Ord. East Granby, Ct., (Turkey Hills Parish in Windsor), 1742; sett. East Granby, Ct., 1742-1755; dism. 1755; became insane and disappeared; d before 1802.

GIDEON MILLS, A.M., b. Windsor, Ct., Aug. 15, 1715, son of Peter, Jr. and Joanna (Porter) Mills; Y. C., 1737, A.B., A.M.; Ord. Simsbury, Ct., Sept. 5, 1744; sett. Simsbury, Ct., 1744-1754; resigned Aug. 1754; inst. West Simsbury, Ct., (now Canton), Feb. 18, 1761; sett. West Simsbury, Ct., 1761-1772; d. West Simsbury, Ct., Aug. 4, 1772, a. 57.

JEDEDIAH MILLS, A.M., b. Windsor, Ct., Mar. 23, 1697, son of Peter, Jr. and Joanna (Porter) Mills; Y. C., 1722, A.B., A.M.; Ord. Huntington, (Ripton), Ct., Feb. 12, 1723/4; sett. Huntington, Ct., 1723-1776; d. Huntington, Ct., Jan. 19, 1776, a. 79.

JONATHAN MILLS, A.M., b. Braintree, Mar. 2, 1702/3, son of Capt. John and Hannah Mills; H. C., 1723, A.B., A.M.; Ord. Bellingham, Feb. 22, 1727; sett. Bellingham, 1727-1737; inst. Harwich, (South Chh.), 1765; sett. Harwich, 1765-1773; d. Harwich, May 21, 1773, a. 70.

SAMUEL JOHN MILLS, A.M., b. Kent, Ct., May 16, 1743, son of John and Jane (Lewis) Mills; Y. C., 1764, A.B., A.M.; Ord. Torrington, Ct., June 28, 1769; sett. Torrington, Ct., 1769-1833; d. Torrington, Ct., May 11, 1833, a. 90.

DANIEL MINER, sett. Grassy Hill, Lyme, Ct., (Separatist Chh.), 1757-1799; d. Lyme, Ct., Apr. 1, 1799.

JEHU MINOR, A.M., b. Woodbury, Ct., June 9, 1743, son of Dea. John and Mary (Judson) Minor; Y. C., 1767, A.B., A.M.; Ord. South Britain, Ct., (Southbury), May 24, 1769, as first minister; sett. South Britain, Ct., 1768-1790; dism. June 1, 1790; inst. South East, N. Y., (Presb. Chh.), Feb. 1, 1792; sett. South East, N. Y., 1791-1808; d. South East, N. Y., July 5, 1808, a. 65.

RICHARDSON MINOR, A.M., bapt. Stonington, Ct., Feb. 25, 1704/5, son of Elnathan and Rebecca Minor; Y. C., 1726, A.B., A.M.; Ord. Trumbull, Ct., (North Stratford Cong. Chh.), Nov. 18, 1730; sett. Trumbull, Ct., 1730-1744; dism. Feb. 21, 1744; became Epis., 1742; d. Salisbury, Eng., 1744, a. 40.

THOMAS MINER, A.M., bapt. Woodbury, Ct., June 25, 1738, son of Thomas and Feda Miner; Y. C., 1769, A.B., A.M.; Ord. Middletown, Ct., (Westfield Society or Little River Parish), Dec. 29,

1773, as the first minister; sett. Middletown, Ct., 1773-1826; d. Middletown, Ct., Apr. 28, 1826, a. 88.

JAMES MINOT, A.M., b. Dorchester, Sept. 14, 1653, son of Capt. John and Lydia (Butler) Minot; H. C., 1675, A.B., A.M.; school-teacher at Dorchester, 1675-1680; sett. Concord, 1681; sett. Stow, 1685-1687; preacher; teacher; physician; J. P.; Capt.; d. Concord, Sept. 20, 1735, a. 83.

DANIEL MITCHELL, A.M., b. North of Ireland, 1707; King James' Coll., U. of Edinburgh, A.M., Feb. 6, 1730; licensed by the Boston Presbytery, 1746; preached at Georgetown, Me., 1747-1748; Ord. Pembroke, N. H., (2nd Chh.), Dec. 3, 1760; sett. Pembroke, N. H., 1760-1776; Presb.; d. Pembroke, N. H., Dec. 16, 1776, a. 69.

EDWARD MITCHELL, b. R. I., 1697; Ord. Smithfield, R. I., 1733; sett. Gloucester, R. I., 1733-1795; Bapt.; d. Gloucester, R. I., Oct. 22, 1795, a. 98.

JONATHAN MITCHELL, A.M., b. Halifax, Yorkshire, England, 1624, son of Matthew and Susan Mitchell; came to Boston, 1635; H. C., 1647, A.B., A.M.; Tutor and Fellow, H. C., 1650-1668; Ord. Cambridge, Aug. 21, 1650; sett. Cambridge, 1650-1668; Election Sermons, 1658, 1667; was called the "matchless Mitchell;" d. Cambridge, July 9, 1668, a. 44.

STEPHEN MIX, A.M., b. New Haven, Ct., Nov. 1, 1672, son of Thomas and Rebecca (Turner) Mix; H. C., 1690, A.B., A.M.; Ord. Wethersfield, Ct., 1694; sett. Wethersfield, Ct., 1694-1738; Ct. Election Sermon, 1735; d. Wethersfield, Ct., Aug. 28, 1738.

AMOS MOODY, A.M., b. Newbury, Nov. 10, 1739, son of John and Hannah (Toppan) Moody; H. C., 1759, A.B., A.M.; Ord. Pelham, N. H., Nov. 20, 1765; sett. Pelham, N. H., 1765-1792; dism. Oct. 24, 1792; Rep. Gen. Ct., N. H., 1793; Magistrate; d. Pelham, N. H., Mar. 22, 1819.

JOHN MOODY, A.M., b. Newbury, prob. Jan. 10, 1705, son of Thomas and Judith (Hale) Moody; H. C., 1727, A.B., A.M.; Ord. Newmarket, N. H., Nov. 25, 1730, as the first minister; sett. Newmarket, N. H., 1730-1778; d. Newmarket, N. H., Oct. 15, 1778, a. 73.

JOSEPH MOODY, A.M., b. York, Me., 1700, son of Rev. Samuel and Hannah (Sewall) Moody; H. C., 1718, A.B., A.M.; Ord. Scotland, Me., (2nd Parish in York), Nov. 29, 1732; sett. Scotland, Me., 1732-1741; dism. Aug. 1741; Town Clerk; County Registrar of Deeds; Judge of Common Pleas, before he was ordained; d. Scotland, Me., Mar. 20, 1753, a. 53.

JOSHUA MOODY, A.M., b. Ipswich, Suffolk, England, 1633, son of William Moodey; came to Ipswich, 1634; H. C., 1653, A.B., A.M.; Fellow, H. C., 1656-1658; Ord. Portsmouth, N. H., July 12, 1671; sett. Portsmouth, N. H., 1658-1684; inst. Boston, (1st Chh.), as asst. min., May 3, 1684; sett. Boston, 1684-1693; sett. Portsmouth, N. H., 1693-1697; chosen President of H. C., 1684, but declined; 4,070 of his ms. sermons are preserved at the Mass. Hist. Soc.; Artillery Election Sermons, 1674, 1685; Election Sermons, 1675, 1692; d. Boston, July 4, 1697, a. 65.

JOSHUA MOODY, A.M., b. Salisbury, Oct. 30, 1686, son of Daniel and Elizabeth Moody; H. C., 1707, A.B., A.M.; sett. Gosport, Isles of Shoals, N. H., 1707-1732; d. Newburyport, Apr. 19, 1768, a. 81.

SAMUEL MOODY, A.M., b. Portsmouth, N. H., ca. 1669, son of Rev. Joshua and Mary (Collins) Moody; H. C., 1689, A.B., A.M.; sett. Hadley, 1693-1694; sett. Newcastle, N. H., 1694-1703; sett. Gosport, Isles of Shoals, N. H., ca. 1698; sett. Portsmouth, N. H., 1716; Justice of the Peace; Justice, Court of Common Pleas, York County, Me.; Major; d. Portland, Me., Apr. 5, 1729, a. ca. 60.

SAMUEL MOODY, A.M., b. Newbury, Jan. 4, 1675/6, son of Sergt. Caleb and Judith (Bradbury) Moody; H. C., 1697, A.B., A.M.; Ord. York, Me., Dec. 20, 1700; sett. York, Me., 1698-1747; Chaplain, at Louisburg, 1745; Election Sermon, 1721; d. York, Me., Nov. 13, 1747, a. 72.

SILAS MOODY, A.M., b. Newbury, Apr. 28, 1742, son of William and Anna (Hale) Moody; H. C., 1761, A.B., A.M.; Ord. Kennebunkport, Me., (Arundel), Jan. 9, 1771; sett. Kennebunkport, Me., 1771-1816; d. Kennebunkport, Me., Apr. 7, 1816.

JONATHAN MOORE, A.M., b. Oxford, July 7, 1739, son of Capt. Elijah and Dorothy (Learned) Moore; H. C., 1761, A.B., A.M.; A.M., (Hon.), Y. C., 1765; Librarian, H. C., 1767-1768; teacher of Greek and Hebrew, H. C., 1761-1763; Ord. Rochester, (Marion), Sept. 7, 1768; sett. Rochester, 1768-1792; dism. because of his liberal theological views, 1792; d. Rochester, (Marion), Apr. 20, 1814, a. 75.

SOLOMON MOOR, A.B., b. Newtown, Limavady, Ireland, 1736; U. of Glasgow, 1758, A.B.; licensed to preach, July 26, 1762; Ord. 1766; came to Halifax, N. S., 1766; inst. New Boston, N. H., Sept. 6, 1768; sett. New Boston, N. H., 1767-1803; Presb.; d. New Boston, N. H., May 28, 1803, a. 67.

THOMAS MOORE, A.M., b. Bolton, June 21, 1745, son of Abraham and Silence (Nichols) Moore; H. C., 1769, A.B., A.M.; Ord. Wiscasset, Me., Aug. 4, 1773; sett. Wiscasset, (Pownalborough, East Parish), 1773-1791; dism. Aug. 4, 1791; d. Wiscasset, Me., 1796.

JOHN MOOREHEAD, b. Newton, near Belfast, Ireland, ca. 1703; U. of Edinburgh; inst. Boston, (Arlington St. Chh.), Mar. 31, 1730, as the first minister; sett. Boston, 1730-1773; his portrait hangs in the Arlington St. Chh.; Presb.; d. Boston, Dec. 2, 1773, a. 70.

JOSEPH MORGAN, A.M., b. Preston, Ct., Nov. 6, 1671, son of Lieut. Joseph and Dorothy (Parke) Morgan; Y. C., 1702, A.B.; A.M., (Hon.), 1720; sett. Greenwich, Ct., 1697-1700; sett. Bedford, N. Y., 1700-1702; sett. East Chester, N. Y., 1702-1704; sett. Greenwich, Ct., (2nd Chh. at Horseneck), 1705-1708; dism. Oct. 17, 1708; sett. Freehold, N. J., 1709-1728; sett. Hopewell, N. J., 1728-1749.

SOLOMON MORGAN, bapt. Groton, Ct., Mar. 24, 1745, son of Dea. Solomon and Mary (Walworth) Morgan; Ord. Voluntown, Ct., (Nazareth Society), Apr. 15, 1772; sett. Voluntown, Ct., 1772-1782; dism. Feb. 26, 1782; inst. Canterbury, Ct., Sept. 30, 1783; sett. Canterbury, Ct., 1783-1797; dism. Mar. 1797; inst. North Canaan, Ct., June 6, 1798; sett. North Canaan, Ct., 1798-1804; d. North Canaan, Ct., Sept. 3, 1804, a. 60.

WILLIAM MORRELL, A.B., Magdalene Coll., Camb., A.B., 1614/5; Ord. by the Bishop of Peterborough, May 24, 1619; was sent out to Massachusetts by the Plymouth Council to superintend the churches established in that Colony, 1623; sett. Weymouth, 1623-1624; came in the Gorges co.; the colony was a failure and broke up in less than a year; Mr. Morrell went to Plymouth where he remained about a year and then returned to England, 1624; published a narrative of his observations, in Latin hexameters and English verse, London, 1625; Anglican.

ISAAC MORRILL, JR., A.M., b. Salisbury, May 20, 1718, son of Isaac and Abigail (Browne) Morrill; H. C., 1737, A.B., A.M.; Ord. Wilmington, May 20, 1741; sett. Wilmington, 1741-1793; Chaplain, French and Indian Wars; Dudleian Lecture, 1776; Convention Sermon, 1778; d. Wilmington, Aug. 17, 1793, a. 75.

MOSES MORRILL, A.M., b. Salisbury, May 1, 1719, son of John and Mary (Stevens) Morrill; H. C., 1737, A.B., A.M.; Ord. Biddeford, Me., Sept. 29, 1742; sett. Biddeford, Me., 1742-1778; d. Biddeford, Me., Feb. 9, 1778, a. 58.

NATHANIEL MORRILL, A.M., b. Salisbury, July 20, 1701, son of Isaac and Abigail (Browne) Morrill; H. C., 1723, A.B., A.M.; Ord. Rye, N. H., Sept. 14, 1726, as the first minister; sett. Rye, N. H., 1726-1734; d. before June 13, 1738.

ROBIE MORRILL, A.M., b. Salisbury, Aug. 28, 1734, son of Abraham and Anna (Clough) Morrill; H. C., 1755, A.B.; A.M., 1759; Ord. Boscawen, N. H., Dec. 29, 1761; sett. Boscawen, N. H., 1761-1766; dism. Dec. 9, 1766; d. Boscawen, N. H., Sept. 23, 1813, a. 79.

SAMUEL MORRILL, A.M., b. Wilmington, Apr. 21, 1744, son of Rev. Isaac Morrill; H. C., 1766, A.B., A.M.; sett. Epping, N. H.; d. Epping, N. H., Sept. 21, 1785.

THEOPHILUS MORRIS, A.B., b. Galway, Ireland, 1705, son of Francis Morris; adm. pensioner, Trinity Coll., Dublin, June 28, 1722, a. 17 yrs.; Trinity Coll., Dublin, 1729, A.B.; inst. West Haven, Ct., Sept. 13, 1740, as missionary for the V.S.P.G.F.P.; sett. West Haven, Ct., 1740-1742; Epis.; returned to England.

JOHN MORRISON, A.B., b. Pathfoot, Scotland, May 22, 1743; U. of Edinburgh, A.B., 1765; arrived at Boston, May 1765;

Ord. Peterborough, N. H., Nov. 26, 1766; sett. Peterborough, N. H., 1766-1772; left Mar. 1772; joined the British army at Boston, 1775; d. Charleston, S. C., Dec. 10, 1782, a. 39.

EBENEZER MORSE, A.M., b. Medfield, Mar. 2, 1718, son of Hon. Joshua and Mary (Partridge) Morse; H. C., 1737, A.B., A.M.; Ord. Boylston, Oct. 26, 1743; sett. Boylston, 1743-1775; dism. Nov. 10, 1775; lawyer and physician; d. Boylston, Nov. 10, 1802, a. 84.

JOHN MORSE, A.M., b. Cambridge; H. C., 1751, A.B., A.M.; Ord. Berwick, Me., (North or 2nd Parish), Apr. 30, 1755; sett. Berwick, Me., 1755-1764; d. Berwick, Me., Nov. 1764.

JOSEPH MORSE, A.M., b. Medfield, May 25, 1671, son of Joseph and Priscilla (Colburn) Morse; H. C., 1695, A.B., A.M.; sett. Weston, 1701-1706; Ord. Canton, Oct. 13, 1717; sett. Canton, 1707-1727; dism. 1726/7; d. Canton, Nov. 29, 1732, a. 61.

JOSHUA MORSE, b. South Kingston, R. I., Apr. 10, 1726; Ord. New London, Ct., (North Bapt. or Montville Parish), May 17, 1751; sett. New London, Ct., (Montville), 1750-1776; removed to Sandisfield, 1779; sett. Sandisfield, 1779-1795; Bapt.; d. Sandisfield, 1795, a. 70.

CHARLES MORTON, A.M., bapt. Pendavy, Cornwall, England, Feb. 15, 1626/7, son of Rev. Nicholas and Elizabeth (Kestle) Morton, of St. Mary Overy's, Southwark; Wadham Coll., Oxford, A.B., 1649; A.M., 1652; Fellow; rector at Blisland, Cornwall, 1656-1662; was suspended for non-conformity, 1662; teacher at Newington Green, Middlesex for 20 years; came to N. E., July 1686; inst. Charlestown, Nov. 5, 1686; sett. Charlestown, 1686-1698; Vice-President, H. C., 1697-1698; d. Charlestown, Apr. 11, 1698, a. 72, s. p.

JAMES MORTON, b. Ireland, 1714; Ord. Blandford, Aug. 1747; sett. Blandford, 1747-1767; dism. June 2, 1767; Presb.; d. Blandford, Oct. 1, 1793, a. 79.

EBENEZER MOSELEY, A.M., b. Hampton, Ct., Feb. 19, 1740/1, son of Rev. Samuel and Bethia (Otis) Moseley; Y. C., 1763, A.B.; A.M., 1768; licensed to preach, June 19, 1765; sett. Brookfield, 1765-1767; Ord. Sept. 1767, as an Indian missionary for the Society of the Propagation of the Gospel in New England and Parts Adjacent; Indian missionary, 1767-1772; at Onohoquaga on the Susquehanna near Binghampton, N. Y.; farmer; member, Committee of Correspondence, 1774; Capt., Am. Rev., 1775-1777; Col., 1791; Rep. Gen. Ct., 1776, 1778, 1783, 1785, 1788-1806, for 20 sessions; deacon, 1788; town clerk, 1797, and many years; d. Hampton, Ct., Mar. 20, 1825, a. 84.

RICHARD MOSELEY, Anglican Chaplain, man-of-war "Salisbury;" sett. Brooklyn, Ct., (Epis. Chh.), 1771-1772; Epis.

SAMUEL MOSELEY, A.M., b. Dorchester, Aug. 15, 1708, son of Ebenezer and Hannah (Weeks) Moseley; H. C., 1729, A.B., A.M.; Ord. Hampton, Ct., (2nd Chh. in Windham), May 15, 1734; sett. Hampton, Ct., 1734-1791; d. Hampton, Ct., July 26, 1791, a. 83.

HUGH MOSHER, b. England, 1633, son of Hugh Mosher; came to N. E., 1636; sett. at Salem; Ensign in the militia, 1669; received a grant of one-fifth of the town of Westerly, R. I., 1676; resided at Newport, R. I., 1660-1668, and at Portsmouth, R. I., 1668-1684; Ord. Tiverton, R. I., (Bapt. Chh. of Tiverton, Little Compton and Dartmouth), 1684; sett. Tiverton, R. I., (Bapt. Chh.), 1684-1694; Bapt.; d. Newport, R. I., 1694.

JOSEPH MOSS., A.M., b. New Haven, Ct., Apr. 7, 1679, son of Joseph and Mary (Alling) Moss; H. C., 1699, A.B.; A.M., Y. C., 1702; Trustee, Y. C., 1730-1732; called to Derby, Ct., Feb. 24, 1706/7; sett. Derby, Ct., 1706-1732; Ct. Election Sermon, 1715; d. Derby, Ct., Jan. 27, 1731/2.

DAVID MOSSOM, b. Greenwich, Kent, England, Mar. 25, 1690, son of Thomas Mossom; matriculated St. John's Coll., Camb., 1705; admitted sizar, St. John's Coll., Camb., June 5, 1705; Ord. London, Eng., June 8, 1718; sett. as Rector at Marblehead, (St. Michael's Chh.), 1718-1727; Rector, St. Peter's Parish, New Kent, Va., 1727-1767; performed the marriage service of George and Martha (Custis) Washington; Epis.; d. St. Peter's Parish, New Kent Co., Va., Jan. 4, 1767, a. 77.

EBENEZER MOULTON, b. Windham, Ct., Dec. 25, 1709, son of Robert and Hannah (Groves) Moulton; Ord. Wales, Nov. 4, 1736; sett. Wales, 1736-1763; sett. Nova Scotia, 1763-1778; Bapt.; d. Wales, 1783.

GEORGE MOXON, A.B., bapt. Wakefield, Yorkshire, England, Apr. 28, 1602, son of James Moxon; Sidney Sussex Coll., Camb., A.B., 1623/4; Ord. as an Anglican clergyman in England, 1626; sett. St. Helen's, Chester, England; cited for non-conformity, 1637; fled to N. E., 1637; sett. Springfield, (1st Chh.), 1637-1651, as the first minsiter; returned to England, 1651, with William Pynchon, Esq.; minister at Newbold-Ashbury, Cheshire, 1653-1661; also at Rushton Spencer, Staffordshire; non-conformist preacher at Congleton, 1667-1687; d. England, Sept. 15, 1687, a. 85.

GEORGE MUIRSON, b. Scotland; Ord. by the Bishop of London, 1705; missionary of the V.S.P.G.F.P. at Greenwich, Ct. and Rye, N. Y., 1705-1707; sett. Stratford, Ct., (Epis. Chh.), 1706-1707; organized the Epis. Chh. at Stratford, Ct., Apr. 1707; Epis.; d. Rye, N. Y., Oct. 12, 1708.

AMOS MUNSON, A.B., b. New Haven, Ct., Apr. 9, 1719, son of Stephen and Lydia (Bassett) Munson; Y. C., 1738, A.B.; licensed to preach, Sept. 30, 1740; sett. Washington, Ct., 1741; never ordained; an original member of the Separatist Chh. at New Haven, Ct., May 1742; d. 1748, a. 29.

SAMUEL MUNSON, A.M., b. New Haven, Ct., Aug. 31, 1745, son of Capt. Samuel and Abigail (Hollinsworth) Munson; Y. C., 1763, A.B., A.M.; Ord. Lenox, Nov. 8, 1770; sett. Lenox, 1770-1792; d. Monroe, Ct., May 14, 1814, a. 69.

STEPHEN MUNSON, A.M., b. New Haven, Ct., Nov. 15, 1704, son of Stephen and Lydia (Bassett) Munson; Y. C., 1725, A.B., A.M.; Ord. Greenwich, Ct., (West or 2nd or Horseneck Chh.), May 29, 1728; sett. Greenwich, Ct., 1728-1730; d. Greenwich, Ct., May 1730, a. 25.

JONATHAN MURDOCK, A.M., b. Westbrook, Ct., Apr. 7, 1745, son of John and Frances (Conkling) Murdock; Y. C., 1766, A.B., A.M.; Ord. Rye, N. Y., 1771; inst. Greenwich, Ct., (2nd Chh.), Oct. 20, 1774; sett. Greenwich, Ct., 1774-1785; dism. Mar. 2, 1785; inst. Bozrah, Ct., Oct. 12, 1786; sett. Bozrah, Ct., 1786-1813; d. Bozrah, Ct., Jan. 17, 1813, a. 68.

JOHN MURRAY, b. Alton, Hampshire, England, Dec. 10, 1741; came to America, 1770; preached at Potter's Farm, N. J., 1770-1772; itinerant preacher in N. E., 1772-1774; Chaplain to R. I. regiments, 1775-1777; Ord. Gloucester, Jan. 1779; re-ord. Dec. 25, 1788; sett. Gloucester, (Universalist Chh.), 1779-1793; inst. Boston, (1st Universalist Chh.), Oct. 23, 1793; sett. Boston, 1793-1809; Universalist; d. Boston, Sept. 3, 1815.

JOHN MURRAY, A.M., b. Antrim, Ireland, May 22, 1742; U. of Edinburgh, 1761, A.B., A.M.; arrived in N. E., 1763; sett. Boothbay, Me., 1763; Ord. Philadelphia, Pa., (2nd Presb. Chh.), May 1765; sett. Philadelphia, Pa., 1765-1766; sett. Boothbay, Me., 1766-1779; removed to Newburyport, 1779; dism. from Boothbay, Me., June 1781; inst. Newburyport, June 4, 1781; sett. Newburyport, (1st Presb. Chh.), 1781-1793; delegate from Boothbay, Me., to the Provincial Congress., 1775; Presb.; d. Newburyport, Mar. 13, 1793, a. 51.

JOHN MYLES, b. Newton, Herefordshire, England, ca. 1621, son of Walter Myles; matriculated at Brazenose Coll., Oxford, Mar. 18, 1635/6, aged 15 years; formed a Baptist Chh. at Ilston, near Swanzey, Wales, Oct. 1, 1649; formed an association of Welsh Bapt. Chhs.; delegate of these churches to a meeting of Bapt. ministers at London, 1651; ejected by the Act of Conformity, 1662; came to N. E. with part of his congregation, 1662; organized a Bapt. Chh. at Rehoboth, 1663; removed to Wannamoisett, (Swansea), Oct. 30, 1667; sett. Swansea, 1663-1675, as the first minister and school master; sett. Boston, (1st Bapt. Chh.), 1675-1679; sett. Swansea, 1680-1683; Bapt.; d. Swansea, Feb. 3, 1683.

SAMUEL MYLES, A.M., son of Rev. John and Ann (Humphrey) Myles; H. C., 1684, A.B., A.M.; A.M., U. of Oxford, 1693; inst. Boston, (Rector of King's Chapel), June 29, 1689; sett. Boston, 1689-1728; laid cornerstone of Christ Chh., Boston, 1723; Epis.; d. Boston, Mar. 4, 1728/9.

JUDAH NASH, A.M., b. Longmeadow, Dec. 31, 1728, son of Timothy and Prudence (Smith) Nash; Y. C., 1748, A.B.; A.M., 1752; Ord. Montague, Nov. 22, 1752; sett. Montague, 1752-1805; d. Montague, Feb. 19, 1805, a. 77.

SAMUEL NASH, A.M., b. Abington, Aug. 4, 1744, son of Samuel and Abigail (Hersey) Nash; Brown U., 1770, A.B., A.M.; Ord. Gray, Me., June 21, 1775; sett. Gray, Me., 1774-1782; dism. 1782; d. Gray, Me., Feb. 1, 1821.

WILLIAM NELSON, A.M., b. Middleborough, July 18, 1741; Brown U., A.M., (Hon.), 1771; Ord. Taunton, (1st Bapt. Chh.), Nov. 12, 1772; sett. Taunton, 1772-1786; Bapt.; d. Taunton, 1806.

ROBERT NESBIT, sett. Becket, (2nd Bapt. Chh.), 1764; Bapt.

ABEL NEWELL, A.M., b. Farmington, Ct., Aug. 15, 1730, son of Dea. Nathaniel and Esther (Hart) Newell; Y. C., 1751, A.B., A.M.; Ord. Goshen, Ct., Aug. 26, 1754; sett. Goshen, Ct., 1754-1781; dism. Feb. 2, 1781; Rep. Gen. Assembly, 1781-1782; d. Charlotte, Vt., Jan. 22, 1813, a. 83.

DANIEL NEWELL, A.M., b. Farmington, Ct., Apr. 18, 1700, son of Ensign Samuel and Mary (Hart) Newell; Y. C., 1718, A.B., A.M.; Ord. Chatham, Ct., (3rd Chh. in Middletown at Portland), Oct. 25, 1721; sett. Chatham, Ct., 1721-1731; d. Chatham, Ct., Sept. 14, 1731, a. 31.

JONATHAN NEWELL, A.M., b. Needham, Dec. 15, 1749, son of Dea. Josiah Newell; H. C., 1770, A.B., A.M.; Ord. Stow, Oct. 11, 1774; sett. Stow, 1774-1830; d. Stow, Oct. 4, 1830.

SAMUEL NEWELL, A.M., b. Southington, Ct., Mar. 1, 1714, son of Samuel and Sarah (Norton) Newell; Y. C., 1739, A.B., A.M.; Ord. Bristol, Ct., (4th Chh. in Farmington), Aug. 12, 1747, as the first minister; sett. Bristol, Ct., 1747-1789; d. Bristol, Ct., Feb. 10, 1789, a. 75.

ANTIPAS NEWMAN, b. England, Oct. 15, 1627, son of Rev. Samuel and Sybil (Featley) Newman; Ord. Wenham, Dec. 10, 1663; sett. Wenham, 1657-1672; d. Wenham, Oct. 15, 1672.

JOHN NEWMAN, A.M., b. Gloucester, Mar. 14, 1716, son of John and Mary (Marshall) Newman; H. C., 1740, A.B., A.M.; Ord. Edgartown, July 29, 1747; sett. Edgartown, 1747-1758; dism. 1758; Justice, Court of Common Pleas, 1761; Col. in the militia; d. Edgartown, Dec. 1, 1763, a. 47.

NOAH NEWMAN, b. England, Jan. 10, 1631, son of Rev. Samuel and Sybil (Featley) Newman; Ord. Rehoboth, Mar. 1668; sett. Rehoboth, 1668-1676; d. Rehoboth, Apr. 16, 1676.

SAMUEL NEWMAN, A.B., b. Banbury, Oxfordshire, England, May 10, 1602, son of Richard Newman; matriculated Magdalen Coll., Oxford, Mar. 3, 1619/20; A.B., St. Edmund's Hall, Oxford, Oct. 17, 1620; Rector at Midhope, Ecclesfield, West Riding, Yorkshire, England, 1625-1635; came to N. E., 1635; inst. Weymouth, Jan. 30, 1638/9, as the first minister; sett. Weymouth, 1639-1643; Ord. Rehoboth, 1644, as the first minister; sett. Rehoboth, (Seekonk), 1644-1663;

named the town Rehoboth; published a Concordance of the Bible, 1643; d. Seekonk, July 5, 1663, a. 61.

JOHN NEWMARCH, A.M., b. Ipswich, Oct. 8, 1672, son of John and Johanna (Burnham) Newmarch; H. C., 1690, A.B., A.M.; Ord. Kittery, Me., (1st Chh.), Nov. 4, 1714; sett. Kittery, Me., 1694-1751; d. Kittery, Me., Jan. 15, 1754.

CHRISTOPHER NEWTON, A.M., bapt. Milford, Ct., Dec. 2, 1716, son of Ezekiel and Abigail Newton; Y. C., 1740, A.B., A.M.; Ord. London, England, July 27, 1755; sett. Huntington, (Ripton), Ct., (Epis. Chh.), 1753-1787; Epis.; d. Huntington, Ct., Feb. 6, 1787, a. 70.

ROGER NEWTON, b. England, son of Samuel Newton; matric. King's Coll., Camb., Easter, 1636; H. C., 1640, but did not graduate; came to N. E., 1638; studied theology at Hartford, Ct., under Rev. Thomas Hooker; Ord. Farmington, Ct., Oct. 13, 1652, as the first minister; sett. Farmington, Ct., 1652-1657; inst. Milford, Ct., Aug. 22, 1660; sett. Milford, Ct., 1660-1683; d. Milford, Ct., June 7, 1683.

ROGER NEWTON, D.D., b. Durham, Ct., May 12, 1737, son of Abner and Mary (Burwell) Newton; Y. C., 1758, A.B., A.M.; S.T.D., Dart. Coll., 1805; Ord. Greenfield, Nov. 18, 1761; sett. Greenfield, 1761-1816; d. Greenfield, Dec. 10, 1816, a. 80.

ELKANAH NICKERSON, said to have been the first minister of the West Harwich Bapt. Chh., formerly the Separatist Chh. which seceded from the Second Chh. in Harwich, 1763; Bapt.

JOSHUA NICKERSON, Ord. Harwich, (Separatist Chh.), Jan. 23, 1749; sett. Harwich, 1749-1756.

SAMUEL NICKERSON, a New Light preacher; succeeded Rev. Joshua Nickerson at Harwich, 1773; sett. Harwich, 1773-1789; the organization disbanded in 1789.

JAMES NICHOLS, A.B., b. Waterbury, Ct., Dec. 1748, son of James and Anna (Porter) Nichols; Y. C., 1771, A.B.; Ord. in England ca. 1772; sett. Goshen, Ct., Northbury, Ct., and New Cambridge, Ct., (now Plymouth and Bristol), 1774-1778; Rector, St. Michael's Chh., Litchfield, Ct., May 1780-1784; Rector, St. James' Chh., Arlington, Vt., 1786-June 1788; suspended from the Epis. ministry, Sept. 2, 1819; Epis.; d. Stafford, N. Y., June 17, 1829, a. 80.

ROBERT BOUCHER NICHOLS, B.C.L., b. West Indes, 1744, son of Isaac Nichols, of Barbados, Gent.; Queen's Coll., Oxford, A.B., 1766; B.C.L., 1778; sett. Salem, (St. Peter's Chh.), 1771-1774; resigned, Dec. 1774; Chaplain in the British Army; returned to England where he was Dean of Middleham; Epis.

CHARLES NICHOLET, came from Va.; preached at Salem, (1st Chh.), 1671-1672; called by the parish, but the church would not concurr; went to England, 1672.

BENJAMIN NILES, b. Lyme, Ct., ca. 1720, son of Ambrose

and Mary Brockway (Mott) Niles; Bapt. minister at Groton, Ct.; Bapt.; d. Groton, Ct., 1763.

HON. NATHANIEL NILES, A.M., b. South Kingston, R. I., Apr. 4, 1741, son of Samuel and Sarah (Niles) Niles; Princeton, 1766, A.B.; A.M.; A.M., (Hon.), H. C., 1722; A.M., (Hon.), Dart. Coll., 1791; preached in several New England towns before the Revolutionary War, but was not ordained; sett. Norwich, Ct., ca. 1775; member, Ct. legislature, 1779-1781; sett. West Fairlee, Orange Co., Vt., 1782-3; Judge, Supreme Court of Vt., 1784-1788; Member of Congress, 1791-1795; Trustee, Dart. Coll., 1793-1820; member, Mass. Hist. Soc.; inventor, theologian, preacher, politician, business man, poet, physician, lawyer and judge; d. West Fairlee, Vt., Oct. 31, 1828.

SAMUEL NILES, A.M., b. New Shoreham, Block Island, R. I., May 1, 1674, son of Capt. Nathaniel and Sarah (Sandys) Niles; H. C., 1699, A.B.; A.M., 1759; sett. Block Island, R. I., Mar. 1700-1702; sett. Kingston, R. I., 1702-1710, (Indian Chh. at Charlestown); Ord. Braintree, (South or 2nd Parish), May 11, 1711; sett. Braintree, 1711-1762; strong Calvinist; d. Braintree, May 1, 1762, a. 88.

SAMUEL NILES, JR., A.B., b. Braintree, Dec. 3, 1743, son of Samuel and Sarah (Niles) Niles; Princeton, 1769, A.B.; Ord. Abington, Sept. 25, 1771; sett. Abington, 1770-1814; d. Abington, Jan. 16, 1814, a. 70.

THOMAS NILES, A.M., b. Colchester, Ct., Sept. 28, 1738, son of John Niles; Y. C., 1758, A.B.; A.M., 1762; Ord. Rumney, N. H., Oct. 21, 1767; sett. Rumney, N. H., 1767-1771; dism. Aug. 20, 1771; d. Rumney, N. H., May 1782, a. 43.

GIDEON NOBLE, A.M., b. Westfield, Mar. 6, 1727/8, son of Ensign Matthew and Joanna (Stebbins) Noble; Y. C., 1755, A.B., A.M.; Ord. Willington, Ct., Nov. 28, 1759; sett. Willington, Ct., 1759-1790; dism. Nov. 1790; d. Willington, Ct., Nov. 13, 1792, a. 65.

OBADIAH NOBLE, A.M., b. Sheffield, Sept. 20, 1739; Princeton, 1763, A.B., A.M.; A.M., (Hon.), Dart. Coll., 1773; Ord. Orford, N. H., Nov. 5, 1771; sett. Orford, N. H., 1771-1777; dism. Dec. 31, 1777; d. Vt., Feb. 19, 1829, a. 90.

OLIVER NOBLE, A.M., b. Hebron, Ct., Mar. 3, 1733/4, son of David and Abigail (Loomis) Noble; Y. C., 1757, A.B., A.M.; Ord. South Coventry, Ct., Jan. 10, 1759; sett. South Coventry, Ct., 1759-1761; dism. June 10, 1761; inst. Newburyport, (5th Parish), Sept. 1, 1762, as the first and only minister of this parish; sett. Newburyport, 1762-1784; dism. Apr. 7, 1784; inst. Newcastle, N. H., Aug. 18, 1784; sett. Newcastle, N. H., 1784-1792; d. Newcastle, N. H., Dec. 15, 1792.

NATHANIEL NORCROSS, A.B., b. England, 1618, son of Jeremiah and Adrean Norcross of Watertown; St. Catherine's Hall, Camb., A.B., 1636/7; came to N. E., with his father, 1638; joined chh. at Salem; chosen minister of the Nashaway plantation, (Lancaster),

1644, but returned to England, 1649/50; Vicar of Walsingham, Norfolk, ca. 1651; ejected 1660; Vicar of St. Mary, Dover, 1653; d. St. Dunstan-in-the-East, London, England, Aug. 10, 1662.

EDWARD NORRIS, A.M., b. Gloucestershire, England, ca. 1584, son of Rev. Edward Norris, Vicar of Tetbury, Gloucestershire; matriculated, Balliol Coll., Oxford, Mar. 30, 1599, a. 15; Magdalen Hall, Oxford, A.B., 1606/7; A.M., 1609; Rector of Anmer, Norfolk, 1624; Ord. Salem, (1st Chh.), Mar. 18, 1639/40; sett. Salem, 1640-1659; Election Sermon, 1646; d. Salem, Dec. 23, 1659, a. 75.

JOHN NORTON, A.M., b. Bishop's Stortford, Hertfordshire, England, May 6, 1606, son of William and Alice (Browest) Norton; Peterhouse, Cambridge, A. B., 1623/4; A.M., 1627; Curate at Bishop's Stortford; Chaplain to Sir William Masham at High Lever, Essex; came to N. E., Oct. 1635; Ord. Ipswich, (1st Chh.), Feb. 20, 1638; sett. Ipswich, 1636-1653; inst. Boston, (1st Chh.), July 23, 1656; sett. Boston, 1653-1663; Election Sermons, 1645, 1657, 1661; Artillery Election Sermon, 1659; active in drawing up "The Platform of Church Discipline," 1646; chief instigator of the persecution of the Quakers in N. E.; Overseer, H. C.; Envoy to England, 1662; d. Boston, Apr. 5, 1663, a. 57.

JOHN NORTON, A.M., b. Ipswich, ca. 1650, son of William and Lucy (Downing) Norton; H. C., 1671, A.B.; A.M., 1716; Ord. Hingham, Nov. 27, 1678; sett. Hingham, 1678-1716; Election Sermon, 1708; d. Hingham, Oct. 3, 1716, a. 65.

JOHN NORTON, A.M., b. Berlin, Ct., Nov. 16, 1715, son of John and Ann (Thompson) Norton; Y. C., 1737, A.B., A.M.; Ord. Deerfield, Nov. 25, 1741, for the chh. at Bernardston; sett. Bernardston, 1741-1745; inst. Chatham, Ct., (5th Chh. in Middletown at East Hampton), Nov. 30, 1748; sett. Chatham, Ct., 1748-1778; Chaplain, French and Indian Wars at Adams; was carried captive to Canada; published an account of his captivity, 1748; d. Chatham, Ct., Mar. 24, 1778, a. 63, of small pox.

SETH NORTON, A.M., b. Farmington, Ct., Aug. 10, 1731, son of Thomas and Elizabeth (Mason) Norton; Y. C., 1751, A.B., A.M.; A.M., (Hon.), H. C., 1756; Ord. Ellington, Ct., July 20, 1757; sett. Ellington, Ct., 1757-1762; d. Ellington, Ct., Jan. 19, 1762, a. 31.

ABRAHAM NOTT, A.M., b. Wethersfield, Ct., Jan. 29, 1696/7, son of John, Jr. and Patience (Miller) Nott: Y. C., 1720, A.B., A.M.; Ord. Saybrook, Ct., (2nd Chh. at Centerbrook), Nov. 16, 1725; sett. Saybrook, Ct., 1722-1756; d. Saybrook, Ct., Jan. 24, 1756, a. 59.

SAMUEL NOWELL, A.M., b. Charlestown. Nov. 12, 1634, son of Hon. Increase and Parnell (Gray) Nowell; H. C., 1653, A.B., A.M.; Fellow or Tutor, 1653; Chaplain, King Philip's War, Narragansett Swamp Fight, Dec. 19, 1675, and in 1676; Assistant, Mass.

Bay Colony, 1680-1686; Artillery Election Sermon, 1678; Commissioner, 1682-1686; Treasurer of the Mass. Bay Colony, 1685-1686; Naval Officer, 1686; Treasurer, H. C., 1682-1686; d. London, England, Sept. 1688.

EDMUND NOYES, A.M., b. Newbury, Mar. 29, 1728, son of Thomas, 3rd and Judith (Marsh) Noyes; H. C., 1747, A.B., A.M.; Ord. Salisbury, (1st Chh.), Nov. 20, 1751; sett. Salisbury, 1751-1809; d. Salisbury, July 12, 1809, a. 81.

JAMES NOYES, b. Choulderton, Wiltshire, England, 1608, son of Rev. William and Anne (Stephens) Noyes; matriculated at Brazenose Coll., Oxford, 1627, but did not graduate; came to N. E., 1634; sett. Medford, 1634-1635; Ord. Newbury, (1st Chh.), May 5, 1635, as the first minister; sett. Newbury, 1635-1656; d. Newbury, Oct. 22, 1656, a. 48.

JAMES NOYES, A.B., b. Newbury, Mar. 11, 1639/40, son of Rev. James and Sarah (Brown) Noyes; H. C., 1659, A.B.; Trustee and Founder of Y. C., 1701; Ord. Stonington, Ct., Sept. 10, 1674, when the church was gathered; sett. Stonington, Ct., 1664-1719; had preached 10 years before the church was gathered; Chaplain, King Philip's War, 1676; d. Stonington, Ct., Dec. 30, 1719, a. 80.

JOSEPH NOYES, A.M., b. Stonington, Ct., Oct. 16, 1688, son of Rev. James, Jr. and Dorothy (Stanton) Noyes; Y. C., 1709, A.B., A.M.; Tutor and Fellow, Y. C., 1710-1715; Ord. New Haven, Ct., July 4, 1716; sett. New Haven, Ct., 1715-1761; d. New Haven, Ct., June 14, 1761, a. 73.

MOSES NOYES, A.B., b. Newbury, Dec. 6, 1643; son of Rev. James and Sarah (Brown) Noyes; H. C., 1659, A.B.; Fellow, Y. C., 1706-1726; Ord. Lyme, Ct., 1693, as the first minister; sett. Lyme, Ct., 1666-1726; preached 27 years before his ordination; Ct. Election Sermon, 1694; d. Lyme, Ct., Nov. 10, 1729, a. 85.

NATHANIEL NOYES, A.B., b. Newburyport, Aug. 12, 1735, son of Dea. Parker and Sarah (Mighill) Noves; Princeton, 1759, A.B.; Ord. South Hampton, N. H., Feb. 23, 1763; sett. South Hampton, N. H., 1763-1800; dism. Dec. 8, 1800; d. Newbury, Dec. 11, 1810, a. 75.

NICHOLAS NOYES, A.M., b. Newbury, Dec. 22, 1647, son of Dea. Nicholas and Mary (Cutting) Noyes; H. C., 1667; A.M., 1716; sett. Haddam, Ct., 1668-1681; Ord. Salem, (1st Chh.), Nov. 14, 1683; sett. Salem, 1682-1717; Chaplain, Great Swamp Fight, King Philip's War, Dec. 19, 1675; Election Sermon. 1698; poet and persecutor of witches; d. Salem, Dec. 13, 1717, a. 70, unm.

EDWARD OAKES. A.M., b. prob. at Tichfield, Hampshire, England, son of Rev. President Urian and Ruth (Ames) Oakes; H. C., 1679, A.B., A.M.; preached at Lancaster, 1680-1681; sett. Branford, Ct., 1682; sett. New London, Ct., 1684-1685; d. Oct. 23, 1689.

JOSIAH OAKES, A.M., b. Boston, May 3, 1689, son of Dr.

Thomas and Martha Oakes; H. C., 1708, A.B., A.M.; Ord. Wellfleet, July 29, 1723; sett. Wellfleet, 1723-1725; left 1727; d. 1733.

PRESIDENT URIAN OAKES, A.M., b. England, 1631, son of Lieut. Edward and Jane Oakes; came to N. E., 1634; H. C., 1649, A.B., A.M.; Fellow, H. C., 1650-1652; Chaplain at Tichford, Hampshire, England, until 1662, when he was silenced for non-conformity; returned to N. E.; Ord. Cambridge, Nov. 8, 1671; sett. Cambridge, 1671-1681; President, H. C., 1675-1681; Artillery Election Sermon, 1672; Election Sermon, 1673; d. Cambridge, July 25, 1681, a. 50.

ELISHA ODLIN, A.M., b. Exeter, N. H., Nov. 16, 1709, son of Rev. John and Elizabeth (Woodbridge) (Clark) Odlin; H. C., 1731, A.B., A.M.; Ord. Amesbury, (1st Chh.), Jan. 25, 1743/4; sett. Amesbury, 1742-1752; d. Amesbury, Jan. 21, 1752, a. 43.

JOHN ODLIN, A.M., b. Boston, Nov. 18, 1681, son of Elisha and Hannah (Bright) Odlin; H. C., 1702, A.B., A.M.; Ord. Exeter, N. H., Nov. 11, 1706; sett. Exeter, N. H., 1706-1754; d. Exeter, N. H., Nov. 20, 1754, a. 73.

WOODBRIDGE ODLIN, A.M., b. Exeter, N. H., Apr. 28, 1718, son of Rev. John and Elizabeth (Woodbridge) (Clark) Odlin; H. C., 1738, A.B., A.M.; Ord. Exeter, N. H., Sept. 28, 1743; sett. Exeter, N. H., 1743-1776; d. Exeter, N. H., Mar. 10, 1776, a. 57.

JOHN OGILVIE, D.D., b. New York City, 1724, of Scottish parents; Y. C., 1748, A.B.; D.D., Aberdeen, 1770; D.D., Columbia, 1770; sett. Norwalk, Ct., 1748-1749; Ord. London, England, June 24, 1749; missionary to the Indians for the V.S.P.G.F.P.; sett. Albany, N. Y., (St. Peter's Chh.), 1750-1763; sett. New York, (Trinity Chh.), 1764-1774; Chaplain in Colonial Wars, 1756-1763; Epis.; d. New York City, Nov. 26, 1774.

JOSEPH O'HARA, came from England, 1728; sett. Providence, R. I., (King's Chh.), Oct. 1728-1729; Epis.

ALLEN OLCOTT, A.M., b. East Hartford, Ct., Oct. 5, 1746, son of Capt. Josiah and Penelope (Beckwith) Olcott; Y. C., 1768, A.B., A.M.; Ord. Farmington, Ct., Jan. 17, 1787; sett. Farmington, Ct., 1781-1791; dism. Aug. 12, 1791, but he had preached since his graduation; d. Manchester, Ct., Apr. 19, 1811, a. 65.

BULKLEY OLCUTT, A.M., b. Bolton, Ct., Oct. 28, 1733, son of Timothy and Eunice (White) Olcutt; Y. C., 1758, A.B.; A.M., 1765; A.M., Dart. Coll., 1786; Ord. Charlestown, N. H., May 28, 1761; sett. Charlestown, N. H., 1761-1793; Trustee, Dart. Coll., 1788; d. Charlestown, N. H., June 26, 1793, a. 59.

JOHN OLIVER, A.B., b. England, 1616, son of Elder Thomas and Ann Oliver; arrived in the "William and Francis," at Boston, June 5, 1632; H. C., 1645, A.B.; minister at Chelsea, 1639/40-1646; sergeant; d. Cambridge, Apr. 12, 1646, a. ca. 30.

THOMAS OLNEY, b. Hertford, England, ca. 1632, son of Thomas and Mary (Small) Olney; came to Providence, R. I., 1654;

Ord. Providence, R. I., (1st Bapt. Chh.), 1668; sett. Providence, R. I., (2nd Bapt. Chh.), 1654-1715; resigned, 1715; Town Clerk, 1664-1715; Assistant, 1669-1679; Member Town Council, 1671-1714; Deputy, 1672-1711; Bapt.; d. Providence, R. I., June 11, 1722.

JAMES OREM, educated in England; Missionary, V.S.P.G.F.P., 1720; sett. Bristol, R. I., (St. Michael's Chh.), 1721-1723; Chaplain, His Majesty's Service, at N. Y.; Epis.

SAMUEL OSBORN, b. Ireland, 1685; educated at Dublin; Ord. Eastham, Sept. 18, 1718; sett. Eastham, 1718-1719; sett. Orleans, (2nd Parish in Eastham), 1719-1738; dism. Nov. 20, 1738; kept a private grammar school in Boston; Arminian in theology; d. Boston, 1774, a. 90.

SYLVANUS OSBORN, A.M., Princeton, 1754, A.B., A.M.; A.M., (Hon.), Y. C., 1757; Ord. Warren, Ct., (2nd Chh. in Kent), Jan. 29, 1757; sett. Warren, Ct., 1757-1771; d. East Greenwich, Ct., 1771.

DAVID OSGOOD, D.D., b. Andover, Oct. 14, 1747, son of Isaac and Elizabeth (Flint) Osgood; H. C., 1771, A.B., A.M.; S.T.D., Y. C., 1797; Ord. Medford, Sept. 14, 1774; sett. Medford, 1774-1822; Artillery Election Sermon, 1788; Convention Sermon, 1798; Dudleian Lecture, 1802; Election Sermon, 1809; d. Medford, Dec. 12, 1822, a. 75.

JAMES OSGOOD, A.M., b. Salem, Aug. 1, 1705, son of Capt. Dea. Peter and Martha (Ayres) Osgood; H. C., 1724, A.B., A.M.; Ord. Stoneham, Sept. 10, 1729, as the first minister of the 1st Chh.; sett. Stoneham, 1728-1746; d. Stoneham, Mar. 2, 1745/6, a. 40.

JOHN OWEN, A.M., b. Braintree, Apr. 13, 1699, son of Nathaniel and Mary Owen; H. C., 1723, A.B., A.M.; Ord. Groton, Ct., (1st Chh.), Nov. 22, 1727; sett. Groton, Ct., 1727-1753; d. Groton, Ct., June 14, 1753, a. 55.

JOHN OXENBRIDGE, A.M., b. Daventry, Northamptonshire, England, Jan. 30, 1608/9, son of Dr. Daniel and Katherine (Harby) Oxenbridge; matriculated Emmanuel Coll., Camb., 1626; Magdalen Hall, Oxford, A.B., 1628; A.M., 1631; Tutor at Magdalen Hall, Oxford, but deprived by Archbishop Laud, 1634; Fellow of Eaton Coll., 1652; sett. Bermuda, 1634-1641; sett. Beverly, England, 1642-1662; lecturer at Berwick-on-Tweed, 1650-1651; silenced 1662; sett. Surinam, 1662-1667; sett. Barbadoes, 1667-1669; inst. Boston, (1st Chh.), Apr. 10, 1670; sett. Boston, 1670-1674; Artillery Election Sermon, 1670; Election Sermon, 1671; d. Boston, Dec. 28, 1674, a. 66.

ELIJAH PACKARD, A.M., b. Bridgewater, Jan. 26, 1725/6, son of Zechariah and Abigail (Davenport) Packard; H. C., 1750, A.B., A.M.; Ord. Plymouth, (2nd or Manomet Chh.), Dec. 26, 1753; sett. Plymouth, 1753-1757; d. near Sheepscott River, Me., Jan. 1766.

JOHN PAGE, A.M., b. Salem, N. H., Oct. 19, 1738; H. C., 1761, A.B., A.M.; Ord. Hawke, N. H., (now Danville), Dec. 21,

1763; sett. Hawke, N. H., 1763-1783; d. Hawke, N. H., Jan. 29, 1783, a. 44.

SOLOMON PAGE, A.M., b. Hampton, N. H., Mar. 16, 1710, son of Samuel and Anne (Marshall) Page; H. C., 1729, A.B.; A.M., 1747; supplied at Hampton, N. H., 1733; "dismissed to the second church in Salisbury, Massachusetts, Dec. 4, 1757;" afterwards went to "Kennebec County;" d. 1788.

ELISHA PAINE, b. Eastham, Dec. 29, 1693, son of Elisha and Rebecca (Doane) Paine; imprisoned 1743, in Ct., for preaching without authority; Bapt. minister, said to have founded the First Bapt. Chh. at Harwich, 1749; sett. Riverhead, L. I., N. Y., (Separatist Chh. of Southold), May 26, 1758.

JOHN PAINE, Ord. Rehoboth, (Separatist Chh.), Aug. 3, 1748.

JOSHUA PAINE, A.M., b. Pomfret, Ct., Mar. 18, 1733/4, son of Seth and Mary Paine; Y. C., 1759, A.B., A.M.; A.M., Dart. Coll., 1792; Ord. Sturbridge, June 17, 1761; sett. Sturbridge, 1761-1799; d. Sturbridge, Dec. 28, 1799, a. 65.

ROBERT PAINE, A.M., b. Ipswich, son of Elder Robert Paine; H. C., 1656, A.B., A.M.; inst. Wells, Me., Sept. 2, 1667; sett. Wells, Me., 1667-1672; 1675; d. ca. 1704.

SETH PAINE, A.M., b. Braintree, Jan. 16, 1701/2, son of John and Deborah (Neal) Paine; Y. C., 1726, A.B., A.M.; Ord. Stafford, Ct., (1st Cong. Chh.), Aug. 7, 1734; sett. Stafford, Ct., 1734-1740; dism. July 24, 1740; became an Epis., 1742, but was not ordained; d. Stafford, Ct., 1753.

SOLOMAN PAYNE, b. Eastham, May 16, 1698, son of Elisha and Rebecca (Doane) Payne; Ord. Canterbury, Ct., (Chh. in the North Society), Sept. 10, 1746; sett. Canterbury, Ct., 1746-1754; d. Canterbury, Ct., Oct. 25, 1754.

THOMAS PAINE, A.M., b. Yarmouth, Apr. 9, 1695, son of James and Bethia (Thacher) Paine; H. C., 1717, A.B., A.M.; Ord. Weymouth, Aug. 19, 1719; sett. Weymouth, 1719-1734; dism. Apr. 15, 1734; father of Robert Treat Paine; d. Quincy, May 31, 1757.

JOHN PALMER, b. Scotland, Ct., 1721; Ord. Scotland, Ct., (Separatist Chh.), May 17, 1749; sett. Scotland, Ct., 1746-1807; d. Scotland, Ct., Aug. 13, 1807, a. 86.

JOSEPH PALMER, A.M., b. Cambridge, Sept. 2, 1729, son of Stephen and Sarah Palmer; H. C., 1747, A.B., A.M.; A.M., (Hon.), Y. C., 1753; Ord. Norton, Jan. 3, 1753; sett. Norton, 1753-1791; d. Norton, Apr. 4, 1791, a. 61.

SAMUEL PALMER, A.M., b. Middleborough, 1707, son of Rev. Thomas and Elizabeth (Sturtevant) Palmer; H. C., 1727, A.B., A.M.; Ord. Falmouth, Nov. 24, 1731; sett. Falmouth, 1731-1775; physician; d. Falmouth, Apr. 13, 1775, a. 68.

SOLOMON PALMER, A.M., b. Branford, Ct., Apr. 6, 1709, son of Daniel and Elizabeth Palmer; Y. C., 1729, A.B., A.M.; Ord.

Huntington, Ct., as a Cong. minister; sett. Cornwall, Ct., 1741-1754; became an Epis.; Ord. London, England, Oct. 1765; sett. New Milford, Ct., and Litchfield, Ct., 1755-1760; sett. Great Barrington, (St. James' Chh.), 1763-1766; sett. Litchfield, Ct., Goshen, Ct., and New Milford, Ct., 1766-1771; missionary, V.S.P.G.F.P.; Epis.; d. Litchfield, Ct., Nov. 2, 1771, a. 63.

THOMAS PALMER, b. 1665, son of William Palmer; Ord. Middleborough, May 2, 1702; sett. Middleborough, 1696-1708; dism. June 2, 1708; physician; d. 1743.

WAIT PALMER, bapt. May 27, 1711, son of William and Grace (Miner) Palmer; Ord. North Stonington, Ct., (Bapt. Chh.), 1743; sett. North Stonington, Ct., 1743-1763; Bapt.

JOSEPH PARKE, A.M., b. Newton, Mar. 12, 1705, son of John and Elizabeth (Miller) Parke; H. C., 1724, A.B., A.M.; Ord. 1730; sett. Westerly, R. I., (Cong. Chh., as minister and Indian missionary), 1733-1777; d. Westerly, R. I., Mar. 1, 1777, a. 72.

PAUL PARKE, b. Preston, Ct., Nov. 18, 1720, son of Hezekiah and Margery (Dyke) Parke; Ord. Preston, Ct., (Separatist-Bapt. Chh.), Mar. 17, 1747; sett. Preston, Ct., 1747-1802; Bapt.; d. Preston, Ct., June 25, 1802.

BENJAMIN PARKER, A.M., b. Bradford, Sept. 17, 1720, son of Benjamin and Lydia (Chamberlain) Parker; H. C., 1737, A.B., A.M.; Ord. Haverhill, (East Chh.), Nov. 28, 1744; sett. Haverhill, 1744-1789; Tory; d. Haverhill, Dec. 1789.

ISAIAH PARKER, b. Westford, Nov. 27, 1752, son of Aaron, Jr. and Dorothy (Fletcher) Parker; Ord. Harvard, (Still River Bapt. Chh.), June 10, 1778; sett. Harvard, 1776-1798; became a Universalist, 1798; sett. Harvard, (1st Universalist Chh.), 1798-1806; Rep. Leg., 1806; physician; Bapt. and Universalist; d. Cavendish, Vt., Jan. 16, 1848, a. 96.

JAMES PARKER, came to Dorchester, ca. 1630; sett. Weymouth, where he was a freeman, 1634, and Deputy to the Gen. Ct., 1639-1642; sett. Portsmouth, N. H., 1642-1646; Barbadoes, 1646-1652; a godly man and a scholar; will made Aug. 21, 1648; d. Barbadoes, 1652.

JONATHAN PARKER, A.M., b. Barnstable, Jan. 1706, son of Daniel and Mary (Lombard) Parker; H. C., 1726, A.B., A.M.; Ord. Plympton, Dec. 22, 1731; sett. Plympton, 1731-1776; d. Plympton, Apr. 24, 1776.

NEHEMIAH PARKER, A.B., b. Shrewsbury, Mar. 26, 1742, son of Stephen, Jr. and Abigail Parker; H. C., 1763, A.B.; Ord. Hubbardston, June 13, 1770; sett. Hubbardston, 1768-1800; dism. June 5, 1800; d. Hubbardston, Aug. 20, 1801, a. 59.

SAMUEL PARKER, A.M., b. Barnstable, 1741; H. C., 1768, A.B., A.M.; Ord. Provincetown, Jan. 20, 1774; sett. Provincetown, 1774-1811; d. Provincetown, Apr. 11, 1811, a. 71.

BISHOP SAMUEL PARKER, D.D., b. Portsmouth, N. H., Aug. 17, 1744, son of Judge William and Elizabeth (Grafton) Parker; H. C., 1764, A.B., A.M.; S.T.D., U. of Pa., 1789; Ord. London, England, Feb. 27, 1774; inst. Boston, (Trinity Chh.), Nov. 2, 1774; sett. Boston, 1774-1804; Artillery Election Sermon, 1791; Election Sermon, 1793; elected Bishop of the Eastern Diocese, Sept. 16, 1804; Epis.; d. Boston, Dec. 6, 1804.

THOMAS PARKER, A.M., b. Newbury, Berkshire, England, June 8, 1595, son of Rev. Robert and Dorothy (Stephens) Parker; an eminent Puritan divine; Trinity Coll., Dublin, 1610-1612; matric., Magdalen Coll., Oxford, 1613; U. of Leyden; U. of Franeker, Ph.M., (i. e. A.M.), 1617; taught school, Newbury, England, 1620-1634; came to N. E., 1634; sett. Ipswich, 1634-1635; Ord. Newbury, May 6, 1635, as the first minister; sett. Newbury, 1635-1677; a noted scholar; cousin to Rev. James Noyes, his colleague at Newbury; d. Newbury, Apr. 24, 1677, a. 82.

THOMAS PARKER, A.M., b. Cambridge, Dec. 17, 1700, son of Capt. Josiah and Elizabeth (Saxton) Parker; H. C., 1718, A.B., A.M.; Ord. Dracut, Mar. 29, 1720/1; sett. Dracut, 1720-1764; d. Dracut, Mar. 18, 1765.

EBENEZER PARKMAN, A.M., b. Boston, Sept. 5, 1703, son of William and Elizabeth (Adams) Parkman; H. C., 1721, A.B., A.M.; Ord. Westborough, Oct. 28, 1724; sett. Westborough, 1724-1782; Convention Sermon, 1761; d. Westborough, Dec. 9, 1782, a. 80.

NOYES PARRIS, A.M., b. Newton, Aug. 22, 1699, son of Rev. Samuel and Dorothy (Noyes) Parris; H. C., 1721, A.B., A.M.; Chaplain at Castle Island, Fort Independence, Boston Harbor; sett. New Jersey; d. 1748.

SAMUEL PARRIS, b. London, England, 1653, son of Thomas Parris, merchant; H. C., but did not graduate; Ord. Danvers, (1st Chh at Salem Village), Nov. 15, 1689; sett. Danvers, 1689-1696; resigned June 1696; sett. Dunstable, Oct. 1, 1707-1712; taught school and supplied pulpits at Stow and Sudbury; was the unhappy instigator of the witchcraft delusion which started in his own home at Danvers; d. Sudbury, Feb. 29, 1719/20, a. 66.

DAVID PARSONS, A.M., b. Northampton, Feb. 1, 1679/80, son of Col. Joseph and Elizabeth (Strong) Parsons; Y. C., 1705, A.B.; A.M., 1707; A.M., H.C., 1715; Ord. Malden, 1709; sett. Malden, 1709-1721; inst. Leicester, Sept. 15, 1721; sett. Leicester, 1721-1735; dism. Mar. 1735; d. Leicester, Oct. 12, 1743, a. 63.

DAVID PARSONS, JR., A.M., b. Malden, Mar. 21, 1712, son of Rev. David and Sarah (Stebbins) Parsons; H. C., 1729, A.B.; A.M., 1733; Ord. Amherst, Nov. 7, 1739; sett. Amherst, 1739-1781; Election Sermon, 1788; d. Amherst, Jan. 1, 1781.

ELIJAH PARSONS, A.M., b. Northampton, Mar. 20, 1747, son of Isaac and Lucina (Strong) Parsons; Y. C., 1768, A.B., A.M.;

Fellow, Y. C., 1814-1821; Ord. East Haddam, Ct., Oct. 28, 1772; sett. East Haddam, Ct., 1772-1827; d. East Haddam, Ct., Jan. 17, 1827, a. 80, s. p.

JONATHAN PARSONS, A.M., b. Westfield, Nov. 30, 1705, son of Dea. Ebenezer and Margaret (Marshfield) Parsons; Y. C., 1729, A.B., A.M.; A.M., Princeton, 1762; Ord. Old Lyme, Ct., (1st Cong. Chh.), Mar. 17, 1730/1; sett. Old Lyme, Ct., 1729-1745; dism. Oct. 1745; inst. Newburyport, (1st Presb. Chh.), Mar. 19, 1745/6; sett. Newburyport, 1746-1776; Presb.; d. Newburyport, July 19, 1776, a. 71.

JOSEPH PARSONS, A.M., b. Northampton, Jan. 28, 1671, son of Col. Joseph and Elizabeth (Strong) Parsons; H. C., 1697, A.B., A.M.; Ord. Lebanon, Ct., Nov. 27, 1700; sett. Lebanon, Ct., 1699-1708; inst. Amesbury, (Rocky Hill Chh., Salisbury), Nov. 26, 1718; sett. Amesbury, 1717-1738; d. Salisbury, Mar. 13, 1739/40, a. 69.

JOSEPH PARSONS, A.M., b. Lebanon, Ct., Oct. 22, 1702, son of Rev. Joseph and Elizabeth (Tompson) Parsons; H. C., 1720, A.B., A.M.; Ord. Bradford, June 8, 1726; sett. Bradford, 1726-1765; Artillery Election Sermon, 1744; Convention Sermon, 1755; Election Sermon, 1759; d. Bradford, May 4, 1765, a. 63.

JOSEPH PARSONS, 3rd., A.M., b. Bradford, Oct. 17, 1733, son of Rev. Joseph, Jr. and Frances (Usher) Parsons; H. C., 1752, A.B., A.M.; Ord. West Brookfield, Nov. 23, 1757; sett. West Brookfield, 1757-1771; d. West Brookfield, Jan. 17, 1771, a. 38.

MOSES PARSONS, A.M., b. Gloucester, June 20, 1716, son of Eben and Lydia (Haskell) Parsons; H. C., 1736, A.B., A.M.; Ord. Newbury, (Byfield Parish), June 20, 1744; sett. Newbury, 1744-1783; orthodox in theology with Arminian tendencies; Election Sermon, 1772; d. Newbury, Dec. 14, 1783, a. 67.

OBEDIAH PARSONS, A.M., b. Gloucester, Apr. 5, 1747, son of Dea. William and Mary (Harraden) Parsons; H. C., 1768, A.B., A.M.; Ord. Gloucester, (Annisquam Parish), Nov. 11. 1772; sett. Gloucester, 1772-1779; dism. Nov. 15, 1779; inst. Lynn, Feb. 4, 1784; sett. Lynn, 1784-1790; dism. Feb. 22, 1790; d. Gloucester, 1801, a. 55.

SAMUEL PARSONS, A.M., b. Salisbury, Sept. 13, 1711, son of Rev. Joseph and Elizabeth (Tompson) Parsons; H. C., 1730, A.B., A.M.; Ord. Rye, N. H., Nov. 3, 1736; sett. Rye, N. H., 1736-1789; d. Rye, N. H., Jan. 4, 1789, a. 77.

WILLIAM PARSONS, A.M., b. Salisbury, Apr. 21, 1716, son of Rev. Joseph and Elizabeth (Tompson) Parsons; H. C., 1735, A.B., A.M.; Ord. South Hampton, N. H., Feb. 22. 1742/3; sett. South Hampton, N. H., 1743-1762; dism. Oct. 6, 1762: sett. Gilmanton, N. H., 1763-1773; d. Gilmanton, N. H., Jan. 31, 1796, a. 80.

RALPH PARTRIDGE, A.M., bapt. Sutton Valence, Kent, England, Apr. 12, 1579, son of Rev. Thomas Partridge; Trinity Coll., Camb., 1599/1600, A.B.; A.M., 1603; Rector at Sutton-by-Dover,

Kent, England, 1619-1625; came to N. E., Nov. 14, 1636; Ord. Duxbury, 1637; sett. Duxbury, 1637-1658; possessed an excellent mind, well versed in theology; practiced medicine; d. Duxbury, 1658.

WILLIAM PARTRIDGE, A.B., b. Hadley, Nov. 16, 1669, son of Hon. Col. Samuel anad Mehitable (Crow) Partridge; H. C., 1689, A.B.; sett. Wethersfield, Ct., (1st Chh.), 1691-1693; prob. not ordained; d. Wethersfield, Ct., Sept. 24, 1693, a. 23.

JOSEPH PATRICK, A.M., b. Western, (now Warren); Y. C., 1769, A.B., A.M.; Ord. Blandford, June 25, 1772; sett. Blandford, 1772; dism. Dec. 1772; Presb.; d. Petersham, Apr. 1783.

WILLIAM PATTEN, A.M., b. Billerica, 1738, son of Nathaniel and Mary Patten; H. C., 1754, A.B., A.M.; A. M., (Hon.), Y. C., 1758; Ord. Halifax, Feb. 1758; sett. Halifax, 1758-1768; sett. Hartford, Ct., (South Chh.), ca. 1768-ca. 1775; d. Roxbury, Jan. 16, 1775, a. 36.

EDWARD PAYSON, A.M., b. Roxbury, June 20, 1657, son of Edward and Mary (Eliot) Payson; H. C., 1677, A.B., A.M.; Ord. Rowley, Oct. 25, 1682; sett. Rowley, 1682-1732; d. Rowley, Aug. 22, 1732, a. 76.

JOHN PAYSON, A.M., b. Walpole, Jan. 6, 1745/6, son of Rev. Phillips and Ann (Swift) Payson; H. C., 1764, A.B., A.M.; Ord. Fitchburg, Jan. 27, 1768; sett. Fitchburg, 1767-1794; dism. May 2, 1794; d. Leominster, May 21, 1804, a. 59.

PHILLIPS PAYSON, A.M., b. Dorchester, Feb. 29, 1704/5, son of Samuel and Mary (Phillips) Payson; H. C., 1724, A.B., A.M.; Ord. Walpole, Sept. 16, 1730; sett. Walpole, 1730-1778; d. Walpole, Jan. 22, 1778, a. 74.

PHILLIPS PAYSON, D.D., b. Walpole, Jan. 18, 1735/6, son of Rev. Phillips and Ann (Swift) Payson; H. C., 1754, A.B., A.M.; S.T.D., 1800; Ord. Chelsea, (1st Chh. now in Revere), Oct. 26, 1757; sett. Chelsea, 1757-1801; Fellow, Am. Acad. Arts and Sciences; Artillery Election Sermon, 1769; Election Sermon, 1778; Dudleian Lecture, 1784; Convention Sermon, 1785; d. Chelsea, Jan. 11, 1801, a. 65.

SAMUEL PAYSON, A.M., b. Walpole, Apr. 26, 1738, son of Rev. Phillips and Ann (Swift) Payson; H. C., 1758, A.B., A.M.; Ord. Lunenburg, Sept. 8, 1762; sett. Lunenburg, 1762-1763; d. Lunenburg, Feb. 14, 1763, a. 24.

OLIVER PEABODY, A.M., b. Boxford, May 7, 1698, son of William and Hannah (Hale) Peabody; H. C., 1721, A.B., A.M.; inst. Natick, (Indian Chh.), Aug. 1, 1721; sett. Natick, 1721-1729; Ord. Cambridge, Dec. 7, 1729; sett. Natick, (1st Cong. Chh.), 1729-1752; Artillery Election Sermon, 1731; d. Natick, Feb. 2, 1752, a. 54.

OLIVER PEABODY, A.M., b. Natick, Jan. 15, 1725/6, son of Rev. Oliver and Hannah (Baxter) Peabody; H. C., 1745, A.B., A.M.; Librarian, H. C., 1748-1750; Ord. Roxbury, Nov. 7, 1750; sett. Roxbury, 1750-1752; d. Roxbury, May 29, 1752, a. 26.

STEPHEN PEABODY, A.M., b. Andover, Nov. 11, 1741, son of John and Sarah (Ingalls) Peabody; H. C., 1769, A.B., A.M.; A.M., (Hon.), Dart. Coll., 1792; Ord. Atkinson, N. H., Nov. 25, 1772, as the first minister; sett. Atkinson, N. H., 1772-1819; d. Atkinson, N. H., May 23, 1819, a. 77.

JEREMIAH PECK, b. London, England, 1628, son of William and Elizabeth Peck; came to Boston, 1637; H. C., 1653-1656, but did not graduate; teacher at Guilford, Ct., 1656-1660; Ord. Old Saybrook, Ct., Sept. 25, 1661; sett. Old Saybrook, Ct., 1661-1666; dism. Jan. 30, 1665/6; sett. Newark, N. J., 1666/7-1674; sett. Elizabethtown, N. J., 1674-1678, as the first minister; sett. West Greenwich, Ct., Sept. 3, 1678-1689; inst. Waterbury, Ct., 1690; sett. Waterbury, Ct., 1690-1699; d. Waterbury, Ct., June 7, 1699, a. 71.

ROBERT PECK, A.M., b. Beccles, Suffolk, England, 1580, son of Robert and Helen (Babbs) Peck; matric., St. Catharine's Hall, Camb.; Magdalene Coll., Camb., A.B., 1598/9; A.M., 1603; Ord. Hingham, Norfolk, England, Jan. 8, 1605; sett. Hingham, England, 1605-1638; came to N. E., 1638; Ord. Hingham, Nov. 28, 1638; sett. Hingham, 1638-1641; returned to Hingham, England, Oct. 27, 1641; sett. Hingham, England, 1646-1656; d. Hingham, England, 1656.

SAMUEL PECK, b. Seekonk, Dec. 2, 1706, son of Capt. Samuel and Rachel Peck; sett. Seekonk, (Elder Peck's Chh.), 1748-1788; Bapt.; d. Rehoboth, Nov. 26, 1788, a. 82.

REUBEN PECKHAM, b. 1709, son of Rev. Timothy and Rachel Peckham; Ord. (prob. at Newport, R. I.) between 1737 and 1740; sett. Hartford, Ct., 1740; sett. Westerly, R. I., ca. 1740-1770; sett. Newmarket, Middlesex County, N. J., 1770; Seventh Day Bapt.; d. after 1780.

TIMOTHY PECKHAM, b. East Greenwich, R. I., Aug. 5, 1681, son of John and Sarah (Newport) Peckham; sett. East Greenwich, R. I., 1734-1752; sett. Newport, R. I., 1752-1757; Bapt.; d. Newport, R. I., Nov. 6, 1757.

WILLIAM PECKHAM, b. Little Compton, R. I., ca. 1647, son of John and Mary (Clarke) Peckham; Ord. Newport, R. I., (1st Bapt. Chh.), Nov. 15, 1711; sett. Newport, R. I., 1711-1732; Deputy, 1696-1698; Bapt.; d. Newport, R. I., June 2, 1734.

PEIRCE, see Pierce.

EDWARD PELL, A.M., b. Boston, July 20, 1711, son of Capt. Edward and Sarah (Clark) Pell; H. C., 1730, A.B., A.M.; Ord. Harwich, Aug. 12, 1747; sett. Harwich, 1747-1752; d. Harwich, Nov. 24, 1752, a. 41.

EBENEZER PEMBERTON, A.M., b. Boston, Feb. 3, 1671/2, son of James and Sarah (Marshall) Pemberton; H. C., 1691, A.B., A.M.; Tutor, H. C., 1697-1700; Fellow, H. C., 1707-1717; Librarian, H. C., 1693-1697; Ord. Boston, (Old South Chh.), Aug. 28, 1700;

sett. Boston, 1699-1717; Artillery Election Sermons, 1701, 1709; Election Sermon, 1710; d. Boston, Feb. 15, 1717/18, a. 45.

EBENEZER PEMBERTON, D.D., b. Boston, Feb. 6, 1704/5, son of Rev. Ebenezer and Mary (Clark) Pemberton; H. C., 1721, A.B., A.M.; S.T.D., Princeton, 1770, (first conferred); Chaplain, Castle William; sett. New York City, (Presb. Chh.), 1727-1753: dism. Oct. 1753; inst. Boston, (New Brick Chh.), Mar. 6, 1754; sett. Boston, 1754-1777; Artillery Election Sermon, 1756; Election Sermon, 1757; Convention Sermon, 1759; Dudleian Lecture, 1766; Fellow, Am. Acad. Arts and Sciences; d. Boston, Sept. 9, 1777, a. 73.

JOHN PENDLETON, Ord. Richmond, R. I., Feb. 11, 1771; Bapt.

JOSEPH PENNIMAN, A.M., b. Braintree, Oct. 5, 1737, son of William and Ruth (Thayer) Penniman; H. C., 1765, A.B.; A.M., 1769; Ord. Bedford, May 22, 1771; sett. Bedford, 1771-1793; dism. Oct. 29, 1793; d. Harvard, 1803.

DANIEL PERKINS, A.M., b. Topsfield, June 15, 1697, son of Capt. Tobijah and Sarah (Denison) Perkins; H. C., 1717, A.B., A.M.; Ord. Bridgewater, Oct. 4, 1721; sett. Bridgewater, 1721-1782; d. Bridgewater, Sept. 29, 1782, a. 86.

NATHAN PERKINS, D.D., b. Lisbon, Ct., May 12, 1748, son of Matthew and Hannah Perkins; Princeton, 1770, A.B.; D.D., 1801; Ord. West Hartford, Ct., (4th Chh. in Hartford), Oct. 14, 1772; sett. West Hartford, Ct., 1772-1838; Ct. Election Sermon, 1808; d. West Hartford, Ct., Jan. 18, 1838, a. 90.

CAPTAIN WILLIAM PERKINS, b. London, England, Aug. 25, 1607, son of William Perkins; matric. Emmanuel Coll., Camb., 1624; came to N. E., 1631; to Ipswich, 1633; freeman at Ipswich, Sept. 3, 1634; resided at Weymouth, 1643-1648; selectman, 1647; Rep. Gen. Ct., 1644; member Anc. & Hon. Art. Co.; sett. Gloucester, 1650-1655; schoolmaster, 1651; sett. Topsfield, 1655-1681, as supply, there being no regularly organized church there at that time; d. Topsfield, May 21, 1682, a. 75.

SAMUEL PERLEY, A.M., b. Ipswich, Aug. 11, 1742, son of Samuel and Ruth (How) Perley; H. C., 1763, A.B., A.M.; Ord. Seabrook, N. H., Jan. 31, 1765, as the first minister; sett. Seabrook, N. H., 1765-1775; dism. May 22, 1775; sett. Newcastle, Me., ca. 1776; inst. Moultonborough, N. H., Oct. 8, 1778, as the first minister; sett. Moultonborough, N. H., 1777-1779; dism. May 1779; inst. Groton, N. H., Oct. 20, 1779, as the first minister; sett. Groton, N. H., 1779-1784; inst. Gray, Me., Sept. 8, 1784; sett. Gray, Me., 1784-1791; dism. May 12, 1791; Moderator of the Salem Presbytery, 1775; J. P., 21 yrs.; Rep. Gen. Ct., 1787; member Constitutional Convention, 1788; Cong. and Presb.; d. Gray, Me., Nov. 28, 1830, a. 89.

DAVID PERRY, A.M., b. Huntington, Ct., July 19, 1746, son of Joshua and Mary (Leavenworth) Perry; Y. C., 1772, A.B.; A.M.,

1776; Ord. Harwinton, Ct., Feb. 16, 1774; sett. Harwinton, Ct., 1773-1783; dism. Dec. 23, 1783; inst. Richmond, Aug. 25, 1784; sett. Richmond, 1784-1817; d. Richmond, June 7, 1817, a. 71.

JOSEPH PERRY, A.M., b. Sherborn, Aug. 15, 1731, son of Joseph and Abigail (Holbrook) Perry; H. C., 1752, A.B., A.M.; A.M., (Hon.), Y. C., 1755; Ord. South Windsor, Ct., (2nd or East Chh. in Windsor), June 11, 1755; sett. South Windsor, Ct., 1755-1783; Ct. Election Sermon, 1775; d. South Windsor, Ct., 1783, a. 50.

ANDREW PETERS, A.M., b. Andover, 1701, son of Samuel and Phoebe (Fry) Peters; H. C., 1723, A.B., A.M.; Ord. Middleton, Nov. 26, 1729; sett. Middleton, 1726-1756; d. Middleton, Oct. 6, 1756, a. 55.

HUGH PETERS, A.M., b. Foy, Cornwall, England, 1599, son of Thomas and Martha (Treffey) Dyrkwood, alias Peters; Trinity Coll., Camb., A.B., 1617/8; A.M., 1622; Ord. London, England, June 18, 1623; lecturer at St. Sepulchre's, London, England, until silenced; colleague of Dr. William Ames of the Separatist English Chh. at Rotterdam, Holland, 1632-1635; came to N. E., Oct. 6, 1635; Overseer, H. C., 1637; Ord. Salem, Dec. 21, 1636; sett. Salem, 1636-1641; left for England, Aug. 3, 1641; Chaplain and Colonel in Oliver Cromwell's army, 1644-1649; official preacher at Whitehall, 1650; tried and executed as a regicide and his head set up on a pike on London Bridge; d. London, Eng., Oct. 16, 1660, a. 61.

SAMUEL ANDREW PETERS, A.M., b. Hebron, Ct., Nov. 20, 1735, son of John and Mary (Marks) Peters; Y. C., 1757, A.B., A.M.; A.M., Columbia U., 1761; (he assumed an LL.D. to which he had no right); Ord. London, England, 1759; sett. Hebron, Ct., (Epis. Chh.), 1759-1775; elected Bishop of Vt., 1794, but never consecrated; Epis.; d. New York City, Apr. 19, 1826, a. 91.

THOMAS PETERS, A.M., b. Foy, Cornwall, England, 1597, son of Thomas and Martha (Treffey) Dyrkwood, alias Peters; Brazenose Coll., Oxford, A.B., 1614; A.M., 1625; Vicar of Mylor, Cornwall, 1628-1643; came to N. E., 1644; sett. Old Saybrook, Ct., 1645-1646, as Chaplain at the Fort and to Col. Fenwick before a church was gathered there; returned to England, 1646; sett. Mylor, Cornwall, 1647-1654; d. Mylor, Cornwall, England, 1654, a. 57.

BENAJAH PHELPS, A.M., b. Hebron, Ct., Mar. 30, 1737, son of Nathaniel, Jr. and Mary (Curtis) Phelps; Y. C., 1761, A.B.; A.M., 1784; Ord. Hartford, Ct., June 5, 1765; sett. Cornwallis, N. S., 1765-1777; inst. Manchester, Ct., 1781; sett. Manchester, Ct., Mar. 1780-1793; resigned, June 19, 1793; d. East Hartford, Ct., Feb. 10, 1817, a. 80.

JOHN PHILLIP, A.M., b. ca. 1585; admitted sizar at Emmanuel Coll., Camb., June 27, 1600; A.B., Emmanuel Coll., Camb., 1603/4; A.M., 1607; Ord. by the Bishop of Norwich, Sept. 24, 1609 (aged 24 years); Rector of Wrentham, Suffolk, England, 1609-1637;

under Bishop Wren was forced to flee to N. E., 1637; sett. Dedham, and prob. occasionally preached, 1637-1641; returned to England, 1641; was one of the Assembly of Divines, 1643; reinstated at Wrentham, Suffolk, England, ca. 1643; sett. Wrentham, Suffolk, Eng., 1643-1662; ejected, 1662; d. Wrentham, Suffolk, England, Sept. 2, 1663.

FRANCIS PHILLIPS, St. John's Coll., Camb.; no matriculation or degrees found; Ord. deacon at London, England, Mar. 4, 1704/5; Chaplain, British Navy, 1711-1712; inst. Stratford, Ct., (Epis. Chh.), Dec. 24, 1712; sett. Stratford, Ct., 1712-1713; minister of the Epis. Chh. in Philadelphia, Pa., 1715; unfrocked; Epis.

GEORGE PHILLIPS, A.M., b. Raynham St. Martin's, Norfolk, England, 1593, son of Christopher Phillips; Gonville & Caius Coll., Camb., A.B., 1613/4; A.M., 1617; Curate at Boxted, Essex, England, 1615-1630; arrived in N. E., June 2, 1630; Ord. Watertown, July 30, 1630, as the first minister of the First Chh.; sett. Watertown, 1630-1644; a liberal; Overseer, H.C., 1642; left a distinguished posterity including Wendell Phillips and Phillips Brooks; d. Watertown, July 1, 1644.

GEORGE PHILLIPS, A.M., b. Rowley, June 3, 1664, son of Rev. Samuel and Sarah (Appleton) Phillips; H. C., 1686, A.B., A.M.; sett. Suffield, Ct., 1692-1694; sett. Brookfield, ca. 1698-1702; Ord. Brookhaven, L. I., N. Y., 1702; sett. Brookhaven, L. I., N. Y., 1702-1739; d. Brookhaven, L. I., N. Y., Apr. 3, 1739.

SAMUEL PHILLIPS, A.M., b. Boxted, Essex, England, 1625, son of Rev. George and —— (Sergeant) Phillips; H. C., 1650, A.B., A.M.; Ord. Rowley, June 1651; sett. Rowley, 1651-1696; Artillery Election Sermon, 1675; Election Sermon, 1678; d. Rowley, Apr. 22, 1696, a. 71.

SAMUEL PHILLIPS, A.M., b. Salem, Feb. 17, 1690/1, son of Samuel and Mary (Emerson) Phillips; H. C., 1708, A.B.; A.M., 1715; Ord. Andover, (South or 2nd Chh.), Oct. 17, 1711, as the first minister; sett. Andover, 1710-1771; Artillery Election Sermon, 1741; Election Sermon, 1750; Convention Sermon, 1753; d. Andover, June 5, 1771, a. 80.

WILLIAM PHIPS, A.M., b. Sherborn, Apr. 17, 1720, son of John and Hannah (Bullen) Phips; H. C., 1746, A.B.; A.M., 1750; Ord. Douglas, Dec. 16, 1747, as the first minister; sett. Douglas, 1747-1765; dism. June 10, 1765; mastered twelve languages; magistrate at Ward (now Auburn) where he helped form the First Chh.; moderator of several county conventions; d. Oxford, Dec. 4, 1798.

THEOPHILUS PICKERING, A.M., b. Salem, Sept. 28, 1700, son of John, Jr. and Sarah (Burrell) Pickering; H. C., 1719, A.B., A.M.; Ord. Essex, (1st Chh.), Oct. 13, 1727; sett. Essex, 1725-1747; d. Essex, Oct. 7, 1747.

PIERCE, and variants:

BENJAMIN PEIRCE, b. Warwick, R. I., son of Azrakim and

Sarah (Heywood) Peirce; Ord. Apponaug, R. I., (Warwick), Dec. 6, 1744; sett. Apponaug, R. I., 1744-1763; Bapt.; d. ca. 1763.

DANIEL PIERCE, sett. New London, Ct., (1st Bapt. or Fort Hill Chh.), 1704; Bapt.

JOHN PEIRCE, b. ca. 1660, son of Capt. Michael and Persis (Eames) Peirce, of Hingham and Scituate; Ord. Swansea, (2nd Chh.), Oct. 19, 1715; sett. Swansea, 1715-1750; Bapt.; d. Swansea, Sept. 8, 1750, a. ca. 90.

NATHAN PEIRCE, b. Rehoboth, Feb. 21, 1716, son of Mial and Judith (Ellis) Peirce; Ord. Rehoboth, (3rd Bapt. Chh.), 1753; sett. Rehoboth, 1753-1793; Bapt.; d. Rehoboth, Apr. 14, 1793, a. 77.

RICHARD PIERCE, A.M., b. Milton, Mar. 29, 1700; H. C., 1724, A.B., A.M.; sett. New Bedford, 1733-1749; d. New Bedford, Mar. 23, 1749, a. 49.

THOMAS PEIRCE, Ord. Newburyport, Mass., for settlement at Scarborough, Me., Nov. 24, 1762; sett. Scarborough, Me., 1762-1775; Presb.; d. Scarborough, Me., Jan. 26, 1775.

JAMES PIERPONT, A.M., b. Roxbury, Jan. 4, 1659/60, son of John and Thankful (Stow) Pierpont; H. C., 1681, A.B., A.M.; Ord. New Haven, Ct., July 2, 1685; sett. New Haven, Ct., 1684-1714; Trustee and Founder of Y. C., 1699; physician; Ct. Election Sermon, 1690; d. New Haven, Ct., Nov. 22, 1714, a. 54.

JONATHAN PIERPONT, A.M., b. Roxbury, June 10, 1665, son of Robert and Sarah (Lynde) Pierpont; H. C., 1685, A.B., A.M.; Fellow, H. C., 1700-1707; Ord. Wakefield, (1st Chh. in Reading), June 26, 1689; sett. Wakefield, 1689-1709; d. Wakefield, (Reading), June 2, 1709, a. 44.

SAMUEL PIERPONT, A.M., b. New Haven, Ct., Dec. 30, 1700, son of Rev. James and Mary (Hooker) Pierpont; Y. C., 1718, A.B., A.M.; Ord. Lyme, Ct., Dec. 12, 1722; sett. Lyme, Ct., 1720/1-1723; drowned in the Connecticut River, Mar. 15, 1723, a. 23.

ABRAHAM PIERSON, A.B., b. Yorkshire, England, ca. 1608; Trinity Coll., Camb., 1632, A.B.; Ord. in England, where he was minister at Newark, Nottinghamshire; came to N. E., 1639; sett. Lynn, Nov. to Dec. 1640; sett. Southampton, L. I., N. Y., 1640-1644; sett. Branford, Ct., 1645-1665; sett. Newark, N. J., 1667-1678; Chaplain, 1654; d. Newark, N. J., Aug. 9, 1678.

PRESIDENT ABRAHAM PIERSON, A.B., b. Lynn, 1641, son of Rev. Abraham and —— (Wheelwright) Pierson; H. C., 1668, A.B.; Ord. Newark, N. J., Mar. 4, 1672; sett. Newark, N. J., 1669-1692; sett. Greenwich, Ct., 1692-1694; inst. Killingworth, Ct., 1694; sett. Killingworth, Ct., (now Clinton), 1694-1707; Trustee and Founder, Y. C., 1700; inducted, President, Y. C., Nov. 11, 1701, served 1701-1707; Ct. Election Sermon, 1700; d. Killingworth, Ct., May 5, 1707.

GEORGE PIGOT, b. Warwick, R. I., son of Rev. George and

Sarah Pigot; (nephew of Dr. Edward Pigot of Warwick); educated in England; Missionary, V.S.P.G.F.P.; sett. Stratford, Ct., (Christ Chh.), 1722-1723; sett. Providence, R. I., (King's Chh.), 1723-1727; sett. Marblehead, (St. Michael's Chh.), 1727-1736; sett. Chaldon, Surrey, England, 1738; Epis.; d. Chaldon, Surrey, England.

JAMES PIKE, A.M., b. Newbury, Mar. 1, 1702/3, son of Joseph and Hannah (Smith) Pike; H. C., 1725, A.B., A.M.; Ord. Somersworth, N. H., Oct. 28, 1730; sett. Somersworth, N. H., 1727-1790; ceased preaching Oct. 31, 1790; d. Somersworth, N. H., Mar. 19, 1792, a. 89.

JOHN PIKE, A.M., b. Salisbury, May 15, 1653, son of Major Robert and Sarah (Sanders) Pike; H. C., 1675, A.B., A.M.; Ord. Dover, N. H., (1st Chh.), Aug. 31, 1681; sett. Dover, N. H., 1678-1709; Chaplain, at Pemaquid, Me., 1694-1695; d. Dover, N. H., Mar. 10, 1709/10, a. 56.

NATHANIEL PITCHER, A.M., b. Dorchester, 1685, prob. son of Nathaniel Pitcher; H. C., 1703, A.B., A.M.; Ord. Scituate, Sept. 14, 1707; sett. Scituate, 1705-1723; d. Scituate, Sept. 27, 1723, a. 38.

TIMOTHY PITKIN, A.M., b. East Hartford, Ct.. Jan. 13, 1726/7, son of Gov. William and Mary (Woodbridge) Pitkin; Y. C., 1747, A.B., A.M.; Tutor, Y. C., 1750-1751; Fellow, Y. C., 1777-1804; Ord. Farmington, Ct., (1st Chh.), June 1752; sett. Farmington, Ct., 1752-1785; dism. June 15, 1785; d. Farmington, Ct., July 8, 1812, a. 86.

PETER PLACE, b. Providence, R. I., son of Enoch and Sarah Place; Ord. Smithfield, R. I., (1st Bapt. Chh.), 1700; sett. Smithfield, R. I. and Gloucester, R. I., 1700-1735; Bapt.; d. Gloucester, R. I., July 6, 1735.

MATTHIAS PLANT, A.B., b. Weston-Jones, Staffordshire, England, 1688; Jesus Coll., Camb., 1712/3, A.B.; Ord. by the Bishop of Ely, as deacon, Dec. 20, 1713; came to N. E., 1721; inst. Newbury (Queen Anne's Chapel), Apr. 29, 1722; sett. Newbury, 1722-1753; inst. Newburyport, (St. Paul's Chh.), July 29, 1751, as Rector; sett. Newburyport, 1740-1753; also minister at the Pond Hill (Epis.) Chh. Amesbury, ca. 1745-1753; Epis.; d. Newbury, Apr. 2, 1753, a. 65.

THOMAS POLLEN, A.M., Gent., b. Lincoln, England, son of Edward Pollen; Corpus Christi Coll.. Oxford, 1720/1, A.B.; A.M., 1723/4; Curate of St. Antholin's Chh., London; Rector of Little Bookham, Surrey, England; sett. Glasgow, Scotland, (Epis. Chh.); came to N. E., May, 1754; sett. Newport, R. I. (Trinity Chh.), May 1754-1760; resigned Nov. 1760; Rector of a parish on the Island of Jamaica; Epis.

BENJAMIN POMEROY, D.D., b. Suffield, Ct., Nov. 19, 1704, son of Capt. Joseph and Hannah (Seymour) Pomeroy; Y. C., 1733, A.B., A.M.; D.D., Dart. Coll., 1774; Trustee, Dart. Coll.; Ord.

Hebron, Ct., Dec. 16, 1735; sett. Hebron, Ct., 1735-1784; Chaplain, French and Indian Wars, 1757-1760; Chaplain, Am. Rev., 1777-1778; d. Hebron, Ct., Dec. 22 1784, a. 80.

SETH POMEROY, A.M., b. Northampton, Sept. 26, 1733, son of Gen. Seth and Mary (Hunt) Pomeroy; Y. C., 1753, A.B. A.M.; A.M., (Hon.), H. C., 1756; Tutor, Y. C.; Ord. Greenfield Hill, Ct., (called Sept. 19, 1757) ; sett. Greenfield Hill, Ct., 1757-1770; d. Greenfield, Hill, Ct., July 1, 1770, a. 37.

DANIEL POND, A.M., b. Wrentham, May 13, 1724, son of John, Jr. and Rachel Pond; H. C., 1745, A.B., A.M.; Ord. Templeton, Dec. 10, 1755, as the first minister; sett. Templeton, 1755-1759; dism. Sept. 2, 1759; teacher at West Medway; liberal; opposed to the Hopkinsian theology; d. Otter Creek, Pa.

JOSEPH POPE, A.M., b. Pomfret Ct., Sept. 28, 1746, son of Joseph and Hannah (Shaw) Pope; H. C., 1770, A.B., A.M.; Ord. Spencer, Oct. 20, 1773; sett. Spencer, 1773-1826; Chaplain, Rev. War; d. Spencer, Mar. 8, 1826.

AARON PORTER, A.M., b. Hadley, July 19, 1689, son of Hon. Samuel and Joanna (Cook) Porter; H. C., 1708, A.B., A.M.; Ord. Medford, Feb. 11, 1713; sett. Medford, 1713-1722; d. Medford, Jan. 23, 1722, a. 33.

JOHN PORTER, A.M., b. Abington, Feb. 2, 1716, son of Samuel and Mary Porter; H. C., 1736, A.B., A.M.; Ord. Brockton, Oct. 15, 1740; sett. Brockton, 1740-1802; d. Brockton, Mar. 12, 1802, a. 87.

NATHANIEL PORTER, D.D., b. Topsfield, Jan. 14, 1745, (bapt. Jan. 3, 1747/8), son of Ezekiel Porter; H. C., 1768, A.B.; A.M., 1772; S.T.D., 1814; S.T.D., Dart. Coll., 1814; Ord. New Durham, N. H., Sept. 8, 1773; sett. New Durham, N. H., 1773-1777; inst. Conway, N. H., Oct. 20, 1778; sett. Conway, N. H., 1778-1815; Chaplain, 1776-1777; d. Fryeburg, Me., Nov. 10, 1836, a. 91.

NEHEMIAH PORTER, A.M., b. Hamilton, Mar. 22, 1720, son of Nehemiah and Hannah (Smith) Porter; H. C., 1745, A.B., A.M.; Ord. Essex, (1st Chh.), Jan. 1749; sett. Essex, 1749-1766; sett. Yarmouth, N. S., 1766-1774; inst. Ashfield, (2nd Chh.), Dec. 21, 1774; sett. Ashfield 1774-1820; was able to enter the pulpit in his one hundredth year and gave the charge to his people at the ordination of his colleague; d. Ashfield, Feb. 29, 1820, a. 99 years, 11 months, 7 days.

SAMUEL PORTER, A.M., b. Hadley, Dec. 2, 1709, son of Samuel and Anna (Colton) Porter; H. C., 1730, A.B., A.M.; Ord. Sherborn, Oct. 23, 1734; sett. Sherborn, 1734-1758; he originated the famous Porter apple; Artillery Election Sermon, 1754; d. Sherborn, Sept. 16, 1758, a. 49.

ELAN POTTER, A.M., b. New Haven, Ct., Jan. 1, 1741/2, son of Dea. Daniel, Jr. and Martha (Ives) Potter; Y. C., 1765, A.B., A.M.; Ord. Shelter Island, L. I., N. Y., June 12, 1766; inst. Enfield,

Ct., (1st Cong. Chh.), Mar. 1, 1769; sett. Enfield, Ct., 1769-1776; dism. Apr. 17, 1776; sett. Southold, L. I., N. Y., Nov. 1792-1794; d. Southold, L. I., N. Y., Jan. 5, 1794, a. 52.

ISAIAH POTTER, A.M., b. Plymouth, Ct., July 23, 1746, son of Dea. Daniel, Jr. and Martha (Ives) Potter; Y. C., 1767, A.B., A.M.; A.M., Dart. Coll., 1780; Ord. Lebanon, N. H., Aug. 25, 1772, as the first minister; sett. Lebanon, N. H., 1772-1816; dism. Aug. 1816; Chaplain at Ticonderoga, 1777; d. Lebanon, N. H., July 2, 1817, a. 70.

LYMAN POTTER, A.M., b. Plymouth, Ct., Mar. 1, 1748, son of Dea. Daniel, Jr. and Martha (Ives) Potter; Y. C., 1772, A.B., A.M.; A.M., Dart. Coll., 1780; Ord. Norwich, Vt., Aug. 31, 1775; sett. Norwich, Vt., 1775-1800; Presb. missionary in Ohio and Pa.; bought a farm at Mingo Bottom, Ohio, where he spent his last days; Vermont Election Sermon, 1787; d. Mingo Bottom, Ohio, July 20, 1827, a. 80.

NATHANIEL POTTER, A.M., b. Elizabeth, N. J.; Princeton, 1753, A.B., A.M.; A.M., (Hon.), H. C., 1758; schoolmaster at Watertown; Ord. Brookline, Nov. 19, 1755; sett. Brookline, 1755-1759; dism. June 17, 1759; d. at sea, 1768.

THOMAS POTWINE, A.M., b. Boston, Oct. 3, 1731, son of John and Mary (Jackson) Potwine; Y. C., 1751, A.B., A.M.; Ord. East Windsor, Ct., (1st Cong. or North Chh.), May 1, 1754, as the first minister; sett. East Windsor, Ct., 1754-1802; d. East Windsor, Ct., Nov. 15, 1802, a. 71.

PETER POWERS, A.M., b. Hollis, N. H., Nov. 29, 1728, as the first white child born in the town, son of Capt. Peter and Anna (Keyes) Powers; H. C., 1754, A.B.; A.M., 1758; A.M., (Hon.), Dart. Coll., 1782; Ord. Norwich, Ct., (3rd or Newent Parish at Lisborn), Dec. 2, 1756; sett. Norwich, Ct., 1756-1765; inst. Haverhill, N. H. and Newbury, Vt., Feb. 27, 1765, as the first minister in Grafton Co., N. H.: sett. Haverhill, N. H. and Newbury, Vt., 1765-1782; inst. Deer Isle, Me., 1785; sett. Deer Isle, Me., 1785-1800; d. Deer Isle, Me., May 13, 1800, a. 71.

WALTER POWERS, perhaps b. Littleton, Oct. 21, 1732, son of Daniel and Martha (Glazier) Powers; Ord. Newtown, N. H., (1st Bapt. Chh. in N. H.), 1755; sett. Newtown, N. H., 1755-1786; Bapt.

PETER PRATT, A.M., b. New London, Ct., July 19, 1716, son of Peter and Mehitable (Watrous) Pratt; Y. C., 1736, A.B., A.M.; Ord. Sharon, Ct., Apr. 30, 1740; sett. Sharon, Ct., 1740-1747; dism. Oct. 13, 1747; clerk of probate, 1755; d. Lebanon, Ct., 1780, a. 64.

CALEB PRENTISS, A.M., b. Cambridge, Nov. 14, 1746, son of Caleb and Lydia (Whittemore) Prentiss; H. C., 1765, A.B., A.M.; Librarian, H. C., 1768-1769; Ord. Wakefield (1st Chh. in Reading), Oct. 25, 1765; sett. Wakefield, 1765-1803; shouldered a musket and marched with a company to Lexington and Concord, 1775; was a moderate Calvinist; d. Wakefield, (Reading), Feb. 7, 1803, a. 56.

JOHN PRENTICE, A.M., b. Newton, 1682, son of Thomas and Sarah (Stanton) Prentice; H. C., 1700, A.B., A.M.; Ord. Lancaster, Mar. 29, 1708; sett. Lancaster, 1705-1746; Election Sermon, 1735; d. Lancaster, Jan. 6, 1747/8, a. 66.

JOSHUA PRENTISS, A.M., b. Cambridge, Apr. 9, 1719, son of Dea. Henry and Elizabeth (Rand) Prentiss; H. C., 1738, A.B., A.M.; Ord. Holliston, May 18, 1743; sett. Holliston, 1743-1784; d. Holliston, Apr. 24, 1788, a. 70.

NATHANIEL PRENTICE, A.M., bapt. Cambridge, Dec. 11, 1698, son of Henry and Mary (Gove) Prentice; H. C., 1715, A.B., A.M.; Ord. Dunstable, 1720; sett. Dunstable, 1720-1737; d. Dunstable, Feb. 27, 1737, a. 38.

OLIVER PRENTICE, Ord. North Stonington, Ct., (Separatist Chh.), May 22, 1753; sett. North Stonington, 1753-1755; d. North Stonington, Ct., Oct. 18, 1755.

SOLOMON PRENTICE, A.M., b. Cambridge, May 11, 1705, son of Solomon and Lydia Prentice; H. C., 1727, A.B., A.M.; Ord. Grafton, Dec. 29, 1731; sett. Grafton, 1731-1747; dism. July 10, 1747; inst. Easton, Nov. 18, 1747; sett. Easton, 1747-1755; became an itinerant "New Light" preacher; in 1750, he attempted to organize a Presbyterian Chh. at Easton, but was not successful; sett. Bellingham; inst. Hull, Mar. 21, 1768; sett. Hull, 1768-1772; d. Grafton, May 22, 1773, a. 68.

THOMAS PRENTICE, A.M., b. Cambridge, Dec. 9, 1702, son of Thomas and Maria (Russell) Prentice; H. C., 1726, A.B., A.M.; Ord. Kennebunkport, Me., (Arundel), Nov. 4, 1730; sett. Kennebunkport, Me., 1729-1738; dism. Sept. 19, 1738; inst. Charlestown, Oct. 3, 1739; sett. Charlestown, 1738-1782; Artillery Election Sermon, 1745; Convention Sermon, 1766; d. Cambridge, June 17, 1782, a. 80.

THOMAS PRENTISS, D.D., b. Holliston, Oct. 27, 1747, son of Rev. Joshua and Mary (Angier) Prentiss; H. C., 1766, A.B., A.M.; S.T.D., 1808; Ord. Medfield, Oct. 30, 1770; sett. Medfield, 1770-1814; Dudleian Lecture, 1800; Convention Sermon, 1803; Chaplain at Roxbury, Rev. War; liberal; d. Medfield, Feb. 28, 1814, a. 67.

BENJAMIN PRESCOTT, A.M., b. Concord, Sept. 16, 1687, son of Capt. Jonathan and Elizabeth (Hoar) Prescott; H. C., 1709, A.B., A.M.; Ord. Peabody, Sept. 23, 1713; sett. Peabody, 1713-1756; resigned Nov. 16, 1756; d. Peabody, May 27, 1777, a. 90.

COMMISSARY ROGER PRICE, A.B., b. Whitefield, Northamptonshire, England, Dec. 6, 1696, son of Rev. William and Elizabeth (Izard) Price; Balliol Coll., Oxford, A.B., 1717/8; Rector of Leigh, Essex, England, 1725-1727; inst. Boston, (King's Chapel, as Rector and B'shop's Commissary), June 25, 1729; sett. Boston, 1729-1746; left Nov. 21, 1746; sett. Hopkinton, (Epis. Chh.), 1748-1752; returned to England; sett. Leigh, Essex, England, 1752-1762; appointed Commissary or superintendent of the Epis. Chhs. of N. E., 1730; laid the corner stone of Trinity Chh., Boston, 1734; Epis.; d. Leigh, Essex, England, Dec. 8, 1762.

JOSEPH PRINCE, b. Boston, Apr. 12, 1723, son of Joseph and Mary (Townsend) Prince; Ord. Barrington, N. H., June 18, 1755; sett. Barrington, N. H., 1755-1768; inst. Candia, N. H., 1782; sett. Candia, N. H., 1782-1789; also preached 3 yrs. at Durham, N. H., 5 at Madbury, N. H., and 13 at Pownalborough, Me.; he was blind from his birth but was a successful minister; d. Newburyport, Jan. 15, 1791, a. 67.

THOMAS PRINCE, A.M., b. Sandwich, May 15, 1687, son of Samuel Prince, Esq.; H. C., 1707, A.B., A.M.; travelled in Europe; preached for several years at Combs, Suffolk, England; Ord. Boston, (Old South Chh.), Oct. 1, 1718; sett. Boston, 1717-1758; author of "Chronological History of New England," 1755; a noted antiquarian and collector of Americana; Artillery Election Sermon, 1721; Election Sermon, 1730; d. Boston, Oct. 22, 1758, a. 72.

THOMAS PRITCHARD, A.B., b. Machynlleth, county Montgomery, Wales, ca. 1677, son of Edward Pritchard; matriculated, Jesus Coll., Camb., Mar. 2, 1698/9, aged 22; Jesus Coll., Camb., 1702, A.B.; came to N. Y., Nov. 30, 1703, as missionary for the V.S.P.G.F.P.; sett. Greenwich, Ct., (Epis. Chh.), Apr. 1704-1705; Vicar of Llangirrig, county Montgomery, 1711; Epis.

JOB PRUDDEN, A.M., bapt. Milford, Ct., Sept. 4, 1715, son of John and Mary (Clark) Prudden; Y. C., 1743, A.B.; A.M., 1763; Ord. New Jersey, May 19, 1747; sett. Milford, Ct., (2nd or Separatist Chh.), 1747-1774; d. Milford, Ct., June 23, 1774, a. 59.

PETER PRUDDEN, b. Kingswalden, Herts., England, 1600; admitted sizar at Emmanuel Coll., Camb., June 20, 1620; arrived at Boston, June 26, 1637; founded New Haven, Ct., 1638, with Rev. John Davenport; Ord. Milford, Ct., Apr. 18, 1640; sett. Milford, Ct., 1639-1656; left a landed estate at Edgton, Yorks., England; d. Milford, Ct., July 6, 1656, a. 56.

EBENEZER PUNDERSON, A.M., b. New Haven, Ct., Sept. 12, 1705, son of Thomas and Lydia (Bradley) Punderson; Y. C., 1726, A.B., A.M.; Ord. Ledyard, Ct., (2nd Cong. Chh. in Groton), Dec. 25, 1729, as the first minister; sett. Ledyard, Ct., 1729-1734; dism. Feb. 5, 1733/4; became an Epis.; Ord. London, England, 1734; sett. Ledyard, Ct., (Epis. Chh.), 1734-1753; sett. Norwich, Ct., (Epis. Chh.), 1736; sett. Hebron, Ct., (Epis. Chh.), 1746-1752; sett. New Haven, Ct., (Trinity Chh.), 1753-1762; sett. Rye, N. Y., 1762-1764; Epis.; d. Rye, N. Y., Sept. 22, 1764, a. 59.

AARON PUTNAM, A.M., b. Reading, Dec. 5, 1733, son of Rev. Daniel and Rebecca (Putnam) Putnam; H. C., 1752, A.B., A.M.; Ord. Pomfret, Ct., (1st Chh.), Mar. 10, 1756; sett. Pomfret, Ct., 1755-1802; resigned May 1802; d. Pomfret, Ct., Oct. 28, 1813, a. 80.

DANIEL PUTNAM, A.B., b. Danvers, Nov. 12, 1696, son of

Capt. Benjamin and Hannah (Holton) Putnam; H. C., 1717, A.B.; Ord. North Reading, (2nd Chh. in Reading), June 29, 1720; sett. North Reading, 1720-1759; d. Reading, June 20, 1759, a. 62.

JOHN RAND, A.M., b. Charlestown, Jan. 24, 1726/7, son of Jonathan and Miliscent (Estabrook) Rand; H. C., 1748, A.B., A.M.; Librarian, H. C., 1753-1755; sett. Tisbury, Jan. 24, 1757-Aug. 12, 1757; Ord. Lyndeborough, N. H., Dec. 7, 1757; sett. Lyndeborough, N. H., 1757-1762; dism. Oct. 8, 1762; removed to Derryfield, N. H., 1765; Justice of the Peace; sett. Bedford, N. H., 1778-1805; d. Bedford, N. H., Oct. 12, 1805, a. 78.

WILLIAM RAND, A.M., b. Charlestown, Mar. 24, 1700, son of William and Persis (Shepard) Rand; H. C., 1721, A.B., A.M.; Ord. Sunderland, May 20, 1724; sett. Sunderland, 1723-1745; inst. Kingston, Sept. 12, 1746; sett. Kingston, 1746-1779; Convention Sermon, 1757; left Sunderland because he did not sympathize with Whitefield; d. Kingston, Mar. 14, 1779, a. 79.

THOMAS RASHLEY, A.M., of Charterhouse, 1629; matriculated at Trinity Coll., Camb., Easter, 1629; A.B., Trinity Coll., Camb., 1632/3; A.M., 1636; Fellow of Trinity Coll., 1633; came to N. E., 1640; member of the First Chh. in Boston, 1640; member of the Artillery Co., 1645; minister at Cape Anne (i. e., Gloucester); sett. as minister at Exeter, N. H., 1645; returned to England; minister at Bishopstoke, Hants., and Barford, Wilts., in 1648; minister at Salisbury Cathedral, in 1652; ejected 1662.

ROBERT RATCLIFFE, B.D., b. 1657, son of Richard Ratcliffe, of Broad-Clist, Devon, England; Exeter Coll., Oxford, 1677, A.B.; A.M., 1680; B.D., 1691; Fellow, 1679-1692; inducted Boston, (Rector of King's Chapel), June 15, 1686; sett. Boston, 1686-1689; returned to England, July 1689; Rector of Stonehouse, Gloucestershire; Rector of Colne Rogers, Gloucestershire, 1694; Epis.

JOB RATHBONE, (Rathbun), b. Stonington, Ct., Jan. 2, 1735/6, son of Rev. Joshua and Mary (Wightman) Rathbone; sett. Canaan, Ct.; sett. Lowville, N. Y., ca. 1765; Rev. Sold.; Bapt.

JOSHUA RATHBONE, b. 1696, son of John and Ann (Dodge) Rathbone; sett. Newport, R. I.; Bapt.; d. 1779.

VALENTINE WIGHTMAN RATHBONE, b. Stonington, Ct., Dec. 1723, son of Rev. Joshua and Mary (Wightman) Rathbone; sett. Stonington Harbor, Ct., (Bapt. Chh.); Ord. Pittsfield, (Bapt. Chh.), 1772; sett. Pittsfield, 1772-1798; sett. Bellingham; Bapt.; d. Bellingham, 1813.

GRINDALL RAWSON, A.M., b. Boston, Jan. 23, 1658/9, son of Colonial Secretary Edward and Rachel (Perne) Rawson; H. C., 1678, A.B., A.M.; Ord. Mendon, Apr. 7, 1684; sett. Mendon, 1680-1715; Chaplain, Canadian campaign, 1690; Artillery Election Sermon, 1703; Election Sermon, 1709; preached and published several sermons for the Indians; d. Mendon, Feb. 6, 1714/5, a. 56.

GRINDALL RAWSON, A.M., b. Mendon, Sept. 6, 1707, son of Rev. Grindall and Susanna (Wilson) Rawson; H. C., 1728, A.B., A.M.; Ord. South Hadley, Oct. 3, 1733; sett. South Hadley, 1733-1741; inst. Hadlyme, Ct., Sept. 18, 1745; sett. Hadlyme, Ct., 1741-1777; d. Hadlyme, Ct., Mar. 29, 1777, a. 69.

GRINDALL RAWSON, A.M., b. Milton, July 29, 1721, son of Pelatiah and Hannah Rawson; H. C., 1741, A.B., A.M.; A.M., (Hon.), Y. C., 1753; Ord. Ware, May 9, 1751; sett. Ware, 1751-1754; resigned Jan. 30, 1754; inst. Yarmouth, Dec. 10, 1755; sett. Yarmouth, 1755-1760; d. Sutton, Nov. 1794, a. 73.

JOHN RAYNER, A.B., (Reiner, Raynor, Reynor, Reyner, etc.), b. Gildersome, Yorkshire, England, ca. 1600, son of Humphrey Rayner; Magdalene Coll., Camb., 1625/6, A.B.; came to N. E., 1635; inst. Plymouth, 1636; sett. Plymouth, 1636-1654; sett. Dover, N. H., 1655-1669; d. Dover, N. H., Apr. 20, 1669, a. 69.

JOHN RAYNER, JR., A.M., b. Plymouth, 1643, son of Rev. John and Frances (Clark) Rayner; H. C., 1663, A.B., A.M.; sett. Mendon, 1667-1668; Ord. Dover, N. H., July 12, 1671; sett. Dover, N. H., 1668-1676; d. Braintree, Dec. 21, 1676, a. 33.

JOHN READ, A.M., b. Fairfield, Ct., Jan. 29, 1679/80, son of William and Deborah (Baldwin) Read; H. C., 1697, A.B.; A.M., 1721; sett. Waterbury, Ct., 1698-1699; sett. East Hartford, Ct., 1699-1702; sett. Windsor, Ct., 1703; sett. Stratford, Ct., 1703-1706; Queen's Attorney, 1712; father of American law; most celebrated attorney of his day; d. Boston, Feb. 7, 1749.

SOLOMON REED, A.M., b. Abington, Oct. 22, 1719, son of Capt. William and Alice Reed; H. C., 1739, A.B., A.M.; Ord. Framingham, (2nd or Separatist Chh.), Jan. 1746/7; sett. Framingham, 1747-1756; sett. Middleborough, (Titicut Separatist Parish), 1756-1785; d. Middleborough, May 7, 1785.

ABNER REEVE, A.M., b. Southold, L. I., N. Y., Feb. 21, 1707/8, son of Thomas and Bethia (Horton) Reeve; Y. C., 1731, A.B.; A.M., 1735; sett. Smithtown, L. I., N. Y., (Presb. Chh.), 1735-1748; Ord. Brookhaven, L. I., N. Y., (Presb. Chh.), Oct. 6, 1755; sett. Brookhaven, L. I., N. Y., 1754-1763; inst. bv covenant, Brattleborough, Vt., July 5, 1770; sett. Brattleborough, Vt., 1767/8-1792; resigned Oct. 3, 1792; d. Brattleborough, Vt., May 16, 1798, a. 90.

EZRA REEVE, A.B., b. Southold, L. I., N. Y., Jan. 27, 1733/4, son of Rev. Abner and Mary Reeve; Y. C., 1757, A.B.; Ord. Mt. Sinai, L. I., N. Y., (Presb. ministry), Oct. 10, 1759; sett. Mt. Sinai, L. I.. N. Y.. 1759-1760; inst. Holland, (South Brimfield), Sept. 13, 1765; sett. Holland, 1765-1818; d. Holland, Apr. 28, 1818, a. 85.

ELISHA REXFORD, A.M., b. New Haven, Ct., Oct. 24, 1737, son of Philip and Anna (Beecher) Rexford; Y. C., 1763, A.B., A.M.; Ord. Monroe, Ct., Jan. 9, 1765, as the first minister; sett. Monroe, Ct., 1765-1808; d. Huntington, Ct., Apr. 3, 1808, a. 71.

GAMALIEL REYNOLDS, b. Norwich, Ct., Nov. 4, 1725, son of Joseph and Hannah (Bingham) Reynolds; Ord. Norwich, Ct., (Bapt. Chh.), Dec. 22, 1762; sett. Norwich, Ct., 1762-1805; Bapt.; d. Norwich, Ct., May 7, 1805, a. 81.

PETER REYNOLDS, A.M., b. Bristol, R. I., Nov. 26, 1700, son of Capt. Peter and Mary (Giles) Reynolds; H. C., 1720, A.B., A.M.; Ord. Enfield, Ct., Nov. 24, 1725; sett. Enfield, Ct., 1724-1768; Ct. Election Sermon, 1757; d. Enfield, Ct., May 11, 1768, a. 68.

CHARLES RHODES, b. Warwick, R. I., Sept. 29, 1719, son of Major John and Catherine (Holden) Rhodes; Ord. Cranston, R. I., July 30, 1764; sett. Cranston, R. I., 1764-1766; mariner and sea captain; Bapt.; d. Warwick, R. I., 1777.

ASAPH RICE, A.M., b. Hardwick, May 9, 1733, son of Beriah and Mary (Goodnow) Rice; H. C., 1752, A.B., A.M.; practiced medicine at Brookfield for some years; Ord. Westminster, Oct. 16, 1765; sett. Westminster, 1765-1815; d. Westminster, Apr. 30, 1816, a. 83.

CALEB RICE, A.M., b. Marlborough, Dec. 13, 1712, son of Dea. Caleb and Mary (Ward) Rice; H. C., 1730, A.B., A.M.; Ord. Sturbridge, Sept. 29, 1736; sett. Sturbridge, 1736-1759; d. Sturbridge, Sept. 2, 1759, a. 47.

JACOB RICE, A.M., b. Westborough, Nov. 27, 1740, son of Jacob and Hannah Rice; H. C., 1765, A.B., A.M.; Ord. Henniker, N. H., June 7, 1769; sett. Henniker, N. H., 1769-1782; dism. Feb. 21, 1782; sett. Brownfield, Me., 1806-1824; d. Brownfield, Me., Feb. 1, 1824, a. 83.

ELISHA RICH, b. Truro, June 4, 1758, son of Zaccheus and Abigail (Harding) Rich; Ord. Chelmsford, (Bapt. Chh.), Oct. 5, 1774; sett. Chelmsford, 1773-1778; sett. Pittsford, Vt.; Bapt.; d. Truro, Aug. 12, 1796.

JOHN RICHARDS, A.M., b. Waterbury, Ct., June 23, 1726, son of Lieut. Thomas and Susanna (Turner) (Reynolds) Richards; Y. C., 1745, A.B., A.M.; A.M., Dart. Coll., 1782; Ord. North Guilford, Ct., Nov. 2, 1748; sett. North Guilford, Ct., 1748-1765; dism. Dec. 24, 1765; sett. Chatham, N. Y., (Cong. Chh.), 1771-1773; called to Piermont, N. H., Feb. 5, 1776; sett. Piermont, N. H., 1776-1802, as the first minister; d. Weybridge, Vt., 1814, a. 88.

GIDEON RICHARDSON, A.M., b. Chelmsford, June 5, 1730, son of Major Josiah and Experience (Wright) Richardson; H. C., 1749, A.B., A.M.; Ord. Wells, Me., Feb. 27, 1754; sett. Wells, Me., 1754-1758; d. Wells, Me., Mar. 17, 1758.

JOHN RICHARDSON, A.M., bapt. Boston, Dec. 26, 1647, son of Amos and Mary Richardson; H. C., 1666, A.B., A.M.; Tutor and Fellow, H. C., 1671-1673; Ord. Newbury, Oct. 20, 1675; sett. Newbury, 1673-1696; Artillery Election Sermon, 1681; d. Newbury, Apr. 27, 1696, a. 50.

DAVID RIPLEY, A.M., b. Scotland, Ct., Feb. 7, 1730/1, son

of David and Lydia (Cary) Ripley; Y. C., 1749, A.B., A.M.; A.M., H.C., 1754; Ord. Abington, Ct., (3rd Chh. in Pomfret), Feb. 21, 1753; sett. Abington, Ct., 1752-1778; dism. Mar. 10, 1778; d. Abington, Ct., Sept. 2, 1785, a. 55.

HEZEKIAH RIPLEY, D.D., b. Scotland, Ct., Feb. 3, 1742/3, son of David and Lydia (Cary) Ripley; Y. C., 1763, A.B., A.M.; D.D., Princeton, 1802; Fellow, Y. C., 1790-1817; Ord. Green Farms, Ct., Feb. 11, 1767; sett. Green Farms, Ct., 1766-1821; Chaplain, Continental Army, 1776-1777; his home was burned by the British, 1779; d. Green Farms, Ct., Nov. 29, 1831, a. 89.

SYLVANUS RIPLEY, A.M., b. Halifax, Sept. 29, 1749, son of Jonathan and Hannah Ripley; Dart. Coll., 1771, A.B., A.M.; Tutor, Dart. Coll., 1772-1782; Trustee, Dart. Coll., 1775-1787; Ord. as a missionary to the Indians, 1771; served as a missionary, 1771-1772; Preceptor, Moor's School (which became Dart. Coll.), 1775-1779; preacher at Dart. Coll., 1779-1787; Prof. of Theology, Dart. Coll., 1782-1787; d. Hanover, N. H., Feb. 5, 1787, a. 37.

AMMI RUHAMAH ROBBINS, A.M., b. Branford, Ct., Aug. 25, 1740, son of Rev. Philemon and Hannah (Foote) Robbins; Y. C., 1760, A.B., A.M.; Ord. Norfolk, Ct., Oct. 28, 1761; sett. Norfolk, Ct., 1761-1813; Chaplain, Rev. War, 1776; Ct. Election Sermon, 1789; Trustee, Williams Coll., 1794-1810; d. Norfolk, Ct., Oct. 31, 1813.

CHANDLER ROBBINS, D.D., b. Branford, Ct., Aug. 24, 1738, son of Rev. Philemon and Hannah (Foote) Robbins; Y. C., 1756, A.B., A.M.; A.M., (Hon.), H. C., 1760; S.T.D., Dart. Coll., 1792; S.T.D., U. of Edinburgh, 1793; Ord. Plymouth, (1st Chh.), Jan. 30, 1760; sett. Plymouth, 1759-1799; Election Sermon, 1791; Anniversary Sermon, 1793; Convention Sermon, 1794; d. Plymouth, June 30, 1799, a. 61.

NATHANIEL ROBBINS, A.M., bapt. West Cambridge, Apr. 17, 1726, son of Thomas and Ruth (Johnson) Robbins; H. C., 1747, A.B., A.M.; A.M., (Hon.), Y. C., 1735; Ord. Milton, Feb. 13, 1750/1; sett. Milton, 1751-1795; Artillery Election Sermon, 1772; d. Milton, May 19, 1795.

PHILEMON ROBBINS, A.M., b. Cambridge, Sept. 19, 1709, son of Nathaniel, Jr. and Hannah (Chandler) Robbins; H. C., 1729, A.B., A.M.; A.M., (Hon.), Y. C., 1733; Ord. Branford, Ct., Feb. 7, 1732; sett. Branford, Ct., 1732-1781; d. Branford, Ct., Aug. 13, 1781.

ROBERT ROBBINS, A.M., b. Wethersfield, Ct., May 23, 1741, son of Jonathan and Sarah (Welles) Robbins; Y. C., 1760, A.B., A.M.; Ord. Chester, Ct., (West Chester Parish of Colchester), Oct. 31, 1764; sett. Chester, Ct., 1763-1804; d. West Chester, Ct., Jan. 22, 1804, a. 63.

JOSEPH ROBERTS, A.M., b. Boston, Jan. 8, 1718/9, son of Joseph and Rachel (Peck) Roberts; H. C., 1741, A.B., A.M.; Ord.

Leicester, Oct. 23, 1754; sett. Leicester, 1754-1762; dism. Dec. 15, 1762; removed to Weston; Rep. Gen. Ct.; d. Weston, Apr. 30, 1811, a. 92, unm.

NATHANIEL ROBERTS, A.M., b. Simsbury, Ct., 1704, son of John Roberts; Y. C., 1732, A.B., A.M.; Ord. Torrington, Ct., Oct. 21, 1741, as the first minister; sett. Torrington, Ct., 1741-1776; d. Torrington, Ct., Mar. 4, 1776, a. 72 .

DAVID ROBINSON, A.M., b. Stratham, N. H., 1716; H. C., 1738, A.B., A.M.; Ord. Newcastle, N. H., Oct. 30, 1748; sett. Newcastle, N. H., 1748-1749; d. Newcastle, N. H., Nov. 18, 1749, a. 33.

JOHN ROBINSON, A.M., b. Dorchester, Mar. 1671, son of Samuel and Mary (Baker) Robinson; H. C., 1695, A.B., A.M.; supply at Lancaster; Ord. Duxbury, Nov. 18, 1702; sett. Duxbury, 1700-1739; d. Lebanon, Ct., Nov. 14, 1745.

JOSEPH ROBY, A.M., b. Boston, May 12, 1724, son of Joseph and Priscilla (Grafton) Roby; H. C., 1742, A.B., A.M.; Ord. Saugus, (2nd Chh. in Lynn), Aug. 1752; sett. Saugus, 1750-1803; d. Saugus, Jan. 31, 1803, a. 80.

CLARK ROGERS, b. West Greenwich, R. I., 1729; inst. Hancock, June 1772; sett. Hancock, 1772-1806; Bapt.; d. Hancock, Jan. 14, 1806, a. 77.

DANIEL ROGERS, JR., A.M., b. Ipswich, Oct. 17, 1706, son of Dr. Daniel (H. C., 1686) and Sarah (Appleton) Rogers; H. C., 1725, A.B., A.M.; Ord. Littleton, Mar. 15, 1731/2; sett. Littleton, 1731-1782; grandson of Rev. John Rogers, President of Harvard College; d. Littleton, Nov. 22, 1782, a. 76.

DANIEL ROGERS, A.M., b. Ipswich, July 28, 1707, son of Rev. John and Martha (Whittingham) Rogers; H. C., 1725, A.B., A.M.; Tutor, H. C., 1732-1741; Ord. York, Me., July 13, 1752; inst. Exeter, N. H., (2nd Chh.), Aug. 31, 1748, as the first minister; sett. Exeter, N. H., 1748-1785; d. Exeter, N. H., Dec. 9, 1785, a. 78.

EZEKIEL ROGERS, A.M., b. Wethersfield, Essex, England, 1590, son of Rev. Richard Rogers; Bennet Coll., Camb., 1604; Christ's Coll., Camb., A.B., 1604/5; A.M., 1608; Chaplain to Sir Francis Barrington, Hatfield Broad Oak, Essex; Rector at Rowley St. Peter, Yorkshire, England, 1621-1638; silenced for non-conformity; came to Rowley, Massachusetts, 1638, bringing his congregation with him; Ord. Rowley, Dec. 3, 1639, as the first minister; sett. Rowley, 1638-1660; physician; Election Sermon, 1643; benefactor of H. C.; d. Rowley, Jan. 23, 1660/1, a. 70.

JAMES ROGERS, b. Westerly, R. I., son of James and Elizabeth Rogers; sett. South Kingston, R. I., (Bapt. Chh.), ca. 1750; Bapt.

PRESIDENT JOHN ROGERS, A.M., b. Coggeshall, Essex, England, Jan. 23, 1630, son of Rev. Nathaniel and Margaret (Crane) Rogers; came to N. E., 1636; H. C., 1649, A.B., A.M.; Ord. Ipswich, July 4, 1656; sett. Ipswich, 1656-1681; physician; fifth President of

Harvard Coll.; inst. Aug. 12, 1683; served, 1683-1684; first graduate of H. C. to become its President; d. Cambridge, July 2, 1684, a. 54.

JOHN ROGERS, b. Milford, Ct., 1648, son of James and Elizabeth (Rowland) Rogers; sett. New London, Ct., 1677-1721; Rogerene or Quaker-Baptist; founder of the sect; d. New London, Ct., Oct. 17, 1721, of small-pox.

JOHN ROGERS, A.M., b. Ipswich, July 7, 1666, son of President John and Elizabeth (Denison) Rogers; H. C., 1684, A.B., A.M.; Ord. Ipswich, Oct. 12, 1692; sett. Ipswich, 1688-1745; Election Sermon, 1706; d. Ipswich, Dec. 28, 1745, a. 79.

JOHN ROGERS, A.M., b. Salem, Nov. 22, 1684, son of Jeremiah Rogers; H. C., 1705, A.B.; A.M., 1744; Ord. Boxford, 1709; sett. Boxford, 1709-1743; d. Leominster, Aug. 17, 1755.

JOHN ROGERS, A.M., b. Ipswich, Jan. 19, 1692, son of Rev. John and Martha (Whittingham) Rogers; H. C., 1711, A.B., A.M.; Librarian, H. C., 1714-1718; Ord. Eliot, Me., (2nd Parish in Kittery), Oct. 25, 1721; sett. Kittery, Me., 1721-1773; d. Eliot, Me., Oct. 16, 1773.

JOHN ROGERS, A.M., b. Boxford, Sept. 24, 1712, son of Rev. John and Susanna (Marston) Rogers; H. C., 1732, A.B., A.M.; Ord. Leominster, (1st Chh.), Sept. 14, 1743; sett. Leominster, 1743-1758; dism. Jan. 28, 1758; sett. Leominster, (2nd Chh., which met at his home), 1762-1787; Unitarian; d. Leominster, Oct. 6, 1789, a. 77.

JOHN ROGERS, A.M., b. Kittery, Me., Aug. 7, 1719, son of Rev. John and Susannah (Whipple) Rogers; H. C., 1739, A.B., A.M.; Ord. Gloucester, (4th Parish), Feb. 1, 1744; sett. Gloucester, 1744-1782; d. Gloucester, Oct. 4, 1782.

JOSHUA ROGERS, Ord. New London, Ct., (2nd Bapt. Chh.), Oct. 11, 1743; sett. New London, Ct., 1743-1756; Bapt.; d. New London, Ct., 1756.

NATHANIEL ROGERS, A.M., b. Haverhill, Suffolk, England, 1598, son of Rev. John and Elizabeth (Gold) Rogers, and a descendant of the martyr; Emmanuel Coll., Camb., A.B., 1617/8; A.M., 1621; Ord. Sept. 20, 1619; Rector at Bocking, Essex, and at Assington, Suffolk, 1630-1636; came to N. E., 1636; Ord. Ipswich, Feb. 20, 1638; sett. Ipswich, 1638-1655; d. Ipswich, July 3, 1655, a. 57.

NATHANIEL ROGERS, A.M., b. Ipswich, Feb. 22, 1669/70, son of President John and Elizabeth (Denison) Rogers; H. C., 1687, A.B., A.M.; Ord. Portsmouth, N. H., May 3, 1699; sett. Portsmouth, N. H., 1699-1723; d. Portsmouth, N. H., Oct. 3, 1723, a. 53.

NATHANIEL ROGERS, A.M., b. Ipswich, Sept. 22, 1701, son of Rev. John, Jr. and Martha (Whittingham) Rogers; H. C., 1721, A.B., A.M.; Ord. Ipswich, Oct. 18, 1727; sett. Ipswich, 1726-1775; d. Ipswich, May 10, 1775, a. 73.

WILLIAM ROGERS, D.D., b. Newport, R. I., July 22, 1751; Brown U., 1769, A.B., A.M.; A.M., U. of Pa., 1773; A.M., Y. C.,

1780; A.M., Princeton, 1786; D.D., U. of Pa., 1790; Principal of the Academy at Newport, R. I., 1769-1770; licensed to preach, 1771; Ord. Philadelphia, Pa., 1772; sett. Philadelphia, Pa., 1772-1775; Chaplain, 1776-1781; Prof., U. of Pa., 1789-1811; member Pa. legislature, 1816-1817; V. P., Religious Hist. Soc. of Phil., 1819; Bapt.; d. Philadelphia, Pa., Apr. 7, 1824.

ROBERT ROGERSON, A.M., b. Portsmouth, England, 1721; St. Paul's School, London, England; A.M., (Hon.), H. C., 1765; sett. Brookline, 1752-1753; inst. Rehoboth, (2nd Parish, now in Attleborough), Feb. 29, 1759; sett. Rehoboth, 1759-1799; d. Rehoboth, Mar. 20, 1799, a. 78.

BENJAMIN ROLFE, A.M., b. Newbury, Sept. 13, 1662, son of Benjamin and Apphia (Hale) Rolfe; H. C., 1684, A.B., A.M.; Ord. Haverhill, Jan. 7, 1693/4; sett. Haverhill, 1689-1708; Chaplain at Falmouth, Me., 1689; d. Haverhill, (killed by the Indians), Aug. 29, 1708, a. 46.

BENAJAH ROOTS, A.M., b. Woodbury, Ct., May 5, 1725, son of John and Ruth (Hickok) Roots; Princeton, 1754, A.B., A.M.; A.M., (Hon.), Y. C., 1784; A.M., (Hon.), Dart. Coll., 1784; Ord. Simsbury, Ct., (1st Cong. Chh.), Aug. 10, 1756; sett. Simsbury, Ct., 1756-1772; inst. West Rutland, Vt., 1774; sett. West Rutland, Vt., Oct. 1773-1784; N. H. Election Sermon, 1779; d. West Rutland, Vt., Mar. 15, 1787, a. 61.

ROBERT ROSS, A.M., Princeton, 1751, A.B., A.M.; A.M., (Hon.), Y. C., 1754; sett. Bridgeport, Ct., (then Stratfield), Nov. 1753-1799; d. Bridgeport, Ct., Aug. 1799.

THOMAS ROSS, b. Westerly, R. I., Sept. 11, 1719, son of William and Ann (Lewis) Ross; sett. Westerly, R. I., (Indian Chh.), fl. 1770; Bapt.

ASHER ROSSETER, A.M., b. Guilford, Ct., Oct. 16, 1715, son of Timothy and Abigail (Penfield) Rosseter; Y. C., 1742, A.B., A.M.; Ord. Preston, Ct., Mar. 14, 1744; sett. Preston, Ct., 1744-1781; d. Preston, Ct., Nov. 17, 1781, a. 66.

ELEAZER ROSSETER, A.M., b. Guilford, Ct., Feb. 4, 1698/9, son of Josiah and Sarah (Sherman) Rosseter; Y. C., 1718, A.B., A.M.; Ord. Stonington, Ct., Dec. 19, 1722; sett. Stonington, Ct., 1722-1762; d. Stonington, Ct., Oct. 11, 1762, a. 64.

DAVID ROUND, b. Swansea, Jan. 28, 1706, son of John and Abigail (Bowen) Round; sett. Rehoboth; sett. Tiverton, R. I., 1752-1775; Bapt.; d. ca. 1775.

NATHANIEL ROUNDS, b. Rehoboth, Feb. 2, 1718, son of Richard and Ann (Martin) Rounds; sett. Rehoboth, (Oak Swamp Bapt. Chh.), 1768-1781; Bapt.; d. Attleborough, July 18, 1781, a. 63.

RICHARD ROUNDS, b. Rehoboth, Mar. 20, 1706, son of Richard and Ann (Martin) Rounds; Ord. Rehoboth, (2nd Bapt.

Chh.), July 13, 1743; sett. Rehoboth, 1743-1749; sett. Rehoboth, (1st Bapt. Chh.), 1749-1768; Bapt.; d. Rehoboth, May 18, 1768, a. 62.

STEPHEN ROWE, A.M., b. Kilfad, Tipperary, Ireland, 1704, son of Michael Rowe; matriculated sizar, Trinity Coll., Dublin, May 21, 1722, aged 18; Trinity Coll., Dublin, A.B., 1726; A.M., 1729; Ord. by the Bishop of Dublin, Ireland, July 5, 1732; inst. Dorchester, S. C., (St. George's Parish), Mar. 19, 1736; sett. Dorchester, S. C., 1736-1741; inst. Boston, (King's Chapel, as asst. Rector), 1741; sett. Boston, 1741-1744; Epis..

DAVID SHERMAN ROWLAND, A.M., b. Fairfield, Ct., Aug. 1719, son of Henry and Tamar (Sherman) Rowland; Y. C., 1743, A.B., A.M.; A.M., Dart. Coll., 1773; Ord. Plainfield, Ct., Mar. 15, 1748; sett. Plainfield, Ct., 1748-1761; dism. May 6, 1761; inst. Providence, R. I., (1st Cong. Chh.), Oct. 1762; sett. Providence, R. I., 1762-1774; dism. Aug. 1774; inst. Windsor, Ct., Mar. 27, 1776; sett. Windsor, Ct., 1774-1794; d. Windsor, Ct., Jan. 13, 1794, a. 75.

JOSEPH ROWLANDSON, A.B., b. England, 1631/2, son of Thomas and Bridget Rowlandson, of Ipswich and Lancaster, Massachusetts; H. C., 1652, A.B.; Ord. Lancaster, Sept. 1660, as the first minister of the First Chh.; sett. Lancaster, 1654-1676; sett. Wethersfield, Ct., 1677-1678; his wife and children were carried captive by the Indians; his wife wrote, "Mary Rowlandson's Narrative," an account of this captivity which has passed through more than forty editions; he published a Fast Day Sermon, 1678; d. Wethersfield, Ct., Nov. 24, 1678, a. ca. 47.

BENJAMIN RUGGLES, A.M., b. Roxbury, Aug. 11, 1676, son of John and Mary (Dyer) Ruggles; H. C., 1693, A.B., A.M.; Ord. Suffield, Ct., Apr. 26, 1698; sett. Suffield, Ct., 1695-1708; d. Roxbury, Sept. 5, 1708.

BENJAMIN RUGGLES, A.M., b. Roxbury, July 4, 1700, son of Capt. Samuel and Martha (Woodbridge) Ruggles; Y. C., 1721, A.B., A.M.; A.M., (Hon.), H. C., 1724; Ord. Lakeville, (West Parish of Middleborough), Nov. 17, 1725; sett. Lakeville, 1725-1753; dism. Dec. 1753; inst. New Braintree, Apr. 18, 1754; sett. New Braintree, 1754-1782; d. New Braintree, May 12, 1782, a. 82.

SAMUEL RUGGLES, A.M., b. Roxbury, Dec. 3, 1681, son of Capt. Samuel and Martha (Woodbridge) Ruggles; H. C., 1702, A.B., A.M.; Ord. Billerica, May 19, 1708; sett. Billerica, 1707-1749; d. Billerica, Mar. 1, 1748/9, a. 67.

THOMAS RUGGLES, A.M., b. Roxbury, Mar. 10, 1670/1, son of Capt. Samuel and Ann (Bright) Ruggles; H. C., 1690, A.B., A.M.; Trustee and Fellow, Y. C., 1711-1728; Ord. Guilford, Ct., Nov. 20, 1695; sett. Guilford, Ct., 1695-1728; d. Guilford, Ct., June 1, 1728.

THOMAS RUGGLES, JR., A.M., b. Guilford, Ct., Nov. 27, 1704, son of Rev. Thomas and Sarah (Fiske) Ruggles; Y. C., 1723,

A.B., A.M.; Fellow, Y. C., 1746-1770; Ord. Guilford, Ct., Mar. 26, 1729; sett. Guilford, Ct., 1729-1770; d. Guilford, Ct., Nov. 20, 1770, a. 66.

TIMOTHY RUGGLES, A.M., b. Roxbury, Nov. 3, 1685, son of Capt. Samuel and Martha (Woodbridge) Ruggles; H. C., 1707, A.B., A.M.; Ord. Marion, (1st Chh. in Rochester), Nov. 22, 1710; sett. Marion, 1710-1768; "an able Divine, and a Faithful Minister. He was much improved in Ecclesiastical Councils." d. Rochester, Oct. 26, 1768, a. 83.

LOUIS RUSMEYER, sett. Newport, R. I., (United Brethren Chh.), 1766-1783; Moravian.

DANIEL RUSSELL, A.M., b. Charlestown, 1642, son of Hon. Richard and Maud (Pitt) Russell; H. C., 1669, A.B., A.M.; Fellow, H. C., 1676; preached at New London, Ct., 1675; sett. Charlestown, 1676-1678; edited an almanac, 1671; d. Charlestown, Jan. 4, 1678/9, a. 36.

DANIEL RUSSELL, A.M., b. Middletown, Ct., June 3, 1702, son of Rev. Noadiah and Mary (Hamlin) Russell; Y. C., 1724, A.B., A.M.; Ord. Rocky Hill, Ct., (3rd Chh. in Wethersfield), June 7, 1727; sett. Rocky Hill, Ct., 1727-1764; d. Rocky Hill, Ct., Sept. 16, 1764, a. 62.

EBENEZER RUSSELL, A.M., b. Branford, Ct., May 4, 1703, son of Rev. Samuel and Abigail (Whiting) Russell; Y. C., 1722, A.B., A.M.; Ord. North Stonington, Ct., Feb. 22, 1727; sett. North Stonington, Ct., 1727-1731; d. North Stonington, Ct., May 22, 1731, a. 28.

JOHN RUSSELL, A.M., b. England, 1626, son of John and Elizabeth Russell of Cambridge, Massachusetts; came to N. E. from Wales, 1632; H. C., 1645, A.B., A.M.; Ord. Wethersfield, Ct., ca. 1649; sett. Wethersfield, Ct., 1649-1659; inst. Hadley, 1659, as the first minister; sett. Hadley, 1659-1692; Election Sermon, 1665; the regicides, Goffe and Whalley, were concealed in his home; d. Hadley, Dec. 10, 1692, a. 65.

JOHN RUSSELL, son of John and Elizabeth Russell of Woburn, Mass.; inst. Boston, (1st Bapt. Chh.), July 28, 1679; sett. Boston, 1679-1680; d. Boston, Dec. 21, 1680.

JONATHAN RUSSELL, A.M., b. Wethersfield, Ct., Sept. 18, 1655, son of Rev. John and Mary (Talcott) Russell; H. C., 1675, A.B., A.M.; Ord. Barnstable, Sept. 19, 1683; sett. Barnstable, 1683-1711; Election Sermon, 1704; d. Barnstable, Feb. 20, 1710/11, a. 55.

JONATHAN RUSSELL, A.M., b. Barnstable, Feb. 24, 1689/90 son of Rev. Jonathan and Martha (Moody) Russell; Y. C., 1708, A.B., A.M.; Ord. Barnstable, Oct. 29, 1712; sett. Barnstable, (East Chh.), 1712-1719; sett. Barnstable, (West Chh.), 1719-1759; d. West Barnstable, Sept. 10, 1759, a. 69.

NOADIAH RUSSELL, A.M., b. New Haven, Ct., July 22, 1659, son of William and Sarah (Davis) Russell; H. C., 1681, A.B.,

A.M.; schoolmaster at Ipswich, 1683-1687; Ord. Middletown, Ct., Oct. 24, 1688; sett. Middletown, Ct., 1688-1713; d. Middletown, Ct., Dec. 3, 1713, a. 53.

NOADIAH RUSSELL, A.M., b. Middletown, Ct., Jan. 24, 1729/30, son of Rev. William and Mary (Pierpont) Russell; Y. C., 1750, A.B., A.M.; preached at Pomfret, Ct., 1753-1756; Ord. Thompson, Ct., Nov. 9, 1757; sett. Thompson, Ct., 1757-1795; d. Mendon, Oct. 27, 1795, a. 66.

SAMUEL RUSSELL, A.M., b. Hadley, Nov. 4, 1660, son of Rev. John and Rebecca (Newbury) Russell; H. C., 1681, A.B., A.M.; Ord. Branford, Ct., Mar. 7, 1687/8, as the first minister; sett. Branford, Ct., 1687-1731; Ct. Election Sermon, 1699; d. Branford, Ct., June 25, 1731, a. 71.

SAMUEL RUSSELL, A.M., b. Branford, Ct., Sept. 28, 1693, son of Rev. Samuel and Abigail (Whiting) Russell; Y. C., 1712, A.B., A.M.; Tutor, Y. C., 1714-1716; Ord. North Guilford, Ct., June 15, 1725; sett. North Guilford, Ct., 1722-1746; d. North Guilford, Ct., Jan. 19, 1745/6, a. 52.

WILLIAM RUSSELL, A.M., b. Middletown, Ct., Nov. 20, 1690, son of Rev. Noadiah and Mary (Hamlin) Russell; Y. C., 1709, A.B., A.M.; Tutor, Y. C., 1713-1714; Fellow, Y. C., 1745-1761; Ord. Middletown, Ct., (1st Chh.), June 1, 1715; sett. Middletown, Ct., 1715-1761; Ct. Election Sermon, 1730; d. Middletown, Ct., June 1, 1761, a. 71.

WILLIAM RUSSELL, A.M., b. Middletown, Ct., July 23, 1723, son of Rev. William and Mary (Pierpont) Russell; Y. C., 1745, A.B., A.M.; Tutor, Y. C., 1749-1750; Ord. Windsor, Ct., (1st Chh.), July 24, 1754; sett. Windsor, Ct., 1750-1775; d. Windsor, Ct., Apr. 17, 1775, a. 52.

HENRY RUST, A.M., b. Ipswich, 1686, son of Lieut. Nathaniel and Joanna (Kinsman) Rust; H. C., 1707, A.B., A.M.; Ord. Stratham, N. H., Apr. 1718; sett. Stratham, N. H., 1717-1749; Arminian; d. Stratham, N. H., Mar. 20, 1749, a. 63.

ROBERT RUTHERFORD, A.M., b. Ireland, 1688; came to Pemaquid, Me. with Col. Dunbar, 1729; preached at Pemaquid and Bristol, Me., 1730-1735; sett. Brunswick and Topsham, Me., May 1735-1742; sett. Georgetown, Me., 1743; Chaplain at St. George's and preached at Thomaston and Warren, Me., 1743-1756; Presb.; d Thomaston, Me., Oct. 18, 1756, a. 68.

ABISHAI SABIN, A.M., b. Pomfret, Ct., Sept. 10, 1735, son of Joshua and Mary (Sabin) Sabin; Y. C., 1759, A.B., A.M.; Ord. Monson, June 23, 1762; sett. Monson, 1762-1771; dism. July 1771; d. Pomfret, Ct., Feb. 4, 1782, a. 47.

RICHARD SACKET, A.M., b. Newton, L. I., N. Y., son of Capt. Joseph and Elizabeth (Betts) Sacket; Y. C., 1709, A.B., A.M.; sett. Greenwich, Ct., (1st Parish), 1714-1716; Ord. West Greenwich,

Ct., Nov. 27, 1717; sett. West Greenwich, Ct., 1716-1727; d. Greenwich, Ct., May 8, 1727.

RICHARD SADLER, b. Worcester, England, ca. 1620, prob. son of Richard Sadler (who came from Worcester, Eng., 1636, to Lynn); admitted pensioner at Emmanuel Coll., Camb., Dec. 30, 1636; matriculated at Emmanuel Coll., Camb., 1637; came to N. E., 1638; sett. at Lynn; returned to England, 1647; Ord. Whixall Chapel, Salop, England, May 10, 1648; lecturer at Ludlow, Shropshire, Eng.; ejected 1662; retired to Whixall, Shropshire, Eng.; d. there, 1675, a. 55.

SETH SAGE, A.M., b. Cromwell, Ct., Feb. 9, 1747/8, son of Dea. Solomon and Hannah (Kirby) Sage; Y. C., 1768, A.B., A.M.; Ord. West Simsbury, Ct., (at Canton Center), July 13, 1774; sett. West Simsbury, Ct., 1774-1778; sett. Colesville, N. Y., (Presb. Chh.), 1800-1807; d. Windsor, N. Y., Feb. 1821, a. 73.

RICHARD SALTER, D.D., b. Boston, July 31, 1721, son of John and Abigail (Durant) Salter; H. C., 1739, A.B., A.M.; S.T.D., Y. C., 1782; Fellow, Y. C., 1771-1780; Ord. Mansfield, Ct., (1st Chh.), June 27, 1744; sett. Mansfield, Ct., 1744-1787; Ct. Election Sermon, 1768; d. Mansfield, Ct., Apr. 14, 1789, a. 68.

GOVERNOR GURDON SALTONSTALL, A.M., b. Haverhill, Mar. 27, 1666, son of Hon. Nathaniel and Elizabeth (Ward) Saltonstall; H. C., 1684, A.B., A.M.; Ord. New London, Ct., Nov. 25, 1691; sett. New London, Ct., 1687-1707; Governor of Connecticut, 1707-1724; Ct. Election Sermon, 1707; d. New London, Ct., Sept. 20, 1724.

EZRA SAMPSON, A.B., b. Lakeville, Feb. 12, 1749, son of Uriah and Ann (White) Sampson; Y. C., 1773, A.B.; Ord. Plympton, Feb. 15, 1775; sett. Plympton, 1775-1796; resigned Apr. 4, 1796; Chaplain, Am. Rev.; Editor, 1801-1805; Judge of the County Court; Unitarian; d. New York City, Dec. 12, 1823, a. 75.

ROBERT SANDEMAN, b. Perth, Scotland, 1718, son-in-law of Rev. John Glas, the founder of the Glasite or Sandemanian sect; came to N. E., Oct. 18, 1764, with Capt. Montgomery; sett. Portsmouth, N. H. and Danbury, Ct., 1764-1771; d. Danbury, Ct., Apr. 2, 1771, a. 53.

DAVID SANFORD, A.M., b. New Milford, Ct., Dec. 11, 1737, son of Elihu and Rachel (Strong) Sanford; Y. C., 1755, A.B., A.M.; Ord. Medway, (West or 2nd Chh.), Apr. 14, 1773; sett. Medway, 1772-1810; Chaplain, Rev. War, 1776, Col. Lemuel Robinson's Regt.; d. Medway, Apr. 7, 1810, a. 73.

ZEDEKIAH SANGER, D.D., b. Sherborn, Oct. 4, 1748, son of Richard and Deborah (Rider) Sanger; H. C., 1771, A.B., A.M.; D.D., Brown U., 1807; Ord. Duxbury, July 3, 1776; sett. Duxbury, 1776-1786; inst. Bridgewater, Dec. 17, 1788; sett. Bridgewater, 1788-1820; Convention Sermon, 1805; Fellow, Am. Acad. Arts and Sciences; prepared youth for college and for the ministry; Preceptor, Bridgewater Academy, 1799-1820; Unitarian; d. Bridgewater, Nov. 17, 1820, a. 73.

SARGENT, and variations.

CHRISTOPHER SARGENT, A.M., b. Amesbury, Aug. 4, 1704, son of Thomas and Mary (Stevens) Sargent; H. C., 1725, A.B., A.M.; Ord. Methuen, Nov. 5, 1729, as the first minister; sett. Methuen, 1729-1783; broad-minded Calvinist; d. Methuen, Mar. 20, 1790, a. 85.

JOHN SERGEANT, A.M., b. Newark, N. J., 1710, son of Jonathan, Jr. and Mary Sergeant; Y. C., 1729, A.B., A.M.; Tutor, 1731-1735; Ord. Deerfield, (for work at Stockbridge), Aug. 31, 1735; inst. Stockbridge, July 1735; sett. Stockbridge, 1734-1749; d. Stockbridge, July 27, 1749, a. 39.

JOHN SERGEANT, b. Stockbridge, 1747, son of Rev. John and Abigail (Williams) Sergeant; Princeton, but did not grad.; sett. as Indian preacher at Stockbridge, 1775-1785; removed to New Stockbridge, N. Y., 1785; Ord. New Stockbridge, N. Y., 1788; sett. New Stockbridge, N. Y., 1785-1824; d. New Stockbridge, N. Y., Sept. 7, 1824, a. 77.

WILLIAM SARGEANT, bapt. Northampton, England, June 20, 1602, son of Roger and Ellen (Marcharmes) Sargeant; came to Charlestown, N. E., 1638; adm. to the First Chh., Charlestown, Mar. 10, 1638/9; lay preacher at Malden, 1648-1650; removed to Barnstable, 1656; a haberdasher by profession; adm. freeman, Plymouth Colony, 1658; d. Barnstable, Dec. 16, 1682.

WINWOOD SERJEANT, b. Bristol, England, ca. 1739; Ord. by the Bishop of Rochester, in England, Dec. 19, 1756; missionary, V.S.P.G.F.P.; sett. Charleston, S. C., (St. Philip's Chh.), 1759; sett. Dorchester, S. C., (St. George's Parish), 1760-1767; sett. Cambridge, (Christ Chh.), Oct. 1767-1774; sett. Kingston, N. H.; sett. Newbury, 1777; returned to England, 1778; Chaplain of a British ship in Boston Harbor, 1775; Epis.; d. Bath, Eng., Sept. 20, 1780.

PETER SAXTON, A.M., b. Bramley, Leeds, Yorkshire, England, son of Christopher Saxton, the chronographer; Trinity Coll., Camb., A.B., 1595/6; A.M., 1603; Ord. York, England, Apr. 18, 1611; Rector of Edlington, Yorkshire, 1614-1640; came to N. E. and succeeded Rev. John Lothrop at Scituate, 1640-1641; returned to England, 1641; Vicar of Leeds, Yorkshire, England, 1646-1651; d. Leeds, Yorkshire, England, Oct. 1, 1651.

JOHN SAYRE, A.B., b. New York City, June 4, 1738, son of John and Esther (Stillwell) Sayre; Columbia U.; sett. Newburg, N. Y., 1767-1773; sett. Fairfield, Ct., 1774-1779; Epis.; d. Maugerville, N. S., Aug. 5, 1784.

JAMES SCALES, A.B., b. Boxford, May 31, 1707, son of James and Sarah (Curtis) Scales; H. C., 1733, A.B.; preached at Canterbury, N. H., 1743-1754; Ord. Hopkinton, N. H., Nov. 23, 1757; sett. Hopkinton, N. H., 1757-1770; dism. July 4, 1770; practiced law; J. P.; d. Hopkinton, N. H., July 26, 1776, a. 69.

WILLIAM SCALES, A.M., b. Bath, Me., Oct. 5, 1742, son of

William and Mary (Ingersoll) Scales; H. C., 1771, A.B., A.M.; preached often but was never settled; d. Lincoln, Me., 1799.

JOHN MARTIN SCHAEFFER, came from Germany; sett. Waldoborough, Me., 1762-1785; Lutheran.

JAMES SCOVILL, A.M., b. Waterbury, Ct., Jan. 27, 1732/3, son of Lieut. William and Hannah (Richards) Scovill; Y. C., 1757, A.B.; A.M., Columbia U., 1761; Ord. London, England, Apr. 1, 1759; missionary, V.S.P.G.F.P., 1759-1783; sett. Waterbury, Ct., 1759-1783; sett. Northbury, Ct., (now Plymouth), 1759-1764; sett. New Cambridge, Ct., (now Bristol), 1759-1764; sett. Westbury, Ct., (now Watertown), 1764-1783; sett. New Brunswick, 1783-1808; Epis.; d. Kingston, Ct., Dec. 19, 1808, a. 76.

WILLIAM SCREVEN, b. Somersetshire, England, 1629; Ord. Boston, (1st Bapt. Chh.), Jan. 11, 1681/2; sett. Kittery, Me., where he organized a Bapt. Chh., Sept. 25, 1682; left after Oct. 9, 1683, for Somerton, S. C., and was minister of a Baptist Chh. there, 1683-1693; removed to Georgetown, S. C.; sett. Georgetown, S. C., 1693-1713; Bapt.; d. Georgetown, S. C., Oct. 10, 1713, a. 84.

SAMUEL SEABURY, A.M., b. Groton, Ct., July 8, 1706, son of Dea. John and Elizabeth (Alden) Seabury; H. C., 1724, A.B., A.M.; Ord. 1731; inst. New London, Ct., (St. James' Chh.), Apr. 10, 1732; sett. New London, Ct., 1732-1743; sett. Hempstead, L. I., N. Y., 1743-1764; Epis.; d. Hempstead, L. I., N. Y., July 15, 1764.

JOB SEAMANS, b. Rehoboth, May 24, 1748, son of Dea. Charles and Hannah Seamans; sett. Sackville, New Brunswick, 1763-1772; Ord. North Attleborough, (North Bapt. Chh.), Dec. 15, 1773; sett. North Attleborough, 1772-1787; dism. Nov. 1787; inst. New London, N. H., Jan. 21, 1789; sett. New London, N. H., 1788-1830; Bapt.; d. New London, N. H., Oct. 4, 1830, a. 83.

JAMES SEARING, A.M., b. Hempstead, L. I., N. Y., Sept. 23, 1704, son of James and Temperance (Williams) Searing; Y. C., 1725, A.B., A.M.; Ord. Newport, R. I., (2nd Cong. Chh.), Apr. 21, 1731; sett. Newport, R. I., 1728-1755; d. Newport, R. I., Jan. 6, 1755, a. 51.

JOHN SEARLE, A.M., b. Northampton, May 14, 1721, son of James and Mary Searle; Y. C., 1745, A.B., A.M.; Ord. Sharon, Ct., Aug. 2, 1749; sett. Sharon, Ct., 1748-1754; dism. June 25, 1754; inst. Stoneham, Jan. 19, 1759; sett. Stoneham, 1759-1776; resigned Apr. 24, 1776; inst. Royalton, Vt., Nov. 19, 1783, as the first minister; sett. Royalton, Vt., 1783-1787; d. Royalton, Vt., July 5, 1787, a. 67.

JONATHAN SEARLE, A.M., b. Rowley, Mar. 15, 1743/4, son of Samuel and Elizabeth (Dickinson) Searle of Byfield; H. C., 1764, A.B., A.M.; Ord. Mason, N. H., Oct. 14, 1772. as the first minister; sett. Mason, N. H., 1772-1781; dism. May 4, 1781; d. Dec. 7, 1812, a. 68.

JONATHAN SEARLE, A.M., b. Rowley, Nov. 16, 1746, son of Dea. William and Jane (Nelson) Searle; H. C., 1765, A.B., A.M.;

A.M., (Hon.), Dart. Coll., 1780; Ord. Salisbury, N. H., Nov. 17, 1773, as the first minister; sett. Salisbury, N. H., 1773-1791; dism. Nov. 8, 1791; d. (Salisbury, N. H.), Dec. 2, 1818, a. 73.

JOHN SECCOMB, A.M., b. Medford, Apr. 25, 1708, son of Capt. Peter and Hannah (Willis) Seccomb; H. C., 1728, A.B., A.M.; Ord. Harvard, Oct. 10, 1733, as the first minister; sett. Harvard, 1733-1757; dism. Sept. 7, 1757; sett. Chester, Nova Scotia, 1761-1792; author of "Father Abbey's Will"; d. Halifax, N. S., Oct. 27, 1792, a. 84.

JOSEPH SECCOMBE, A.M., b. Boston, June 14, 1706, son of John and Mehitable (Simmons) Seccombe; H. C., 1731, A.B., A.M.; Ord. Kingston, N. H., Nov. 23, 1737; sett. Kingston, N. H., 1737-1760; d. Kingston, N. H., Sept. 15, 1760, a. 54.

NICHOLAS SEVER, A.M., b. Roxbury, Apr. 15, 1680, son of Caleb and Sarah (Inglesby) Seaver; H. C. 1701, A.B., A.M.; Tutor, H. C., 1716-1728; Fellow, H. C., 1725-1728; Ord. Dover, N. H., Apr. 11, 1711; sett. Dover, N. H., 1711-1715; dism. 1715, because of an impediment in his speech; Judge, Plymouth County, Mass.; d. Kingston, Apr. 7, 1764, a. 83.

HENRY SEWALL, b. Coventry, England, 1614, son of Henry and Anne (Hunt) Sewall; arrived at Boston in the "Ellen and Dorcas," 1634; freeman, May 17, 1637; returned to England 1647-1659; Deputy, Gen. Ct., Mass., 1661-1663; 1668-1670; sett. Warwick, Hants., Tamworth, Bishopstoke and North Baddesly, near Romsey, where he was a minister; father of Chief-Justice Samuel Sewall; d. Newbury, May 16, 1700, a. 86.

JOSEPH SEWALL, D.D., b. Boston, Aug. 15, 1688, son of Chief Justice Samuel and Hannah (Hull) Sewall; H. C., 1707, A.B., A.M.; S.T.D., U. of Glasgow, 1731; Fellow, H. C., 1728-1765; chosen President of H. C., 1724, but declined; Ord. Boston, (Old South Chh.), Sept. 16, 1713; sett. Boston, 1713-1769; Artillery Election Sermon, 1714; Election Sermon, 1724; d. Boston, June 27, 1769, a. 81.

WILLIAM SEWARD, A.M., b. Durham, Ct., July 27, 1712, son of Dea. William and Damaris (Punderson) Seward; Y. C., 1734, A.B., A.M.; Ord. Killingworth, Ct., (North Chh.), Jan. 18, 1737/8; sett. Killingworth, Ct., 1738-1782; d. Killingworth, Ct., Feb. 5, 1782, a. 70.

WILLIAM SEWARD, A.M., b. North Killingworth, Ct., Nov. 19, 1747, son of Rev. William and Concurrence (Stevens) Seward; Y. C., 1769, A.B., A.M.; Ord. Greenwich, Ct., (Stanwich Society), Feb. 25, 1773; sett. Greenwich, Ct., 1773-1794; dism. Feb. 1794; Chaplain, Col. Waterbury's Reg., Rev. War, 1775; d. Fishkill, N. Y., July 15, 1822, a. 75.

RICHARD SEYMOUR, of Berry-Pomeroy, Devonshire, England; preached at St. George's Island, Me., Aug. 9, 1607; at Sagadahoc, Me., Aug. 19, 1607; Chaplain of the unfortunate Gilbert and Popham expedition, 1608; assistant of the Colony; supposed to have been the first ordained Protestant preacher in America north of Virginia; Epis.

BENJAMIN SHATTUCK, A.M., b. Watertown, July 30, 1687, son of William and Susannah (Randall) Shattuck; H. C., 1709, A.B., A.M.; Ord. Littleton, Dec. 25, 1717; sett. Littleton, 1717-1730; dism. Aug. 24, 1730; d. Littleton, 1763. (Wor. Reg. Deeds, 35:439).

BEZALEEL SHAW, A.M., b. Bridgewater, 1738, son of Rev. John and Sarah (Angier) Shaw; H. C., 1762, A.B., A.M.; Ord. Nantucket, (1st Cong. Chh.), Nov. 25, 1767; sett. Nantucket, 1767-1796; d. Nantucket, Feb. 28, 1796, a. 57.

JOHN SHAW, A.M., b. Bridgewater, Apr. 13, 1708, son of Joseph and Judith (Whitmarsh) Shaw; H. C., 1729, A.B., A.M.; Ord. Bridgewater, Nov. 17, 1731; sett. Bridgewater, 1731-1791; d. Bridgewater, Apr. 20, 1791, a. 83.

JOHN SHAW, A.M., b. Bridgewater, Sept. 14, 1748, son of Rev. John and Sarah (Angier) Shaw; H. C., 1772, A.B., A.M.; Ord. Haverhill, Mar. 12, 1777; sett. Haverhill, 1777-1794; d. Haverhill, Sept. 29, 1794, a. 46.

OAKES SHAW, A.M., b. Bridgewater, June 29, 1736, son of Rev. John and Sarah (Angier) Shaw; H. C., 1758, A.B., A.M.; Ord. Barnstable, (West Chh.), Oct. 1, 1760; sett. Barnstable, 1760-1807; father of Hon. Lemuel Shaw, H. C., 1800, Chief Justice of the Supreme Court of Mass.; d. Barnstable, Feb. 11, 1807, a. 71.

WILLIAM SHAW, (perhaps b. ca. 1685, son of Brian Shaw, of Mavesyn Ridware, Co. Stafford, Eng.; matric., Oriel Coll., Oxford, Mar. 19, 1700/1, a. 15); inst. Marblehead, (St. Michael's Chh.), July 20, 1715, as Rector; sett. Marblehead, 1715-1718; Epis.

WILLIAM SHAW, D.D., b. Bridgewater, Jan. 15, 1741, son of Rev. John and Sarah (Angier) Shaw; H. C., 1762, A.B., A.M.; S.T.D., 1815; Ord. Marshfield, (1st Chh.), Apr. 2, 1766; sett. Marshfield, 1766-1816; d. Marshfield, June 1, 1816.

BENJAMIN SHELDON, b. Providence, R. I., 1720, son of Timothy and Rebecca Sheldon; sett. Tiverton, R. I., 1752-1775; Bapt.; d. Tiverton, R. I., Dec. 31, 1781.

JEREMIAH SHEPARD, A.M., b. Cambridge, Aug. 11, 1648, son of Rev. Thomas and Margaret (Boradel) Shepard; H. C., 1669, A.B., A.M.; sett. Rowley, 1673-1678; sett. Essex, 1679-1680; Ord. Lynn, Oct. 6, 1680; sett. Lynn, 1680-1720; Rep. Gen. Ct., 1689; Election Sermon, 1715; d. Lynn, June 2, 1720, a. 72.

NATHANIEL SHEPARD, b. Norton, Feb. 13, 1713, son of Isaac and Elizabeth (Fuller) Shepard; Ord. Attleborough, (North Chh.), Jan. 20, 1747/8; sett. Attleborough, 1748-1752; d. Attleborough, Apr. 14, 1752, a. 40.

SAMUEL SHEPARD, A.M., b. Cambridge, Oct. 18, 1641, son of Rev. Thomas and Joanna (Hooker) Shepard; H. C., 1658, A.B.,

A.M.; Fellow, H. C., 1660-1663; Ord. Rowley, Nov. 15, 1665; sett. Rowley, 1665-1668; d. Rowley, Apr. 7, 1668, a. 26.

SAMUEL SHEPARD, b. Salisbury, June 22, 1739, son of Israel and Mary (True) Shepard; Ord. Stratham, N. H., (Bapt. Chh.), Sept. 25, 1771; sett. Stratham, N. H., (united Bapt. churches of Stratham, Brentwood, Nottingham and Epping), 1770-1815; physician; Bapt.; d. Brentwood, N. H., Nov. 4, 1815, a. 77.

THOMAS SHEPARD, A.M., b. Towcester, Northamptonshire, England, Nov. 5, 1605, (the day of the "Gun-powder Plot"), son of William Shepard; Emmanuel Coll., Camb., A.B., 1623/4; A.M., 1627; Ord. at Peterborough, July 13, 1627; lecturer at Earles Colne, Essex, 3 yrs.; Chaplain to Sir Richard Darley, Knt.; sett. Buttercrambe, Yorkshire, 1 yr.; was silenced and unfrocked; came to N. E., 1635; Ord. Cambridge, Feb. 1, 1635/6; sett. Cambridge, 1636-1649; Election Sermon, 1637; d. Cambridge, Aug. 25, 1649, a. 44.

THOMAS SHEPARD, JR., A.M., b. London, England, Apr. 5, 1635, son of Rev. Thomas and Margaret (Toutville) Shepard; came to N. E., 1635; H. C., 1653, A.B., A.M.; Fellow, H. C., 1654-1673; Ord. Charlestown, Apr. 13, 1659; sett. Charlestown, 1659-1677; Artillery Election Sermon, 1663; Election Sermon, 1672; d. Charlestown, Dec. 22, 1677, a. 43.

THOMAS SHEPARD, 3rd., A.M., b. Charlestown, July 5, 1658, son of Rev. Thomas and Anna (Tyng) Shepard; H. C., 1676, A.B., A.M.; Ord. Charlestown, May 5, 1680, as successor to his father; sett. Charlestown, 1680-1685; d. Charlestown, June 8, 1685, a. 27.

JAMES SHERMAN, b. Milford, Ct., 1645, son of Rev. John and Abigail Sherman; Ord. Sudbury, 1678; sett. Sudbury, 1678-1705; dism. May 22, 1705; later became a physician at Elizabeth, N. J., and at Salem; d. Sudbury, Mar. 3, 1718.

JOHN SHERMAN, b. Dedham, Essex, England, Dec. 26, 1613, son of Edmund and Grace (Makin) Sherman; matriculated sizar at St. Catharine's Hall, Camb., Easter, 1631; declined to subscribe for his degree; (another John Sherman, not this one, was A.B., Trinity Coll., Camb., 1629/30; A.M., 1633); came to N. E., 1634; sett. New Haven, Ct., 1636-1644; sett. Branford, Ct., 1645; Ord. Watertown, 1647; sett. Watertown, 1647-1685; Mass. Convention Sermon, 1682; Fellow, H. C., where he gave lectures for 30 years; his sermons were distinguished for beauty of style and language; he was a recognized authority in astronomy; by two wives he was the father of twenty-six children; Overseer, H.C., 1678-1685; d. Watertown, Aug. 8, 1685, a. 72.

JOSIAH SHERMAN, A.M., b. Watertown, Apr. 29, 1729, son of William and Mehitable (Wellington) Sherman; Princeton, 1754, A.B., A.M.; A.M., (Hon.), H. C., 1758; A.M., (Hon.), Y. C., 1765; Ord. Woburn, Jan. 28, 1756; sett. Woburn, 1756-1775; sett. Milford, Ct., (Separatist Chh.), Aug. 1775-June 1781; Artillery Election Sermon, 1760; d. Woburn, Nov. 24, 1789.

NATHANIEL SHERMAN, A.M., b. Newton, Mar. 5, 1724, son of William and Mehitable (Wellington) Sherman; Princeton, 1753, A.B., A.M.; Ord. Bedford, Feb. 18, 1756; sett. Bedford, 1756-1768; dism. Mar. 20, 1768; inst. Mt. Carmel, Ct., May 18, 1768; sett. Mt. Carmel, Ct., 1768-1797; d. East Windsor, Ct., July 18, 1797, a. 74.

JACOB SHERWIN, A.B., b. Hebron, Ct., Mar. 31, 1736, son of Jacob and Hannah (Phelps) Sherwin; Y. C., 1759, A.B.; Ord. Ashfield, (2nd Chh.), Feb. 23, 1763; sett. Ashfield, 1763-1774; dism. May 17, 1774; inst. Sunderland, Vt., (2nd Chh.), Mar. 18, 1790; sett. Sunderland, Vt., 1790-1803; J. P.; Town Clerk; d. Sunderland, Vt., Jan. 7, 1803, a. 67.

JOHN SHERWOOD, b. Stratfield, Ct., Sept. 22, 1705, son of Samuel and Rebecca (Burr) Sherwood; Ord. Stratfield, Ct., (Bapt. Chh.), Dec. 1757; sett. Stratfield, Ct., 1757-1767; Capt., Stratfield military co., 1747; Bapt.; d. Stratfield, Sept. 17, 1779, a. 74.

SAMUEL SHERWOOD, A.M., b. Fairfield, Ct., Feb. 10, 1729/30, son of Capt. Dea. Samuel and Jane (Burr) Sherwood; Y. C., 1749, A.B., A.M.; A.M., Princeton, 1755; Ord. Weston, Ct., (Northfield), Aug. 17, 1757, as the first minister; sett. Weston, Ct., 1757-1783; d. Weston, Ct., May 25, 1783, a. 54.

SAMUEL SHIVERICK, sett. Marion, (1st Chh. in Rochester), 1683-1687; sett. Falmouth, (1st Chh.), 1700-1707; a Huguenot minister who escaped from the Catholic persecution of the Protestants in France.

MATTHEW SHORT, A.M., b. Newbury, Mar. 14, 1687/8, son of Henry and Sarah (Whipple) Short; H. C., 1707, A.B., A.M.; Ord. Attleborough, Nov. 12, 1712; sett. Attleborough, 1712-1715; dism. May 3, 1715; sett. Saco and Biddeford, Me., 1716-1722; inst. Easton, 1723; sett. Easton, 1723-1731; d. Easton, Apr. 16, 1731, a. 44.

GEORGE SHOVE, b. England, 1634, son of Rev. Edward and Margery Shove; (Rev. Edward Shove, King's Coll., Camb., A.B., 1625; A.M., 1629; sailed from England in 1638, as assistant to Rev. Ezekiel Rogers, founder and first minister at Rowley; but Mr. Shove died on the voyage to America); H. C., 1650-1652, but did not graduate; Ord. Taunton, Nov. 17, 1665; sett. Taunton, 1665-1687; d. Taunton, Apr. 21, 1687.

SETH SHOVE, A.M., b. Taunton, Dec. 10, 1667, son of Rev. George and Hopestill (Newman) Shove; H. C., 1687, A.B., A.M.; sett. Simsbury, Ct., 1691-1695; Ord. Danbury, Ct., Oct. 13, 1697, as the first minister; sett. Danbury, Ct., 1696-1735; d. Danbury, Ct., Oct. 3, 1735, a. 68.

WILLIAM SHURTLEFF, A.M., b. Plymouth, Apr. 4, 1689, son of William and Susanna (Lothrop) Shurtleff; H. C., 1707, A.B., A.M.; Ord. Newcastle, N. H., 1712; sett. Newcastle, N. H., 1712-1732; inst. Portsmouth, N. H., (South Parish), Feb. 21, 1733; sett.

Portsmouth, N. H., 1733-1747; d. Portsmouth, N. H., May 9, 1747, a. 58.

DANIEL SHUTE, D.D., b. Malden, July 19, 1722, son of John and Mary (Wayte) Shute; H. C., 1743, A.B., A.M.; S.T.D., 1790; Ord. South Hingham, Dec. 10, 1746; sett. Hingham, 1746-1802; appointed Chaplain of Col. Joseph Williams' Regt., 1758, by Gov. Pownal; Artillery Election Sermon, 1767; Election Sermon, 1768; Convention Sermon, 1783; member of the Constitutional Convention, 1780; ratified the Constitution of the United States, 1788; liberal; Unitarian; d. Hingham, Aug. 30, 1802.

ELIJAH SILL, A.M., b. Lyme, Ct., Nov. 8, 1724, son of Joseph and Phoebe (Lord) Sill; Y. C., 1748, A.B., A.M.; Ord. Sherman, Ct., (North Chh. in New Fairfield), Oct. 16, 1751; sett. Sherman, Ct., 1751-1779; dism. Oct. 5, 1779; inst. Dorset, Vt., Sept. 22, 1784; sett. Dorset, Vt., 1784-1789; also preached in N. Y. state; Vt. Election Sermon, 1788; d. Burlington, N. Y., 1792, a. 68.

ROBERT SILLIMAN, A.M., b. Fairfield, Ct., Sept. 26, 1716, son of Robert, Jr. and Ruth (Treadwell) Silliman; Y. C., 1737, A.B., A.M.; Ord. New Canaan, Ct., Feb. 3, 1742; sett. New Canaan, Ct., 1741-1771; dism. Aug. 28, 1771; inst. Chester, Ct., Jan. 29, 1772; sett. Chester, Ct., 1772-1781; d. Norwalk, Ct., Apr. 9, 1781, a. 65.

JAMES SIMONS, sett. Charlestown, R. I., (Indian Chh.), ca. 1750; Bapt.

SAMUEL SKELTON, A.M., bapt. Coningsby, Lincolnshire, England, Feb. 26, 1592/3, son of Rev. William Skelton; Clare Hall, Camb., A.B., 1611/2; A.M., 1615; Rector of Sempringham, Lincolnshire, 1615-1620; Chaplain to the Earl of Lincoln, ca. 1629; came to Salem, New England, 1629; Ord. Salem, July 20, 1629; sett. Salem, 1629-1634; d. Salem, Aug. 2, 1634.

ISAAC SKILLMAN, D.D., b. New Jersey, 1740; Princeton, 1766, A.B.; A.M., Brown U., 1774; D.D., Brown U., 1798; Ord. New York City, (1st Bapt. Chh.); inst. Boston, (2nd Bapt. Chh.), Sept. 1773; sett. Boston, 1773-1787; dism. Oct. 7, 1787; sett. Salem, N. J., 1790-1799; Bapt.; d. Salem, N. J., June 8, 1799, a. 59.

THOMAS SKINNER, A.M., b. Chelsea, 1709, son of Thomas and Mehitable (Durant) Skinner; H. C., 1732, A.B., A.M.; Ord. Colchester, Ct., (West Chester Parish), Apr. 16, 1740; sett. Colchester, Ct., 1740-1762; d. Colchester, Ct., Oct. 10, 1762, a. 54.

JOHN SMALLEY, D.D., b. Columbia, Ct., June 4, 1734, son of Benjamin and Mary (Baker) Smalley; Y. C., 1756, A.B., A.M.; S.T.D., Princeton, 1800; Ord. New Britain, Ct., (1st Chh.), Apr. 19, 1758; sett. New Britain, Ct., (Berlin), 1757-1820; Ct. Election Sermon, 1800; d. New Britain, Ct., June 1, 1820, a. 86.

AARON SMITH, A.M., b. Ipswich, Oct. 25, 1713, son of Daniel and Elizabeth (Paine) Smith; H. C., 1735, A.B.; A.M., 1739;

Ord. Marlborough, June 11, 1740; sett. Marlborough, 1740-1778; dism. Apr. 29, 1778; d. Wayland, Mar. 25, 1781, a. 67.

COTTON MATHER SMITH, A.M., b. Suffield, Ct., Oct. 26, 1731, son of Dea. Samuel and Jerusha (Mather) Smith; Y. C., 1751, A.B., A.M.; Ord. Sharon, Ct., (1st Chh.), Aug. 28, 1755; sett. Sharon, Ct., 1754-1806; Chaplain at Ticonderoga and at Canada, 1775; d. Sharon, Ct., Nov. 27, 1806, a. 76.

EBENEZER SMITH, b. Hadley, Oct. 4, 1734, son of Chileab and Sarah (Moody) Smith; Ord. Ashfield, Aug. 20, 1761; sett. Ashfield, 1761-1798; Bapt.

*ELIPHALET SMITH, Cong. minister; bapt. 1770, at Brentwood, N. H., by Rev. Hezekiah Smith, D.D.; sett. Deerfield, N. H., (Bapt. Chh.); removed to Lincoln Co., Me.

ELIAS SMITH, A.M., b. Reading, Aug. 8, 1731, son of Benjamin and Elizabeth (Burnap) Smith; H. C., 1753, A.B., A.M.; Ord. Middleton, Jan. 10, 1759; sett. Middleton, 1759-1791; Trustee of Phillips' Academy; d. Middleton, Oct. 17, 1792, a. 61.

FREDERICK SMITH, sett. Newport, R. I., (United Brethren Chh.), ca. 1763; Moravian.

HENRY SMITH, A.M., b. Norwich, England, 1588; matric. Sidney Sussex Coll., Camb., 1617; Magdalene Coll., Camb., A.B., 1621/2; A.M., 1625; Ord by the Bishop of Peterborough, June 8, 1623; sett. Watertown, 1636/7; sett. Wethersfield, Ct., 1641-1648, as the first minister; d. Wethersfield, Ct., 1648.

HEZEKIAH SMITH, D.D., b. Long Island, N. Y., Apr. 21, 1737, son of Peter and Rebecca (Nichols) Smith; Princeton, 1762, A.B., A.M.; A.M., Brown U., 1769; A.M., Y. C., 1772; D.D., Brown U., 1797; Fellow, Brown U., 1765-1805; Ord. Charleston, S. C., Sept. 20, 1763; inst. Haverhill, (1st Bapt. Chh.), Nov. 12, 1766; sett. Haverhill, 1765-1805; Chaplain, Rev. War; Bapt.; d. Haverhill, Jan. 24, 1805, a. 67.

ISAAC SMITH, A.M., b. Sterling, Ct., Nov. 30, 1744, son of Lemuel and Martha (Coit) Smith; Princeton, 1770, A.B., A.M.; A.M., (Hon.), Dart. Coll., 1785; Ord. Gilmanton, N. H., (Cong. Chh.), Nov. 30, 1774; sett. Gilmanton, N. H., 1774-1817; d. Gilmanton, N. H., Mar. 25, 1817, a. 72.

JEDEDIAH SMITH, A.M., b. Suffield, Jan. 31, 1726/7, son of Ebenezer and Christiana Smith; Y. C., 1750, A.B.; A.M., 1754; Ord. Granville, (East or 1st Chh.), Dec. 1, 1756; sett. Granville, 1756-1776; dism. Apr. 16, 1776; d. Natchez, Miss., Sept. 2, 1776, a. 50.

JOHN SMITH, b. England, 1614, son of Thomas Smith of Brinspittae, Dorsetshire, England; came to N. E., 1630; sett. Barnstable, 1653-1659, as supply; on Sept. 1661, he was minister of a Separatist Chh. at Barnstable which was closed by a council which met June 4, 1662; removed to Long Island, N. Y., and New Jersey; returned to Sandwich; Ord. Sandwich, 1675; sett. Sandwich, 1673-1688; member

Lieut. Dimock's military co., Barnstable, 1643; Rep. Gen. Ct., Plymouth Colony, 1656-1657; deputy, N. J., Assembly, 1669, 1671, 1672; assistant, N. J., 1670-1671; d. Sandwich, Oct. 2, 171-.

JOHN SMITH, A.B., b. Plainfield, Ct., 1745; Princeton, 1770, A.B.; Ord. Dighton, Apr. 22, 1772; sett. Dighton, 1772-1800; d. Kentucky, ca. 1820, a. 75.

JOHN SMITH, D.D., b. Rowley, Dec. 21, 1752, son of John and Elizabeth (Palmer) Smith; Dart. Coll., 1773, A.B., A.M.; A.M., Y. C., 1777; A.M., (Hon.), H. C., 1780; D.D., Brown U., 1803; Preceptor, Moor's School, 1773-1774; Tutor, 1774-1778; Prof. of Latin, Greek and Hebrew, Dart. Coll., 1778-1809; Librarian, 1779-1809; minister, Coll. Chh., 1782-1805; Trustee, 1788-1809; d. Hanover, N. H., Apr. 30, 1809, a. 56.

JOSEPH SMITH, A.B., b. Hadley, 1674, son of Lieut. Dea. Philip and Rebecca (Foote) Smith; H. C., 1695, A.B.; sett. Brookfield, 1702-1705; Ord. Cohanzy, N. J., May 10, 1709; sett. Cohanzy, N. J., 1708-1713; inst. Middletown, Ct., (2nd Chh. at Cromwell), Jan. 5, 1714/5, as the first minister; sett. Cromwell, Ct., 1715-1736; d. Middletown, Ct., Sept. 8, 1736.

MATTHEW SMITH, Ord. North Stonington, Ct., (Separatist Chh.), Dec. 10, 1746; sett. North Stonington, Ct., 1743-1749; excommunicated, Aug. 3, 1749.

NEHEMIAH SMITH, b. England, 1605; freeman, Plymouth Colony, 1637/8; proprietor at Marshfield, 1653; sett. New London, Ct., 1653; sett. Norwich, Ct.; d. 1686.

PETER THACHER SMITH, A.M., b. Portland, Me., June 14, 1731, son of Rev. Thomas and Sarah (Tyng) Smith; H. C., 1753, A.B., A.M.; Ord. Windham, Me., Sept. 22, 1762; sett. Windham, Me., 1761-1790; d. Windham, Me., Oct. 26, 1826, a. 95.

RALPH SMITH, A.B., bapt. Gainsford, Durham, England, Apr. 5, 1590, son of Ralph and Catharine (Matthewson) Smith; Christ's Coll., Camb., A.B., 1613/4; came to N. E., in the "Talbot," 1629; Ord. Plymouth, 1629; sett. Plymouth, 1629-1637; remained at Plymouth, 1637-1645; sett. Manchester, 1645-1650; d. Boston, Mar. 1, 1660/1.

SAMUEL SMITH, A.M., b. Glastonbury, Ct., Feb. 20, 1691/2, son of Samuel and Jane (Tudor) Smith; Y. C., 1713, A.B., A.M.; Tutor; Ord. Columbia, Ct., (2nd Chh. in Lebanon), 1720; sett. Columbia, Ct., 1720-1724; dism. Dec. 24, 1724; d. Columbia, Ct., May 27, 1725.

THOMAS SMITH, A.M., b. Boston, Mar. 10, 1702, son of Thomas, Esq. and Mary (Corwin) Smith; H. C., 1720, A.B., A.M.; Ord. Portland, Me., (1st Parish and 1st Chh. in Falmouth, now Portland), Mar. 8, 1726/7; sett. Portland, (Falmouth), 1726-1795; d. Portland, Me., May 23, 1795, a. 93.

THOMAS SMITH, A.M., b. Barnstable, Feb. 6, 1706/7, son

of Joseph and Ann (Fuller) Smith; H. C., 1725, A.B., A.M.; Ord. Yarmouth, Apr. 16, 1729; sett. Yarmouth, 1729-1754; inst. Pembroke, Dec. 4, 1754; sett. Pembroke, 1754-1788; d. Pembroke, July 7, 1788, a. 81.

TITUS SMITH, A.B., b. South Hadley, June 4, 1734, son of Dea. John and Elizabeth (Smith) Smith; Y. C., 1764, A.B.; Ord. Apr. 24, 1765, as missionary to the Indians; sett. Onohoguaga; sett. Granby, 1768; sett. Danbury, Ct., 1770-1773; re-ordained at Boston as a Sandemanian Elder; d. Halifax, N. S., Sept. 15, 1807, a. 73.

WILLIAM SMITH, A.M., b. Charlestown, Jan. 29, 1706/7, son of Capt. William and Abigail (Fowle) Smith; H. C., 1725, A.B., A.M.; Ord. Weymouth, (1st Chh.), Dec. 4, 1734; sett. Weymouth, 1734-1783; his dau. Abigail Smith married President John Adams and was the mother of President John Quincy Adams; d. Weymouth, Sept. 17, 1783, a. 77.

JOSEPH SNOW, JR., b. Bridgewater, Mar. 26, 1715, son of Dea. Joseph and Elizabeth (Field) Snow; Ord. Providence, R. I., (Beneficent Cong. Chh.), Feb. 1747; sett. Providence, R. I., 1745-1803; d. Providence, R. I., Apr. 10, 1803, a. 89.

JOHN SOUTHMAYD, A.B., b. Middletown, Ct., Aug. 23, 1676, son of Capt. William Southmayd; H. C., 1697, A.B.; Ord. Waterbury, Ct., May 30, 1705; sett. Waterbury, Ct., 1699-1755; d. Waterbury, Ct., Nov. 14, 1755.

EBENEZER SPARHAWK, A.M., b. Brighton, June 15, 1738, son of Noah and Priscilla (Brown) Sparhawk; H. C., 1756, A.B., A.M.; teacher, 1756-1760; Ord. Templeton, Nov. 18, 1761; sett. Templeton, 1761-1805; d Templeton, Nov. 25, 1805.

JOHN SPARHAWK, A.M., b. Cambridge, 1672, son of Nathaniel and Patience (Newman) Sparhawk; H. C., 1689, A.B., A.M.; Ord. Bristol, R. I., June 12, 1695; sett. Bristol, R. I., 1693-1718; d. Bristol, R. I., Apr. 29, 1718, a. 45.

JOHN SPARHAWK, A.M., b. Bristol, R. I., Sept. 1713, son of Rev. John Sparhawk; H. C., 1731, A.B., A.M.; Ord. Salem, Dec. 8, 1736; sett. Salem, 1736-1755; d. Salem, Apr. 30, 1755, a. 42.

NATHANIEL SPARHAWK, A.M., b. Cambridge, 1694, son of Dea. Nathaniel and Abigail (Gates) Sparhawk; H. C., 1715, A.B., A.M.; Ord. Lynnfield, Aug. 17, 1720; sett. Lynnfield, 1720-1731; dism. July 1, 1731; d. Lynnfield, May 7, 1732, a. 38.

SAMPSON SPAULDING, A.M., b. Chelmsford, June 7, 1711, son of John and Mary (Barrett) Spaulding; H. C., 1732, A.B., A.M.; Ord. Tewksbury, Nov. 23, 1737; sett. Tewksbury, 1737-1796; d. Tewksbury, Dec. 15, 1796, a. 86.

SAMUEL SPEAR, A.M., b. Braintree, July 6, 1696, son of Samuel and Elizabeth (Daniel) Spear; H. C., 1715, A.B., A.M.; school teacher at Truro; sett. Provincetown, 1717-1741; d. 1748.

DAVID SPRAGUE, b. Hingham, Apr. 12, 1707, son of David

and Sarah (Jordon) Sprague; Ord. Westerly, R. I., (Bapt. Chh.), July 12, 1739; sett. Scituate, R. I., 1737-1740; sett. North Kingston, R. I., 1740-1750; sett. South Kingston, R. I., 1750; sett. Exeter, R. I., (Bapt. Chh. which he founded), 1750-1754; sett. New Shoreham, Block Island, R. I., Aug. 28, 1759-1766; sett. Exeter, R. I., 1766-1777; Bapt.; d. Exeter, R. I., 1777, a. 70.

JONATHAN SPRAGUE, b. Hingham, May 28, 1648, son of William and Miliscent (Eames) Sprague; Ord. Providence, R. I., 1685; preached 1685-1741; Deputy, 1695-1714; J. P., 1701-1703; Speaker, 1703; Bapt.; d. Smithfield, R. I., Sept. 1741, a. 93.

SOLOMON SPRAGUE, b. Scituate, R. I., Apr. 2, 1730, son of David and Experience (Crandall) Sprague; Ord. Exeter, R. I., June 1, 1769; sett. Exeter, R. I., 1769-1794; physician; Bapt.; d. Exeter, R. I., Feb. 26, 1794.

ALPHEUS SPRING, A.B., b. Watertown, May 10, 1739, son of Henry and Keziah (Converse) Spring; Princeton, 1766, A.B.; Ord. Eliot, Me., (2nd Parish of Kittery), June 29, 1768; sett. Eliot, Me., 1768-1791; d. Eliot, Me., June 14, 1791.

JAMES SPROAT, D.D., b. Middleborough, Apr. 11, 1722, son of Lieut. Ebenezer and Experience Sproat; Y. C., 1741, A.B.; A.M., 1757; S.T.D., Princeton, 1780; Ord. Guilford, Ct., (4th Cong. Chh.), Aug. 23, 1743; sett. Guilford, Ct., 1743-1767; dism. Oct. 18, 1767; inst. Philadelphia, Pa., (2nd Presb. Chh.), Mar. 30, 1769; sett. Philadelphia, Pa., 1769-1793; Cong. and Presb.; d. Philadelphia, Pa., Oct. 18, 1793, a. 72.

JOSEPH STACY, A.M., b. Cambridge, 1694, son of Thomas and Hannah (Hicks) Stacy; H. C., 1719, A.B., A.M.; Ord. Kingston, Nov. 2, 1720; sett. Kingston, 1720-1741; d. Kingston, Aug. 25, 1741, a. 47.

ROBERT STANTON, A.M., b. Stonington, Ct., Dec. 7, 1689, son of Robert and Joanna (Gardner) Stanton; H. C., 1712, A.B., A.M.; Ord. Salem, (East or 2nd Chh.), Apr. 8, 1719; sett. Salem, 1719-1727; d. Salem, May 3, 1727, a. 37.

JOHN STAPLES, A.B., b. Taunton, son of Dea. Seth Staples; Princeton, 1765, A.B.; Ord. Canterbury, Ct., (2nd Chh., Westminster Society), Apr. 17, 1772; sett. Canterbury, Ct., 1772-1804; d. Canterbury, Ct., Feb. 15, 1804.

PETER STARR, A.M., b. Danbury, Ct., Sept. 1744, son of Samuel and Abigail (Dibble) Starr; Y. C., 1764, A.B., A.M.; Fellow, Y. C., 1813-1818; Ord. Warren, Ct., Mar. 18, 1772; sett. Warren, Ct., 1771-1829; d. Warren, Ct., July 17, 1829, a. 85.

DAVID STEARNS, A.M., b. Watertown, Dec. 24, 1709, son of John and Abigail (Fiske) Stearns; H. C., 1728, A.B., A.M.; Ord. Lunenburg, Apr. 18, 1733; sett. Lunenburg, 1733-1761; d. Lunenburg, Mar. 9, 1761.

EBENEZER STEARNS, bapt. Lexington, July 8, 1711, son of

Isaac and Elizabeth (Stone) Stearns; taxed at Stoughton, 1739-1749; resident at Douglas, 1750-1760; Ord. Easton, (Bapt. Chh.), July 21, 1762; sett. Easton, 1761-1766; inst. Nobleborough, Me., (Bapt. Chh.), 1768; later sett. Whitefield, Me.; Bapt.

 JOSIAH STEARNS, A.M., b. Billerica, Jan. 20, 1731/2, son of John and Esther (Johnson) Stearns; H. C., 1751, A.B., A.M.; Ord. Epping, N. H., Mar. 8, 1758; sett. Epping, N. H., 1758-1788; d. Epping, N. H., July 25, 1788, a. 56.

 SHUBAEL STEARNS, b. Boston, Jan. 28, 1705/6, son of Shubael and Rebecca (Laneford) Stearns; was a Separatist preacher, 1745-1751; Ord. Tolland, Ct., (Bapt. ministry), May 20, 1751; sett. N. E. as a missionary preacher, 1751-1754; missionary at Hampshire and Berkeley Counties, Va., and at Guilford County, N. C.; Bapt.; d. Sandy Creek, N. C., Nov. 20, 1771.

 ELIPHALET STEELE, A.M., b. West Hartford, Ct., June 26, 1742, son of Eliphalet and Catharine (Marshfield) Steele; Y. C., 1764, A.B., A.M.; Ord. Egremont, June 28, 1770; sett. Egremont, 1770-1794; dism. Apr. 29, 1794; inst. Paris, N. Y., July 15, 1795; sett. Paris, N. Y., 1795-1817; many of Mr. Steele's people at Egremont sympathized with Shays's Rebellion while Mr. Steele did not; d. Paris, N. Y., Oct. 7, 1817, a. 76.

 STEPHEN STEEL, A.M., b. Hartford, Ct., 1696/7, son of Lieut. James, Jr. and Sarah (Barnard) Steel; Y. C., 1718, A.B., A.M.; Ord. Tolland, Ct., 1723; sett. Tolland, Ct., 1719-1758; Ct. Election Sermon, 1743; d. Tolland, Ct., Dec. 4, 1759, a. 63.

 BENJAMIN STEVENS, D.D., b. Charlestown, May 4, 1721, son of Rev. Joseph Stevens; H. C., 1740, A.B., A.M.; S.T.D., 1785; Ord. Kittery, Me., (1st Chh.), May 1, 1751; sett. Kittery, Me., 1751-1791; Mass. Election Sermon, 1761; Dudleian Lecture, 1772; Convention Sermon, 1775; d. Kittery, Me., May 18, 1791, a. 70.

 JOSEPH STEVENS, A.M., b. Andover, June 20, 1682, son of Dea. John and Mary (Ingalls) Stevens; H. C., 1703, A.B., A.M.; Tutor, 1711-1714; Fellow, 1712-1713; Ord. Charlestown, Oct. 13, 1713; sett. Charlestown, 1713-1721; Artillery Election Sermon, 1715; d. Charlestown, Nov. 16, 1721, a. 39, of small pox.

 PHINEAS STEVENS, A.M., b. Andover, May 13, 1716, son of Ebenezer and Sarah (Sprague) Stevens; H. C., 1734, A.B., A.M.; Ord. Boscawen, N. H., Oct. 29, 1740; sett. Boscawen, N. H., 1740-1755; d. Boscawen, N. H., Jan. 19, 1755, a. 38.

 THOMAS STEVENS, b. Plainfield, Ct., son of Capt. Thomas Stevens; Ord. Plainfield, Ct., (Separatist Chh.), Sept. 11, 1746; sett. Plainfield, Ct., 1746-1755; d. Plainfield, Ct., Nov. 15, 1755.

 TIMOTHY STEVENS, A.M., b. Roxbury, Jan. 28, 1666, son of Timothy and Sarah (Davis) Stevens; H. C., 1687, A.B., A.M.; Ord. Glastonbury, Ct., Oct. 1693, as the first minister; sett. Glastonbury Ct., 1692-1726; d. Glastonbury, Ct., Apr. 14, 1726, a. 60.

ABEL STILES, A.M., b. Windsor, Ct., 1708, son of John and Ruth (Bancroft) Stiles; Y. C., 1733, A.B., A.M.; Tutor, Y. C., 1736-1737; Ord. Woodstock, Ct., (1st Chh.), July 23, 1737; sett. Woodstock, Ct., (1st Chh.), 1737-1760; sett. Woodstock, Ct., (North Chh.), 1760-1783; uncle of President Stiles; d. Woodstock, Ct., July 25, 1783, a. 75.

PRESIDENT EZRA STILES, D.D., LL.D., b. North Haven, Ct., Nov. 29, 1727, son of Rev. Isaac and Kezia (Taylor) Stiles; Y. C., 1746, A.B., A.M.; Hon. degrees: A.M., H. C., 1754; S.T.D., U. of Edinburgh, 1765; S.T.D., Dart Coll, 1780; S.T.D., Princeton, 1784; LL.D., Princeton, 1784; Tutor, Y. C., 1749-1755; Professor of Ecclesiastical History and President, Y. C., 1778-1795; Ord. Newport, R. I., (1st Cong. Chh.), Oct. 22, 1755; sett. Newport, R. I., 1755-1776; inst. Dighton, (Anti-Pedobaptist Cong. Chh.), Mar. 14, 1776; sett. Dighton, 1776-1777; left May 22, 1777; sett. Portsmouth, N. H., (1st Chh.), 1777-June 1778; Fellow, Am. Acad. Arts and Sciences; member Am. Phil. Soc. and Mass. Hist. Soc.; Ct. Election Sermon, 1783; d. New Haven, Ct., May 12, 1795, a. 67.

ISAAC STILES, A.M., b. Windsor, Ct., July 30, 1697, son of John and Ruth (Bancroft) Stiles; Y. C., 1722, A.B., A.M.; Ord. North Haven, Ct., Nov. 11, 1724; sett. North Haven, Ct., 1724-1760; Ct. Election Sermon, 1742; d. North Haven, Ct., May 14, 1760, a. 63.

SAMUEL STILLMAN, D.D., b. Philadelphia, Pa., Feb. 27, 1737; A.M., (Hon.), U. of Pa., 1761; A.M., (Hon.), H. C., 1761; A.M., (Hon.), Brown U., 1769; S.T.D., Brown U., 1788; Trustee and Fellow, Brown U., 1764-1807; Ord. Charleston, S. C., Feb. 26, 1759; sett. James Island, S. C., 1759-1761; sett. Bordentown, N. J., (Bapt. Chh.), 2 years; Boston, (2nd Bapt. Chh.), 1 year; inst. Boston, (1st Bapt. Chh.), Jan. 9, 1765; sett. Boston, 1765-1807; member Am. Phil. Soc., 1768; Artillery Election Sermon, 1770; Election Sermon, 1779; Bapt.; d. Boston, Mar. 12, 1807, a. 70.

DANIEL STIMPSON, A.M., b. Weston, Feb. 2, 1731, son of James and Sarah (Cutter) Stimpson; H. C., 1759, A.B., A.M.; Ord. Winchendon, Dec. 15, 1762; sett. Winchendon, 1762-1768; d. Winchendon, July 20, 1768, a. 37.

JOSEPH STIMPSON, A.M., b. Charlestown, 1700, son of Andrew and Abigail Stimpson; H. C., 1720, A.B., A.M.; Ord. Malden, (South Chh. at Everett), Sept. 24, 1735; sett. Malden, 1735-1744; d. Malden, 1752, a. 52.

ANTHONY STODDARD, A.M., b. Northampton, Aug. 9, 1678, son of Rev. Solomon and Esther (Warham) Stoddard; H. C., 1697, A.B.; A.M., 1715; Trustee, Y. C., 1738; Ord. Woodbury, Ct., (1st Chh.), May 27, 1702; sett. Woodbury, Ct., 1700-1760; Ct. Election Sermon, 1716; d. Woodbury, Ct., Sept. 6, 1760.

SAMSON STODDARD, A.M., b. Boston, ca. 1680, son of Samson Stoddard; H. C., 1701, A.B., A.M.; Ord. Chelmsford, Nov. 6,

1706; sett. Chelmsford, 1706-1740; Artillery Election Sermon, 1713; d. Chelmsford, Aug. 23, 1740, a. 60.

SIMEON STODDARD, A.M., b. Woodbury, Ct., Mar. 1, 1734/5, son of Capt. Dea. Gideon and Olive (Curtiss) Stoddard; Y. C., 1755, A.B., A.M.; Ord. Chester, Ct., (4th Chh. in Saybrook), Oct. 31, 1759; sett. Chester, Ct., 1759-1765; d. Chester, Ct., Oct. 27, 1765, a. 31.

SOLOMON STODDARD, A.M., b. Boston, Sept. 27, 1643, son of Anthony, Esq. and Lucy (Downing) Stoddard; H. C., 1662, A.B., A.M.; first Librarian of H. C., 1667-1672; Fellow, 1666-1667; Ord. Northampton, Sept. 11, 1672; sett. Northampton, 1669-1729; Election Sermon, 1703; a leading minister of Massachusetts for 30 years; liberal; grandfather of Rev. Jonathan Edwards; d. Northampton, Feb. 11, 1728/9, a. 86.

ELIAB STONE, A.M., b. Framingham, May 5, 1737, son of Micah and Abigail (Stone) Stone; H. C., 1758, A.B., A.M.; Ord. North Reading, May 20, 1761; sett. North Reading, 1761-1822; d. North Reading, Aug. 31, 1822, a. 85.

ISAAC STONE, A.M., b. Shrewsbury, Mar. 6, 1747/8, son of Dea. Jonas and Rachel (Fiske) Stone; H. C., 1770, A.B., A.M.; Ord. Douglas, Oct. 30, 1771; sett. Douglas, 1771-1805; dism. Oct. 28, 1805; d. Oxford, Feb. 25, 1837, a. 89.

JAMES STONE, A.M., b. Newton, June 8, 1704, son of Hon. Ebenezer and Margaret (Trowbridge) Stone; H. C., 1724, A.B., A.M.; Ord. Holliston, Nov. 20, 1728; sett. Holliston, 1728-1742; d. Holliston, July 28, 1742, a. 38.

NATHAN STONE, A.M., b. Brewster, Feb. 18, 1707/8, son of Rev. Nathaniel and Reliance (Hinckley) Stone; H. C., 1726, A.B., A.M.; Ord. Southborough, Oct. 21, 1730; sett. Southborough, 1730-1781; d. Southborough, May 31, 1781, a. 74.

NATHAN STONE, A.M., b. Southborough, Sept. 30, 1737, son of Rev. Nathan and Judith (Fox) Stone; H. C., 1762, A.B., A.M.; Ord. Dennis, Oct. 17, 1764; sett. Dennis, 1764-1804; member Southborough Military Co., 1757; d. Dennis, Apr. 26, 1804.

NATHANIEL STONE, A.M., b. Watertown, Apr. 1667, son of Dea. Simon and Mary (Whipple) Stone; H. C., 1690, A.B.; A.M., 1725; Ord. Brewster, (Harwich), Oct. 16, 1700; sett. Brewster, 1700-1755; Election Sermon, 1720; d. Brewster, Feb. 8, 1755, a. 87.

SAMUEL STONE, A.M., b. Hertford, England, July 30, 1602, son of John Stone; Emmanuel Coll., Camb., A.B., 1623/4; A.M., 1627; Ord. by the Bishop of Peterborough, July 8, 1626; Curate at Stisted, Essex, 1623-1630; suspended for non-conformity; Lecturer at Towcester, Northamptonshire, England, 1630; came to N. E., 1633; Ord. Cambridge, Oct. 11, 1633; sett. Cambridge, 1633-1636, as the first minister; sett. Hartford, Ct., 1636-1663; Chaplain in Major John

Mason's expedition against the Pequot Indians, 1637; d. Hartford, Ct., July 26, 1663.

TIMOTHY STONE, A.M., b. Guilford, Ct., July 23, 1742, son of Col. Dea. Timothy and Rachel (Norton) Stone; Y. C., 1763, A.B., A.M.; Ord. Goshen, Ct., (Lebanon), Sept. 30, 1767; sett. Goshen, Ct., 1767-1797; Ct. Election Sermon, 1792; d. Goshen, Ct., May 12, 1797, a. 54.

SETH STORER, A.M., b. Saco, Me., May 26, 1702, son of Col. Joseph and Hannah Storer of Wells, Me.; H. C., 1720, A.B., A.M.; Ord. Watertown, July 22, 1724; sett. Watertown, 1724-1774; d. Watertown, Nov. 27, 1774, a. 73.

ANDREW STORRS, A.M., b. Mansfield, Ct., Dec. 20, 1735, son of Capt. Samuel and Mary (Warner) Storrs; Y. C., 1760, A.B., A.M.; A.M., (Hon.), H. C., 1765; Ord. Northbury, Ct., Nov. 27, 1765; sett. Northbury, Ct., 1765-1785; d. Northbury, Ct., Mar. 2, 1785, a. 50.

ELEAZER STORRS, A.M., b. Mansfield, Ct., Nov. 24, 1738; son of Huckins and Eunice (Porter) Storrs; Y. C., 1762, A.B., A.M.; Ord. Sandisfield, Feb. 26, 1766; sett. Sandisfield, 1766-1797; dism. Apr. 26, 1797; d. Sandisfield, Dec. 24, 1810, a. 72.

ISAAC STORY, A.B., b. Boston, Sept. 9, 1749, son of William, Esq. and Joanna (Appleton) Story; Princeton, 1768, A.B.; Ord. Marblehead, (2nd Chh.), May 1, 1771; sett. Marblehead, 1771-1802; dism. Feb. 4, 1802; d. Marblehead, Oct. 23, 1816, a. 67.

JONATHAN STORY, Ord. Preston, Ct., (Separatist Chh.), 1752; sett. Preston, Ct., 1752-1756.

GOVERNOR WILLIAM STOUGHTON, A.M., b. England, Sept. 30, 1631, son of Hon. Israel Stoughton of Dorchester; in New England by 1632; H. C., 1650, A.B.; A.M., Oxford U.; Fellow, New College, Oxford; minister in the county of Sussesx, England; ejected 1662; returned to Dorchester, Massachusetts, 1662; Election Sermon, 1668; was called to 1st Chh. in Cambridge, but declined; Magistrate, 1671; Agent for the Province, in England; member of the Council; Justice of the Superior Court; Chief Justice of a special tribunal for witchcraft trials, 1692; Lieut. Gov., 1692-1701; Commander in Chief, 1694-1699, 1700; two portraits exist of him, one owned by the Boston Athenaeum, and another by Harvard University; d. Dorchester, July 7, 1701, a. 70, s. p.

SAMUEL STOW, A.M., b. Kent, England, ca. 1622, son of John and Elizabeth (Biggs) Stow; came to N. E., 1634; H. C., 1645, A.B., A.M.; sett. Middletown, Ct., 1653-1660; sett. Simsbury, Ct., 1682-1686; d. Middletown, Ct., May 8, 1704, a. 82.

NICHOLAS STREET, A.M., Gent., bapt. Bridgewater, Somersetshire, England, Jan. 26, 1602/3, son of Nicholas, Esq. and Susanna (Gilbert) Street; matric. Oxford U., Nov. 2, 1621, aet. 18; Pembroke Coll., Oxford, A.B., 1624/5; A.M., Emmanuel Coll., Camb., 1636;

came in the "Susan and Ellen," 1635; Ord. Taunton, Jan. 17, 1640/1; sett. Taunton, 1637-1659; inst. New Haven, Ct., Nov. 26, 1659; sett. New Haven, Ct., 1659-1674; d. New Haven, Ct., Apr. 22, 1674.

NICHOLAS STREET, A.M., b. Wallingford, Ct., Feb. 21, 1730, son of Capt. Elnathan and Damaris (Hull) Street; Y. C., 1751, A.B., A.M.; Ord. East Haven, Ct., Oct. 8, 1755; sett. East Haven, Ct., 1755-1806; d. East Haven, Ct., Oct. 3, 1806, a. 77.

SAMUEL STREET, A.B., b. England, 1635, son of Rev. Nicholas Street of Taunton; H. C., 1664, A.B.; Ord. Wallingford, Ct., 1674; sett. Wallingford, Ct., 1672-1717; d. Wallingford, Ct., Jan. 16, 1717, a. 82.

ADAMS STREETER, b. Framingham, Dec. 31, 1735, son of Stephen and Catharine (Adams) Streeter; Ord. Douglas, (1st Bapt. Chh.), Nov. 24, 1774; sett. Douglas, 1774-1781; sett. Boston, (1st Universalist Chh.), 1781-1786; Bapt. and Universalist; d. Smithfield, R. I., Sept. 14, 1786.

JOHN STRICKLAND, JR., A.M., b. Hadley, Sept. 14, 1741, son of John and Tabitha (Hastings) Strickland; Y. C., 1761, A.B.; A.M., 1765; Ord. Oakham, Apr. 1, 1768; sett. Oakham, (1st Chh., Presb.), 1768-1773; dism. June 2, 1773; inst. Hudson, N. H., (Nottingham West), (Presb. Chh.), July 13, 1774; sett. Hudson, N. H., 1774-1782; dism. Oct. 24, 1782; inst. Turner, Me., Nov. 20, 1784; sett. Turner, Me., 1784-1797; dism. May 18, 1797; inst. Andover, Me., (Cong. Chh.), Mar. 12, 1806; sett. Andover, Me., 1806-1823; d. Andover, Me., Oct. 4, 1823, a. 82.

BENJAMIN STRONG, A.B., b. Woodbury, Ct., June 10, 1710, son of Adino and Eunice Strong; Y. C., 1734, A.B.; Ord. Stanwich, Ct., June 18, 1735; sett. Stanwich, Ct., 1735-1767; dism. Mar. 31, 1767; d. Stanwich, Ct., Feb. 1775.

CYPRIAN STRONG, D.D., b. Farmington, Ct., May 26, 1743, son of Capt. Asahel and Ruth (Hooker) Strong; Y. C., 1763, A.B.; A.M., 1767; A.M., Dart. Coll., 1797; S.T.D., Y. C., 1803; Ord. Portland, Ct., Aug. 19, 1767; sett. Portland, Ct., 1767-1811; Ct. Election Sermon, 1799; d. Portland, Ct., Nov. 17, 1811, a. 68.

JOB STRONG, A.M., b. Northampton, Nov. 14, 1721, son of Lieut. Nathaniel and Penelope (Phillips) Strong; Y. C., 1747, A.B., A.M.; Ord. Portsmouth, N. H., (South Parish), June 28, 1749; sett. Portsmouth, N. H., 1749-1751; d. Portsmouth, N. H., Sept. 30, 1751, a. 29.

JOSEPH STRONG, A.M., b. Coventry, Ct., Mar. 19, 1728/9, son of Dea. Joseph and Elizabeth (Strong) Strong; Y. C., 1749, A.B., A.M.; Ord. Granby, Ct., (Salmon Brook), Nov. 1, 1752; sett. Granby, Ct., 1752-1779; dism. Dec. 26, 1779; inst. Williamsburg, Dec. 26, 1781; sett. Williamsburg, 1781-1803; Chaplain, Ct. troops on Long Island, 1776; Election Sermon, 1802; d. Goshen, Jan. 1, 1803, a. 74.

JOSEPH STRONG, D.D., b. Coventry, Ct., Sept. 21, 1753, son

of Rev. Nathan and Esther (Meacham) Strong; Y. C., 1772, A.B., A.M.; Princeton, DD., 1807; Fellow, Y. C., 1806-1826; Ord. Norwich, Ct., (1st Chh.), Mar. 18, 1778; sett. Norwich, Ct., 1778-1834; d. Norwich, Ct., Dec. 18, 1834, a. 82.

NATHAN STRONG, A.M., b. Woodbury, Ct., Apr. 12, 1717, son of Elnathan and Patience (Jenner) Strong; Y. C., 1742, A.B., A.M.; Ord. Coventry, Ct., Oct. 9, 1745; sett. Coventry, Ct., 1745-1795; Ct. Election Sermon, 1790; d. Coventry, Ct., Nov. 7, 1795, a. 79.

NATHAN STRONG, D.D., b. Coventry, Ct., Oct. 5, 1748, son of Rev. Nathan and Esther (Meacham) Strong; Y. C., 1769, A.B., A.M.; Tutor, Y. C., 1772-1773; D.D., Princeton, 1801; Fellow, Y. C., 1804-1809; Ord. Hartford, Ct., (1st Chh.), Jan. 5, 1774; sett. Hartford, Ct., 1773-1816; Chaplain, Col. Samuel Wyllys' Regt., 1776; d. Hartford, Ct., Dec. 25, 1816, a. 69.

NEHEMIAH STRONG, A.M., b. Northampton, Feb. 24, 1728/9, son of Nehemiah and Hannah (French) Strong; Y. C., 1755, A.B., A.M.; Tutor, Y. C., 1757-1760; Ord. East Granby, Ct., (Turkey Hills, Parish of Windsor), Jan. 21, 1761; sett. East Granby, Ct., 1760-1767; dism. June 23, 1767; Prof. of Mathematics and Natural Philosophy and Astronomy, Y. C., 1770-1781; resigned Dec. 14, 1781; d. Bridgeport, Ct., Aug. 13, 1807, a. 79.

THOMAS STRONG, A.M., b. Northampton, 1715, son of Jonathan and Mehitable (Stebbins) Strong; Y. C., 1740, A.B., A.M.; Ord. New Marlborough, Nov. 1, 1744; sett. New Marlborough, 1744-1777; uncle of Gov. Caleb Strong; d. New Marlborough, Aug. 23, 1777, a. 63.

ROBERT STURGEON, came from Ireland; sett. Watertown, (Independent Chh.), 1721-1722; dism. by an ecclesiastical council, May 1, 1722; sett. Wilton, Ct., 1726-1732; sett. Bedford, N. Y., (Presb. Chh.), 1732-1743.

CLEMENT SUMNER, A.M., b. Hebron, Ct., July 15, 1731, son of Dr. William and Hannah (Hunt) Sumner; Y. C., 1758, A.B; A.M., 1763; Ord. Keene, N. H., June 11, 1761; sett. Keene, N. H., 1761-1772; dism. Apr. 30, 1772; sett. Thetford, Vt., 1773-1775; Tory; sett. on a farm in Swanzey, N. H.; supplied the Universalist Chh., Keene, N. H.; d. Keene, N. H., Mar. 22, 1795, a. 63.

JOHN SUMNER, A.M., b. Roxbury, Aug. 1, 1705, son of Edward and Elizabeth (Clap) Sumner; H. C., 1723, A.B., A.M.; supply at Wellfleet, 1727; d. Spencer, 1787, a. 83.

JOSEPH SUMNER, D.D., b. Pomfret, Ct., Jan. 30, 1740, son of Samuel and Elizabeth (Griffin) Sumner; Y. C., 1759, A.B., A.M.; A.M., (Hon.), Dart. Coll., 1782; S.T.D., H. C., 1814; S.T.D., College of South Carolina, 1814; Ord. Shrewsbury, Jan. 23, 1762; sett. Shrewsbury, 1762-1824; liberal; d. Shrewsbury, Dec. 9, 1824, a. 85.

JOSEPH SWAIN, A.M., b. Reading, Feb. 18, 1722/3, son of

John and Mary (Perkins) Swain; H. C., 1744, A.B., A.M.; Ord. Wenham, Oct. 24, 1750; sett. Wenham, 1750-1792; Chaplain, French and Indian Wars; d. Wenham, June 29, 1792, a. 70.

JOSIAH SWAN, A.M., b. Charlestown, Mar. 18, 1711/2, son of Capt. Ebenezer and Prudence (Foster) Swan; H. C., 1733, A.B., A.M.; Ord. Dunstable, Dec. 27, 1738; sett. Dunstable, 1738-1746; dism. 1746, because of a division of the town by the Massachusetts-New Hampshire boundary line; became a schoolmaster at Lancaster; d. Leominster, July 1780.

RICHARD SWEET, son of John and Elizabeth Sweet; sett. North Kingston, R. I., (Bapt. Chh.), 1710-1740; Bapt.; d. North Kingston, R. I., 1740.

ELEAZER SWEETLAND, A.B., b. Hebron, Ct., May 5, 1751, son of Aaron and Anne (Hutchinson) Sweetland; Dart. Coll., 1774, A.B.; Ord. East Haddam, Ct., May 21, 1776; sett. East Haddam, Ct., 1776-1777; d. East Haddam, Ct., Mar. 25, 1777.

JOB SWIFT, D.D., b. Sandwich, June 17, 1743, son of Josiah and Abigail Swift; Y. C., 1765, A.B., A.M.; A.M., (Hon.), Dart. Coll., 1790; S.T.D., Williams Coll., 1803; Trustee, Dart. Coll., 1788-1801; Trustee, Williams Coll., 1794-1802; Ord. Richmond, Oct. 14, 1767; sett. Richmond, 1767-1774; dism. Dec. 27, 1774; sett. Amenia, N. Y., 1775-1783; sett. Manchester, Vt., 1783-1786; inst. Bennington, Vt., May 31, 1786; sett. Bennington, Vt., 1786-1801; dism. June 7, 1801; Chaplain, Rev. War; d. Enosburg, Vt., Oct. 20, 1804, a. 60.

JOHN SWIFT, A.M., b. Milton, Mar. 14, 1678/9, son of Thomas and Elizabeth (Vose) Swift; H. C., 1697, A.B., A.M.; Ord. Framingham, Oct. 8, 1701; sett. Framingham, 1701-1745; Artillery Election Sermon, 1726; Election Sermon, 1732; a charter member of the Marlborough Ministerial Association, June 5, 1725; d. Framingham, Apr. 24, 1745, a. 67.

JOHN SWIFT, JR., A.M., b. Framingham, Jan. 14, 1713/4, son of Rev. John and Sarah (Tileston) Swift; H. C., 1733, A.B., A.M.; Ord. Acton, Nov. 8, 1738; sett. Acton, 1738-1775; d. Acton, Nov. 7, 1775, a. 61, of small pox.

SETH SWIFT, A.M., b. Kent, Ct., Oct. 30, 1749, son of Josiah and Abigail Swift; Y. C., 1774, A.B., A.M.; Trustee, Williams Coll., 1793-1807; Ord. Williamsburg, May 26, 1779; sett. Williamsburg, 1776-1807; d. Williamsburg, Feb. 13, 1807, a. 58.

THOMAS SYMMES, A.M., b. Bradford, Jan. 31, 1677/8, son of Rev. Zechariah and Susanna (Graves) Symmes; H. C., 1698, A.B., A.M.; Ord. Boxford, Dec. 30, 1702, as the first minister; sett. Boxford, 1701-1708; dism. May 21, 1708; inst. Bradford, Dec. 1708; sett. Bradford, 1708-1725; Artillery Election Sermon, 1720; d. Bradford, Oct. 6, 1725, a. 47.

TIMOTHY SYMMES, A.M., b. Scituate, May 27, 1714, son of Timothy and Elizabeth Symmes; H. C., 1733, A.B., A.M.; Ord.

Millington, Ct., (East Haddam), Dec. 1736; sett. Millington, Ct., 1736-1743; sett. Ipswich, 1752-1756; d. Ipswich, Apr. 6, 1756, a. 41.

WILLIAM SYMMES, D.D., b. Charlestown, Nov. 1728, son of William and Ruth (Converse) Symmes; H. C., 1750, A.B., A.M.; S.T.D., 1803; Tutor, H. C., 1755-1758; Ord. Andover, Nov. 1, 1758; sett. Andover, 1757-1807; Election Sermon, 1785; Dudleian Lecture, 1786; Arminian and Arian in theology; d. Andover, May 3, 1809, a. 80.

ZECHARIAH SYMMES, A.M., b. Canterbury, Kent, England, Apr. 5, 1599, son of Rev. William Symmes, B.D.; Emmanuel Coll., Camb., A.B., 1620/1; A.M., 1624; Lecturer at St. Antholin's, London, 1621-1625; Rector at Dunstable, England, 1625-1632; came to N. E., 1634; Ord. Charlestown, Dec. 22, 1634; sett. Charlestown, 1634-1671; Election Sermon, 1648; d. Charlestown, Jan. 28, 1670/1, a. 72.

ZECHARIAH SYMMES, JR., A.M., b. Charlestown, Jan. 9, 1637/8, son of Zechariah and Sarah Symmes; H. C., 1657, A.B., A.M.; Fellow, H. C., 1657-1663; sett. Rehoboth, 1661-1666; Ord. Bradford, Dec. 27, 1682, as the first minister; sett. Bradford, 1668-1708; d. Bradford, (Haverhill), Mar. 22, 1707/8, a. 71.

PHILIP TABER, sett. Tiverton, R. I., 1720-1752; Bapt.; d. Tiverton, R. I., Nov. 1752.

MOSES TAFT, A.M., b. Mendon, July 20, 1727, son of Eleazer and Rachel (Thayer) Taft; H. C., 1751, A.B., A.M.; Ord. Randolph, Aug. 26, 1752; sett. Randolph, 1752-1791; d. Randolph, Nov. 11, 1791, a. 64.

BARNABAS TAYLOR, A.M., b. Yarmouth; H. C., 1721, A.B., A.M.; Ord. Bristol, R. I., (Cong. Chh.), Dec. 24, 1729; sett. Bristol, R. I., 1729-1740; dism. June 3, 1740.

EDWARD TAYLOR, A.M., b. Sketelby, Leicestershire, England, ca. 1642; came to N. E., 1668; H. C., 1671, A.B.; A.M., 1720; Ord. Westfield, Aug. 27, 1679, as the first minister; sett. Westfield, 1671-1729; physician; d. Westfield, June 24, 1729, a. 86.

HEZEKIAH TAYLOR, A.M., b. Grafton, Nov. 16, 1748, son of Hezekiah and Abigail (Hunt) Taylor; H. C., 1772, A.B.; A.M., 1797; Ord. Newfane, Vt., June 30, 1774; sett. Newfane, Vt., 1774-1811; retired May 1811; d. Newfane, Vt., Aug. 23, 1814, a. 66.

JAMES TAYLOR, A.M., b. Westport, Ct., July 12, 1729, son of Capt. John and Hannah (Stewart) Taylor; Y. C., 1754, A.B., A.M.; Ord. New Fairfield, Ct., (Southern Parish), Mar. 29, 1758; sett. New Fairfield, Ct., 1758-1764; dism. June 5, 1764; sett. Deerfield, 1768; sett. Buckland, 1780; d. Buckland, July 7, 1785, a. 56.

JOHN TAYLOR, A.M., b. Boston, Aug. 30, 1704, son of John and Ann (Winslow) Taylor; H. C., 1721, A.B., A.M.; Ord. Milton, Nov. 13, 1728; sett. Milton, 1728-1750; Artillery Election Sermon, 1745; d. Milton, Jan. 26, 1749/50, a. 46.

JOSEPH TAYLOR, A.M., bapt. Cambridge, 1651, son of John and Katherine Taylor; H. C., 1669, A.B., A.M.; sett. New Haven,

Ct., 1673-1679; Ord. Southampton, L. I., N. Y., Mar. 1680; sett. Southampton, L. I., N. Y., 1679-1682; d. Southampton, L. I., N. Y., Apr. 4, 1682.

NATHANIEL TAYLOR, A.M., b. Danbury, Ct., Aug. 27, 1722, son of Daniel Taylor; Y. C., 1745, A.B., A.M.; Fellow, Y. C., 1774-1800; Ord. New Milford, Ct., June 29, 1748; sett. New Milford, Ct., 1748-1800; Chaplain at Crown Point, 1762; d. New Milford, Ct., Dec. 9, 1800, a. 79.

WILLIAM TENNENT, 3rd., A.M., b. Freehold, N. J., 1740, son of Rev. William Tennent, Jr.; Princeton, 1758, A.B., A.M.; A.M., (Hon.), H. C., 1763; Ord. as Presb., 1762; inst. Norwalk, Ct., (1st Cong. Chh.), Nov. 1765; sett. Norwalk, Ct., 1765-1772; sett. Charleston, S. C., (Independent Chh.), 1772-1777; member S. C. Provincial Congress; Presb.; d. Santee, S. C., Aug. 11, 1777, a. 37.

WILLIAM MACKAY TENNENT, D.D., son of Rev. Charles Tennent; Princeton, 1763, A.B.; Trustee, Princeton, 1785-1808; D.D., Y. C., 1794; Ord. Greenfield, Ct., (Cong. Chh.), June 17, 1772; sett. Greenfield, Ct., 1772-1781; sett. Abington, Pa., (Presb. Chh.), 1781-1810; Moderator, Gen. Assembly of the Presb. Chh.; Presb.; d. Abington, Pa., Dec. 1810.

DAVID TENNEY, A.M., b. Georgetown, Apr. 4, 1749, son of Lieut. John and Rose (Chandler) Tenney; H. C., 1768, A.B., A.M.; Ord. Barrington, N. H., Sept. 18. 1771; sett. Barrington, N. H., 1771-1778; d. Durham, N. H., Oct. 26, 1778, a. 29.

SAMUEL TERRY, A.M., b. Enfield, Ct., Mar. 26, 1690. son of Samuel and Hannah (Morgan) Terry; H. C., 1710, A.B., A.M.; called to Barrington, R. I., Apr. 21, 1718; sett. Barrington, R. I., 1718-1726; dism. Aug. 16, 1726; sett. Uxbridge, 1728; schoolmaster at Mendon, 1733; sett. Union, Ct., 1734-1735; removed to Hebron, Ct.

JOSIAH THACHER, A.B., b. Lebanon, Ct.; Princeton, 1760, A.B.; Ord. Gorham, Me., Oct. 28, 1767; sett. Gorham, Me., 1767-1781; dism. Apr. 28, 1781; appointed Judge of the Court of Common Pleas, 1784-1799; d. Gorham, Me., Dec. 25, 1799.

OXENBRIDGE THACHER, A.M., b. Milton, May 17, 1681, son of Rev. Peter and Theodora (Oxenbridge) Thacher; H. C., 1698, A.B., A.M.; preached at Canton, 1700-1707; became a merchant in Boston; Deputy to the General Court, 1733-1736; J. P.; d. Milton, Oct. 29, 1772.

PETER THACHER, A.M., b. Salem, July 18, 1651, son of Rev. Thomas and Elizabeth (Partridge) Thacher; H. C., 1671, A.B., A.M.; Fellow, H. C., 1674-1676; Ord. Milton. June 1, 1681; sett. Milton, 1680-1727; Artillery Election Sermon, 1695; Election Sermon, 1711; Convention Sermon, 1724; d. Milton, Dec. 17, 1727, a. 76.

PETER THACHER, A.M., bapt. Boston, Aug. 26, 1677, son of Thomas and Mary (Savage) Thacher; H. C., 1696, A.B., A.M.; Ord. Weymouth, Nov. 26, 1707; sett. Weymouth, 1707-1718; dism.

Feb. 23, 1718/9; inst. Boston, (New North Chh.), Jan. 28, 1719/20; sett. Boston, 1720-1739; Artillery Election Sermon, 1712; Election Sermon, 1726; d. Boston, Feb. 26, 1738/9, a. 62.

PETER THACHER, A.M., b. Milton, Oct. 6, 1688, son of Rev. Peter and Theodora (Oxenbridge) Thacher; H. C., 1706, A.B., A.M.; Ord. Middleborough, Nov. 2, 1709; sett. Middleborough, 1707-1744; d. Middleborough, Apr. 22, 1744, a. 55.

PETER THACHER, A.M., b. Middleborough, Jan. 25, 1715/6, son of Rev. Peter and Mary (Prince) Thacher; H. C., 1737, A.B., A.M.; Ord. Attleborough, (East Chh.), Nov. 30, 1748, as the first minister; sett. Attleborough, 1743-1784; dism. Oct. 26, 1784; d. Attleborough, Sept. 13, 1785, a. 70.

PETER THACHER, D.D., b. Milton, Mar. 21, 1752, son of Oxenbridge Thacher; H. C., 1769, A.B., A.M.; S.T.D., U. of Edinburgh, 1791; Ord. Malden, Sept. 19, 1770; sett. Malden, 1770-1784; dism. Dec. 8, 1784; inst. Boston, (Brattle St. Chh.), Jan. 12, 1785; sett. Boston, 1785-1802; Artillery Election Sermon, 1793; Convention Sermon, 1802; Fellow, Am. Acad. Arts and Sciences; Member Mass. Hist. Soc.; declared by Whitefield to be the ablest preacher in the Colonies; d. Savannah, Ga., Dec. 16, 1802, a. 51.

RALPH THACHER, b. Duxbury, 1647, son of Rev. Thomas and Elizabeth (Partridge) Thacher; Ord. Chilmark, 1697; sett. Chilmark, 1697-1714; Constable and Town Clerk of Duxbury before he settled in Chilmark; d. Lebanon, Ct., after 1715.

ROLAND THACHER, A.M., b. Barnstable, Aug. 23, 1710, son of Hon. Capt. John and Desire (Sturgis) (Dimmock) Thacher; H. C., 1733, A.B., A.M.; Ord. Wareham, Dec. 26, 1739; sett. Wareham, 1739-1774; d. Wareham, Feb. 18, 1775, a. 64.

THOMAS THACHER, b. Milton Clevedon, Somersetshire, England, May 1, 1620, son of Rev. Peter and Ann (Allwood) Thacher; (his father was the Rector of St. Edmund's, Salisbury); arrived in Boston, June 4, 1635; educated by President Charles Chauncy of H. C.; Ord. Weymouth, Jan. 2, 1644/5; sett. Weymouth, 1644-1669; inst. Boston, (Old South Chh.), Feb. 16, 1669/70, as the first minister; sett. Boston, 1670-1678; Artillery Election Sermons, 1654, 1670; his portrait is owned by the Old South Assn. in Boston; physician; d. Boston, Oct. 15, 1678, a. 58.

JOSEPH THAXTER, A.M., b. Hingham, Apr. 23, 1744, son of Dea. Joseph and Mary (Leavitt) Thaxter; H. C., 1768, A.B., A.M.; Ord. Edgartown, Martha's Vineyard, 1780; sett. Edgartown, 1780-1827; fought at Bunker Hill and Concord Bridge; Chaplain, 1776, at Bunker Hill, White Plains, etc.; Chaplain at the laying of the corner stone of the Bunker Hill monument, 1824; Unitarian; d. Edgartown, July 18, 1827, a. 83.

ALEXANDER THAYER, D.D.. b. Mendon, Jan. 25, 1743/4, son of William and Abigail (Sumner) Thayer; Princeton, 1765, A.B.,

A.M.; D.D.; Ord. Paxton, Nov. 28, 1770; sett. Paxton, 1770-1782; dism. Aug. 14, 1782; d. Holliston, Sept. 25, 1807, a. 64.

EBENEZER THAYER, A.M., b. Boston, Feb. 1, 1689, son of Nathaniel and Deborah Thayer; H. C., 1708, A.B., A.M.; taught school in Boston, 1709-1710; Ord. West Roxbury, Nov. 12, 1712; sett. West Roxbury, 1712-1730; Artillery Election Sermon, 1724; Election Sermon, 1725; d. West Roxbury, Mar. 6, 1733.

EBENEZER THAYER, A.M., b. Braintree, July 16, 1734, son of Nathaniel and Ruth (Eliot) Thayer; H. C., 1753, A.B., A.M.; Tutor, H. C., 1760-1766; Ord. Hampton, N. H., Sept. 17, 1766; sett. Hampton, N. H., 1766-1792; d. Hampton, N. H., Sept. 6, 1792 a. 58.

EZRA THAYER, A.M., b. Bellingham, Apr. 28, 1733, son of Dea. Jonathan and Elizabeth (Alden) Thayer; H.C., 1754, A.B., A.M.; Ord. Ware, Jan. 10, 1759; sett. Ware, 1759-1775; d. Ware, Feb. 12, 1775.

THOMPSON, see Tompson.

CHARLES THOMPSON, A.M., b. Amwell, N. J., Apr. 14, 1748; Brown U., 1769, A.B., A.M.; Trustee, Brown U., 1795-1803; Ord. Warren, R. I., (Bapt. Chh.), July 3, 1771; sett. Warren, R. I., 1770-1778; sett. Ashford, Ct., 1778-1779; sett. Swansea, (1st Chh.), 1779-1802; Chaplain, Continental army, 1775-1778; Bapt.; d. Charlton, May 1, 1803 a. 56.

EBENEZER THOMPSON, A.M., b. West Haven, Ct., June 21, 1712, son of Joseph and Elizabeth (Smith) Thompson; Y. C., 1733, A.B., A.M.; lay reader, Simsbury, Ct., (Epis. Chh.), 1740-1743; Ord. England, 1743; sett. Scituate, (St. Andrew's Chh.), 1743-1775; sett. Marshfield, (Epis. Chapel), 1745-1775; Epis.; d. Scituate, Nov. 28, 1775, a. 64.

THOMAS THOMPSON, b. Ireland, 1704; Edinburgh; Ord. Tyrone, Ireland; inst. Derry, N. H., (Londonderry), Oct. 1733; sett. Derry, N. H., 1733-1738; Presb.; d. Derry, N. H., Sept. 22, 1738, a. 34.

THOMAS THORNTON, A.M., b. Yorkshire, England, 1609, son of John and Grace (Withers) Thornton, of Bidforth, Yorks.; educated in England, (perhaps at Trinity Coll., Camb., A.B., 1623/4; A.M., 1627); silenced and ejected, 1662; came to N. E., 1662; Ord. Yarmouth, 1667; sett. Yarmouth, 1662-1692; only physician in Yarmouth from 1670, until old age forced him to retire; d. Boston, Feb. 15, 1700/1, a. 91.

AMOS THROOP, A.M., bapt. Bristol, R. I., June 7, 1702, son of John and Rebecca Throop; H. C., 1721, A.B., A.M.; Ord. Woodstock, Ct., May 24, 1727; sett. Woodstock, Ct., (1st Chh.), 1727-1735; d. Woodstock, Ct., Sept. 10, 1735, a. 34.

BENJAMIN THROOP, A.M., b. Bristol, R. I., June 9, 1712, son of Capt. William, Jr. and Elizabeth Throop; Y. C., 1734, A.B., A.M.; Ord. Bozrah, Ct., (4th Chh. in Norwich), Jan. 3, 1738/9, as the first minister; sett. Bozrah, Ct., 1739-1785; Ct. Election Sermon, 1758; d. Bozrah, Ct., (New Concord), Sept. 16, 1785, a. 74.

GEORGE TROOP, prob. b. Bristol, R. I., June 12, 1757, son of Thomas and Elizabeth Throop; Ord. Otis, 1772; sett. Otis, (Loudon), 1772-1775; was the only minister of the First Chh. of Otis, which was disbanded by an ecclesiastical council in 1775; Chaplain, Rev. War, 1776.

WILLIAM THROOP, A.M., b. Bristol, R. I., Aug. 22, 1720, son of William and Elizabeth Throop; Y. C., 1743, A.B., A.M.; A.M., Princeton, 1755; Ord. Mansfield, Ct., (2nd or North Chh. at Storrs), Oct. 11, 1744, as the first minister; sett. Storrs, Ct., 1744-1747; dism. Jan. 15, 1746/7; inst. Southold, L. I., N. Y., Sept. 21, 1748; sett. Southold, L. I., N. Y., 1748-1756; d. Southold, L. I., N. Y., Sept. 29, 1756, a. 36.

DAVID THURSTON, A.B., b. Wrentham, May 6, 1726, son of Daniel and Deborah (Pond) Thurston; Princeton, 1751, A.B.; Ord. Medway, (West Chh.), June 23, 1752; sett. Medway, 1752-1769; resigned Feb. 22, 1769; farmer at Oxford and Sutton; d. Sutton, May 5, 1777, a. 50.

GARDNER THURSTON, b. Newport, R. I., Nov. 14, 1721, son of Edward and Elizabeth Thurston; Ord. Newport, R. I., (2nd Bapt. Chh.), Apr. 29, 1759; sett. Newport, R. I., 1748-1802; largest congregation and meeting house of Baptists in N. E.; Bapt.; d. Newport, R. I., May 23, 1802, a. 81.

PARDON TILLINGHAST, b. Seven Cliffs, near Beach Head, Sussex, England, ca. 1622; came to Providence, R. I., 1645; Ord. Providence, R. I., (1st Bapt. Chh.), 1681; sett. Providence, R. I., 1681-1718; Deputy, 1672-1700; member Town Council, 1688-1707; Bapt.; d. Providence, R. I., Jan. 29, 1718, a. 96.

PELATIAH TINGLEY, A.M., b. Attleborough, 1735, son of Timothy Tingley; Y. C., 1761, A.B.; A.M., 1765; sett. Gorham, Me., (Cong. Chh.), 1765-1766; Ord. Sanford, Me., (Calvinist Bapt. Chh.), Oct. 21, 1772; sett. Sanford, Me., 1772-1782; sett. Waterboro, Me., 1782-1821; Free Will Bapt.; d. Waterboro, Me., Sept. 3, 1821, a. 86.

SAMUEL TOBEY, A.M., b. Sandwich, 1715, son of Samuel and Abiah (Fish) Tobey; H. C., 1733, A.B., A.M.; Ord. Berkley, Nov. 23, 1737; sett. Berkley, 1737-1781; d. Berkely, Feb. 13, 1781.

ZACCHEUS TOBEY, Ord. New Bedford, (Bapt. Chh.), 1792; sett. New Bedford, 1774-1792.

ABRAHAM TODD, A.M., b. New Haven, Ct., Feb. 18, 1709/10, son of Jonah and Hannah (Clark) Todd; Y. C., 1727, A.B., A.M.; Ord. West Greenwich, Ct., 1733; sett. West Greenwich, Ct., 1732-1772; dism. July 1772; sett. Madison, Ct., 1730-1731; sett. Derby, Ct., 1732; d. West Greenwich, Ct., Dec. 17, 1772, a. 63.

JONATHAN TODD, A.M., b. New Haven, Ct., Mar. 9, 1712/13, son of Jonathan and Sarah (Morrison) Todd; Y. C., 1732,

A.B., A.M.; Ord. Madison, Ct., (East Guilford), Oct. 24, 1733; sett. Madison, Ct., 1733-1791; Ct. Election Sermon, 1749; d. East Guilford, Ct., Feb. 24, 1791, s. p.

SAMUEL TODD, A.M., b. North Haven, Ct., Mar. 6, 1716/7, son of Samuel and Susannah (Tolles) Todd; Y. C., 1734, A.B., A.M.; Ord. Plymouth, Ct., (Northbury), May 7, 1740; sett. Plymouth, Ct., 1740-1764; inst. North Adams, Nov. 1766; sett. North Adams, 1766-1778; dism. Jan. 1778; sett. Grafton, N. H., 1782-1789; Chaplain, Am. Rev.; d. Orford, N. H., June 10, 1789, a. 73.

BENJAMIN TOMPSON, A.B., b. Braintree, July 14, 1642, son of Rev. William and Abigail (Collins) Tompson; H. C., 1662, A.B.; taught school in Boston, 1667-1670/1; at Charlestown; and at Braintree, 1678-1700, and 1703-1714; among his pupils who became famous was Cotton Mather who wrote of him with affection and praise in his Magnalia Christi; he preached occasionally but probably was not ordained; he wrote poetry, and was also an excellent physician; d. Roxbury, Apr. 10, 1714, a. 72.

EDWARD TOMPSON, A.B., b. Braintree, Apr. 20, 1665, son of Ens. Dea. Samuel and Sarah (Shepard) Tompson; H. C., 1684, A.B.; teacher at Newbury, 1684-1687; sett. Simsbury, Ct., 1687-1691; sett. Newbury, 1691-1695; Ord. Marshfield, (1st Chh.), Oct. 14, 1696; sett. Marshfield, 1696-1705; d. Marshfield, Mar. 16, 1704/5, a. 40.

JOHN TOMPSON, A.M., b. Scarborough, Me., Oct. 3, 1740, son of Rev. William and Anna (Hubbard) Tompson; H. C., 1765, A.B., A.M.; Ord. Portland, Me., Oct. 26, 1768; sett. Standish, Me., 1768-1783; dism. Apr. 7, 1783; inst. South Berwick, Me., (1st Parish in Berwick), May 7, 1783; sett. South Berwick, Me., 1783-1828; d. Berwick, Me., Dec. 21, 1828, a. 88.

SAMUEL TOMPSON, A.M., b. Newbury, Sept. 1, 1691, son of Rev. Edward and Sarah Tompson; H. C., 1710, A.B., A.M.; Ord. Gloucester, (2nd Chh.), Nov. 28, 1716; sett. Gloucester, 1712-1724; d. Gloucester, Dec. 8, 1724.

WILLIAM TOMPSON, A.B., b. Winwich, Lancashire, England, 1598; Brazenose Coll., Oxford, A.B., 1621/2; preacher at Winwich several years before coming to N. E., in 1637; sett. York, Me., 1637-1639; Ord. Quincy, (1st Chh. in Braintree), Nov. 19, 1639, as the first minister; sett. Quincy, (1st Chh.), 1639-1659; missionary to Va., 1642-1643; d. Quincy, (Braintree), Dec. 10, 1666, a. 68.

WILLIAM TOMPSON, JR., A.B., b. Lancashire, England, ca. 1633, son of Rev. William and Abigail (Collins) Tompson; H. C., 1653, A.B.; sett. Springfield, 1654-1656; sett. New London, Ct., 1657-1661, as an Indian preacher for the "Society for Propagating the Gospel in New England;" sett. Mystic, Ct., 1659; sett. New London, Ct., 1659-1663; sett. Surry Co., Va., Sept. 1665; d. Pixford Bay, Surry Co., Va., after June 29, 1665.

WILLIAM TOMPSON, A.M., b. Marshfield, Apr. 26, 1697, son of Rev. Edward and Sarah Tompson; H. C., 1718, A.B., A.M.; Ord. Scarborough, Me., (1st Parish at Black Point), June 26, 1728; sett. Scarborough, Me., 1727-1759; also preached at Dunstan, Me., (2nd or Blue Point Parish), 1727-1743; d. Scarborough, Me., Feb. 13, 1759, a. 62.

AMOS TOPPAN, A.M., b. Newbury, Feb. 7, 1735/6, son of Samuel, Jr. and Dorothy (Moody) Toppan; H. C., 1758, A.B., A.M.; Ord. Kingston, N. H., Aug. 18, 1762; sett. Kingston, N. H., 1761-1771; d. Kingston, N. H., June 23, 1771, a. 35.

BENJAMIN TOPPAN, A.M., b. Newbury, Feb. 28, 1720, son of Samuel and Abigail (Wigglesworth) Toppan; H. C., 1742, A.B., A.M.; Ord. Manchester, Dec. 11, 1745; sett. Manchester, 1744-1790; d. Manchester, May 6, 1790, a. 69.

BEZALEEL TOPPAN, A.M., b. Newbury, Mar. 5, 1705, son of Rev. Christopher and Sarah (Angier) Toppan; H. C., 1722, A.B., A.M.; sett. Concord, N. H., 1725; sett. Salem; d. 1762, a. 57.

CHRISTOPHER TOPPAN, A.M., b. Newbury, Dec. 15, 1671, son of Dr. Peter and Jane (Batt) Toppan; H. C., 1691, A.B., A.M.; Ord. Newbury, Sept. 9, 1696; sett. Newbury, 1695-1747; physician; d. Newbury, July 23, 1747, a. 76.

DAVID TOPPAN, D.D., b. Manchester, Apr. 21, 1753, son of Rev. Benjamin and Elizabeth (March) Toppan; H. C., 1771, A.B., A.M.; A.M., (Hon.), Dart. Coll., 1786; S.T.D., H. C., 1794; Ord. West Newbury, (2nd Chh.), Apr. 18, 1774; sett. West Newbury, 1774-1792; Hollis Professor of Divinity, H. C., June 1792; Fellow, Am. Acad. Arts and Sciences; Election Sermon, 1792; Convention Sermon, 1797; d. Cambridge, Aug. 27, 1803.

JOSEPH TORREY, A.M., b. Weymouth, Oct. 19, 1707, son of Ens. Joseph and Elizabeth (Symmes) Torrey; H. C., 1728, A.B., A.M.; Ord. South Kingston, R. I., (Cong. Chh.), May 17, 1732; sett. South Kingston, R. I., 1732-1791; physician; d. South Kingston, R. I., Nov. 25, 1791, a. 85.

JOSIAH TORREY, A.M., b. Boston, Feb. 9, 1680/1, son of Joseph and Sarah (Wilson) Torrey; H. C., 1698, A.B., A.M.; Ord. Tisbury, Oct. 18, 1704; sett. Tisbury, 1701-1723; also preached to the Indians; d. Tisbury, Oct. 7, 1723, a. 43.

SAMUEL TORREY, b. Combe St. Nicholas, England, 1632, son of Capt. William and Jane (Haviland) Torrey; came to N. E., 1640; H. C., 1653-1656, but did not graduate; Ord. Weymouth, Feb. 14, 1664/5; sett. Weymouth, 1656-1707; chosen President of H. C., but declined, 1684; Artillery Election Sermon, 1669; Election Sermons, 1674, 1683, 1695; an excellent preacher; d. Weymouth, Apr. 21, 1707, a 75, s. p.

THOMAS TOUSEY, A.B., b. Wethersfield, Ct., 1690, son of Thomas Tousey; Y. C., 1707, A.B.; Ord. Newtown, Ct., Oct. 19,

1715; sett. Newtown, Ct., 1713-1724; dism. Mar. 1724; Capt., 1727; J. P., 1728; Rep.; d. Newtown, Ct., Mar. 14, 1761, a. 71.

EBENEZER TOWNSEND, had been a member of a New Light Chh. in Newmarket, N. H., 1756; Ord. Gorham, Me., (2nd Chh.), Apr. 4, 1759, (first lay ord. in Me.) ; sett. Gorham, Me., 1759-1762; an uneducated and humble man but a faithful preacher; d. Gorham, Me., Sept. 22, 1762.

JONATHAN TOWNSEND, A.M., b. Boston, (or Lynn), Jan. 1, 1697/8, son of Jonathan and Elizabeth (Walton) Townsend; H. C., 1716, A.B., A.M.; Ord. Needham, Mar. 23, 1720; sett. Needham, 1720-1762; Convention Sermon, 1758; d. Needham, Sept. 30, 1762, a. 65.

JONATHAN TOWNSEND, JR., A.M., b. Needham, 1721, son of Rev. Jonathan and Mary (Sugars) Townsend; H. C., 1741, A.B., A.M.; Ord. Medfield, Oct. 23, 1745; sett. Medfield, 1745-1769; d. Dedham, 1776, of small pox.

SOLOMON TOWNSEND, A.M., b. Boston, Aug. 25, 1715, son of Solomon and Esther (Sugars) Townsend; H. C., 1735, A.B., A.M.; Ord. Barrington, R. I., 1743; sett. Barrington, R. I., 1743-1796; d. Barrington, R. I., Dec. 25, 1796, a. 81.

JEREMIAH TRACY, JR., Ord. Newent, Ct., (Separatist Chh.), 1746; sett. Newent, Ct., 1746-1753.

STEPHEN TRACY, A.M., b. Norwich, Ct.; Princeton, 1770, A.B., A.M.; A.M., (Hon.), Dart. Coll., 1792; Ord. Peru, Apr. 1772; sett. Peru, 1772-1776; dism. May 1776; inst. Huntington, May 23, 1781; sett. Huntington, 1781-1799; dism. Jan. 1, 1799.

NATHANIEL TRASK, A.M., b. Lexington, Mar. 18, 1722/3, son of Nathaniel and Anna (Raymond) Trask; H. C., 1742, A.B., A.M.; Ord. Brentwood, N. H., Dec. 2, 1747; sett. Brentwood, N. H., 1747-1789; d. Brentwood, N. H., Dec. 12, 1789, a. 67.

JAMES TREADWAY, A.M., b. Colchester, Ct., son of James and Sarah (Munn) Treadway; Y. C., 1759, A.B., A.M.; preached at East Granby, Ct., 1771; Ord. Weathersfield, Vt., 1779; sett. Weathersfield, Vt., 1779-1783; d. Me. after 1814.

JOHN TREADWELL, A.M., b. Ipswich, Sept. 20, 1738, son of John and Hannah (Boardman) Treadwell; H. C., 1758, A.B., A.M.; Ord. Lynn, Mar. 2, 1763; sett. Lynn, 1763-1782; Rep.; Senator; Judge of Common Pleas; d. Salem, Jan. 5, 1811.

RICHARD TREAT, A.M., b. Glastonbury, Ct., May 14, 1694, son of Lieut. Thomas and Dorothy (Bulkley) Treat; Y. C., 1719, A.B., A.M.; Ord. Brimfield, Nov. 18, 1724; sett. Brimfield, 1723-1734; dism. Mar. 25, 1734; d. Sheffield, ca. 1757.

SALMON TREAT, A.M., b. Wethersfield, Ct., ca. 1673, son of Lieut. James and Rebecca (Lattimer) Treat; H. C., 1694, A.B.; A.M., Y. C., 1702; sett. Greenwich, Ct., (1st Chh.), 1695-1697; Ord.

Preston, Ct., Nov. 16, 1698; sett. Preston, Ct., 1697-1744; resigned, Mar. 14, 1743/4; d. Preston, Ct., Jan. 6, 1762.

SAMUEL TREAT, A.M., bapt. Milford, Ct., Sept. 3, 1648, son of Gov. Robert and Jane (Tapp) Treat of Ct. (eldest of 21 sons); H. C., 1669, A.B., A.M.; Ord. Eastham, Mar. 17, 1675; sett. Eastham, 1672-1717; taught the Indians; Election Sermon, 1713; Plymouth Election Sermon, 1678; d. Eastham, Mar. 18, 1716/7, a. 69.

JOHN TROUTBEC, A.M., b. Blencoe, Dacre, Cumberland, England, son of George Troutbeck; Queen's Coll., Oxford, 1741, A.B., A.M.; licensed by the Bishop of London, May 7, 1754; missionary for the V.S.P.G.F.P.; sett. Hopkinton, (Epis. Chapel), 1752-1769; appointed Chaplain of the Frigate, "Rose," 1769; inst. Boston, (King's Chapel, as King's Lecturer), 1755; sett. Boston, 1755-1775; went to Halifax, N. S., 1775, and returned to England; Epis.; d. Blencowe, England, 1779.

CALEB TROWBRIDGE, A.M., b. Newton, Nov. 17, 1692, son of Lieut. Dea. James and Margaret (Atherton) Trowbridge; H. C., 1710, A.B., A.M.; Ord. Groton, Mar. 2, 1714/5; sett. Groton, 1715-1760; d. Groton, Sept. 9, 1760, a. 68.

HENRY TRUE, A.M., b. Salisbury, Feb. 27, 1725/6, son of Dea. Jabez and Sarah (Tappan) True; H. C., 1750, A.B., A.M.; Ord. Hampstead, N. H., June 24, 1752; sett. Hampstead, N. H., 1752-1782; d. Hampstead, N. H., May 22, 1782, a. 56.

BENJAMIN TRUMBULL, D.D., b. Hebron, Ct., Dec. 19, 1735, son of Benjamin and Mary (Brown) Trumbull; Y. C., 1759, A.B., A.M.; S.T.D., Y. C., 1796; Ord. North Haven, Ct., Dec. 24, 1760; sett. North Haven, Ct., 1760-1820; Chaplain, Gen. Wooster's Regt., 1775-1776; Ct. Election Sermon, 1801; d. North Haven, Ct., Feb. 2, 1820, a. 85.

JOHN TRUMBULL, A.M., bapt. Suffield, Ct., Apr. 23, 1715, son of John and Elizabeth (Winchell) Trumbull; Y. C., 1735, A.B., A.M.; Fellow, Y. C., 1772-1787; Ord. Watertown, Ct., Jan. 16, 1739/40; sett. Watertown, Ct., 1739-1787; Ct. Election Sermon, 1782; d. Watertown, Ct., Dec. 13, 1787, a. 73.

JOHN TUCK, A.M., b. Hampton, N. H., Aug. 23, 1702, son of Dea. John and Bethia (Hobbs) Tucke; H. C., 1723, A.B., A.M.; Ord. Gosport, Isles of Shoals, N. H., July 26, 1732, as the first and only minister ordained on the island; sett. Gosport, N. H., 1732-1773; physician; d. Gosport, N. H., Aug. 12, 1773, a. 70.

JOHN TUCK, JR., A.M., b. Gosport, Isles of Shoals, N. H., Aug. 7, 1741, son of Rev. John and Mary (Dole) Tuck; H. C., 1758, A.B., A.M.; Ord. Epsom, N. H., Sept. 23, 1761; sett. Epsom, N. H., 1761-1774; Chaplain, Rev. War; d. Salem, N. Y., Feb. 9, 1777, a. 35, of small pox.

JOHN TUCKER, D.D., b. Amesbury, Sept. 19, 1719, son of Benjamin and Alice (Davis) Tucker; H. C., 1741, A.B., A.M.;

S.T.D., 1787; Ord. Newbury, (1st Chh.), Nov. 20, 1745; sett. Newbury, 1745-1792; Convention Sermon, 1768; Election Sermon, 1771; Dudleian Lecture, 1778; liberal; d. Newbury, Mar. 22, 1792, a. 73.

SAMUEL TUDOR, A.M., b. Windsor, Ct., Mar. 8, 1704/5, son of Samuel and Abigail (Filley) Tudor; Y. C., 1728, A.B., A.M.; Ord. Windsor, Ct., (Poquonnoc), Jan. 1740; sett. Windsor, Ct., 1740-1757; d. Windsor, Ct., Sept. 21, 1757, a. 53.

JOHN TUFTS, A.M., b. Medford, Feb. 26, 1688/9, son of Peter and Mercy (Cotton) Tufts; H. C., 1708, A.B., A.M.; Ord. West Newbury, (1st Chh.), June 30, 1714; sett. West Newbury, 1714-1738; d. Amesbury, Aug. 17, 1752.

JOSHUA TUFTS, A.M., b. Newbury, Oct. 4, 1716, son of Rev. John and Sarah (Bradstreet) Tufts; H. C., 1736, A.B., A.M.; Ord. Litchfield, N. H., Dec. 9, 1741; sett. Litchfield, N. H., 1741-1744; sett. Edgartown, 1759-1760; sett. Cumberland, N. S.; d. 1766.

ELDAD TUPPER, b. Sandwich, May 31, 1674, son of Capt. Thomas, Jr. and Martha (Mayhew) Tupper; appointed to act for the Indians; prob. not ordained; d. Sandwich, Sept. 15, 1750.

ELISHA TUPPER, b. Sandwich, July 17, 1707, son of Rev. Eldad and Martha (Wheaton) Tupper; sett. Mattapoisett, (Rochester), 1736-1739; sett. Sandwich, (Indian Chh. at Herring Pond), 1739-1787; d. Sandwich, 1787, a. 80.

CAPTAIN THOMAS TUPPER, b. Sandwich, England, 1578; came to Lynn, 1635; removed to Sandwich, 1637; Captain; Deputy to the Gen. Court for 19 years; sett. Sandwich, (Indian Chh. at Herring Pond), 1658-1676, as the first minister; Indian missionary; d. Bourne, Mar. 28, 1675/6, a. 98.

CAPTAIN THOMAS TUPPER, JR., b. Sandwich, Jan. 16, 1638, son of Capt. Thomas and Anne Tupper; sett. Sandwich, (Indian Chh. at Herring Pond), 1676-1706; Indian missionary; member Council of War; Town Clerk; Selectman, 14 years; Deputy to the Gen. Court, 8 years; d. Sandwich, May 1706.

CALEB TURNER, A.M., b. Mansfield, Ct., May 9, 1733, son of Philip and Mary Turner; Y. C., 1758, A.B., A.M.; Ord. Lakeville, July 25, 1761; sett. Lakeville, 1760-1801; d. Lakeville, Sept. 11, 1803, a. 71.

CHARLES TURNER, A.M., b. Scituate, Sept. 3, 1732, son of Charles and Eunice (James) Turner; H. C., 1752, A.B., A.M.; Ord. Duxbury, July 23. 1755; sett. Duxbury, 1755-1775; Election Sermon, 1773; d. Turner, Me., 1813, a. 81.

DAVID TURNER, A.M., b. Scituate, 1693, son of Thomas and Hannah (Jenkins) Turner; H. C., 1718, A.B., A.M.; Ord. Rehoboth, (2nd Cong. Precinct), Nov. 29, 1721; sett. Rehoboth, 1721-1757; physician; d. Rehoboth, Aug. 9, 1757, a. 63.

EBENEZER TURRELL, A.M., b. Boston, Feb. 5, 1701, son of Samuel and Lydia (Stoddard) Turrell; H. C., 1721, A.B., A.M.;

Ord. Medford, Nov. 25, 1724; sett. Medford, 1724-1778; d. Medford, Dec. 5, 1778, a. 76.

MOSES TUTTLE, A.M., b. New Haven, Ct., June 25, 1715, son of John and Hannah (Humiston) Tuttle; Y. C., 1745, A.B., A.M.; Ord. Granville, 1746/7; sett. Granville, 1747-1754; sett. Kent Co., Del., (Presb. Chh.), 1756-1762; d. Southold, L. I., N. Y., Nov. 21, 1785, a. 71.

ANDREW TYLER, A.M., b. Boston, Aug. 20, 1719, son of Andrew Tyler, Esq.; H. C., 1738, A.B., A.M.; Ord. Westwood, Nov. 30, 1743; sett. Westwood, 1743-1772; dism. Dec. 17, 1772; Royalist; d. Boston, May 3, 1775.

JOHN TYLER, A.M., b. Wallingford, Ct., Aug. 15, 1742, son of John and Mary (Doolittle) Tyler; Y. C., 1765, A.B.; A.B., Columbia U., 1767; A.M., Columbia U., 1769; Ord. London, 1768; sett. Norwich, Ct., (Christ Chh., Epis., as Rector), 1768-1823; Epis.; d. Norwich, Ct., Jan. 20, 1823, a. 81.

CALEB UPHAM, A.M., b. Malden, Oct. 17, 1723, son of Ebenezer and Elizabeth (Blanchard) Upham; H. C., 1744, A.B., A.M.; Ord. Truro, Oct. 29, 1755; sett. Truro, 1755-1786; d. Truro, Apr. 9, 1786, a. 63.

EDWARD UPHAM, A.M., b. Malden, Mar. 26, 1709/10, son of James and Dorothy (Wigglesworth) Upham; H. C., 1734, A.B., A.M.; A.M., (Hon.), Brown U., 1769; Fellow and Trustee Brown U., 1764-1789; Ord. West Springfield, (1st Bapt. Chh.), Oct. 15, 1740; sett. West Springfield, 1740-1749; inst. Newport, R. I., (1st Bapt. Chh.), 1748; sett. Newport, R. I., 1748-1771; sett. West Springfield, (2nd Bapt. Chh.), 1771-1797; liberal; open communion Bapt.; Arminian; d. West Springfield, Oct. 5, 1797, a. 87.

TIMOTHY UPHAM, A.M., b. Malden, Feb. 9, 1747/8, son of Timothy and Mary (Cheever) Upham; H. C., 1768, A.B., A.M.; Ord. Deerfield, N. H., Dec. 9, 1772, as the first minister; sett. Deerfield, N. H., 1772-1811; d. Deerfield, N. H., Feb. 21, 1811, a. 63.

JOHN URQUEHART, came from Scotland to N. E., 1774; sett. Warren, Me., 1775-1783; sett. Topsham, Me., 1783-1785; inst. Ellsworth, Me., 1785; sett. Ellsworth, Me., 1785-1790; left the state; Presb.

JAMES USHER, A.M., b. Bristol, R. I., Sept. 20, 1733, son of Rev. John and Elizabeth Usher; Y. C., 1753, A.B., A.M.; sett. Hebron, Ct., (Epis. Chh.), 1757; was sailing for England to take orders when he was captured by the French, 1757; Epis.; d. Bayonne, France, 1757, a. 24, s. p.

JOHN USHER, A.B., b. (Boston), June 1695, son of Gov. John and Elizabeth (Allen) Usher of N. H.; H. C., 1719, A.B.; Ord. 1722; Missionary, V.S.P.G.F.P.; sett. Bristol, R. I., (St. Michael's Chh.), 1723-1775; Epis.; d. Bristol, R. I., Apr. 30, 1775

JOHN USHER, A.M., b. Bristol, R. I., Sept. 27, 1723, son of

Rev. John and Elizabeth Usher; H. C., 1743, A.B., A.M.; A.M., (Hon.), Brown U., 1794; Ord. 1793; sett. Bristol, R. I., (St. Michael's Chh.), 1792-1800; lawyer; lay reader; clergyman; Epis.; d. Bristol, R. I., July 5, 1804, a. 81.

THOMAS USTWICK, A.M., b. New York City, Aug. 30, 1753, son of Stephen and Jane (Ruland) Ustwick; Brown U., 1771, A.B., A.M.; sett. Stamford, Ct., (Bapt. Chh.), 1775-1776; Ord. Ashford, Ct., (Bapt. Chh.), Aug. 5, 1777; sett. Ashford, Ct., (Bapt. Chh.), 1776-1779; sett. Grafton, (Bapt. Chh.), 1779-1780; sett. Philadelphia, Pa., (1st Bapt. Chh.), 1781-1802; Bapt.; d. Burlington, N. J., Apr. 18, 1803.

RICHARD ULTEY, sett. Newport, R. I., (United Brethren Chh.), 1758; Moravian.

LAURENT VANDENBOSCH, arrived at Boston, 1685; sett. Boston, (French Protestant Chh.), 1685-1686; minister of the Huguenot Chh., Staten Island, N. Y.; sett. North Sassafra and Shrewsbury Parishes, Cecil County, Maryland, 1692-1696; St. Paul's Chh., Kent County, Maryland, Sept. 1693-1696; Huguenot; Epis.; d. St. Paul's Parish, Kent County, Maryland, 1696.

JAMES VARNEY, A.M., b. Boston, Aug. 8, 1706, son of James and Jane Varney; H. C., 1725, A.B., A.M.; Ord. Wilmington, Oct. 24, 1733; sett. Wilmington, 1733-1739; dism. Apr. 5, 1739; d. 1783.

WILLIAM VAUGHAN, Ord. Newport, R. I., (1st Bapt. Chh.), 1648; sett. Newport, R. I., (1st Bapt. Chh.), 1648-1656; sett. Newport, R. I., (2nd Bapt. Chh.), 1656-1677; freeman, 1655; Bapt.; d. Newport, R. I., before Sept. 2, 1677.

JOHN VEAZIE, A.M., b. Braintree, Nov. 12, 1681, son of Solomon and Elizabeth (Sanders) Veazie; H. C., 1700, A.B., A.M.; schoolmaster at Braintree, 1701-1703; preached at Quincy, July 9, 1704; at Medfield, Sept. 1705; Sewall laments the early death of this "young hopeful minister;" d. July 3, 1707.

SAMUEL VEAZIE, A.M., b. Braintree, Jan. 8, 1711, son of Samuel and Deborah (Wales) Veazie; H. C., 1736, A.B., A.M.; Ord. Duxbury, Oct. 31, 1739; sett. Duxbury, 1739-1750; inst. Hull, Apr. 1753; sett. Hull, 1753-1767; d. 1797.

COMMISSARY WILLIAM VEAZIE, A.M., b. Braintree, Aug. 10, 1674, son of Ens. William and Mary Veazie; H. C., 1693, A.B., A.M.; A.M., Oxford U., 1697; Ord. London, England, Aug. 16, 1697; sett. New York City, (Trinity Chh., as Rector), 1697-1746; appointed Commissary, 1712; preached often at Boston (King's Chapel); he was the first minister of the first Epis. Chh. in N. Y. City; Epis.; d. New York City, July 18, 1746, a. 72.

JONATHAN VICKERY, son of George and Rebecca (Phipeny) Vickery; sett. Chatham, 1699-1702; executor of his father's estate, July 29, 1679; drowned at Chatham, Apr. 30, 1702.

ROGER VIETS, A.B., b. East Granby, Ct., Mar. 9, 1737/8, son

of John and Lois (Phelps) Viets; Y. C., 1758, A.B.; Ord. London, England, Mar. 1763; sett. Simsbury, Ct., (Epis. Chh.), 1763-1786; inst. Digby, N. S., Aug. 28, 1786; sett. Digby, N. S., 1786-1811; Epis.; d. Digby, N. S., Aug. 11, 1811, a. 74.

JONATHAN VINAL, A.M., bapt. Scituate, Apr. 17, 1743, son of Capt. Israel and Jemima (Pope) Vinal; H. C., 1751, A.B., A.M.; preached but was not settled; d. 1777.

WILLIAM VINAL, A.M., b. Boston, May 20, 1718, son of Elijah and Elizabeth (Ellis) Vinal; H. C., 1739, A.B., A.M.; Ord. Newport, R. I., (1st Cong. Chh.), Oct. 29, 1746; sett. Newport, R. I., 1746-1768; dism. Sept. 21, 1768; d. 1781, a. 63.

JOHN WADE, A.M., b. Ipswich, Feb. 15, 1674/5, son of Hon. Col. Thomas and Elizabeth (Coggswell) Wade; H. C., 1693, A.B., A.M.; Chaplain and physician of the Garrison at Brunswick, Me., 1696; Ord. South Berwick, Me., (1st Parish in Berwick), Nov. 18, 1702; sett. South Berwick, Me., 1699-1703; physician; d. Berwick, Me., Nov. 13, 1703.

NOAH WADHAMS, A.B., b. Wethersfield, Ct., May 17, 1726, son of Noah and Anne (Hurlburt) Wadhams; Princeton, 1754, A.B.; sett. New Preston, Ct., 1757-1768, as the first minister; d. Plymouth, Ct., May 22, 1806.

PRESIDENT BENJAMIN WADSWORTH, A.M., b. Milton, Feb. 28, 1669/70, son of Capt. Samuel and Abigail (Lindall) Wadsworth; H. C., 1690, A.B., A.M.; Fellow, H. C., 1697-1707; 1712-1725; Ord. Boston, (1st Chh.), Sept. 8, 1696; sett. Boston, 1693-1725; dism. June 16, 1725; inst. President, H. C., July 7, 1725; served as President, 1725-1736; Artillery Election Sermon, 1700; Election Sermon, 1716; d. Cambridge, Mar. 12, 1736/7, a. 67.

BENJAMIN WADSWORTH, D.D., b. Milton, July 18, 1750, son of Dea. Benjamin and Esther (Tucker) Wadsworth; H. C., 1769, A.B., A.M.; S.T.D., 1816; Ord. Danvers, Dec. 23, 1772; sett. Danvers, 1772-1826; d. Danvers, Jan. 18, 1826, a. 76.

DANIEL WADSWORTH, A.M., b. Farmington, Ct., Nov. 14, 1704, son of Dea. John, Jr. and Elizabeth (Stanley) Wadsworth; Y. C., 1726, A.B., A.M.; Ord. Hartford, Ct., (1st Chh.), Sept. 28, 1732; sett. Hartford, Ct., 1732-1747; d. Hartford, Ct., Nov. 12, 1747, a. 43.

EBENEZER WADSWORTH, b. Milton, ca. 1725, son of Recompense and Sarah (Morey) Wadsworth; Ord. Grafton, (Separatist Chh.), Mar. 20, 1751; sett. Grafton, 1751-1767.

JOHN WADSWORTH, A.M., b. Milton, Aug. 6. 1703, son of Dea. John and Elizabeth (Vose) Wadsworth; H. C., 1723, A.B., A.M.; Ord. Canterbury, Ct., Sept. 3, 1729; sett. Canterbury, Ct., 1729-1741; dism. May 27, 1741; sett. Palmer; sett. Coos, N. H.; d. Milton, June 15, 1766, a. 63.

SAMUEL WADSWORTH, b. Milton, July 23, 1720, son of

Dea. John and Elizabeth (Vose) Wadsworth; Ord. Killingly, Ct., (3rd Chh. at South Killingly), June 3, 1747; sett. Killingly, Ct., 1746-1762; d. Milton, May 11, 1762, a. 42.

SAMUEL WAKEMAN, bapt. England, June 7, 1635, son of Capt. John and Elizabeth (Hopkinson) Wakeman; H. C., 1655, but did not graduate; Ord. Fairfield, Ct., Sept. 30, 1665; sett. Fairfield, Ct., 1665-1692; Ct. Election Sermon, 1685; d. Fairfield, Ct., Mar. 8, 1692.

WILLIAM WALDRON, A.M., b. Portsmouth, N. H., Nov. 4, 1697, son of Capt. Richard and Elinor (Vaughan) Waldron; H. C., 1717, A.B., A.M.; Ord. Boston, (New Brick Chh.), May 22, 1722, as the first minister; sett. Boston, 1721-1727; Artillery Election Sermon, 1727; d. Boston, Sept. 11, 1727, a. 30.

ATHERTON WALES, A.M., b. Braintree, Mar. 8, 1704, son of Elder Nathaniel and Joanna Wales; H. C., 1726, A.B., A.M.; sett. Marshfield, (2nd Chh.), 1739-1795; d. Marshfield, 1795.

JOHN WALES, A.M., b. Braintree, May 25, 1699, son of Elder Nathaniel and Joanna Wales; H. C., 1728, A.B., A.M.; Ord. Raynham, Oct. 20, 1731; sett. Raynham, 1731-1765; d. Raynham, Feb. 23, 1765, a. 66.

SAMUEL WALES, D.D., b. Raynham, Mar. 2, 1747/8, son of Rev. John and Hazadiah (Leonard) Wales; Y. C., 1767, A.B., A.M.; S.T.D., 1782; S.T.D., Princeton, 1784; Tutor, Y. C., 1769-1770; Ord. Milford, Ct., (1st Chh.), Dec. 19, 1770; sett. Milford, Ct., 1770-1781; induct. Livingston Professor of Divinity, Y. C., June 12, 1782; served, 1782-1793; Chaplain, Rev. War, 1776; Ct. Election Sermon, 1785; d. New Haven, Ct., Feb. 18, 1794, a. 46.

JOHN WALLEY, A.M., b. Boston, Oct. 6, 1716, son of the Hon. John and Bethia (Eyer) Walley; H. C., 1734, A.B., A.M.; Ord. Ipswich, (2nd or South Chh.), Nov. 4, 1747; sett. Ipswich, 1747-1764; dism. Feb. 22, 1764; inst. Bolton, May 1773; sett. Bolton, 1773-1783; dism. Jan. 31, 1783; d. Roxbury, Mar. 2, 1784, s. p.

THOMAS WALLEY, b. 1618, son of Robert Walley; (a Rev. Thomas Walley received an A.B. at Pembroke Coll., Oxford, 1657); Rector of William and Mary's Parish, Whitehall, London; ejected for non-conformity; came to N. E., 1663; Ord. Barnstable, 1663; sett. Barnstable, 1663-1678; d. Barnstable, Mar. 24, 1678/9, a. 61.

TIMOTHY WALKER, A.M., b. Woburn, July 27, 1705, son of Samuel and Judith (Howard) Walker; H. C., 1725, A.B., A.M.; Ord. Concord, N. H., Nov. 18, 1730, as the first minister; sett. Concord, N. H., 1730-1782; visited England twice as an agent for the town of Concord, N. H.; d. Concord, N. H., Sept. 1, 1782, a. 77.

ZACHARIAH WALKER, b. Boston, Sept. 15, 1637, son of Robert Walker; H. C., 1653-1655, but did not graduate; sett. Jamaica, L. I., N. Y., 1662-1668; Ord. Woodbury, Ct., (2nd Chh. in Stratford), May 5, 1670, as the first minister; sett. Woodbury, Ct., 1668-1700; d. Woodbury, Ct., Jan. 20, 1699/1700.

NATHANIEL WALTER, A.M., b. Roxbury, Aug. 15, 1711, son of Rev. Nehemiah and Sarah (Mather) Walter; H. C., 1729, A.B., A.M.; Ord. West Roxbury, July 10, 1734; sett. West Roxbury, 1734-1776; Artillery Election Sermon, 1746; French interpreter for Gen. Pepperell at the siege of Louisburg in 1745; d. West Roxbury, Mar. 11, 1776.

NEHEMIAH WALTER, A.M., b. Youghall, Ireland, Dec. 1663, son of Thomas Walter of Lancashire, England; came to N. E., 1679; H. C., 1684; A.B., A.M.; Fellow, H. C., 1692-1703; Ord. Roxbury, Oct. 17, 1688; sett. Roxbury, 1688-1750; Artillery Election Sermons, 1697, 1711; Convention Sermon, 1723; d. Roxbury, Sept. 17, 1750, a. 86.

THOMAS WALTER, A.M., b. Roxbury, Dec. 13, 1696, son of Rev. Nehemiah and Sarah (Mather) Walter; H. C., 1713, A.B., A.M.; Ord. Roxbury, Oct. 19, 1718; sett. Roxbury, 1718-1725; d. Roxbury, Jan. 10, 1724/5, a. 28.

WILLIAM WALTER, D.D., b. West Roxbury, Oct. 7, 1737, son of Rev. Nathaniel and Rebecca (Abbott) Walter; H. C., 1756, A.B., A.M.; D.D., King's Coll., Aberdeen, 1784; Ord. England, 1764; inst. Boston, (Trinity Chh.), Oct. 1763, as asst. minister; as Rector, July 22, 1764; sett. Boston, 1763-1775; left Mar. 17, 1775; sett. Christ Church, Shelburne, N. S., 1783-1791, as the first minister; inst. Boston, (Christ Chh.), May 29, 1792; sett. Boston, 1792-1800; Tory; Epis.; d. Boston, Dec. 5, 1800.

JOSEPH WALTON, b. Newcastle, N. H.; a cooper; Ruling Elder and preacher, Portsmouth, N. H., (3rd or Independent Chh.), 1771-1789; Ord. Portsmouth, N. H., (Independent Chh.), Sept. 22, 1789; sett. Portsmouth, N. H., 1771-1822; d. Portsmouth, N. H., Jan. 10, 1822.

WILLIAM WALTON, A.M., b. England; Emmanuel Coll., Camb., A.B., 1621/2; A.M., 1623; Vicar of Seaton, Devonshire, 1626; came to Hingham, N. E., 1635; freeman, Mar. 3, 1635/6; sett. Marblehead, 1638-1668, as a missionary preacher; first minister at Marblehead; d. Marblehead, Oct. 1668, (bur. Oct. 9).

EDMUND WARD, A.M., b. Guilford, Ct., Sept. 22, 1706, son of Capt. Andrew, Jr. and Deborah (Joy) Ward; Y. C., 1727, A.B., A.M.; Ord. Guilford, Ct., (4th Society), Sept. 21, 1733; sett. Guilford, Ct., 1729-1734; became an Epis.; Rep. Gen. Ct., 1759-1761; Epis.; d. Guilford, Ct., Nov. 15, 1779, a. 73.

EPHRAIM WARD, A.M., b. Newton, Mar. 21, 1741, son of Dea. Ephraim and Mary (Haven) (Stone) Ward; H. C., 1763, A.B., A.M.; Ord. West Brookfield, Oct. 23, 1771; sett. West Brookfield, 1771-1818; d. West Brookfield, Feb. 9, 1818, a. 77.

JOHN WARD, A.M., b. Haverhill, Suffolk, England, Nov. 5, 1606, son of Rev. Nathaniel Ward; Emmanuel Coll., Camb., A.B., 1626/7; A.M., 1630; Rector of Hadleigh, Essex, 1633-1639; came to

N. E., 1639; Ord. Haverhill, Oct. 24, 1645, as the first minister; sett. Haverhill, 1641-1693; physician; Dr. Mather says he preached an excellent sermon in his 87th year; d. Haverhill, Dec. 27, 1693, a. 87.

NATHAN WARD, A.M., b. Newton, Apr. 11, 1721, son of Joseph and Esther (Kenrick) Ward; A.M., (Hon.), Dart. Coll.; Ord. Newton, (Separatist Chh.), Jan. 17, 1753; sett. Newton, 1753-1758; dism. Apr. 1758; sett. Newcastle, Me., 1760-1763; Ord. at Newburyport, July 10, 1765, for service at Plymouth, N. H.; sett. Plymouth, N. H., 1765-1788; New Light preacher; d. Plymouth, N. H., June 15, 1804, a. 83.

NATHANIEL WARD, A.M., b. Haverhill, Suffolk, England, 1578, son of Rev. John Ward, a distinguished Puritan divine; Emmanuel Coll., Camb., A.B., 1599/1600; A.M., 1603; admitted to Lincoln's Inn, May 15, 1607, and nominated a barrister, Oct. 17, 1615; Chaplain to the British merchants at Elbing, 1620-1624; Curate at St. James' Chh., Duke's Place, Picadilly, London, 1626-1628; Rector of Stondon Massey, Essex, England, 1628-1633; suspended; came to N. E., 1634; Ord. Ipswich, June 1634, as the first minister; sett. Ipswich, 1634-1637; returned to England, 1646, where he became minister at Shenfield, Essex, 1648-1652; joined the Rev. John Cotton in framing the code of laws established in N. E., 1639; Election Sermon, 1641; author of the "Simple Cobbler of Agawam," 1647; d. Shenfield, Essex, England, Oct. 1653.

ROBERT WARD, A.M., b. Charlestown, Sept. 23, 1694, son of Robert and Margaret (Peachie) Ward; H. C., 1719, A.B., A.M.; Ord. Wenham, Jan. 25, 1721/2; sett. Wenham, 1722-1732; d. Wenham, July 19, 1732, a. 37.

JOHN WARHAM, A.M., b. 1595; St. Mary's Hall, Oxford, A.B., 1614; A.M., 1618; Ord. by the Bishop of Exeter at Silferton, Devon, May 23, 1619; minister at Exeter, Devonshire, England; Ord. Plymouth, England, Mar. 30, 1630, for service in N. E.; came in the "Mary and John," 1630, to Dorchester; sett. Dorchester, 1630-1635, as junior minister; sett. Windsor, Ct., 1636-1669, as the first minister; administered the Lord's Supper for others but refused to partake himself; d. Windsor, Ct., Apr. 1, 1670.

NOADIAH WARNER, A.M., b. East Haddam, Ct., Jan. 12, 1728/9, son of John and Mehitable (Chapman) (Richardson) Warner; Y. C., 1759, A.B., A.M.; Ord. Danbury, Ct., (1st Chh.), Feb. 13, 1764; sett. Danbury, Ct., 1762-1768; dism. Feb. 24, 1768; farmer at Newtown; d. Newtown, Ct., Feb. 2, 1794, a. 66.

JOHN WARREN, A.M., b. Roxbury, Sept. 18, 1704, son of Joseph and Deborah Warren; H. C., 1725, A.B.. A.M.; Ord. Wenham, Sept. 10, 1733; sett. Wenham, 1733-1749; d. Wenham, July 19, 1749, a. 45.

THOMAS WATERHOUSE, A.B., b. London, England, ca. 1600, son of Edward Waterhouse; matric. Emmanuel Coll., Camb., 1631; Charterhouse, Camb., A.B., 1634/5; sett. Coddenham, Herts.,

England; came to N. E., 1639; schoolmaster at Dorchester, 1639-1642; preached occasionally; returned to England, 1642; Vicar of Ash Bocking, Suffolk, 1652-1662; ejected 1662; Rector of Little Hallingbury, Essex, 1658-1669; d. Creeting, Suffolk, England, 1679/80, a. 80.

SIMON WATERMAN, A.M., b. Bozrah, Ct., Jan. 3, 1736/7, son of Nehemiah Waterman; Y. C., 1759, A.B., A.M.; Ord. Wells, Ct., (Separatist Chh. of Wallingford), Oct. 7, 1761; sett. Wells, Ct., 1761-1787; dism. June 7, 1787; inst. Plymouth, Ct., Aug. 29, 1787; sett. Plymouth, Ct., 1787-1809; dism. Nov. 15, 1809; d. New York City, Nov. 19, 1813, a. 77.

TIMOTHY WATERS, sett. Wallingford, Ct., (Bapt. Chh.), 1735-1750; Bapt.

CALEB WATSON, A.M., b. Roxbury, July 29, 1641, son of John and Alice Watson; H. C., 1661, A.B., A.M.; sett. Hadley, 1665-1673; sett. Hartford, Ct., 1674-1696; sett. Farmington, Ct., 1697-1701; schoolmaster and preacher though never ordained; d. Windsor, Ct., 1725/6.

WILLIAM WAY, sett. Freetown, 1704-1707; dism. Jan. 21, 1706/7; schoolmaster and minister; prob. not ordained.

BENJAMIN WEBB, A.M., b. Braintree, Dec. 13, 1695, son of Benjamin and Susanna (Ballentine) Webb; H. C., 1715, A.B., A.M.; Ord. Eastham, 1720; sett. Eastham, 1720-1746; d. Eastham, Aug. 21, 1746, a. 50.

JOHN WEBB, A.M., b. Braintree, Aug. 21, 1687, son of John and Bethia (Adams) Webb; H. C., 1708, A.B., A.M.; Chaplain, Castle William, Boston Harbor; Ord. Boston, (New North Chh.), Oct. 20, 1714, as the first minister; sett. Boston, 1714-1750; Artillery Election Sermon, 1719; Election Sermon, 1738; d. Boston, Apr. 16, 1750, a. 63.

JOSEPH WEBB, A.M., b. Boston, May 10, 1666, son of Joseph and Grace Webb; H. C., 1684, A.B., A.M.; Fellow, Y. C.; sett. Derby, Ct., 1688-1690; Ord. Fairfield, Ct., Aug. 15, 1698; sett. Fairfield, Ct., 1698-1732; Ct. Election Sermon, 1701; d. Stratford, Ct., Sept. 19, 1732, a. 66.

NATHAN WEBB, A.M., b. Braintree, Apr. 9, 1705, son of Benjamin and Susanna (Ballentine) Webb; H. C., 1725, A.B., A.M.; Ord. Uxbridge, Feb. 3, 1730/1; sett. Uxbridge, 1731-1772; d. Uxbridge, Mar. 16, 1772, a. 67.

ELISHA WEBSTER, A.M., b. West Hartford, Ct., Nov. 12, 1713, son of Capt. John and Abiel (Steel) Webster; Y. C., 1738, A.B., A.M.; Ord. Canaan, Ct., Oct. 1, 1740, as the first minister; sett. Canaan, Ct., 1740-1752; dism. Oct. 14, 1752; d. Southington, Ct., Jan. 29, 1788, a. 75.

NICHOLAS WEBSTER, A.B., b. Gloucester, Oct. 9, 1673, son of Dr. John and Ann (Batt) Webster; H. C., 1695, A.B.; sett. Manchester, 1698-1715; minister and physician; d. Gloucester, Dec. 22, 1717.

PELATIAH WEBSTER, A.M., b. Lebanon, Ct., Nov. 24, 1726, son of Pelatiah and Joanna (Smith) Webster; Y. C., 1746, A.B., A.M.; Ord. Greenwich, Dec. 20, 1749; sett. Greenwich, 1749-1755; dism. Oct. 1755; became a merchant; resided at Philadelphia, Pa.; d. Philadelphia, Pa., Sept. 10, 1795, a. 69.

SAMUEL WEBSTER, D.D., b. Bradford, Aug. 16, 1718, son of Samuel and Mary (Kimball) Webster; H. C., 1737, A.B., A.M.; S.T.D., 1792; Ord. Salisbury, Aug. 12, 1741; sett. Salisbury, 1741-1796; Election Sermon, 1777; Convention Sermon, 1779; d. Salisbury, July 18, 1796, a. 78.

SAMUEL WEBSTER, A.M., b. Salisbury, Sept. 16, 1743, son of Rev. Dr. Samuel and Elizabeth (Whiting) Webster; H. C., 1762, A.B., A.M.; Ord. Temple, N. H., Oct. 2, 1771; sett. Temple, N. H., 1771-1777; member Committee of Safety, 1775; Chaplain of a N. H. Regt., 1775; d. Aug. 4, 1777, a. 33.

GEORGE WEEKS, bapt. Dorchester, Nov. 2, 1664, son of William Weeks; missionary to the Indians at Harwich, where he died 1745.

JOSHUA WINGATE WEEKS, A.M., b. Hampton, N. H., 1738, son of Col. Dr. John and Martha (Wingate) Weeks, of Greenland, N. H.; H. C., 1758, A.B., A.M.; Ord. in England, 1763; sett. Marblehead, (St. Michael's Chh.), 1763-1775; sett. Annapolis Royal, N. S., 1779; sett. New York, N. Y., 1779-1780; sett. Preston, N. S., 1793; sett. Greysborough, N. S., 1795; Loyalist; Epis.; d. Annapolis, Halifax, N. S., 1806, a. 68.

DANIEL WELCH, A.M., b. Windham, Ct., Mar. 20, 1725/6, son of Thomas and Hannah (Abbe) Welch; Y. C., 1749, A.B., A.M.; Ord. Mansfield, Ct., (2nd or North Parish at Storrs), Jan. 29, 1752; sett. Storrs, Ct., 1752-1782; d. Mansfield, Ct., Apr. 28, 1782, a. 56.

NATHANIEL WELCH, A.B., b. Charlestown, Sept. 9, 1665, son of Thomas and Elizabeth (Upham) Welch; H. C., 1687, A.B.; sett. Enfield, Ct., 1687-1689; not ordained; d. Enfield, Ct., July 10, 1689, a. 23.

EZRA WELD, A.M., b. Pomfret, Ct., June 13, 1736, son of John and Esther (Waldo) Weld; Y. C., 1759, A.B., A.M.; Ord. Braintree, Nov. 17, 1762; sett. Braintree, 1762-1816; d. Braintree, Jan. 16, 1816, a. 80.

HABIJAH SAVAGE WELD, A.M., b. Dunstable, Sept. 2, 1702, son of Rev. Thomas and Hannah (Tyng) (Savage) Weld; H. C., 1723, A.B., A.M.; teacher at Martha's Vineyard and Woburn, 1725-1726; Ord. Attleborough, Oct. 1, 1727; sett. Attleborough, 1727-1782; d. Attleborough, May 14, 1782, a. 80.

THOMAS WELDE, A.M., bapt. Sudbury, Suffolk, England, July 15, 1595, son of Edmund and Amy (Brewster) Welde; Trinity

Coll., Camb., A.B., 1613/4; A.M., 1618; Ord. Peterborough, Mar. 2, 1617/8; Vicar of Haverhill, Suffolk, England; Vicar of Terling, Essex, 1624-1631; ejected; arrived at Boston, N. E., in the "William and Francis," June 5, 1632; inst. Roxbury, July 1632, as the first minister; sett. Roxbury, 1632-1641; returned to England, 1641, as agent for the Colony; Rector of St. Mary's Chh., Gateshead Parish, Newcastle, Durham, England, 1649-1660; co-author with the Rev. Richard Mather of the "Bay Psalm Book," 1639; d. London, England, Mar. 23, 1660/1.

THOMAS WELD, A.M., b. Roxbury, June 12, 1653, son of Thomas, Jr. and Dorothy (Whiting) Weld; H. C., 1671, A.B., A.M.; Ord. Dunstable, Dec. 16, 1685; sett. Dunstable, 1679-1702; Rep. Gen. Ct., 1689; d. (killed by the Indians), Dunstable, June 9, 1702, a. 49.

THOMAS WELD, A.M., b. Roxbury, Nov. 1702, son of Edmund and Elizabeth (White) Weld; H. C., 1723, A.B., A.M.; Ord. Upton, Jan. 4, 1738; sett. Upton, 1738-1744; sett. Middleborough, (1st Parish), 1744-1749; dism. Jan. 8, 1749; at Middleborough with three quarters of the parish and sixteen members of the church, he held the meeting house, ministerial lands and parsonage; d. as a Chaplain in the French and Indian War, 1755.

JAMES WELLMAN, A.M., b. Lynnfield, May 10, 1723, son of Abraham, Jr. and Elizabeth (Taylor) Wellman; H. C., 1744, A.B., A.M.; A.M., (Hon.), Dart. Coll., 1792; Ord. Millbury, Oct. 7, 1747; sett. Millbury, 1747-1760; dism. June 22, 1760; inst. Cornish, N. H., and Windsor, Vt., Sept. 29, 1768; sett. Windsor, Vt., 1768-1774; sett. Cornish, N. H., 1768-1785; dism. Oct. 1785; d. Cornish, N. H., Dec. 18, 1808, a. 85.

NOAH WELLS, D.D., b. Colchester, Ct., Jan. 25, 1718, son of Noah, Jr. and Sarah (Wyatt) Welles; Y. C., 1741, A.B., A.M.; S.T.D., Princeton, 1774; S.T.D., Y. C., 1774; Tutor, Y. C., 1745-1746; Fellow, Y. C., 1774-1776; Ord. Stamford, Ct., (1st Chh.), Dec. 31, 1746; sett. Stamford, Ct., 1746-1776; Chaplain, Am. Rev.; Ct. Election Sermon, 1764; d. Stamford, Ct., Dec. 31, 1776, a. 58.

RUFUS WELLS, A.B., b. Deerfield, Sept. 29, 1743, son of Dr. Thomas and Sarah (Hawks) Wells; H. C., 1764, A.B.; Ord. Whatley, Sept. 25, 1771; sett. Whatley, 1771-1834; d. Whatley, Nov. 8, 1834, a. 91.

SAMUEL WELLES, A.M., b. Wethersfield, Ct., Dec. 24, 1689, son of Capt. Samuel, Jr. and Ruth (Rice) Welles; Y. C., 1707, A.B., A.M.; Ord. Lebanon, Ct., Dec. 5, 1711; sett. Lebanon, Ct., 1711-1722; dism. Dec. 4, 1722; Mass. House Rep., 1727-1734; J. P., 1729; member Council, 1735-1748; Judge Common Pleas, 1755-1770; d. Boston, May 20, 1770, a. 81.

THOMAS WELLS, A.M., b. Ipswich, Jan. 11, 1646/7, son of Dea. Thomas and Abigail (Warner) Wells; A.M., (Hon.), H. C., 1703; preached at Kittery Point, Me., 1670; Ord. Amesbury, 1672, as the first minister; sett. Amesbury, 1672-1734; d. Amesbury, July 10, 1734, a. 87.

WHITMAN WELSH, A.M., b. Milford, Ct., June 5, 1738, son of Thomas and Sarah (Whitman) Welsh; Y. C., 1762, A.B., A.M.; Ord. Williamstown, Oct. 1765; sett. Williamstown, 1765-1776; marched to Canada, 1776, as Chaplain; d. Quebec, Apr. 8, 1776, a. 38, of small pox.

WILLIAM WELSTEED, A.M., b. Boston, 1695; bapt. June 28, 1696, son of the Hon. William Welsteed; H. C., 1716, A.B., A.M.; Librarian, H. C., 1718-1720; Tutor, H. C., 1720-1728; Fellow, H. C.; Ord. Boston, (New Brick Chh.), Mar. 27, 1728; sett. Boston, 1728-1753; Artillery Election Sermon, 1729; Convention Sermon, 1750; Election Sermon, 1751; d. Boston, Sept. 29, 1753, a. 58.

JOHN WENBOURNE, b. Boston, Sept. 21, 1638, son of William and Elizabeth Wenbourne; H. C., 1656-1659, but did not graduate; sett. Manchester, 1667-1689; prob. went to S. C.; d. 1707.

ELDER WILLIAM WENTWORTH, bapt. Alford, England, Mar. 15, 1615/6, son of William and Susanna Carter (Fleming) Wentworth; Ord. Dover, N. H., (as Ruling Elder), Mar. 10, 1655/6; preached at Dover, N. H., South Berwick, Me., and Salmon Falls, 1655-1690; preached at Exeter, N. H., 1690-1693; d. Exeter, N. H., after 1693.

SAMUEL WEST, D.D., b. Yarmouth, Mar. 3, 1729/30, son of Dr. Sackville and Ruth (Jenkins) West; H. C., 1754, A.B., A.M.; S.T.D., 1793; supply, Tisbury, 1757-1759; Ord. New Bedford, June 3, 1761; sett. New Bedford, 1761-1803; Chaplain, Rev. War; Member Constitutional Convention of Mass.; Fellow, Am. Acad. of Arts and Sciences; Member Am. Phil. Soc.; Election Sermon, 1776; Dudleian Lecture, 1782; Unitarian; d. Tiverton, R. I., Sept. 24, 1807.

SAMUEL WEST, D.D., b. Martha's Vineyard, Nov. 19, 1738, son of Rev. Thomas West of Rochester; H. C., 1761, A.B., A.M.; S.T.D., Dart. Coll., 1798; Chaplain, Fort Pownall on the Penobscot, Me., 1761-1763; Ord. Needham, Apr. 25, 1764; sett. Needham, 1764-1789; dism. Jan. 12, 1789; inst. Boston, (Hollis St. Chh.), Mar. 12, 1789; sett. Boston, 1789-1808; Election Sermon, 1786; Artillery Election Sermon, 1784; Unitarian; d. Boston, Apr. 10, 1808, a. 70.

STEPHEN WEST, D.D., b. Tolland, Ct., Nov. 2, 1735, son of Judge Zebulon and Mary (Delano) West; Y. C., 1755, A.B.; S.T.D., Dart. Coll., 1792; Trustee and Vice-President, Williams College. 19 years; Ord. Stockbridge, June 15, 1759; sett. Stockbridge, 1758-1818; Arminian; d. Stockbridge, May 13, 1819, a. 83.

THOMAS WEST, A.M., b. Martha's Vineyard, 1708, son of Abner and Jean (Look) West; H. C., 1730, A.B.; A.M., 1759; sett. Martha's Vineyard, 1742-1748; sett. Rochester, (3rd Chh.), 1748-1790; d. Rochester, July 14, 1790, a. 82.

WILLIAM WETHERELL, A.M., b. Yorkshire, England,

1600; Corpus Christi Coll., Camb., A.B., 1622/3; A.M., 1626; came to N. E., 1635; schoolmaster at Charlestown, 1635-1638; removed to Duxbury, 1638; Ord. Norwell, (2nd or South Chh. in Scituate), Sept. 2, 1645, as the first minister; sett. Norwell, 1644-1684; d. Norwell, Apr. 9, 1684, a. 84.

IZRAHIAH WETMORE, A.M., b. Stratford, Ct., Aug. 30, 1728, son of Izrahiah and Sarah (Booth) Wetmore; Y. C., 1748, A.B., A.M.; Ord. Stratford, Ct., (1st Chh.), May 16, 1753; sett. Stratford, Ct., 1753-1780; resigned Apr. 1, 1780; inst. Trumbull, Ct., Oct. 13, 1785; sett. Trumbull, Ct., 1785-1798; Ct. Election Sermon, 1773; d. Trumbull, Ct., Aug. 3, 1798, a. 70.

JAMES WETMORE, A.M., b. Middletown, Ct., Dec. 25, 1695, son of Izrahiah and Rachel (Stow) Wetmore; Y. C., 1714, A.B., A.M.; Ord. North Haven, Ct., (Cong. Chh.), Nov. 1718; sett. North Haven, Ct., 1718-1722; became an Epis.; Ord. London, England, July 25, 1723; asst. minister, New York City, (Trinity Chh.), 1723-1726; Rector, (Christ Chh.), Rye, N. Y., 1726-1760; Epis.; d. Rye, N. Y., May 15, 1760, a. 64.

NOAH WETMORE, A.M., b. Middlefield, Ct., Apr. 16, 1730, son of Samuel and Hannah (Hubbard) Wetmore; Y. C., 1757, A.B., A.M.; Ord. Bethel, Ct., Nov. 25, 1760; sett. Bethel, Ct., 1760-1784; dism. Nov. 2, 1784; inst. Setauket, L. I., N. Y., (Presb. Chh.), Apr. 13, 1786; sett. Setauket, L. I., N. Y., 1786-1796; d Setauket, L. I., N. Y., Mar. 9, 1796, a. 66.

H. WHEATLEY, minister of Narragansett Chh., Kingston, R. I., 1713-1714; Epis.

EPHRAIM WHEATON, b. Rehoboth, Oct. 20, 1659, son of Robert and Alice (Bowen) Wheaton; Ord. Swansea, (1st Bapt. Chh.), 1704; sett. Swansea, 1704-1734; Bapt.; d. Swansea, Apr. 26, 1734, a. 75.

GEORGE WHEATON, A.B., b. Mansfield, July 6, 1751, son of Dr. George and Elizabeth (Morey) Wheaton; H. C., 1769, A.B.; Ord. Claremont, N. H., (1st Cong. Chh.), Feb. 19, 1772, as the first minister; sett. Claremont, N. H., 1772-1773; d. Mansfield, June 24, 1773, a. 21.

JOSEPH WHEELER, A.M., b. Concord, Mar. 18, 1735/6, son of Joseph and Abigail (Butterfield) Wheeler; H. C., 1757, A.B., A.M.; Ord. Harvard, Dec. 12, 1759; sett. Harvard, 1759-1768; dism. July 28, 1768; pvt. in Col. Asa Whitcomb's regt. on the Lexington alarm; member Committee of Correspondence, 1775; Rep. Legislature, 1775; Registrar of Probate, Worcester Co., 1776-1793; Justice of the Peace and Quorum, 1776-1793; removed to Worcester, Aug. 17, 1781; County Treasurer; d. Worcester, Feb. 10, 1793, a. 58.

WILLIAM WILLARD WHEELER, A.M., b. Concord, Dec. 24, 1734, son of William Wheeler; H. C., 1755, A.B., A.M.; Ord. in England, 1767; sett. Georgetown, Me., 1768-1772; left Apr. 1772; sett.

Newport, R. I., (Trinity Chh.), 1772-1783; sett. Scituate, (St. Andrew's Chh.), 1783-1810; sett. Marshfield, (Trinity Chh.), 1783-1810; sett. Taunton, 1786-1799; Epis.; d. Scituate, Jan. 14, 1810, a. 75.

PRESIDENT ELEAZER WHEELOCK, D.D., b. Windham, Ct., Apr. 22, 1711, son of Dea. Ralph and Ruth (Huntington) Wheelock; Y. C., 1733, A.B., A.M.; S.T.D., U. of Edinburgh, 1767; Ord. Columbia, Ct., (3rd Chh. in Lebanon), June 4, 1735; sett. Columbia, Ct., 1735-1770; dism. Aug. 15, 1770; first President of Dartmouth College, 1769-1779; d. Hanover, N. H., Apr. 24, 1779, a. 68.

RALPH WHEELOCK, A.M., b. Shropshire, England, 1600; Clare Hall, Camb., A.B., 1626/7; A.M., 1631; Ord. deacon by the Bishop of Peterborough, Sept. 20, 1629; came to N. E., 1637; resided first at Watertown and Dedham; a founder of the First Chh. in Dedham, 1638; Deputy Gen. Ct., 1639, 1640, from Dedham; preached at Dedham and Medfield; admitted freeman, 1638; founder of Medfield, 1650; Rep. Gen. Ct., from Medfield, 1653, 1663, 1664, 1666 and 1667; appointed, Sept. 27, 1642, by the Gen. Ct., Clerk of the writs, and one of the commissioners to end small causes, in Dedham; authorized to "solemnize marriages," Oct. 1645; great-grand-father of Rev. Eleazer Wheelock, D.D., founder and first president of Dart. Coll. who was the father of Rev. John Wheelock, D.D., the second president of Dart. Coll.; d. Medfield, Jan. 11, 1683/4, a. 84.

JOHN WHEELWRIGHT, A.M., b. Saleby, Lincolnshire, England, 1594, son of Robert and Katherine (Mawer) Wheelwright; Sidney-Sussex Coll., Camb., 1614/5, A.B.; A.M., 1618; Ord. priest by the Bishop of Peterborough, Dec. 20, 1619; Vicar of Bilsby, Lincolnshire, England, 1623-1633; suspended for non-conformity; came to N. E., 1636; sett. Braintree, 1636-1637; as a result of a sermon preached in Boston, he was convicted of sedition and sentenced to banishment, Mar. 1636/7; sentence revoked, 1644; sett. Exeter, N. H., 1638-1642, as the first minister; sett. Wells, Me., 1643-1644; inst. Hampton, N. H., June 24, 1647; sett. Hampton, N. H., 1647-1659; dism. May 4, 1659; was in England 1656-1662; inst. Salisbury, Dec. 9, 1662; sett. Salisbury, 1662-1679; his portrait is owned by the Commonwealth of Massachusetts; d. Salisbury, Nov. 15, 1679.

JOSEPH WHIPPLE, A.M., b. Ipswich, July 31, 1701, son of Matthew and Martha (Thyng) Whipple; H. C., 1720, A.B., A.M.; Ord. Hampton Falls, N. H., Jan. 15, 1727; sett. Hampton Falls, N. H., 1727-1757; d. Hampton Falls, N. H., Feb. 17, 1757, a. 56.

DANIEL WHITE, sett. Newport, R. I., (2nd Bapt. Chh.), 1724-1728; a meeting house was erected for him in 1724; by 1728, only one member remained, so he sold the meeting house and left; sett. Philadelphia, Pa., 1728; Bapt.

DAVID WHITE, A.M., b. Hatfield, July 1, 1710, son of Dea. John and Hannah (Wells) White; Y. C., 1730, A.B., A.M.; Ord. Hardwick, Nov. 17, 1736; sett. Hardwick, 1736-1784; d. Hardwick, Jan. 6, 1784, a. 74.

EBENEZER WHITE, A.B., b. Dorchester, July 3, 1685, son of James and Sarah (Baker) White; H. C., 1704, A.B.; Ord. Attleborough, Oct. 17, 1716; sett. Attleborough, 1715-1726; had preached here 1710-1711; d. Attleborough, Sept. 4, 1726, a. 41.

EBENEZER WHITE, A.M., b. Weymouth, Dec. 21, 1709, son of Dea. Thomas and Mary (White) White; Y. C., 1733, A.B., A.M.; Ord. Danbury, Ct., (1st Chh.), Mar. 10, 1735/6; sett. Danbury, Ct., 1736-1764; dism. Mar. 30, 1764; sett. Danbury, Ct., (2nd Chh., Separatist), 1764-1779; d. Danbury, Ct., Sept. 11, 1779, a. 70.

EBENEZER WHITE, A.M., b. Brookline, Mar. 29, 1714, son of Dea. Benjamin and Margaret (Weld) White; H. C., 1733, A.B., A.M.; Ord. Mansfield, Feb. 23, 1737; sett. Mansfield, 1737-1761; d. Mansfield, Jan. 18, 1761.

EBENEZER RUSSELL WHITE, A.M., b. Danbury, Ct., Dec. 22, 1743, son of Rev. Ebenezer and Mary (Moss) White; Y. C., 1760, A.B., A.M.; Tutor, Y. C., 1762-1765; Ord. Danbury, Ct., (Separatist Chh.), 1767; sett. Danbury, Ct., 1768-1774; became a Sandemanian; postmaster; d. Danbury, Ct., May 4, 1825, a. 82.

JOHN WHITE, A.M., b. Brookline, July 18, 1669, son of Lieut. John and Elizabeth (Bowles) White; H. C., 1685, A.B., A.M.; Chaplain to Gov. Sir William Phips; Rep. Gen. Ct., 20 years; Fellow, H. C., 1697; Treasurer, H. C., 1713-1721; d. Dec. 11, 1721, unm.

JOHN WHITE, A.M., b. Brookline, 1677, son of Joseph and Hannah (Scarborough) White; H. C., 1698, A.B., A.M.; Chaplain at Saco, 1702; Ord. Gloucester, (1st Chh.), Apr. 21, 1703; sett. Gloucester, 1702-1760; d. Gloucester, Jan. 16, 1760, a. 83.

JOSEPH MOSS WHITE, A.M., b. Danbury, Ct., Sept. 13, 1741, son of Rev. Ebenezer and Mary (Moss) White; Y. C., 1760, A.B., A.M.; sett. Danbury, Ct., as a Sandemanian preacher, 1764-1769; land surveyor, 1769; member Constitutional Convention, 1788; d. Danbury, Ct., July 10, 1822, a. 81.

STEPHEN WHITE, A.M., b. Middletown, Ct., (Cromwell), June 8, 1718, son of Capt. John and Susannah (Alling) White; Y. C., 1736, A.B., A.M.; Ord. Windham, Ct., Dec. 24, 1740; sett. Windham, Ct., 1740-1794; Ct. Election Sermon, 1763; d. Windham, Ct., Jan. 9, 1794, a. 76.

THOMAS WHITE, A.M., b. Hatfield, July 10, 1701, son of Capt. Daniel and Sarah (Bissell) White; Y. C., 1720, A.B., A.M.; Ord. Bolton, Ct., (1st Chh.), Oct. 26, 1726, as the first minister; sett. Bolton, Ct., 1726-1763; d. Bolton, Ct., Feb. 22, 1763, a. 62.

TIMOTHY WHITE, A.M., b. Haverhill, Nov. 13, 1700, son of John, Jr. and Lydia (Gilman) White; H. C., 1720, A.B., A.M.; sett. Nantucket, May 9, 1725-May 1750, as the first minister, but may not have been ordained; d. Haverhill, Feb. 24, 1765, a. 65.

GEORGE WHITEFIELD, A.B., b. Gloucester, England, Dec. 16, 1714, son of Thomas Whitefield, of St. Marie de Crypt, Gloucestershire; Pembroke, Coll., Oxford, 1736, A.B.; Ord. as an Anglican priest, 1736; Chaplain to the Countess of Huntington, 1748; preached 34 years; crossed the Atlantic 13 times and preached more than 18,000 sermons; came to Massachusetts in 1734, his first sermon being before 3,000 people in the Brattle St. Chh., Boston; said to have preached to 25,000 people on Boston Common, but his figures were often inaccurate; Epis.; d. Sept. 30, 1770, and was buried at his request under the pulpit of the First Presb. Chh. in Newburyport.

HENRY WHITEFIELD, B.D., b. England, 1597, son of Thomas and Mildred (Manning) Whitefield, of East Sheen and Mortlake, Surrey; matric. New College, Oxford, 1610; A.B., A.M., B.D.; Vicar of Ockham, Surrey, England, 1616-1636; landed at New Haven, Ct., July 1639; sett. Guilford, Ct., 1639-1650; returned to England, 1650; sett. Winchester, England, 1650-1657; d. Winchester, England, ca. 1660.

JOHN WHITING, A.M., b. England, 1635, son of Hon. William and Susanna Whiting, of Hartford, Ct.; H. C., 1653, A.B., A.M.; sett. Salem, (1st Chh., as asst. minister), 1657-1659; Ord. Hartford, Ct., (1st Chh.), 1660; sett. Hartford, Ct., 1660-1669; inst. Hartford, Ct., (2nd Chh.), Feb. 12, 1669/70; sett. Hartford, Ct., (2nd. Chh.), 1670-1689; Ct. Election Sermon, 1686; d. Hartford, Ct., Sept. 8, 1689.

JOHN WHITING, A.M., b. Billerica, July 1, 1664, son of Rev. Samuel and Dorcas (Chester) Whiting; H. C., 1685, A.B., A.M.; Ord. Lancaster, Dec. 3, 1690; sett. Lancaster, 1688-1697; slain by the Indians at Lancaster, Sept. 11, 1697, a. 33.

JOHN WHITING, A.M., b. Lynn, June 20, 1681/2, son of Rev. Joseph and Sarah (Danforth) Whiting; H. C., 1700, A.B., A.M.; Librarian, H. C., 1703-1706; Tutor, H. C., 1706-1712; Fellow, H. C., 1711-1712; Ord. Concord, May 14, 1712; sett. Concord, 1711-1737; Chaplain at Port Royal, 1710; d. Concord, May 4, 1752, a. 71.

JOSEPH WHITING, A.M., b. Lynn, Apr. 6, 1641, son of Rev. Samuel and Elizabeth (St. John) Whiting; H. C., 1661, A.B., A.M.; Fellow, 1664-1666; Ord. Lynn, Oct. 6, 1680; sett. Lynn, 1680-1682; sett. Southampton, L. I., N. Y., 1682-1723; d. Southampton, L. I., N. Y., Apr. 7, 1723, a. 82.

SAMUEL WHITING, A.M., b. Boston, Lincolnshire, England, Nov. 20, 1597, son of John Whiting, Esq., Mayor (1600-1608) of Boston, England; Emmanuel Coll., Camb., A.B., 1616/7; A.M., 1620; Ord. priest by the Bishop of Peterborough, May 4, 1621; Chaplain to Sir Roger Townshend, Bart. and to Sir Nathaniel Bacon, Knt.; Curate at Lynn, Norfolk, 1621-1624; Rector of Skirbeck, Lincolnshire, 1625-1636; silenced for non-conformity; came to N. E., Apr. 1636; Ord. Lynn, Nov. 8, 1636; sett. Lynn, 1636-1679; Artillery Election Sermon, 1660; d. Lynn, Dec. 11, 1679, a. 82.

SAMUEL WHITING, JR., A.M., b. Skirbeck, Lincolnshire, England, Mar. 25, 1633, son of the Rev. Samuel and Elizabeth (St.

John) Whiting; H. C., 1653, A.B., A.M.; Ord. Billerica, Nov. 11, 1663, as the first minister; sett. Billerica, 1658-1713; Artillery Election Sermon, 1682; d. Billerica, Feb. 28, 1712/3, a. 79.

SAMUEL WHITING, b. Hartford, Ct., Apr. 22, 1670, son of the Rev. John and Sybil (Collins) Whiting; studied under Rev. James Fitch of Norwich, Ct.; Ord. Windham, Ct., Dec. 4, 1700, as the first minister; sett. Windham, Ct., 1693-1725; d. Enfield, Ct., Sept. 27, 1725, a. 55.

SAMUEL WHITING, A.M., b. Wrentham, Jan. 28, 1750, son of Joseph and Mary (Clark) Whiting of Franklin; H. C., 1769, A.B., A.M.; A.M., (Hon.), Y. C., 1772; Ord. Rockingham, Vt., Oct. 27, 1773; sett. Rockingham, Vt., 1773-1809; dism. May 18, 1809; sett. Chester, Vt., 1773-1778; d. Rockingham, Vt., May 16, 1819, a. 69.

ELNATHAN WHITMAN, A.M., b. Fairfield, Ct., Jan. 16, 1708/9, son of Rev. Samuel and Sarah (Stoddard) Whitman; Y. C., 1726, A.B., A.M.; Tutor, Y. C., 1728-1732; 1748-1774; Fellow, Y. C., 1748-1774; Ord. Hartford, Ct., (2nd Chh.), Nov. 29, 1732; sett. Hartford, Ct., 1732-1777; Ct. Election Sermon, 1745; d. Hartford, Ct., Mar. 4, 1777, a. 68.

SAMUEL WHITMAN, A.M., b. Hull, 1676, son of Rev. Zechariah and Sarah (Alcock) Whitman; H. C., 1696, A.B., A.M.; Trustee and Fellow, Y. C., 1724-1746; Secretary of the Board of Trustees, Y. C.; preached at Lancaster and Salem; Ord. Farmington, Ct., Dec. 10, 1706; sett. Farmington, Ct., 1705-1751; Ct. Election Sermon, 1714; d. Farmington, Ct., July 31, 1751.

ZECHARIAH WHITMAN, A.B., b. Weymouth, 1644, son of Dea. Ens. John and Ruth Whitman; H. C., 1668, A.B.; Ord. Hull, Oct. 13, 1670; sett. Hull, 1670-1725; d. Hull, Nov. 5, 1726, a. 82.

AARON WHITNEY, A.M., b. Littleton, Mar. 14, 1714, son of Moses, Jr. and Elizabeth Whitney; H. C., 1737, A.B., A.M.; Ord. Petersham Dec. 1738; sett. Petersham, 1738-1774; dism. as a Tory, 1774; d. Petersham, Sept. 8, 1779.

JOSIAH WHITNEY, D.D., b. Plainfield, Ct., Aug. 11, 1731, son of Col. David and Elizabeth (Warren) Whitney; Y. C., 1752, A.B., A.M.; Fellow, Y. C.; S.T.D., H. C., 1802; Ord. Brooklyn, Ct., (2nd Chh. in Pomfret), Feb. 4, 1756; sett Brooklyn, Ct., 1755-1824; Ct. Election Sermon, 1788; d. Brooklyn, Ct., Oct. 20, 1824, a. 93.

PETER WHITNEY, A.M., b. Petersham, Sept. 6, 1744, son of Rev. Aaron and Alice (Baker) Whitney; H. C., 1762, A.B., A.M.; Ord. Northborough, Nov. 4, 1767; sett. Northborough, 1767-1816; member Mass. Hist. Soc.; author of a History of Worcester County, 1793; d. Northborough, Feb. 19, 1816, a. 72.

PHINEAS WHITNEY, A.M., b. Weston, Apr. 23, 1740, son of William and Hannah (Harrington) Whitney; H. C., 1759, A.B., A.M.; Ord. Shirley, Feb. 25, 1762; sett. Shirley, 1762-1819; Arminian; d. Shirley, Dec. 13, 1819.

NATHANIEL WHITTAKER, A.B., b. Long Island, N. Y., Feb. 22, 1732; Princeton, 1752, A.B.; inst. Chelsea, Ct., (Norwich), Feb. 25, 1761; sett. Chelsea, Ct., 1761-1769; inst. Salem, (3rd Chh.), July 28, 1769; sett. Salem, 1769-1784; dism. Feb. 26, 1784; inst. Norridgewock, Me., Sept. 10, 1784; sett. Norridgewock, Me., 1784-1789; Presb.; d. Va., Jan. 21, 1795.

CHAUNCY WHITTELSEY, A.M., b. Wallingford, Ct., Oct. 8, 1717, son of Rev. Samuel and Sarah (Chauncy) Whittelsey; Y. C., 1738, A.B., A.M.; Tutor, Y. C., 1739-1745; Ord. New Haven, Ct., (1st Chh.), Mar. 1, 1758; sett. New Haven, Ct., 1758-1787; J. P., 1753-1757; Ct. Election Sermon, 1778; d. New Haven Ct., July 24, 1787, a. 70.

SAMUEL WHITTELSEY, A.M., b. Saybrook, Ct., 1686, son of John and Ruth (Dudley) Whittelsey; Y. C., 1705, A.B., A.M.; Trustee, Y. C., 1732-1752; Ord. Wallingford, Ct., May 17, 1710; sett. Wallingford, Ct., 1708-1752; Ct. Election Sermon, 1731; d. Wallingford, Ct., Apr. 15, 1752, a. 67.

SAMUEL WHITTELSEY, JR., A.M., b. Wallingford, Ct., July 10, 1713, son of Rev. Samuel and Sarah (Chauncy) Whittelsey; Y. C., 1729, A.B., A.M.; A.M., (Hon.), H. C., 1732; Tutor, Y. C., 1732-1738; Ord. Milford, Ct., (2nd Chh.), Nov 9, 1737; sett. Milford, Ct., 1737-1768; d. Milford, Ct., Oct. 22, 1768, a. 56.

AARON WHITTEMORE, A.M., b. Concord, Dec. 13, 1711, son of Benjamin and Esther (Brooks) Whittemore; H. C., 1734, A.B., A.M.; Ord. Pembroke, N. H., Mar. 1, 1736/7; sett. Pembroke, N. H., 1737-1767; Lieut.; d. Pembroke, N. H., Nov. 16, 1767, a. 55.

WILLIAM WHITWELL, A.M., b. Boston, Dec. 27, 1737, son of William and Rebecca (Keen) Whitwell; Princeton, 1758, A.B., A.M.; A.M., (Hon.), H. C., 1762; Ord. Marblehead, (1st Chh.), Aug. 25, 1762; sett. Marblehead, 1762-1781; d. Marblehead, Nov. 8, 1781, a. 45.

ANTHONY WIBIRD, A.M., b. Portsmouth, N. H., 1728, son of John and Elizabeth (Fitch) Wibird; H. C., 1747, A.B., A.M.; Ord. Quincy, (1st Chh. in Braintree), Feb. 5, 1755; sett. Quincy, 1755-1800; supplied at Amesbury, 1752; Unitarian; d. Quincy, June 4, 1800, a. 72, unm.

WILLIAM WICKENDON, came from Salem to Providence, R. I., 1639; Ord. Providence, R. I., (1st Bapt. Chh.), 1647; sett. Providence, R. I., 1647-1669; Commissioner, 1651-1655; Deputy, 1664-1666; Bapt.; d. Providence, R. I., Feb. 23, 1669/70.

EDWARD WIGGLESWORTH, D.D., b. Malden, 1693, son of Rev. Michael and Sybil (Sparhawk) Wigglesworth; H. C., 1710, A.B., A.M.; S.T.D., U. of Edinburgh, 1730; taught school in Boston, 1714-1721; he and his clerical descendants to the present day, generation after generation, have stood at the top of their classes in scholarship at Harvard College; he preached often but was never settled; Hollis

Professor of Divinity, H. C., 1721-1765; Convention Sermon, 1748; Dudleian Lecture, 1757; Fellow, H. C., 1724-1765; d. Cambridge, Jan. 16, 1765.

EDWARD WIGGLESWORTH, JR., D.D., b. Cambridge, Feb. 7, 1731/2, son of Rev. Dr. Edward and Rebecca (Coolidge) Wigglesworth; H. C., 1749, A.B., A.M.; S.T.D., 1786; A.M., (Hon.), Y. C., 1752; Tutor, H. C., 1764-1765; Hollis Professor of Divinity, H. C., 1765-1794; Fellow, H. C., 1779-1792; Fellow, Am. Acad. Arts & Sciences; Dudleian Lecture, 1787; d. Cambridge, June 17, 1794.

MICHAEL WIGGLESWORTH, A.M., b. Yorkshire, England, Oct. 18, 1631, son of Edward Wigglesworth; H. C., 1651, A.B., A.M.; Fellow, 1652-1654; Ord. Malden, Sept. 7, 1656; sett. Malden, 1654-1705; Election Sermon, 1686; Artillery Election Sermon, 1696; author of the poem, "The Day of Doom;" physician; d. Malden, June 10, 1705, a. 73.

SAMUEL WIGGLESWORTH, A.M., b. Malden, Feb. 4, 1688, son of Rev. Michael and Martha Wigglesworth; H. C., 1707, A.B., A.M.; Ord. Hamilton, Oct. 27, 1714; sett. Hamilton, 1714-1768; Election Sermon, 1733; Convention Sermon, 1751; Dudleian Lecture, 1760; physician; d. Hamilton, Sept. 3, 1768, a. 80.

ELNATHAN WIGHT, b. Medfield, Dec. 23, 1715, son of Joseph and Mercy Wight; Ord. Bellingham, (1st Bapt. Chh.), Jan. 14, 1755; sett. Bellingham, 1755-1761; Bapt.; d. Bellingham, Nov. 6, 1761, a. 46.

JABEZ WIGHT, A.M., b. Dedham, July 12, 1701, son of Joseph and Mary (Stearns) Wight; H. C., 1721, A.B., A.M.; Ord. Preston, Ct., (5th Society in Norwich), Oct. 27, 1726; sett. Preston, Ct., 1726-1782; d. Preston, Ct., Sept. 11, 1782, a. 82.

JOHN WIGHT, A.M., b. Dedham, Apr. 22, 1699, son of Daniel and Annah (Dewing) Wight; H. C., 1721, A.B., A.M.; sett. Bristol, R. I., 1728-1740; Ord. Windham, Me., (New Marblehead Parish), Dec. 14, 1743; sett. Windham, Me., 1743-1753; d. Windham, Me., May 8, 1753, a. 54.

DANIEL WIGHTMAN, b. Narrangansett, R. I., Jan. 2, 1668, son of George, Sr. and Elizabeth (Updike) Wightman; Ord. Newport, R. I., (2nd Bapt. Chh.), 1704; sett. Newport, R. I., 1701-1750; Bapt.; d. Newport, R. I., Aug. 31, 1750, a. 82.

JAMES WIGHTMAN, (prob. b. Narragansett, R. I., Feb. 17, ———, son of John and Jane (Bentley) Wightman); Ord. North Kingston, R. I., 1750; sett. North Kingston, R. I., 1750-1791; Bapt.; d. North Kingston, R. I., 1791.

TIMOTHY WIGHTMAN, b. Groton, Ct., Nov. 19, 1719, son of Rev. Valentine and Hannah (Holmes) Wightman; Ord. Groton, Ct., (Bapt. Chh.), May 20, 1756; sett. Groton, Ct., 1754-1796; Bapt.; d. Groton, Ct., Nov. 14, 1796.

VALENTINE WIGHTMAN, b. North Kingston, R. I.,

Apr. 16, 1681, son of George and Elizabeth (Updike) Wightman; Ord. Groton, Ct., (1st Bapt. Chh. in Ct.), 1710; sett. Groton, Ct., 1705-1747; Bapt.; d. Groton, Ct., June 9, 1747, a. 66.

ISAAC WILCOX, Ord. Westerly, R. I., (3rd Chh. of Christ, or Wilcox Chh.), Feb. 14, 1771, as the first minister.

BENJAMIN WILDMAN, A.M., b. Danbury, Ct., 1737, son of Jonathan Wildman; Y. C., 1758, A.B., A.M.; Ord. Southbury, Ct., Oct. 22, 1766; sett. Southbury, Ct., 1766-1812; d. Southbury, Ct., Aug. 2, 1812, a. 76.

DANIEL WILKINS, A.M., bapt. Middleton, May 18, 1710, son of John and Abigail Wilkins; H. C., 1736, A.B; A.M., 1744; Ord. Amherst, N. H., Sept. 23, 1741; sett. Amherst, N. H., 1741-1783; d. Amherst, N. H., Feb. 11, 1783, a. 73.

JOHN WILLARD, D.D., b. Biddeford, Me., Jan. 28, 1733, son of Rev. Samuel and Abigail (Wright) Willard; H. C., 1751, A.B., A.M.; S.T.D., Y. C., 1803; Ord. Stafford, Ct., (1st Chh.), Mar. 23, 1757; sett. Stafford, Ct., 1757-1807; d. Stafford, Ct., Feb. 16, 1807.

PRESIDENT JOSEPH WILLARD, D.D., LL.D., b. Biddeford, Me., Dec. 29, 1738, son of Rev. Samuel and Abigail (Wright) Willard; H. C., 1765, A.B., A.M.; S.T.D., 1785; LL.D., Y. C., 1791; Tutor, H. C., 1766-1772; Fellow, H. C., 1768-1772; Ord. Beverly, Nov. 25, 1772; sett. Beverly, 1772-1781; President of Harvard College, inst. Dec. 19, 1781; served, 1781-1804; Convention Sermon, 1784; Dudleian Lecture, 1785; Vice-Pres., Am. Acad. Arts & Sciences; Member Am. Phil. Soc.; Member Koen. Gesellsch. wissensch., Goettingen; d. Cambridge, Sept. 25, 1804.

JOSEPH WILLARD, A.M., b. Grafton, Dec. 27, 1741, son of Benjamin and Sarah (Brooks) Willard; H. C., 1765, A.B., A.M.; A.B., (Hon.), Y. C., 1765; Ord. Mendon, Apr. 19, 1769; sett. Mendon, 1769-1782; dism. Dec. 4, 1782; inst. Boxborough, Nov. 2, 1785; sett. Boxborough, 1785-1828; resigned Dec. 1823; soldier in Col. A. Williams' regt., 1759; his four brothers were the famous clock-makers; Universalist; d. Boxborough, Sept. 1828, a. 87.

JOSEPH WILLARD, A.M., b. Saybrook, Ct., July 23, 1696, son of Samuel and Sarah (Clark) Willard; Y. C., 1714, A.B., A.M.; A.M., (Hon.), H. C., 1723; Ord. Sunderland, Jan. 1, 1718/9; sett. Sunderland, 1718-1721; sett. Rutland, July 2, 1721-1723; killed by the Indians at Rutland, Aug. 14, 1723.

HON. JOSIAH WILLARD, A.M., b. Boston, June 21, 1681, son of President Samuel and Eunice (Tyng) Willard; H. C., 1698, A.B., A.M.; Librarian, H. C., 1701-1702; Tutor, H. C., 1703-1706; preacher; visited West Indes and Europe; J. P.; sea captain; Secretary of the Province of Mass., 1717-1756; Judge of Probate, 1728-1745; d. Boston, Dec. 7, 1756.

PRESIDENT SAMUEL WILLARD, A.M., b. Concord, Jan. 31, 1639/40, son of Major Simon and Mary (Sharpe) Willard; H. C.,

1659, A.B., A.M.; Fellow, H. C., 1692-1707; Ord. Groton, July 13, 1664; sett. Groton, 1663-1676; inst. Boston, (Old South Chh.), Mar. 31, 1678; sett. Boston, 1676-1707; Vice-President of Harvard College, but acting President, inst., Sept. 6, 1701; served 1701-1707; author of the famous "Body of Divinity;" Artillery Election Sermons, 1686, 1699; Election Sermons, 1682, 1694; d. Boston, Sept. 12, 1707, a. 67.

SAMUEL WILLARD, A.M., b. Kingston, Jamaica, West Indes, 1705, son of Major John and Frances (Sherburne) Willard; H. C., 1723, A.B., A.M.; Ord. Biddeford, Me., Sept. 30, 1730; sett. Biddeford, Me., 1730-1741; d. Kittery, Me., Oct. 25, 1741.

ABRAHAM WILLIAMS, A.M., b. Marlborough, Feb. 25, 1726/7, son of Abraham and Elizabeth (Breck) Williams; H. C., 1744, A.B., A.M.; Ord. Sandwich, June 14, 1749; sett. Sandwich, 1749-1784; Fellow, Am. Acad. Arts & Sciences; Election Sermon, 1762; d. Sandwich, Aug. 8, 1784, a. 58.

CHESTER WILLIAMS, A.M., b. Pomfret, Ct., May 29, 1718, son of Rev. Ebenezer and Penelope (Chester) Williams; Y. C., 1735, A.B., A.M.; Tutor, Y. C., 1738-1740; Ord. Hadley, Jan. 21, 1740/1; sett. Hadley, 1740-1753; d. Hadley, Oct. 13, 1753, a. 36.

EBENEZER WILLIAMS, A.M., b. Roxbury, Aug. 12, 1690, son of Samuel and Sarah (May) Williams; H. C., 1709, A.B., A.M.; Fellow, Y. C., 1731-1748; Ord. Pomfret, Ct., (1st Chh.), Oct. 26, 1715; sett. Pomfret, Ct., 1713-1753; d. Pomfret, Ct., Mar. 28, 1753, a. 63.

EBENEZER WILLIAMS, A.M., b. Roxbury, June 13, 1738, son of Capt. John and Elizabeth (Williams) Williams; H. C., 1760, A.B., A.M.; Ord. Falmouth, Me., (present 1st Chh. in Falmouth, formerly the 3rd Parish at New Casco), Nov. 6, 1765; sett. Falmouth, Me., 1765-1799; d. Falmouth, Me., Feb. 25, 1799.

ELEAZER WILLIAMS, A.M., b. Deerfield, July 1, 1688, son of Rev. John and Eunice (Mather) Williams; H. C., 1708, A.B., A.M.; Ord. Mansfield, Ct., Oct. 18, 1710, as the first minister; sett. Mansfield, Ct., 1710-1742; Ct. Election Sermon, 1723; d. Mansfield, Ct., Sept. 21, 1742, a. 54.

ELIPHALET WILLIAMS, D.D., b. Lebanon, Ct., Feb. 4, 1726/7, son of Rev. Dr. Solomon and Mary (Porter) Williams; Y. C., 1743, A.B., A.M.; A.M., (Hon.), H. C., 1771; S.T.D., Y. C., 1782; Fellow, Y. C., 1769-1801; Ord. East Hartford, Ct., (3rd Chh. in Hartford), Mar. 30, 1748; sett. East Hartford, Ct., 1748-1803; Ct. Election Sermon, 1769; d. East Hartford, Ct., June 29, 1803, a. 77.

PRESIDENT ELISHA WILLIAMS, A.M., b. Hatfield, Aug. 24, 1694, son of Rev. William and Eliza (Cotton) Williams; H. C., 1711, A.B., A.M.; Ord. Newington, Ct., (2nd Chh. in Wethersfield), Oct. 17, 1722, as the first minister; sett. Newington, Ct., 1722-1726; Rector (or President), Y. C., 1726-1739; Rep. Gen. Assembly; Judge,

Superior Court of Ct.; Colonel; Chaplain, Cape Breton Expedition, 1746; d. Wethersfield, Ct. July 24, 1755, a. 61.

JOHN WILLIAMS, A.M., b. Roxbury, Dec. 10, 1664, son of Dea. Samuel and Theoda (Park) Williams; H. C., 1683, A.B., A.M.; taught school at Dorchester, 1684-1685; Ord. Deerfield Oct. 17, 1688, as the first minister; sett. Deerfield, 1686-1729; Convention Sermon, 1728; he with his oldest son and daughter, Eunice, were carried captive to Canada, 1704; the trip was about 300 miles; they were released, 1706; his wife was massacred at Deerfield at the time of their capture; he published a narrative of his captivity called, "The Redeemed Captive," 1706; d. Deerfield, June 12 1729, a. 65.

NATHAN WILLIAMS, D.D., b. Longmeadow, Oct. 28, 1735, son of Rev. Dr. Stephen and Abigail (Davenport) Williams; Y. C., 1755, A.B., A.M.; Tutor Y. C., 1756-1760; Fellow, Y. C., 1788-1808; D.D., Princeton, 1794; Ord. Tolland, Ct., Apr. 30, 1760; sett. Tolland, Ct., 1759-1829; Ct. Election Sermon, 1780; d. Tolland, Ct., Apr. 15, 1829, a. 94.

NATHANIEL WILLIAMS, A.M., b. Boston, Aug. 25, 1675, son of Dea. Nathaniel and Mary (Oliver) Williams; H. C. 1693, A.B., A.M.; Ord. Cambridge, (Harvard College Chapel), Aug. 16, 1698; sett. Barbadoes, West Indes, 1698-1700; taught school in Boston, 1703-1736; chosen Rector (or President), Y. C., 1723, but declined; preacher and physician; d. Boston, Jan. 10, 1737/8.

NEHEMIAH WILLIAMS, A.M., b. Hadley, Feb. 24, 1749, son of Rev. Chester and Sarah (Porter) Williams; H. C. 1769, A.B., A.M.; A.B., (Hon.), Y. C., 1769; Ord. Brimfield, Feb. 9, 1775; sett. Brimfield, 1775-1796; Fellow, Am. Acad. Arts and Sciences; d. Brimfield, Nov. 26, 1796, a. 47.

ROGER WILLIAMS, A.B., b. ca. 1600, son of James and Alice (Pemberton) Williams; Pembroke Coll., Camb., A.B., 1626/7; Chaplain to Sir William Masham of Otes, High Laver, Essex, 1629-1630; came to N. E., 1630; Ord. Salem, Apr. 12, 1631; sett. Plymouth, 1631-1633; sett. Salem, 1633-1635; dism. Oct. 19, 1635; founded Providence, R. I., 1636; established the Baptist Church in America, 1636; sett. Providence, R. I., (1st Bapt. Chh.), 1636-1643; went to England and there received a charter for the settlement of Providence Plantations, 1654-1657; Deputy Gov. of R. I., 1667; author of "Bloody Tenant of Persecution," 1647, and "Bloody Tenant, Yet More Bloody," 1652; Bapt.; d. Providence, R. I., Apr. 1683.

SAMUEL WILLIAMS, LL.D., b. Waltham, Apr. 23, 1743, son of Rev. Warham and Abigail (Leonard) Williams; H. C. 1761, A.B., A.M.; LL.D., U. of Edinburgh, 1785; LL.D., Y. C., 1786; Ord. Bradford, Nov. 20, 1765; sett. Bradford, 1765-1780; Fellow, Am. Acad. Arts and Sciences; Member Am. Phil. Soc.; Hollis Prof. of Mathematics and Natural Phil., H. C., 1780-1788; supply, Rutland, Vt., 1789-1795, and for 2 years at Burlington; author of a Natural and Civil History of Vermont; d. Rutland, Vt., Jan. 2, 1817, a. 74.

SIMEON WILLIAMS, A.M., b. Easton, June 19, 1743, son of Dea. Simeon and Zipporah (Crane) Williams; Princeton, 1765, A.B., A.M.; A.M., (Hon.), H. C., 1769; Ord. South Weymouth, Oct. 26, 1768; sett. South Weymouth, 1768-1819; d. South Weymouth, May 31, 1819, a. 76.

SIMON WILLIAMS, A.B., b. Trim, Co. Meath, Ireland, Feb. 19, 1729; Princeton, 1763, A.B.; Ord. Windham N. H., (by the Presbytery), Dec. 1766; sett. Windham, N. H., 1766-1793; d. Windham, N. H., Nov. 10, 1793, a. 64.

SOLOMON WILLIAMS, D.D., b. Hatfield, June 4, 1700, son of Rev. William and Christian (Stoddard) Williams; H. C., 1719, A.B., A.M.; S.T.D., Y. C., 1773; Fellow, Y. C., 1749-1769; Ord. Lebanon, Ct., (1st Chh.), Dec. 5, 1722; sett. Lebanon, Ct., 1722-1776; Ct. Election Sermon, 1741; d. Lebanon, Ct., Feb. 29, 1776, a. 76.

SOLOMON WILLIAMS, A.M., b. East Hartford, Ct., July 13, 1752, son of Rev. Dr. Eliphalet and Mary (Williams) Williams; Y. C., 1770, A.B., A.M.; Tutor, Y. C., 1773-1775; sett. Lebanon, Ct., 1776-1778; Ord. Northampton, June 4, 1778; sett. Northampton, 1778-1834; d. Northampton, Nov. 9, 1834, a. 83.

STEPHEN WILLIAMS, D.D., b. Deerfield, May 14, 1693, son of Rev. John and Eunice (Mather) Williams; H. C., 1713, A.B., A.M.; S.T.D., Dart. Coll., 1773; Ord. Longmeadow, Oct. 17, 1716; sett. Longmeadow, 1714-1782; Convention Sermon, 1754; was carried captive with his father to Canada, 1704; in 1734, he established an Indian mission at Stockbridge; served as Chaplain at Louisburg, 1745; in the Northern army, 1756; d. Longmeadow, June 10, 1782, a. 90.

STEPHEN WILLIAMS, A.M., b. Longmeadow, Jan. 26, 1721/2, son of Rev. Dr. Stephen and Abigail (Davenport) Williams; Y. C., 1741, A.B., A.M.; Ord. Woodstock, Ct., (West Chh.), June 24, 1747; sett. West Woodstock, Ct., 1747-1795; d. Woodstock, Ct., May 6, 1795, a. 74.

WARHAM WILLIAMS, A.M., b. Deerfield, Sept. 7, 1699, son of Rev. John and Eunice (Mather) Williams; H. C., 1719, A.B., A.M.; Ord. Waltham, June 11, 1723; sett. Waltham, 1723-1751; carried captive to Canada with his father, 1704; d. Waltham, June 22, 1751, a. 52.

WARHAM WILLIAMS, A.M., b. Longmeadow, Jan. 7, 1725/6, son of Rev. Dr. Stephen and Abigail (Davenport) Williams; Y. C., 1745, A.B., A.M.; Tutor, Y. C., 1746-1750; Fellow and Secretary, Y. C.; Ord. Northford, Ct., June 13, 1750, as the first minister; sett. Northford, Ct., 1749-1788; d. Northford, Ct., Apr. 4, 1788, a. 63.

WILLIAM WILLIAMS, A.M., b. Newton, Feb. 2, 1665, son of Capt. Isaac and Martha (Parke) Williams; H. C.. 1683, A.B., A.M.; Ord. Hatfield, 1685 or 1686; sett. Hatfield, 1685-1741; Election Sermon, 1719; Convention Sermon, 1726; d. Hatfield, Aug. 29, 1741, a. 76.

WILLIAM WILLIAMS, JR., A.M., b. Hatfield, May 11, 1688, son of Rev. William and Eliza (Cotton) Williams; H. C., 1705, A.B., A.M.; Ord. Weston, Nov. 1, 1709; sett. Weston, 1709-1750; dism. Oct. 24, 1750; Artillery Election Sermon, 1737; Election Sermon, 1741; d. Weston, Mar. 6, 1760, a. 72.

WILLIAM WILLIAMS, A.M., b. Hilltown, Pa., 1752, son of John and Ann (White) Williams; Brown U., 1769, A.B., A.M.; Fellow, Brown U., 1789-1818; teacher, Warren, R. I., 1769-1773; founder, Wrentham Academy, 1773; principal; Ord. West Wrentham, (1st Bapt. Chh.), July 3, 1776; sett. West Wrentham, 1773-1823; Bapt.; d. West Wrentham, Sept. 22, 1823, a. 71.

ELIAKIM WILLIS, A.M., b. Dartmouth, Jan. 9, 1713/4, son of Samuel and Mehitable (Gifford) Willis; H. C., 1735, A.B., A.M.; Ord. Malden, (South Chh.), Oct. 25, 1752; sett. Malden, (South Chh.), 1751-1792; sett. Malden, (1st and 2nd Chhs., united), 1792-1801; d. Malden, Mar. 14, 1801, a. 87.

HENRY WILLIS, A.M., b. Windsor, Ct., Oct. 14, 1690, son of Lieut. Joshua and Hannah (Buckland) Willis; Y. C., 1715, A.B., A.M.; Ord. Franklin, Ct., (2nd Chh. in Norwich), Oct. 8, 1718, as the first minister; sett. Franklin, Ct., 1717-1750; resigned, Jan. 23, 1749/50; d. Norwich, Ct., Sept. 3, 1758, a. 68.

NOAH WILLISTON, A.M., b. Springfield, July 3, 1734, son of Joseph and Hannah (Stebbins) Williston; Y. C., 1757, A.B., A.M.; Ord. West Haven, Ct., June 11, 1760; sett. West Haven, Ct., 1760-1811; d. West Haven, Ct., Nov. 10, 1811, a. 78.

BLISS WILLOUGHBY, Ord. Newent, Ct., (Separatist Chh., Norwich), 1753; sett. Newent, Ct., 1753-1764; went to England as agent for the Separatist Chhs. in 1756; became a Bapt., 1764, and from 1768 on was a leader of the Baptists at Shaftsbury, Vt.; Bapt..

EBENEZER WILLOUGHBY, son of Bliss Willoughby; preached with his father at Shaftsbury, Vt.; Bapt.

JONATHAN WILLOUGHBY, b. prob. Portsmouth, Hants., England, son of Deputy-Gov. Francis and Mary Willoughby of Ct.; H. C., 1651-1654, but did not graduate; sett. Wethersfield, Ct., Sept. 26, 1664-1666; sett. Haddam, Ct., 1666.

JOHN WILSON, A.M., b. Windsor, England, Dec. 1588, son of Rev. Dr. William and Isabel (Woodhall) Wilson; King's Coll., Camb., A.B., 1609/10; A.M., 1613; Fellow, King's College, Camb., 1608-1610; sett. Sudbury, Suffolk, England, 1620-1630; came to N. E., 1630; Ord. Boston, (1st Chh.), Nov. 22, 1632, as the first minister; sett. Boston, 1630-1667; Chaplain, Pequot War, 1637; Artillery Election Sermon, 1638; d. Boston, Aug. 7, 1667, a. 78.

JOHN WILSON, JR., A.M., b. London, England, Sept. 1621, son of Rev. John and Elizabeth (Mansfield) Wilson, of Boston, N. E.; H. C., 1642, A.B., A.M.; Ord. Dorchester, 1649, as "coadjutor" to Rev. Richard Mather; sett. Dorchester, 1649-1651; Ord. Medfield,

Oct. 12, 1652, as the first minister; sett. Medfield, 1651-1691; Artillery Election Sermon, 1668; physician and school master at Medfield for nearly forty years; d. Medfield, Aug. 23, 1691, a. 70.

JOHN WILSON, 3rd., b. Medfield, June 18, 1660, son of Rev. John and Sarah (Hooker) Wilson; H. C., but did not remain long; educated by his father; preached at New Haven, Ct., for more than a year, 1682; preached at Medfield as an asst. to his father, 1682-1691; removed to Braintree, 1692; physician; Rep. Gen. Ct., 1698; Captain, Braintree military company, 1696; J. P., 1700; d. Braintree, 1728.

JOHN WILSON, A.M., b. Medfield, May 31, 1686, son of Dr. John and Sarah (Newton) Wilson; H. C., 1705, A.B., A.M.; sett. Barrington, R. I., 1710-1713; d. Barrington, R. I., 1713, a. 27.

JOHN WILSON, A.B., b. Ulster, Ireland, 1703; graduated at the U. of Edinburgh; came to N. E., 1729; inst. Auburn, (Chester), N. H., (Presb. Chh.), 1734; sett. Auburn, N. H., 1734-1779; d. Chester, N. H., Feb. 1, 1779, a. 76.

ELHANAN WINCHESTER, b. Brockline, Sept. 30, 1751, son of Dea. Elhanan and Sarah (Belcher) Winchester; Ord. Rehoboth, (Bapt. Chh.), Sept. 4, 1771; sett. Rehoboth, 1771-1773; inst. Hull, Aug. 16, 1773; sett. Hull, 1773; sett. Grafton, (Bapt. Chh.), 1773-1777; sett. South Carolina, 1777-1780; in 1781, he became a Universalist; sett. Philadelphia, Pa., (1st Universalist Chh.), 1781-1787; went to England; sett. London, England, (Univ. Chh.), 1787-1794; returned to Boston, July 1794; Bapt. and Universalist; d. Hartford, Ct., Apr. 18, 1797, a. 46.

JONATHAN WINCHESTER, A.M., b. Brookline, Apr. 21, 1717, son of Henry and Frances (White) Winchester; H. C., 1737, A.B., A.M.; Ord. Ashburnham, Apr. 23, 1760; sett. Ashburnham, 1760-1767; d. Ashburnham, Nov. 27, 1767, a. 50.

PAINE WINGATE, A.M., b. Hampton, N. H., Sept. 19, 1703, son of Col. Joshua and Mary (Lunt) (Paine) Wingate; H. C., 1723, A.B., A.M.; Ord. Amesbury, (2nd or West Chh.), June 3, 1726; sett. Amesbury, 1726-1786; d. Amesbury, Feb. 19, 1786, a. 83.

PAINE WINGATE, JR., A.M., b. Amesbury, May 14, 1739, son of Rev. Paine and Mary (Balch) Wingate; H. C., 1759, A.B., A.M.; Ord. Hampton Falls, N. H., Dec. 14, 1763; sett. Hampton Falls, N. H., 1763-1776; dism. Mar. 16, 1776; removed to Stratham, N. H.; delegate to the Continental Congress; member state legislature; Rep. and Senator in Congress; Judge of the Superior Court, 1796-1809; d. Stratham, N. H., Mar. 7, 1838, a. 98.

JOSEPH WINSHIP, A.M., bapt. Arlington, May 28, 1738, son of Dea. John and Elizabeth (Wyeth) Winship; H. C., 1762, A.B., A.M.; Ord. Woolwich, Me., June 12, 1765; sett. Woolwich, Me., 1764-1817; d. Woolwich, Me., Sept. 29, 1824.

EDWARD WINSLOW, A.M., b. Boston, Nov. 8, 1722, son of Joshua and Elizabeth (Savage) Winslow; H. C., 1741, A.B., A.M.;

sett. Stratford, Ct., 1754-1763; sett. Quincy, (Christ Chh.), Dec. 1763-1777; left Jan. 1, 1777; Epis.; d. New York City, 1780.

JOHN WINSOR, b. Smithfield, R. I., Mar. 2, 1723, son of Joshua and Deborah (Harding) Winsor; Ord. Smithfield, R. I., Oct. 27, 1756; sett. Smithfield, R. I., (Bapt. Chh. united with Gloucester, R. I. Bapt. Chh.), 1756-1811; Bapt.; d. Smithfield, R. I., 1811, a. 88.

JOSEPH WINSOR, b. Providence, R. I., Oct. 4, 1713, son of Rev. Samuel and Mercy (Harding) Winsor; Ord. Gloucester, R. I., Oct. 31, 1763; sett. Gloucester, R. I., 1763-1802; Bapt.; d. Gloucester, R.I., summer 1802, a. 89.

JOSHUA WINSOR, b. Providence, R. I., May 25, 1682, son of Samuel and Mercy (Williams) (Waterman) Winsor; Ord. Smithfield, R. I., (1st Bapt. Chh.), 1718; sett. Smithfield, R. I., 1718-1750; Bapt.; d. Smithfield, R. I., Oct. 10, 1752.

SAMUEL WINSOR, b. Providence, R. I., Nov. 18, 1677, son of Samuel and Mercy (Williams) (Waterman) Winsor; Ord. Providence, R. I., (1st Bapt. Chh.), 1733; sett. Providence, R. I., 1733-1758; Bapt.; d. Providence, R. I., Nov. 17, 1758.

SAMUEL WINSOR, b. Providence, R. I., Nov. 1, 1722, son of Rev. Samuel and Mary (Harding) Winsor; Ord. Providence, R. I., (1st Bapt. Chh.), June 21, 1759; sett. Providence, R. I., 1759-1771; withdrew May 30, 1771 to Johnston; sett. Johnston, R. I., 1771-1802; Bapt.; d. Johnston, R. I., Jan. 1802.

FRANCIS WINTER, A.M., b. Boston, Dec. 4, 1740, son of William and Abigail (Gatcomb) Winter; H. C., 1765, A.B., A.M.; Ord. Bath, Me., (2nd Chh. of Christ in Georgetown), June 1, 1768; sett. Bath, Me., 1767-1787; dism. Jan. 1787; magistrate; Rep. Gen. Ct.; liberal; d. Bath, Me., Dec. 20, 1826, a. 86.

JEREMIAH WISE, A.M., bapt. Roxbury, Nov. 2, 1679, son of Rev. John and Abigail (Gardner) Wise; H. C., 1700, A.B., A.M.; Ord. South Berwick, Me., (1st Parish in Berwick), Nov. 26, 1707; sett. South Berwick, Me., 1703-1755; Election Sermon, 1729; d. Berwick, Me., Jan. 21, 1756, a. 76.

JOHN WISE, A.M., b. Roxbury, Aug. 15, 1652, son of Joseph and Mary (Thompson) Wise; H. C., 1673, A.B., A.M.; sett. Hatfield, 1677-1678; Ord. Essex, Aug. 12, 1683, as the first minister; sett. Essex, 1680-1725; opponent of taxation without representation; strong defender of the freedom of the church; Chaplain, King Philip's War; Chaplain, Canadian Expedition, 1690; Rep. Gen. Ct., 1689; d. Essex, Apr. 8, 1725, a. 72.

ICHABOD WISWALL, b. Dorchester, 1637, son of Elder Thomas and Elizabeth Wiswall: H. C., 1651, but did not graduate; Ord. Duxbury, 1676; sett. Duxbury, 1676-1700; a proficient astronomer; an enemy of Gov. Andros; d. Duxbury, July 23, 1700, a. 63.

JOHN WISWALL, A.M., b. Boston, Apr. 15, 1731, son of Peleg and Elizabeth (Rogers) Wiswall; H. C., 1749, A.B., A.M.;

Ord. Falmouth, Me., (3rd Parish at New Casco, now the 1st Chh.), Nov. 3, 1756; sett. Falmouth, Me., 1756-1763; became an Epis.; Ord. by Bishop of London, 1764; sett. Portland, Me., (Epis. Chh.), 1763-1775; Tory; went to England; sett. Cornwallis, N. S., 1781-1812; Epis.; d. 1812.

SAMUEL WISWALL, A.M., b. Dorchester, Sept. 2, 1679, son of Enoch and Elizabeth (Oliver) Wiswall; H. C., 1701, A.B., A.M.; Ord. Edgartown, 1713; sett. Edgartown, 1713-1746; d. Edgartown, Dec. 23, 1746, a. 68.

MATHER WITHINGTON, A.B., b. Dorchester, Nov. 13, 1714, son of Ebenezer and Katharine (Mather) Withington; H. C., 1732, A.B.; taught school at Cape Ann; preacher; astronomer; mathematician; d. Dorchester, Apr. 28, 1736, unm.

ABRAHAM WOOD, A.M., b. Sudbury, Sept. 15, 1748, son of Cornelius and Mary (Eaton) Wood; H. C., 1767, A.B., A.M.; Ord. Chesterfield, N. H., Dec. 31, 1772; sett. Chesterfield, N. H., 1772-1823; d. Chesterfield, N. H., Oct. 18, 1823, a. 75.

JABEZ WOOD, b. Middleborough; Ord. Swansea, Sept. 5, 1751; sett. Swansea, 1751-1779; dism. 1779; Bapt.; d. Vermont, 1794.

ASHBEL WOODBRIDGE, A.M., bapt. Hartford, Ct., June 10, 1704, son of Rev. Timothy and Mehitable (Willis) Woodbridge; Y. C., 1724, A.B., A.M.; Fellow, Y. C., 1755-1758; Ord. Glastonbury, Ct., Oct. 23, 1728; sett. Glastonbury, Ct., 1728-1758; Chaplain, 1746; Ct. Election Sermon, 1752; d. Glastonbury, Ct., Aug. 6, 1758, a. 54.

BENJAMIN WOODBRIDGE, D.D., b. Stanton, Wiltshire, England, 1622, son of Rev. John and Dorothy (Parker) Woodbridge; came to N. E., 1634, with his brother Rev. John Woodbridge; H. C., 1642, A.B., A.M.; A.M., Magdalen Coll., Oxford, 1648; S.T.D., Oxford U.; sett. Salisbury, England, 1648-1652; sett. Newbury, England, 1652-1665; silenced 1662; returned to N. E.; sett. Amesbury, 1666-1669; returned to England; d. Ingelfield, Berkshire, England, Nov. 1, 1684, a. 62.

BENJAMIN WOODBRIDGE, son of Rev. John and Mercy (Dudley) Woodbridge; H. C., but did not graduate; Ord. Windsor, Ct., Mar. 18, 1669/70; sett. Windsor, Ct., 1670-1681; sett. Bristol, R. I., 1681-1686, as the first minister; sett. Kittery, Me., 1688; sett. Portsmouth, N. H., 1691; sett. Newcastle, N. H., 1694; sett. Medford, 1698-1710; d. Medford, Jan. 15, 1709/10.

BENJAMIN WOODBRIDGE, A.M., b. West Springfield, June 15, 1712, son of Rev. John and Jemima (Eliot) Woodbridge; Y. C., 1740, A.B., A.M.; Ord. Woodbridge, Ct., (formerly Amity), Nov. 3, 1742, as the first minister; sett. Woodbridge, Ct., 1742-1785; d. Amity, Ct., Dec. 24, 1785, a. 73.

DUDLEY WOODBRIDGE, A.B., b. Killingworth, Ct., ca. 1675, son of Rev. John and Abigail (Leete) Woodbridge; H. C., 1694,

A.B.; Ord. Simsbury, Ct., Nov. 10, 1697; sett. Simsbury, 1695-1710; d. Simsbury, Ct., Aug. 3, 1710.

DUDLEY WOODBRIDGE, A.M., b. Groton, Ct., Apr. 21, 1705, son of Rev. Ephraim and Hannah (Morgan) Woodbridge; H. C., 1724, A.B., A.M.; preached at Groton, Ct., 1725-1727, but prob. not ordained; physician at Stonington, Ct.; d. Stonington, Ct., Oct. 4, 1790.

EPHRAIM WOODBRIDGE, A.M., b. Wethersfield, Ct., June 1680, son of Rev. John and Abigail (Leete) Woodbridge; H. C., 1701, A.B., A.M.; Ord. Groton, Ct., Nov. 29, 1704, as the first minister; sett. Groton, Ct., 1704-1724; d. Groton, Ct., Dec. 1, 1725.

EPHRAIM WOODBRIDGE, A.M., b. Groton, Ct., June 20, 1746, son of Capt. Paul and Sarah (Goodridge) Woodbridge; Y. C., 1765, A.B; A.M., 1774; Ord. New London, Ct., (1st Chh.), Oct. 11, 1769; sett. New London, Ct., 1769-1776; d. New London, Ct., Sept. 6, 1776, a. 31.

JOHN WOODBRIDGE, b. Stanton, Wiltshire, England, 1613/4, son of Rev. John and Dorothy (Parker) Woodbridge; Oxford U., but did not graduate; came to N. E., 1634; Ord. Rowley, Oct. 24, 1645, for service at Andover; sett. Andover, 1645-1648, as the first minister; returned to England where he preached at Andover, Wiltshire and at Burford St. Martin's, Wiltshire, but was ejected, 1662; came back to N. E.; sett. Newbury, 1663-1670; town clerk at Newbury, 1635-1638; taught school in Boston, 1643-1644; member, Anc. & Hon. Art. Co.; Deputy; Magistrate, 1678-1679; Assistant, 1683-1684; Justice of the Peace; Chaplain in England; his portrait may be seen at the Boston Athenaeum; d. Newbury, Mar. 17, 1694/5, a. 82.

JOHN WOODBRIDGE, A.B., b. Andover, ca. 1644, son of Rev. John and Mercy (Dudley) Woodbridge; H. C., 1664, A.B.; Ord. Killingworth, Ct., (now Clinton), Apr. 17, 1669/70, as the first minister; sett. Killingworth, Ct., 1666-1679; left Jan. 6 1678/9; inst. Wethersfield, Ct., 1679; sett. Wethersfield, Ct., 1679-1691; d. Wethersfield, Ct., 1691, a. 47.

JOHN WOODBRIDGE, 3rd., A.B., b. Killingworth, Ct., June 10, 1678, son of Rev. John, Jr. and Abigail (Leete) Woodbridge; H. C., 1694, A.B.; Ord. West Springfield, June 16, 1698; sett. West Springfield, 1698-1718; d. West Springfield, June 10, 1718, a. 40.

JOHN WOODBRIDGE, 4th., A.M., b. West Springfield, Dec. 25, 1702, son of Rev. John, 3rd. and Jemima (Eliot) Woodbridge; Y. C., 1726, A.B., A.M.; Ord. Windsor, Ct., (Poquonock), 1728; sett. Windsor, Ct., 1728-1737; inst. South Hadley, Apr. 21, 1742; sett. South Hadley, 1742-1783; d. South Hadley, Sept. 10, 1783, a. 81.

SAMUEL WOODBRIDGE, A.M., b. Bristol, R. I., 1683, son of Rev. Benjamin and Mary (Ward) Woodbridge; H. C., 1701, A.B., A.M.; Ord. East Hartford, Ct., (3rd Chh. in Hartford), Mar. 30, 1705, as the first minister; sett. East Hartford, Ct., 1705-1746; Ct. Election Sermon, 1724; d. East Hartford, Ct., June 9, 1746, a. 63.

SAMUEL WOODBRIDGE, A.M., b. Glastonbury, Ct., Jan. 23, 1739/40, son of Rev. Ashbel and Jerusha (Pitkin) Woodbridge; Y. C., 1763, A.B., A.M.; Ord. Eastbury, Ct., (Buckingham), June 25, 1766; sett. Buckingham, Ct., 1766-1768; dism. June 28, 1768; farmer; Chaplain, Rev. War; d. West Hartland, Ct., July 23, 1797, a. 57.

TIMOTHY WOODBRIDGE, A.M., b. Burford St. Martin's, Wiltshire, England, 1656, son of Rev. John and Mercy (Dudley) Woodbridge; H. C., 1675, A.B., A.M.; Founder, Trustee and Fellow, Y. C., 1700-1732; Ord. Hartford, Ct., (1st Chh.), Nov. 18, 1685; sett. Hartford, Ct., 1683-1732; sett. Kittery, Me., 1680-1682; Ct. Election Sermons, 1698, 1727; d. Hartford, Ct., Apr. 30, 1732.

TIMOTHY WOODBRIDGE, JR., A.M., bapt. Hartford, Ct., Oct. 3, 1686, son of Rev. Timothy and Mehitable (Wyllys) Woodbridge; Y. C., 1706, A.B., A.M.; Ord. Simsbury, Ct., Nov. 13, 1712; sett. Simsbury, Ct., 1710-1742; Ct. Election Sermons, 1734, 1739; d. Simsbury, Ct., Aug. 28, 1742, a. 56.

TIMOTHY WOODBRIDGE, 3rd., A.M., b. Simsbury, Ct., 1713, son of Rev. Timothy, Jr. and Dorothy (Lamb) Woodbridge; Y. C., 1732, A.B., A.M.; Tutor, Y. C.; Ord. Hatfield, 1740; sett. Hatfield, 1740-1770; d. Hatfield, June 3, 1770, a. 58.

JOSEPH WOODMAN, A.B., b. Newbury, Aug. 22, 1748, son of John and Anna (Adams) Woodman; Princeton, 1766, A.B.; Ord. Sanbornton, N. H., Nov. 13, 1771, as the first minister; sett. Sanbornton, N. H., 1771-1806; dism. Nov. 13, 1806; N. H. Election Sermon, 1802; d. Sanbornton, N. H., Sept. 28, 1807, a. 59.

WILLIAM WOODROP, (possibly the William Woodrop, son of John Woodrop, of Yarmouth, Norfolk, England, Gent.; matriculated pensioner at Corpus Christi Coll., Camb., Easter, 1660; admitted Gray's Inn, Jan. 28, 1660/1); a non-conformist clergyman driven from his church in England, 1662; preached at Lancaster, and Cotton Mather, in his Magnalia Christi, recorded him as being minister there; returned to England, July 12, 1687.

JOHN WOODWARD, A.M., b. Dedham, Dec. 7, 1671, son of Peter and Mehitable Woodward; H. C., 1693, A.B., A.M.; Ord. Norwich, Ct., Dec. 6, 1699; sett. Norwich, Ct., 1699-1716; dism. Sept. 13, 1716; Ct. Election Sermon, 1712; d. New Haven, Ct., Feb. 14, 1746/7.

SAMUEL WOODWARD, A.M., b. Newton, Feb. 1, 1726/7, son of Dea. Ebenezer and Mindwell (Stone) Woodward; H. C., 1748, A.B., A.M.; Ord. Weston, Sept. 25, 1751; sett. Weston, 1751-1782; Artillery Election Sermon, 1782; d. Weston, Oct. 5, 1782, a. 56.

FRANCIS WOOSTER, JR., b. Bradford, June 7, 1698, son of Francis and Mary (Cheney) Worcester; Ord. Sandwich, (Separatist Chh. at Scusset), June 18, 1735; sett. Sandwich, 1735-1749; d. Hollis, N. H., Oct. 14, 1783, a. 85.

WILLIAM WORCESTER, (bapt. Watford, Northants., England, Oct. 5, 1595, son of Rev. William Worcester Vicar of Watford); matriculated sizar, St. John's Coll., Camb., Easter, 1620; Ord. deacon by the Bishop of Peterborough, Dec. 22, 1622; inst. Olney, Bucks., England, July 26, 1624; Vicar of Olney, Bucks., England, 1624-1636; came to N. E., 1639; freeman, 1640; sett. Salisbury, 1639-1662, as the first minister; d. Salisbury, Oct. 28, 1662.

PETER WORDEN, 5th., b. Westerly, R. I., June 5, 1728, son of Peter, 4th. and Rebecca (Richmond) Worden; Ord. Warwick, R. I., May 21, 1751; sett. Warwick, R. I., and Coventry, R. I., 1751-1770; sett. Cheshire, Mar. 1770-1808; Bapt.; d. Cheshire, Feb. 21, 1808, a. 80.

WILLIAM WORTHINGTON, A.M., b. Hartford, Ct., Dec. 5, 1695, son of William and Mehitable (Graves) Worthington; Y. C., 1716, A.B., A.M.; preached at North Stonington, Ct., 1720-1724; Ord. Westbrook, Ct., (Saybrook), June 29, 1726; sett. Westbrook, Ct., 1724-1756; Ct. Election Sermon, 1744; d. Saybrook, Ct., Nov. 16, 1756, a. 61.

EBENEZER WRIGHT, A.M., b. Wethersfield, Ct., Oct. 2, 1706, son of Thomas and Prudence (Deming) Wright; Y. C., 1724, A.B., A.M.; Ord. Stamford, Ct., (1st Chh.), May 7, 1732; sett. Stamford, Ct., 1732-1746; d. Stamford, Ct., May 5, 1746, a. 40.

ELIPHALET WRIGHT, b. Windham, Ct., Feb. 27, 1728/9, son of Ebenezer and Sarah (Huntington) Wright; Ord. Killingly, Ct., (South or Separatist Chh.), May 16, 1765; sett. Killingly, Ct., 1764-1784; d. Killingly, Ct., Aug. 4, 1784, a. 56.

JOB WRIGHT, A.M., bapt. Northampton, Oct. 16, 1737, son of Dea. Stephen and Esther (Cook) Wright; Y. C., 1757, A.B., A.M.; Ord. Bernardston, July 1, 1761; sett. Bernardston, 1761-1782; dism. Mar. 13, 1782; Justice of the Peace, 1789-1797; d. Bernardston, Jan. 24, 1823, a. 85.

JOHN WYETH, A.M., bapt. Cambridge, Mar. 6, 1743, son of John and Elizabeth (Hancock) Wyeth; H. C., 1760, A.B., A.M.; Ord. Gloucester, (Annisquam Parish), Feb. 5, 1766; sett. Gloucester, 1766-1768; dism. May 17, 1768; practiced law; d. Gloucester, Feb. 2, 1811, a. 68.

EBENEZER WYMAN, A.M., b. Woburn, May 5, 1707, son of Jacob and Elizabeth (Richardson) Wyman; H. C., 1731, A.B., A.M.; Ord. Union, Ct., Dec. 13, 1738; sett. Union, Ct., 1738-1746; d. Union, Ct., Jan. 9, 1746, a. 38.

THOMAS YARRELL, sett. Newport, R. I., (United Brethren Chh.), 1758-1763; Moravian.

NATHAN YOUNG, sett. Scituate, R. I., (Chh. at Foster), ca. 1754-1756; Bapt.

JOHN YOUNGLOVE, b. ca. 1637, son of Samuel and Margaret Younglove, of Ipswich; prob. studied at H. C.; visited Bermuda, 1663-1664; preached at Brookfield, 1667-1674; schoolmaster at Hadley, 1674-1678 and 1688-1689; freeman, 1676; sett. Suffield, Ct., 1679-1690; d. Suffield, Ct., June 3, 1690.

ABBREVIATIONS:

a. age
adm. admitted
asst. min. assistant minister
b. born
bapt. baptized
Bapt. Baptist
ca. about
Camb. Cambridge University
Chh. church
coll. college
Columbia King's College or Columbia U.
Cong. Congregationalist
Ct. Connecticut
d. died
Dart. Dartmouth College
dea. deacon
dism. dismissed
ed. educated
Eng. England
Epis. Episcopalian
grad. graduated
H. C. Harvard College
inst. installed
M. merged
matric. matriculated
min. minister
ord. ordained
pres. President
Presb. Presbyterian
Princeton College of New Jersey or Princeton University
ret. returned
sett. settled as minister
S.T.D. Doctor of Divinity
U. University
Unit. Unitarian
X. extinct
Y. C. Yale College
yrs. years

Notes:

The degrees A.B. and B.A., A.M. and M.A., are given as A.B. and A.M. respectively for simplification.

All ministers listed are Congregational unless otherwise designated.

All place names are in Massachusetts unless otherwise evident or designated.

The ages given on grave stones, in obituaries, church and vital records vary greatly, are proverbially inaccurate, and as given in this work should be accepted only as approximate.

THE COLONIAL CHURCHES OF NEW ENGLAND AND THEIR CLERGY

ABINGTON, Mass. Dec. 13, 1712.
First Congregational Church.
1712-1749. Samuel Brown
1750-1770. Ezekiel Dodge
1771-1814. Samuel Niles
ABINGTON, Ct. Jan. 31, 1753.
First Congregational Church.
1753-1778. David Ripley
ACKWORTH, N. H. Mar. 12, 1773.
First Congregational Church.
Supplies to 1789.
ACTON, Mass. Nov. 8, 1738. X.
First Congregational Parish.
Unitarian.
1738-1775. John Swift
ADAMS, Mass. 1766. X.
First Congregational Church.
1766-1778. Samuel Todd
AGAWAM, Mass. Nov. 10, 1762.
First Congregational Church.
1762-1819. Sylvanus Griswold
AGAWAM, Mass. 1771. X.
Second Baptist Church.
1771-1797. Edward Upham
AMESBURY, Mass. 1672. X.
First Congregational Church.
1672-1734. Thomas Wells
1722-1743. Edmund March
1744-1752. Elisha Odlin
1754-1784. Thomas Hibbert
AMESBURY, Mass. Nov. 19, 1718.X.
Rock Hill Congregational Church.
1718-1738. Joseph Parsons
1741-1796. Samuel Worcester, D.D.
AMESBURY, Mass. 1745. X.
King George III's Chapel.
Episcopal.
1745-1753. Matthias Plant
1760-1768. Edward Bass, D.D.
1768-1778. Moses Badger
AMHERST, Mass. Nov. 7, 1729.
First Congregational Church.
1735-1781. David Parsons, Jr.
AMHERST, N. H. Sept. 12, 1741.
First Congregational Church.
1741-1783. Daniel Wilkins
ANDOVER, Mass. Oct. 10, 1711.
South Congregational Church.
1711-1771. Samuel Phillips
1772-1809. Jonathan French
ANDOVER, Ct. Feb. 15, 1748/9.
First Congregational Church.
1748-1791. Samuel Lockwood, D.D.
APPLEDORE, Me. 1650. X.
(See Gosport, N. H.).

APPONAUG, R. I. Dec. 6, 1744.
Baptist Church.
1744-1763. Benjamin Peirce
ARLINGTON, Mass. Oct. 8, 1733.
First Congregational Parish.
Unitarian.
1739-1783. Samuel Cooke
ASHBURNHAM, Mass. Apr. 23, 1760
First Congregational Church.
1760-1767. Jonathan Winchester
1768-1823. John Cushing, D.D.
ASHBY, Mass. June 12, 1776.
First Congregational Parish.
Unitarian.
Supplies to 1778.
ASHFIELD, Mass. July 1761. X.
First Baptist Church.
1761-1798. Ebenezer Smith
ASHFIELD, Mass. Feb. 22, 1763.
Second Church, Congregational.
1763-1774. Jacob Sherwin
1774-1820. Nehemiah Porter
ASHFORD, Ct. Nov. 26, 1718.
First Congregational Church.
1716-1742. James Hale
1742-1751. John Bass
1757-1764. Timothy Allen
1768-1782. James Messenger
ASHFORD, Ct. 1774.
First Baptist Church.
1776-1779. Thomas Ustwick
ATHOL, Mass. Aug. 29, 1750.
First Congregational Church.
Unitarian.
1750-1782. James Humphrey
ATKINSON, N. H. Nov. 25, 1772.
First Congregational Church.
1772-1819. Stephen Peabody
ATTLEBOROUGH, Mass. 1739. X.
Episcopal Chapel.
1739-1754. John Checkley
ATTLEBOROUGH, Mass.
June 6, 1743.
East Congregational Church.
1743-1784. Peter Thacher
ATTLEBOROUGH, Mass. 1747. X.
North Congregational Church.
1747-1752. Nathanael Shepard
ATTLEBOROUGH, Mass.
July 3, 1765. X.
First Baptist Church.
1765-1769. Elihu Daggett
AUBURN, N. H. 1734.
Second or West Parish of Chester.
Presbyterian-Congregational.
1734-1779. John Wilson

AUBURN, Mass. Jan. 25, 1776.
First Congregational Church.
Supplies to 1784.
BARNSTABLE, Mass. Oct. 11, 1639.
Congregational Church of the East Precinct. Unitarian.
1639-1653. John Lothrop
1640-1646. John Mayo
1663-1678. Thomas Walley
1683-1711. Jonathan Russell
1712-1719. Jonathan Russell, Jr.
1725-1770. Joseph Greene.
1771-1783. Timothy Hilliard
BARNSTABLE, Mass. Oct. 11, 1639.
Congregational Church of the West Precinct.
1639-1653. John Lothrop
1640-1646. John Mayo
1663-1678. Thomas Walley
1683-1711. Jonathan Russell
1712-1759. Jonathan Russell, Jr.
1760-1807. Oakes Shaw.
BARNSTABLE, Mass. 1662. X.
Second Congregational Church.
1662-1662. John Smith
BARNSTABLE, Mass. May 10, 1750.
Separatist Church. X.
1750-1760. Nathaniel Ewer
BARRE, Mass. July 29, 1753.
First Congregational Parish.
    Both church and parish became Unitarian.
1752-1766. Thomas Frink
1767-1801. Josiah Dana
BARRINGTON, R. I. 1717.
First Congregational Church.
1710-1713. John Wilson
1718-1726. Samuel Terry
1728-1740. Peleg Heath
1743-1796. Solomon Townsend
BARRINGTON, N. H.
            June 18, 1755. X.
First Congregational Church.
1755-1768. Joseph Prince
1771-1778. David Tenney
BATH, Me. 1762. X.
First Congregational Church.
1767-1787. Francis Winter
BECKET, Mass. Dec. 28, 1758.
First Congregational Society.
1759-1764. Ebenezer Martin
1771-1788. Zadoc Hunn
BECKET, Mass. 1764.
Second Church, Baptist.
ca. 1764. Robert Nesbit
BEDFORD, Mass. July 15, 1730.
First Congregational Parish.
    Unitarian.

1730-1754. Nicholas Bowes
1756-1768. Nathaniel Sherman
1771-1793. Joseph Penniman
BEDFORD, N. H. Aug. 15, 1749.
First Presbyterian Church.
1757-1778. John Houston
BELCHERTOWN, Mass. 1737.
First Congregational Church.
1739-1752. Edward Billings
1756-1814. Justus Forward
BELLINGHAM, Mass.
            Feb. 22, 1727. X.
First Congregational Church.
1727-1737. Jonathan Mills
BELLINGHAM, Mass. Jan. 23, 1737/8
First Baptist Church.
1755-1761. Elnathan Wight
1766-1797. Noah Alden
BENNINGTON, Vt. Dec. 3, 1762.
First Congregational Church.
(First Church in Vermont).
1763-1778. Jedediah Dewey
BERKLEY, Mass. Nov. 2, 1737.
First Congregational Church.
1737-1781. Samuel Tobey
BERLIN, Ct. Feb. 9, 1775.
First Congregational Church.
(Worthington Society)
1775-1780. Jonathan Bird
BERNARDSTON, Mass. 1740.
First Congregational Church.
    Both Church and Parish became Unitarian.
1741-1745. John Norton.
1761-1782. Job Wright
BERWICK, Me. Apr. 3, 1755. X.
First Congregational Church.
1755-1764. John Morse
1765-1797. Matthew Merriam
BERWICK, Me. June 28, 1768.
First Baptist Church.
ca. 1768. Joshua Emery
BETHANY, Ct. Oct. 12, 1763.
First Congregational Church.
1763-1804. Stephen Hawley
BETHEL, Ct. Nov. 25, 1760.
First Congregational Church.
1760-1784. Noah Wetmore
BETHLEM, Ct. Mar. 27, 1739.
First Congregational Church.
1740-1790. Joseph Bellamy, D.D.
BEVERLY, Mass. Sept. 20, 1667.
First Congregational Parish.
    Entire Church and Parish became Unitarian.
1667-1720. John Hale
1701-1729. Thomas Blowers

1729-1773. Joseph Champney
1772-1781. Joseph Willard
BEVERLY, Mass. Dec. 25, 1715.
North or Second Congregational
 Church.
1715-1775. John Chipman
1771-1780. Enos Hitchcock
BIDDEFORD, Me. Sept. 30, 1730. X.
First Congregational Church.
1717-1721. Matthew Short
1723-1726. John Eveleth
1727-1728. Marston Cabot
1729-1729. John Moody
1730-1741. Samuel Willard
1742-1778. Moses Morrill
BILLERICA, Mass. Nov. 11, 1663.
First Congregational Parish.
 Both Church and Parish became
 Unitarian.
1658-1713. Samuel Whiting, Jr.
1707-1749. Samuel Ruggles
1747-1760. John Chandler
1763-1823. Henry Cummings, D.D.
BLACKSTONE, Mass.
 Sept. 14, 1768. X.
Chestnut Hill Congregational Church.
 Unitarian.
1768-1773. Benjamin Balch.
BLANDFORD, Mass. 1735.
First Presbyterian Church.
 Congregational.
1744-1746. William McClenathan
1747-1767. James Morton
1772-1772. Joseph Patrick
BLOOMFIELD, Ct. Feb. 15, 1737/8.
First Congregational Church.
1737-1783. Hezekiah Bissell
BLUE HILL, Me. Oct. 7, 1772.
First Congregational Church.
Supplies to 1796.
BOLTON, Ct. Oct. 27, 1725.
First Congregational Church.
1725-1763. Thomas White
1763-1812. George Colton
BOLTON, Mass. Nov. 4, 1738.
First Congregational Parish.
 Both Church and Parish became
 Unitarian.
1741-1771. Thomas Goss
1773-1783. John Walley
BOLTON, Mass. 1770. M.
Second Congregational Church.
 Merged with the First Church.
1770-1780. Thomas Goss
BOOTHBAY, Me. Apr. 12, 1767. X.
First Presbyterian Church.
 Congregational.
1766-1779. John Murray

BOSCAWEN, N. H. Oct. 8, 1740.
First Congregational Church.
1740-1755. Phineas Stevens
1761-1766. Robie Morrill
1768-1774. Nathaniel Merrill
BOSTON, Mass. July 30, 1630.
First Church in Boston.
 The entire Church and Parish became
 Unitarian.
1630-1667. John Wilson
1633-1652. John Cotton
1656-1663. John Norton
1668-1670. John Davenport
1668-1710. James Allen
1670-1674. John Oxenbridge
1684-1693. Joshua Moody
1693-1697. John Bailey
1695-1725. Benjamin Wadsworth
1705-1715. Thomas Bridge
1717-1769. Thomas Foxcroft
1727-1787. Charles Chauncy, D.D.
BOSTON, Mass. June 5, 1650.
Second Church, Congregational.
 The entire Church and Parish became
 Unitarian.
1655-1673. John Mayo
1664-1723. Increase Mather, D.D.
1684-1728. Cotton Mather, D.D.
1723-1748. Joshua Gee
1732-1741. Samuel Mather, D.D.
1747-1768. Samuel Checkley, Jr.
1768-1816. John Lathrop, D.D.
BOSTON, Mass. May 28, 1665.
First Baptist Church.
1665-1676. Thomas Gould
1675-1679. John Myles
1679-1680. John Russell
1681-1689. Isaac Hull
1684-1702. John Emblen
1708-1728. Ellis Callender
1718-1738. Elisha Callender
1739-1767. Jeremiah Condy
1765-1807. Samuel Stillman, D.D.
BOSTON, Mass. May 12, 1669.
Old South Church, Congregational.
1670-1673. Thomas Thacher
1678-1707. Samuel Willard
1700-1717. Ebenezer Pemberton
1713-1769. Samuel Sewall, D.D.
1718-1758. Thomas Prince
1761-1763. Alexander Cumming
1766-1769. Samuel Blair, D.D.
1771-1775. John Bacon
BOSTON, Mass. 1686. X.
French Huguenot Church.
1685-1686. Laurent Vandenbosch
1687-1688. David de Bonrepos
1696-1696. Daniel Bondet

1696-1715. Pierre Daille
1715-1748. Andrew Le Mercier
BOSTON, Mass. June 15, 1686.
King's Chapel.
Episcopal, Congregational, Unitarian.
This was the first Episcopal Church in New England and became the first Unitarian Church in America.
1686-1689. Robert Ratcliffe
1689-1689. Robert Clark
1689-1728. Samuel Myles
1693-1696. George Hatton
1699-1706. Christopher Bridge
1709-1729. Henry Harris
1729-1746. Roger Price
1731-1736. Thomas Harward
1741-1744. Addington Davenport
1741-1776. Henry Caner, D.D.
1747-1755. Charles Brockwell
1775-1775. James Troutbec
BOSTON, Mass. Dec. 12, 1698. X.
Brattle Street Church, Congregational.
The entire Church and Parish became Unitarian.
1699-1747. Benjamin Colman, D.D.
1716-1743. William Cooper
1746-1783. Samuel Cooper, D.D.
BOSTON, Mass. May 5, 1714. X.
New North Church, Congregational.
The entire Church and Parish became Unitarian.
1714-1750. John Webb
1720-1739. Peter Thacher
1742-1772. Andrew Eliot, D.D.
BOSTON, Mass. Apr. 15, 1717. M.
New South Church, Congregational.
The entire Church and Parish became **Unitarian.**
1719-1769. Samuel Checkley
1766-1772. Penuel Bowen
1773-1775. Joseph Howe
BOSTON, Mass. May 23, 1722. M.
New Brick Church, Congregational.
Merged with the Second Church. Unitarian.
1722-1727. William Waldron
1728-1753. William Welsted
1738-1752. Ellis Gray
1754-1777. Ebenezer Pemberton, D.D.
BOSTON, Mass. Sept. 5, 1722.
Christ Church, Episcopal.
1723-1765. Timothy Cutler, D.D.
1760-1767. James Greaton
1768-1775. Mather Byles, Jr., D.D.
BOSTON, Mass. 1729.
Arlington Street Church, Presbyterian.
The entire Church and Parish became Unitarian.

1729-1773. John Moorhead
BOSTON, Mass. June 18, 1732. M.
Hollis Street Church, Congregational.
The entire Church and Parish became Unitarian.
1732-1777. Mather Byles, D.D.
BOSTON, Mass. Apr. 15, 1734.
Trinity Church, Episcopal.
1740-1746. Addington Davenport
1747-1767. William Hooper
1763-1775. William Walter, D.D.
1774-1804. Samuel Parker, D.D.
BOSTON, Mass. Jan. 3, 1737. X.
West Church, Congregational.
The entire Church and Parish became Unitarian.
1737-1746. William Hooper
1747-1766. Jonathan Mayhew, D.D.
1767-1804. Simeon Howard, D.D.
BOSTON, Mass. July 19, 1742. M.
Tenth Congregational Society.
Merger with the Second Church in Boston, Unitarian.
1742-1785. Samuel Mather, D.D.
BOSTON, Mass. July 27, 1743.
Second Baptist Church.
1743-1765. Ephraim Bound
1770-1772. John Davis
1773-1787. Isaac Skillman, D.D.
BOSTON, Mass. Feb. 17, 1748. X.
Eleventh Congregational Society.
1748-1785. Andrew Croswell
BOSTON, Mass. 1764. X.
Sandemanian Society.
BOXBOROUGH, Mass. 1775/6. X.
First Congregational Parish. Universalist.
Supplies to 1785.
BOXFORD, Mass. Dec. 30, 1702.
East Congregational Parish.
1702-1708. Thomas Symmes
1709-1743. John Rogers
1759-1793. Eliezur Holyoke
BOXFORD, Mass. Dec. 9, 1736.
Second or West Congregational Church.
1736-1772. John Cushing
1774-1786. Moses Hale
BOYLSTON, Mass. Oct. 6, 1743. X.
First Congregational Parish. Unitarian.
1743-1775. Ebenezer Morse
BOZRAH, Ct. Jan. 3, 1738/9.
First Congregational Church.
1739-1785. Benjamin Throop
BOZRAH, Ct. 1746.
Separatist Church at Norwich Plains. (See Newent Separatist Church).

242

BRAINTREE, Mass. Sept. 10, 1707.
First Congregational Church.
1707-1710. Hugh Adams
1711-1762. Samuel Niles
1762-1811. Ezra Weld
BRANFORD, Ct. 1647.
First Congregational Church.
1644-1646. John Sherman
1647-1665. Abraham Pierson
1667-1673. John Bowers
1680-1684. Samuel Mather
1687-1731. Samuel Russell
1732-1781. Philemon Robbins
BRATTLEBOROUGH, Vt.
July 5, 1770.
First or West Congregational Church.
1767-1792. Abner Reeve
BRENTWOOD, N. H. Dec. 2, 1747.
First Congregational Church.
1748-1789. Nathaniel Trask
BRENTWOOD, N. H. July, 1752. M.
Second Congregational Church.
United with the First Church, Jan. 7, 1756.
BRENTWOOD, N. H. May 2, 1771.
First Baptist Church.
1771-1815. Samuel Shepard.
BREWSTER, Mass. Oct. 16, 1700.
First Congregational Parish.
The entire Church and Parish became Unitarian.
1700-1755. Nathaniel Stone
1748-1791. Isaiah Dunster
BRIDGEPORT, Ct. June 13, 1695.
First Congregational Church.
1690-1714. Charles Chauncy
1715-1747. Samuel Cooke
1749-1751. Lyman Hall
1747-1799. Robert Ross
BRIDGEWATER, Mass. July 9, 1718.
First Congregational Society.
The entire Church and Parish became Unitarian.
1717-1730. Benjamin Allen
1731-1791. John Shaw
BRIDGEWATER, Mass. 1748.
Trinity Church, Episcopal.
Supplies.
BRIGHTON, Mass. 1737.
First Congregational Parish
Both Church and Parish became Unitarian.
Supplies to 1784.
BRIMFIELD, Mass. Nov. 18, 1724.
First Congregational Church.
1723-1734. Richard Treat
1735-1776. James Bridgham
1775-1796. Nehemiah Williams

BRISTOL, R. I. 1680.
First Congregational Church.
1681-1686. Benjamin Woodbridge
1687-1691. Samuel Lee
1693-1718. John Sparhawk
1721-1729. Nathaniel Cotton
1728-1740. John Wight
1729-1740. Barnabas Taylor
1740-1775. John Burt
BRISTOL, R. I. 1719.
St. Michael's Church, Episcopal.
1720-1721. James McSparran, D.D.
1721-1723. James Orem
1723-1775. John Usher
BRISTOL, Ct. Aug. 12, 1747.
First Congregational Church.
New Cambridge Society.
1747-1789. Samuel Newell
BRISTOL, Ct. 1759.
Trinity Church, Episcopal.
1759-1764. James Scovill
1774-1778. James Nichols
BRISTOL, Me. 1766.
First Presbyterian Church.
Congregational.
1772-1795. Alexander McLean
BROCKTON, Mass. Oct. 15, 1740.
First Congregational Church.
1740-1802. John Porter
BROOKFIELD, Mass. Oct. 17, 1717.
First Congregational Society.
Unitarian.
1716-1747. Thomas Cheney
1749-1755. Elisha Harding
1758-1799. Nathan Fiske, D.D.
BROOKFIELD, Ct. Sept. 28, 1757.
First Congregational Church.
1757-1796. Thomas Brooks
BROOKLINE, Mass. Oct. 26, 1717.
First Congregational Parish.
The entire Church and Parish became Unitarian.
1718-1747. James Allen
1748-1751. Cotton Brown
1755-1759. Nathaniel Potter
1760-1796. Joseph Jackson
BROOKLYN, Ct. Nov. 21, 1734.
First Congregational Society.
Unitarian.
1735-1754. Ephraim Avery
1755-1824. Josiah Whitney, D.D.
BROOKLYN, Ct. 1771.
Episcopal Church.
1771-1772. Richard Moseley
1772-1815. Daniel Fogg, Jr.
BRUNSWICK, Me. 1747.

First Presbyterian Church.
Congregational.
1735-1742. Robert Rutherford
1747-1760. Robert Dunlap
1762-1788. John Miller
BUCKINGHAM, Ct. 1727.
First Congregational Church.
1731-1733. Jonathan Hubbard
1735-1739. Chileab Brainard
1739-1742. Nehemiah Brainard
1744-1765. Isaac Chalker
1766-1768. Samuel Woodbridge
1769-1805. James Eells
BURLINGTON, Mass. Oct. 29, 1735.
First Congregational Church.
1735-1748. Supply Clap
1751-1774. Thomas Jones
1774-1813. John Marrett
BUXTON, Me. Mar. 16, 1763.
First Congregational Church.
1760-1818. Paul Coffin, D.D.
CAMBRIDGE, Mass. Oct. 11, 1633.
First Congregational Parish.
Unitarian.
1633-1636. Thomas Hooker
1633-1636. Samuel Stone
1636-1649. Thomas Shepard
1650-1668. Jonathan Mitchell
1671-1681. Urian Oakes
1682-1692. Nathaniel Gookin
1696-1717. William Brattle
1717-1784. Nathaniel Appleton, D.D.
CAMBRIDGE, Mass. Apr. 1751. X.
First Baptist Church.
1751-1753. Nathaniel Draper
CAMBRIDGE, MASS. Oct. 15, 1761.
Christ Church, Episcopal.
1761-1765. East Apthorp, D.D.
1767-1774. Winwood Sarjeant
CAMPTON, N. H. June 1, 1774.
First Congregational Church.
1774-1792. Selden Church
CANDIA, N. H. June 1771.
First Congregational Church.
1771-1780. David Jewett
CANTERBURY, Ct. June 13, 1711.
First Congregational Church.
1711-1727. Samuel Estabrook
1729-1741. John Wadsworth
1744-1771. James Cogswell, D.D.
CANTERBURY, Ct. Sept. 10, 1746. X.
Separatist Church, North Society.
1746-1754. Solomon Paine
1759-1768. Joseph Marshall
CANTERBURY, Ct. 1750. X.
First Baptist Church.
ca. 1750. Benjamin Herrington

CANTERBURY, N. H. 1760.
First Congregational Church.
1756-1756. Robert Cutler
1761-1779. Abiel Foster
CANTERBURY, Ct. Dec. 20, 1770.
Westminster Congregational Church.
1772-1804. John Staples
CANTON, Mass. Oct. 13, 1717.
First Congregational Parish.
Both Church and Parish became
Unitarian.
1717-1727. Joseph Morse
1727-1733. Samuel Dunbar
CANTON, Mass. 1755. X.
The English Church, Episcopal.
1755-1763. Ebenezer Miller, D.D.
1763-1767. Edward Winslow
1767-1776. William Clark
CANTON CENTER, Ct. May 1750.
First Congregational Church.
1750-1751. Evander Morrison
1761-1772. Gideon Mills
1774-1778. Seth Sage
CARLISLE, Mass. 1758.
First Congregational Society.
Unitarian.
Supplies to 1781.
CARVER, Mass. 1732.
North Congregational Church.
1733-1743. Othniel Campbell
1746-1804. John Howland
CASCO, Me. 1637. X.
Spurwink Episcopal Church.
(First Church in Maine).
1637-1640. Richard Gibson
1640-1675. Robert Jordon
CENTERBROOK, Ct. Nov. 16, 1725.
First Congregational Church.
1722-1756. Abraham Nott.
1757-1773. Stephen Holmes
1775-1785. Benjamin Dunning
CHARLEMONT, Mass. 1767. X.
First Congregational Church.
1765-1779. Jonathan Leavitt
CHARLESTOWN, Mass. Nov. 2, 1632
First Congregational Church.
1632-1636. Thomas James
1634-1671. Zechariah Symmes
1637-1638. John Harvard
1639-1651. Thomas Allen
1639-1677. Thomas Shepard, Jr.
1680-1685. Thomas Shepard, 3rd.
1685-1698. Charles Morton
1698-1741. Simon Bradstreet
1713-1721. Joseph Stevens
1724-1774. Hull Abbot
1739-1782. Thomas Prentice

CHARLESTOWN, R. I. 1702. X.
Indian Congregational Church.
1702-1710. Samuel Niles
CHARLESTOWN, R. I. Sept. 17, 1708.
Seventh Day Baptist Church.
1708-1720. John Maxson
1712-1719. Joseph Clark
1719-1748. John Maxson, Jr.
1739-1750. Joseph Maxson
1727-1773. Thomas Hiscox
1773-1793. Joshua Clark
CHARLESTOWN, R. I. 1750. X.
Indian Baptist Church.
ca. 1750. James Simons
ca. 1770. Thomas Ross
CHARLESTOWN, N. H. Dec. 4, 1754.
First Congregational Church.
Both Church and Parish became
 Unitarian.
1754-1756. John Dennis
1761-1793. Bulkley Olcutt
CHARLTON, Mass. Apr. 16, 1761. X.
First Congregational Society.
 Unitarian.
1761-1776. Caleb Curtiss
CHARLTON, Mass. July 13, 1762. X.
First Baptist Church.
1763-1791. Nathaniel Green
CHATHAM, Mass. June 15, 1720.
First Congregational Church.
1699-1702. Jonathan Vickery
1703-1706. Gershom Hall
1706-1708. John Latimer
1711-1715. Hugh Adams
1718-1748. Joseph Lord
1749-1782. Stephen Emery
CHELMSFORD, Mass. Nov. 15, 1655.
First Congregational Society.
Both Church and Parish became
 Unitarian.
1655-1676. John Fisk
1677-1704. Thomas Clarke
1708-1740. Samson Stoddard
1741-1792. Ebenezer Bridge
CHELMSFORD, Mass. Oct. 22, 1771.
First Baptist Church.
1773-1778. Elisha Rich
CHELSEA, Ct. 1760. X.
First Congregational Church.
1761-1769. Nathaniel Whittaker
1771-1778. Ephraim Judson
CHESHIRE, Ct. Dec. 9, 1724.
First Congregational Church.
1722-1766. Samuel Hall
1767-1813. John Foot
CHESHIRE, Ct. 1760.

St. Paul's Church, Episcopal.
ca. 1760. Joseph Moss,
 lay reader.
CHESHIRE, Mass. Aug. 28, 1769.
First Baptist Church.
1770-1808. Peter Worden
CHESHIRE, Mass. Sept. 21, 1771.
Lanesborough Baptist Church.
1771-1804. Nathan Mason
CHESTER, Ct. Sept. 15, 1742.
First Congregational Church.
1742-1751. Jared Harrison
1759-1765. Simeon Stoddard
1767-1770. Elijah Mason
1772-1781. Robert Silliman
CHESTER, N. H. Oct. 20, 1731.
First Congregational Church.
1731-1734. Moses Hale
1736-1796. Ebenezer Flagg
CHESTER, Mass. Dec. 20, 1769. X.
First Congregational Church.
1769-1814. Aaron Bascom
CHESTER, Vt. 1773.
First Congregational Church.
1773-1778. Samuel Whiting
CHESTERFIELD, Mass. Oct. 30, 1764
First Congregational Church.
1764-1774. Benjamin Mills
CHESTERFIELD, N. H. 1771. X.
First Congregational Church.
1772-1823. Abraham Wood
CHICOPEE, Mass. Sept. 27, 1752.
First Congregational Church.
1752-1813. John McKinstry
CHILMARK, Mass. 1693. X.
Indian Baptist Church.
Native preachers.
CHILMARK, Mass. 1715. X.
First Congregational Church.
1687-1714. Ralph Thacher
1715-1746. William Homes
1746-1776. Andrew Boardman
1776-1782. Timothy Fuller
CLAREMONT, N. H. 1770.
First Congregational Church.
1772-1773. George Wheaton
1774-1785. Augustine Hibberd
CLAREMONT, N. H. Nov. 1773.
Union Church, Episcopal.
1773-1785. Ranna Cossit
CLINTON, Ct. 1667.
First Congregational Church.
1666-1679. John Woodbridge
1682-1691. James Bailey
1691-1693. Warham Mather
1694-1707. Abraham Pierson
1709-1763. Jared Eliot, F.R.S.
1764-1777. Eliphalet Huntington

COHASSET, Mass. Dec. 12, 1721.
First Congregational Society.
Both Church and Parish became
Unitarian.
1721-1740. Nathaniel Hobart
1741-1746. John Fowle
1747-1791. John Brown
COLCHESTER, Ct. Dec. 20, 1703.
First Congregational Church.
1703-1731. John Bulkley
1732-1787. Ephraim Little
COLCHESTER, Ct. 1743. X.
Separatist Church.
ca. 1743. Jabez Jones
COLRAIN, Mass. 1750.
First Presbyterian Church.
Congregational.
1753-1761. Alexander McDowell
1769-1773. Daniel McClallen
COLUMBIA, Ct. 1720.
First Congregational Church.
1720-1724. Samuel Smith
1725-1739. William Gager
1735-1770. Eleazer Wheelock, D.D.
1772-1807. Thomas Brockway
CONCORD, Mass. July 5, 1636.
First Congregational Parish.
Both Church and Parish became
Unitarian.
1636-1659. Peter Bulkley
1636-1644. John Jones
1659-1696. Edward Bulkley
1667-1711. Joseph Estabrook
1712-1737. John Whiting
1739-1764. Daniel Bliss
1765-1776. William Emerson
CONCORD, Mass. Dec. 12, 1745. X.
West or Black Horse Church.
Separatist Congregational.
CONCORD, N. H. Nov. 18, 1730.
First Congregational Church.
1730-1782. Timothy Walker
CONWAY, Mass. July 14, 1768.
First Congregational Church.
1769-1826. John Emerson
CORNISH, N. H. Sept. 29, 1768.
First Congregational Church.
1768-1785. James Wellman
CORNWALL Ct. 1740.
First Congregational Church.
1741-1754. Solomon Palmer
1755-1786. Hezekiah Gold
CORNWALL, Ct. 1761.
Episcopal Church.
1761-1766. Thomas Davies
COVENTRY, Ct. Oct. 9, 1745.
North Congregational Church.
1745-1795. Nathan Strong

COVENTRY, R. I. May 21, 1751.
First Baptist Church.
1751-1771. Peter Worden
1763-1770. Timothy Greene
CRANSTON, R. I. July 12, 1764.
First Baptist Church.
ca. 1764. Elisha Green
CROMWELL, Ct. Jan. 5, 1714/5.
First Congregational Church.
1703-1711. David Deming
1715-1736. Joseph Smith
1738-1776. Edward Eells
CUMBERLAND, R. I. 1749.
First Baptist Church.
1749-1774. Josias Cook
1752-1773. Nathaniel Cook
1772-1806. Abner Ballou
CUMMINGTON, Mass. 1772. X.
First Congregational Church.
Supplies to 1779.
DANBURY, Ct. 1696.
First Congregational Church.
1697-1735. Seth Shove
1732-1732. Abraham Todd
1736-1764. Ebenezer White
1762-1768. Noadiah Warner
1769-1776. Ebenezer Baldwin
1770-1773. Titus Smith
DANBURY, Ct. 1764.
Second Church, Separatist.
1764-1779. Ebenezer White
1767-1774. Ebenezer Russell White
DANBURY, Ct. 1764.
Sandemanian Church.
1764-1769. Joseph Moss White
1769-1772. Theophilus Chamberlain
DANVERS, Mass. Oct. 1671.
First Congregational Church.
1671-1680. James Bailey
1680-1683. George Burroughs
1685-1688. Deodat Lawson
1689-1696. Samuel Parris
1698-1715. Joseph Green
1716-1769. Peter Clark
1772-1826. Benjamin Wadsworth DD.
DANVILLE, N. H. Dec. 21, 1763. X.
First Congregational Church.
1763-1783. John Page
DARIEN, Ct. June 6, 1744.
First Congregational Church.
1744-1806. Moses Mather, D.D.
DARTMOUTH, Mass.
See Tiverton, R. I.
DEDHAM, Mass. Nov. 8, 1638.
First Congregational Church.
Both Church and Parish became
Unitarian.
1637-1671. John Allin

1673-1685. William Adams
1693-1723. Joseph Belcher
1724-1755. Samuel Dexter
1756-1803. Jason Haven
DEDHAM, Mass. 1768.
St. Paul's Church, Episcopal.
1767-1777. William Clark
DEERFIELD, Mass. Oct. 17, 1688.
First Congregational Church.
Both Church and Parish became
Unitarian.
1686-1729. John Williams
1732-1780. Jonathan Ashley
DEERFIELD, N. H. 1770.
First Baptist Church.
1770-1776. Eliphalet Smith
DEERFIELD, N. H. Dec. 9, 1772.
First Congregational Church.
1772-1811. Timothy Upham
DEER ISLE, Me. Aug. 1773.
First Congregational Church.
Supplies to 1785.
DENNIS, Mass. June 22, 1727.   X.
First Congregational Church.
Unitarian.
1727-1763. Josiah Dennis
1764-1804. Nathan Stone
DERBY, Ct. Nov. 18, 1673.
First Congregational Church.
1673-1687. John Bowers
1688-1690. Joseph Webb
1693-1706. John James
1706-1732. Joseph Moss
1733-1787. Daniel Humphreys
DERBY, Ct. 1736.
St. James' Church, Episcopal.
1736-1740. Jonathan Arnold
1743-1747. John Lyon
1749-1820. Richard Mansfield, D.D.
DERRY, N. H. 1719.
First Presbyterian Church.
Congregational.
1719-1729. James McGregore
1729-1735. Matthew Clark
1733-1738. Thomas Thompson
1740-1791. William Davidson
DIGHTON, Mass. 1710.
First Congregational Church.
1710-1777. Nathaniel Fisher
1772-1800. John Smith
DIGHTON, Mass. 1769.
Pedo-Baptist Congregational Society.
Both Church and Parish became
Unitarian.
1776-1777. Ezra Stiles, D.D., LL.D.
DIGHTON, Mass. Dec. 2, 1772.
First or West Baptist Church.
1772-1810. Enoch Goff

DORCHESTER, Mass. June 6, 1630.
First Congregational Parish.
Entire Church and Parish became
Unitarian.
1630-1635. John Warham
1630-1636. John Maverick
1636-1669. Richard Mather
1640-1641. Jonathan Burr
1649-1651. John Wilson, Jr.
1671-1680. Josiah Flynt
1681-1729. John Danforth
1729-1773. Jonathan Bowman
1774-1793. Moses Everett
DOUGLAS, Mass. Nov. 11, 1747.
First Congregational Church.
1747-1765. William Phips
1771-1805. Isaac Stone
DOUGLAS, Mass. Nov. 24, 1774.   X.
First Baptist Church.
1774-1784. Adam Streeter
DOVER, N. H. Dec. 1638.
First Congregational Church.
1633-1635. William Leverich
1637-1638. George Burdett
1638-1641. Hanserd Knollys
1640-1642. Thomas Larkham
1642-1655. Daniel Maud
1655-1669. John Rayner
1671-1676. John Rayner, Jr.
1681-1710. John Pike
1711-1715. Nicholas Sever
1717-1769. Jonathan Cushing
1767-1786. Jeremv Belknap, D.D.
DOVER, Mass. Nov. 7, 1762.
First Congregational Parish.
Both Church and Parish became
Unitarian.
1762-1811. Benjamin Caryl
DRACUT, Mass. Mar. 29, 1721.   X.
First Congregational Parish.
Unitarian.
1720-1765. Thomas Parker
1765-1781. Nathan Davis
DRESDEN, Me.
See Pownalborough.
DUBLIN, N. H. June 10, 1772.
First Congregational Society.
Both Church and Parish became
Unitarian.
1772-1776. Joseph Farrar
DUDLEY, Mass. 1732.
First Congregational Church.
1735-1743. Perley Howe
1744-1790. Charles Gleason
DUDLEY, Mass. 1744.   X.
Baptist Church.
See Webster.

DUNSTABLE, Mass. Dec. 16, 1685. X.
First Congregational Parish.
Universalist.
1679-1702. Thomas Weld
1703-1708. Samuel Hunt
1708-1712. Samuel Parris
1720-1737. Nathaniel Prentice
1738-1746. Josiah Swan
1757-1774. Josiah Goodhue
DUNSTABLE, Mass. 1747. X.
Separatist Congregational Church.
1747-1751. Samuel Bird
DUNSTAN, Me. Nov. 7, 1744. X.
First Congregational Parish.
Unitarian.
1744-1776. Richard Elvins
DURHAM, Ct. Feb. 7, 1711.
First Congregational Church.
1706-1756. Nathaniel Chauncy
1756-1797. Eliezur Goodrich, D.D.
DURHAM, N. H. Mar. 26, 1718
First Congregational Church.
1656-1657. Seth Fletcher
1660-1662. Joseph Hull
1684-1717. John Buss
1718-1739. Hugh Adams
1742-1748. Nicholas Gilman
1749-1778. John Adams
DUXBURY, Mass. 1632.
First Congregational Parish.
The entire Church and Parish became
Unitarian.
1632-1637. William Brewster
1637-1658. Ralph Partridge
1663-1675. John Holmes
1676-1700. Ichabod Wiswall
1702-1738. John Robinson
1739-1750. Samuel Veazie
1755-1775. Charles Turner
1776-1786. Zedekiah Sanger, D.D.
EAST BRIDGEWATER, Mass.
Feb. 28, 1723.
First Congregational Parish.
Both Church and Parish became
Unitarian.
1724-1787. John Angier
1767-1805. Samuel Angier
EAST CANAAN, Ct. Dec. 5, 1769.
First Congregational Church.
1770-1775. Asahel Hart
EAST GRANBY, Ct. 1737.
Turkey Hills Congregational Parish.
1742-1755. Ebenezer Mills
1760-1767. Nehemiah Strong
1773-1774. Abel Forward
1776-1785. Aaron Jordon Booge
EAST GREENWICH, R. I. 1700.
First Baptist Church.

1743-1747. Daniel Fisk
1753-1792. John Gorton
EAST GREENWICH, R. I. 1734.
Baptist Church.
1734-1752. Timothy Peckham
1758-1794. Philip Jenkins
EAST GREENWICH, R. I. 1774.
Catholic Congregational Society.
Supplies to 1815.
EAST HADDAM, Ct. May 3, 1704.
First Congregational Church.
1704-1749. Stephen Hosmer
1751-1771. Joseph Fowler
1772-1827. Elijah Parsons
1776-1777. Eleazer Sweetland
EASTHAM, Mass. 1643/4. X.
First Congregational Church.
1646-1655. John Mayo
1655-1670. Thomas Crosby
1673-1717. Samuel Treat
1718-1719. Samuel Osborn
1720-1746. Benjamin Webb
1751-1794. Edward Cheever
EAST HAMPTON, Ct. 1650. X
First Congregational Church.
1650-1696. Thomas James
EAST HAMPTON, Ct. Nov. 30, 1748.
First Congregational Church.
1748-1778. John Norton
EAST HARTFORD, Ct. Mar. 30, 1705
First Congregational Church.
1699-1702. John Read
1705-1746. Samuel Woodbridge
1748-1803. Eliphalet Williams, D.D.
EAST HARTLAND, Ct. May 1, 1768.
First Congregational Church.
1768-1772. Starling Graves
1773-1815. Aaron Church
EAST HAVEN, Ct. Oct. 8, 1711.
First Congregational Church.
1704-1754. James Hemingway
1755-1806. Nicholas Street
EAST KINGSTON, N. H.
Nov. 14, 1739.
First Congregational Church.
1739-1772. Peter Coffin.
EAST LYME, Ct. Jan. 12, 1749. X.
Separatist Church.
1749-1752. Ebenezer Mack
EAST LYME, Ct. 1752.
First Baptist Church.
1752-1768. Ebenezer Mack
1774-1810. Jason Lee
EASTON, Mass. 1713.
First Congregational Parish.
Unitarian.
1723-1731. Matthew Short
1731-1744. Joseph Belcher

1747-1755. Solomon Prentice
1755-1756. George Farrar
1763-1782. Archibald Campbell
EASTON, Mass. 1750. X.
Presbyterian Church.
1750-1755. Solomon Prentice
EASTON, Mass. July 21, 1762. X.
First Baptist Church.
1762-1766. Ebenezer Stearns
1766-1794. Esek Carr
EASTON, Ct. Dec. 14, 1763.
First Congregational Church.
1763-1810. James Johnson
EAST PROVIDENCE, R. I. 1643.
First Congregational Church.
(Formerly Seekonk, Mass.)
1644-1663. Samuel Newman
1668-1676. Noah Newman
1679-1693. Samuel Angier
1693-1720. Thomas Greenwood
1720-1766. John Greenwood
1759-1764. John Carns
1766-1783. Ephraim Hyde
EAST WESTMORELAND, N. H.
First Baptist Church. 1771.
1773-1800. Ebenezer Bailey
EAST WINDSOR, Ct. May 1, 1754.
North Congregational Church.
1754-1803. Thomas Potwine
EAST WOODSTOCK, Ct. 1759.
East Congregational Church.
1760-1783. Abel Stiles
EDGARTOWN, Mass. July 1641. X.
First Congregational Parish.
Unitarian.
1642-1657. Thomas Mayhew, Jr.
1658-1681. Gov. Thomas Mayhew
1664-1667. John Cotton, Jr.
1681-1682. Deodat Lawson
1684-1717. Jonathan Dunham
1713-1746. Samuel Wiswall
1747-1758. John Newman
1759-1760. Joshua Tufts
1761-1778. Samuel Kingsbsury
EGREMONT, Mass. Feb. 20, 1770. X.
First Congregational Church
1770-1794. Eliphalet Steele
ELIOT, Me. June 22, 1721.
First Congregational Church.
1721-1773. John Rogers
1768-1791. Alpheus Spring
ELLINGTON, Ct. 1730.
First Congregational Church.
1730-1749. John McKinstry
1749-1756. Nathaniel Huntington
1757-1762. Seth Norton
1765-1780. John Bliss

ENFIELD, Ct. June 3, 1699.
First Congregational Church.
1687-1689. Nathaniel Welch
1697-1724. Nathaniel Collins
1724-1768. Peter Reynolds
1769-1776. Elan Potter
ENFIELD, Ct. Aug. 20, 1762.
Separatist Church.
1762-1787. Nathaniel Collins
EPPING, N. H. Dec. 9, 1747.
First Congregational Church.
1747-1755. Robert Cutler
1758-1788. Josiah Stearns
EPSOM, N. H. Sept. 23, 1761. X.
First Congregational Church.
1761-1774. John Tuck
ESSEX, Mass. Sept. 9, 1681.
First Congregational Church.
1680-1725. John Wise
1725-1747. Theophilus Pickering
1749-1766. Nehemiah Porter
1774-1779. John Cleaveland
ESSEX, Mass. May 22, 1746. M.
Second Congregational Church.
1746-1774. John Cleaveland
EVERETT, Mass. Apr. 18, 1734. M.
South Congregational Parish in Malden.
1735-1744. Joseph Stimpson
1747-1750. Aaron Cleaveland
1751-1792. Eliakim Willis
EXETER, N. H. 1638. X.
First Congregational Church.
1638-1642. John Wheelwright
1650-1683. Samuel Dudley
1684-1690. John Cotton, 3rd.
EXETER, N. H. Sept. 18, 1698.
The Congregational Church.
1698-1705. John Clark
1706-1754. John Odlin
1743-1776. Woodbridge Odlin
EXETER, N. H. June 7, 1744. X.
Second Congregational Church.
1748-1785. Daniel Rogers
EXETER, R. I. 1750.
First Baptist Church.
1750-1754. David Sprague
1766-1777. David Sprague
1769-1794. Solomon Sprague
FAIRFIELD, Ct. 1643.
First Congregational Church.
1643-1665. John Jones
1665-1692. Samuel Wakeman
1698-1732. Joseph Webb
1733-1773. Noah Hobart
1774-1805. Andrew Eliot

FAIRFIELD, Ct. 1722.
Episcopal Church.
1722-1723. George Pigot
1727-1744. Henry Caner, D.D.
1747-1773. Joseph Lamson
1774-1779. John Sayre
FALL RIVER, Mass. Sept. 30, 1747. X.
First Congregational Church.
1747-1776. Silas Brett
FALMOUTH, Mass. Oct. 10, 1708.
First Congregational Church.
1700-1707. Samuel Shiverick
1707-1723. Joseph Metcalf
1724-1730. Josiah Marshall
1731-1775. Samuel Palmer
1775-1778. Zebulon Butler
FALMOUTH, Me. 1754. Dormant.
First Congregational Church.
1755-1763. John Wiswell
1765-1799. Ebenezer Williams
FARMINGTON, Ct. Oct. 13, 1652.
First Congregational Church.
1652-1657. Roger Newton
1661-1697. Samuel Hooker
1697-1701. Caleb Watson
1705-1751. Samuel Whitman
1752-1785. Timothy Pitkin
FITCHBURG, Mass. Jan. 7, 1768.
First Congregational Parish.
Both Church and Parish became
   Unitarian.
1768-1794. John Payson
FITZWILLIAM, N. H.
            Mar. 27, 1771. X.
First Congregational Society.
   Unitarian.
1771-1799. Benjamin Brigham
FOSTER, R. I. 1745.
First Baptist Church.
1745-1756. Nathan Young
FRAMINGHAM, Mass. Oct. 8, 1701.
First Congregational Parish.
   Unitarian.
1701-1745. John Swift
1746-1775. Matthew Bridge
FRAMINGHAM, Mass. Oct. 1746. M.
Separatist Church.
1747-1757. Solomon Reed
FRAMINGHAM, Mass. 1763. X.
First Baptist Church.
Supplies to 1792.
FRANCESTOWN, N. H.
            Jan. 27, 1773.
First Presbyterian Parish.
Became Congregational and later
   Unitarian.
1773-1781. Samuel Cotton
FRANKLIN, Ct. Oct. 8, 1718.

First Congregational Church.
1717-1750. Henry Willis
1753-1782. John Ellis
1771-1778. Ephraim Judson
FRANKLIN, Ct. Oct. 27, 1747. X.
Separatist Church at Norwich Farms.
1747-1759. Thomas Denison
FRANKLIN, Mass. Feb. 16, 1738.
First Congregational Society.
1738-1754. Elias Haven
1760-1763. Caleb Barnum
1769-1827. Nathaniel Emmons, D.D.
FREETOWN, Mass. 1704. X.
First Congregational Church.
1704-1707. William Way
1710-1711. Joseph Avery
1713-1717. Jonathan Dodson
1717-1721. Thomas Craighead
1747-1776. Silas Brett
FREETOWN, Mass. 1720. X.
Episcopal Church.
Supplied by Dr. James McSparran and
   others.
FREETOWN, Mass. Sept. 13, 1775. X.
First Calvinistic Baptist Church.
1776-1784. Abner Lewis
FRYEBURG, Me. Aug. 21, 1775.
First Congregational Church.
1775-1805. William Fessenden
GARDINER, Me. 1771. X.
St. Ann's Church, Episcopal.
Lay supplies.
GAY HEAD, Mass. 1663. X.
Indian Baptist Church.
Native preachers.
GEORGETOWN, Mass. Nov. 17, 1706
Byfield Congregational Parish.
1706-1744. Moses Hale
1744-1783. Moses Parsons
GEORGETOWN, Mass. Oct. 4, 1732.
First Congregational Church.
1732-1788. James Chandler
GEORGETOWN, Mass. 1754.
First Baptist Church of Rowley.
1770-1772. Eliphaz Chapman
GEORGETOWN, Me. 1739. X.
First Presbyterian Church.
   Congregational.
1739-1742. William McClanathan
1742-1742. Robert Rutherford
1742-1744. William McClanathan
1747-1748. Daniel Mitchell
1748-1753. Alexander Boyd
1765-1810. Ezekiel Emerson
GILEAD, Ct. Apr. 1, 1752.
Gilead Congregational Society of
   Hebron.
1752-1797. Elijah Lathrop

GILMANTON, N. H.
  Nov. 16, 1773. X.
First Baptist Church.
Supplies to 1786.
GILMANTON, N. H.
  Nov. 30, 1774. X.
First Congregational Church.
1763-1773. William Parsons
1774-1817. Isaac Smith
GILSUM, N. H. Oct. 27, 1772.
First Congregational Church.
Supplies to 1794.
GLASTONBURY, Ct. July 1692.
First Congregational Church.
1692-1725. Timothy Stevens
1728-1758. Ashbel Woodbridge
1758-1791. John Eells
GLOUCESTER, Mass. 1642.
First Congregational Parish.
Both Church and Parish became
  Unitarian.
1642-1650. Richard Blinman
1650-1655. William Perkins
1663-1700. John Emerson
1703-1760. John White
1751-1775. Samuel Chandler
1776-1804. Eli Forbes, D.D.
GLOUCESTER, Mass. Oct. 4, 1716. X.
Second Congregational Church.
  Universalist.
1712-1724. Samuel Tompson
1725-1777. Richard Jaques
1770-1820. Daniel Fuller
GLOUCESTER. Mass. June 11, 1728.
Annisquam or Third Congregational
  Parish, Universalist.
1728-1762. Benjamin Bradstreet
1766-1768. John Wyeth
1772-1779. Obediah Parsons
GLOUCESTER. Mass. Oct. 27, 1743 X
Fourth Congregational Parish.
  Universalist.
1744-1782. John Rogers.
GLOUCESTER. R. I. 1700.
First Baptist Church.
1700-1735. Peter Place
1733-1795. Edward Mitchell
1742-1763. Thomas Knowlton
1756-1811. John Winsor
1763-1802. Joseph Winsor
GOFFSTOWN. N. H. Oct. 30, 1771.
First Congregational Church.
1771-1774. Joseph Currier
GORHAM. Me. Dec. 26. 1750.
First Congregational Church.
1750-1764. Solomon Lombard
1767-1779. Josiah Thacher

GORHAM, Me. Jan. 25, 1758. M.
Second Congregational Church.
1759-1762. Ebenezer Townsend
GORHAM, Me. June 20, 1768.
First Baptist Church.
Supplies.
GOSHEN, Ct. Nov. 1740.
First Congregational Church.
1740-1753. Stephen Heaton
1754-1781. Abel Newell
GOSHEN, Ct. 1767. X.
Episcopal Church.
1767-1771. Solomon Palmer
1774-1778. James Nichols
GOSPORT, N. H. July 26, 1732. X.
First Congregational Church.
1650-1662. John Brock
1662-1665. Joseph Hull
1672-1692. Samuel Belcher
1694-1703. Samuel Moody
1707-1732. Joshua Moody
1732-1773. John Tuck
1773-1775. Jeremiah Shaw
GRAFTON, Mass. 1671. X.
Hassanamesit Indian Congregational
  Church.
Native preachers.
GRAFTON, Mass. Dec. 28, 1731.
The Congregational Society.
  Unitarian.
1731-1747. Solomon Prentiss
1750-1772. Aaron Hutchinson
1774-1787. Daniel Grosvenor
GRAFTON. Mass. Mar. 20, 1751. X.
Separatist Church.
1751-1767. Ebenezer Wadsworth
GRAFTON, MASS. June 17, 1767. X.
First Baptist Church.
1773-1777. Elhanan Winchester
GRANBY, Ct. 1739.
First Congregational Church.
1740-1742. Eli Colton
1745-1747. David Sherman Rowland
1747-1748. Isaac Burr
1750-1751. Aaron Brown
1752-1779. Joseph Strong
GRANBY, Mass. Oct. 3, 1762.
First Congregational Parish.
1762-1784. Simon Bachus
GRANVILLE, Mass. 1747.
First Congregational Church.
1747-1754. Moses Tuttle
1756-1776. Jedediah Smith
GRAY. Me. Aug. 1774. X.
First Congregational Church.
1774-1782. Samuel Nash

GREAT BARRINGTON, Mass.
Dec. 28, 1743.
First Congregational Church.
1743-1769. Samuel Hopkins, D.D.
GREAT BARRINGTON, Mass.
Sept. 21, 1762.
St. James's Church, Episcopal.
1763-1766. Solomon Palmer
1770-1793. Gideon Bostwick
GREEN FARMS, Ct. Oct. 26, 1715.
First Congregational Church.
1712-1741. Daniel Chapman
1742-1766. Daniel Buckingham
1766-1821. Hezekiah Ripley, D.D.
GREENFIELD, Mass. Mar. 28, 1754.
First Congregational Church.
1754-1757. Edward Billings
1761-1816. Roger Newton, D.D.
GREENFIELD HILL, Ct.
May 18, 1726.
First Congregational Church.
1726-1756. John Goodsell
1757-1770. Seth Pomeroy
1772-1781. William M. Tennent, D.D.
GREENLAND, N. H. July 1706.
First Congregational Church.
1707-1760. William Allen
1756-1804. Samuel Macclintock, D.D.
GREENWICH OLD TOWN, Ct.
Feb. 2, 1669/70.
First Congregational Church.
1669-1673. Eliphalet Jones
1673-1676. William Leverich
1678-1689. Jeremiah Peck
1691-1694. Abraham Pierson
1695-1697. Salmon Treat
1697-1700. Joseph Morgan
1700-1708. Nathaniel Bowers
1709-1710. John Jones
1715-1717. Richard Sackett
1728-1739. Ebenezer Gould
1730-1746. Ephraim Bostwick
1763-1769. Ebenezer Davenport
GREENWICH, Ct. 1705.
Episcopal Church.
1704-1705. Thomas Pritchard
1705-1708. George Muirson
1710-1719. Christopher Bridge
1722-1726. Robert Jenney, LL.D.
1726-1747. James Wetmore
1748-1799. Ebenezer Dibblee, D.D.
GREENWICH, Ct. Nov. 3, 1773.
First Baptist Church.
Supplies to 1785.
GREENWICH, Mass. Dec. 20, 1749.
First Congregational Church.
1749-1755. Pelatiah Webster
1760-1786. Robert Cutler

GRISWOLD, Ct. Nov. 20, 1720.
First Congregational Church.
1720-1761. Hezekiah Lord
1762-1808. Levi Hart, D.D.
GROTON, Mass. July 16, 1664.
First Congregational Church.
Both Church and Parish became Unitarian.
1662-1663. John Miller
1662-1676. Samuel Willard
1678-1690. Gershom Hobart
1691-1693. Samuel Carter
1706-1712. Dudley Bradstreet
1712-1760. Caleb Trowbridge
1761-1775. Samuel Dana
GROTON, Ct. Nov. 29, 1704.
First Congregational Church.
1704-1724. Ephraim Woodbridge
1725-1727. Dudley Woodbridge
1727-1753. John Owen
1754-1757. Samuel Kirtland
1758-1768. Jonathan Barber
1769-1798. Aaron Kinne
GROTON, Ct. 1705.
First Baptist Church in Connecticut.
1705-1747. Valentine Wightman
1747-1756. Daniel Fisk
1756-1796. Timothy Wightman
GROTON, Ct. 1750. X.
Separatist Church.
1750-1797. Parke Avery
GROTON, Ct. 1763.
Second Baptist Church.
ca. 1763. Benjamin Niles
1765-1818. Silas Burrows
GROVELAND, Mass. June 7, 1727.
First Congregational Church.
1727-1792. William Balch
GUILFORD, Ct. June 19, 1643.
First Congregational Church.
1639-1650. Henry Whitefield
1643-1659. John Higginson
1664-1694. Joseph Eliot
1695-1728. Thomas Ruggles
1729-1770. Thomas Ruggles, Jr.
1757-1800. Amos Fowler
GUILFORD, Ct. Sept. 21, 1733. X.
Second Congregational Church.
1729-1734. Edmund Ward
1735-1741. Joseph Lamb
1743-1767. James Sproat, D.D.
1771-1775. Daniel Brewer
GUILFORD, Ct. 1764.
Episcopal Church.
1764-1767. Bela Hubbard, D.D.
GUILFORD, Vt. 1770. X.
First Congregational Church.
1774-1776. Ebenezer Gurley

HADDAM, Ct. 1696.
First Congregational Church.
1668-1681. Nicholas Noyes
1683-1692. John James
1691-1715. Jeremiah Hobart
1714-1738. Phinehas Fisk
1739-1746. Aaron Cleaveland
1749-1753. Joshua Elderkin
1756-1803. Eleazer May
HADDAM, Ct. Sept. 14, 1740.
Haddam Neck Congregational Church.
1740-1761. Benjamin Bowers
1762-1783. Benjamin Boardman
HADDAM, Ct. Aug. 18, 1775.
East Plains Congregational Church.
Supplies to 1797.
HADLEY, Mass. Nov. 22, 1659.
First Congregational Church.
1659-1692. John Russell, Jr.
1695-1745. Isaac Chauncy
1740-1753. Chester Williams
1755-1811. Samuel Hopkins, D.D.
HADLYME, Ct. June 26, 1745.
First Congregational Church.
1741-1777. Grindall Rawson
HALIFAX, Mass. Oct. 16, 1734.
First Congregational Church.
1735-1756. John Cotton
1758-1768. William Patten
1769-1801. Ephraim Briggs
HALLOWELL, Me. 1772. X.
First Congregational Church.
Supplies to 1786.
HAMILTON, Mass. Oct. 12, 1714.
First Congregational Church.
1714-1768. Samuel Wigglesworth
1771-1823. Manasseh Cutler, D.D.
HAMPSTEAD, N. H. June 3, 1752.
First Congregational Church.
1752-1782. Henry True
HAMPTON, N. H. 1638.
First Congregational Church.
(Oldest Church in New Hampshire.)
1638-1641. Stephen Bachiller
1639-1661. Timothy Dalton
1647-1659. John Wheelwright
1659-1686. Seaborn Cotton
1696-1710. John Cotton
1710-1734. Nathaniel Gookin
1734-1765. Ward Cotton
1765-1792. Ebenezer Thayer
HAMPTON, Ct. June 5, 1723.
First Congregational Church.
1723-1733. William Billings
1734-1791. Samuel Moseley
HAMPTON FALLS, N. H.
     Dec. 13, 1711. X.

First Congregational Society.
Unitarian.
1712-1726. Theophilus Cotton
1727-1757. Joseph Whipple
1757-1762. Josiah Bayley
1763-1776. Paine Wingate, Jr.
HANCOCK, Mass. June 1772. X.
First Baptist Church.
1772-1806. Clark Rogers
HANOVER, Mass. 1726.
St. Andrew's Church, Episcopal.
1726-1730. Charles Brockwell
1733-1736. Addington Davenport
1743-1775. Ebenezer Thompson
1775-1776. Edward Winslow
HANOVER, Mass. Dec. 5, 1728.
First Congregational Church.
1728-1756. Benjamin Bass
1756-1779. Samuel Baldwin
HANOVER, Ct. May 13, 1766.
First Congregational Church.
1765-1766. Timothy Stone
1768-1832. Andrew Lee, D.D.
HANOVER, N. H. Jan. 23, 1771.
First Presbyterian Church.
Congregational.
1771-1779. Eleazer Wheelock, D.D.
HANOVER, N. H. July 17, 1771.
First Congregational Church.
1772-1809. Eden Burroughs, D.D.
HANSON, Mass. Aug. 31, 1748.
First Congregational Church.
1748-1803. Gad Hitchcok, D.D.
HARDWICK, Mass. Oct. 20, 1736.
First Congregational Church.
Both Church and Parish became
  Unitarian.
It is now Universalist.
1736-1784. David White
HARDWICK, Mass. 1750. X.
Separatist Church, Congregational.
(Removed to Bennington. Vt., 1761,
where it became the first church in the
state of Vermont.)
HARPSWELL, Me. 1753. X.
First Congregational Church.
1753-1764. Elisha Eaton
1761-1822. Samuel Eaton
HARTFORD, Ct. 1636.
First Congregational Church.
1636-1647. Thomas Hooker
1636-1663. Samuel Stone
1660-1669. John Whiting
1664-1679. Joseph Haynes
1679-1682. Isaac Foster
1683-1732. Timothy Woodbridge
1732-1747. Daniel Wadsworth

1747-1772. Edward Dorr
1773-1816. Nathan Strong, D.D.
HARTFORD, Ct. Feb. 12, 1669/70.
Second Congregational Church.
1669-1689. John Whiting
1694-1731. Thomas Buckingham
1732-1777. Elnathan Whitman
HARTFORD, Ct. ca. 1737. X.
First Baptist Church.
1737-1740. Reuben Peckham
HARVARD, Mass. Oct. 10, 1733.
First Congregational Church.
Both Church and Parish became
    Unitarian.
1733-1757. John Seccombe
1759-1768. Joseph Wheeler
1769-1777. Daniel Johnson
HARVARD, Mass. June 29, 1751. X.
Separatist Church.
1760-1780. Shadrack Ireland
HARVARD, Mass. June 27, 1776.
First Baptist Church.
1776-1798. Isaiah Parker
HARWICH, Mass. Nov. 6, 1747.
First Congregational Church.
1747-1752. Edward Pell
1762-1765. Benjamin Crocker
1765-1773. Jonathan Mills
HARWICH, Mass. Jan. 23, 1749. X.
Separatist Church.
1749-1757. Joshua Nickerson
HARWICH, Mass. Dec. 11, 1751. X.
Separatist Church.
1751-1756. Richard Chase
HARWICH, Mass. Sept. 29, 1757.
Baptist Religious Society.
1756-1777. Richard Chase
HARWINTON, Ct. Oct. 4, 1738.
First Congregational Church.
1737-1774. Andrew Bartholomew
1774-1783. David Perry
HATFIELD, Mass. Apr. 1, 1671.
First Congregational Church.
1669-1679. Hope Atherton
1682-1685. Nathaniel Chauncy
1685-1741. William Williams
1740-1770. Timothy Woodbridge
1772-1828. Joseph Lyman, D.D.
HAVERHILL, Mass. 1641.
First Congregational Parish.
    Unitarian.
1641-1693. John Ward
1639-1708. Benjamin Rolfe
1711-1715. Joshua Gardner
1719-1742. John Brown
1743-1774. Edward Barnard

HAVERHILL, Mass. Dec. 27, 1682.
First Church in Bradford.
    Congregational.
1668-1708. Zachariah Symmes
1708-1725. Thomas Symmes
1726-1765. Joseph Parsons
1765-1780. Samuel Williams
HAVERHILL, Mass. Nov. 4, 1730.
North or Second Parish.
(See Plaistow, N. H.).
HAVERHILL, Mass. Oct. 22, 1735. X.
Third Congregational Parish.
    Universalist.
1735-1761. Samuel Bachellor
1771-1801. Phinehas Adams
HAVERHILL, Mass. Nov. 28, 1744. X.
Fourth or East Congregational Parish.
1744-1789. Benjamin Parker
HAVERHILL, Mass. May 9, 1765.
First Baptist Church.
1765-1806. Hezekiah Smith, D.D.
HAVERHILL, N. H. Sept. 1764. X.
First Congregational Church.
1765-1784. Peter Powers
HEBRON, Ct. Nov. 19, 1717.
First Congregational Church.
1717-1734. John Bliss
1735-1784. Benjamin Pomeroy, D.D.
HEBRON, Ct. 1735.
Episcopal Church.
1734-1742. John Bliss
1745-1745. Barzillai Dean
1746-1752. Ebenezer Punderson
1748-1751. Jonathan Colton
1752-1757. Matthew Graves
1757-1757. John Usher
1759-1775. Samuel Andrew Peters
HENNIKER, N. H. June 7, 1769.
First Congregational Church.
1769-1782. Jacob Rice
HILLSBOROUGH, N. H.
    Oct. 12, 1769. X.
First Congregational Church.
1772-1803. Jonathan Barnes
HINGHAM, Mass. Sept. 18, 1635.
First Congregational Parish.
The entire Church and Parish became
    Unitarian.
1635-1679. Peter Hobart
1638-1641. Robert Peck
1678-1716. John Norton
1718-1787. Ebenezer Gay, D.D.
HINGHAM, Mass. Mar. 25, 1745.
Second Congregational Church.
The entire Church and Parish became
    Unitarian.
1746-1802. Daniel Shute, D.D.

254

HINSDALE, N. H. Aug. 17, 1763.
First Congregational Church.
1763-1810. Bunker Gay
HOLDEN, Mass. Dec. 22, 1742.
First Congregational Church.
1742-1773. Joseph Davis
1774-1824. Joseph Avery
HOLLAND, Mass. Sept. 13, 1765.
First Congregational Church.
1765-1818. Ezra Reeve
HOLLIS, N. H. Apr. 20, 1743.
First Congregational Church.
1743-1801. Daniel Emerson
HOLLISTON, Mass. Nov. 20, 1728.
First Congregational Church.
1724-1742. James Stone
1743-1784. Joshua Prentiss
HOPKINTON, R. I. Sept. 17, 1708.
Seventh Day Baptist Church.
(Churches at Westerly, Charlestown
and Hopkinton, R. I.),
1708-1720. John Maxson
1712-1719. Joseph Clark
1719-1748. John Maxson, Jr.
1739-1750. Joseph Maxson
1727-1773. Thomas Hiscox
1773-1793. Joshua Clark
HOPKINTON, Mass. Sept. 2, 1724.
First Congregational Church.
1724-1772. Samuel Barrett, Jr.
1772-1788. Elijah Fitch
HOPKINTON, Mass. 1750. X.
St. Paul's Church, Episcopal.
1748-1752. Roger Price
1752-1769. John Troutbec
HOPKINTON, N. H. Nov. 23, 1757.
First Congregational Church.
1757-1770. James Scales
1773-1786. Elijah Fletcher
HUBBARDSTON, Mass. Feb. 14, 1770
First Congregational Church.
Both Church and Parish became
Unitarian.
1768-1800. Nehemiah Parker
HUDSON, N. H. Nov. 30, 1737.
First Congregational Church.
1737-1796. Nathaniel Merrill
HUDSON, N. H. July 13, 1774.
First Presbyterian Church.
Congregational.
1774-1783. John Strickland
HULL. Mass. 1670. X.
First Congregational Church.
1670-1726. Zachariah Whitman
1725-1746. Ezra Carpenter
1753-1767. Samuel Veazie
1768-1772. Solomon Prentice
1773-1773. Elhanan Winchester, Jr.

HUNTINGTON, Ct. Feb. 12, 1723/4.
First Congregational Church.
1724-1776. Jedediah Mills
1773-1816. David Ely, D.D.
HUNTINGTON, Ct. 1740.
Episcopal Church.
1740-1754. Samuel Johnson, D.D.
1755-1787. Christopher Newton
HYANNIS, Mass. June 20, 1771.
First Baptist Church.
1771-1794. Enoch Eldredge
IPSWICH, Mass. June 1634.
First Congregational Parish.
1634-1637. Nathaniel Ward
1638-1655. John Norton
1638-1653. Nathaniel Rogers
1655-1685. Thomas Cobbett
1656-1704. William Hubbard
1656-1681. John Rogers
1686-1689. John Denison
1688-1745. John Rogers, Jr.
1703-1725. Jabez Fitch
1726-1775. Nathaniel Rogers
1752-1756. Timothy Symmes
1775-1806. Levi Frisbie
IPSWICH. Mass. July 22, 1747. M.
Second or South Congregational
Church.
1747-1764. John Walley
1765-1827. Joseph Dana, D.D.
IPSWICH, Mass. Nov. 15, 1749.
Linebrook Congregational Parish.
1749-1779. George Lesslie
JAMAICA PLAIN. Mass.
Dec. 11, 1770.
First Congregational Society.
Both Church and Parish became
Unitarian.
1772-1786. William Gordon, D.D.
JOHNSTON, R. I. May 30, 1771.
First Baptist Church.
1771-1802. Samuel Winsor, Jr.
KEENE, N. H. Oct. 18, 1738.
First Congregational Church.
1738-1747. Jacob Bacon
1753-1760. Ezra Carpenter
1761-1772. Clement Sumner
KENNEBUNK. Me. May 14, 1751.
First Congregational Parish.
Both Church and Parish became
Unitarian.
1751-1800. Daniel Little
KENNEBUNKPORT Me.
Nov. 4, 1730. X.
First Congregational Parish.
1719-1729. John Eveleth
1729-1738. Thomas Prentice

1741-1768. John Hovey
1771-1816. Silas Moody
KENSINGTON, Ct. Dec. 10, 1712.
First Congregational Church.
1712-1750. William Burnham
1756-1776. Samuel Clarke
KENSINGTON, N. H. Oct. 6, 1737.
First Congregational Church.
1737-1789. Jeremiah Fogg
KENT, Ct. Apr. 29, 1741.
First Congregational Church.
1741-1755. Cyrus Marsh
1758-1811. Joel Bordwell
KENT, Ct. 1761. X.
Episcopal Church.
1761-1766. Thomas Davies
KILLINGLY, Ct. Jan. 3, 1746/7. X.
Separatist Church.
1747-1762. Samuel Wadsworth
1764-1784. Eliphalet Wright
KILLINGWORTH, Ct.
Jan. 18, 1737/8.
First Congregational Church.
1738-1782. William Seward
KILLINGWORTH, Ct. 1764.
Episcopal Church.
1764-1767. Bela Hubbard, D.D.
KINGSTON, Mass. 1720.
First Congregational Parish.
Both Church and Parish became Unitarian.
1720-1741. Joseph Stacey
1742-1745. Thaddeus Maccarty
1746-1779. William Rand
KINGSTON, N. H. Sept. 23, 1725.
First Congregational Church.
1707-1717. Benjamin Choate
1725-1737. Ward Clark
1737-1760. Joseph Seccombe
1762-1771. Amos Toppan
KITTERY, Me. Sept. 25, 1682. X.
First Baptist Church.
1682-1683. William Scriven
KITTERY POINT, Me. Nov. 4, 1714.
First Congregational Church.
1699-1754. John Newmarch
1751-1791. Benjamin Stevens, D.D.
KITTERY, Me. 1729. X.
Gowell's Hill Congregational Church.
1729-1734. John Eveleth
KITTERY, Me. Sept. 19, 1750. X.
Spruce Creek Congregational Church.
1743-1743. Timothy Brown
1750-1778. Josiah Chase
LAKEVILLE, Mass. Oct. 6, 1725.
First Congregational Church.
1725-1753. Benjamin Ruggles
1761-1801. Caleb Turner

LAKEVILLE, Mass. Nov. 16, 1757. X
First Baptist Church, Christian.
1753-1793. Ebenezer Hinds
LANCASTER, Mass. 1653.
First Congregational Church.
The entire Church and Parish became Unitarian.
1654-1676. Joseph Rowlandson
1690-1697. John Whiting
1701-1704. Andrew Gardner
1708-1748. John Prentice
1748-1795. Timothy Harrington
LANESBOROUGH, Mass.
Mar. 28, 1764.
First Congregational Church.
1764-1822. Daniel Collins
LANESBOROUGH, Mass.
Oct. 6, 1767.
St. Luke's Church, Episcopal
1770-1793. Gideon Bostwick
LEBANON, Ct. Nov. 27, 1700.
First Congregational Church.
1699-1708. Joseph Parsons
1711-1722. Samuel Welles
1722-1776. Solomon Williams, D.D.
1776-1778. Solomon Williams, Jr.
LEBANON, Ct. Nov. 26, 1729.
Goshen Congregational Church.
1728-1766. Jacob Eliot
1767-1797. Timothy Stone
LEBANON, Me. June 23, 1765.
First Congregational Church.
1765-1812. Isaac Hasey
LEBANON, N. H. Sept. 27, 1768.
First Congregational Church.
1772-1817. Isaiah Potter
LEBANON, N. H. 1771. X.
First Baptist Church.
1771-1784. Jedediah Hibberd
LEBANON, Ct. May 31, 1775.
Exeter Congregational Parish.
1775-1812. John Gurley
LEDYARD, Ct. Oct. 1729. X.
First Congregational Church.
1729-1734. Ebenezer Punderson
1736-1746. Andrew Croswell
LEDYARD, Ct. 1734.
Episcopal Church.
1734-1753. Ebenezer Punderson
1754-1754. Aaron Cleaveland
LEDYARD, Ct. June 10, 1748.
Second Congregational Church.
1748-1772. Jacob Johnson
LEICESTER, Mass. Mar. 30, 1721.
First Congregational Church.
1721-1735. David Parsons
1736-1754. David Goddard

1754-1762. Joseph Roberts
1763-1794. Benjamin Conklin
LEICESTER, Mass. Sept. 28, 1738.
Greenville Baptist Church.
1738-1773. Thomas Green
1776-1782. Benjamin Foster, D.D.
LEMPSTER, N. H. Nov. 1761.
First Congregational Church.
Supplies to 1782.
LENOX, Mass. 1769.
First Congregational Church.
1770-1792. Samuel Munson
LEOMINSTER, Mass. Sept. 14, 1743.
First Congregational Society.
Both Church and Parish became
Unitarian.
1743-1758. John Rogers
1762-1814. Francis Gardner
LEOMINSTER, Mass. 1762. M.
Second Congregational Church.
Unitarian.
1762-1787. John Rogers
LEVERETT, Mass. July 16, 1767.
First Baptist Church.
(At North Leverett).
LEVERETT, Mass. Oct. 10, 1774.
First Congregational Church.
Supplies to 1784.
LEXINGTON, Mass. Oct. 21, 1696.
First Congregational Society.
Entire Church and Parish became
Unitarian.
1692-1697. Benjamin Estabrook
1698-1752. John Hancock
1734-1739. Ebenezer Hancock
1755-1805. Jonas Clarke
LINCOLN, Mass. Aug. 10, 1747.
First Congregational Church.
1748-1780. William Lawrence
LISBON, Ct. Dec. 10, 1723.
First or Newent Congregational
Church.
1723-1753. Daniel Kirtland
1756-1765. Peter Powers
1771-1782. Joel Benedict, D.D.
LITCHFIELD, Ct. June 19, 1723.
First Congregational Church.
1723-1752. Timothy Collins
1753-1810. Judah Champion
LITCHFIELD, Ct. 1755.
St. Michael's Episcopal Church.
1755-1760. Solomon Palmer
1761-1766. Thomas Davies
1766-1771. Solomon Palmer
LITCHFIELD, N. H. Dec. 9, 1741. X.
First Congregational Church.
1741-1744. Joshua Tufts
1765-1781. Samuel Cotton

LITTLE COMPTON, R. I. 1704.
First Congregational Church.
1697-1700. Eliphalet Adams
1701-1701. John Clarke
1704-1748. Richard Billings
1749-1785. Jonathan Ellis
1753-1763. Timothy Brown
LITTLETON, Mass. Dec. 25, 1717.
First Congregational Church.
Both Church and Parish became
Unitarian.
1717-1730. Benjamin Shattuck
1731-1782 Daniel Rogers
LONDONDERRY, N. H. 1735.
West or Second Presbyterian Church.
1736-1777. David McGregore
LONGMEADOW, Mass. Oct. 17, 1716
First Congregational Church.
1714-1782. Stephen Williams, D.D.
LUNENBURG, Mass.
May 15, 1728. X.
First Congregational Society.
Unitarian.
1728-1732. Andrew Gardner, Jr.
1733-1761. David Stearns
1762-1763. Samuel Payson
1764-1801. Zabdiel Adams
LYME, Ct. Jan. 22, 1729/30.
North Congregational or Hamburg
Parish.
1730-1794. George Beckwith
LYME, Ct. Dec. 25, 1746. X.
Separatist Church.
1746-1759. John Fuller
LYME, Ct. 1750. X.
First Baptist Church.
ca. 1750. Mr. Cooley
LYME, Ct. 1755. X.
Separatist Church at Grassy Hill.
1757-1799. Daniel Miner
LYME, N. H. May 22, 1771.
First Presbyterian Church.
Congregational.
1773-1810. William Conant
LYNDEBOROUGH, N. H.
Dec. 5, 1757.
First Congregational Church.
1757-1762. John Rand
1768-1809. Sewall Goodridge
LYNN, Mass. Aug. 1632.
First Congregational Church.
1632-1636. Stephen Bachiller
1636-1679. Samuel Whiting
1637-1655. Thomas Cobbett
1680-1682. Joseph Whiting
1680-1720. Jeremiah Shepard
1720-1761. Nathaniel Henchman
1763-1782. John Treadwell

LYNNFIELD CENTER, Mass.
    Aug. 17, 1720.
First Congregational Church.
    Unitarian-Universalist.
1720-1731. Nathaniel Sparhawk
1731-1755. Stephen Chase
1755-1777. Benjamin Adams
MACHIAS, Me. 1782.
First Congregational Church.
1771-1794. James Lyon
MADBURY, N. H. 1758.   X.
First Congregational Parish.
1758-1770. Samuel Hyde
1770-1772. Eliphaz Chapman
MADBURY, N. H. 1768.
Baptist Church.
MADISON, Ct. Nov. 25, 1707.
First Congregational Church
1707-1731. John Hart
1730-1731. Abraham Todd
1733-1791. Jonathan Todd
MALDEN, Mass. May 11, 1649.
First Congregational Parish.
    Universalist.
1650-1652. Marmaduke Matthews
1654-1705. Michael Wigglesworth
1663-1669. Benjamin Bunker
1674-1678. Benjamin Blakeman
1681-1686. Thomas Cheever
1709-1721. David Parsons
1721-1767. Joseph Emerson
1770-1785. Peter Thacher, D.D.
MANCHESTER, Mass. Nov. 7, 1716.
First Congregational Church
1716-1743. Ames Cheever
1744-1790. Benjamin Toppan
MANSFIELD, Ct. Oct. 18, 1710.
First Congregational Church
1710-1742. Eleazer Williams
1744-1787. Richard Salter, D.D.
MANSFIELD, Mass. Aug. 31, 1731. X.
First Congregational Parish.
    Unitarian.
1731-1761. Ebenezer White
1761-1808. Roland Green
MANSFIELD, Ct. Oct. 9, 1745.   X.
Separatist Church.
1743-1745. Oliver Grant
1746-1746. Thomas Marsh
1746-1775. John Hovey
MARBLEHEAD, Mass. Aug. 13, 1684.
First Congregational Church
1668-1724. Samuel Cheever
1716-1770. John Barnard
1762-1781. William Whitwell
MARBLEHEAD, Mass. 1715.
St. Michael's Episcopal Church.
1715-1717. William Shaw

1718-1727. David Mossom
1728-1738. George Pigot
1740-1749. Alexander Malcolm
1753-1762. Peter Bours
1763-1776. Joshua Wingate Weeks
MARBLEHEAD, Mass. Apr. 16, 1716.
Second Congregational Church.
The entire Church and Parish became
    Unitarian.
1716-1737. Edward Holyoke
1738-1771. Simon Bradstreet
1771-1802. Isaac Story
MARION, Mass. Oct. 13, 1703.
First Congregational Society.
1683-1687. Samuel Shiverick
1687-1709. Samuel Arnold, Jr.
1710-1768. Timothy Ruggles
1768-1792. Jonathan Moore
MARLBOROUGH, Mass. Oct. 3, 1666.
First Congregational Church.
1665-1701. William Brinsmead
1704-1731. Robert Breck
1733-1735. Benjamin Kent
1740-1778. Aaron Smith
MARLBOROUGH, Ct. May 21, 1749.
First Congregational Church.
1749-1761. Elijah Mason
1762-1773. Benjamin Dunning
1776-1797. David Huntington
MARSHFIELD, Mass. 1632.
First Congregational Church.
1641-1642. Richard Blinman
1642-1656. Edward Bulkley
1657-1693. Samuel Arnold
1696-1705. Edward Tompson
1707-1739. James Gardner
1740-1752. Samuel Hill
1753-1759. Joseph Green
1759-1763. Thomas Browne
1766-1816. William Shaw, D.D.
MARSHFIELD, Mass. 1738/9.
Second Congregational Church.
Both Church and Parish became
    Unitarian.
1739-1795. Atherton Wales
MARSHFIELD, Mass. 1745.   X.
Trinity Church, Episcopal.
1745-1775. Ebenezer Thompson
1775-1810. William Willard Wheeler
MARTHA'S VINEYARD, Mass.
    1642.   X.
Missionaries to the Indian Churches.
1642-1657. Thomas Mayhew, Jr.
1658-1681. Gov. Thomas Mayhew
1673-1689. John Mayhew
1694-1758. Experience Mayhew
1767-1806. Zachariah Mayhew

MASHPEE, Mass. Aug. 17, 1670. X.
Indian Congregational Church.
1670-1685. Richard Bourn
1685-1725. Native preachers.
1729-1742. Joseph Bourn
1742-1758. Native preachers.
1758-1807. Gideon Hawley
MASON, N. H. Oct. 13, 1772.
First Congregational Church.
1772-1781. Jonathan Searle
MATTAPOISETT, Mass.
July 28, 1736.
First Congregational Church.
1740-1768. Ivory Hovey, Jr.
1772-1836. Lemuel LeBaron
MEDFIELD, Mass. 1651.
First Congregational Parish.
Both Church and Parish became
Unitarian.
1651-1691. John Wilson, Jr.
1697-1745. Joseph Baxter
1745-1769. Jonathan Townsend
1770-1814. Thomas Prentiss, D.D.
MEDFORD, Mass. Feb. 11, 1713.
First Congregational Parish.
Both Church and Parish became
Unitarian.
1713-1722. Aaron Porter
1724-1778. Ebenezer Turrell
1774-1822. David Osgood, D.D.
MENDON, Mass. Dec. 1, 1669.
First Congregational Parish.
Both Church and Parish became
Unitarian.
1668-1668. John Rayner
1669-1675. Joseph Emerson
1680-1715. Grindall Rawson
1716-1768. Joseph Dorr
1769-1782. Joseph Willard
MERIDEN, Ct. Oct. 22, 1729.
First Congregational Church.
1729-1767. Theophilus Hall
1769-1786. John Hubbard
MERRIMAC, Mass. May 19, 1726.
Second Congregational Church in
Amesbury.
1726-1786. Pain Wingate
MERRIMAC, N. H. Sept. 5, 1772.
First Congregational Church.
1772-1821. Jacob Burnap, D.D.
METHUEN, Mass. Oct. 29, 1729.
First Congregational Church.
1729-1783. Christopher Sargeant
METHUEN, Mass. Apr. 16, 1766. M.
Second Congregational Church.
1772-1777. Eliphaz Chapman
MIDDLEBOROUGH, Mass. 1665. X.

Assawampsett Indian Congregational
Church.
Native preachers.
MIDDLEBOROUGH, Mass. 1665. X.
Nemasket Indian Congregational
Church.
Native preachers.
MIDDLEBOROUGH, Mass. 1665. X.
Titicut Indian Congregational Church.
Native preachers.
MIDDLEBOROUGH, Mass.
Dec. 26, 1694.
First Congregational Church.
1678-1695. Samuel Fuller
1696-1708. Thomas Palmer
1707-1744. Peter Thacher, D.D.
1744-1748. Thomas Weld
1748-1777. Sylvanus Conant
MIDDLEBOROUGH, Mass. 1744. M.
Second Congregational Parish.
1744-1748. Sylvanus Conant
MIDDLEBOROUGH, Mass.
Feb. 4, 1748/9. X.
Titicut Independent Separatist Church.
1748-1756. Isaac Bachus
MIDDLEBOROUGH, Mass.
May 11, 1749.
North Titicut Congregational Church.
1756-1785. Solomon Reed
MIDDLEBOROUGH, Mass. 1751. X.
Second Separatist Church.
1751-1756. James Mead
MIDDLEBOROUGH, Mass.
First Baptist Church. Jan. 16, 1756.
1756-1806. Isaac Bachus
MIDDLEBOROUGH, Mass.
Aug. 4, 1761.
Third Calvinistic Baptist Church.
1761-1763. Ebenezer Jones
1771-1789. Asa Hunt
MIDDLEFIELD, Ct. Oct. 10, 1747.
First Congregational Church.
1747-1756. Ebenezer Gould
1764-1770. Joseph Denison
1771-1785. Abner Benedict
MIDDLETON, Mass. Oct. 22, 1729.
First Congregational Parish.
Universalist.
1729-1756. Andrew Peters
1759-1791. Elias Smith
MIDDLETOWN, Ct. Nov. 4, 1668.
First Congregational Church.
1653-1660. Samuel Stow
1664-1684. Nathaniel Collins
1688-1713. Noadiah Russell
1715-1761. William Russell
1762-1806. Enoch Huntington

MIDDLETOWN, Ct. Oct. 28, 1747.
South Congregational Church.
1747-1792. Ebenezer Frothingham
MIDDLETOWN, Ct. 1750.
Christ Church, Episcopal.
1752-1760. Ichabod Camp
1764-1799. Abraham Jarvis, D.D.
MIDDLETOWN, Ct. Dec. 28, 1773.
Third Congregational Church.
1773-1826. Thomas Miner
MILFORD, Ct. Aug. 22, 1639.
First Congregational Church.
1639-1656. Peter Prudden
1660-1683. Roger Newton
1685-1738. Samuel Andrew
1737-1768. Samuel Whittelsey
1770-1781. Samuel Wales, D.D.
MILFORD, Mass. Apr. 5, 1741.
First Congregational Church.
1742-1792. Amariah Frost
MILFORD, Ct. May 1747.
Separatist Church.
1747-1774. Job Prudden
1775-1781. Josiah Sherman
MILFORD, Mass. May 31, 1749. X.
Separatist Church.
1749-1750. Samuel Hovey
MILLBURY, Mass. Sept. 10, 1747.
First Congregational Church.
1747-1760. James Wellman
1764-1792. Ebenezer Chaplin
MILLINGTON, Ct. Nov. 20, 1745.
First Congregational Church.
1736-1743. Timothy Symmes
1745-1766. Hobart Estabrook
1767-1773. Diodate Johnson
MILLIS, Mass. Oct. 7, 1714.
First Congregational Church.
1715-1722. David Deming
1724-1795. Nathan Bucknam
MILTON, Mass. Apr. 24, 1678.
First Congregational Parish.
Both Church and Parish became
Unitarian.
1681-1727. Peter Thacher
1728-1750. John Taylor
1751-1795. Nathaniel Robbins
MONROE, Ct. Dec. 14, 1764.
First Congregational Church.
1765-1808. Elisha Rexford
MONSON, Mass. June 23, 1762.
First Congregational Church.
1762-1772. Abishai Sabin
1773-1805. Jesse Ives
MONSON, Mass. 1768. X.
First Baptist Church.
1770-1813. Seth Clark
MONTAGUE, Mass. Nov. 22, 1752.

First Congregational Church.
1752-1805. Judah Nash
MONTEREY, Mass. Sept. 25, 1750.
First Congregational Church.
1750-1784. Adonijah Bidwell
MONTVILLE, Ct. Oct. 3, 1722.
First Congregational Church.
1722-1740. James Hillhouse
1739-1783. David Jewett
MONTVILLE, Ct. 1747. X.
Chesterfield Baptist Church.
1747-1750. Jedediah Hyde
1750-1779. Joshua Morse
MONTVILLE, Ct. Jan. 5, 1769. X.
Chesterfield Congregational Church.
1768-1772. James Beckwith
MORRIS, Ct. 1768.
First Congregational Church.
1772-1781. George Beckwith, Jr.
MOUNT CARMEL, Ct. Jan. 26, 1764.
First Congregational Church.
1768-1797. Nathaniel Sherman
NANTUCKET, Mass. 1728.
First Congregational Church.
1725-1750. Timothy White
1761-1766. Joseph Mayhew
1767-1796. Bezaleel Shaw
NASHUA, N. H. Dec. 16, 1685.
First Congregational Church.
1685-1702. Thomas Weld
1703-1708. Samuel Hunt
1708-1712. Samuel Parris
1720-1737. Nathaniel Prentice
1738-1746. Josiah Swan
1767-1818. Joseph Kidder
NATICK, Mass. 1660. X.
Indian Congregational Church.
1650-1690. John Eliot
1650-1668. John Eliot, Jr.
1685-1718. Daniel Gookin
NATICK, Mass. Dec. 3, 1729. X.
English and Indian Church.
Congregational.
1721-1752. Oliver Peabody
NATICK, Mass. Mar. 1753. X.
English and Indian Congregational
Church.
1753-1799. Stephen Badger
NEEDHAM, Mass. Mar. 20, 1720.
First Congregational Parish.
Entire Church and Parish became
Unitarian.
1720-1762. Jonathan Townsend
1764-1789. Stephen West, D.D.
NEW BEDFORD, Mass. 1708.
First Congregational Society.
Both Church and Parish became
Unitarian.

1708-1730. Samuel Hunt
1733-1749. Richard Pierce
1751-1759. Israel Cheever
1761-1803. Samuel West, D.D.
NEW BEDFORD, Mass. Oct. 7, 1774.
First Baptist Church.
ca. 1774. Zaccheus Tobey
NEW BOSTON, N. H. Sept. 6, 1768.
First Presbyterian Church.
1768-1803. Solomon Moor
NEW BRAINTREE, Mass.
                      Apr. 18, 1754.
First Congregational Church.
1754-1782. Benjamin Ruggles
NEW BRITAIN, Ct. Apr. 19, 1758.
First Congregational Church.
1757-1820. John Smalley, D.D.
NEWBURY, Mass. May 6, 1635.
First Congregational Church.
1635-1656. James Noyes
1635-1677. Thomas Parker
1663-1670. John Woodbridge
1675-1696. John Richardson
1696-1747. Christopher Toppan
1745-1792. John Tucker, D.D.
NEWBURY, Mass. 1682.   X.
First Baptist Church.
NEWBURY, Mass.
                    Feb. 27, 1711/2. X.
Queen Anne's Chapel, Episcopal.
1712-1714. Thomas Lambton
1715-1720. Henry Lucas
1722-1740. Matthias Plant
NEWBURY, Vt. Jan. 24, 1765.
First Congregational Church.
1765-1784. Peter Powers
NEWBURYPORT, Mass.
                    Jan. 12, 1725/6.
First Congregational Church.
Entire Church and Parish became
    Unitarian.
1725-1767. John Lowell
1768-1808. Thomas Cary
NEWBURYPORT, Mass. 1740.
St. Paul's Church, Episcopal.
1740-1753. Matthias Plant
1752-1803. Edward Bass, D.D.
NEWBURYPORT, Mass.
                    Jan. 3, 1745/6.
First Presbyterian Church.
1746-1776. Jonathan Parsons
NEWBURYPORT, Mass.
                    Apr. 17, 1761. X.
Fifth Congregational Parish.
1762-1784. Oliver Noble
NEWBURYPORT, Mass.
                    Mar. 4, 1768.

North Congregational Church.
1768-1773. Christopher Bridge Marsh
NEW CANAAN, Ct. June 20, 1733.
First Congregational Church.
1732-1741. John Eells
1741-1771. Robert Silliman
NEWCASTLE, N. H. Nov. 8, 1704.
First Congregational Church.
1703-1712. John Emerson
1712-1732. William Shurtleff
1732-1748. John Blunt
1748-1749. David Robinson
1750-1778. Stephen Chase
NEWCASTLE, Me. 1754.   X.
First Presbyterian Church.
    Congregational.
1753-1758. Alexander Boyd
NEW CHESHIRE, Ct. Sept. 27, 1749.
First Congregational Church.
1749-1751. Lyman Hall
NEW DURHAM, N. H.
                    Sept. 8, 1773. X.
First Congregational Church.
1773-1777. Nathaniel Porter, D.D.
NEWENT, Ct. 1746.   X.
Separatist Church of Lisbon.
1746-1753. Jeremiah Tracy, Jr.
1753-1764. Bliss Willoughby
NEW FAIRFIELD, Ct. Nov. 9, 1742.
First Congregational Church.
1742-1745. Samuel Buell, D.D.
1742-1753. Benjah Case
1758-1764. James Taylor
NEW FAIRFIELD, Ct. 1761.
Episcopal Church.
1761-1766. Thomas Davies
NEWFANE, Vt. June 30, 1774.
First Congregational Church.
1774-1811. Hezekiah Taylor
NEWFIELDS, N. H. 1730.   X.
First Congregational Church.
1730-1778. John Moody
NEW GLOUCESTER, Me.
                    Jan. 16, 1765.
First Congregational Church.
1765-1792. Samuel Foxcroft
NEW HARTFORD, Ct.
                    Oct. 10, 1739. X.
First Congregational Church.
1739-1794. Jonathan Marsh
NEW HAVEN, Ct. Aug. 22, 1639.
First Congregational Church.
1636-1642. Thomas James
1639-1640. Samuel Eaton
1639-1667. John Davenport
1644-1656. William Hooke
1659-1674. Nicholas Street
1673-1676. Joseph Taylor

1676-1682. John Harriman
1684-1714. James Pierpont
1715-1761. Joseph Noyes
1758-1787. Chauncy Whittelsey
NEW HAVEN, Ct. May 7, 1742.
United Congregational Society.
1751-1768. Samuel Bird
1769-1795. Jonathan Edwards, D.D.
NEW HAVEN, Ct. 1755.
Trinity Church, Episcopal.
1753-1762. Ebenezer Punderson
1763-1763. Solomon Palmer
1767-1791. Bela Hubbard, D.D.
NEW HAVEN, Ct. June 30, 1757.
Congregational Church in Yale
 College.
1755-1780. Naphtali Daggett, D.D.
NEW HAVEN, Ct. Feb. 3, 1773.
Fair Haven Congregational Church.
1772-1784. Allyn Mather
NEWINGTON, N. H. Nov. 16, 1715.
First Congregational Church.
1710-1783. Joseph Adams
NEWINGTON, Ct. Oct. 17, 1722.
First Congregational Church.
1722-1726. Elisha Williams
1726-1745. Simon Bachus
1747-1803. Joshua Belden
NEW IPSWICH, N. H. Oct. 21, 1760.
First Congregational Church.
1760-1809. Stephen Farrar
NEW LONDON, Ct. 1642.
First Congregational Church.
1650-1657. Richard Blinman
1659-1660. William Tompson, Jr.
1660-1660. Gershom Bulkley
1666-1683. Simon Bradstreet
1684-1685. Edward Oakes
1687-1707. Gurdon Saltonstall
1709-1753. Eliphalet Adams
1753-1756. William Adams
1757-1768. Mather Byles, Jr., D.D.
1769-1776. Ephraim Woodbridge
NEW LONDON, Ct. 1677. X.
Rogerene Baptist Church.
1677-1726. John Rogers
NEW LONDON, Ct. Sept. 25, 1725.
St. James's Church, Episcopal.
1732-1743. Samuel Seabury
1748-1778. Matthew Graves
NEW LONDON, Ct. Mar. 6, 1743. X.
Separatist Church.
1743-1744. James Davenport
NEW LONDON, Ct. 1770. X.
Indian Baptist Church.
NEWMARKET PLAINS, N. H.
Separatist Church. Dec. 1773. X.
1773-1797. Nathaniel Ewers

NEW MARLBOROUGH, Mass.
 Oct. 31, 1744.
First Congregational Church.
1744-1777. Thomas Strong
NEW MILFORD, Ct. Nov. 21, 1716.
First Congregational Church.
1712-1744. Daniel Boardman
1748-1800. Nathaniel Taylor
NEW MILFORD, Ct. 1755.
Episcopal Church.
1755-1760. Solomon Palmer
1761-1766. Thomas Davies
1767-1786. Richard Samuel Clarke
NEWPORT, R. I. 1640. X.
First Congregational Church.
1640-1642. Robert Lenthal
NEWPORT, R. I. 1644.
First Baptist Church.
1644-1676. John Clark
1648-1656. William Vaughan
1652-1682. Obadiah Holmes
1690-1694. Richard Dingley
1711-1732. William Peckham
1726-1732. John Comer
1731-1748. John Callender
1748-1771. Edward Upham
1771-1778. Erasmus Kelly
1785-1787. Benjamin Foster, D.D.
NEWPORT, R. I. 1655.
Second Baptist Church.
1655-1656. Thomas Baker
1656-1667. William Vaughan
1679-1700. John Harden
1700-1736. James Clark
1701-1750. Daniel Wightman
1731-1759. Nicholas Eyres
1759-1802. Gardner Thurston
NEWPORT, R. I. Dec. 23, 1671.
Third Baptist Church.
(First Sabbatarian Baptist Church in
 America.)
1671-1704. William Hiscox
1704-1717. William Gibson
1715-1737. Joseph Crandal
1754-1778. John Maxson
1775-1778. Ebenezer David
NEWPORT, R. I. Oct. 1700.
Trinity Church, Episcopal.
1700-1701. David Bethune
1701-1704. John Lockyer
1704-1750. James Honeyman
1750-1754. Jeremiah Leaming, D.D.
1754-1760. Thomas Pollen
1760-1771. Marmaduke Browne
1771-1779. George Bissett
1772-1783. William Willard Wheeler
1729-1731. George Berkeley, D.D.

NEWPORT, R. I. Nov. 3, 1720.
First Congregational Church.
1695-1745. Nathaniel Clap
1740-1743. Joseph Gardner
1744-1745. Jonathan Helyer
1746-1768. William Vinal
1770-1803. Samuel Hopkins, D.D.
NEWPORT, R. I. 1724. X.
Fourth Baptist Church.
1724-1728. Daniel White
NEWPORT, R. I. Apr. 11, 1728.
Second Congregational Church.
1728-1730. John Adams
1731-1755. James Searing
1754-1756. Samuel Fayerweather
1755-1776. Ezra Stiles, D.D., LL.D.
NEWPORT, R. I. 1758.
Moravian or United Brethren Church.
1758-1758. Richard Ultey
1758-1765 Thomas Yarrell
1763-1763. Frederick Smith
1766-1783. Louis Rusmyer
NEWPORT, R. I. Mar. 4, 1770. X.
Fifth Baptist Church.
(Existed only a year.)
NEWPORT, R. I. Apr. 14, 1771.
Sixth Baptist Church.
ca. 1771. Henry Dawson
NEW PRESTON, Ct. 1757.
First Congregational Church.
1757-1768. Noah Wadhams
1769-1806. Jeremiah Day
NEW PRESTON, Ct. 1764.
St. Andrew's Church, Episcopal.
1764-1766. Thomas Davies
NEW SALEM, Mass. Dec. 15, 1742.
The Congregational Society.
Entire Church and Parish became Unitarian.
1742-1792. Samuel Kendall
NEW SALEM, Mass. Jan. 24, 1772. X.
First Baptist Church.
1772-1790. Samuel Bigelow
NEW SHOREHAM, R. I. 1759.
First Baptist Church.
1759-1766. David Sprague
NEW SHOREHAM, R. I. Oct. 3, 1772.
First Congregational Church.
1700-1702. Samuel Niles
1756-1758. Samuel Maxwell
Supplies.
NEWTON, Mass. July 20, 1664.
1664-1668. John Eliot, Jr.
1672-1712. Nehemiah Hobart
1714-1757. John Cotton
1758-1780. Jonas Merriam

NEWTON, Mass. Jan. 17, 1750. X.
Separatist Church.
1750-1780. Jonathan Hyde
NEWTON, Mass. Jan. 17, 1753. X.
Separatist Church.
1753-1758. Nathan Ward
NEWTON, N. H. 1755. X.
First Baptist Church.
1755-1786. Walter Powers
NEWTON, N. H. Jan. 17, 1759. X.
First Congregational Church.
1759-1791. Jonathan Eames
NEWTOWN, Ct. Oct. 19, 1715.
First Congregational Church.
1711-1712. Phinehas Fish
1713-1724. Thomas Tousey
1725-1732. John Beach
1732-1743. Elisha Kent
1743-1776. David Judson
NEWTOWN, Ct. 1732.
Trinity Church, Episcopal.
1732-1782. John Beach
NEWTOWN, Ct. 1770. X.
Sandemanian Church.
NIANTIC, Ct. Nov. 25, 1724.
First Congregational Church.
1719-1761. George Griswold
NOBLEBOROUGH, Me. 1768. X.
First Baptist Church.
ca. 1768. Ebenezer Stearns
NORFOLK, Ct. Dec. 24, 1760.
First Congregational Church.
1761-1810. Ammi Ruhamah Robbins
NORTHAMPTON, Mass. June 18, 1661.
First Congregational Church.
1658-1669. Eleazer Mather
1662-1672. Joseph Eliot
1672-1729. Solomon Stoddard
1729-1750. Jonathan Edwards
1753-1777. John Hooker
NORTH ANDOVER, Mass. Oct. 24, 1645.
First Congregational Church.
Both Church and Parish became Unitarian.
1645-1647. John Woodbridge
1648-1697. Francis Dane
1682-1718. Thomas Barnard
1719-1757. John Barnard
1758-1807. William Symmes, D.D.
NORTH ATTLEBOROUGH, Mass. Nov. 12, 1712.
First Congregational Church.
1712-1715. Matthew Short
1715-1726. Ebenezer White
1727-1782. Habijah Weld

NORTH ATTLEBOROUGH, Mass.
North Baptist Church.   1769.
1767-1769. Abraham Bloss
1773-1787. Job Seamans
NORTHBOROUGH, Mass.
                    May 26, 1746.
First Congregational Church.
Entire Church and Parish became
  Unitarian.
1746-1767. John Martyn
1767-1816. Peter Whitney
NORTH BRANFORD, Ct.
                    May 18, 1724.
First Congregational Church.
1727-1772. Jonathan Merrick
1769-1808. Samuel Eells
NORTH BROOKFIELD, Mass.
                    May 28, 1752.
First Congregational Church.
1752-1776. Eli Forbes, D.D.
1776-1795. Joseph Appleton
NORTHFIELD, Mass. Aug. 1718.
First Congregational Society.
Both Church and Parish became
  Unitarian.
1718-1748. Benjamin Doolittle
1750-1794. John Hubbard
NORTHFORD, Ct. June 13, 1750.
First Congregational Church.
1749-1788. Warham Williams
NORTH GROTON, Ct.
Separatist Church. Nov. 14, 1751. X.
1751-1755. Nathaniel Brown, Jr.
ca. 1755. Park Allyn
ca. 1765. Peter Allyn
ca. 1775. Paul Allyn
NORTH GUILFORD, Ct.
                    June 15, 1725.
First Congregational Church.
1722-1746. Samuel Russell
1748-1765. John Richards
1766-1808. Thomas Wells Bray
NORTH HAMPTON, N. H.
                    Oct. 31, 1739.
First Congregational Church.
1739-1766. Nathaniel Gookin
1767-1774. Joseph Stacy Hastings
NORTH HAVEN, Ct. Nov. 1718.
First Congregational Church.
1718-1722. James Wetmore
1724-1760. Isaac Stiles
1760-1820. Benjamin Trumbull, D.D.
NORTH HAVEN, Ct. 1750.
Episcopal Church.
1755-1762. Ebenezer Punderson
1762-1786. Samuel Andrews
1763-1763. Solomon Palmer

NORTH KINGSTON, R. I. 1666.
First Baptist Church.
1660-1710. Thomas Baker
1710-1740. Richard Sweet
1750-1791. James Wightman
NORTH KINGSTON, R. I. 1707.
St. Paul's Episcopal Church.
1706-1709. Christopher Bridge
1717-1718. William Guy
1721-1757. James McSparran, D.D.
1760-1774. Samuel Fayerweather
NORTH KINGSTON, R. I. 1750. X.
Baptist Church.
ca. 1750. Benjamin Herrington
ca. 1760. Samuel Albro
NORTH MADISON, Ct. June 8, 1757.
First Congregational Church.
1757 1765. Richard Ely
NORTH PROVIDENCE, R. I.
First Baptist Church. June 23, 1765.
1765-1782. Ezekiel Angell
NORTH READING, Mass.
                    June 29, 1720. X.
First Congregational Parish.
  Universalist.
1720-1759. Daniel Putnam
1761-1822. Eliab Stone
NORTH STONINGTON, Ct.
                    Feb. 27, 1727.
North Congregational Church.
1727-1731. Ebenezer Russell
1732-1781. Joseph Fish
NORTH STONINGTON. Ct.
Separatist Church. Dec. 10, 1743. X.
1743-1749. Matthew Smith
1753-1755. Oliver Prentice
1759-1780. Nathan Avery
NORTH STONINGTON, Ct. 1743.
First Baptist Church.
1743-1763. Wait Palmer
1750-1764. Stephen Babcock
1768-1795. Eleazer Brown, 3rd.
NORTH STONINGTON, Ct. 1765.
Second Baptist Church.
1765-1818. Simeon Brown
NORTH WINDSOR, Ct.
                    Sept. 2, 1761. X.
First Congregational Church.
1766-1794. Theodore Hinsdale
NORTH YARMOUTH, Me.
                    Nov. 18, 1730.
First Congregational Church.
1727-1729. Samuel Seabury
1730-1735. Ammi Ruhamah Cutter
1736-1763. Nicholas Loring
1764-1769. Edward Brooks
1769-1809. Tristram Gilman

NORTON, Mass. Oct. 28, 1714.
First Congregational Parish.
Both Church and Parish became
 Unitarian.
1714-1749. Joseph Avery
1753-1791. Joseph Palmer
NORTON, Mass. Sept. 7, 1748. X.
Separatist Church.
1748-1761. William Carpenter
NORTON, Mass. Apr. 1, 1761. X.
First Baptist Church.
1761-1768. William Carpenter
1769-1786. William Nelson
NORWALK, Ct. 1652.
First Congregational Church.
1652-1693. Thomas Hanford
1695-1727. Stephen Buckingham
1727-1778. Moses Dickenson
1765-1772. William Tennent
NORWALK, Ct. 1737.
St. Paul's Episcopal Church.
1737-1744. Henry Caner, D.D.
1738-1745. Richard Caner
1747-1773. Joseph Lamson
1749-1751. John Ogilvie, D.D.
1751-1756. John Fowle
1756-1758. Ebenezer Dibblee, D.D.
1758-1776. Jeremiah Leaming, D.D.
NORWELL, Mass. Feb. 2, 1642.
First Congregational Parish.
Entire Church and Parish became
 Unitarian.
1645-1684. William Wetherell
1680-1689. Thomas Mighill
1694-1698. Deodat Lawson
1704-1750. Nathaniel Eells
1751-1754. Jonathan Dorby
1754-1811. David Barnes, D.D.
NORWICH, Ct. 1660.
First Congregational Church.
1660-1702. James Fitch
1696-1699. Henry Flynt
1699-1716. John Woodward
1716-1784. Benjamin Lord, D.D.
NORWICH, Ct. 1736.
Christ Church, Episcopal.
1736-1753. Ebenezer Punderson
1768-1823. John Tyler
NORWICH, Ct. Oct. 30, 1747. X.
Bean Hill Separatist Church.
1747-1757. Jedediah Hyde
1759-1762. John Fuller
1762-1805. Gamaliel Reynolds
NORWICH, Vt. Aug. 31, 1775. X.
First Congregational Church.
1775-1800. Lyman Potter
NORWOOD, Mass. June 23, 1736.
First Congregational Church.

1736-1774. Thomas Balch
1776-1812. Jabez Chickering
NOTTINGHAM, N. H.
 Nov. 3, 1742. X.
First Congregational Church.
1742-1749. Stephen Emery
1758-1770. Benjamin Butler
NOTTINGHAM, N. H. May 3, 1771.
First Baptist Church.
1771-1815. Samuel Shepard
OAKHAM, Mass. Aug. 28, 1766. X.
First Presbyterian Church.
The Parish became Congregational
 and later Unitarian.
1766-1773. John Strickland
OLD LYME, Ct. 1693.
First Congregational Church.
1666-1726. Moses Noyes
1720-1723. Samuel Pierpont
1729-1745. Jonathan Parsons
1746-1786. Stephen Johnson
OLD SAYBROOK, Ct. 1646.
First Congregational Church.
1636-1639. John Higginson
1645-1646. Thomas Peters
1646-1660. James Fitch
1661-1666. Jeremiah Peck
1670-1709. Thomas Buckingham
1709-1732. Azariah Mather
1736-1784. William Hart
ORFORD, N. H. Aug. 27, 1770.
First Presbyterian Church.
Became Congregational, 1786.
1771-1777. Oliver Noble
ORLEANS, Mass 1719. X.
First Congregational Church.
1718-1738. Samuel Osborn
1739-1772. Joseph Crocker
1772-1807. Jonathan Bascom
OTIS, Mass. 1772. X.
First Congregational Church.
1772-1775. George Throop
OXFORD, Mass. 1686. X.
French Protestant Church.
1686-1696. Daniel Bondet
1699-1704. James Labourie
OXFORD, Mass. Jan. 18, 1720/1.
First Congregational Church.
1721-1761. John Campbell
1764-1782. Joseph Bowman
OXFORD, Ct. Jan. 9, 1745/6.
First Congregational Church.
1745-1763. Jonathan Lyman
1764-1779. David Brownson
PALMER, Mass. Dec. 1730.
First Presbyterian Church.
 Congregational.
1730-1748. John Harvey

1753-1756. Robert Burns
1761-1811. Moses Baldwin
PAWTUCKET, R. I. 1754.
First Baptist Church.
1754-1759. Maturin Ballou
PAXTON, Mass. Sept. 3, 1767.
First Congregational Church.
1767-1769. Silas Bigelow
1770-1782. Alexander Thayer
PEABODY, Mass. Sept. 23, 1713.
First Congregational Church.
1713-1756. Benjamin Prescott
1759-1792. Nathan Holt
PELHAM, Mass. 1743. X.
First Presbyterian Church.
The Parish became Congregational and later Unitarian.
1742-1755. Robert Abercrombie
1760-1771. Richard Crouch Graham
PELHAM, N. H. Nov. 13, 1751.
First Congregational Church.
1751-1765. James Hobbs
1765-1792. Amos Moody
PEMBROKE, Mass. Dec. 3, 1712.
First Congregational Parish.
Entire Church and Parish became Unitarian.
1712-1753. Daniel Lewis
1754-1786. Thomas Smith
PEMBROKE, N. H. Mar. 1, 1736/7.
First Congregational Church.
1737-1767. Aaron Whitman
1768-1775. Jacob Emery
PEMBROKE, N. H. Dec. 3, 1760. M.
First Presbyterian Church.
Became Congregational, 1807.
1760-1776. Daniel Mitchell
PEPPERELL, Mass. Jan. 29, 1746/7.
First Congregational Parish.
Both Church and Parish became Unitarian.
1746-1775. Joseph Emerson
PERU, Mass. June 1770.
First Congregational Church.
1772-1776. Stephen Tracy
PETERBOROUGH, N. H. Nov. 26, 1766.
The Congregational Society.
Began as a Presbyterian Church, then became Congregational, and finally both Church and Parish became Unitarian.
1766-1772. John Morrison
PETERSHAM, Mass. Oct. 1738.
First Congregational Society.
Entire Church and Parish became Unitarian.
1738-1777. Aaron Whitney

PETERSHAM, Mass. 1768. X.
First Baptist Church.
Supplies until 1778.
PIERMONT, N. H. 1771.
First Congregational Church.
1776-1802. John Richards
PITTSFIELD, Mass. Feb. 7, 1764.
First Congregational Church.
1763-1810. Thomas Allen
PITTSFIELD, Mass. 1772.
First Baptist Church.
1772-1798. Valentine Rathbun
PLAINFIELD, Ct. Jan. 3, 1705/6.
First Congregational Church.
1699-1748. Joseph Coit
1748-1761. David Sherman Rowland
1769-1777. John Fuller
PLAINFIELD, Ct. Sept. 11, 1746. M.
Separatist Church.
United with the First Church, 1769.
1746-1755. Thomas Stevens
1758-1769. Alexander Miller
PLAINFIELD, N. H. July 10. 1765.
First Congregational Church.
1773-1790. Abraham Carpenter
PLAISTOW, N. H. Nov. 4, 1730. X.
First Congregational Church.
1730-1764. James Cushing
1765-1801. Gyles Merrill
PLYMOUTH, Mass. Dec. 11, 1620.
First Congregational Parish.
Both Church and Parish became Unitarian.
(This is the first church to be planted in New England, and is today the oldest Protestant church with a continuous history in the Western Hemisphere.)
1620-1629. William Brewster
1629-1636. Ralph Smith
1631-1634. Roger Williams
1636-1654. John Ravner
1638-1641. Charles Chauncy
1669-1699. John Cotton, Jr.
1699-1723. Ephraim Little
1724-1755. Nathaniel Leonard
1760-1799. Chandler Robbins, D.D.
PLYMOUTH, Mass. Nov. 8, 1738.
Manomet Congregational Church.
1738-1749. Jonathan Ellis
1753-1757. Elijah Packard
1770-1803. Ivory Hovey
PLYMOUTH, Ct. May 7, 1740.
First Congregational Church.
1740-1764. Samuel Todd
1765-1785. Andrew Storrs

PLYMOUTH, Mass. Nov. 7, 1744. M.
Third Congregational Church.
1744-1748. Thomas Frink
1749-1776. Jacob Bacon
PLYMOUTH, Ct. 1749.
Episcopal Church.
1749-1755. Richard Mansfield, D.D.
1759-1764. James Scovill
1774-1778. James Nichols
PLYMOUTH, N. H. Apr. 16, 1764.
First Congregational Church.
1765-1798. Nathan Ward
PLYMPTON, Mass. Oct. 27, 1698.
First Congregational Church.
1698-1732. Isaac Cushman
1731-1776. Jonathan Parker
1775-1796. Ezra Sampson
POMFRET, Ct. Oct. 26, 1715.
First Congregational Church.
1713-1753. Ebenezer Williams
1753-1756. Noadiah Russell
1756-1802. Aaron Putnam
PORTLAND, Me. Mar. 8, 1726/7.
First Congregational Parish.
Both Church and Parish became Unitarian.
1674-1690. George Burroughs
1721-1722. Jonathan Pierpont
1727-1795. Thomas Smith
1764-1814. Samuel Deane, D.D.
PORTLAND, Ct. Oct. 25, 1721.
First Congregational Church.
1721-1731. Daniel Newell
1733-1766. Moses Bartlett
1767-1811. Cyprian Strong, D.D.
PORTLAND, Me. Nov. 4, 1763.
St. Paul's Church, Episcopal.
1763-1775. John Wiswell
PORTSMOUTH. N. H. 1640. X.
Episcopal Church.
1640-1643. Richard Gibson
PORTSMOUTH, N. H. July 12, 1671.
First Congregational Church.
1658-1697. Joshua Moody
1699-1723. Nathaniel Rogers
1725-1746. Jabez Fitch
1747-1774. Samuel Langdon, D.D.
PORTSMOUTH, N. H. Mar. 23, 1715.
Second Congregational Church.
Both Church and Parish became Unitarian.
1715-1732. John Emerson
1733-1747. William Shurtleff
1749-1751. Job Strong
1752-1806. Samuel Haven, D.D.
PORTSMOUTH, N. H. 1734.
Queens' Chapel, Episcopal.
(Now St. John's Church).

1736-1772. Arthur Browne
1755-1760. Marmaduke Browne
PORTSMOUTH, N. H.
Oct. 14, 1758. X.
Independent Church, Baptist.
1761-1770. Samuel Drown
PORTSMOUTH, N. H. 1764. X.
Sandemanian Church.
1764-1771. Robert Sandeman
POWNAL, Vt. 1772.
First Baptist Church.
1772-1774. Benjamin Gardner
POWNALBOROUGH, Me. 1763. X.
St. John's Church, Episcopal.
1763-1775. Jacob Bailey
PRESTON, Ct. Nov. 16, 1698.
First Congregational Church.
1697-1744. Salmon Treat
1744-1781. Asher Rosseter
PRESTON, Ct. Oct. 27, 1726. X.
Fifth Congregational Church in Norwich.
1726-1782. Jabez Wight
PRESTON, Ct. Mar. 17, 1747. X.
Baptist Church.
1747-1802. Paul Parke
PRESTON, Ct. 1752. X.
Separatist Church.
1752-1765. Jonathan Story
PRINCETON, Mass.
Aug. 12, 1764. X.
First Congregational Church.
Both Church and Parish became Unitarian.
1767-1776. Timothy Fuller
PROSPECT, Ct. 1770. X.
Separatist Church.
1770-1780. Benjamin Beach
PROVIDENCE. R. I. 1639.
First Baptist Church in America.
1639-1643. Roger Williams
1639-1659. Ezekiel Holliman
1642-1650. Chad Brown
1647-1669. William Wickendon
1654-1700. Gregory Dexter
1681-1718. Pardon Tillinghast
1719-1726. Ebenezer Jenkes
1726-1732. James Brown
1733-1758. Samuel Winsor
1733-1740. Thomas Burlingham
1759-1771. Samuel Winsor, Jr.
1771-1791. James Manning, D.D.
PROVIDENCE, R. I. 1654. X.
Second Baptist Church.
1645-1715. Thomas Olney

PROVIDENCE, R. I. 1720.
First Congregational Church.
Both Church and Parish became Unitarian.
1728-1747. Josiah Cotton
1752-1758. John Bass
1763-1774. David Sherman Rowland
PROVIDENCE, R. I. 1722.
King's Church, Episcopal.
(Now St. John's Cathedral.)
1723-1727. George Pigot
1728-1729. Joseph O'Hara
1730-1736. Arthur Browne
1739-1754. John Checkley
1755-1776. John Graves
PROVIDENCE, R. I. 1743.
Beneficent Congregational Church.
1743-1803. Joseph Snow
PROVIDENCE, R. I. 1752.
Baptist Church.
1752-1754. Maturin Ballou
PROVINCETOWN, Mass. 1714. X.
First Congregational Church.
1717-1741. Samuel Spear
1773-1811. Samuel Parker
PUTNAM, Ct. Oct. 19, 1715.
First Congregational Church.
1715-1741. John Fiske
1746-1753. Perley Howe
1753-1775. Aaron Brown
QUINCY, Mass. Sept. 17, 1639.
First Congregational Society.
Entire Church and Parish became Unitarian.
1636-1637. John Wheelwright
1639-1659. William Tompson
1640-1668. Henry Flynt
1672-1708. Moses Fiske
1709-1726. Joseph Marsh
1726-1744. John Hancock
1745-1753. Lemuel Briant
1755-1800. Anthony Wibird
QUINCY, Mass. Apr. 22, 1704.
Christ Church, Episcopal.
1702-1704. William Barclay
1711-1713. Thomas Eager
1715-1715. Henry Lucas
1727-1763. Ebenezer Miller, D.D.
1763-1777. Edward Winslow
RANDOLPH, Mass. May 28, 1731.
First Congregational Church.
1731-1750. Elisha Eaton
1752-1791. Moses Taft
RAYNHAM, Mass. Oct. 19, 1731.
First Congregational Church.
1731-1765. John Wales
1766-1812. Perez Fobes, LL.D.

READING, Mass. Feb. 8, 1770.
First Congregational Church.
1770-1782. Thomas Haven
REDDING, Ct. 1732.
Episcopal Church.
1732-1782. John Beach
REDDING, Ct. Mar. 21, 1733.
First Congregational Church.
1733-1749. Nathaniel Hunn
1753-1810. Nathaniel Bartlett
REHOBOTH, Mass. Nov. 29, 1721.
First Congregational Church.
1721-1757. David Turner
1759-1799. Robert Rogerson
REHOBOTH, Mass. Jan. 20, 1732.
First Baptist or Oak Swamp Church.
1732-1734. John Comer
1736-1742. Nathaniel Millard
1745-1749. Samuel Maxwell
1749-1768. Richard Round.
REHOBOTH, Mass. July 13, 1743. X.
Second Baptist or Round's Church.
1743-1749. Richard Round
REHOBOTH, Mass. Aug. 3, 1748. X.
Separatist Church.
1748-1748. John Paine
REHOBOTH, Mass. 1748. X.
Elder Peck's Baptist Church.
1748-1788. Samuel Peck
REHOBOTH, Mass. Feb. 8, 1753.
Third Baptist Church.
1755-1781. Daniel Martin
1753-1793. Nathan Pierce
REHOBOTH, Mass. 1753. X.
Fourth Baptist Church.
REHOBOTH, Mass. Nov. 10, 1762. X.
Fifth Baptist Church.
1762-1804. John Hix
1773-1804. Jacob Hix
REHOBOTH, Mass. Sept. 4, 1771. X.
Sixth Baptist Church.
1771-1778. Elhanan Winchester
REHOBOTH, Mass. Jan. 20, 1773. X.
Seventh Baptist Church.
1773-1809. Jacob Hix
REVERE, Mass. Oct. 19, 1715. X.
First Congregational Church.
Both Church and Parish became Unitarian.
1715-1749. Thomas Cheever
1748-1754. William McClenachen
1757-1801. Phillips Payson, D.D.
RICHMOND, Mass. 1765.
First Congregational Church.
1767-1774. Job Swift, D.D.
RICHMOND, R. I. 1723.
First Baptist Church.
ca. 1771. John Pendleton

RICHMOND, N. H. 1770. X.
First Baptist Church.
1770-1790. Maturin Ballou
RICHMOND, Mass. 1770. X.
First Baptist Church.
Supplies.
RIDGEBURY, Ct. Jan. 18, 1769.
First Congregational Church.
1769-1804. Samuel Camp
RIDGEFIELD, Ct. 1712.
First Congregational Church.
1713-1738. Thomas Hawley
1739-1778. Jonathan Ingersoll
RINDGE, N. H. Nov. 6, 1765.
First Congregational Church.
1765-1780. Seth Deane
ROCHESTER, N. H. Sept. 18, 1737.
First Congregational Church.
1737-1760. Amos Main
1760-1764. Samuel Hill
1766-1775. Avery Hall
1776-1825. Joseph Haven
ROCHESTER, Mass. 1753.
First Congregational Church.
1748-1790. Thomas West
ROCKINGHAM, Vt. Oct. 12, 1773. X.
First Congregational Church.
1773-1809. Samuel Whiting
ROCKPORT, Mass. Feb. 13, 1755.
First Congregational Church.
1755-1805. Ebenezer Cleaveland
ROCKY HILL, Ct. June 7, 1727.
First Congregational Church.
1727-1764. Daniel Russell
1765-1776. Burrage Merriam
ROWE, Mass. 1770.
First Congregational Church.
Both Church and Parish became Unitarian.
1770-1781. Cornelius Jones
ROWLEY, Mass. Dec. 3, 1639.
First Congregational Church.
1639-1661. Ezekiel Rogers
1639-1641. John Miller
1648-1650. John Brock
1651-1696. Samuel Phillips
1682-1732. Edward Payson
1729-1774. Jedediah Jewett
ROXBURY, Mass. 1631/2.
First Congregational Church.
Entire Church and Parish became Unitarian.
1632-1641. Thomas Welde
1632-1690. John Eliot
1650-1674. Samuel Danforth
1688-1750. Nehemiah Walter
1718-1725. Thomas Walter
1750-1752. Oliver Peabody
1753-1775. Amos Adams
ROXBURY, Ct. 1740.
Episcopal Church.
1740-1760. John Beach
1761-1767. Thomas Davies
ROXBURY, Ct. June 1744.
First Congregational Church.
1744-1794. Thomas Canfield
ROYALSTON, Mass. Oct. 13, 1766.
First Congregational Church.
1768-1818. Joseph Lee
ROYALSTON, Mass. May 5, 1768.
First Baptist Church.
1770-1786. Whitman Jacobs
RUMNEY, N. H. Oct. 21, 1767. X.
First Congregational Parish.
1767-1771. Thomas Niles
RUTLAND, Mass. June 7, 1720.
First Congregational Church.
1721-1723. Joseph Willard
1727-1740. Thomas Frink
1742-1792. Joseph Buckminster
RUTLAND, Vt. Oct. 20, 1773.
First or West Congregational Church.
1773-1784. Benajah Roots
RYE, N. H. July 10, 1726.
First Congregational Church.
1726-1734. Nathaniel Morrill
1736-1789. Samuel Parsons
SACO, Me. 1640. X.
First Congregational Parish.
1640-1646. Thomas Jenner
1653-1653. George Barlow
1653-1659. Robert Booth
1661-1675. Seth Fletcher
1685-1688. William Milburne
SACO, Me. Oct. 13, 1762. X.
First Congregational Church.
1762-1798. John Fairfield
SALEM, Mass. Aug. 6, 1629.
First Congregational Society.
Entire Church and Parish became Unitarian.
1629-1630. Francis Higginson
1629-1634. Samuel Skelton
1631-1635. Roger Williams
1636-1641. Hugh Peters
1637-1640. John Fiske
1640-1659. Edward Norris
1660-1708. John Higginson
1683-1717. Nicholas Noyes
1714-1717. George Curwin
1718-1735. Samuel Fiske
1736-1755. John Sparhawk
1755-1776. Thomas Barnard
1772-1779. Asa Dunbar

SALEM, Mass. Nov. 14, 1718.
Second Congregational Church.
Entire Church and Parish became Unitarian.
1719-1727. Robert Stanton
1728-1736. William Jennison
1737-1788. James Diman
SALEM, Ct. 1719.
First Congregational Church.
1719-1749. Joseph Lovett
1775-1776. David Huntington
SALEM, Mass. May 4, 1735.
Third Congregational Church.
1736-1745. Samuel Fiske
1745-1762. Dudley Leavitt
1763-1766. John Huntington
1769-1784. Nathaniel Whittaker
SALEM, Mass. Oct. 8, 1738.
St. Peter's Episcopal Church.
1738-1746. Charles Brockwell
1747-1780. William McGilchrist
1771-1774. Robert Boucher Nichols
SALEM, N. H. Jan. 16, 1740.
First Congregational Church.
1740-1798. Abner Bayley
SALEM, Mass. Mar. 30, 1772. M.
North Congregational Church.
Entire Church and Parish became Unitarian.
1773-1814. Thomas Barnard, D.D.
SALEM, Mass. Feb. 14, 1775.
South Congregational Church.
1774-1814. Daniel Hopkins, D.D.
SALISBURY, Mass. 1639. X.
First or East Congregational Church.
1639-1662. William Worcester
1662-1679. John Wheelwright
1682-1696. James Alling
1696-1752. Caleb Cushing
1751-1809. Edmund Noyes
SALISBURY, Ct. Nov. 22, 1744.
First Congregational Church.
1744-1788. Jonathan Lee
SALISBURY, Ct. 1761.
Episcopal Church.
1761-1766. Thomas Davies
SALISBURY, N. H. Nov. 17, 1773.
First Congregational Church.
1773-1791. Jonathan Searle
SANBORNTON. N. H. Nov. 13, 1771.
First Congregational Church.
1771-1806. Joseph Woodman
SANDISFIELD, Mass. Feb. 24, 1756.
First Congregational Church.
1756-1761. Cornelius Jones
1766-1798. Eleazer Storrs
SANDOWN, N. H. Nov. 28, 1759.

First Congregational Church.
1759-1780. Josiah Cotton
SANDWICH, Mass. 1638.
First Congregational Parish. Unitarian.
1638-1654. William Leveritch
1658-1688. John Smith
1691-1722. Rowland Cotton
1722-1746. Benjamin Fessenden
1749-1784. Abraham Williams
SANDWICH, Mass. 1658. X.
Indian Congregational Church.
1658-1676. Capt. Thomas Tupper
1676-1706. Thomas Tupper, Jr.
1706-1750. Eldad Tupper
1739-1787. Elisha Tupper
SANDWICH, Mass. June 18, 1735. X.
Second Congregational Church.
1735-1749. Francis Wooster, Jr.
SANFORD, Me. Sept. 16, 1772.
First Baptist Church.
1772-1782. Pelatiah Tingley
SAUGUS, Mass. Dec. 5, 1732.
First Congregational Parish.
Unitarian-Universalist.
1739-1748. Edward Cheever
1750-1803. Joseph Roby
SAYBROOK, Ct. 1760.
First Baptist Church.
ca. 1760. Eliphalet Lester
SCARBOROUGH, Me. Sept. 1727.
First Congregational Church.
1719-1720. Hugh Campbell
1722-1725. Hugh Henry
1728-1759. William Tompson
1762-1775. Thomas Peirce
1775-1831. Thomas Lancaster
SCITUATE, Mass. Jan. 18, 1634.
First Congregational Parish.
Both Church and Parish became Unitarian.
1634-1639. John Lothrop
1640-1641. Peter Saxton
1640-1654. Charles Chauncy
1654-1659. Henry Dunster
1660-1678. Nicholas Baker
1691-1705. Jeremiah Cushing
1707-1723. Nathan Pitcher
1724-1761. Shearjashub Bourne
1763-1780. Ebenezer Grosvenor
SCITUATE, R. I. 1727.
First Baptist Church.
1727-1744. Samuel Fiske
1737-1740. David Sprague
1738-1755. James Colvin
1759-1768. Maturin Ballou
1762-1792. Reuben Hopkins

SCOTLAND, Me. 1732.
First Congregational Church.
1732-1741. Joseph Moody
1742-1751. Samuel Chandler
1754-1794. Samuel Lankton
SCOTLAND, Ct. Oct. 22, 1735.
First Congregational Church.
1735-1771. Ebenezer Devotion
1772-1804. James Cogswell, D.D.
SCOTLAND, Ct. May 17, 1749. X.
Separatist Church.
1749-1807. John Palmer
SEABROOK, N. H. Nov. 1764. X.
First Presbyterian Church.
Congregational.
1765-1775. Samuel Perley
SHAFTSBURY, Vt. 1768.
First Baptist Church in Vermont.
ca. 1768. Bliss Willoughby
ca. 1774. Ebenezer Willoughby
SHARON, Ct. Apr. 30, 1740.
First Congregational Church.
1740-1747. Peter Pratt
1748-1754. John Searle
1754-1806. Cotton Mather Smith
SHARON, Mass. Jan. 25, 1741/2.
First Congregational Parish.
Unitarian.
1741-1797. Philip Curtis
SHARON, Ct. 1761.
Episcopal Church.
1761-1766. Thomas Davies
SHEFFIELD, Mass. Oct. 22, 1735.
First Congregational Church.
1735-1765. Jonathan Hubbard
1771-1785. John Keep
SHELBURNE, Mass. 1770.
First Congregational Church.
1773-1788. Robert Hubbard
SHERBORN, Mass. Mar. 26, 1685.
First Congregational Church.
Both Church and Parish became Unitarian.
1680-1718. Daniel Gookin, Jr.
1712-1731. Daniel Baker
1734-1758. Samuel Porter
1759-1770. Samuel Locke, D.D.
1770-1816. Elijah Brown
SHERMAN, Ct. Mar. 28, 1744.
First Congregational Church.
1744-1746. Thomas Lewis
1751-1779. Elijah Sill
SHIRLEY, Mass. Feb. 25, 1753.
First Congregational Church.
Both Church and Parish became Unitarian.
1762-1819. Phinehas Whitney
SHREWSBURY, Mass. Dec. 4, 1723.

First Congregational Church.
1723-1760. Job Cushing
1762-1824. Joseph Sumner, D. D.
SHUTESBURY, Mass. Oct. 27, 1742.
First Congregational Church.
1742-1778. Abraham Hill
SIMSBURY, Ct. Mar. 3, 1696/7.
First Congregational Church.
1682-1686. Samuel Stow
1687-1691. Edward Tompson
1691-1695. Seth Shove
1695-1710. Dudley Woodbridge
1710-1742. Timothy Woodbridge
1744-1754. Gideon Mills
1756-1772. Benajah Roots
1774-1778. Seth Sage
SIMSBURY, Ct. 1740.
St. Andrew's Episcopal Church.
1740-1743. Ebenezer Thompson
1747-1777. William Gibbs
1763-1786. Roger Viets
SMITHFIELD, R. I. 1685. X.
Baptist Church.
1685-1741. Jonathan Sprague
SMITHFIELD, R. I. 1700.
First Baptist Church of Smithfield and Gloucester.
1700-1735. Peter Place
1718-1750. Joshua Winsor
1756-1811. John Winsor
SOMERS, Ct. Mar. 15, 1727.
First Congregational Church.
1727-1747. Samuel Allis
1748-1761. Freegrace Leavitt
1773-1801. Charles Backus, D.D.
SOMERS, Ct. 1769.
Separatist Church.
1769-1774. Mr. Ely
SOMERSWORTH, N. H.
Oct. 28, 1730.
First Congregational Church.
1730-1790. James Pike
SOUTHAMPTON, Mass. June 8, 1743
First Congregational Church.
1743-1803. Jonathan Judd
SOUTH BERWICK, Me. June 4, 1702
First Congregational Church.
1702-1703. John Wade
1707-1755. Jeremiah Wise
1756-1777. Jacob Foster
SOUTHBOROUGH, Mass.
Oct. 21, 1730. X.
First Congregational Parish.
Unitarian.
1730-1781. Nathan Stone
SOUTH BRITAIN, Ct. May 24, 1769.
First Congregational Church.
1768-1790. Jehu Minor

SOUTHBURY, Ct. Jan. 17, 1732/3.
First Congregational Church.
1733-1774. John Graham
1767-1768. Ichabod Lewis
1766-1812. Benjamin Wildman
SOUTH CANAAN, Ct. Mar. 1741.
First Congregational Church.
1740-1752. Elisha Webster
1752-1803. Daniel Farrand
SOUTH COVENTRY, Ct. 1712.
First Congregational Church.
1714-1752. Joseph Meacham
1759-1761. Oliver Noble
1763-1794. Joseph Huntington, D.D.
SOUTH HADLEY, Mass.
Oct. 3, 1733.
First Congregational Church.
1733-1741. Grindall Rawson
1742-1783. John Woodbridge
SOUTH HAMPTON, N. H.
Feb. 22, 1743. X.
First Congregational Church.
1743-1762. William Parsons
1763-1801. Nathaniel Noyes
SOUTHINGTON, Ct. Nov. 13, 1726.
First Congregational Church.
1724-1726. Daniel Buck
1726-1755. Jeremiah Curtis
1756-1774. Benjamin Chapman
SOUTHINGTON, Ct. 1750. X.
First Baptist Church.
1750-1784. John Merriman
SOUTH KILLINGLY, Ct. 1746.
Breakneck Hill Congregational Chh.
1746-1755. Nehemiah Barker
1760-1763. Eden Burroughs, D.D.
1764-1777. Eliphalet Huntington
SOUTH KINGSTON, R. I. 1725. X.
First Baptist Church.
1725-1750. Daniel Everit
SOUTH KINGSTON, R. I.
May 17, 1732.
First Congregational Church.
1732-1791. Joseph Torrey
SOUTH KINGSTON, R. I. ca. 1750.
Baptist Church.
ca. 1750. James Rogers
SOUTH PORTLAND, Me.
Nov. 10, 1734.
First Congregational Church.
1730-1754. Benjamin Allen
1756-1797. Ephraim Clark
SOUTH PORTLAND, Me.
Nov. 15, 1739. X.
First Presbyterian Church.
1739-1742. William McClanachan
SOUTHWICK, Mass. Aug. 17, 1773.
The Congregational Church.

1773-1786. Abel Forward
SOUTH WINDSOR, Ct. May 28, 1698
First Congregational Church.
1694-1758. Timothy Edwards
1755-1783. Joseph Perry
SPENCER, Mass. May 17, 1744.
First Congregational Church.
1744-1772. Joshua Eaton
1773-1826. Joseph Pope
SPRAGUE, Ct. 1766.
The Congregational Society.
1766-1770. Jesse Ives
SPRINGFIELD, Mass. 1637.
First Congregational Church.
1637-1652. George Moxon
1661-1692. Pelatiah Glover
1694-1733. Daniel Brewer
1734-1784. Robert Breck
STAFFORD, Ct. May 22, 1723.
First Congregational Church.
1723-1731. John Graham
1734-1740. Seth Paine
1744-1756. Eli Colton
1757-1807. John Willard, D.D.
STAFFORD, Ct. June 5, 1755.
First Baptist Church.
1755-1765. Noah Alden
STAMFORD, Ct. May 1641.
First Congregational Church.
1641-1644. Richard Denton
1644-1694. John Bishop
1692-1731. John Davenport
1732-1746. Ebenezer Wright
1746-1776. Noah Wells, D.D.
STAMFORD, Ct. 1747.
Episcopal Church.
1748-1799. Ebenezer Dibblee, D.D.
STAMFORD, Ct. 1773.
First Baptist Church.
1773-1775. Ebenezer Ferris
1775-1776. Thomas Ustwick
STANDISH, Me. May 11, 1769.
First Congregational Parish.
Unitarian.
1768-1783. John Tompson
STANWICH, Ct. June 17, 1735.
First Congregational Church.
1735-1767. Benjamin Strong
1773-1794. William Seward
STERLING, Mass. Dec. 19, 1742.
First Congregational Society.
Entire Church and Parish became
Unitarian.
1744-1774. John Mellen
STERLING, Ct. Feb. 13, 1772. X.
Nazareth Congregational Society.
1772-1782. Solomon Morgan

STERLING, Mass. Nov. 1774. X.
Second Congregational Society.
1774-1784. John Mellen
STOCKBRIDGE, Mass. Oct. 18, 1734.
First Congregational Church.
1734-1749. John Sergeant
1751-1758. Jonathan Edwards
1759-1819. Stephen West, D.D.
STONEHAM, Mass. July 2, 1729.
First Congregational Church.
1729-1746. James Osgood
1746-1757. John Carnes
1759-1776. John Searl
STONINGTON, Ct. June 3, 1674. X.
First Congregational Church.
1660-1662. Zechariah Brigden
1663-1719. James Noyes
1722-1762. Eleazer Rosseter
1762-1781. Nathaniel Eells
STONINGTON, Ct. July 14, 1733. X.
East Congregational Church.
1733-1781. Nathaniel Eells
STONINGTON HARBOR, Ct. 1772.
Third Baptist Church of Stonington.
1772-1772. Valentine W i g h t m a n Rathburn
STORRS, Ct. Oct. 11, 1744.
The Congregational Church.
1744-1747. William Throop
1752-1782. Daniel Welch
STOUGHTON, Mass. Aug. 10, 1744.
First Congregational Parish.
Unitarian-Universalist.
1746-1799. Jedediah Adams
STOW, Mass. 1700.
First Congregational Parish.
Both Church and Parish became Unitarian.
1700-1718. John Eveleth
1718-1775. John Gardner
1774-1828. Jonathan Newell
STRATFIELD, Ct. 1751.
First Baptist Church.
1757-1767. John Sherwood
ca. 1767. Benjamin Coles
STRATFORD, Ct. 1640.
First Congregational Church.
1640-1665. Adam Blakeman
1665-1703. Israel Chauncy
1703-1706. John Read
1709-1719. Timothy Cutler, D.D.
1722-1752. Hezekiah Gold
1753-1780. Israhiah Wetmore
STRATFORD, Ct. Apr. 1707.
Christ Church, Episcopal.
1706-1707. George Muirson
1712-1713. Francis Phillips
1722-1723. George Pigot
1723-1754. Samuel Johnson, D.D.
1727-1744. Henry Caner, D.D.
1747-1773. Joseph Lamson
1754-1763. Edward Winslow
1764-1772. Samuel Johnson, D.D.
1767-1777. Ebenezer Kneeland
STRATFORD, N. H. 1773. X.
First Congregational Church.
1773-1775. Clement Sumner
STRATHAM, N. H. 1718.
First Congregational Church.
1718-1749. Henry Rust
1747-1785. Joseph Adams
STRATHAM, N. H. July 18, 1770.
First Baptist Church.
1772-1815. Samuel Smith
STURBRIDGE, Mass. Sept. 29, 1736.
First Congregational Church.
1736-1759. Caleb Rice
1761-1799. Joshua Paine
STURBRIDGE, Mass. Nov. 1747. X.
Separatist Church.
1747-1749. John Blunt
STURBRIDGE, Mass. June 1749.
Fiskdale Baptist Church.
1750-1755. John Blunt
STURBRIDGE, Mass. Sept. 27, 1768. X.
Second Baptist Church.
1768-1775. William Ewing
SUDBURY, Mass. Feb. 11, 1723.
First Congregational Society.
Unitarian.
1723-1772. Israel Loring
1772-1816. Jacob Bigelow
SUFFIELD, Ct. Apr. 26, 1698.
First Congregational Church.
1679-1690. John Younglove
1692-1694. George Phillips
1695-1708. Benjamin Ruggles
1710-1741. Ebenezer Devotion
1742-1796. Ebenezer Gay, D.D.
SUFFIELD, Ct. Apr. 18, 1750. X.
Separatist Church.
1742-1763. Joseph Hastings
SUFFIELD, Ct. June 29, 1763. X.
Separatist Church.
1763-1775. Israel Holly
SUFFIELD, Ct. 1763.
First Baptist Church.
1763-1785. Joseph Hastings
1775-1811. John Hastings
SUNDERLAND, Mass. Jan. 1, 1718/9.
First Congregational Church.
1719-1721. Joseph Willard
1723-1745. William Rand
1747-1797. Joseph Ashley

273

SURRY, N. H. June 12, 1769.
First Congregational Church.
Supplies to 1781.
SUTTON, Mass. Nov. 9, 1720.
First Congregational Church.
1720-1728. John McKinstry
1729-1789. David Hall, D.D.
SUTTON, Mass. Sept. 16, 1735. X.
First Baptist Church
1737-1775. Benjamin Marsh
1737-1738. Thomas Green
SUTTON, Mass. Jan. 31, 1751. X.
Separatist Church.
1751-1765. Ezekiel Cole
SUTTON, Mass. Apr. 27, 1765.
Second Baptist Church.
1768-1772. Jeremian Barstow
SWANSEA, Mass. 1663.
First Baptist Church.
1663-1683. John Myles
1685-1716. Capt. Samuel Luther
1704-1734. Ephraim Wheaton
1733-1739. Samuel Maxwell
1742-1748. Benjamin Herrington
1750-1779. Jabez Wood
SWANSEA, Mass. 1693.
Baptist Church of Christ.
Christian.
1693-1706. Thomas Barnes
1709-1748. Joseph Mason
1715-1750. John Pierce
1738-1775. Job Mason
1752-1804. Russell Mason
SWANSEA, Mass. 1720. X.
Episcopal Church.
Supplies.
SWANZEY, N. H. Nov. 4, 1741.
First Congregational Church.
1741-1748. Timothy Harrington
1753-1769. Ezra Carpenter
1769-1798. Edward Goddard
TAUNTON, Mass. 1637.
First Congregational Society.
Both Church and Parish became
Unitarian.
1637-1644. William Hooke
1637-1659. Nicholas Street
1665-1687. George Shove
1687-1727. Samuel Danforth
1729-1738. Thomas Clap
1742-1765. Josiah Crocker
1769-1776. Caleb Barnum
TAUNTON, Mass. 1740.
St. Thomas's Episcopal Church.
1765-1770. John Lyon
TAUNTON, Mass. 1769.
First Baptist Church.
1769-1785. William Nelson

TEMPLE, N. H. Oct. 2, 1771.
First Congregational Church.
1771-1777. Samuel Webster
TEMPLETON, Mass. Dec. 10, 1755.
First Congregational Church.
Both Church and Parish became
Unitarian.
1755-1759. Daniel Pond
1761-1805. Ebenezer Sparhawk
TEWKSBURY, Mass. Nov. 23, 1737.
First Congregational Church.
1737-1796. Samson Spaulding
THETFORD, Vt. 1773.
First Congregational Church.
1773-1775. Clement Sumner
THOMASTON, Me. 1742. X.
First Presbyterian Church.
1743-1756. Robert Rutherford
THOMPSON, Ct. Jan. 1729/30.
First Congregational Church.
1730-1756. Marston Cabot
1757-1795. Noadiah Russell
THOMPSON, Ct. 1750. X.
First Baptist Church.
1750-1770. Whitman Jacobs
1773-1773. Parson Crosby
THOMPSON, Ct. 1773.
Second Baptist Church.
1773-1773. John Martin
TIVERTON, R. I. 1684.
Baptist Church of Dartmouth, Tiverton and Little Compton.
1676-1695. John Cooke
1684-1713. Hugh Mosher
1698-1720. Aaron Davis
1720-1752. Philip Taber
1752-1775. David Rounds
1752-1775. Benjamin Sheldon
1775-1800. Peleg Burroughs
TIVERTON, R. I. 1720. X.
Episcopal Church.
1720-1721. James McSparran, D.D.
TIVERTON, R. I. Aug. 20, 1746.
First Congregational Church.
1746-1778 Othniel Campbell
TOLLAND, Ct. 1717.
First Congregational Church.
1719-1758. Stephen Steele
1759-1829. Nathan Williams, D.D.
TOPSFIELD, Mass. Nov. 4, 1663.
First Congregational Church.
1663-1671. Thomas Gilbert
1672-1680. Jeremiah Hobart
1684-1725. Joseph Green
1728-1774. John Emerson
TOPSHAM, Me. 1771. X.
First Presbyterian Church.

Became Congregational and later
   Unitarian.
Supplies to 1789.
TORRINGTON, Ct. Oct. 21, 1741.
First Congregational Church.
1741-1776. Nathaniel Roberts
1776-1783. Noah Merwin
TORRINGTON, Ct. 1769.
Torringford Congregational Church.
1769-1833. Samuel John Mills
TOWNSEND, Mass. Oct. 16, 1734. X.
First Congregational Parish.
   Unitarian.
1734-1760. Phinehas Hemenway
1761-1797. Samuel Dix
TRUMBULL, Ct. Nov. 18, 1730.
First Congregational Church.
1730-1744. Richardson Minor
1747-1785. James Beebe
TRURO, Mass. Nov. 1, 1711. X.
First Congregational Church.
   Unitarian.
1711-1754. John Avery
1755-1786. Caleb Upham
TYNGSBOROUGH, Mass.
               June 10, 1755.
First Congregational Parish.
   Unitarian.
Supplies to 1790.
UNION, Ct. Dec. 13, 1738.
First Congregational Church.
1734-1735. Samuel Terry
1735-1736. Jacob Bacon
1738-1746. Ebenezer Wyman
1749-1758. Caleb Hitchcock
1759-1783. Ezra Horton
UPTON, Mass. Jan. 18, 1735.
First Congregational Church.
1738-1744. Thomas Weld
1750-1795. Elisha Fish
UPTON, Mass. 1751. X.
First Baptist Church.
1751-1765. Abraham Bloss.
UPTON, Mass. 1770.
Baptist Church.
   Became Unitarian.
1770-1770. Mr. Boise
UXBRIDGE, Mass. Jan. 6, 1730/1.
First Congregational Society.
Both Church and Parish became
   Unitarian.
1731-1772. Nathan Webb.
1774-1781. Hezekiah Chapman
VASSALBOROUGH, Me. 1775. X.
First Congregational Church.
1775-1775. William Scales
VERNON, Ct. Nov. 24, 1762.

First Congregational Church.
1762-1817. Ebenezer Kellogg
VOLUNTOWN, Ct. Oct. 15, 1723.
First Presbyterian Church.
   Congregational.
1723-1770. Samuel Dorrance
VOLUNTOWN, Ct. Apr. 17, 1751.
Separatist Church of Voluntown and
   Plainfield.
1751-1798. Alexander Miller
WAKEFIELD, Mass. Nov. 5, 1645.
First Congregational Church.
1645-1648. Henry Green
1648-1662. Samuel Haugh
1662-1688. John Brock
1689-1709. Jonathan Pierpont
1712-1732. Richard Brown
1733-1765. William Hobby
1765-1803. Caleb Prentice
WALDEBOROUGH, Me. 1762.
First Lutheran Church.
   Congregational.
1762-1785. John Martin Schaeffer
WALES, Mass. Nov. 4, 1736.
Wales Baptist Church.
1736-1763. Ebenezer Moulton
1765-1769. James Mellen
1773-1826. Elijah Codding
WALLINGFORD, Ct. 1674/5.
First Congregational Church.
1672-1717. Samuel Street
1708-1752. Samuel Whittelsey
1758-1789. James Dana, D.D.
WALLINGFORD, Ct. 1735. X.
Baptist Church.
1735-1750. Timothy Waters
WALLINGFORD, Ct. 1742.
Union Church, Episcopal.
1752-1760. Ichabod Camp
1762-1786. Samuel Andrews
WALPOLE, Mass. July 2, 1730.
First Congregational Society.
Both Church and Parish became
   Unitarian.
1728-1729. Joseph Belcher
1730-1778. Phillips Payson
WALPOLE, N. H. June 10, 1761.
Town Congregational Society.
   Unitarian.
1761-1764. Jonathan Leavitt
1767-1813. Thomas Fessenden
WALTHAM, Mass. Feb. 4, 1696.
First Congregational Parish.
Entire Church and Parish became
   Unitarian.
1697-1719. Samuel Angier
1723-1751. Warham Williams
1752-1809. Jacob Cushing, D.D.

WARE, Mass. May 9, 1751.
First Congregational Church.
1751-1754. Grindall Rawson
1769-1775. Ezra Thayer
WAREHAM, MASS. Dec. 25, 1739.
First Congregational Church.
1739-1775. Rowland Thacher
1775-1779. Josiah Cotton
WARNER, N. H. Feb. 5, 1772.
First Congregational Church.
1772-1801. William Kelley
WARREN, Mass. 1743.
First Congregational Church.
1744-1784. Isaac Jones
WARREN, R. I. Oct. 15, 1764.
First Baptist Church.
1764-1770. James Manning, D.D.
1770-1778. Charles Thompson
WARREN, Ct. Sept. 1756.
First Congregational Church.
1757-1771. Sylvanus Osborn
1771-1829. Peter Starr
WARREN, Me. 1747. X.
Presbyterian Church at Fort St. George's.
1747-1756. Robert Rutherford
WARREN, Me. 1775. X.
First Presbyterian Church.
Congregational.
1775-1783. John Urquehart
WARWICK, R. I. 1641. X.
Quaker-Baptist Church.
1641-1677. Samuel Gorton
WARWICK, R. I. 1721. X.
Episcopal Church at Coweset.
1722-1739. James McSparran, D.D.
1739-1754. John Checkley
1763-1783. John Graves
WARWICK, R. I. 1725.
First Baptist Church.
1725-1752. Manasseh Martyn
1744-1752. John Hammett
Francis Bates
WARWICK, R. I. June 16, 1757. X.
Baptist Church.
1757-1785. Charles Holden
WARWICK, Mass. Sept. 24, 1760.
First Congregational Parish.
Both Church and Parish became Unitarian.
1760-1777. Lemuel Hedge
WASHINGTON, Ct. Sept. 1, 1742.
Judea Congregational Society.
1742-1747. Reuben Judd
1748-1793. Daniel Brinsmade
WASHINGTON, Ct. 1762.
St. John's Episcopal Church.
1762-1766. Thomas Davies

WASHINGTON, Mass. 1772. X.
First Congregational Church.
1773-1820. William Gay Ballantine
WATERBURY, Ct. Aug. 26, 1683.
First Congregational Church.
1690-1699. Jeremiah Peck
1699-1755. John Southmayd
1740-1797. Mark Leavenworth
WATERBURY, Ct. 1742.
Episcopal Church.
1737-1740. Jonathan Arnold
1740-1742. Theophilus Morris
1743-1747. John Lyon
1749-1755. Richard Mansfield, D.D.
1759-1783. James Scovill
WATERFORD, Ct. Mar. 28, 1726. X.
First Baptist Church.
1726-1774. Stephen Gorton
WATERFORD, Ct. Oct. 11, 1743.
Second Baptist Church.
1743-1756. Joshua Rogers
1748-1777. Nathaniel Howard
1767-1827. Zadock Darrow
WATERTOWN, Mass. July 30, 1630.
First Congregational Parish.
Unitarian.
1630-1644. George Phillips
1639-1650. John Knowles
1647-1685. John Sherman
1686-1692. John Bailey
1687-1689. Thomas Bailey
1690-1723. Henry Gibbs
1724-1774. Seth Storer.
WATERTOWN, Mass. 1721. X.
Independent Congregational Church.
1721-1722. Robert Sturgeon
WATERTOWN, Ct. Jan. 16, 1739/40.
First Congregational Church.
1739-1787. John Trumbull
WATERTOWN, Ct. 1764.
Episcopal Church.
1764-1783. James Scovill
WAYLAND, Mass. Aug. 1640.
First Congregational Parish.
Unitarian.
1640-1678. Edmund Browne
1678-1705. James Sherman
1706-1723. Israel Loring
1723-1760. William Cooke
1761-1801. Josiah Bridge
WEATHERSFIELD, Vt. 1775.
First Congregational Church.
Supplies to 1783.
WEBSTER, Mass. 1744. X.
Baptist Church of Dudley and Webster.
Supplies to 1772; then extinct.

276

WELLESLEY, Mass. 1773.
First Congregational Church.
Supplies to 1798.
WELLFLEET, Mass. July 29, 1723.
First Congregational Church.
1723-1725. Josiah Oakes
1730-1786. Isaiah Lewis
WELLS, Me. 1643. X.
First Congregational Parish.
1643-1647. John Wheelwright
1654-1660. Seth Fletcher
1664-1667. Joseph Emerson
1667-1667. Jeremiah Hobart
1667-1672. Robert Paine
1672-1682. John Buss
1683-1688. Percival Green
1689-1690. Richard Martyn
1692-1693. John Hancock
WELLS, Me. Oct. 29, 1701.
First Congregational Church.
1698-1724. Samuel Emery
1725-1752. Samuel Jefferds
1754-1758. Gideon Richardson
1759-1811. Moses Hemenway, D.D.
WELLS, Ct. Apr. 3, 1759. X.
Wallingford Separatist Church.
1761-1787. Simon Waterman
WENDELL, Mass. Nov. 20, 1774.
First Congregational Church.
Supplies to 1783.
WENHAM, Mass. Oct. 8, 1644. X.
First Congregational Church.
1640-1655. John Fisk
WENHAM, Mass. Dec. 10, 1663.
The Congregational Church.
1663-1672. Antipas Newman
1673-1720. Joseph Gerrish
1722-1732. Robert Ward
1733-1749. John Warren
1750-1792. Joseph Swain
WEST AVON, Ct. Nov. 20, 1751.
First Congregational Church.
1751-1767. Ebenezer Booge
1769-1826. Rufus Hawley
WESTBOROUGH, Mass.
Oct. 28, 1724.
First Congregational Society.
Unitarian.
1724-1782. Ebenezer Parkman
WEST BRIDGEWATER, Mass. 1651.
First Congregational Society.
Entire Church and Parish became
Unitarian.
1663-1719. James Keith
1721-1782. Daniel Perkins
WEST BRIDGEWATER, Mass.
Jan. 8, 1749. X.
Separatist Church.

WESTBROOK, Ct. June 29, 1726.
First Congregational Church.
1724-1756. William Worthington
1757-1802. John Devotion
WESTBROOK, Me. Apr. 8, 1765. X.
First Congregational Church.
1765-1797. Thomas Browne
WEST BROOKFIELD, Mass.
Nov. 23, 1757.
First Congregational Church.
1757-1771. Joseph Parsons
1771-1816. Ephraim Ward
WESTCHESTER, Ct. Dec. 17, 1729.
First Congregational Church.
1729-1739. Judah Lewis
1740-1762. Thomas Skinner
1763-1804. Robert Robbins
WESTERLY, R. I. Sept. 17, 1708.
Seventh Day Baptist Church.
1708-1720. John Maxson
1712-1719. Joseph Clark
1719-1748. John Maxson, Jr.
1739-1750. Joseph Maxson
1727-1773. Thomas Hiscox
1773-1793. Joshua Clark
WESTERLY, R. I. 1721. X.
Episcopal Church.
Supplied by missionaries from the
Narragansett Church.
WESTERLY, R. I. 1733. X.
First Congregational Church.
1733-1777. Joseph Park
WESTERLY, R. I. 1740. X.
Baptist Church.
1740-1770. Reuben Peckham
WESTERLY, R. I. Apr. 5, 1750.
First Baptist Church.
1750-1764. Stephen Babcock
WESTERLY, R. I. Feb. 14, 1771. X.
Wilcox Baptist Church.
ca. 1771. Isaac Wilcox
WESTERLY, R. I. 1775.
Second Baptist Church.
1775-1784. Oliver Babcock
WESTFIELD, Mass. Aug. 27, 1679.
First Congregational Church.
1671-1729. Edward Taylor
1726-1740. Nehemiah Bull
1741-1776. John Ballantine
WESTFIELD, Mass. 1748.
Separatist Church.
(Became the First Congregational
Church in the State of Vermont.)
1748-1765. Jedediah Dewey
WESTFORD, Mass. Nov. 15, 1727.
First Congregational Parish.
Unitarian.
1727-1779. Willard Hall

WESTFORD, Ct. Feb. 11, 1768.
First Congregational Church.
1768-1777. Ebenezer Martin
WEST GREENWICH, Ct. 1705.
Horseneck Congregational Church.
1705-1707. Joseph Morgan
1717-1727. Richard Sackett
1728-1730. Stephen Monson
1732-1772. Abraham Todd
1774-1785. Jonathan Murdock
WESTHAMPTON, Mass. 1774.
First Congregational Church.
Supplies to 1779.
WEST HARTFORD, Ct.
Feb. 24, 1713/4.
First Congregational Church.
1713-1759. Benjamin Colton
1757-1770. Nathaniel Hooker
1772-1838. Nathan Perkins, D.D.
WEST HAVEN, Ct. Mar. 20, 1719/20.
First Congregational Church.
1720-1722. Samuel Johnson, D.D.
1725-1734. Jonathan Arnold
1738-1742. Timothy Allen
1742-1758. Nathan Birdseye
1760-1811. Noah Williston
WEST HAVEN, Ct. 1736.
Episcopal Church.
1736-1740. Jonathan Arnold
1740-1742. Theophilus Morris
1749-1755. Richard Mansfield, D.D.
WEST MEDWAY, Mass. Oct. 4, 1750.
First Congregational Church.
1752-1769. David Thurston
1773-1807. David Sanford
WESTMINSTER, Mass. Oct. 20, 1742.
First Congregational Church.
1742-1757. Elisha Marsh
1765-1815. Asaph Rice
WESTMINSTER, Vt. June 11, 1767.
First Congregational Church.
1767-1769. Jesse Goodell
1774-1785. Joseph Bullen
WESTMORELAND, N. H.
Nov. 7, 1764.
United Congregational Church.
1764-1775. William Goddard
1776-1777. Jeremiah Barnard
WEST NEWBURY, Mass.
Oct. 28, 1698.
First Congregational Church.
1698-1714. Samuel Belcher
1714-1738. John Tufts
1739-1752. Thomas Barnard
1752-1779. Moses Hale
WEST NEWBURY, Mass.
Sept. 1, 1731.
Second Congregational Church.

1731-1772. William Johnson
1774-1792. David Toppan, D.D.
WESTON, Mass. Nov. 2, 1709.
First Congregational Parish.
Both Church and Parish became
Unitarian.
1709-1750. William Williams
1751-1782. Samuel Woodward
WESTON, Ct. Aug. 17, 1757.
First Congregational Church.
1757-1783. Samuel Sherwood
WEST ROXBURY, Mass.
Nov. 2, 1712.
First Congregational Parish.
Both Church and Parish became
Unitarian.
1712-1730. Ebenezer Thayer
1734-1776. Nathaniel Walter
1773-1783. Thomas Abbot
WEST SPRINGFIELD, Mass.
June 1698.
First Congregational Church.
1698-1718. John Woodbridge
1720-1755. Samuel Hopkins
1756-1820. Joseph Lathrop, D.D.
WEST SPRINGFIELD, Mass.
First Baptist Church. 1740. X.
1740-1748. Edward Upham
WEST STAFFORD, Ct. Oct. 31, 1764.
First Congregational Church.
1764-1807. Isaac Foster
WEST SUFFIELD, Ct. 1744.
First Congregational Church.
1746-1796. John Graham
WEST TISBURY, Mass. 1673.
First Congregational Church.
1673-1689. John Mayhew
1701-1723. Josiah Torrey
1727-1752. Nathaniel Hancock
1757-1757. John Rand
1760-1781. George Daman
WEST TISBURY, Mass. 1680. X.
Indian Congregational Church.
Supplied by missionaries from Martha's Vineyard
WESTWOOD, Mass. June 4, 1735.
First Congregational Parish.
Entire Church and Parish became
Unitarian.
1735-1743. Josiah Dwight
1743-1772. Andrew Tyler
WEST WOODSTOCK, Ct.
July 24, 1747.
West Congregational Church.
1747-1795. Stephen Williams
WETHERSFIELD, Ct. 1641.
First Congregational Church.
1641-1648. Henry Smith

1649-1659. John Russell
1659-1663. John Cotton
1663-1664. Joseph Haynes
1664-1666. Jonathan Willoughby
1666-1667. Gershom Bulkley
1677-1678. Joseph Rowlandson
1679-1691. John Woodbridge
1691-1693. William Partridge
1694-1738. Stephen Mix
1739-1772. James Lockwood
1774-1821. John Marsh, D.D.
WEYMOUTH, Mass. July 1635.
First Congregational Church.
1635-1639. Joseph Hull
1636-1640. Thomas Jenner
1637-1639. Robert Lenthal
1639-1644. Samuel Newman
1644-1669. Thomas Thacher
1656-1707. Samuel Torrey
1707-1718. Peter Thacher
1719-1734. Thomas Paine
1734-1783. William Smith
1769-1771. James Blake
WEYMOUTH, Mass. Sept. 18, 1723.
South Congregational Church.
1723-1766. James Bayley
1768-1819. Simeon Williams
WHATLEY, Mass. Aug. 21, 1771.
First Congregational Church.
1771-1834. Rufus Wells
WILBRAHAM, Mass. June 24, 1741.
First Congregational Church.
1741-1776. Noah Merrick
WILLIAMSBURG, Mass.
                                                 July 3, 1771.
First Congregational Church.
1773-1777. Amos Butler
WILLIAMSTOWN, Mass. Mar. 1765.
First Congregational Church.
1765-1776. Whitman Welsh
1776-1807. Seth Swift
WILLINGTON, Ct. Sept. 11, 1726.
First Congregational Church.
1728-1758. Daniel Fuller
1759-1790. Gideon Noble
WILMINGTON, Mass. Oct. 24, 1753.
First Congregational Church.
1733-1739. James Varney
1741-1793. Isaac Morrill
WILTON, Ct. June 20, 1726.
First Congregational Church.
1726-1732. Robert Sturgeon
1732-1767. William Gaylord
1768-1786. Isaac Lewis, D.D.
WILTON CENTRE, N. H.
                                           Dec. 14, 1763.
First Congregational Church.

Both Church and Parish became Unitarian.
1763-1778. Jonathan Livermore
WINCHENDON, Mass.
                               Dec. 15, 1762.
First Congregational Churlh.
1762-1768. Daniel Stimpson
1769-1799. Joseph Brown
WINCHESTER, N. H. Nov. 24, 1736.
First Congregational Church.
1736-1747. Joseph Ashley
1764-1777. Micah Lawrence
WINCHESTER, Ct. Oct. 30, 1771.
First Congregational Church.
1772-1789. Joshua Knapp
WINDHAM, Ct. Dec. 10, 1700.
First Congregational Church.
1693-1725. Samuel Whiting
1726-1739. Thomas Clap
1740-1794. Stephen White
WINDHAM, Ct. Oct. 7, 1747.
Separatist Church.
1747-1747. Elihu Marsh
WINDHAM, Me. Dec. 14, 1743.
First Congregational Church.
1739-1742. Nicholas Hodge
1743-1753. John Wight
1761-1790. Peter Thacher Smith
WINDHAM, N. H. 1742.
First Presbyterian Church.
1747-1752. William Johnston
1760-1765. John Kinkead
1766-1793. Simon Williams
WINDSOR, Ct. 1635.
First Congregational Church.
1635-1670. John Warham
1639-1644. Ephraim Hewett
1667-1680. Nathaniel Chauncy
1682-1728. Samuel Mather
1710-1747. Jonathan Marsh, D.D.
1747-1751. Isaac Burr
1750-1775. William Russell
1774-1794. David Sherman Rowland
WINDSOR, Ct. 1669.   X.
Second Congregational Church.
1668-1680. Benjamin Woodbridge
WINDSOR, Ct. 1728.
Poquonack Congregational Church.
                          Universalist.
1728-1737. John Woodbridge
1740-1757. Samuel Tudor
1771-1787. Dan Foster
WINDSOR, Vt. Sept. 29, 1768.
First Congregational Church.
1768-1774. James Wellman
WINDSOR, Mass. Mar. 25, 1772.
First Congregational Church.
1773-1777. David Avery

WISCASSET, Me. Apr. 3, 1773.
First Congregational Church.
1773-1791. Thomas Moore
WOBURN, Mass. Aug. 14, 1642.
First Congregational Church.
1642-1684. Thomas Carter
1679-1703. Jabez Fox
1703-1756. John Fox
1729-1754. Edward Jackson
1756-1775. Josiah Sherman
WOBURN, Mass. Sept. 17, 1747. M.
Third Congregational Church.
1747-1756. Josiah Cotton
WOLCOTT, Ct. Nov. 15, 1773.
First Congregational Church.
1773-1791. Alexander Gillet
WOODBRIDGE, Ct. Nov. 2, 1742.
First Congregational Church.
1742-1785. Benjamin Woodbridge
WOODBURY, Ct. May 5, 1670.
First Congregational Church.
1668-1700. Zachariah Walker
1700-1760. Anthony Stoddard
1760-1813. Noah Benedict
WOODBURY, Ct. 1761.
St. Paul's Episcopal Church.
1761-1766. Thomas Davies
1771-1789. John Rutgers Marshall
WOODSTOCK, Ct. 1690.
First Congregational Church.
1690-1726. Josiah Dwight
1727-1735. Amos Throop
1737-1760. Abel Stiles
1763-1777. Abiel Leonard, D.D.
WOODSTOCK, Ct. Feb. 1766.
First Baptist Church.
1766-1790. Biel Ledoyt
WOOLWICH, Me. June 12, 1765.
First Congregational Church.
1764-1824. Josiah Winship
WORCESTER, Mass. 1718. X.
First Presbyterian Church.
1725-1725. Edward FitzGerald
1725-1736. William Johnston

WORCESTER, Mass. 1719.
First Congregational Church.
1719-1722. Andrew Gardner
1725-1745. Isaac Burr
1747-1784. Thaddeus Maccarty
WORTHINGTON, Mass.
Apr. 1, 1771.
First Congregational Church.
1771-1781. Jonathan Huntington
WRENTHAM, Mass. Apr. 13, 1692.
First Congregational Church.
1669-1719. Samuel Man
1719-1751. Henry Messenger
1750-1784. Joseph Bean
WRENTHAM, Mass. 1769.
First Baptist Church.
1773-1823. William Williams
YARMOUTH, Mass. Nov. 3, 1639.
First Congregational Church.
1639-1643. Marmaduke Matthews
1647-1662. John Miller
1662-1692. Thomas Thornton
1693-1705. John Cotton
1708-1726. Daniel Greenleaf
1729-1754. Thomas Smith
1755-1760. Grindall Rawson
1762-1768. Joseph Green, Jr.
1769-1828. Timothy Alden
YARMOUTH, Mass. 1640. X.
Second Congregational Church.
1640-1646. Joseph Hull
YORK, Me. Dec. 3, 1673.
First Congregational Church.
(This is the oldest church now existing in Maine.)
1637-1639. William Tompson
1662-1692. Shubael Dummer
1692-1693. John Hancock
1698-1747. Samuel Moody
1749-1798. Isaac Lyman

www.ingramcontent.com/pod-product-compliance
Lightning Source LLC
Chambersburg PA
CBHW071241230426
43668CB00011B/1529